BOOKS BY PETER GAY

The Bourgeois Experience: Victoria to Freud
Volume III   The Cultivation of Hatred (1993)

Reading Freud: Explorations and Entertainments (1990)

Freud: A Life for Our Time (1988)

A Godless Jew:
Freud, Atheism, and the Making of Psychoanalysis (1987)

The Bourgeois Experience: Victoria to Freud
Volume II   The Tender Passion (1986)

Freud for Historians (1985)

The Bourgeois Experience: Victoria to Freud
Volume I   Education of the Senses (1984)

Freud, Jews and Other Germans:
Masters and Victims in Modernist Culture (1978)

Art and Act: On Causes in History—Manet, Gropius, Mondrian (1976)

Style in History (1974)

Modern Europe (1973), with R. K. Webb

The Bridge of Criticism: Dialogues on the Enlightenment (1970)

The Enlightenment: An Interpretation
Vol. II   The Science of Freedom (1969)

Weimar Culture: The Outsider as Insider (1968)

A Loss of Mastery: Puritan Historians in Colonial America (1966)

The Enlightenment: An Interpretation
Vol. I   The Rise of Modern Paganism (1966)

The Party of Humanity: Essays in the French Enlightenment (1964)

Voltaire's Politics: The Poet as Realist (1959)

The Dilemma of Democratic Socialism:
Eduard Bernstein's Challenge to Marx (1952)

The Naked Heart

The Bourgeois Experience

VICTORIA TO FREUD

VOLUME IV

The Naked Heart

PETER GAY

W · W · NORTON & COMPANY · NEW YORK · LONDON

First published as a Norton paperback 1996

The text of this book is composed in Bembo,
with the display set in Centaur.
Composition and Manufacturing by The Haddon Craftsmen, Inc.

ISBN 0-393-03813-0
ISBN 0-393-31515-0 pbk.

W. W. Norton & Company, Inc., 500 Fifth Avenue, New York, N.Y. 10110
W. W. Norton & Company Ltd., 10 Coptic Steet, London WC1A 1PU

1 2 3 4 5 6 7 8 9 0

Contents

The illustrations will be found following pages 116 and 244.

Our age is bewailed as the age of Introversion. Must that needs be evil?
We, it seems, are critical; we are embarrassed with second thoughts; we
cannot enjoy any thing for hankering to know whereof the pleasure con-
sists; we are lined with eyes; we see with our feet; the time is infected with
Hamlet's unhappiness,—"Sicklied o'er with the pale cast of thought."
Is it so bad then? Sight is the last thing to be pitied. Would we be blind?
                              —Emerson, *"The American Scholar" (1837)*

Je peux commencer Mon coeur mis à nu *n'importe où, n'importe*
comment, et le continuer au jour le jour, suivant l'inspiration du jour et
de la circonstance, pourvu que l'inspiration soit vive.
                              —Baudelaire, *"Mon coeur mis à nu" (after 1861)*

Der Psychologe . . . wird . . . verlangen dürfen, dass die Psychologie
wieder als Herrin der Wissenschaften anerkannt werde, zu deren Dienste
und Vorbereitung die übrigen Wissenschaften da sind. Denn Psychologie
ist nunmehr wieder der Weg zu den Grundproblemen.
                              —Nietzsche, Jenseits von Gut und Böse *(1886)*

The Naked Heart

Introduction

The nineteenth century was intensely preoccupied with the self, to the point of neurosis. During the very decades of the most sustained campaign for mastery of the world ever undertaken, bourgeois devoted much delightful and perhaps even more anxious time to introspection. It was while scientists and sociologists, physicians and reformers launched their concerted assaults on ignorance, poverty, and disease that novelists, painters, biographers, and even historians made self-exploration their cardinal business. Edgar Allan Poe promised instant glory to the one who would write "a very small book—'my heart laid bare.'" He never did write it; nor did Charles Baudelaire, who adopted Poe's proposal and took some stabs at it.[1] But there were swarms of bourgeois in the century who shared their naked heart with their contemporaries.

As was to be expected, specialists in human nature supplied invaluable clues to the search for the self. Illustrious Victorian names tumble over one another. Philosophers from Hegel to Nietzsche intensified the explorations first undertaken by the ancient Greeks and pointed the enterprise in unexpected directions. Psychologists like Wilhelm Wundt and Jean Martin Charcot made their discipline far more responsive to observation than it had ever been and tried to earn it a reputation for being a science of man. In the writings of that astonishing genius William James, advances in psychological understanding blended with original departures in introspective philosophy. Around the turn of the century, Sigmund Freud began to revolutionize the way we think of the mind at work, although he had to wait for the 1920s before his theories penetrated into general culture, until now everyone, including the most impassioned anti-Freudian, speaks Freud. In his double role as scientist and polemicist, more disposed to intensify middle-class anxieties than to allay them, Karl Marx made the mentality of the bourgeoisie his special concern. But, important as these figures were, this book is only marginally about them. Rather, it deals mainly with ordinary bourgeois, with readers of biographies, histories, and novels as much as their authors, with obscure as much as well-known diarists and letter writers. Whenever possible, I have focused on whatever traces of their thoughts and feelings middle-class men and women left behind, or whatever I have been able to infer. And among these thoughts and feelings a preoccupation with the self loomed large.

Solemn commentators found this fixation problematic but beyond control. In the late 1790s, Immanuel Kant had already observed that "from the day that humans started speaking through the 'I,' they have brought their beloved self to light wherever they could, and egotism is advancing irresistibly." The nineteenth century amply confirmed Kant's diagnosis. John Stuart Mill noted that "self-consciousness" had been the "daemon of the man of genius of our time from Wordsworth to Byron, from Goethe to Chateaubriand," and provided the age with "so much of its cheerful and its mournful wisdom." He need not have confined his observation to the most conspicuous autobiographical writers of the age; by mid-century the attempt to hide or reveal, at least to understand, the secret life of the self had grown into a favorite, and wholly serious, indoor sport. In 1805, William Wordsworth in a self-regarding mood had thought it "a thing unprecedented in Literary history that a man should talk so much about himself."[2] A few decades later, such talk was commonplace. The probing tone of nineteenth-century fiction and the increasing scientific attention lavished on dreams, drug addiction, madness, and deviant sexual passions were so many symptoms of inwardness on the march.

Impressive evidence lurks everywhere, perhaps most concentrated in an eloquent statement by Turgenev: in 1859, in his novel *On the Eve,* he has a leading character, no doubt speaking for his author, confess to excessive self-absorption. But then, at once apologetic and sardonic, he adds that he does not think himself a rarity: many people are "always studying themselves in disgusting detail, feeling their pulses with every sensation that they experience and then reporting to themselves: 'That's how I feel, and that's what I think.' What a useful, sensible sort of occupation."[3] No doubt, by the second half of the century, preoccupation with the state of one's nerves, already lively before, had grown into something of an obsession.[4] Historians have taken Freud's psychoanalytic techniques and theories of the mind as pivotal moments in the transition of Victorian culture to the twentieth century. So they were, but they also represent the culmination of a century-long effort to map inner space.

Writers, whether novelists, poets, or editorialists, spread the cult of self-awareness to the reading middle classes. Artists, too, painters and sculptors and, in their wordless way, composers, professed a heartfelt interest in the secret needs and conflicting emotions concealed beneath civilized surfaces. It is common, said Ralph Waldo Emerson in a much quoted address, "The American Scholar," in 1837—the year that Queen Victoria acceded to the throne—to bewail the time as "the age of Introversion," an age "embarrassed with second thoughts" and "infected with Hamlet's unhappiness." But Emerson refused to be dismayed: "Sight is the last thing to be pitied. Would we be blind?" He thought the age of introversion "a very good one, if we but know what to do with it."[5] As the years went by, more and more bourgeois wondered whether they knew.

In time, then, so-called ordinary bourgeois massively joined the pilgrimage to the interior with their intimate diaries, confessional journals, and confidential correspondence, with their love letters and religious ruminations. But it was necessarily men of words—and women—who laid out the agenda for the rest. Praising the diagnostic virtues of phrenology, Poe singled out as its "most direct, and, perhaps, most salutary" effect, *"self-examination and self-knowledge."* At mid-century, in *Pendennis,* William Makepeace Thackeray was a little more quizzical about the possible consequences of self-scrutiny: "I doubt whether the wisest of us know what our own motives are, and whether some of the actions of which we are the very proudest will not surprise us when we trace them, as we shall some day, to their source."[6] Introspection seemed as risky as it was seductive.

In fact, from the beginning of the century, the fashion of intense self-scrutiny had not only its enthusiasts but its detractors, and this contest of strongly held views provided the Victorian century with some of its most interesting tensions.* While a broad spectrum of cultural critics, ranging from Karl Marx to Matthew Arnold, denigrated bourgeois for leading an empty inner life and for submitting everything to the calculus of materialistic advantage, other critics worried over bourgeois introspection as the symptom of a modern sickness. From his early years, Johann Wolfgang von Goethe, for one, had repeatedly voiced a manly distrust of concentration on the self as a descent into morbid subjectivity; the "great, so significant-sounding task, *Know thyself,*" he summed up his reservations in 1823, "has always seemed suspect to me." After all, "man knows himself only in so far as he knows the world." In the same mood, Benjamin Disraeli, speaking as a novelist, wanted self-disclosure to be severely rationed. Reflecting on a sequence of youthful novels, he confided to his diary around 1836, "This trilogy is the secret history of my feelings—I shall write no more about myself."[7] There could be, it seemed, too much self-disclosure.

Goethe and Disraeli had their successors. "That mania of personal analysis

---

*I should note that I shall be using "Victorian" and "nineteenth-century" as synonyms throughout this book.

has become a malady in our time," lamented the eminent French psychologist Théodule Ribot decades later. Even the old Emerson had grown anxious. No longer so buoyant as he had been when he wrote "The American Scholar," he described current self-awareness with a metaphor deliberately chosen for its harshness: "The young men were born with knives in their brain, a tendency to introversion, self-dissection, anatomizing of motives."[8] In short, however, stimulating, Hamlet was proving a most uncomfortable companion, but, it seemed, an inescapable one.

It is obvious that baring the heart has been a seductive, if often troubling, pursuit since remote antiquity. Through the centuries, the all-too-familiar inscription over the entrance of the temple at Delphi, *Know thyself,* which so worried Goethe, had been read as an invitation to self-scrutiny. In his role as philosophical gadfly, Socrates had deliberately turned away from the metaphysical and cosmological program of his predecessors; focusing attention on the human condition, he anticipated by over two millennia Alexander Pope's celebrated injunction to eschew theological theorizing and recognize that the proper study of mankind is man, a study that involved learning to know the race by learning to know oneself.

Inwardness, of course, had never quite disappeared from human concerns. Its history is long, and its greatest protagonists are only too well known, ranging from Plato to Marcus Aurelius, from St. Augustine's *Confessions* to Montaigne's *Essais* and beyond. The rise of eighteenth-century sensibility, of which Goethe's *Werther* remains the most dramatic exemplar, antedated the nineteenth century by decades, but left its mark on the Victorians. "My good friend, quoth I—, as sure as I am I—and you are you—." The narrator in *Tristram Shandy,* that mid-eighteenth-century classic in comic psychology, is speaking to a post office commissary. "—And who are you?" replies the commissary. "—Don't puzzle me; said I." Indeed, many years before Victorians began to worry over it, this fixation could seem a little eccentric, even perverse. "I was too accustomed," confessed the Pietistic "beautiful soul" in Goethe's *Wilhelm Meisters Lehrjahre,* "to occupy myself with myself."[9] What makes the Victorians' self-scrutiny important, then, is not that they invented introspection or were the first to brood about it but that they made it available, almost inescapable, to a wide public. And most of the Victorians cultivating their inner selves were bourgeois.

"Bourgeois": the term is one of those capacious baskets for generalizations that appear to gather up more precise information than in fact they do.[10] Much nineteenth-century invective, developed at a time when class distinctions grew increasingly clear-cut and increasingly contested, reduced "bourgeois" to little more than a derisive epithet. Such social critics as William Morris denounced their age for being "oppressed with bourgeoisdom and philistinism." In actuality, the meaning of "bourgeois" is too diverse, the signals it sends too contradictory, to deserve such a fate. British Victorians liked to speak in a cautious plural about the "middle classes," and their prudence captures a significant part of the truth. Nineteenth-century names that deliberately confounded traditional categories, oxymorons like "money aristocracy" or "starched-collar proletariat," attest to the complexities concealed behind global class names.

So do the gaps separating industrial barons on the edge of ennoblement from petty bank clerks, professional men from small merchants, professors from minor public servants, rentiers from shop owners—bourgeois all. Old money smelled different from new money, but in both situations money was not everything. The Victorian bourgeoisie had more than one hierarchy of prestige; the esteem attached to an admired poet or an eminent academic was at least partially independent of income. The linguistic subdivisions introduced in country after country cast a glaring light on these divisions: the Germans differentiated between the bourgeoisie of property and that of education—*Besitzbürgertum* and *Bildungsbürgertum*—while the French had their *grande,* their *bonne,* their *petite bourgeoisie.* Not satisfied, close observers sliced the territory occupied by the middle classes even more finely. Certain codes, like the Prussian law, might tersely define the estate of the middle classes—the *Bürgerstand*—as all persons neither noble nor peasant, but economic and social realities subverted these grand simplicities. It is almost unnecessary to remark that bourgeois styles of living and thinking varied with social aspirations and opportunities, further highlighting the fissures separating one segment of the bourgeoisie from others.

And yet, while very different futures awaited bourgeois high and low, they did share ways of thinking about themselves that made them just that—bourgeois. They were enemies and allies. In 1820, Prince Metternich, writing to Czar Alexander I about the middling orders, astutely observed that "this intermediate class" assumes "all sorts of disguises, uniting and subdividing as occasion offers, helping each other in the hour of danger, and the next day depriving each other of all their conquests." In large part, their self-definition was negative, conceived in opposition to estates above and below them, and many of their confident-sounding claims to middle-class excellence had a defensive ring about them.

One reason for this defensiveness was the crucial fact, of which nineteenth-century bourgeois were well aware, that they remained a distinct and recognizable minority. Historians of urban life have estimated that the middle classes made up some 12 or, at best, 15 percent of most city populations. To be surrounded, virtually swamped, by a sea of proletarians supplied compelling incentives to class solidarity, however compromised by actual mobility on the margins. A handful of magnates could hope to marry, or otherwise buy their way, into the aristocracy; a far larger handful of petty bourgeois feared that they could sink into the masses of the toiling poor. But most bourgeois remained more or less firmly fixed within solid middling incomes, habits, and values. And their ideology consisted not merely of thrift, punctuality, and self-restraint but also of a commitment to an inner honesty that should clarify, if possible enrich, their inner life.

This book seeks to chart the fascinating spectacle of nineteenth-century bourgeois struggling for inwardness. It was a time when the art of listening to music and poetry developed into a posture almost religious in its ardor and when romantic notions of love secured a vast, largely uncritical public. It was a time, too, when autobiographies and self-portraits, biographies, histories, and novels exploring character exploded into sizable domestic industries and when intimate letters and diaries grew more common and more candid than ever. And it was a time when disturbers of the bourgeois peace like Marx, Nietzsche, and Freud complicated the way the self perceives, and responds to, the world.

There remains a disturbing question: what is the self that Victorian bourgeois seemed so intent on discovering and defining? In recent years, it has become fashionable to stress the sheer subjectivity of all perception, including self-perception, and to view the self as an evolving invention. In this view, to talk or write about the self, to paint it, to exhibit it in public or private, even to think about it, is never simply to report what is plainly already there, but to *create* a self through the very act of recording.* This assault on the very possibility of dependable knowledge about the inner life amounts to a drastic redefinition of the self. True, it seems an understandable reaction to a naive realism that purports to grasp the inner or the outer world directly, without any interference from wishes, passions, or the constraints of language, as though one could infallibly see these worlds through a window that is altogether transparent. Historians have toyed with modern perceptions of perception: Carl Becker's relativist motto, "every man his own historian," which slyly intimates that every interpretation of the past is as good as any other, has long enjoyed a certain vogue. But for my part, I find this claim for the instability of the self and the relativity of all knowledge justified only within the strictest limits. It may function as a useful caution against arrogance and the delusion that our knowledge of others, or ourselves, is easy. Turning Gertrude Stein's famous dismissal of Oakland on its head, I have done my writing, in this book as in others, on the

---

*I shall return to this theme when I analyze autobiographies; see below, pp. 104–6.

conviction that when we study the past, even the past of minds, there *is* a there there.

I have worked with the assumption, then, that the self is not a fiction but an amalgam of stable and unstable elements and that, however elusive to the researcher, it can be known. That is why I have turned to Freud, who saw the mind as an enigma to be solved. To him, it was the outcome of the cooperation—as well as competition—of necessity and reason, of nature and nurture. And his version of how endowment and experience, often at war with one another, sculpt the mind has proved most fruitful in my work.

This is not the place for a primer of psychoanalytic theory. But a sketch of its essential logic may not be out of place. Fundamental to Freud's theory of mind is that it is part of nature, quite as orderly, quite as subject to causal pressures, as any physical entity. The mental phenomena that often appear uncaused, illogical, downright senseless must have a meaning. For the psychoanalyst and, I would argue, for the historian, any expression, no matter how banal or absurd—a dream, a fantasy, a slip of the tongue, a symptom, a linguistic habit—is a message waiting to be deciphered. The impression that so much of mental life is beyond understanding is an intelligible misperception springing from an unwillingness to delve beneath surfaces. The connections we fail to see have been driven into a realm of the mind, the unconscious, to which the investigator has at best indirect access. Some mental material has been lodged in that unconscious from the beginning, but most of it has been pushed underground by defensive mechanisms, of which repression is only the best known. As a wishing animal that wants only gratification, if possible instantly, the human animal needs to defend itself against its most longed-for pleasures, both sexual and aggressive, pleasures unacceptable without at least some controls. It is first the society of the child—its parents, siblings, teachers, priests—and internalized prohibitions acquired from a wider world that sets limits on passions. The less one knows about one's demanding appetites, the better. In short—and this is particularly relevant to the historian—the individual's imperious desires and the needs of civilization are usually at odds. All education, whatever else it might be, is also a stringent imposition of unwelcome boundaries.

The human self, then, as Freud saw it, is an organism in conflict, much of it played out on the larger stage on which historians have conventionally concentrated. Contrary to its reputation, the thought of Freud and his successors in no way slights the influence on mental development of family, politics, religion, or economic competition and, in turn, the influence of the individual on his—or her—environment. Freud recognized that those significant portions of the mental organization he called the ego and the superego are continuously enmeshed with outside forces, busily learning, or refusing to learn, their lessons.

Thus ideals and fears, incentives and threats help to shape the self as much as do the instinctual urges that spring from profoundly buried inner reservoirs. It is often forgotten that psychoanalysts recognize even the much maligned Oedipus complex as responding to external pressures. This is how Freud saw human nature, and this, I am convinced, is how people are and how they were.

Freud is not popular among historians. But, though aware of this hostility, I repeat that I have found the psychoanalytic perspective immensely valuable, and so, I believe, will others. It has guided me to the questions I have asked of the past as much as, perhaps even more than, to the answers it has supplied. As I have insisted in *Freud for Historians,* published in 1985, all historians are psychologists and depend for the most part on prosaic generalizations about human behavior. These may do much toward understanding historic figures, but normally they stop short just when things get interesting and call for deeper explanations. Historical portraits that remain on the level of manifest experience without exploring the hidden reaches of the mind miss much that is worth capturing. This volume, the fourth in a series of five, deals with the inner life, Freud's favored domain.

So was the time span of these books, the long nineteenth century, Freud's chosen laboratory. There are historians who have grudgingly admitted that perhaps Freud could offer valuable testimony to the times in which he lived and the class to which he belonged. I am not comfortable with this restriction: I would argue that his view of human nature is relevant to earlier times and more remote cultures than his own. The widely accepted portrait of his patients as idle, upper-class and upper-middle-class Jewish Viennese housewives is a caricature. His repertory of analysands included men as much as women, gentiles as much as Jews, aristocrats as well as commoners, Britons, Americans, Russians, Frenchwomen as well as Austrians. But this much is true enough: the applicability of Freud's view of human character is particularly striking among the population that makes up my subjects. He knew them intimately.

In the chapters that follow, external facts—books, paintings, letters, economic conflicts, social and political developments, in a word, real men and women and the conditions of their making—will occupy center stage as they encounter open or secret support for their desires or no less open or secret resistances to them. It will emerge that there is nothing in the Freudian dispensation to undermine these historical realities, everything that respects their complexities.

BOURGEOIS EXPERIENCES, IV

The Art of Listening

In 1847, the American artist William Sidney Mount solidified his reputation as a genre painter with a canvas he called *The Power of Music*. It depicts a shirt-sleeved fiddler playing in a barn to an attentive audience of two men. But outside, hidden from the improvised concert by the half-closed barn door, he has a third listener, a black man, hat in hand, rapt. His axe and jug beside him, he has paused to drink in the sounds reaching him at his humble vantage point. The scene is a tribute to the art of listening.

Mount plainly favored this sort of subject. From a musical family, himself an accomplished violinist, composer of songs, inventor of a reasonably priced violin, and collector of folk tunes, he liked to paint rustics taking in a musical turn after a sleigh ride or a fetching young couple actively enjoying a fiddler's tune. In 1828, in a youthful self-portrait—he was then twenty-one—he defined himself staring solemnly at the viewer, holding a wooden flute as his personal emblem. And two years before he painted *The Power of Music,* he had rehearsed its composition, virtually its theme, with *Dance of the Haymakers*. Harvesters are dancing in a barn, while outside a black boy beats rhythm with two sticks as he watches the merrymakers.[1]

Read on its surface, *The Power of Music* is what it purports to be: a gently amusing set piece, inviting a benevolent smile. Mount thought that black musicians, whom he painted without a hint of condescension, added to "the humor of the scene."[2] On another level, the painting may serve as a commentary on a society half slave and half free: though quite unaware of it, the amateur violinist is performing for a segregated audience. *The Power of Music,* though, yields a still deeper meaning. The intent silence of the white listeners and even more the quiet, almost beatific smile on the black farm laborer's face, both pointed up by the title Mount chose for his canvas, attest to the theme of this book: the ascent of inwardness in the Victorian age.

Placing a high value on the insinuating qualities of music was, of course, not a nineteenth-century invention. The title of Mount's painting resonates with many centuries of awe before the grip of music on the mind. Homer's Sirens, with their irresistible melodies, and the mythical Orpheus, who soothed the gods of the underworld with his lyre, leave no doubt that by the time Plato proscribed musical modes that would reduce citizens to effeminacy, the impact of auditory sensations on performers and listeners alike was thoroughly familiar. When, around 1823, Heinrich Heine wrote *Die Loreley,* probably his best-known poem, he was reviving an old fable about the seductive female who, perched on a steep cliff overlooking the Rhine, lures to their death infatuated boatmen unable to resist her song.* Many poets, we know, have celebrated the compelling force of music across the centuries. For Shakespeare—to cite only the greatest of them—music was sweet and most eloquent, the food of love; the man who has no music in him, he tells us, is fit only for treasons, stratagems, and spoils. And the romantics were almost on principle susceptible to what Thomas De Quincey significantly called "the deep voluptuous enjoyment of music." Leigh Hunt noted that Lord Byron listened to music "with an air of romantic regret." It was a pose more than an authentic response but, it seems, an attitude almost required for a poet of his stripe.[3] What the Victorians did with the power of music, as with inwardness in general, was to democratize it.

This was certainly not a simple feat of the nineteenth-century bourgeois will. Many social impulses flowed together to elevate secular music from mere enter-tainment into an invitation to ecstasy. Since the late Renaissance, and intensify-ing in tempo during the eighteenth century, there had been a marked refine-ment of manners among the respectable classes. Those who could afford it gradually moved away from the unmediated expression of emotional needs toward the management and delay of gratification. Eighteenth-century moral weeklies strained to teach good bourgeois the blessings of forbearance and kindliness to lesser beings like women, children, or the poor. Long since, the middle classes had learned to eat with a fork instead of their fingers, and now in the age of the Enlightenment they were instructed how to polish their conduct and acquire a measure of finesse in the higher reaches of culture. Samuel Rich-ardson's best-selling novel of the early 1740s, *Pamela; or, Virtue Rewarded,* fore-shadowed a storm of sensibility to come.

It reached gale force in the 1760s and 1770s, when a vogue for tender,

---

*So was Dante Gabriel Rossetti, when, in 1865, he painted *The Merciless Lady.* A lovely young woman plying her instrument diverts the attention of a handsome young man from a woman who is desperately grasping his hand and glaring at the seductive singer as she is about to lose him to the pitiless musician.

sentimental tales swept reading and listening publics especially in Western countries. Jean Jacques Rousseau's vastly popular *La Nouvelle Héloïse,* or Henry Mackenzie's lachrymose *The Man of Feeling,* taught a generation to shed delicious tears about doomed love and the sad lot of unfortunates. The view that music is the most expressive of the arts could only benefit, among audiences no less than among theorists. In the France of those years, operagoers found themselves prey to unexpected moments of melting sentiment as they absorbed the music of Christian Willibald Gluck, music that reached for emotional effects with almost uncanny skill. In 1785, in a treatise on the "poetics of music," the French aesthetician B. G. D. de Lacépède extolled music's capacity to turn listeners toward self-contemplation.[4]

Other theorists, with the English and Germans taking the lead, had been making equally ambitious claims for music all along. For decades they had been preaching what the Germans called *Affektenlehre,* the doctrine that it is the business of music to stir the feelings of composer, performer, and audience alike. They analyzed the affective messages sent by major and minor keys, by rhythms, harmonies, and melodies, and by cunningly produced crescendos. In his famous *General History of Music,* launched in the late 1770s, Dr. Charles Burney defined music as "the art of pleasing by the succession and combination of agreeable sounds," and granted every hearer "a right to give way to his feelings, and be pleased or dissatisfied without knowledge, experience, or the fiat of critics."[5] In retrospect, the respect that Burney and other writers on music displayed for listeners' emotional absorption read like rehearsals for romantic inwardness. In such an atmosphere, piety toward music could only prosper.

It prospered literally in a world of growing affluence among the middle classes. By the time of the French Revolution, a consumer society had emerged as homely products like toys, affordable tableware and furniture, to say nothing of more high-flying ventures like literary periodicals, began to supply an apparently insatiable appetite. From mid-century on, thousands of households made themselves proud possessors of a clavichord or, later, of a new, more powerful and flexible instrument, the fortepiano. Aristocrats with their private orchestras were not the only patrons of musical parties; well-to-do bourgeois mounted family entertainments with the lady of the house, or one of her daughters, at the keyboard, or held more showy musical soirées, as lofty sentiments flowed freely.

After 1815, once the shadow of Napoleon had been lifted from Europe, this demand for goods other than bare necessities mounted at unprecedented rates. By the 1830s and 1840s, it had become almost banal to call the age an age of transition, and all, except for a few gloomy prophets like Thomas Carlyle, used the epithet as a term of praise. In 1825—to cite a single but appropriate witness from a vast array of testimony—M. P. Lahalle, a little-known French writer on musical life, noted with high approval that "the mass of pleasures has increased in proportion to the mass of wealth" and that "a life more comfortable, more delicate, more varied in feelings or more contemplative, has become the lot of all classes of society." And it was, to Lahalle's mind, music that had developed into "the privileged art of this century. It has profited from the favor that poetry has lost."[6]

Lahalle's verdict is far too sweeping, even a little naive. But it was supported by an impressive array of economic facts. Urbanization, industrialization, the rise of a world market, and the modern sophistication of banking and commerce exacted an often exorbitant price, especially among skilled artisans threatened by the new machinery, and among the working poor exposed to the ravages of bad harvests and economic fluctuations. And the erratic business cycles did not spare even solid bourgeois agonizing reversals of fortune. Yet the beneficiaries of innovation—and there were more and more of them as the century progressed—saw their income and, with that, their leisure thriving almost out of recognition in the Victorian years. This meant more time, money, and energy for luxuries, however modest, and the devout enjoyment of music ranked high among them.

While social and economic developments fostered piety toward music during the nineteenth century, right through the age of the Enlightenment most secular performances had been mere accompaniments to sociability. To be sure, sensitive eighteenth-century patrons, often themselves accomplished amateur musicians—Prince Karl Lichnowsky, Mozart's pupil and Beethoven's Maecenas, comes readily to mind—imposed courtesy for composer and performer in their private concerts and, when provoked, sternly enforced silent listening.[7] But it took decades before these civilized attitudes were elevated into a general cultural ideal. Most eighteenth-century musical performers had provided an agreeable backdrop for flirting, gossiping, dining. No doubt, Mozart drew on his own experience for the supper scene in the second act of *Don Giovanni*, when he has the Don entertain his guests with orchestras enlivening the party.[8] Musical events at the mansions of thriving bourgeois and munificent aristocrats were occasions for gregariousness and gallantry, often screens for seduction.

The brightly lit opera houses were noisier still. A handful of music lovers conscientiously followed the action onstage with a libretto, but most of the audience chatted as liveried servants hawked carafes of wine and oranges—during the performance. Many arrived late and left early, often as audibly as they had come. And for those in the market for them, prostitutes lurked in the remote reaches of the upper balconies. In the 1740s, the French novelist Jacques Rochette de La Morlière had an aristocratic character make a point of despising those who go to musical events to listen. That, he sneered, was "bourgeois"; nothing, he thought, was "so damnable as listening to a work like a street merchant or some provincial just off the boat." Down to the end of the eighteenth century, Stendhal recorded in the 1820s after things had been changing, Roman audiences would use "the opera-house as a kind of club and general centre for conversation."[9]

And not the opera house alone. Around 1766, the French artist Michel Barthélemy Ollivier painted the ten-year-old Mozart at the keyboard as a select party of stylishly dressed "listeners" pays far more attention to a lavishly laid-out lunch than to the music.[10] These were the years when, in Vienna and elsewhere, concerts were often held in restaurants. No wonder that Mozart should find the rare moment of silence, that ultimate accolade to the power of music, so exceptional that he explicitly commented on it. Still, he cherished noise quite as much, when it was appreciative. In April 1781, after giving a triumphant concert in Vienna, he reported to his father on the applause that had poured over him. "But I must add that what pleased and surprised me most was the astonishing silentium—and in the midst of playing the screaming of 'bravo.' Surely for Vienna, where there are so many, and so many good, pianists, this is honor enough."[11] He would have taken unbroken silence as a sign of disapproval.

Stendhal would attribute the same sentiments to Gioacchino Rossini several decades later. In his biography of the composer, he reports that when in 1813 *Tancredi* premiered in Venice, Rossini was too worried about the public's possible response to take his usual place at the piano. But after "the first *allegro* of the overture" was "so well received" that "every corner of the house echoed with clapping and cheering," he "screwed up sufficient courage to edge into his seat." Scholars have shown this anecdote to be apocryphal, but the fact that Stendhal could make it up testifies to the current conviction that composers needed to have audiences respond audibly, even in the middle of a number.[12] The qualities that music lovers still professed to value most highly were fidelity to nature and an apt rendering of the text—honorable aims both, but still far short of the quasi-religious experience that the nineteenth century came to demand.

Philosophers provided alibis for the shallow, sociable view of what music should mean. In 1751, in his celebrated *Discours préliminaire* to Denis Diderot's *Encyclopédie,* Jean Le Rond d'Alembert placed music below painting, sculpture, and poetry in the "last rank" of the imitative arts. Its task was to follow nature in both its soothing and its strident manifestations. For d'Alembert, then, as for many others, music at its best followed a distinct literary program. "Any music that paints nothing is mere noise." A quarter of a century later, in 1776, in his *General History of Music*—a work of deep learning, diligent scholarship, and honest affection—Dr. Burney could still define music as "an innocent luxury, unnecessary indeed, to our existence, but a great gratification and improvement of the sense of hearing." It provided a "tranquil pleasure short of rapture" in which "intellect and sensation are equally concerned." In the same decade, the influential German aesthetician Johann Georg Sulzer took the same line in his bulky *Allgemeine Theorie der schönen Künste;* he classified concert music among entertainments, and described concertos, symphonies, sonatas, and solos as offering "a lively and not unpleasant noise, or a civil and entertaining chatter, but not one that engages the heart."[13] The conviction that, on the contrary, making and hearing music engages the heart more surely than any other human experience had to wait for the romantics.*

It was inevitable that such casual attitudes should survive well into the nineteenth century. In 1805, at the Stuttgart court, the highly regarded composer and violinist Louis Spohr had to bite his lip as his noble audience played cards during his performance. And as he made ready for a recital at the court of Braunschweig, the duchess, unwilling to be distracted from *her* card game, enjoined Spohr from playing forte.[14] Although annoyed, he did not go on strike. In fact, the suavest among the musicians of the day learned to accommodate themselves to such survivals of condescending boorishness. In 1812, Rossini surrendered to them by including in his opera *Ciro in Babilonia* an *aria del sorbetto,* "Chi disprezza gl'infelici." That "sherbet aria" was accurately named; Rossini designed this number, literally and deliberately monotonous, for a minor singer to give the audience time and opportunity to converse and spoon ices. As late as 1822, the countess of Blessington, who knew the fashionable musical world in London intimately, noted tartly, "The fine ladies come to see, and to be seen; to excite admiration, and to flirt; and for the latter objects there are worse situations in the world than an Opera box."[15] She was blaming the women, but there is no evidence that music-loving men silenced them.

By the time of Lady Blessington's strictures, E. T. A. Hoffmann's classic

---

*While, as will emerge, the romantics made the most extravagant claims for music, they were not wholly of one mind on this issue. In his *Génie du Christianisme,* Chateaubriand vehemently criticized "modern music"—he meant secular music—for its failure to "express the truth of the passions." He chose love songs as an example: they "imitate the voluptuousness of the senses, but are false in their morals or when they touch on the soul." (*Génie du Christianisme* [1802; 2 vol. ed. Pierre Reboul, 1966], II, 483). True, Chateaubriand was making a tendentious case in behalf of devout religious music. But the point remains that he saw no higher powers at work in music as such.

denunciations of bad manners at musical performances were a decade old. Irritated and outspoken, he denounced good bourgeois at private musicales, the very people proud of their musical refinement, for keeping quiet only during the intermission. The start of the performance, he charged, was a signal to launch a flow of talk. Certainly, he noted sarcastically, the card players tolerated the musical noise graciously. Let a musician flee a prattling social evening to play his instrument in a remote room: the company will run after him to "listen, which is to say, to keep gabbling with the utmost energy."* Public concerts, too, Hoffmann thought, provided splendid opportunities for exchanging the news and flattering the ladies.[16]

For all its tendentiousness, this collective portrait has strong claims on the historian's attention. Hoffmann was a man of many talents—lawyer, judge, caricaturist, composer, music critic, author of haunting tales—and he testified to the power, and the travail, of music in his time with unrivaled expressiveness. It speaks to his cast of mind that many of his celebrated novellas and novels have music for their theme and musicians for their protagonist. In one of them, Hoffmann has Gluck, twenty-two years after his death, appearing to the narrator as an eccentric stranger who plays and sings his *Armida* to perfection from blank pages and in the end, dressed in the court attire of his day, dramatically reveals his identity: "I am Gluck." In another, he has the soprano taking the role of Donna Anna in Mozart's *Don Giovanni* singing to, and mysteriously visiting, the narrator sitting alone in a visitors' box and then, just as mysteriously, dying in the middle of the night as he sits shuddering in his room. In yet another, he has the ailing young singer Antonia, who knows she must die if she ever sings again, violate the injunction and pay the penalty in full. Above all, he has Kapellmeister Johannes Kreisler, the mad musician who is saner than all comfortable *Bürger* put together, raging and rebelling against them—in vain. "I ask, and with justice," Hoffmann bitterly inquired, "who is better off: the public servant, the merchant, the man living off his income who eats and drinks

*Hoffmann, *Kreisleriana,* 2nd ser., no. 1, "Brief des Barons Wallborn an den Kapellmeister Kreisler" (1814), *Werke,* ed. Herbert Kraft and Manfred Wacker, 4 vols. (1967), I, 236. Once again Lady Blessington's comments are apposite: "A real lover of music, would I am persuaded, seldom enter the pit of the Opera; and the boxes never, unless indeed the fair sex were banished from both. A murmur of voices never ceases in the first, and in the second, even in the midst of the most exquisite solo or duet you are deafened by the shrill repetitions from the ladies, of, 'how very fine,' 'quite charming,' 'this passage is divine.' . . . The dear sex think it quite sufficient to give their applause to the music, without giving their attention. Indeed this feeling seems to pervade the greater proportion, if not the whole of the audiences; for, in the finest part of an exquisite quartette, admirably executed, the applause has sometimes been so loud as to interrupt the performance, which has been drowned in noise." Blessington, *The Magic Lantern; or, Sketches of Scenes in the Metropolis* (1822), 55–56.

well, goes for drives as is proper, and whom everyone reverently salutes, or the artist who must wretchedly make do in his fantastical world?"[17]

It is telling for the tensions plaguing nineteenth-century middle-class culture that Kreisler, crusader against the philistine, should become a favorite icon for the Victorian avant-garde, who fancied themselves at war with the bourgeoisie.* The fury of his polemics attests that while the modern art of listening as the most privileged form of introspection was acquiring forceful partisans, it had not yet conquered. In fact, to judge from continuing complaints about inattentive and unmannerly audiences, that art was never perfectly mastered. Old habits died hard. One evening in 1822, still a young man, Hector Berlioz sat in the Paris opera next to a man humming the words of the aria being sung onstage, and he recalled the episode in his memoirs without comment.[18] What is more, the raucous transports that purists were coming to disdain as symptoms of ignorance and ill breeding were not always wholly unwelcome to performers. In Vienna as late as 1860, a reviewer noted that when the opera orchestra played the overture to Luigi Cherubini's *Anacreon,* the performance of the violins aroused such fervor in the hall that the last bars of the "charming" piece were "covered over with noise and applause"—and no one objected.[19] But worshipful silence, little known in the eighteenth century, gradually established itself as the standard in the nineteenth, a standard that composers and conductors, performers and listeners set up and tried to enforce.

There is a certain irony in the romantics' relentless warfare against the unmusical middle classes. Critics of bourgeois culture were acting as educators of the very public they despised. Good listening presupposed a mannerliness and silent inwardness that could be learned. And the nineteenth century produced a small army of single-minded preceptors struggling to train listeners in requisite introspective postures. Their repetitiousness attests to failure upon failure but, at the same time, to an increasingly solemn commitment by concert-going audiences to civilize themselves—and their neighbors.

One of the first among the pedagogues teaching musical manners was Goethe. Presiding over the court theater in the duchy of Weimar, he protested that spectators and listeners, mainly students from the nearby University of Jena, were disgracing theatrical and musical performances with untimely manifestations of pleasure or displeasure. He wanted boisterous "irregularities" like hissing or shouts of "vivat!" stopped, and got them stopped. "With us," he wrote

---

*This so-called great war between the vulgar bourgeoisie, who loved money and hated art, and the avant-garde painters, poets, architects—and composers—for whom Hoffmann supplied much ammunition, was far more complex an affair than he, and his admirers, liked to think.

severely in 1803 to the public official in charge, "no sign of impatience is permitted to occur. Disapproval may draw attention to itself only through silence, approval only through applause," and he meant applause that did not interrupt the performance. What is more, "no actor can be called out, there must be no call to have an aria repeated."[20]

Not long after, a virtuous civic organization took up the cause of self-discipline in Frankfurt, Goethe's hometown. The *Museum,* as it christened itself, was established in 1808, by bourgeois and for bourgeois. A home for the muses, it was not a museum but a private association with limited membership designed to overcome the "poverty-stricken onesidedness" and triviality of local entertainment by promoting a variety of artistic events and improving discussions. In its original statutes, the directors provided guidelines to proper conduct at lectures and concerts: "During literary or musical performances everyone is asked to refrain from speaking. Applause, too, expresses itself better through attentiveness than the clapping of hands. Signs of disapproval are not to be expected from the discretion of the society.—Dogs are not tolerated."[21]

The records of the *Museum* reveal that these arduous prescriptions required frequent reiteration. As late as 1893, a printed program requested members of the audience, "especially in the boxes, not to leave their seats during, or before the conclusion of, a piece." Four years later, the direction, responding to further complaints, urgently appealed to the ladies to "enter the hall without hats." Plainly, the task of training bourgeois in the art of listening was unending. Nor were audiences the only ones needing instruction in respectful silence; musicians, too, were often deficient in the necessary decorum. In 1842, in one among innumerable reminders, the reviewer of a concert by the New York Philharmonic sternly observed that it would contribute to the "dignity as well as the permanency of the society" if "the members of the orchestra refrain from all unnecessary conversation whilst in their places."[22]

Naturally the educators, in the lead German conductors and performers who carried their demanding etiquette across the civilized world, were often frustrated by their listeners' unsublimated need for instant self-expression. Faced with noisy interruptions, conductors would stop the orchestra, scowl at the audience, and at times even lecture it. In 1857, the New York Philharmonic chided the public in its annual report: "We must necessarily insist upon musical good manners. The inattention and heedless talking and disturbance of but a limited number of our audience are proving a serious annoyance to our Philharmonic performances." Mature listeners, the management insinuated, could, and should, take matters into their own hands. "The remedy for this, after all, lies rather with the audience itself than the society authorities. If each little neighborhood would take care of itself, and promptly frown down the few chance disturbers of its pleasures, perfect order would soon be secured. We hope this will be done." In a fit of national self-doubt, the report added, "In foreign audiences it is effectively done."[23]

Had they known of very similar controversies and complaints in Europe, the managers of the Philharmonic might have been less self-denigrating. As late as 1888, two anonymous Dutch concertgoers argued out the question of permissible behavior at public performances in the pages of the *Algemeen Handelsblad*, a liberal Amsterdam daily that local bourgeois found congenial. The first wanted concerts to be less stuffy than they had become: after all music, though surely important, should take second place to audiences' having a good time. To that end, he proposed to permit smoking in the hall once again, allow waiters to circulate taking orders for drinks, and let people talk at will. The second, indignant at such heresies, objected to the noise people were making during performances and to those inconsiderate enough to leave before the end. Clearly the Dutch public needed to be educated in the art of silent listening, and it was the first conductor of the Concertgebouw Orchestra, Willem Kes, who from 1888 on made it his business to purify long-standing habits.[24]

Even the Germans were less disciplined than their religion of music demanded. In 1860, commenting on the conduct of Berliners at the performances of the visiting Italian opera, a critic derided those who attended for strictly nonmusical reasons. There is the rich boxholder who is in love with one of the singers and carries an expensive bouquet for her. There is the man who puts in an appearance only to be seen. "He sits in a conspicuous seat with gigantic opera glasses and is the terror of the whole neighborhood. Unmusical as a dog, he barks and howls his applause in the most tender sustained passages and spoils most arias for the dilettantes sitting near him."[25] This is satire, but there was much to satirize, even in Europe.

In view of this blemished record, it was only natural for reviewers to take special note of the occasions when listeners showed themselves on their best behavior. As early as March 1819, the London *Morning Chronicle* reported that at a recent concert of the Royal Philharmonic orchestra, an audience "of the most select kind," all of it "distinguished by a pure love of excellent music," preserved "silence and attention" during the whole evening. In November 1825, when a touring European opera company performed Rossini's *Il Barbiere di Siviglia* in New York, sung mainly in Italian, well-dressed patrons paid this unaccustomed musical experience the tribute it deserved. "When the orchestra began the overture," a reviewer was pleased to report the next day, "a most gratifying silence was immediately produced, and continued through the performance." Indeed, "the attention was constant, intelligent, and eminently flattering to the artists who were the objects of it."[26] Decades later music critics, obviously not spoiled, still thought exemplary behavior worth an approving comment. "There was no idea of chatter," a reporter wrote about the opening concert at Carnegie Hall, on May 5, 1891. He welcomed the absence of dandies and was gratified to observe that "all was quiet, dignified, soft, slow and noiseless, as became the dedication of a great temple."[27]

But there seemed no way of driving all unbelievers from the temple of music. Frowning down the sinners was never quite enough, and music lovers were usually grateful if the din at least abated. In 1896, in Chicago, the reviewer of a concert led by the pioneering American conductor Theodore Thomas, noted with evident gratification that the playing of the "chef d'oeuvre," Beethoven's *Eroica,* "was received and followed with the closest attention and there was noticeably less conversation than on previous occasions." He speculated that this was probably because the weather had been inclement, so that "few beyond the truly musical were present." This was a shrewd conjecture. By the late Victorian days, the dogma of silent attention had not yet taken hold among boxholders. Preserving in a more democratic age aristocratic styles of conduct in the opera house, they seem to have been the chief culprits. In 1891, the directors of the Metropolitan Opera posted this blunt notice in each box: "Many complaints having been made to the directors of the Opera House of the annoyance produced by the talking in the boxes during the performance, the Board requests that it be discontinued."[28] The less affluent, less snobbish concertgoer sitting in the orchestra and the poverty-stricken music student standing in the top balcony were far more likely to have developed listening into a high art.

Virtually frozen in their seats as they reveled in the spell of sounds, scarcely breathing, consumed with guilt if they rustled with their program, good nineteenth-century listeners controlled their appreciation until the designated moment for emotional explosion had arrived. When, in 1876, Jacques Offenbach gave his American farewell concert at Gilmore Gardens in midtown Manhattan, an enormous arena that could hold an audience of more than eight thousand, listeners overpowered him with their affection—but at the proper moments. "My pieces were encored and encored twice—*bissés et trissés*—with the most strenuous enthusiasm," Offenbach wrote home to his wife. "I tried to put on my overcoat and my hat, to climb down from the stage and implore these amiable Yankees with a look. In vain. They clapped their hands in a frenzy, slapped their canes against the seats and broke the benches until I returned to my pulpit." Once their call for an encore had been gratified, those amiable Yankees showed themselves suitably tamed to breathe in the encore to come. "There was a roar of satisfaction for a moment, and then the most complete silence reigned in the hall during the performance of the piece."[29] This reminiscence sounds like a bit of self-advertising, but in fact concert audiences, at least in the United States, whether excessively pleased or excessively displeased, did break furniture to express their feelings.[30]

The nineteenth-century campaign to raise music to this lonely, sacred eminence was an exacting one, almost against nature.[31] Undivided silent attention to a musical performance does violence to basic human impulses, among the most devout listeners as among the unlettered. That is why the clamor for uncompromising sublimation of the urge to become actively involved proved all the more difficult to enforce: it ran directly counter to a fundamental, very enjoyable experience. Just as many visitors to a museum cannot resist the itch to run their fingers over paintings and sculptures—Freud once said that looking is a substitute for touching—listeners to music, even educated listeners, are tempted to hum along with the tune or sway to the beat, tap their feet or drum their fingers, shake their head or conduct the orchestra from their seat, to say nothing of gratifying the itch to explain their ineffable responses to whoever sits next to them. Listening awakens the urge to mimic marked rhythms, march-like sonorities, stirring crescendos.

Music virtually enforces these primitive physical appetites precisely because its effects travel back to the deepest taproots of human experience. It stimulates barely disguised erotic sensations and revives memories of early agreeable stimuli that call out for repetition: a mother singing her infant to sleep, a father gently rocking the cradle, a parent affectionately reading to a child, a tune heard in cherished, enveloping company. The emotional intensity of listening to music with its aura of direct wordless communication and its vague cognitive boundaries, vaguer by far than those drawn by a poem or a novel, seems to reawaken the early, somehow unforgotten delights that merging with a loving adult can provide.

In themselves, emotional exhibitions are so many homages to the power of music. At moments of highest excitement, Hoffmann's spokesman, Johannes Kreisler, would act out, with passionate gestures and wild exclamations, the bliss and the melancholy that music making released in him. Yet the romantic ideal of decorum decreed that if music was to lift reverent listeners to their finest self, it could do so only if they remained mute, virtually unconscious of the world around them as they concentrated on inspiring sounds. This also explains why serious listeners' irritation with distractions is more than a snobbish sense of their superiority over the uncouth. It almost literally takes them away from themselves. "A shrill-toned, yapping female voice in a near-by box";—I am borrowing Stendhal's enumeration—"or over-heating in the auditorium; or a neighbour leaning back luxuriously in his own seat and communicating a series of steady, maddeningly regular jerks to your own," all act as direct interferences with a deeply regressive communion with one's past.[32]

The nineteenth-century ideal of self-control for the sake of exquisite, if postponed, psychological rewards required a far-reaching reshuffling of the traditional ranking of the arts. Leonardo da Vinci had called music the younger sister of painting, and until late in the eighteenth century, such a verdict had remained largely uncontested. We recall d'Alembert's ranking of the arts, in which music occupied the bottom rung of the ladder. Kant, though he can be quoted on several sides of the argument, ultimately defined music with some condescension as "a play of pleasant sensations" and remained faithful to the time-honored hierarchies. But during the early romantic years, scholars, poets, and novelists subverted the tradition. They elevated music to equality with its sister arts and even attempted to establish its superiority to them. Music lovers might have recalled Shelley's famous claim that poets are the unacknowledged legislators of the world to make the counterclaim that composers, for their part, deserve reverence as the high priests of a new dispensation that provided its devotees with glimpses of the inner life that no other artist could give, not even a poet.

An array of nineteenth-century cultural phenomena, which had little in common except giving unprecedented public exposure to the worship of music, accompanied and reinforced this evolution. The cult of virtuosos like Niccolò Paganini and Franz Liszt, a collective mania that responsible music critics derided as the vulgar overvaluation of mere entertainers, was one of these. The virtual deification of Beethoven, which the same critics thought highly appropriate, was another. By whatever byways it reached the general public, this was the new faith that prompted M. P. Lahalle in 1825 to call music "the privileged art of this century." A few years earlier, a far more considerable figure, Arthur Schopenhauer, had already given this revised ranking of the arts his imprimatur. Music, "the wonderful art of sounds," he wrote in *Die Welt als Wille und Vorstellung,* stands apart from, and above, all the other arts. Its lucid and lovely language, which penetrates to the very core of humanity, is one that everyone understands. The composer, a veritable somnambulist whose reason does not grasp what he is doing, "reveals the innermost essence of the world and imparts the deepest wisdom." Music, he found it necessary to repeat, is never satisfied with the bare surfaces of things, but expresses the very being— *"das An-sich"*—behind all appearance: "the will itself." And he exclaimed over the expressive devices at the composer's disposal. "How wonderful is the effect of *major* and *minor!*"[33] Before many years had gone by, enthusiastic devotees of the religion of music following in Schopenhauer's wake had a majority of the educated public with them.

As we have seen, the romantics had been pioneers in showing the way to this revaluation, and the German romantics were in the vanguard. The short-lived but widely read critic and novelist Wilhelm Heinrich Wackenroder, who died in 1798 at twenty-five, apostrophized his readers in his *Fantasien über die Kunst:* "Let us therefore convert our life into a work of art, and we may boldly assert that we are then already immortal on this earth." And the work of art he had in mind was music, "the most wonderful of them all." It does nothing less than "describe human feelings in a superhuman way." Clothed "in golden clouds of airy harmonies," it shows humans "all the movements of their hearts" in the most spiritual way possible. Wackenroder and his admirers anticipated by decades Walter Pater's aphorism, now badly overworked, that all art constantly aspires toward the condition of music. Their language pervaded German romanticism. For Friedrich Schelling, architecture was "congealed music," while Novalis called poetry "nothing but inward painting and music."[34] E. T. A. Hoffmann's irritated criticism of the musically uncivilized bourgeois amounted to the same celebration with other means.

All these outpourings show a secular religion in the making.[35] That easy, soon banal habit of likening a concert hall to a temple documents that such hyperbole flourished mightily through the century. The religion of music, and its associated art, dance, triumphed almost without resistance, as metaphor and more than a metaphor. In the 1840s, when the celebrated ballerina Fanny Elssler performed in Boston, Margaret Fuller is reported to have whispered to Ralph Waldo Emerson sitting next to her, "This is poetry," to which Emerson whispered back, "No, Margaret. It is religion." Listeners eagerly did their part in worshiping at this modern shrine. Starting in 1848, a troupe of twenty-five German instrumentalists, the Germania Music Society, superbly trained and imbued with a sense of mission to bring their country's classics to the Americans, toured the United States for several years. Suitably impressed, the *New York Herald* noted in reviewing one of its concerts that "the audience appeared as though awed through the whole performance by the sublimity of sounds" so "sensitively expressed" that they seemed to make for "more rapture" than a "supernatural agency" might create.[36]

Some audiences, to be sure, especially in the provinces, were less restrained and, it appeared, incorrigible. At times the conductor of the Germania Music Society felt compelled to stop the concert in protest against loud conversation. Still, by the mid-1860s, Cosima Wagner could take the new doctrine as well established. "Our art—I dare say it—is religion," she wrote King Ludwig II; "its bearers are martyrs."[37] Religious terms came to be routinely enlisted as the highest possible praise. In 1903, the celebrated German conductor Hans Richter, an orthodox Wagnerian, could exclaim to a friend after conducting the *Ring des Nibelungen* at Covent Garden that the English audience had been "the most delightful and most pleasing" part of his experience: "What a devotional—*weihevolle*—silence *during,* and what an enthusiasm *after* each act!"[38]

It requires an exercise of the historical imagination to read this promotion of music to the summit of the arts as authentic, indeed as desperately sincere. Endlessly reiterated, the ideology was spread in essays, stories, and reviews of the most ordinary concerts. The very fact that it drew on a small reservoir of handy similes only tightened its hold on the public mood. It was revealing of that emerging mood that Wackenroder, before 1800, could call his slim collection of connected essays *Herzergiessungen eines kunstliebenden Klosterbruders,* the "effusions," literally the "heart outpourings," of an "art-loving monk." Wackenroder was no Catholic; quite the contrary, his unbounded enthusiasms did not violate the strict Pietist principles with which he had grown up. But, laboring to express the inexpressible, he found the image of the contemplative, unworldly monk the most acceptable vehicle for his "heart outpourings."

To be sure, reviewers trained in music could subject compositions to sober commentary, none more competently than E. T. A. Hoffmann. The late romantic Robert Schumann, as spirited and original a critic as the early Victorian age produced, subjected compositions old and new to the most searching analyses. But not all their fellow romantics greeted these exercises in technical judgment with unmixed delight. Did they not have it on Wordsworth's authority that we murder to dissect?[39] Stendhal recalled concerts with extravagant exclamatory phrases like "blaze of joy" or "musical frenzy" or "uncontrollable delight." Berlioz, as thoroughly versed a professional musician as the century produced, sprinkled his memoirs with excited moments of discovering "that sublime art," in himself "mystical and passionate" feelings, and the insight that this magic had something erotic about it.[40]*

Indeed, with time, the romantics developed a quasi-official vocabulary that

---

*Prominent among nineteenth-century writers who recognized the erotic basis of musical pleasure was Thomas DeQuincey. "If he [the reader] is not (as most are) deafer than the grave to every *deep* note that sighs upwards from the Delphic caves of human life, he will know that the rapture of life (or anything which by approach can merit that name) does not arise, unless as perfect music arises, music of Mozart or Beethoven, by the confluence of the mighty and terrific discords with the subtle concords. Not by contrast, or as reciprocal foils, do these elements act—which is the feeble conception of many—but by union. They are the sexual forces in music; 'male and female created he them'; and these mighty antagonists do not put forth their hostilities by repulsion, but by deepest attraction." "Vision of Life" (1845), *Selected Writings,* ed. Philip Van Doren Stern (1937; ed. 1949), 887.

music lovers were expected to employ, whether they meant it or not. In 1825, the German critic and historian Ludwig Rellstab visited the ailing Beethoven and informed him that he had recently heard his E-flat major quartet, the first of Beethoven's last quartets. Beethoven was briefly pleased and then worried. "It is so difficult that they most likely played it badly! Did it go well at all?" he asked. And then, with rising anxiety, "How did you like it?" To which Rellstab, who had privately dismissed the magnificent opus 127 as showing Beethoven's earlier genius in ruins, dutifully replied, "I was profoundly and devoutly moved to the very core of my heart."[41] He knew not what to feel, but what to say. Flattery has smoothed tensions inherent in human intercourse from the beginning of civilization, but Rellstab's kind of blandishment, a salute to inwardness in the age of Beethoven, had a distinctly modern air about it.

In fact, on the great subject of music, Hoffmann himself took some of the highest flights of lyrical prose the romantic age produced, even in articles loaded with musical examples and theoretical excursions. His most frequently quoted manifesto in behalf of celestial music appears in a review of Beethoven's Fifth Symphony. When we speak of music as an independent art, he wrote, we must mean instrumental music, which "disdains every aid, every admixture of other arts." It alone can "purely express its characteristic nature." Music "is the most romantic of all the arts—one might almost say, the only *purely* romantic." It "discloses to humanity an unknown domain, a world that has nothing in common with the outer world of the senses that surrounds it." In that barely discovered world, music "leaves behind all feelings that can be determined through concepts to surrender itself to the inexpressible."[42]

Hoffmann readily conceded that the "magic power" of music embroidered with texts, as in opera, works like a miraculous elixir. He had, after all, committed more than one opera himself. "Music clothes every passion—love, hatred, fury, despair, etc.—in the purple luster of romanticism." But what he called "the indefinite longing that is the essence of romanticism" was to Hoffmann's mind beyond the grasp of song. Instrumental music alone "irresistibly sweeps away the listener to the marvelous spiritual realm of the infinite." At its most successful, pure organized sound, the symphony above all, lends human life a touch of the divine.[43] This text is a remarkable rhetorical performance, gathering up in tight compass the key words that the nineteenth-century champions of inwardness employed to conjure up untapped sources of secret emotions: "romantic," "unknown," "inexpressible," "infinite," "magic." Later commentaries, by Hoffmann and many others, were variations on these governing themes.

For their part, the French, reluctant to desert the pleasures of opera on behalf of more ethereal blessings, were slow to join the fashion for "pure" music.

Until the Bourbon Restoration, audiences considered Haydn and Beethoven, even Mozart, too obscure and too complicated to be truly enjoyable. Around 1817, Stendhal, that avid operagoer, put it bluntly: "The cultivation of the instrumental department has ruined music." Playing is easier than singing and has, for half a century, "corrupted the taste of the lovers of the vocal."[44] Lahalle's defense of absolute music, dating from 1825, was, at least in France, a bold step into the future. What is the true nature of music? Lahalle asked, and replied, "Let us close our eyes and listen!" That experiment works best "when I suppress the human voice," and when "the imagination is influenced neither by a program nor by any ornamentation." Composers and performers of "descriptive music" who employ special instruments and sounds are like madmen who think they are portraying a storm or a battle when they have merely broken the furniture of their apartment and scattered it around. No doubt, music and poetry can form an alliance, but they always remain distinct in essence: "Poetry acts on the senses through the intelligence and the imagination, while music acts on the imagination and the intelligence through the senses." To combine the two is to sacrifice the latter to the former.[45]

A few years later, the French concert-going public was ready to listen. Berlioz organized performances to provide public exposure to his orchestral works, while the orchestra of the Conservatoire discovered Beethoven. In 1829, in an important appreciation, Berlioz anticipated the rising orthodoxy of reverent attention as he described listening to Beethoven's difficult late, C sharp minor quartet: he found the experience a nightmare that brought tears of anguish and terror to his eyes.[46] Some time after this, George Sand told Liszt, "The music of Meyerbeer creates only images, that of Beethoven gives birth to feelings and ideas. Meyerbeer has a magnificent spectacle pass before your eyes; he places his personages before you. Beethoven makes you enter once again into the most intimate depths of the self; everything you have felt, experienced, your loves, your suffering, your dreams, all are revived by the breath of his genius and throw you into an infinite reverie."[47] The most intimate depths of the self creating an infinite reverie—a German romantic could not have said it better.

Berlioz's confession proves that the magnetism of music could make sensitive music lovers weep. "Good God!" exclaimed the French romantic poet Antoine Fontaney in the mid-1830s, in the privacy of his diary. "What charm there is in music! I could almost cry!"[48] The German pianist and conductor Karl Halle, better known in his English incarnation as Sir Charles Hallé, a seasoned professional musician, would shed tears as he listened to Jenny Lind, "the Swedish Nightingale," and over the "affecting scenes" of the operas he was conducting. The "beauty of the music" was too much for his composure. And that prolific neoclassical painter Jean Auguste Dominique Ingres, an amateur violinist far more energetic than talented, sobbed as he played Mozart sonatas with Hallé at the piano. So did the audience, Hallé recalled, "though not tears of delight."[49]

Musicians, then, far from too hardened to permit themselves such expressive gestures, reveled in them. In 1892, writing from Detroit to his "beloved friend" the music publisher and concert agent Albert Gutmann, the German pianist Alfred Grünfeld fondly recalled their last encounter, "as I played for you, as a farewell, the F-minor fantasy of Chopin. Seeing you weep, I could not forget this impression for a long long time."[50] When Grünfeld wrote this letter, such memories might be indelible, but they had been platitudes for years, the official attitude not merely of professional makers of music but of the most pedestrian bourgeois listener.

Berlioz exhibits the exalted—and selective—ideology of tears in one vivid scene. He recalled that he had once heard Liszt ruining Beethoven's Moonlight Sonata with extraneous trills, tremolos, and embellishments. But in a later recital, Liszt showed himself more pious as he performed the same piece for a small group of friends. It was late in the afternoon, and the lamp was going out. Berlioz welcomed that: he thought the dim twilight would be right for the opening adagio movement from the C-sharp minor sonata. But Liszt went him one better: he asked that all lights be extinguished and the fireplace covered. Then, in total darkness, Berlioz remembered, "after a moment's pause, rose in its sublime simplicity the noble elegy he had once so strangely disfigured; not a note, not an accent was added to the notes and the accents of the author. It was the shade of Beethoven, conjured up by the virtuoso to whose voice we were listening. We all trembled in silence, and when the last chord had sounded no one spoke—we were in tears."[51] The lesson was plain: a true music lover does not waste his emotions on self-advertising virtuosity; only the real thing will penetrate the defenses of his inner self.

The prominence of Beethoven in these anecdotes is striking; it is impossible to exaggerate his share in fostering the nineteenth-century art of listening. The romantics' promotion of absolute music to the place of honor in humanity's quest for its soul was accompanied, and fueled, by a corresponding promotion of the composer.[52] When they paid their respects to the genius, who is not enslaved to the rules and differs in kind from the merely talented practitioner, they were breathing life into an idealization familiar from the days of the Renaissance. To the divine Michelangelo they joined that towering contemporary figure, the divine Beethoven. He seemed the embodiment of the romantic genius. Like Wordsworth's Newton, he had voyaged through strange seas of thought alone.

Thinking chiefly of Beethoven, the romantics hailed the genius as both human and more than human. He feels what everyone feels, but, vibrating to melodies to which others are deaf, feels it more keenly than ordinary mortals—more keenly and more productively. For, infinitely superior to the inarticulate mass of men and women, he lends his feelings memorable shape. The composer of genius pours out his self to the world, nourishing others with his soul's blood. Wagner in the throes of composing described his state as somnambulism.[53] None of this implied naive, untutored spontaneity. Hoffmann, for one, took care to emphasize that while Beethoven governs the "inner realm of sounds as absolute sovereign," he does so with an inspiring respect for musical structure, with the "careful prudence"—*Besonnenheit*—"inseparable from the true genius and nourished by the continuous study of art."[54] Schumann, for another, consistently argued that inspiration cannot dispense with craftsmanship.

This insistence on coupling the intuitive insights of the genius with his prudence throws dazzling light on nineteenth-century inwardness.* It reveals that to the romantics, aesthetic subjectivity consisted of two closely allied but distinct mental operations: the musical—or painterly or poetic—idea welling up from the unconscious, and the schooled introspection that allows the creator to criticize, revise, and refine his creation. Inspiration has always elicited awe; it seems to appear from nowhere or, better, from a mysterious wellspring to which the creator knows he must attend but cannot identify. In comparison, the work of self-criticism seems a mundane feature of all-too-human craftsmanship. But, wherever one ranks conscious control on the ladder of human excellence, however plainly it is linked to the outside world as an internalization of teachers' precepts and reviewers' complaints, it *is* a mental act, no enemy to inwardness. The point remained that the romantics were confident that the bulk of mediocre bourgeois music lovers, hampered by severely limited horizons, could never adequately respond either to inspiration or to craftsmanship. The more sublime of Beethoven's compositions, the fruit of a marriage between his indwelling gifts and his arduous training, must be beyond them. Later generations would be more liberal in their assessment of bourgeois capacities for inwardness, even in music. It was, after all, around them everywhere.

Among the witnesses to the spreading new ideology of listening, and among its most agreeable agents, the practitioners of the sister art of painting were perhaps the most telling. In 1867, Winslow Homer dramatized the intimacy of the two arts with *The Studio:* two musicians are playing side by side in a painter's

---

*It will reappear several times in the course of these pages, first of all as a prominent tenet in romantic aesthetics. See below, esp. p. 50.

studio, one the cello, the other the violin, using their easels as music stands. On the floor, Homer has cunningly put sheet music with "W. A. Mozart" legible at the top. And in 1885, Henri Fantin-Latour's homage to music, *Autour du piano,* grouped several musician friends around Emmanuel Chabrier at the keyboard.

At times, a measure of wishful thinking seems to have governed these nine-teenth-century canvases, depicting as a fact what was only an aspiration. In *Le Concert,* Jacques Tissot shows the hall of a magnificent, brightly lit mansion; a richly dressed cosmopolitan audience, sitting in easy chairs or standing on an elegantly curving staircase, crowds around the celebrated violinist Madame Neruda. Some are still chatting with one another as the soloist makes ready to play. But talk is clearly about to cease: when *Le Concert* was first exhibited at the Royal Academy of Arts, in 1875, it bore the title *Hush.* Thus, allying themselves with conductors of symphony orchestras or indignant listeners in the concert hall, painters helped to hush listeners, whether bourgeois or aristocrats, by posing them in a variety of, or readiness for, devotional postures.

Artists did not confine their celebration of spiritual engrossment to music making; Sir Lawrence Alma-Tadema, for one, painted scenes in which listeners give their earnest attention to a reading from Homer or some other favorite poet.[55] But musical moments remained a favorite subject for depicting soulful-ness in action. Many painters found their preoccupation with respectful audi-ences easy and natural; they consorted with performers and, often, cultivated musical talents of their own. The versatile William Sidney Mount, in short, was far from alone. It has not escaped his biographers that James McNeill Whistler liked to give his canvases suggestive musical titles—nocturnes, and symphonies. And it is well known that in 1842 Ingres, that impassioned violinist whose interest in music never flagged, painted *Cherubini and the Muse of Lyric Poetry,* his accolade to a composer he admired and, more, to an art he cherished. The aged Cherubini, deep in thought, is seated, his right hand touching his temple, while a young woman in classical garb holds her hand over his head in blessing. Again, Eugène Delacroix, for years the intimate of Berlioz and Liszt, was a lifelong, indefatigable concertgoer.[56] And E. T. A. Hoffmann long wavered among three careers: painting, writing, composing. In an age of increasingly severe specialization, Victorian artists were among the last Renaissance men.

The knowledgeable involvement of nineteenth-century painters with com-posers and performers lent their canvases an atmospheric authenticity. True, musical subjects had been a staple for centuries: cavaliers serenading Venuses, St. Cecilia at the keyboard, angels massed in a celestial concert singing to the greater glory of God. So had still lifes caressing handsome instruments with the light gleaming on the rich wood of a viola da gamba. And Dutch genre painters had featured music makers as they captured convivial concerts, carousing peasants, feasting bourgeois, or handsome ladies under melodious amorous siege. The originality of nineteenth-century painters lay not in their choice of music and musicians but in the way they imported a religious aura into their depictions of secular concerts private and public.

Many of these Victorian canvases have been casualties of time and harsh critical verdicts, but their very mediocrity made them all the more effective agents for the art of listening. At mid-century, the Belgian artist Edouard Jean Conrad Hamman, whose paintings of famous composers were widely reproduced, did a *Mozart in Vienna*. The composer is at the keyboard, surrounded by a cultivated audience clearly spellbound by his performance; a woman sitting behind him manifests her thoughtful concentration by supporting her chin in her hand. By this time, listening had developed beyond appropriate ritual words to appropriate ritual gestures. It is hardly necessary to point out that Hamman's painting is an anachronistic fantasy, a projection of nineteenth-century ideals on an eighteenth-century scene; in his time, Mozart had not enlisted such devotion. Again, the German painter August Borckmann, who in the 1880s achieved prominence with a series of pictures on music, painted an odd concoction, *Beethoven and the Rasumowsky Quartette*. It reads almost like a test in which viewers are asked to identify inaccuracies: an idealized Beethoven stands in the middle of a handsome room conducting a string quartet, while behind him a woman plies the piano. But what matters here is Borckmann's audience; men and women are visibly absorbed in the music that this impossible aggregation is offering them.

Most canvases about listening were not quite so absurd. There was the once famous classic of popular art, Lionello Balestrieri's *A Beethoven Sonata*. Exhibited in 1900 at the Paris World's Fair and awarded a gold medal, it traveled from country to country in engravings. In a smallish, sparsely furnished room, a violinist and a pianist at an upright are playing for a silent audience of five. To leave no doubt about the object of their worship, Balestrieri has included a plaster cast of Beethoven's death mask hanging beside the piano. Each listener displays a distinct reverential attitude. One sits hands in his pockets, intent; another is bent forward, head in hands. By this time, listeners living up to the sacred task of listening by covering their eyes probably outranked those who were merely silent.

As they offered these portrayals of inwardness, artists increasingly put the spotlight on the listener. In the age of flamboyant virtuosos—from the 1830s until after mid-century—they could hardly afford to neglect the performer altogether. But even when they focused on the performer, his—or her—impact on an invisible audience was strongly implied by the musician's transfigured, or diabolical, expression. Delacroix's somber portrait of 1831, *Paganini Playing the*

Violin, is a study in the demonic; a wizard is bewitching his listeners. Delacroix has the emaciated violinist standing in dim light, dressed in black except for the startling white accents of his shirt and collar; he is playing with his eyes closed and looks as though the rumor that he had sold his soul to the devil might well be true. There were times, it seems, when the deity of music was Satan.[57] Liszt, too, was depicted as a maker of magic who enslaves his audience. While the artists who did his portrait did not belong to a single school, they developed predictable conventions inviting predictable responses. They liked to place him at the keyboard, displaying the famous profile of which he was justly proud, looking slightly upward, unseeing, as though receiving a message inaudible to lesser mortals. And almost unconsciously, he seems to be transmitting that message to the listeners who have come under his spell.

In the best-known of these exercises in virtuoso worship, Josef Danhauser's *Liszt's Moment of Consecration* of 1840, Liszt is actually staring at an object that others, too, can see: an over-life-size bust of Beethoven. A large and complex composition, the canvas is a farrago of quotations and imaginary conviviality. Liszt's audience is French, while the rosy-tinted, cloudy skyscape outside the window says "Vienna." So does the ornate grand piano built by Conrad Graf, once Beethoven's piano maker, who had commissioned the painting. His name plaque is conspicuous above the pianist's right hand: this solemn depiction of a consecrated musical moment intersects with the self-promoting advertising needs of commercial culture. The sheet music scattered about intimates that Liszt is playing one of his own compositions. His audience consists of a distinguished assembly of writers and performers, all of them entranced, each absorbed in the recital in characteristic fashion: Paganini and Rossini, the two professional musicians in the room, stand in the background, quietly observing the incomparable keyboard sorcerer; Victor Hugo, standing behind George Sand, leans on her wing chair, a half-closed pamphlet held negligently; for her part Sand, in trousers, is stretched out to full length, the cigar dangling in her left hand forgotten, her right hand reaching over to her neighbor, Alexandre Dumas *père,* as if to seek his hand in companionship or warn him to be silent. Dumas himself holds a closed book on his lap and glances at Liszt with a rather inscrutable look, apparently astonished at the witchcraft that is holding him, the great talker, silent for once.

As is only appropriate, the most intimately involved of the listeners is Liszt's mistress, the countess Marie d'Agoult. Seated on a floor cushion, her back to the viewer, she is leaning against the piano and oblivious of everything but the music and the musician. And that musician seems aware only of Beethoven as he communes with his idol. Danhauser has tried to capture each figure, performer and listeners alike, alone with ineffable thoughts, transfiguring a conversation piece into a devotional scene, complete with deity, high priest, and pious communicants.[58]

Later in the century, painters would become even more emphatic about the art of listening as they virtually dispensed with the performer. The protagonist of Arthur Hughes's provocatively titled *Memories* is a richly dressed young woman listening to an unobtrusive violinist who sits on a remote window seat. Facing the viewer directly, she is on her knees with an open, erotically suggestive, jewel box by her left hand. Her large eyes, dark pools of unfathomable musings, are wide, almost staring. Plainly, she has been stimulated by the music to think thoughts about far-away, very important events. Again, in a subtle drawing, *Le Concert,* Daumier focuses on a single listener, a middle-aged man shown frontally, slumped in an upholstered chair. His arms lie relaxed, his eyes are open but dreaming, as a violinist and pianist play a duet in the background. And in Alma-Tadema's *An Audience* of 1881, two thoughtful young women appear at half length, one of them with her hands folded and the other with her lips pressed together. The painter refuses to specify what they are listening to, but that they are listening with all their might is inscribed on their faces.

From such somewhat elusive testimonials, it was but a step to a remarkable psychological study by the Belgian artist Fernand Khnopff. His *En écoutant du Schumann* of 1883, places his listener, a woman sitting bolt upright, into the middle of a tastefully appointed bourgeois interior, her face hidden behind a hand reaching to her temple. Only the right arm and hand of the pianist on whose performance she is fixed are barely visible at deep left. For Khnopff, the art of listening has replaced the art of playing. It is interesting to note that while a majority of the protagonists in these canvases are women, men too are shown responding to the rituals of inwardness. The dominant ideology of the nineteenth century took women to be more sensitive, more passive, more receptive than the male.[59] But men, even manly men, were far from immune to music's charms.

Wagner's *Festspielhaus* in Bayreuth stands as the supreme monument to the lengths to which devout lovers of music could drive the art of listening in the Victorian decades. The Wagnerians elevated—their opponents said, debased— the experience of music into a cult, a cult strangely able to arouse both Teutonic fervor and soulful inwardness. Opened in 1876 with the *Ring* cycle, after years of single-minded planning, shameless fund-raising, and envenomed controversy, Bayreuth was designed, and widely received, as a shrine to which select spirits made pilgrimages as to a Mecca of music. Contemptuous of what they derided as the histrionic vulgarities of foreign composers, they came to hear not operas but the hallowed German Music of the Future. Numbers of them displayed their emotional engagement with fits of trembling, of weeping, even of fainting.

With these displays in mind, observers domestic and foreign identified Wagner's temple to narcissism—his narcissism—as a milestone in the spiritual education of music lovers. In 1910, in its article on applause, the *Encyclopaedia Britannica* summed up what was by then conventional wisdom: "The reverential spirit which abolished applause in church, has tended to spread to the theatre and the concert room, largely under the influence of the quasi-religious atmosphere of the Wagner performances at Baireuth."[60] The paradox of the ideology of listening, which imposed on audiences the most rigorous suppression of activity but could be a spur to action, was more acute at Bayreuth than it had been—and would be—anywhere else. There were times, it turned out, when sublimation did not have sublime results.

Articulate, angry, in no way disposed to forgive the slights that Wagner had visited on them, his antagonists disparaged the Bayreuth spirit as a supreme perversion. Not all their hostility sprang from pique; the partisans of Brahms, in particular, rejected Wagner's musical metaphysics as a false religion, a self-indulgent heresy. They found Bayreuth redolent with an erotic adulation almost unconcealed, the atmosphere drenched in incense to the Master. For Elizabet von Herzogenberg, an intelligent, gifted amateur musician and an outspoken, sarcastic Brahmsian, the Bayreuth festival was seduction posing as salvation. The faithful, she charged, "attend 'Parsifal' the way Catholics on Good Friday attend holy graves; for them it has become a divine service." To her mind "the whole gang" of Wagner's acolytes was "in an unnaturally elevated, hysterically rapturous condition, like Ribera's saints with their uplifted eyes."[61] Her assault may sound intemperate, but it is certain that when Cosima Wagner identified music with religion, she had her husband's music in mind.

Of course, Wagner had not been the first to equate music with religion. As we have seen, facile metaphors like "piety" or "temple" had disfigured journalism for decades. But the Wagnerites took this language literally. In the 1880s, Nietzsche, disappointed in what he considered Wagner's betrayal of his ideals and no longer his admiring partisan, drastically drew the consequences and denounced Wagner as a "despairing *décadent,* grown rotten." To Nietzsche's mind, the spirit of this self-advertising and self-glorifying manipulator of human souls had infected music with a deadly disease and "conducted the *very last* campaign of war and reaction against the spirit of the Enlightenment."[62] This belated romantic, he believed, was also the most unhealthy and the most dangerous.

No doubt the arena of which Wagner had long dreamt, and had the architect Gottfried Semper design for him, encouraged, virtually forced, listeners to listen, and nothing else. Writing to Wagner in 1865, when the *Festspielhaus* was still a utopian fantasy, Ludwig II of Bavaria, whose infatuation with Wagner's vision cost him much anxiety and more money, greeted the idea of Bayreuth in his characteristic organ tones: it must be entered only by "the consecrated, the art-inflamed. Only your holy sounds may fill its halls."[63] His hyperbole anticipated the reality. The *Festspielhaus* was built of wood, with simple wooden seats, guaranteeing resonant acoustics and allowing no architectural decor to interfere with the listener's rapture. Deliberately echoing the amphitheaters of ancient Greece, where music had been an integral part of an all-embracing ritual, the auditorium did away with center aisles and, more important, with boxes; all that mattered were the sounds and sights that Wagner had conjured up. Other innovations underscored these aids to rapt concentration: the *Festspielhaus* was the first opera auditorium to douse all the lights, and it consigned both orchestra and conductor to a deep pit, rendering both invisible to the audience. Neither players plying their instruments nor the kapellmeister waving his baton could distract worshipers from Wagner's total work of art.

The political intentions of Wagner, including his chauvinistic ideology proposing to cleanse German music of such alien admixtures as Jewish and French compositions, were blatant enough. But the impact of Bayreuth on the history of inwardness remains ambiguous. On the one hand, it worked to push the experience of listening beyond the intensity available to ordinary mortals. On the other hand, it robbed true believers of their clear sense of separate selfhood. Like other crowds, only more decorously, participants in the Bayreuth ambiance surrendered their individuality for a shared spiritual bath and a collective adoration of the genius who had brought them there.

Driven to fever pitch, the Wagnerites sometimes even exceeded the rigorous standards that the Bayreuth establishment had laid down. In 1888, Cosima Wagner, who had presided over the grail since her husband's death five years earlier, complained of the "temple guardians" who were (as the Germans say) more papist than the pope. "They're the ones who hiss when a naive audience at the end of the second act of *Parsifal* gives a cheer." Such a sign of approval, she thought, was "as necessary to those poor people who have wholly surrendered themselves as a sip of water is to a thirsting animal."[64] Richard Wagner's widow was not noted for her sense of humor, but in her lofty and irritable way, she found the zealots amusing. Though herself among the chief architects of the Bayreuth doctrine, she dimly sensed that extremist demands for *Innerlichkeit* could reduce sublimation to a distasteful mixture of self-aggrandizing snobbishness and self-abasing idolatry. In music, that most romantic of the arts, as in literature, philosophy, or politics, the triumph of inwardness proved a threat to bourgeois minds as much as a blessing.

⟡ ONE ⟡

The Re-enchantment of the World

T he prophets, poets, and propagandists of the nineteenth-century quest for
the naked heart were the romantics. They explored its possibilities and complicated its outlines; they refined its vocabulary and more or less unwittingly
shaped the bourgeoisie's perception of the self for decades ahead. The stakes
were high: leading romantics saw it as their historic mission to re-enchant the
world. They felt an urgent need to restore the sense of wonder and mystery that
eighteenth-century deists, skeptics, and atheists—Voltaire and Hume and Holbach and their fellow mutineers against faith—had attempted to erase with their
bloodless scientism, impious insults, and shallow witticisms. The Enlightenment had, romantics charged, damaged the inner life almost beyond repair.
Theirs was a brave effort. Disenchanted with disenchantment, they worked to
undo the secularization of the world that had been the dismal accomplishment
of their fathers' generations.

But they rarely acted in concert; the romantics wrote their novels and recited
their poems, painted their canvases and composed their music in intensely
personal ways. No wonder their first historians were already tempted to define
their style of thinking as the style that defies definition. As early as 1836, Søren
Kierkegaard protested "against the view that romanticism can be com-
prehended in one concept, for romanticism implies overflowing all boundaries."[1] Still, while the romantics' differences of outlook call for fine discriminations, one common element dominated their work: in powerful, often
programmatic ways, they turned to the interior. The young Coleridge once
reproached his friend Robert Southey with pleading "for the Wisdom of mak-

ing Self an undiverging Center," but it did not take him long to practice what he had denounced.[2]

So did the other romantics, from the outset. In 1798, the poet Friedrich von Hardenberg—known to the world by his pseudonym, Novalis—famously, if a little obscurely, set down the romantic program in one of his notebooks: "The world must be romanticized. Thus one rediscovers the original meaning." To romanticize is nothing but to enhance one's powers. "The lower self is identified with a better self in this operation." Some years later, Hegel, no romantic, summed up this assignment more succinctly: "The true contents of the romantic are absolute inwardness" and its corresponding form, "spiritual subjectivity"—*absolute Innerlichkeit* and *geistige Subjektivität.*[3]

The romantics' individualistic ways of celebrating the inner life, though, guaranteed that their inwardness added up to a multifarious banquet of sentiments and convictions.* All attempts to reduce romanticism to an easy formula are mocked by the imp of the particular. It differed from country to country, generation to generation, often romantic to romantic. In early 1825, the French painter and critic Etienne Jean Delécluze, a liberal who knew everyone and numbered the arch-romantic Stendhal among his friends, gave up in resignation. "All those who take the name of romantic differ so much in their opinions, start from principles so different, and arrive at conclusions so opposite from each other that it is truly impossible to extract a basic idea from all this chaos."[4] He had company in his bewilderment, but his resignation, if understandable, was premature. It is true that far from being an army of zealots, or even a school, the romantics created a mood rather than a movement. But the mood made history.

When romantics did try to construct a movement, they failed. In the late 1790s, a small clan of promising German critics and scholars, poets and novelists established an informal but ardent partnership in Jena and Berlin. They came before the public in May 1798, with the first issue of the *Athenäum*. Its editors and animating spirits were the learned brothers Schlegel, who launched their ideological aphorisms in that influential but short-lived periodical and enlisted other exploratory romantics like Novalis as contributors.† The two were a remarkable pair. The elder, August Wilhelm, born in 1767, was through his long life a popular lecturer and prolific author on the history and theory of

---

*It is telling that some historians of the period, despairing of finding unity amidst such diversity, should have adopted a plural: romanticisms.

†Novalis contributed essays, reviews, poems, and fragments. Other *Athenäum* authors included the novelist, poet, playwright, and translator Ludwig Tieck; the theologian Friedrich Daniel Ernst Schleiermacher with "ethical rhapsodies"; and the philosophers Friedrich Wilhelm Joseph von Schelling and Johann Gottlieb Fichte.

literature and the brilliant translator of Shakespeare, whom he made into an arch-romantic. Wearied by years of wandering, he settled at the University of Bonn after the Napoleonic Wars and retreated from the contemporary world to the study of Sanskrit. His brother Friedrich, five years his junior, was almost as scholarly as August Wilhelm, but more volatile in temper and more original in spirit, a provocative editor, aphorist, and, in his brother's wake, orientalist. In their own judgment, they were, with their co-authors at the *Athenäum,* "authentically revolutionary,"[5] constituting a family of precocious talents, and engaged in what they hailed as the long overdue restoration of the inner life to thought and literature.

Bound together by fervent friendships, the little band was tested by clashes of temperament and erotic rivalries—tested and found wanting. The women among them were as brilliant as the men, though, hampered by social conventions, not so productive. They were also a source of strain: anything but reticent, they did not get on easily with one another.* Appointments in distant cities, discordant personalities, disagreements over literary questions soon scattered the friends. Friedrich Schlegel's announced ideal of "symphilosophizing" proved utopian, in fact against the romantic grain; extravagant emotional overvaluations generated lasting estrangements.† So did conflicting religious commitments: in 1808, after years of vacillation, Friedrich Schlegel converted to Roman Catholicism while his brother, fighting off similar seductions, sturdily reaffirmed his Protestantism. Romantic individualism was an exhilarating ideal but, quite as much, a powerful obstacle to forming an enduring party. Its accent on the subjective sphere took its toll on social cohesion.

The most prominent English romantics whom hindsight has thrown together—Keats, Shelley and Byron, Coleridge, Wordsworth and Scott—provide equally persuasive evidence for such haunting divisions. Although Wordsworth and Coleridge kept up a troubled friendship, they had little truck with the others except to criticize them. Keats denigrated Byron as unoriginal and heartless; Byron derided Keats and rejected much of Wordsworth's finest poetry as puerile stuff. Wordsworth had mixed feelings about Shelley's verse, was cool to Keats, and denounced Byron as vicious. Shelley was an atheist and a republican; Coleridge, after a radical phase, a loyal upholder of church and state. Wordsworth was ambivalent about the greatest eighteenth-century neoclassi-

---

*The most remarkable intelligence among these women, August Wilhelm Schlegel's wife, Caroline, who had already weathered some searing amorous adventures before she married him, left her husband to join, and marry, another romantic, the philosopher Schelling.

†They reverberate with erotic overtones: when, late in 1797, Schleiermacher moved in with Friedrich Schlegel for a time, the two with heavy jocularity called their intimacy a marriage.

cist poet, Alexander Pope, Coleridge appreciated merely his wit, Byron enthusiastically hailed him as his ancestor. The arch-romantic Sir Walter Scott was delighted with a publisher's commission to edit the works, and write the life, of that most unromantic Restoration dramatist and critic John Dryden, whom he much admired. In 1815, amidst this confusion, Coleridge said it all: the notion of a "*new school* of poetry" was a "fiction."[6]

Such diversity also separated romantics in France and elsewhere. Benjamin Constant, novelist and political philosopher, was an advanced liberal; François René de Chateaubriand, the celebrated poet, novelist, and autobiographer, a moderate royalist—most of the time. Théodore Géricault made himself, in Jules Michelet's words, "the Correggio of suffering," an epithet borne out by his stunning and gruesome *Raft of the Medusa,* which depicts shipwrecked survivors desperately signaling to a ship on the distant horizon; while Eugène Delacroix, as political an artist as Géricault, also drew inspiration from history and the Orient.[7] Romantic painters everywhere mingled dream and reality, politics and religion in unique mixtures. Only Caspar David Friedrich could have painted his symbolic landscapes. And romantic composers resembled no one but themselves: Berlioz did not sound like Schumann or Schubert like Meyerbeer.

It was typical for their insistence on being themselves at all costs that some romantics refused to choose between public and private spheres and found their fixation on the self no obstacle to active intervention in the world. Chateaubriand punctuated his literary career with that of a diplomat; Benjamin Constant, perhaps best known for his self-lacerating romance *Adolphe,* was an influential political activist; Novalis, that quintessential unworldly poet, worked as a trained mining administrator; E. T. A. Hoffmann, as we have already seen, writer, composer, painter, and music critic, the embodiment of the romantic imagination, was a hardworking and respected judge.

To complicate definitions further, many romantics cordially despised one another, and at times said so in print. August Wilhelm Schlegel was the target of much heartfelt abuse. Constant denounced him as a bore, coward, and egotist. Stendhal called him a miserable pedant, a mere translator who fancied himself a thinker.[8] In 1816, William Hazlitt opened his review of Schlegel's major work, the *Vorlesungen über dramatische Kunst und Litteratur,* with the curt statement "The book is German." He did not mean it as a compliment but thought all German romantics, not Schlegel alone, pompous in the extreme; encumbered with "a large apparatus" of metaphysical absurdities, he wrote, "their pretensions have always much exceeded their performance."[9] Some of these dislikes sprang from private resentments; others were doctrinaire judgments drawing on vague notions about national character. But they disclose incurable tensions in what posterity has rashly described as a united army of rebels rising up together against moribund neoclassical doctrines in the arts and literature.

The notion that romanticism might be defined by pitting it against classicism was born in the romantic era and has enjoyed a long run. Goethe claimed paternity; August Wilhelm Schlegel and, following him, Madame de Staël, enlisted the notion in their effort to understand, and advance, the romantics' cause. Chateaubriand took it as fundamental; so did Stendhal.* But this stab at clarification, though far from meaningless, was quickly subverted: Byron felt uncomfortable with it, and in 1824 the young Victor Hugo exclaimed, "Romanticism, classicism—what do these names matter?" He soon changed his mind, but in 1833 the English novelist Edward Bulwer-Lytton noted that "the style of Byron is at once classical and romantic," and "even a Shelley, whom some would style emphatically of the Romantic School, has formed himself on the model of the Classic."[10] It was a shrewd point and had been in the air for some time. Goethe, of all people, once famously defined the romantic as sick and the classical as healthy, but for much of the time, he wrote like a romantic and served German romantics as a much admired exemplar.

Similar conundrums confound the romantics' timetable. Setting aside some early tentative manifestations, one may date the origins of English and German romanticism with deceptive precision from 1798, the year of Wordsworth and Coleridge's *Lyrical Ballads* and of the Schlegels' *Athenäum*. But in France neoclassicism fought off romantic tendencies tenaciously; it was kept alive by the Revolution and survived the reign of its supreme sponsor, Napoleon I. Not without protests: in her novels and polemics Madame de Staël made defiant romantic statements, and so did the young Chateaubriand. In 1824, Louis Simon Auger, permanent secretary of the Académie française and ardent defender of time-honored classical ideals in literature, launched a venomous attack on the romantics, but was relieved to find that "the sect is new and still counts only a few avowed initiates."[11] If it was dangerous at all, he thought, that was because its devotees were young and fervent. The most spectacular founding statements of French romanticism, then, were not issued until 1827, with Victor Hugo's preface to *Cromwell,* and 1830, when Hugo's tragedy *Hernani* prompted noisy battles in the audience between the supporters and the opponents of unconventional romantic drama.

---

*Romanticism, to Stendhal, was modern, authentic, alive; classicism, remote, artificial, dead. The romantics, he wrote, produce literary works that give people the greatest possible pleasure; the classicists, in contrast, "would have given the greatest pleasure to their great-grandparents." *Racine et Shakespeare. Etude sur le romanticisme* (1970), 71. For Chateaubriand, see *Mémoires d'outre-tombe* (1849–50; ed. Maurice Levaillant and Georges Moulinier, 2 vols., 1951; 3rd ed., 1957), I, 272.

By that time, the romantic impulse had been largely exhausted in England and the German states; most of its votaries were dead or unproductive or had shifted their attention to esoteric scholarship. The romantic epochs in other countries—in Scandinavia and Italy or in the United States—also followed distinctive rhythms of their own, each virtually impossible to coordinate with the others. At the same time, romantics in one country left their mark on eager disciples abroad. Coleridge the sage is unthinkable without his close reading of German romantic philosophers, notably Schelling, the aesthetician, theologian, and philosopher of Nature whom we shall meet again; Goethe, Edgar Allan Poe, and many others were enamored of Byron's poetry; Delacroix confessed a debt to an English friend, the precocious landscapist Richard Bonington; the verse of Charles Augustin Sainte-Beuve, France's most penetrating critic, openly derived from the English lake poets; Beethoven reshaped the musical life of the nations, even of resistant France. In short, a period with a reputation for championing the unfettered individual exemplified that ideal in its dizzying variety.

Yet, in the end, what would matter more to nineteenth-century culture than the romantics' diversity was what appeared as their single, largely irresistible romantic message: an obsession with the deeper reaches of the feelings. More passionately and consistently than their predecessors, the romantics experienced and interpreted the self, pursuing it to its most secret hiding places. Freud was no romantic, but the self-analysis he launched in the mid-1890s reads like a late fulfillment of the romantic program. Obviously, the romantics did not invent the modern self; that had been in the making at least since Montaigne. But they left a potent legacy to the century as models of self-reflection in solitude or as feeling individuals responding to the world in the domains of politics, religion, or love.

I. The Imagination Unleashed

The notion of a coherent romantic movement may be untenable, at best a convenience. But the sense that romantics mounted a massive collective rebellion against the Enlightenment is far from fanciful. While the likes of Stendhal, Hazlitt, or Shelley proudly claimed the heritage of the eighteenth century, many of their fellows rejected what they saw as its repellent subversive agenda. To make this case at all plausible, it became necessary to invent a disagreeable stick figure: the coffee house pundit who spouts an arrogant and shallow doctrine characterized by unbounded faith in reason, irresponsible optimism, and sovereign disregard of historical development. This required romantics to repress the Enlightenment's sympathetic view of passion, its pessimistic streak, and its touches of political realism.* No doubt, the romantics who distanced themselves from the philosophes had good reasons, but they were no less unjust to the philosophes than the philosophes had been to the Christians.

True, in the hands of free spirits like Byron or Constant, romantic self-exploration liberated energies that subverted traditional ways of thinking. Still, most romantics found that they could not live with the dominant Enlightened ideal, the autonomous self making its way in an indifferent nature. Self-determination and daring declarations of intellectual independence generated a frightening vacuum where there had been faith. Adrift in a world from which the divine father had disappeared, then, romantics rejected the philosophes' critical spirit and retreated to a safer posture supported by sacred books and sacred paternal figures. Some of them reveled in the heady sense that they were making all things new. But more of them eagerly returned to old verities or, estranged from the doctrines of their fathers but desperately in want of spiritual shelter, constructed authoritarian doctrines of their own.

Rage at the Enlightenment's work of demolition pervaded romantic declarations both published and unpublished. To Friedrich Schlegel, Paris, widely recognized as the headquarters of the philosophes, was the "new Sodom." Such biblical echoes made for favorite romantic epithets: in 1805, Coleridge derided France as a "Babylon, the mother of whoredoms in morality, philosophy, and taste," and it was the France of the Enlightenment he was calling these names. Three years later, his friend Wordsworth showed himself quite as emphatic; in *The Convention of Cintra,* he denounced "the pestilential philosophisms of France," most especially the "paradoxical reveries of Rousseau, and the flippancies of Voltaire." The "process of depoeticization," wrote August Wilhelm Schlegel, "has lasted long enough; it is high time that air, fire, water, earth be poeticized once again." Deploying a vivid metaphor, Novalis reproached the philosophes, imbued with a heretical hatred of all religion, with having "disfigured the infinite creative music of the universe into the monotonous clatter of a gigantic mill." The philosophical German artist Philipp Otto Runge, who wrote as much as he painted, thought it "a shame how many splendid human beings have had to succumb to the miserable mentality of the so-called Enlightenment and philosophy." In 1816, in *The Statesman's Manual,* Coleridge urged

---

*This derisive definition of the Enlightenment's thought, in short, overlooked Hume's skepticism epitomized in his emphatic (if overstated) dictum that reason is, and ought to be, the slave of the passions; kidnapped Rousseau's worship of nature by labeling it "pre-romanticism"; stripped the Enlightenment of Diderot's romantic version of science, Christoph Martin Wieland's slyly erotic novels, Voltaire's tough-minded realism about politics and human nature—and then complained about the philosophes' naive rationalism. That is definition by larceny.

the upper classes of England to turn away from the prophets of unbelief and return to the religion of their fathers.[1] Even among those like John Stuart Mill who deplored this rejection of the Enlightenment, it became a commonplace that the romantic search for faith was a widespread, powerful impulse.

Friedrich Schlegel was exemplary among the romantic rebels against the eighteenth century. Just before 1800, as a young critic, he sought recruits for a campaign against "Enlightenment Berlinism"—*Aufklärungsberlinism*—and found them.[2] The war against Voltaire and his allies occupied him the rest of his life. In a series of lectures dating from 1804 to 1806, he dismissed Enlightenment thought with contempt. Ranking schools of thought, he placed scientific empiricism, the stance most congenial to the philosophes, on the lowest rung of the ladder, and put materialism, to which much of the late Enlightenment had committed itself, just above it. Skepticism and pantheism, two views well represented among the philosophes, fared only marginally better in Schlegel's hierarchy; only Idealism, almost as spiritual as religion, found his full approval.[3] That much for the enemies of enchantment!

Many among Schlegel's fellow romantics shared his truculent vision as they repudiated their faithless fathers. In truth, though making a fetish of originality, they carried more eighteenth-century baggage than they liked to think.[4] Hence their agenda is shadowed by incurable ambiguities. Their struggle between perceptiveness and tendentiousness is perhaps most obtrusive in their cherished tenet, the creative nature of the imagination. The "Imagination," Wordsworth wrote, "in truth,

> Is but another name for absolute strength
> And clearest insight, amplitude of mind,
> And reason in her most exalted mood.[5]

This romantic tribute to creativity was less than wholly creative. Like others before them, the philosophes had admiringly quoted the ancients on the madness that attends artistic genius and the frenzy that forces open the gates to inspiration. Voltaire, though a well-informed and admiring popularizer of Newtonian science, lamented the decay of poetry and the ascendancy of prose in his time.*

---

*In a letter of 1735, he worried over the "banishment" in a rationalistic age, of "sentiment, imagination, and the graces," terms that would, of course, acquire considerably more intensity among the romantics. Voltaire to Pierre Robert de Cornier de Cideville, April 16, 1735, *Correspondance*, ed. Theodore Besterman, 13 vols. (1971–93), I, 586. This is not the place to expound

Nor was Voltaire the first to celebrate the imagination. From the beginning of his century, essayists, poets, and philosophers had sung its pleasures. Joseph Addison devoted eleven numbers of his *Spectator* to hailing the imagination as "the very Life and highest Perfection of Poetry," which has "something in it like Creation." And near the end of the century as near its beginning, in some much quoted paragraphs of the *Kritik der Urteilskraft,* Kant offered lyrical tributes to unconditioned imaginative freedom. The most prestigious representative of the *Aufklärung* (no one, not even the most exasperated critics of the Enlightenment, ever called *him* shallow), he hailed *"Genius"* as "the talent (natural gift) that gives rules to art," a talent in every way "opposed to the *spirit of imitation.*" Genius draws inspiration from the creative unconscious: "The author of a product that he owes to his genius does not know himself just how his ideas for it have come to him." Kant was no romantic, and emphatically separated passion from the perception of beauty. But among the romantics perhaps only Keats, for whom the two were essentially one, surpassed him in his fervor for human imaginative powers: "I am certain," Keats wrote in 1817, "of nothing but of the holiness of the Heart's affections and the truth of Imagination—what the imagination seizes as Beauty must be truth—whether it existed before or not." In a telling metaphor, he compared the imagination to "Adam's dream—he awoke and found it truth."[6] But his joyful discovery was not new.

Occasionally romantics did acknowledge a debt to their antagonists. Coleridge, for one, recorded his obligations to Kant and others: "There you will trace or if you are on the hunt, track me." Even so, romantics were on solid ground as they claimed credit for their obsession with the creative imagination. They surpassed the eighteenth century's high regard for its importance by underscoring its pivotal role in all mental activity. "Nothing great," wrote Coleridge in one of his lay sermons, "was ever atchieved without enthusiasm," and enthusiasm is the mental state that liberates the imagination.[7] Was it not indispensable to the making of poems, paintings, and symphonies—works in which the romantics excelled—and, indeed, of humbler human artifacts?

As aggressive secularists, the philosophes had devoted themselves to demystifying the world. The enigmas that had baffled the finest minds of the past and

---

the history of the imagination in the age of the Enlightenment. That history would include eighteenth-century theorists from Addison to the Earl of Shaftesbury to Mark Akenside's important verse treatise of 1744, *The Pleasures of Imagination,* to the ambitious German thinker Johann Nicolaus Tetens, who in 1776 and 1777 distinguished fancy from imagination and discriminated among various levels of imaginative activity. At its highest level, he insisted, the imagination is not just a curator who rearranges the paintings in his museum but "is itself a painter and invents and makes new pictures." *Philosophische Versuche über die menschliche Natur und ihre Entwicklung,* 2 vols. (1776–77), I, 107.

reduced them to pious awe were, for them, unsolved scientific questions. The human psyche is part of nature and calls for the sort of researches that natural philosophers—we call them physicists, chemists, and biologists today—were conducting with such stunning results. Newton, to Voltaire and the other philosophes the greatest man who ever lived, had set the pattern for researchers to follow, and they hoped that a Newton of the mind might be hovering in the wings. That is why they were so enamored of the psychological theory of association, the view that thoughts arise from sense impressions that are linked to one another. Canonized in 1749 in David Hartley's influential *Observations on Man,* the theory enabled them to dispense with religious hypotheses about supernatural agencies at work in the human psyche. The poet or painter who depicts a mythological beast not in nature—a centaur or a unicorn—is exercising his talents by combining images already stored in the recesses of his mind.

For all their protests in behalf of the endangered state of poetry, the philosophes did not find this somewhat pedestrian view of mental activity at all distressing. Originality was not one of their icons.* And, lending particular point to their prosaic vision, they were disposed to distrust fictions as appealing hoaxes, diverting lies, primitive forms of expression to be outgrown. The future belonged to science, not to agreeable fabrications. In 1754, the abbé Nicolas Trublet, a minor French essayist, made this preconception explicit in a remarkable prophecy: "As reason is perfected, judgment will more and more be preferred to imagination, and, consequently, poets will be less appreciated. The first writers, it is said, were poets. I can well believe it; they could hardly be anything else. The last writers will be philosophers." This was an extreme statement, but it soon became a commonplace. In 1800, immersed in Enlightened views of human nature, the French student of primitive societies Joseph Marie de Gérando noted that the first faculty the observer must investigate in "savages" is the imagination, since it is "always the first faculty to develop."[8] The implication was inescapable: as savagery is superseded by civilization, the imagination will yield primacy of place to reason.

This denigration of the imaginative faculty infuriated the romantics and confirmed their sense of distance from the thought of the previous century. They could accept—in fact, insisted on—the idea that the imagination is most alive in children, primitives, and, for that matter, the insane. But it did not follow that it must be discarded as the child grows into an adult, the savage into a civilized being, the madman into a sane person. The imagination remained the essential

---

*Pope was speaking for the dominant intellectual temper of the Enlightenment when he famously defined "true wit" as "nature to advantage dressed / What oft was thought but ne'er so well expressed," thus depreciating novelty for its own sake.

food of poets, composers, painters, anyone endowed with sensitivity, all their lives. It is notorious how often the romantics extolled the innocence, the innate perceptiveness, of those not yet spoiled by society. Did Wordsworth not famously assert that he would "rather be / A Pagan suckled in a creed outworn"? Two important German romantic novels published around the turn of the century sent the same message: the protagonist of Friedrich Hölderlin's *Hyperion* calls the child "a divine being as long as it has not been dipped into the chamaeleon dye of men," and longs, in Hölderlin's characteristically yearning tone, that "one might become like children, so that the golden time of innocence might return." And in *Lucinde*—to which we will come back—Friedrich Schlegel has the hero ask his mistress in the midst of sexual arousal, "Are we not children?"[9]

The alienation of the early nineteenth century from the Enlightenment's history of the human mind as an overcoming of childish fancy was only reinforced by the aggressive manner that its heirs carried this tendentious scheme into the romantic era. In his youthful essay on Milton, published in 1825, Thomas Babington Macaulay flatly asserted, "We think that, as civilisation advances, poetry almost necessarily declines." No doubt, "the vocabulary of an enlightened society is philosophical, that of a half-civilized people is poetical." Macaulay sounded as though these bald assertions were truths accepted by all. He had in fact been anticipated in 1820 by the satirical novelist Thomas Love Peacock, who characterized the contemporary poet as "a semi-barbarian in a civilized community. He lives in the days that are past. His ideas, thoughts, feelings, associations, are all with barbarous manners, obsolete customs, and exploded superstitions. The march of his intellect is like that of a crab, backward." Thus "in whatever degree poetry is cultivated, it must necessarily be to the neglect of some branch of useful study; and it is a lamentable spectacle to see minds, capable of better things, running to seed in the specious indolence of these empty aimless mockeries of intellectual exertion."[10] Poetry, that luxuriant outgrowth of the imagination, had no future in an age of science. Subjective musings must give way to objective knowledge.

Peacock's amusing essay has a claim to attention apart from its interest as a document of the anti-romantic style in the romantic decades. It provoked his friend Shelley to a defense of poetry that will occupy us later, the most impassioned plea for the creative imagination the age was to produce. As an atheist and a political radical, Shelley necessarily appreciated the critical work of the Enlightenment: "The exertions of Locke, Hume, Gibbon, Voltaire, Rousseau, and their disciples, in favour of oppressed and deluded humanity, are entitled to the gratitude of mankind." He found it "easy to calculate" how much worse off the world would have been if they had never lived: "A little more nonsense would have been talked for a century or two; and perhaps a few more men, women and children, burnt as heretics." But if the great poets and painters of the past had never been born, the loss would have exceeded all imagination; the very sciences now being exalted "over the direct expression of the inventive and creative faculty" would never have been born either.[11]

Most fellow romantics rejected even the limited continuity with the Enlightenment that Shelley was prepared to see in his generation. Certainly William Blake, years before Shelley's *Defence of Poetry,* had emphatically refused to compromise with the philosophes' scientific world view. Less controlled than other poets, he put his case with characteristic intemperance. He had read Bacon, Locke, and Newton and Edmund Burke's book on the sublime with "Contempt & Abhorrence." They "mock Inspiration & Vision." Where was the imagination, where were inspiration and vision, in their philosophy? No doubt: "Meer Enthusiasm is the All in All!"[12] Insanity is preferable to the empty, fashionable philosophy of the time; anything but rationalism![13]

Blake, the eccentric and mystic, fits nowhere easily, not even under the capacious tent of romanticism.[14] Typically, Wordsworth thought him an interesting madman, but many romantics sounded much like Blake. For Thomas De Quincey, the opium eater, "the mere understanding" was "the meanest faculty in the human mind, and the most to be distrusted." Earlier, in a letter of 1791, the young Coleridge argued that "Reason is feasted, Imagination is starved: whilst Reason is luxuriating in it's proper Paradise, Imagination is wearily travelling over a dreary desart." Ten years later, he triumphantly announced that he had "overthrown the doctrine of Association, as taught by Hartley, and with it all the irreligious metaphysics of modern Infidels." He would continue to crusade against "the monstrous puerilities of CONDILLAC and CONDORCET," detestable men who "uniformly put the negation of a power for the possession of a power—& called the want of imagination, Judgment, & the never being moved to Rapture Philosophy!"[15] The imagination unleashed was the trump card the romantics played against the so-called Age of Reason.

While romantics in Britain and, later, in France were polemicizing against the passion for reason, Friedrich and August Wilhelm Schlegel provided the rationale for their love affair with the creative imagination. Curiously enough, the Schlegels, though spirited propagandists for the nonrational inner life as a privileged source of artistic vitality, contributed virtually nothing to the rapidly growing store of romantic literature. They were theorists of the imagination, rarely its practitioners, preferring the epigram, the lecture, the treatise to the novel or the poem. Both were industrious practical critics, whose verdicts on dramas, poems, and novels ancient and modern remain among the most interesting appraisals produced in the romantic decades. Both were impressive philologists with a scholarly grasp on exotic, to say nothing of the ancient, languages. Not even the single striking work of fiction in their vast output, Friedrich Schlegel's *Lucinde,* was much of an exception.[16] Published in 1799, when he was twenty-seven, it was a manifesto in the shape of a novel. In the vulgar sense of that word, *Lucinde* was "romantic" enough in origin and tenor. Emerging from the passionate conversations about literary theory, literary history, and the nature of love that German romantics had carried on in Jena and Berlin, it translated a real love affair into an ostensible fiction. In 1797, Schlegel had fallen in love with a married woman, Moses Mendelssohn's daughter Dorothea Veit. Intelligent and literary, she had obeyed paternal fiat, married a decent soul, and smarted under her boring existence. Though the mother of two gifted boys, nothing could hold her back once she had been smitten with Schlegel, that brilliant critic seven years her junior. She left her husband, filed for divorce, joined her lover, and eventually married him. *Lucinde* was the only child of that union.*

Although the Schlegel brothers edited the *Athenäum* together, each played a distinct role in fostering the romantic atmosphere just beginning to spread. Friedrich, mercurial, imaginative, alternating between feverish productivity and indolence, made glittering aphorisms and cloudy fragments—he liked them largely because they saved him the agony of composing a real book. August Wilhelm, for his part, vain and pedantic, was a splendid translator, an intelligent and independent-minded reader, and a scholarly student of Sanskrit. The romantic ideas he popularized largely bore his brother's signature, but his activity mattered to the diffusion of romanticism, particularly after Friedrich Schlegel, as a Catholic convert, was consumed by the religious interpretation of the world.

In the brothers' analysis of creativity, the imagination naturally holds pride of place. On a visit to France in 1803, Friedrich Schlegel produced the accepted responses: he noted with chauvinistic disdain and patriotic self-congratulation that the French sadly, and strangely, lacked what the Germans so gloriously possessed: *Phantasie.* In France, "one finds everything for sensuality, but nothing for the imagination," a devastating aberration. "Because the imagination is silent, the senses must be incessantly kept busy." Hence everything in France is spectacle. No wonder they had never produced a Shakespeare, to Friedrich Schlegel "the very center, the core of the romantic imagination." What is art, he asked rhetorically late in life, "but the imagination become visible and as it were corporeally emerging in shape and word and sound?" This "mobile,

---

*See below, pp. 91–93.

multiform, ever inventive imagination" is humanity's "dangerous asset."[17]

Astute foreign readers like Stendhal and Hazlitt were quick to point out that, at least in countries devoted to rational discourse or common sense, such vaporous and grandiloquent pronouncements could only compromise, perhaps ruin, the theoretical message of the German romantics, no matter how erudite and perceptive they might seem. But Friedrich Schlegel chose his adjectives for the blessed imagination—"restless, pensive, and creative"—with some care. Though awed by the mysterious power of creativity, he included "pensive"— *sinnend*—among its attributes to suggest that he was capable of discriminating judgments.[18] Much like the great E. T. A. Hoffmann, he doubted that unaided inspiration can produce masterpieces. The sober instruments of reflection, self-knowledge, and technical competence are needed to force the spontaneous idea into artistic form.

True, Schlegel believed that art and literature subsist on free play; on his way to France, traveling through lovely German forests, he mused on the "feeling of romantic freedom."[19] His longing for breathing space in the creative domain and his impatience with the fetters that classical doctrines and uncritical ancestor worship imposed on the artist were insistent, at times desperate. And that longing and that impatience took shape, as they did in others, in deep distaste for the scientific determinism that had been the hallmark of the secular Enlightenment. But, it is worth reiterating, Friedrich Schlegel was not calling for unregulated spontaneity. For the romantics, to dethrone reason was not to banish it from the kingdom of the imaginative arts.

On the great matter of the free imagination, August Wilhelm Schlegel was, we have seen, in his younger brother's camp. But he was no mere echo. "Poetry, if I may say so," he wrote, "is the speculation of the imagination."[20] But, like his brother, he recognized that the creative inwardness is not simply irrational, and stressed the need for both prudence and clarity, qualities that enthusiastic admirers of great works find so hard to achieve. In the true poet, like Shakespeare, the two faces of inwardness blend into one.

Shakespeare, of course, had embodied this felicitous synthesis of intuition and thinking more admirably than any other writer. As his accomplished translator and interpreter, Schlegel could count on a respectful hearing even in England, though his bardolatry raised some eyebrows there. Shakespeare, he wrote, had displayed an "outstanding cultivation of mental powers, practiced art, maturely considered and worthy intentions."[21] In short, this arch-romantic theorist was prepared to countenance a sizable share of experience, reflection, and practice in the making of great art. Genius, he insisted as he reviewed Kant's pronouncements on the matter, must combine fancy and understanding, imagination and reason, intuition and craftsmanship.

Still, though respectful to intellect and competence, the romantics remained convinced that the imagination does not just weave variations on preexisting materials; it invents fresh images and metaphors, hears hitherto unfathomed harmonies. Their confrontation with the philosophes on this issue was more consequential than a psychologists' quarrel of technical interest, more drastic than a marginal departure from the association psychology that had dominated the Enlightenment. It allowed the romantics to depict humans—or at least the artists among them—as approaching divinity. The very stature of the self was at issue. If the philosophes were right, the human mind is nothing better than a passive instrument responding to external stimuli even in high art and literature. If the romantics were right, the self contributes to the making of the external world, including, of course, the works of the imagination. The adjectives the romantics lavished on the imaginative human animal—"promethean," "god-like" and the all-purpose "creative," lent almost scriptural weight—trembled on the edge of a religious view of humanity.

Since commerce in romantic ideas was authentic free trade, the German view of the creative imagination made its way across Europe. For some six years early in the century, August Wilhelm Schlegel was linked, intellectually though not romantically, with the formidable Madame de Staël. In her spacious château at Coppet on the Lake of Geneva, she gathered some of the most interesting minds of the epoch to work in their studies, read their manuscripts aloud, quarrel with each other, and—the chosen few, not including Schlegel—make love to the hostess. In De l'Allemagne, in which she singled out the Germans as Europe's most poetic nation and Schlegel as Germany's first critic, she adapted his romantic pronouncements to her own, more moderate ways of thinking. She restated his indictment of French neoclassicism and of the Enlightenment's empiricist psychology; she exhaustively explored, and exceeded, his enthusiasm for enthusiasm. Half a century earlier, Montesquieu had traced modern liberty to the forests of Germany. Now Madame de Staël acquainted France, Britain, even the remote United States, where she, too, had faithful readers, with the splendors of German inwardness.

Madame de Staël was a fashionable novelist and opinionated commentator on the current scene: with some justice, Napoleon's censors treated her book on Germany as a political challenge. De l'Allemagne amounted to a courageous quarrel with the emperor; quickly suppressed in 1810, it did not become generally available until three years later. But once it appeared—first in England and a year later, after Napoleon's fall, in France—it aroused the kind of controversy that is calculated to secure ideas a wide hearing. Madame de Staël was unusual among the circle she had gathered at Coppet with her admiration for Schiller and her skepticism about Goethe and, thus, never satisfied with being a mere transmission belt, secured considerable independence from the German romantics who had been her tutors. But whatever she borrowed and whatever was her own, *De l'Allemagne* was read not just as an assault on a dictator but, more important, as an authoritative textbook of romantic attitudes.

In his own fashion, Coleridge was quite as effective as Madame de Staël as an exporter of German romantic notions about the imagination. Some of his most widely read works of prose, notably the *Biographia Literaria* of 1817, are largely disguised, if well-selected, anthologies. They swarm with extended passages taken, often without acknowledgment, from German literary critics and philosophers. Coleridge was, to be sure, far more than a plagiarist who happened to know German. He was precociously erudite, steeped in ancient and modern thought, forever in search of a coherent account of creativity, an astonishing, voluble talker who practically made free association into a principle of conversation—his conversation.[22] For all his intermittent involvement in public affairs, his life was the inner life. As he told a friend in 1796, "I do not *like* history. Metaphysics and poetry and 'facts of mind' . . . are my darling studies."[23] This overpowering preoccupation with the self, this concentration on the facts of mind dominates his poetry, which at its best has a hallucinatory quality, all the more haunting because he left some of it unfinished. *Kubla Khan* records a glittering opium vision; *The Rime of the Ancient Mariner* is laden with obscure religious symbolism. These poems are romantic in subject matter and treatment and radically private in origins. No one but Coleridge could have written them.

Still, the distinctions that Coleridge drew between fancy and imagination, and between levels of the imagination, were sheer borrowings from August Wilhelm Schlegel and, even more, from Schelling. For Schelling, aesthetics is the master discipline. Before Keats, he equated beauty with truth; before Shelley, he hailed the poet as the discoverer and supreme interpreter of nature. In Schelling's romantic thought, the imagination ranks highest among human endowments. But—once again—Schelling insisted that it must do its creative work with the support of conscious artistry: Shakespeare, for Schelling as for other romantics the supreme proof for his theories, had been a superb artisan as much as an intuitive genius.

Coleridge's version of this romantic philosophizing is an extraordinary amalgam of hidden quotations, elaborate paraphrases, and novel formulations. The great poet is original; far from reflecting current taste, he creates it. As a genius, he lives on a plane higher than that occupied by mere talents. And what distinguishes him is that he alone can so "represent familiar objects as to awaken in the minds of others a kindred feeling concerning them."[24] The man of talent has fancy; the genius, imagination. Fancy is subject to the laws of association; the "primary IMAGINATION" is "a repetition in the finite mind of the eternal act of creation in the infinite I Am."[25] Endowed with commanding powers, the genius lets his unconscious do the creative work—this is in fact the definition of genius. But in addition to imaginative freedom, he needs and has method. For all that, Coleridge never lost sight of the enemy: the Enlightenment's view of mental operations, with its pernicious sense of the mind parasitic on borrowed energy.

The creative inner life, then, Coleridge felt compelled to believe, is far richer than ever dawned on the Enlightenment. Philosophy "is employed on objects of the INNER SENSE," and so is poetry. It was this inner sense that interested him, and plagued him. He needed to understand "the mind's self-experience in the act of thinking." Only an elite of explorers could hope to discover the source of "highest and intuitive knowledge." It alone could "acquire the philosophic imagination, the sacred power of self-intuition, who within themselves can interpret and understand the symbol." And he hailed the "men in all ages, who have been impelled as by an instinct to propose their own nature as a problem, and who devote their attempts to its solution."* He praised these rare explorers in general terms, but he was identifying himself with them. Few philosophical poets have found their own nature quite so enigmatic, and so endlessly fascinating, as Coleridge. As he wrestled with it, his search for originality seduced him into coining rebarbative neologisms: "desynonymize" and "esemplastic."[26] Awkward and teutonic, at the obscure end of the stylistic range he could command, these strained coinages raised more problems than they solved.

Shelley's *Defence of Poetry*, though lucidity itself, was problematic in another way: through hyperbole. Indulging his enviable oratorical powers, Shelley piled up claim upon claim for the unrivaled position of the poet in history. He was in good company: it became a cliché in romantic literature to eulogize poets of the past as leaders of their culture or its martyrs and, in imitation of the ancients, to invoke the muse of poetry as an aid to their inspiration. But in his time few poets made the case for the creative powers of the imagination more earnestly, more ferociously even, than Shelley. At his most energetic, not even Victor Hugo could equal Shelley in this sublime self-regard.

To be a poet, Shelley wrote, "is to apprehend the true and the beautiful." Participating in the eternal, the infinite, and the one, he is "a nightingale, who

*Biographia Literaria; or, Biographical Sketches of My Literary Life and Opinions, 2 vols. (1815), in The Collected Works of Samuel Taylor Coleridge, ed. Kathleen Coburn et al., 16 vols. (1969–92), VII, 250, 241–42 [ch. 12], 89 [ch. 5]. As he put it in one of his most convoluted metaphors: these explorers will recognize "that the wings of the air-sylph are forming within the skin of the caterpillar; those only, who feel in their own spirits the same instinct, which impels the chrysalis of the horned fly to leave room in its involucrum for antennae yet to come." Ibid., 242 [ch. 12].

sits in darkness and sings to cheer its own solitude with sweet sounds; his auditors are as men entranced by the melody of an unseen musician, who feel that they are moved and softened, yet know not whence or why." Better, far better, poets "are not only the authors of language and of music, of the dance, and architecture, and statuary, and painting: they are the institutors of laws, and the founders of civil society, and the inventors of the arts of life." Poetry, which Shelley defined straightforwardly as "the expression of the imagination," is the all-powerful teacher. It "lifts the veil from the hidden beauty of the world and makes familiar objects be as if they were not familiar," and "creates new materials of knowledge and power and pleasure." It is "something divine," the "centre and the circumference of knowledge," which "turns all things to loveliness."[27]

In his transports, it apparently never occurred to Shelley to ask why, if poets have done all these things, their legislative powers had remained unacknowledged through the centuries. But while Shelley's fanciful historical survey is a tendentious fiction, his *Defence of Poetry* documents a new mood that mortals more ordinary than Shelley were beginning to share. His reversal of time-honored hierarchies had radical implications. In lavishing tributes to the historic role of these devotees of the inner life, he was proposing to enlarge the space that the self could, and should, occupy in human existence. In elevating poets above all others, above scientists, statesmen, and saints, Shelley was working to secularize the traditional view of the self as the child of God. The commanding place once occupied by the priest (or the saint) was now to be taken by the poet.

Shelley's rhetorical fireworks attest that a romantic did not need to be conventionally religious to work for the restoration of enchantment to the world. They attest, too, that even though Shelley's extravagant claim for the poet as secular savior was aristocratic in its vision of the gifted few, it was in its poetic way a democratic move. What really counted in life on Shelley's showing was not birth or fortune but that imponderable, incalculable inner endowment—genius. Thus Shelley's manifesto spoke for inwardness the way that Napoleon advocating careers open to talent had spoken for life in society. It was therefore a political statement, a plea for the restitution of *Innerlichkeit* to a world from which magic had fled.

2. The Self in Politics

Stirred by the historic earth tremors around them, the first generation of romantics played passionately at radical politics. They toasted the French Revolution, provoked local censors, joined reform clubs their governments put under surveillance. But most of them sooner or later—the Germans sooner—defected from such risky adventures. The French romantics were, as will soon emerge, the most visible exception. "Every literary work," wrote Victor Hugo in 1833, "is an act," and he meant a political act.[1] Few romantics outside France would have endorsed this assertive maxim. The pronouncements on political issues they continued to permit themselves were driven not by some well-grounded pressure for reform or the hunt for influence but by utopian longings, religious commitments, weariness with a world incurably corrupt, or the urge to flee to their chosen vocation—art, music, poetry. And even as they mused on political issues, most of them proudly defined their vocation to be reaching for a higher inwardness.

There were in their time, and later, lively disputes over what constitutes rational political thinking: one romantic's moderation was the fanaticism of another. All politics, after all, harbors an expressive dimension; the pursuit of interests, whether one's own or that of one's class, can never exhaust its sources of energy. Even Machiavelli, that notorious technician of power, had been moved by openly confessed private motives. But more often than that of others, the politics of the romantics was drowned in self-regarding passions. In the heat of sincerest political excitement, their response to events proved of greater moment to them than the events themselves. The French Revolution, Napoleon's dictatorship, the repressive ordinances of the British or central European governments meant less to them than how they felt—felt, rather than thought—about them.

The political cultures maturing in the romantic decades signified drastic departures from what had traditionally done duty for politics: cabals and conspiracies among the few near the throne alternating with food riots and occasional uprisings. In days past—still very much days present in the German states and farther south and east—rulers had given no house room to legal opposition, but damned any effort to organize criticism of entrenched power as sedition. The punishment for politicians out of favor had once been the scaffold or, more recently, disgrace—which meant, concretely, exile to the boredom and futility of provincial domesticity. But eighteenth-century Britain and the newly

formed United States, even if both still resounded with oratory denouncing
"faction," had begun to experiment with the give-and-take of political parties
competing for office. And the French Revolution, though marred by the
deadly sport of mutual denunciation, put political education on the agenda.
Parties, still maligned but increasingly domesticated, were shedding the reproach of factionalism. Thus politics evolved into a serious game played under
well-understood rules, including the convention that losers must remain free to
resume efforts in the contest for power.[2]

The cultivation of politics had far-reaching social consequences. As the rational, pacific pursuit of influence, it called for open channels of communication
between governors and governed, substantial latitude for dissenting views on
contested issues, and institutions, however narrowly restricted, for popular participation: fundamental laws, legislatures, elections at least relatively free of
intimidation and fraud. Yet this invitation to active citizenship was precisely
what many romantics came to reject.

To be sure, not all of the romantics' withdrawal from politics was of their
making. During these turbulent decades, governments clamped tight controls
on discontent by suspending civil rights and jailing inconvenient critics. Cowed
by this atmosphere, rebellious romantics tethered their reformist, to say nothing
of their revolutionary, sentiments and exercised self-censorship. In 1794, when
William Wordsworth, then a self-confessed subversive, professed himself one of
"that odious class of men called democrats" who disapprove of monarchies and
aristocracies, his brother Richard reined him in: "I hope you will be cautious in
writing or expressing your political opinions. By the suspension of the Habeas
Corpus Acts the Ministers have great powers."[3] To trade extremist politics for
safe conservatism, or to abandon politics altogether for nature, scholarship, or
religion, to collect folk tales or study Sanskrit instead of signing petitions
seemed only sensible.

But the need for self-protective prudence was not the main reason for romantic retreats from radicalism. An intensifying disillusionment with the sanguinary course of the French Revolution and, later, the aggressive posture of
Napoleonic France provided legitimate grounds for disavowing dreams of
changing the world through action. Yet neither fear of repression nor dismay at
demagogues who had betrayed sacred liberty, fraternity, and equality, nor even
the toll that growing older usually takes on youthful activism, can fully explain
the romantics' disowning their early ideals, or politics altogether.* The roman-

---

*Whether romantics exchanged the cause of movement for the cause of stability or whether
they became wholly unpolitical, in both instances they achieved political effects. Conservatism is,

tic cult of the self had in itself important repercussions for its votaries: talking and writing about politics, many romantics were indulging in little more than emphatic self-expression. As we shall see, they transformed revolutions, wars, censorship, economic misery, social legislation into so much autobiography.

Not all romantics saw themselves quite that way. Confessed solipsists apart, a number of them liked to experience themselves as earnestly involved in public affairs, though in their distinctive imaginative manner. If they found precious little poetry in politics, they discovered that politics could provide significant impulses for poetry. In 1818, in one of his lectures on the English poets, worth quoting at some length, Hazlitt brilliantly documented this linkage. He thought it profound, nothing less than historic. The school of poetry headed by Wordsworth, he said, "had its origin in the French revolution, or rather in those sentiments and opinions which produced that revolution." Toward the end of the eighteenth century, poetry had degenerated into insipid and mechanical routine. "It wanted something to stir it up, and it found that something in the principles of the French revolution." The results were stunning. "The change in the belles-lettres was as complete, and to many persons as startling, as the change in politics, with which it went hand in hand. There was a mighty ferment in the heads of statesmen and poets, kings and people. According to the prevailing notions, all was to be natural and new. Nothing that was established was to be tolerated. All the common-place figures of poetry, tropes, allegories, personifications, with the whole heathen mythology, were instantly discarded; a classical allusion was considered as a piece of antiquated foppery; capital letters were no more allowed in print, than letters-patent of nobility were permitted in real life; kings and queens were dethroned from their rank and station in legitimate tragedy or epic poetry, as they were decapitated elsewhere; rhyme was looked upon as a relic of the feudal system, and regular metre was abolished along with regular government. Authority and fashion, elegance or arrangement, were hooted out of countenance, as pedantry and prejudice."[4]

As Hazlitt saw it, this cooperation of politics with poetry, astonishing in its intimacy, produced a kind of democratic anarchy and, among imaginative writers, an utter self-centeredness. The new poet "is jealous of all excellence but his own," slow to admire but insistent on being admired. "He tolerates only what he himself creates; he sympathizes only with what can enter into no competition with him." In short, "he sees nothing but himself and the universe," and "his egotism is in some respects a madness."[5] Hazlitt proffered this amusing

---

after all, as political a stance as radicalism. And the romantics who eschewed politics altogether served the powers that be; their apathy proved to be a form of political action.

characterization in all seriousness. And it does felicitously encapsulate a salient
quality of the romantics' style: the pressure of the world on their work filtered
through their narcissistic way of referring public issues back to intimate needs
and fantasies and the essentially literary nature of their social engagement. But,
as will become apparent, Hazlitt's social history of recent poetry works better
with some romantics than with others.* Virtually every generalization about
the romantics can claim only the most limited validity; they were unanimous
about very little, least of all about their attitude to public affairs.

The French, propelled into the arena by their history, were the most political
romantics of all. They wrote their autobiographies on the barricades, in legislatures, for partisan journals. Political activity, at least energetic political talk,
made an integral part of their self-definition. As men of letters following Rousseau, who had asserted half a century earlier that everything is at bottom linked
to politics, they welcomed their public vocation as a grand destiny. Like most of
their contemporaries, they believed that the world is ruled, and changed, by
ideas. Hence ideas felicitously expressed are not the lackeys of power but its
arbiters. Marx's challenge to this consensus, his demotion of ideas to a super-
structure shaped by, rather than shaping, society, was still in the future.

The upheavals that had punctuated French history for decades appeared to
confirm the alliance between thought and action. It seemed obvious that the
Revolution had been almost literally the child of subversive Enlightenment
propagandists. Counterrevolutionaries made much of this: the overturn of the
monarchy, the assault on Christianity, the judicial murder of the king and
queen, the Terror, had been, they liked to say, the philosophes' fault. In his
rather paranoid *Mémoires pour servir à l'histoire du jacobinisme* of 1798, the first
attempt to analyze the causes of the Revolution, the abbé Barruel had blamed it
on a conspiracy of freemasons and philosophes led by three haters of Christianity—Frederick II of Prussia, d'Alembert, and Voltaire.

Voltaire's haggard face haunted the French romantics, even those who were
not Barruel's disciples. In admiration or abhorrence, they saw him, indisputably
France's most conspicuous eighteenth-century man of letters, as an exemplar of
the politician with a pen. Not without justice: he had meddled in public controversies openly or covertly but always intelligently, proving a shrewd critic of
institutions and an impassioned campaigner to set injustices right. But not all
French romantics thanked him for it. In 1821, visiting Sans Souci, Frederick the
Great's château in Postdam, Chateaubriand mused that the Prussian king and
his sometime friend Voltaire had been "two figures bizarrely linked, who will

*See below, esp. pp. 62, 66–67.

live: the latter destroyed a society with the philosophy that served the first to found a kingdom." A decade later, in 1833, another romantic, Alfred de Musset, apostrophized a hideously smiling Voltaire in love with death. He had been the sapper who had labored night and day to undermine the great edifice that had collapsed on them all.[6] As men of words, the romantics could only salute, however wryly, the most effective man of words modern France had produced. And Diderot's intentions for his *Encyclopédie* could only sustain the sense of their own power, or at least of their opportunities: as chief editor of that supposedly innocuous enterprise, he had frankly advertised his aim of changing the general way of thinking. They thought that he had fulfilled his program; to their mind, the Revolution had been the *Encyclopédie* in action.

In truth, the French revolutionaries had driven this emerging ideology of the poet as legislator, one-tenth reality and nine-tenths fantasy, beyond the limits of most men's imaginations. Those to be principal actors in the sanguinary events to come had arrived in Paris with an epic poem or a tragedy in their back pockets, and had enacted their literary theatricals on the public stage—for good or ill. Theirs, more than any other, had been a revolution that lived off words, off pamphlets and manifestoes, newspaper editorials and carefully rehearsed speeches—words that had changed minds and made history.[7] Granted, the revolution had proved an uncertain benefit to literary men. The poet André Chénier, discovered by the romantics only a quarter of a century later, had been guillotined, and some of his fellows had barely escaped the same fate. But their travail merely served to show how much poetry—and poets—matter.

So did Napoleon I, in his authoritarian way. Quite unintentionally he underscored the political influence of writers by the attention he paid to their publications, and by such personal interventions as his campaign against Madame de Staël's *De l'Allemagne*. Voltaire, Chénier, Madame de Staël, then, were heroes and heroines of the pen the romantics could scarcely ignore. Napoleon's dictatorship had only whetted their appetites by refusing to gratify them. But while he could arrest and distort the political education of the French, he could not uproot it.

No wonder, then, that once Napoleon was securely out of the way, political rhetoric exploded. Poets, playwrights, and novelists, finding their voices at least partially unencumbered after Waterloo, leaped into the great debate over the future of France. The charter of 1815 that would serve as their country's constitution until the July Revolution of 1830 ended the Restoration regime still hesitated to grant political opinions free range, but the press laws enacted in 1819 were decidedly more liberal. Accordingly newspapers and periodicals identified with a distinct party sprang up to satisfy the pent-up demand. French romantic poets and dramatists wrote editorials, and many found their first audience as journalists. The influential daily *Le Globe,* launched in September 1824, amassed a distinguished roster of young romantics and their ideological allies, including that gifted, prolific critic Sainte-Beuve and Adolphe Thiers, then at the beginning of his long, stormy career as a historian and politician.

Goethe was one among many cultivated Europeans who read the *Globe* faithfully through its seven-year existence. More than any other paper, it helped to define the meaning of French romanticism. Significantly, though founded as a literary journal engaged in the romantics' campaign to break the stranglehold of the neoclassical theory of drama, it turned political three years later and became the voice of the moderate liberals.[8] In the years that romantics secured a foothold in French literary consciousness, public debate was over fundamentals, and they became involved as a matter of course. So inward a poet as Alphonse de Lamartine, celebrated for his moody, melancholy verses, moved into conspicuous though rather pathetic public service as head of the provisional government after the February Revolution in 1848. It may not have been bliss to be alive in France during that second dawn, but it was at least exhilarating.

Precisely the restrictions imposed upon public criticism by the chicanery practiced during the Restoration and the uncertainty over the shifting boundaries of permitted speech spurred French romantics to ever more daring pronouncements. The unpredictable combination of openings and frustrations changing from crisis to crisis tantalized them. Incorrigible individualists, they agreed only on their right to express themselves with little reserve. For the rest, they were scattered across the political map, attending salons or joining circles of the like-minded; their partisan stance ranged from nostalgia for the Old Regime to nostalgia for Napoleon, from support for the charter to daydreams about untried constitutional arrangements. In those years, Victor Hugo was a royalist and Chateaubriand a temperate monarchist; Stendhal a Bonapartist and Benjamin Constant a liberal. Whatever their perspective, French romantics were pleased to accept the invitation to political combat that the Bourbon Restoration offered them. In these circumstances, it was natural for Hugo to sound like Shelley before him, and grandly call the poet "God's spokesman to princes."[9] Animated by the sense of a new world dawning, prodded by the grandiose schemes of Henri Saint-Simon and his followers for a new industrial age, they saw little cause for excessive modesty about their own importance.

The chances that the Restoration regime gave for political participation proved an exciting release from passivity. But not all romantics welcomed it, certainly not all the time. They never degenerated into mindless men of action but remained sensitive cultivators of the inner life, and their appetite for action was often shadowed by their brooding over its pointlessness. Persuaded that their world was out of joint, some of them, Hamlet-like, cursed that they had been born to set it right. From Chateaubriand to Alfred de Vigny, from Benjamin Constant to Alfred de Musset, they lamented—or, at times, caressed—what they called the *mal du siècle,* a besetting despondency and aimlessness. This modern malady drove them to offer incompatible diagnoses and diverse prescriptions, but they tended to see it as a real threat. The unhealthy excess of cynicism among the sophisticated, the philistinism of the bourgeois, the bewildering legacy left by a quarter century of turmoil, and, above all, the decay of religious belief were symptoms they detected everywhere.

No doubt, this morbid analysis was a form of action, designed to cure contemporaries of their malaise by pinpointing its causes. The ineffectual characters who dominated French romantic novels and poems, prone to defeat, failure, even suicide, were not models but warnings. After all, some among these young diagnosticians had a future as political theorists and government officials. Although French romantics experienced wrenching tensions between their private and their public selves, many found ways of living with both. But they could do so largely because their politics never lost a certain literary flavor, and literature never its hold on their lives. Looking back at Paris during Frédéric Chopin's life there, the perceptive English musicologist H. R. Haweis noted that "about 1832, the effervescence of the first years of the July Revolution seemed to pass naturally into questions of art and literature, and as the French are occasionally tired of blood but never of glory, the great battle of the Romantic and Classical schools was fought out in the bloodless arena of the arts."[10] The self-expressive element in romantic politics never waned, not even in France.

The first decades of Victor Hugo's long career document the fertile coexistence of private and public life among France's romantics, and the primacy of the aesthetic. As an apprentice poet in the early 1820s, rapidly gaining ascendancy over his peers with his powerful and musical diction, Hugo was a suave conformist, writing verses that royalty could, and did, reward. Louis XVIII was his king, the charter his constitution, Catholicism his religion—that was all he then needed to know. He felt at home among young men who, in Sainte-Beuve's acid words, professed to be "Christians of good breeding and vague sentiments."[11] A royal gift of five hundred francs, a gesture equally welcome as financial support and as a sign of high favor, cemented Hugo's loyalty. The accession in 1824 of the king's younger brother as Charles X, less interested in poetry and more in piety, at first changed nothing for him. A worthy successor at least in this, the new monarch kept Hugo's support warm by awarding him the coveted *Légion d'honneur.*

But Hugo was a quick study and a restless soul. The literary battles of French romantics against neoclassical orthodoxy, and his new friends around the *Globe,* propelled him to the left in politics and religion alike. By 1827, with his unorthodox drama *Cromwell,* he had landed firmly in the camp of the opposition. Three years later, in the preface to *Hernani,* he trumpeted his newfound radicalism without reserve. Addressing chiefly the youth, he noted that while romanticism was still poorly defined, its true meaning was unmistakable: "From its militant aspect, it is nothing but *liberalism* in literature." It was a rallying cry intended for more than poets: "Liberty in the arts, liberty in society: that is the double aim toward which all consistent and logical spirits must tend in step."[12] Hugo was proclaiming—and demonstrating—that in France many roads, including the theater, led to politics.

There was something of the careerist in Hugo's shifting alliances, but his political convictions drew on sources deeper than opportunism.* In his years of rapid evolution, Hugo discovered his principal good cause: abolition of the death penalty. As a youth traveling with his family, he had seen the rotting corpses of convicted criminals hanging from trees by the roadside; as an adolescent, he had watched with horror a young girl, a thief, being branded on the shoulder in a Paris public square and her scream haunted him all his life. In 1828, the year after *Cromwell,* he published a gripping novella, *Le Dernier Jour d'un condamné,* which meticulously records the last hours of a murderer awaiting the guillotine.[13] These scenes, real and imagined, roused private devils in him, devils that the French political system permitted him to enlist in a dramatic agenda for reform, an agenda in which the drama, with Hugo in the leading role, held pride of place.

The experience of the German romantics was far more exiguous and virtually compelled them to keep their distance from politics. Actually, only a handful among them ever took the way *to* politics. Germans had not been so fortunate as their western neighbors. Split into some three hundred units, most of them of duodecimo size, the Germanies were a collection of absolute regimes unencumbered by guaranteed rights or working representative bodies. Governed by princes as authoritarian as they chose to be, these states were at worst petty dictatorships, at best disciplined extended families. The churches were firmly under the ruler's thumb; the aristocracy, a solid support; culture high and low, under close official superintendence. It was only fitting that German subjects should call their prince the father of their country—*Landesvater;* the most they could hope for from that surrogate paternal authority was a benevolent

---

*These energies never slackened and eventually drove him into exile in protest against Louis Napoleon's coup of December 1851.

disposition. Reform-minded German bourgeois pinned their hopes on bureau-crats, those well-educated, devoted, and authoritative public servants who ad-ministered their domains by following the rational rules they themselves had defined.

In this climate, German legal scholars developed political theories that pro-vided little more than grounds for submissive allegiance to the local dynasty. The baneful metaphor of the state as an organism into which all institutions—the churches, the military, the nobility, the universities, the schools, the bu-reaucracy—were solidly integrated offered no purchase to the kind of educa-tion that raises subjects into citizens. It seemed almost as though the most prominent carriers of high German culture—poets or novelists, scholars or playwrights—men who had traveled abroad and read the foreign newspapers, had made a tacit pact with the authorities to secure space for their idiosyncratic religious views or irregular sexual escapades in return for abstention from criti-cism of the state.[14] No political tradition could grow on so barren a soil.

Germans were not altogether unaware of their plight. In 1801, in perhaps the most depressed poem he ever wrote, Friedrich Schiller greeted the advent of the new century by asking where freedom can be found in a murderous world steadily at war. His despairing reply was that one must flee "the pressures of life" by seeking the "holy quiet domains of the heart." Freedom exists only in the realm of dreams, and the beautiful blooms only in song.* But the situation that Schiller, driven by activist impulses, found most disheartening, many prominent German romantics welcomed. The year before this lament for the fatal confinement of freedom, Friedrich Schlegel had enjoined his readers in a published fragment, "Do not squander faith and love in the political world, but sacrifice your innermost to the divine world of science and art in the holy fire stream of eternal cultivation."[15] He was speaking for his romantic friends.

Two decades later, after revolutions and wars had reshaped central Europe forever, Schlegel remained loyal to this antipolitical stance: "Doubtless the essential problem of the age, its goal and vocation," he wrote in 1822, "the destination it must reach and the task it must solve, lies in a sphere quite different from the political unrest, party formations, and battles of the pres-ent."[16] This pronouncement points in two directions, underscoring once again the complexities of romantic politics. On the one hand, as Britain, France, and the United States were discovering, the party spirit Schlegel condemned was providing a sturdy foundation for politics. At the same time, Schlegel's demo-

---

*"In des Herzens heilig stille Räume / Mußt du fliehen aus des Lebens Drang. / Freiheit ist nur in dem Reich der Träume, / Und das Schöne blüht nur im Gesang."

tion of politics was anything but disinterested. It suited his missionary efforts to help undo the secular work of the Enlightenment and of the French Revolution.

He had pursued that cause for years. "Nothing is needed more in our time than a spiritual counterweight to the Revolution," he noted in 1800.[17] After moving to Vienna in 1808, the year of his conversion to Catholicism, he lectured on literature and philosophy and edited newspapers mouthing the Hapsburg line. The Austrian government soon enlisted his sharp pen, and for several heady years he found himself near the center of power as he wrote memoranda for Prince Metternich, the architect of the European order after Napoleon's fall, joined Austrian delegations at international conferences, and drafted a constitution for a Germany of the post-Napoleonic age. This was not just lucrative and flattering employment; Schlegel had persuaded himself that arch-Catholic Austria was the only authentic empire in Europe, showing the way toward an idealized Germanic kingdom.

During this career, which abruptly ended in 1818 as he lost his posts, he hoped to yoke literary to practical life.[18] But in reality, the gap between literature and politics continued as unbridgeable as before. Friedrich von Gentz, a hardheaded conservative who had translated Burke's *Reflections on the Revolution in France* into German, saw this clearly. Schlegel, he wrote in 1816, "was never suited for practical business; for several years now, his religious—or better: clerical—rage has made him into a total fool." Still, as we have seen, a presumably unpolitical posture could serve reactionary politics. Even so, despite years of partisan activity, Schlegel refused to recognize his factiousness. When his brother, now estranged from him, hinted at it, he waxed indignant. "I am firm in the inner conviction," he frostily replied, "that I stand, and live, far removed from, wholly beyond the sphere of, all present-day parties."[19]

However self-serving, this declaration reveals Friedrich Schlegel's true colors. For all his devoted service to Metternich, he was committed to the life of introspection first and last. As early as 1798, he had admitted to his brother that in the fragments he was about to publish, the number of political paragraphs compared to the Christian ones was "paltry."[20] Paltry they would remain. Across more than three decades, Friedrich Schlegel wrote his brother hundreds of letters, some of them little treatises, naturally filled with the kind of gossip suitable to family correspondence: reports on debts, infatuations, suicidal fantasies. But such intimate themes, and comments on literature and publishing, engrossed Schlegel's attention. He had much to say about Dante but not about Danton. A political animal would have written very different letters.

Since he lectured on the events of the day, one can carpenter together a rudimentary political platform from Friedrich Schlegel's writings. After he had discarded his youthful infatuation with the French Revolution, he urged the emancipation of the Jews and a return of the Roman Catholic Church to its position of influence in Germany.[21] Between 1820 and 1823, in a series of articles promisingly titled "The Signature of the Age," he elaborated his mature thinking about the state. But this, Schlegel insisted, was merely a theoretical exercise, a "purely intellectual discussion," analyzing the "sickly" condition of his time.[22]

At bottom, then, Schlegel's political theory is an antipolitical theory, in tune with his conviction that partisanship deserves little attention and that pious reconciliation is humanity's cardinal need. Short of anarchy, which the state must combat, "the strength of faith and love" alone and not "partisan struggles" will conquer. Having suffered revolutions from below and above, Europe in the 1820s was, he said, facing a "revolution of the middle" that "threatens it with a new terrible crisis and a general convulsion." Like his former chief, Metternich, Schlegel regarded the bourgeoisie as the truly revolutionary element in European society—an unconscious compliment (only partly warranted) intended as a stern reproach. Germany, he added, is relatively calm only because "most governments have seriously worked to restore, or revive, old corporate institutions in German fashion." Other states, though, forgetful of their history and infatuated with such constitutional devices as representative bodies, are vulnerable to anarchy. "The truly new can emerge only from the truly old." The state, then, stands as the overarching guardian of "eternal and essential" institutions like "the church and the schools, the family and the gild." The whole is not a mechanism but—predictably—an organism, something the post-revolutionary age has failed to understand.[23]

Schlegel aimed his critique not solely at subversive liberals. He saw two parties of "self-appointed world improvers and saviors": revolutionaries driven by the lust to destroy and utopian enemies of the revolution who, having designed a perfect world, want to force everyone into docility. Both extremists share a view of the state as "an all-directing and all-governing law machine." What is needed is not a passive third party in the middle that would feebly yield to fanatics. A government should govern, when it does govern, forcefully, but in general as little as possible. The state may be "an armed corporate body for peace," but "the true inner and spiritual peace can enter the minds of men only through religion."[24] Schlegel's ideal state, then, serves Christianity, which alone can cure the modern sickness of unbelief. Unalterably opposed to making a religion of politics, Schlegel made a politics of religion.*

---

*Novalis, the most solipsistic and politically regressive among the German romantics, developed a similar "political" theory. He longed for a medieval past, far more imagined than real, for a

And so, virtually, did Coleridge in his later years. The trajectory of English romantics thinking about politics, though of course distinct, bore striking resemblances to that of German *Romantiker*. True, their political culture was far more highly developed than its German counterparts and their spectrum of attitudes toward activism far wider. But for all their opportunities—their parliament, burgeoning political parties, problems of industrialization crying out for remedial action, and relative freedom of speech partially restored after the hysteria of the anti-French crusade—such articulate English romantics as Coleridge fled politics in the German manner.

In the late 1790s, after a vigorous and outspoken radical phase, Coleridge returned to what he extolled as the havens that the Anglican Church and traditional social institutions could best provide. He justified criticizing his government's repressive policies by his fear that they were making the very radicals they hoped to stifle. As for himself, he wished "to be a good man & a Christian." These were the thin conclusions in which this erudite, tormented talker persisted as he longed for the consolations of faith and of certainty. Reason, and reasoning, had little to do with it. "My opinion is thus," he wrote a friend in 1801, "that deep Thinking is attainable only by a man of deep Feeling, and that all Truth is a species of Revelation." In a lay sermon of 1817, he summed up the conservatism he had been preaching for years: "To the Feudal system we owe the forms, to the Church the substance of our liberty."[25] Hazlitt's epithet for Coleridge, whose genius he had once admired, is telling. The *Rime of the Ancient Mariner,* which he called Coleridge's "most remarkable performance," was "high German"—for Hazlitt, we know, never a term of praise.[26]

But Coleridge was not all of English romanticism. In 1818, we recall, Hazlitt derided his country's new poets as egotists on principle, inspired by the French Revolution yet so self-obsessed that they saw only themselves and the universe—in that order. But at least one romantic text published just two years later, Shelley's *Prometheus Unbound,* suggests that Hazlitt's character sketch fits some romantic contemporaries less well than others. In the preface, Shelley acknowledged himself to be possessed by "a passion for reforming the world." Some critics have hinted that his difficult and ambitious verse drama was little better than a narcissistic explosion dressed up as an elaborate classical allegory.

---

golden time when all had lived contentedly within the unifying embrace of Christendom, and the paternal care of such as Prussia's king and queen (his only comfort in these radical times), a "heavenly couple" benevolently governing their adoring subjects. But these political fantasies, unabashedly aesthetic, nostalgic, at times downright childlike, were no more than auxiliaries for Novalis's mission: the voyage to the interior.

But it is more appropriately read as a splendid fable about man's liberation through love, a grandiose political vision that transcends its author's self-centeredness.

Another poet whose work Hazlitt knew well, Lord Byron, lends support to this more nuanced perception of English romanticism. Byron's political streak is undeniable; he might have been more active in public life, and more effective, if gossip about his private affairs had not driven him into exile. The maiden speech he delivered in the House of Lords in late February 1812 is a sample of what he might have done if he had stayed—and not got bored. England was racked with devastating technological unemployment and appalling destitution, and the only remedy the government could devise was to take revenge on Luddite weavers who were destroying the machines that were throwing them out of work. Eloquently Byron denounced the bill that would make frame breaking a capital crime. "I was born for opposition," he wrote a week later, elated with his rhetorical triumph.[27] But from Italy he could express his opposition only with verbal abuse in satirical poems and in letters to his friends. Still, as everyone knows, he was not content with mere words, and died in the service of an appealing cause, Greek independence from the Ottomans. He probably did more for liberalism by dying than by living on.

Yet William Wordsworth's subordination of politics to poetry was more characteristic of English romanticism than Byron's fascination with it. As a child, Wordsworth had enjoyed "unconscious intercourse with beauty," and his engagement with public issues proved as subjective an experience as his awe before nature. Even so, politics retained its interest for him; in 1831, when John Stuart Mill visited Wordsworth, then sixty-one, he was surprised to find him extremely well informed. His verse, Mill noted, gave no indication that "real life and the pursuits of men" concerned him in the slightest, but "these very subjects occupy the greater part of his thoughts, & he talks on no subject more instructively than on states of society & forms of government."[28]

Wordsworth no doubt talked well about states and governments, but even his discovery of politics had been a tribute to his utterly romantic sensibility. In the summer of 1790, still a Cambridge undergraduate, he had undertaken a strenuous walking tour on the Continent accompanied by a classmate, and on French soil on his way to the Alps he happened to witness the first-anniversary celebration of the taking of the Bastille. Wordsworth warmed to the event. To see a "whole nation mad with joy," he wrote his sister, Dorothy, impressed him deeply.[29] His reaction was characteristically self-referential, at least in retrospect:

> How sweet at such a time, with such delight
> On every side, in prime of youthful strength

> To feel a Poet's tender melancholy
> And fond conceit of sadness.[30]

He returned to England filled with revolutionary sentiments. An enthusiast
intent on grounding his opinions on solid information, he spent his time reading political tracts and attending debates in the House of Commons, and when
he went back to France late in 1791, he was pleased to find cogent reasons to
support the Revolution.

They were a poet's reasons, literally picturesque. In a memorable passage in
the *Prelude,* he recalled his chief instructor in revolutionary principles, a French
officer named Beaupuy, with whom he happened

> One day to meet a hunger-bitten girl
> Who crept along fitting her languid self
> Unto a heifer's motion—by a cord
> Tied to her arm, and picking thus from the lane
> Its sustenance, while the girl with her two hands
> Was busy knitting in a heartless mood
> Of solitude—and at the sight my friend
> In agitation said, "Tis against that
> Which we are fighting."

Wordsworth, by then an ardent radical, could only agree:

> I with him believed
> Devoutly that a spirit was abroad
> Which could not be withstood, that poverty,
> At least like this, would in a little time
> Be found no more.[31]

One can hardly fault Wordsworth's humane impulse as he watched the hunger-
bitten girl creeping along with her heifer, but he was plainly not engaged in
tough-minded analysis. As a poet enmeshed in politics, he rejected abstract
theorizing in favor of listening to his emotions face to face with concrete
experiences.

To be sure, Wordsworth neither intended nor advertised the *Prelude* as an
exercise in political argument. He candidly labeled it an "autobiographical
poem" tracing the "growth of a poet's mind," in which he reflected with sorely
gained distance on excited times past. In the version of the poem he completed
in 1805 but left in his desk, he traced the evolution of his political opinions

through the crucial years of the French Revolution down to the fall of Robespierre in late July 1794 and beyond. Though imbued with revolutionary ideals
and scathing about his own government's anti-French campaign, he had found
his faith shaken by the Terror. The French, declared enemies of oppression
everywhere, were becoming oppressors in their turn. But he yielded up his
radicalism with visible reluctance. The execution of King Louis XVI on January 21, 1793, a parricide that cost the revolutionaries many of their foreign
sympathizers, did not diminish Wordsworth's wholehearted commitment to
radical republicanism. There were times, he wrote (but did not publish), when
compassion is out of place and liberty must borrow the arms of despotism.

But in the *Prelude* of 1805, writing from a recently acquired patriotic perspective yet trying to recapture earlier thoughts and feelings, he anatomized his
enthusiasms and his "juvenile errors."[32] But this was more than emotion recol-
lected in tranquility. Books 9 and 10 rise to a penetrating self-analysis as he
records his sojourn in France in 1792, reading revolutionary pamphlets but also
consorting with royalists about to emigrate. Honestly he reports the way that
complex, often confusing events evoked complex, often confused responses in
him.

The times gave Wordsworth and his friends much to talk about. "How
gravely and earnestly used Samuel Taylor Coleridge and William Wordsworth
and my uncle Southey also to discuss the affairs of the nation," Sara Coleridge,
the poet's daughter, was to recall, "as if it all came home to their business and
bosoms, as if it were their private concern!"[33] One may take this reminiscence
as the record of an absorbed interest in important news from home and abroad.
But it suggests, more subtly, these romantics' subjective reception of that news;
they took it as an opportunity to feel their own pulse as it quickened at historic
events. And it serves as a reminder that Wordsworth's overworked comment
on his youthful revolutionary attitudes—"Bliss was it in that dawn to be alive, /
But to be young was very Heaven"—was a typical inward look. To be blissful
and in heaven is not the stuff of which practical politics is made, but an instructive comment on the romantic self in politics.

In 1798, after years of provocation, as Wordsworth remembered them, he
finally turned against the Revolution. Lamenting France's invasion of Switzer-
land as changing "a war of self-defence / For one of conquest," he reacted in
expected ways, examining the state of his feelings:

> I read her doom,
> With anger vexed, with disappointment sore,
> But not dismayed, nor taking to the shame
> Of a false prophet.[34]

Wordsworth never breaks his contract with his readers, never fails to inform them just where he stands, or in what direction he is moving—emotionally.

In old age, Wordsworth portrayed his evolution as a voyage from rash impulse to good sense: "I went over to Paris at the time of the revolution in 1792 or 1793," he said, "and so was *pretty hot in it;* but I found Mr. J. Watt there before me, and quite as warm in the same cause. We thus both began life as ardent and thoughtless radicals; but we have both become, in the course of our lives, as all sensible men, I think, have done, good sober-minded Conservatives."[35] His insistence that he had "given twelve hours thought to the conditions and prospects of society, for one to poetry," which John Stuart Mill found so remarkable, is well known. Still, his sober conservatism was no more firmly grounded than his thoughtless radicalism had been, in fact most probably less well. His mounting outrage at the violence of the French Revolution, his patriotic hatred of Napoleon, and his rediscovery of the English nation were all matched among more prosaic compatriots. But his Toryism was too extravagant to be simply rational; he prized his subjectivity at the expense of political reflection.

To be sure, his paternalistic sympathies with the poor and oppressed, the subject of some of his most moving verse, never diminished, but there was not a reformist cause that the elderly poet did not find grounds for panicked alarm. He opposed legislation against cruelty to animals and wrote a sequence of semi-religious sonnets defending the death penalty. And his attitude toward the Great Reform Act of 1832, which widened the franchise and reduced electoral corruption, was pure hysteria. "My heart aches at the thought of what we are now threatened with." He predicted a calamitous future, wholeheartedly seconding the anxiety of the influential and irreconcilable Tory magnate Lord Lonsdale: since the "reformed Parliament cannot be altered for the better, nothing can prevent an explosion and the entire overthrow of the Institutions of the Country." Resorting to complicated and lurid metaphors, he charged that while the British constitution had grown organically, "under the Protection of Providence," as a "skin grows to, with, and for the human body," the newly empowered ministers "would flay this body, and present us, instead of its natural Skin, with a garment made to order, which, if it be not rejected, will prove such a Shirt as in the Fable, drove Hercules to madness and self-destruction." In an access of charity, he begged God to forgive the writers of the Reform Bill, who had "already gone so far towards committing a greater political crime than any recorded in History."[36]

Wordsworth's liberal contemporaries were disposed to call this shift hard names. Mary Shelley recorded in her diary that she and her husband had read part of Wordsworth's *Excursion* as a pathetic confession of weakness and dependency: "He is a slave." Perhaps the most memorable denunciation came in 1845, when Wordsworth still had five years to live, with Robert Browning's harsh, and excessive, accusation that he had sold his birthright for a "handful of silver" and a "riband to stick in his coat."[37] More to the point, though arguably still overemphatic, was Hazlitt's judgment in his review of *The Excursion* that Wordsworth had never been anything but an autobiographer, a poet who "may be said to create his own materials; his thoughts are his real subjects." The "power of his mind preys upon itself. It is as if there were nothing but himself and the universe. He lives in the busy solitude of his own heart; in the deep silence of thought." How different this egotism from Shakespeare's ability to be "nothing in himself," and to be "all that others were"![38]

This comment reminds us that the great philosophical poem on which Wordsworth labored all his life and never completed was to be called "The Recluse."[39] It recalls, too, Keats's much quoted rejection of the "wordsworth-ian or egotistical sublime," as he sought for the poetical impersonality that "has no self."[40] No doubt the romantics dealt with their inwardness and its links to the outside world in the most varied ways. And in itself their idealism and their indignation were not new; political thinkers have been animated by such gen-erous emotions all the way from Plato to Voltaire. What set them apart from their predecessors was the sustained cultivation of the responsive self in the public as much as in the private domain.

3. Heart Religion

Keats's comment on the Wordsworthian egotistical sublime captures a principal ingredient in the romantic mentality—including, it must be said, Keats's own—its dual, intertwined absorption in the aesthetic and the subjective. This was by no means the monopoly of Wordsworth and his admirers: as Thomas Babington Macaulay observed of the most visible among the English romantics, "Lord Byron never wrote without some reference, direct or indirect, to him-self"; he was "himself the beginning, the middle, and the end of all his own poetry, the hero of every tale, the chief object in every landscape."[1] The ro-mantics' infatuation with the self was a mental aphrodisiac; decades before Oscar Wilde observed that to love oneself is the beginning of a lifelong ro-mance, they proved that the re-enchantment of the world often began with self-enchantment before the mirror.

Not surprisingly, this potent amalgam of aestheticism and subjectivity found its most concentrated expression in the romantics' way with religion. "Religion is so beautiful, that almost necessarily it decorates the works where it is introduced, however weakly; its grandeur, wisdom, sweetness and usefulness have, I should say, a literary attraction."[2] This is the voice of the Italian playwright and novelist Alessandro Manzoni. Despite a dramatic conversion to the faith into which he had been born, he long held on to a tincture of doubt and an ironic anticlericalism, but one element that sustained his recaptured piety was the sheer comeliness of Roman Catholicism. And Protestant romantic poets in Sweden no less than Catholics in Spain basked in the beauties of true faith.

The romantics were no more at one about the great matter of religion than about politics, but they generated an identifiable style of thinking. To be sure, as we have seen, Shelley called himself "atheos" as well as "demokratikos" and "philanthropos"; Stendhal was a skeptic, and Fichte, as a young professor of philosophy at Jena, was convicted of propagating atheism. But none of these mutineers could weaken, let alone eradicate, the current of piety that largely dominated the romantics' world view. The commanding majority, persuaded that the Enlightenment had denied humans starved for transcendence the nourishment that only belief in—even better, love for—God can provide, felt impelled to undo the damage the philosophes had left behind.

This sense of a great rescue mission organized romantic polemics in unexpected domains: they enlisted even their claims for the creative imagination in their efforts to restore religion to the heart of human concerns. Man's "faith in God," Friedrich Schleiermacher wrote in 1799, "depends on the direction of the imagination."[3] Romantics had no doubt that the notorious *mal du siècle,* that *"general inner disharmony"* which Friedrich Schlegel diagnosed in company with other romantics, was the fault of unbelievers.[4] Skeptics, deists, and atheists had rejected the sublime truths and the restraining hand of faith, and calamity had followed. Nothing seemed more obvious.

The prodigious outpourings of the Dutch philologist, historian, conservative propagandist, and influential poet Willem Bilderdijk offer evidence that this religious crusade was not confined to the capitals of romanticism.[5] The only Dutch-speaking writer enjoying an international reputation, Bilderdijk made war on the rationalistic spirit of his age in everything he wrote. Endorsing a literal-minded Calvinism, he expended his formidable verbal resources extolling inward feeling at the expense of reason, and called a romantic's curse upon his unbelieving race: "I sing the doom of the primeval world," he wrote in 1808,

> And of that race, with hell and devils leagued
> In deeds iniquitous, which dared to tempt
> Heav'ns Majesty, and, impious, sought to scale
> The battlements of Paradise.[6]

Other romantics, in the Netherlands and elsewhere, shared Bilderdijk's convictions and often his rage, but fell short of his pugilistic powers.

While, as we have noted, some pious romantics invented new doctrines, more of them, intent on breathing vigor into moribund forms, preferred to adapt time-honored dispensations to modern demands. They found the quest for a religion of the heart exceedingly congenial; zestfully they leaped into the age-old struggle, ever renewed, between frozen ritual and vital faith. Most romantics disdained battles over fine points of theology as a waste of time; some even refused high posts in their church as a betrayal of their innermost convictions. And even those romantics who remained loyal, converted, or returned to traditional churches did not stake their case on confessional tenets or tangible institutions. Rather, they passionately sought the spirit that gives life. Born as a Jew, Heine once described, at once poignantly and cynically, the act of conversion to Christianity as a passport to Western civilization. Just as poignantly, though less cynically, romantics reveled in baptisms and re-baptisms, usually a wrenching emotional rather than carefully calculated step. Jews turned Christian; Protestants, Catholic; tepid believers, zealot. Intent on sharing the inner peace that had cleansed their soul, they became missionaries to save others. The romantic move toward inwardness was not always a lonely business.

Some cardinal texts in this campaign were written around the turn of the century: Novalis's *Die Christenheit oder Europa,* though not published until 1826, in 1799; Schleiermacher's polemic *Reden über die Religion* in the same year; Chateaubriand's *Génie du Christianisme* in 1802. The last of these is probably the most spectacular among them, certainly the most revealing. A bulky but polished treatise, it was an astonishing production for its dashing and adventurous author. From a prestigious, conspicuously pious family long settled in Brittany, Chateaubriand had been intended for the priesthood, lost his vocation, served a tour of duty as an officer in the French army, and traveled in the United States, which provided him with incomparable materials for exotic tales about romantic Indians. After his return, though at first far from hostile to the aims of the Revolution, he joined the emigration of French nobles, thus avoiding the fate of his family: prison and the guillotine. For some years, he lived a life of near destitution and intense reading in England—a romantic figure before the advent of French romanticism. In 1800, he came home, drafts of his defense of Christianity in his baggage.

His book became an instant best-seller and for decades remained a handy storehouse to be pillaged for sermons, lessons in Catholic seminaries, and by literary imitators.[7] On its first appearance, one witness recalled, "not a woman in Paris slept. People grabbed it, people stole a copy. Then what an awakening, what chatter, what palpitations! *Quoi!* that is Christianity, we all said, but it's

delicious." It tells much about Chateaubriand's culture that women should
have been his most enthusiastic readers. But men were not immune. Victor
Hugo recalled how the *Génie du Christianisme* had dazzled him with its "music
and color," its picturesque blend of cathedral architecture and tales from the
Bible.[8] Critics of the book—and it had many—worried about all this delicious-
ness. They admitted that Chateaubriand had painted beguiling word pictures
and told touching stories, but they wondered if these could stand up to responsible criticism. Not a few questioned the author's sincerity. Had he not started
on the book in London sensing that it might catch the reemerging fashion for
religion after the dry decades of faithless *lumières* and Revolution? Had he not
published it opportunely while the First Consul, Napoleon Bonaparte, was
concluding a concordat with Rome? Had he not, as recently as 1797, published
an essay on revolutions that had virtually proclaimed the bankruptcy of Christianity?

But if Chateaubriand was an opportunist, he was an opportunist who believed his own press releases. He had good reason for claiming that he had put
into the text everything he had in his heart.[9] Certainly, as his subsequent career
would amply show, Chateaubriand did not lack civic courage. But he was not
above correcting the facts: introducing the first edition of the *Génie du Christianisme,* he attributed its genesis to an appeal from his dying mother to return to
the faith. The book was a "mausoleum a son had built his mother." And the
sister who had conveyed this message to him, he reported, had died from the
consequences of her imprisonment before he received her letter. "These two
voices from the tomb, that death which served as interpreter of death, struck
me. I became a Christian. I did not yield, I admit, to great supernatural enlightenment; my conviction arose from the heart. I wept, and I believed."[10] This
lachrymose bit of pseudo-autobiography was all too convenient, prettier than
the reality. Actually his sister had died more than a year after his mother. And in
1799, Chateaubriand had candidly called the treatise in progress an "occasional
work"—*oeuvre de circonstance*—and hoped for a publishing success. Shrewdly
assessing his strengths as a writer, he observed that he was making "every effort
to banish polemics or theology, and to make reading it as agreeable as that of a
novel."[11] He wanted his readers to weep and to believe—and buy his book.

In short, Chateaubriand was confident that the most effective way of enticing the reading public—and this makes the *Génie du Christianisme* so informative a witness to the romantic age—was to turn religion into a sentimental and
appealing personal matter. Its author presented himself as one wounded soul
thirsting after beauty, speaking to others. This, to repeat, was not pure pose, but
however authentic the *Génie* as a confessional text, its true origins were more
remote, more obscure than Chateaubriand made them out to be.[12] It was almost

transparently a distillation of early memories revived and enlivened by recent events, a childhood atmosphere translated into theological propaganda, a work of regression astutely exploited.

There was, of course, nothing particularly original about Christian convictions springing from deep inward sources. Memorable figures from St. Paul to St. Augustine, from Luther to Pascal, had been propelled into making immortal defenses of piety by overpowering intimate experiences. But romantics like Chateaubriand offered private episodes not merely as the impetus for conversion to religion but as compelling evidence for its validity. In their consistent and emphatic assertion of the self's supremacy, romantic believers, unlike most of their devout ancestors, thought their personal testimony sufficient.

Chateaubriand's argument—if that is the right word—is quickly summarized: not that Christianity is beautiful because it is true; it is true because it is beautiful. He loaded his text with long passages of erudition, usually dubious, and with comparisons, no less dubious, between Christianity and other, naturally inferior religions. Chapters on ornaments and festivals jostle chapters on tombs from the ancient Egyptians to the medieval Christians, chapters on missions and chivalrous orders, chapters on Catholic doctrine. None of them forbidding, all of them eminently digestible, they read like a strenuously informal gallery talk by a genial guide. And they all point to the ineffable loveliness of Catholic Christianity: the celestial harmonies of religious chants, the sublimity of the Cross as a symbol, the sentiments that prove the immortality of the soul. Significantly, Chateaubriand titled the two central parts of the *Génie* "Poetics of Christianity" and "Beaux-Arts and Literature." His heart is in poetry—devout poetry. He finds it important that "the Bible is more beautiful than Homer," a judgment he pursues with meticulously drawn parallels through two chapters.[13] Whether readers found this sort of thing persuasive rather than merely pleasing depended on their willingness to set aside traditional exegesis in favor of a vague but thrilling adoration of the beauties of Christ and of Christianity.

This assertive turn to aesthetic piety exercised considerable power over the French public, but its influence was even more marked in the German states. Their romantics had fewer repairs to make in the crumbling structure of belief: in their culture, prophets of disenchantment had been few and relatively uninfluential. The musty aroma of Pietism, that curious blend of severe morality, intimate self-examination, and infatuation with the body of Christ, continued to hang over late-eighteenth-century German thinkers. Hölderlin, Schleiermacher, and Novalis came out of a Pietist environment, and their training left permanent deposits in their poetic, often sensual religiosity. But Pietists or not, German romantics rejected materialism or atheism as sheer aberrations, almost beyond the bounds of the thinkable. Around 1800, not even the most liberal German state could have imagined a constitution modeled on that of the United States, a founding document that had remained ostentatiously silent about the deity, even by implication.

No wonder that an eighteenth-century German deist like the philosopher and orientalist Hermann Samuel Reimarus should remain an isolated and, outside his intimate circle in Hamburg, little-known figure. His rationalistic readings ridiculing Scriptures for absurdities and contradictions and his fragmentary code of a natural religion could not be published in his lifetime, and made virtually no impact on German debates on matters of faith. And Lessing, that freest, most critical of spirits, devised a creed of his own—heterodox, humane, idiosyncratic, and antidogmatic, to be sure, yet announcing the progressive revelation of religious truths in the world. Even Kant, the great *Aufklärer,* had smuggled elements of original sin—he called it "radical evil"—into what he dubbed religion within the bounds of reason alone. And yet, even though German enlightened thinking stopped short of the radical skepticism of a Hume or the outright atheism of a Holbach, its stabs at reasoned faiths could not satisfy the appetites of German romantics hungering for more substantial fare.

No doubt quite sincerely, the religious food the German romantics craved was for the spirit. But much of their exalted spirituality was a thinly veiled expression of their inner erotic life. They made no secret of this: without apology, in devout language, they yearned for, and recalled, sexual experiences. There was, for the most part, nothing coarse about their earthy religiosity. After all, most of its readers deplored Friedrich Schlegel's *Lucinde* as a scandalous departure from more decorous confessions.* But German romantic religion was, even so, carnal enough.

The first step toward this worldly unworldliness was to link the aesthetic to the sacred. "In its essence," Hölderlin wrote, "all religion is poetic."[14] He was summing up the core of German romanticism. In his unfinished novel, *Hyperion,* he used simple, striking metaphors to make the link: "The first child of divine beauty is art," and "the second daughter of beauty is religion. Religion is love of beauty." Surely, "without such a love of beauty, without such a religion, every state is a wizened skeleton without love and spirit, and all thinking and acting a tree without a top." Hölderlin was speaking of Athens, but he meant his definition of religion to have general application. In *Hyperion,* the Athenians, beautiful and whole, stand tall as an ideal for Germans who sadly fall short of the pattern. Love is religion, religion is love. Novalis underscored this identification in a celebrated aphorism: "Love is the final purpose of *world*

*See below, pp. 91–93.

history.'[15] This was subjectivity raised to metaphysical dimensions.

German romantic religion, then, treated outward forms as mere vessels; they cherished feelings deep enough to reach down to the wellsprings of instinctual drives. The most self-willed German romantics hesitated to desert traditional dispensations and hailed the advent of Christianity as the moment when divine love had entered the world. But they considered a believer's fate of having been born into one confession rather than another something of an accident; each church, with its doctrines and rituals, is simply a particular manifestation of a universal truth.

Friedrich Schlegel, at least before his conversion to Rome, voiced this aesthetic pantheism most expressively. In 1798, he described his love Dorothea Veit to his friend Novalis as "but a sketch, but in a great style throughout. Her whole essence is religion, although she knows nothing of it."[16] What mattered to him was not to whom she prayed—she would, in her three decades with Schlegel, convert twice, first from Judaism to Protestantism and then, with her husband, to Catholicism—but her way of living within, and exuding, a religious aura. Her lover fondly saw her displaying a delectable devout sensibility, displaying it, we know from *Lucinde,* everywhere, whether on walks or in bed.

This was the sort of praise to which Novalis could respond, must even have found rather tepid. The last years of his short life—he died in 1801, at twenty-eight, of consumption—were at once darkened and inspired by an obsession with the loss of his fiancée, Sophie von Kühn. She must have been a charming and precocious girl, with whom Novalis had become infatuated when she was thirteen. But two years later, in March 1797, just after her fifteenth birthday, she died. The journal Novalis kept during these shattering days records incessant, painful brooding about her and frequent pilgrimages to her grave to bring flowers and, weeping, to commune with her. Elation and depression visited him in turn. One May evening in the cemetery, he felt "indescribably joyful" and experienced "flashing moments of enthusiasm." Centuries were like moments; "her presence was palpable—all the time I believed she would appear."[17] He allowed these near-hallucinations to govern his feelings, his thoughts, his poetry for the four years that remained to him. Still, in late 1798, though he kept the candle of his cult of Sophie burning bright, Novalis became engaged to be married again.

His great lyrics *Hymnen an die Nacht* were one tribute to Sophie; his determination to join her, to confound night and day, death and life, were another. "Life," he wrote in the *Blüthenstaub* fragments he contributed to the *Athenäum* in 1798, "is the beginning of death. Life exists for the sake of death." The wish for suicide was rarely out of his mind. "The authentic philosophical act is self-killing," he observed in one of his unpublished thought experiments; "that is the real beginning of all philosophy." Yet by no means all among Novalis's thoughts of love were purely spiritual, or spiritual at all. Shortly after Sophie von Kühn's death, he candidly confided his lustful musings to his private journal: "Early, sensual stirrings," or, a few days later, "sensual fantasies." Again, in May, "Lasciviousness was active from early in the day until the afternoon," or some days after, "much lasciviousness." He yearned to rejoin his fiancée's body as much as her soul.[18]

The cult of Sophie von Kühn became enmeshed with Novalis's religion as he coupled her name with that of Jesus. He saw his faith, which tells of Christ's triumph over death, through the lenses of his all-consuming bereavement. Bringing uncharacteristic intensity to a characteristic romantic maneuver—we have seen it before and will see it again—Novalis made erotic love and emotional religion into virtual Siamese twins, with the boundaries between them porous. "I have religion for little Sophie—not love," he wrote in an unpublished fragment, only to complicate the matter instantly: "Absolute love, independent of the heart, founded on faith, is religion." Again, "Love can merge into religion through absolute will." And he jotted down some suggestive notions, presumably for later use: "All absolute feeling is religious. / Religion of the beautiful. Artist's religion. / Consequences from that."[19] Drawing some of these consequences in his poems and his unfinished novel *Heinrich von Ofterdingen,* he mingled the spiritual and the erotic. The last *Hymn to the Night,* titled "Longing for death," concludes with an ecstatic verse about descending to the sweet bride, to Jesus the beloved. A dream breaks our bonds and lowers us into the father's lap.[20] Novalis's romantic fantasies were a closet drama of love and death, with a single actor on stage.

Novalis freely acknowledged the power that extreme subjectivity exercised over him. "The imagination puts the world of the future either in the heights or in the depths, or in the migration of souls into us. We dream of traveling through the universe—Is that universe not *in us?* We do not know the depths of our spirit—the mysterious path goes to the interior. Eternity with its worlds—past and future—is in us, or nowhere."[21] Novalis had studied Fichte to good purpose; the philosophy of the Ego and of absolute Idealism, the view that the self creates the world, strongly appealed to him. But his accolade to the powers of the imagination—eternity is in us, or nowhere—had grounds more passionate than philosophical reflection. The exaltation of an inner world at the expense of external reality could scarcely go further than Novalis pushed it. His practical experience of administering salt mines seemed far away.

While other German romantics stopped short of making overt sexuality and inward piety live in open concubinage, they shared Novalis's conviction that religion is in essence a matter of feeling. Among testimonials to this literally self-centered religiosity, Friedrich Schleiermacher's *Reden über die Religion* proved the most trenchant and the most quotable. Writing to his close friend in Berlin, the intelligent Jewish hostess Henriette Herz, who rivaled her competitors with her gift for friendship and surpassed them with her beauty, he called his faith, in a charming pun, a *"heart religion"—Herzreligion—*"so through and through that I have room for no other."*

Once Schleiermacher, an obscure preacher in Berlin, had published his stirring battle call against unbelief, he was obscure no longer. His manifesto proved so provocative largely because it did not aim at the expected targets, the godless philosophes. Schleiermacher despised the French for their "frivolous indifference" and their "witty levity." But he preferred to concentrate on educated Germans who rarely thought about God, or justified him with arguments drawn from ethics or metaphysics. The point to be established was the autonomy of religion. It did not require sophisticated debates over the nature of the Deity, abstruse researches into proofs for immortality, or moral speculations: true belief cannot be a collection of notions about God. In fact, those who know the most are not necessarily the most pious. "If you would only read between the lines!" Modern scholasticism is simply irrelevant. The essence of religion "is neither thinking nor acting, but intuition and feeling."[22] While in later life, Schleiermacher would show himself a formidable scholar, theologian, and academic administrator, in this early romantic statement, the most influential book he ever wrote, his anti-intellectualism was uncompromising. "Intuition without feeling is nothing."[23] So is feeling without intuition—and so is reason without both.

For Schleiermacher, then, an authentic religious sense consists of a pious receptivity, an almost sexual opening up to God. The religious moment is a moment of ecstasy, "modest and tender like a virginal kiss, sacred and fruitful like a bridal embrace." Schleiermacher chose his erotic metaphors more felicitously than he knew. The "higher and divine activity" of the soul "flies" toward that moment. "I embrace it not like a shadow but like the sacred being itself. I lie on the bosom of the infinite world; I am at this moment its soul, for I feel all its forces and its infinite life like my own; at this moment it is my body, for I penetrate its muscles and its members like my own."[24] Religion is contemplative surrender to, or incorporation of, the divine, a seductive coupling of self-abasement and self-glorification that is literally amorous.

*Friedrich Wilhelm Kantzenbach, *Friedrich Daniel Ernst Schleiermacher in Selbstzeugnissen und Bilddokumenten* (1967), 50. The punning meaning of this declaration is lost in translation. In calling his religion "Herzreligion," Schleiermacher not only defines it as religion of the heart but hints at the influence of his friend Henriette Herz on his thinking.

One consequence Schleiermacher drew from this theology was that religion must eschew all sectarianism. "To love the world spirit and joyfully to watch his work is the goal of our religion, and there is no fear in love"—or hate. Religion demands an abiding aesthetic affection that acknowledges God as the Great Sculptor. Yielding to feeling and intuition, the believer discovers the "harmony of the universe" that God has made, that "wonderful and grand unity in his eternal work of art."[25] The Divine Artist stands preeminent among all artists not merely with his gift for creating unmatched beauty but with his supreme ability to resolve the conflicts to which imperfect humans are heir.

It is only fair to add that although Schleiermacher's theology was, much like Novalis's, supremely subjective almost by definition, it was not solipsistic. Its inwardness reached out to others. "From its wanderings through the whole domain of humanity, religion returns with a sharpened sense and a better formed judgment into its own self." While one's "most essential and dearest home" is "the innermost life," we "find material for religion" by joining "humanity" in love. Only the one who grasps the infinite in all its manifestations can be called truly religious. Schleiermacher praised the ancient Greeks for having understood this truth: they knew that love, humility, joy, longing after God, all deserve the name of piety. "To become one with the Infinite in the midst of finitude and to be eternal in one moment—that is the immortality of religion."[26] The broad appeal of Schleiermacher's populist theology is easy to understand: no learning is needed.

The romantics' cult of Nature, then, was religion of the heart projected on the outside world, a humble egotism.* Feelings of swooning impotence and grandiose omnipotence took their turn. Spread across the romantic landscape, this cult found diverse, though predictable, local expressions. The Germans made a philosophy of it; the French, tales about improbably sensitive and well-spoken savages; the English, poetry. All these forms of faith matter to the historian of nineteenth-century bourgeois culture, for it was on the ground of Nature that the disenchanters and the re-enchanters of the world fought out their great duel most implacably.

The severe intellectual style of the Enlightenment had at once involved humans in, and separated them from, nature. It involved them by treating them as beings subject to laws that the sciences of man and society are called to discover: the determinism that governs the orbits of the planets or the growth of trees also governs all human phenomena. The philosophes' critical spirit, which

---

*As below, in the relevant pages on art, I shall capitalize "Nature" when a romantic gives it a religious tinge.

they saw scoring its most spectacular triumphs in the natural sciences, literally held nothing sacred. This view amounted to the denial that there is anything divine about the body or, even more important, about the soul—or, as they preferred to conceptualize it, the mind. The biblical saga about man being made in God's image was only one of the discredited fairy tales that the devout apparently could not live without.

At the same time—and this is often overlooked—the scientific cast of mind separated humans from nature in their capacity as investigators, whether of the world or of the self. It held that as detectives tracking nature's riddles, they must concentrate on discovering and testing objective truths. The findings of science are independent of human wishes. Knowledge is superior to ignorance, but whatever the impulsions driving scientists to their work, their results are ethically neutral. From this perspective, the Enlightenment sturdily rejected the fond expectation that nature exists to give life meaning and value. It does not acquire significance only when humans swim in its ambiance and adore its splendor. Rather it exists, and must be known, for its own sake. To make the very life of nature dependent on the observer is to project human sentiments into entities where they do not belong, or to identify observers with the object from which, for science's sake, they should carefully detach themselves.

The romantics had no quarrel with the philosophes' definition of humans as dual beings at once enmeshed in and divorced from nature, but they reversed the signs from approval to alarm. They thought the human condition a scandal, especially in modern times, and held centuries of corrosive unbelief that the Enlightenment had driven to fatal extremes directly responsible for it. The devilish subverters of the true faith had alienated humanity from Nature by denying its God-given endowment, which, however vicious the philosophes' efforts to efface it, must still glow in the embers of the modern soul. And precisely this alienation had entangled modern man with Nature, though in its lowest forms, as lustful appetites. If it was at all appropriate to speak of the human animal, that epithet correctly described the consequences of the philosophes' destructive project of lowering man to the level of beasts—or, if the eighteenth-century materialists had had their way, of a machine. That epithet of Friedrich Schlegel's for Paris, "the modern Sodom," points up the romantic rejection of the eighteenth-century celebration of the worldly. The moral neutrality of the sciences that the philosophes had toasted as a liberation from prejudice and superstition was, for the romantics, a symptom of this degradation.

But where the philosophes had spread havoc, the romantics saw salvation; their hope for climbing out of the pit of modern godlessness lay in worshiping Nature. It was there that they might glimpse the traces of divinity: in its works

as much as in its word. Coleridge earnestly reminded his readers of that "revelation of God—the great book of his servant Nature."[27] Other romantics took
humble, daily things—brooks and hills, animals and birds, songs and the laughter of children—as so many lessons in natural piety. Wordsworth said it best in
1798, in the aptly titled "The Tables Turned." The poet invites his friend,
probably the disputatious Hazlitt, to leave his books and instead notice the sun,
the green fields, the woodlands and listen to the birds: "Let Nature be your
teacher." She has, after all, "a world of ready wealth," to bless minds and hearts
with cheerful and spontaneous wisdom:

> One impulse from a vernal wood
> May teach you more of man,
> Of moral evil and of good,
> Than all the sages can.

There is nothing mild-mannered in Wordsworth's love of Nature; it issues in
an attack on deadly rationalism:

> Sweet is the lore which Nature brings;
> Our meddling intellect
> Mis-shapes the beauteous forms of things.
> We murder to dissect.

A whole world of thought unfolds in these two deceptively simple quatrains.
They disparage the analytical spirit, that mainstay of the Enlightenment which,
as the assassin of higher truths, had attempted to undermine the salutary teachings Nature has in store for those who know how to read the eloquent vernal
wood.*
   The romantics had of course not invented the theological contention that the
merest glance at the works of God in Nature is bound to generate or intensify
piety. This proof for the existence and beneficence of God and for the truth of
religion had long enjoyed considerable prestige as a respectable weapon in the
armory of religious apologetics. What lent originality to the romantic appeal to

---

*These romantic teachings are not "scientific," not frozen in formulas, but aesthetic and ethical:
they speak to the worshiper of Nature with their appealing beauty and purity. It was in Wordsworth's spirit, and in his presence, that in December 1817, during the much reported dinner at
Benjamin Haydon's, Keats and Lamb sarcastically toasted the health of Newton, who had destroyed the poetry of the rainbow, and had added a coda: "confusion to mathematics!" See
Marjorie Hope Nicolson, *Newton Demands the Muse: Newton's "Opticks" and the Eighteenth Century
Poets* (1946), 1–2.

Nature was that it assigned the worshiper a leading role in the making of this creed. Not content with marveling at the superhuman competence and superhuman versatility of the divine artificer, devout romantics resonated with Nature's hallowed rhythms, rhythms they could gather into themselves only after they had truly learned to see, hear, smell—and respond. In romantic religion, the most far-ranging exploration of the blessed universe must eventually lead back to the self.

This theology of Nature, though, was as risky for the pious as it was exhilarating, and early-nineteenth-century Christians were sensitive to that. They could hardly overlook that the appeal to God's omnipresence had in the past served a small army of dubious believers. Most insidious of all, they thought, the pantheists, those evasive atheists in the garb of enthusiasts, had used that appeal as a favorite debating point. If God is everywhere and in all things, the essential distance between sinful humans and their divine judge is blurred, and key tenets of Christian doctrine—providence, divine sovereignty, original sin—must lose all reason for existence. Yet romantics, including theologians, regularly toyed with this seductive pagan faith. In the early 1830s, looking back, Heinrich Heine said flatly, "We do not talk about it, but pantheism is the open secret of Germany," its "hidden religion," professed by "our greatest thinkers, our best artists."[28]

One can see why: to its devotees, pantheism seemed far nobler than sectarianism and eliminated the need for worrying technical issues in theology or tortured apologies for contradictions in Holy Scriptures. It permitted those thirsting for God to revel in religion as love, or religion as poetry. Some of Hölderlin's most rapturous outpourings, redolent with a devout pantheism, were far from isolated. The young Schlegel brothers, Novalis, and Schelling had read deeply in Spinoza, the most celebrated—or, rather, the most notorious—of modern pantheists, and they had woven his *Ethics,* like his *Political-Theological Tractate,* into the texture of their thought. Schelling's *Naturphilosophie,* which preached the identity of Nature and Spirit, looked suspiciously like an elaborate metaphysical structure camouflaging pantheistic notions with high-flown verbiage.

The venomous quarrels over the philosophy of Spinoza that erupted in German philosophical and literary circles in the 1780s exposed pantheism not merely as a threat to sectarian Christianity but, among anxious theologians, to all faith. Through much of the century, Spinoza, known mainly through tendentious denigrations, seemed the most dangerous of all seducers: the plausible atheist. His terse formula, God or Nature, was read as a clever invitation to desert religion altogether. It was only when Lessing, and after him Goethe, discovered Spinoza that he came to be called the thinker drunk with God.

Then Spinoza the impecunious Jewish lens grinder living a life of unblemished probity, the uncompromising thinker who bravely courted expulsion from his religious community, the philosopher who preached rationality and tolerance, became for his few but fervent admirers a secular saint. "He does not prove the Existence of God," wrote Goethe. "Existence is God. And if others scold him for that and call him Atheum, I should call and praise him as theissimum, indeed christianissimum."[29] This last epithet was a dubious compliment: Spinoza was no Christian. But Goethe's praise was a manifesto for his culture. It made Spinoza respectable for those inclined to romantic religiosity.

Schleiermacher was still more idolatrous, more instructive, and more pathetic. In *Reden über die Religion,* he reverently reminded his readers of "the spirit of holy, rejected Spinosa!" In his lyrical portrait, he expounded the pantheist's cult of Nature: the identity of God and universe; the exclusive love for the Infinite; the capacity of extraordinary individuals to make themselves into the pure reflection of the world.[30] In his systematic writings on *Naturphilosophie,* Schelling would not express the religious worship of nature any more clearly, but at far greater length.

The best way to read Schelling is to read Goethe. Early conscious of his gifts, vastly ambitious, an alert and critical reader of Kant and Fichte intent on constructing his own system, Schelling had impressed Goethe, who in 1798 secured a professorship for the twenty-three-year-old at the University of Jena. In the five years he spent there, Schelling was an intimate of his patron's who fully shared his enthusiasm for Nature. For Schelling the study of Nature was the study of the World Spirit at work; any phenomenon in physics or geology or chemistry provided a key to the Eternal. His method of "intellectual intuition," as Schelling called it, a kind of poetical philosophizing, could only appeal to Goethe, who repeatedly disavowed any gift for formal philosophy but read widely in it and, for all his disclaimers, wrote philosophical poems. If Schelling, who perpetrated some forgettable verse of his own, had possessed Goethe's gifts, it is these poems he might have written.

Goethe, as everyone knows, was too protean a genius to be captured by any category. Poet, novelist, playwright, autobiographer, translator, sketcher, editor, theater director, travel writer, literary historian, art critic, public servant, student of the natural sciences, cultural monument, he was, with equal competence and originality, romantic and classicist alike. But when he apostrophized or investigated Nature, he was a romantic to the core. Goethe the scientist was no armchair enthusiast; his correspondence documents his delight, unwearied with the years, in his direct observation of nature in all its dizzying variety. He gathered thousands of geological specimens in the mines in the Weimar duchy, in the Italian countryside, or near favorite Bohemian spas. He botanized in fields and forests as enthusiastically as in his study he perused naturalists' treatises with a skeptical eye. He stared at skulls of animals and humans until he made a discovery—the intermaxillary bone in the human upper jaw—that secured him a place in the history of comparative anatomy. He set up untold numbers of experiments to determine the nature of light and colors, and took greater pride in his work on optics, he told his faithful Eckermann, than in anything else he had ever done, including his dramas. An obsessive collector, he turned his house in Weimar into a museum of natural objects as much as of etchings and plaster casts.

But he pursued all his exacting researches intent on vindicating a romantic view of the universe. "What more can humans gain in life," he asked rhetorically, "than have God-Nature reveal itself to them?"[31] The study of Nature was the royal road to glorious revelations. "There are only two true religions, the one that recognizes and worships the holy that lives in us and around us quite formlessly, the other that acknowledges it in its most beautiful form. Everything between these two is idolatry."[32] Goethe's Nature is a vast organism in which human beings, precisely like all other natural phenomena, form an essential element. Each person, each rock, each plant, each animal is a witness equally touched by divinity. "I treat bones as a text," he wrote a friend in the midst of his anatomical studies, "to which all of life and all that is human can be attached."[33]

Goethe knew that profuse Nature offers too many texts for one lifetime, but he tried to read as many of them as humanly possible, never forgetting his ideological program. He picked up pieces of granite to surprise Nature's patient way of evolving from phase to phase. He amassed plants and, in search of the single primal plant—Urpflanze—from which all others must have sprung through wonderful metamorphoses, he firmly rejected Carl von Linné's efforts at classifying them.[34] He investigated the skeletal remains of animals and humans to confirm his conjecture that both must have originated in a single ancestor, thus reinforcing his sense of Nature at once miraculous and methodical, mysterious but orderly. And he labored for years over his theory of colors to prove Newton wrong.[35] The moral pathos of his campaign to discredit Newton's *Opticks* is only too transparent. Nature, Goethe said sternly, trying to put Newton in his place, does not make white light, the noblest of phenomena, into a mere composite of colors!

As a romantic scientist, Goethe took a characteristic interest not only in the "sensuous" but also in the "ethical" significance of color.[36] The study of Nature matters above all because it reveals the deep connections that unite, and the ethical-religious values that govern, the universe. As the small child yearns to merge with its mother, so did Goethe seek to merge with Mother Nature; his apostrophes to her bountiful breasts were not routine poetic clichés. In decisive conflict with contemporary scientists intent on separating the observer from the observed, Goethe placed humanity at the center of his researches. That is why he detested the contrivances of modern science: the telescope, the microscope, the mathematical formula. To his mind, they interfere with the unmediated, pious experience of God-Nature; far from being aids to understanding, they are repellent instruments of torture.

Seeing, then, was for Goethe not a passive registration of cold, external reality but an act that makes a difference to what is seen. "One can say that with every attentive look at the world, we are already theorizing."[37] More: in a terse quatrain in his work on colors, he revived an ancient mystical pantheistic belief that only like recognizes like: "If the eye were not akin to the sun, / It could never see the sun. / If God's own power were not in us, / How should the divine enchant us?"[38] These comments on the affinities of the mind to nature were cousins to older insights about the pressure of desire on perception. Shakespeare had already recognized that a wish can be father to the thought; other astute psychologists had long known that private preconceptions or cultural styles influence what observers observe.

Coleridge put this case for the romantics: "we receive but what we give, / And in our Life alone does Nature live." If we are to behold anything more worthy than "that inanimate cold World *allow'd* / To the poor loveless ever-anxious Crowd," then "from the Soul itself must issue forth / A Light, a Glory, a fair luminous cloud / Enveloping the Earth!"[39] The quarrel between the heirs of the Enlightenment and the romantics was over this crucial issue. What the natural scientists in Goethe's, Schelling's, and Coleridge's day were deploring as a liability that investigators must train themselves to overcome, the romantics took to be humanity's greatest asset in the quest for the divine in the world. As we have seen, many of them made a God unknown to any existing church. But fighting for the re-enchantment of the world, they were as devout as any Christian.

Some romantics, of course, found it perfectly logical to be churchgoers and philosophical worshipers of Nature at the same time. In the later decades of his long life—he lived to be eighty, his best work some forty years behind him—Wordsworth was among the most clerical of citizens the romantic age produced. But this is not the religion by which he will be remembered. It was precisely during his early years, when he had no more use for church than he had for kings, that he wrote poems that made him the unforgettable spokesman for romantic religiosity. He had many critics in his lifetime, and not for his apostasy from radicalism alone. No poet, it seems, was parodied more often, and more effectively, than Wordsworth. But in his finest work, he set a standard for the adoration of Nature that no other poet, including Goethe, was able to surpass.

During the mid-Victorian years, in a memorable passage of his *Autobiography*, John Stuart Mill paid tribute to Wordsworth's poetry for rescuing him from a profound, prolonged depression: it had proved "a medicine for my state of mind" in expressing "not mere outward beauty, but states of feeling, and of thought coloured by feeling, under the excitement of beauty." Reading the best of Wordsworth, Mill was not converted to religion of any sort. But he responded, more intelligently than many others had done before him, to Wordsworth's "love of rural objects and natural scenery," aware that the poet had written "not only without turning away from, but with a greatly increased interest in the common feelings and common destiny of human beings."[40]

Mill's last comment is of particular interest, since it should have silenced shallow readers who reduced Wordsworth to the poet of the great outdoors. That he was supremely the poet of nature—or, to retain our usage, of Nature— is beyond cavil. But his Nature emphatically embraced human nature. In *Lyrical Ballads,* that epoch-making volume of 1798 and in its revised edition two years later, Wordsworth devoted loving attention to people, often of humble station, and to their mental states. He saw them all as teachers: aged peasants, discharged soldiers, children, vagrants, even idiots. In the successive versions of the *Prelude,* he turned his sensibility on the person he thought he could examine most closely: himself. Nature, he wrote, tutored him

> To look with feelings of fraternal love
> Upon those unassuming things that hold
> A silent station in this beauteous world.[41]

What his identification with all manners of people could teach him, much like flowers and mountains, was the supremacy of Nature, the melody of the universe.

In lines from *Tintern Abbey* that are deservedly often quoted and deserve to be quoted again, Wordsworth rehearsed his faith by beautifully recording its resonance in himself:

> And I have felt
> A presence that disturbs me with the joy
> Of elevated thoughts; a sense sublime
> Of something far more deeply interfused,
> Whose dwelling is the light of setting suns,
> And the round ocean and the living air,

And the blue sky, and in the minds of man:
A motion and a spirit, that impels
All thinking things, all objects of all thought,
And rolls through all things.

Wordsworth tartly rejected the proposition—he took it as a reproach—that he was a pure pantheist. The matter is difficult: though widely read and reflective and for years subjected to the torrent of Coleridge's learned conversation, Wordsworth was never fully explicit about matters of philosophy, let alone theology. But his imprecision only makes him all the more representative of the romantic mood. He was far from being a fanatical subverter of reason, but he believed that those religious at heart could turn the profane into the sacred without rationalistic cogitation and teach others to join them. In the end, romanticism was a vast exercise in shared solitude, a solitude shared through love.

4. The Bourgeois Egotistical Sublime

It is a striking irony that the romantics, that loose and quarrelsome family of cultural elitists, left a legacy of emotional individualism to a bourgeois culture that most of them professed to despise. The romantic egotistical sublime broadened out into a bourgeois egotistical sublime—a very banquet of unintended consequences splendidly exemplifying Hegel's cunning of history. After all, apart from a handful of pioneering malcontents like the young Goethe's Werther, the romantics had been the first writers and artists in history to make sustained war upon the bourgeoisie. They had little use for the applause of the middle-class consumer. E. T. A. Hoffmann, we recall, did not hesitate to depict solid burghers as boors and madmen as the only truly civilized people in his uncivilized age. And Stendhal complained—really, boasted—that he did not expect his literary gifts to be recognized for another two or three generations. By and large, romantics were content to share the outpourings of their rich inner life with what Stendhal called the happy few. They created, and their followers spread, that plausible but largely inaccurate legend that the century was dominated by a war to the death between a revolutionary avant-garde and the hopeless proper bourgeoisie. Yet, while the romantics were not Victorians in disguise and would appear to be most implausible teachers for the nineteenth-century middle classes, that is precisely what they became.

The romantics' self-perception gave little inkling of their future impact. For all of Shelley's and Hugo's boasts, they harbored few illusions about being sovereign shapers of thought and taste. Their moments of noisy triumph were rare: that raucous Paris premiere of Hugo's *Hernani* in 1830 was a signal but exceptional event in the history of romantic cultural politics. For the most part, they caressed the opposite illusion, declaring themselves with aggressive pathos to be embattled, persecuted victims of philistines and hypocrites. In a swamp of mediocrities, they held high the standards of originality and creativeness. In any event, Shelley himself had conceded that he and his fellows, legislators to the world, were unacknowledged. And yet, defying this strategic modesty, the romantics' celebration of the self was to leave its irrevocable imprint on the cultural landscape of bourgeois Victorians.

The conduit leading beyond the romantics' select audience to the respectable masses was romantic love. Its raffish parentage and metaphysical pretensions did not prevent that love from emerging as a powerful agent disseminating a new sense of self as picturesque as it was effective. We recall that romantic religion was virtually indistinguishable from romantic love, as numbers of romantics sanctified erotic affections. Their high-flown vocabulary and claims to spirituality could not hide the sensual core of their love for God or Nature. Not content with amassing the amorous record that gave gossips inexhaustible material, romantics sublimated love into an ideology.

Among the most intensive, certainly the most amusing, explorations of love as an exercise of the imagination was doubtless Stendhal's highly subjective *De l'amour.* As a faithful devotee of the Enlightenment, Stendhal billed his book as a scientific study. Love, he argued, is the product of an emotional reconstruction that the lover performs on his chosen object. "Crystallization," the mental sleight of hand necessary to all infatuation, amounts to a radical self-deception: the lover "underrates his own good qualities and overrates the smallest favors his beloved bestows."[1] Desire transforms reality to make it serve the demands of erotic needs. Even disillusionment, which must always come, cannot permanently cure the fevers of the amorous imagination. Love is born, triumphs, and dies in the lover's mind, only to be reborn as a new object comes into view.

Shelley, no less imaginative than Stendhal in theorizing about romantic love, paid quite as fervent a tribute to love's inwardness. He first publicly expounded his views in 1813, at twenty-one, in a note to *Queen Mab:* love springs from "the *perception* of loveliness." An erudite modern Platonist—he translated Plato's dialogue on love, the *Symposium,* to good purpose—he persuaded himself that "the nature of Love and Friendship is very little understood," and set out to clarify both. This was not disinterested research; from the days of his sexual awakening, as he frankly admitted, Shelley pursued the phantom of love with women as much as in his poems.[2]

It was an anarchist's pursuit. In Shelley's view, the "despotism of positive institutions" is bound to ruin love. It "withers under constraint; its very essence is liberty; it is compatible neither with obedience, jealousy, nor fear; it is there most pure, perfect, and unlimited, where its votaries live in confidence, equality, and unreserve." He saved his most cutting invective for the laws that dictate lifelong marriage, as "odious" a "usurpation" as ever devised to cripple human happiness. "The present system of constraint does no more in the majority of instances than make hypocrites or open enemies." Love must be protected from the prison that is marriage, which is bound to corrode love's essence. That is why romantics and their epigones could agree with Shelley, in all seriousness, that "prostitution is the legitimate offspring of marriage and its accompanying errors."[3]

These verbal onslaughts were not mere provocations by a self-confident rebel intent on shocking the philistines. Shelley was searching for the grounds of true happiness, which can spring from love alone. "We are born into the world," he wrote around 1815, "and there is something within us which, from the instant that we live, more and more thirsts after its likeness." This is not quite narcissism: Shelley, conveniently oblivious to his own erotic record, was as severe with egotistical and promiscuous lovers as with the upholders of Christian respectability. Nor must love degenerate into brute sensuality: in 1818, Shelley analyzed love as composed of several intertwined strands, including the aesthetic and the ethical. "The act itself" he curtly dismissed as "nothing." True love is governed by three considerations: the beloved should be "as perfect and beautiful as possible, both in body and in mind"; the sexual act should be enjoyed temperately, lest it be debased into "a diseased habit, equally pernicious to body and mind"; intercourse "ought to be indulged *according to nature.*"[4] For Shelley, love calls for admiration, respect, and care, for a genuine mutuality that can be realized only in free unions.

Love has, of course, been most variously defined through the ages, as a semireligious experience or an animal-like coupling, as a disease akin to madness or the supreme cure for loneliness and longing.[5] The eighteenth century, which the romantics rarely lost from sight in their polemics, had done nothing to dissolve the tensions between love and duty, passion and marriage; the Enlightenment had developed theories of sex, but not of love. With spirited vulgarity, Diderot had defined love as "the voluptuous rubbing of two intestines."[6]

It was largely to discredit such nonconformist or coarse views of human relations that late-eighteenth-century German thinkers elevated friendship above love. The sensitive protagonist of *Woldemar,* Friedrich Heinrich Jacobi's well-received novel of the late 1770s, oscillates between two women and marries the one who means less to him than the other, on the startling ground that had he chosen the idealized friend of his soul, he would have committed an abomination like incest. A certain horror of sensuality, and an identification with the sacred mother who must remain unspotted even in one's fantasies, resonates in this sort of thinking.

Radically dissatisfied with these defensive maneuvers, German romantics instead proposed a love that would spring from a harmony between body and mind. A century before Freud would offer a theoretical justification for it, Friedrich Schlegel and his friend Schleiermacher analyzed true love as the confluence of two currents: the affectionate and the passionate. Affection without passion is friendship, passion without affection is lust. The philosophes, in the romantics' disdainful estimation, had never risen to this high standard; nor were married couples of their own day living up to it. They were too cold, too formal, Schlegel objected, not truthful enough to their feelings, ever to approach, let alone reach, the ideal. "Nearly all marriages are only concubinage," nothing better than "provisional experiments and distant approximations to a real marriage," which consists of "several persons becoming just one." This was, Schlegel conceded, "a pretty thought, whose realization, however, appears to experience many and great difficulties." In sum, "What is called a happy marriage is to love what a correct poem is to improvised singing."[7] The rigid rule followed in Christian states that makes even the most miserable marriage indissoluble for life is a powerful obstacle to authentic unions.

Another obstacle, no less powerful, Schlegel observed, is men's self-serving conviction that women are less intelligent and competent than men, are passive and submissive by nature. Since Schlegel's views on women evolved, it is easy to extract conflicting positions from his writings. But on balance he was a worthy contemporary for Mary Wollstonecraft, whose feminist classic of 1792, *Vindication of the Rights of Woman,* brilliantly tried to discredit male claims to superiority. As Schlegel canvassed with Novalis the burning issue of male and female nature, and often agreed with him, Schlegel never flirted with the antique cliché "In man there is reason; in woman, feeling," to which Novalis apparently subscribed.[8] Schlegel acknowledged that because she bears children, woman's destiny must differ from man's. But the other "feminine" qualities that most men and slavish women take to be inexpungeable—domesticity, dependency, piety—have actually been imposed by long-standing cultural habits. Women can and should be strong and independent, just as men can and should be yielding and emotional. And the two sexes shall be joined in equal sensuality leavened by commitment. "I can no longer say, my love or your love. Both are equal to each other and completely one, as much love as counter-love. It is marriage, eternal unity, and connection of our spirits."[9] That is how Schlegel summed up the matter in the canonical text of romantic love, his novel *Lucinde*.

As intricately designed as a nest of Chinese boxes, *Lucinde* is, as we have seen, a roman à clef. Lightly disguising reality, the novel dramatizes the wordy love affair of Friedrich Schlegel and Dorothea Veit; it shows them arousing each other with provocative letters and conversations about life, longing, and death as they stand lightly clad in a pavilion to look at the rising sun. Schlegel's venture into fiction proved to be the first among the outrages that romantics would inflict on respectable society. "It is said," the author's worried mother wrote to her older son August Wilhelm, "that he is living with a person, a Jewess." She feared that her "Fritz has already shown himself to me with his novel (the Lucinde!) as someone without religion and without good principles."[10] It was an early warning that the romantics were dangerously distancing themselves from the customs, or at least the professions, of their class.

But more than a scandal, *Lucinde* was a symptom of romantic bids for freedom. Its protagonists are two aesthetic souls who find each other, and themselves, through their mutual passion. Despite some titillating hints at their erotic excitement, their love provided abundant opportunities for high-flown talk. A determined assault on what this couple and their circle damned as boring bourgeois notions of marriage, the novel preaches a refined sensuality, the sanctity of the body, and the debts of the mind to Eros. Schlegel wanted to show lovemaking elevated by philosophizing, philosophizing humanized by lovemaking. "It was not your lips alone for which I yearned, or for your eyes, or for your body," the hero tells the heroine, "but it was a romantic confusion of all these things, a wondrous mixture of the most diverse memories and longings."[11] Here, if anywhere, is the hold of *Lucinde* on the history of culture. Its author perceptively denigrated his foray into literature as "frivolous."[12] But it helped to define the romantic conception of love, which, suitably tamed, was to reverberate so powerfully in the inner life of the Victorians.

In a loyal defense of *Lucinde,* Schleiermacher made Schlegel's ideas his own. "The divine plant of love is for once pictured in its complete form, and not in torn-off blossoms and leaves." The novel shows "love whole and in one piece, the most spiritual and the most sensual, not just in one work and in the same person side by side, but linked in the most intimate way in every utterance and every trait. Here the One cannot be separated from the Other; in the most sensual you clearly see the spiritual at the same time." Sensuality, "with its living presence, documents that it really is what it professes to be, namely a worthy and indispensable element in love."[13] As Shelley's counterpart at least in this—like Shelley, he had translated Plato's *Symposium*—Schleiermacher the theologian could take this unorthodox stance because to him the body is no less holy, no less a guarantor of religious truth, than the soul. It hardly needs reiteration that in this romantic theory a free choice of one's partner is the cardinal prerequisite for love. No calculation, whether financial or tribal, should be permitted to disturb the hallowed precincts.

All this was esoteric to a degree. In confining his hopes for an appreciative public to the happy few, Stendhal read the vagaries of the exploding mass market with fair realism. And the way that romantics conducted themselves produced very different, but equally intractable, problems for the nineteenth-century middle classes; they found many of the romantics' lives nothing less than shocking. Frau Schlegel's indignation at her Friedrich's wayward love life should occasion no surprise. But it is of historical importance that, real though it was, romantics overstated their estrangement from the bourgeoisie. Consider Byron: separating from his wife after damaging stories about his character and conduct were circulating, Byron decided to leave England. He charged that he was being avoided at parties, hissed in the House of Lords, abused in the press, insulted in the streets. But contemporary evidence discredits this report; Byron's nightmarish imaginings reflected his state of mind more accurately than it did public attitudes.[14]

Still, even though his sense of being ostracized was at least partly the work of guilt-ridden fantasies, that did not make Byron eligible as a model for the respectable. He was reported in polite and literary society—we do not know how far rumors about him penetrated beyond his circle—to have committed incest with his half sister, sodomized his wife, conducted a string of love affairs with women of all ranks, and varied them with homosexual flings. His promiscuity seemed almost superhuman. In England and later in Italy, women threw themselves at him or wrote for assignations to save him from his sadness and his impiety, and he was disposed to accept their invitations.[15] A bookkeeper, a businessman, a professor could aspire to such libertinism only in his most far-fetched dreams and perhaps privately admire (though publicly censure) from afar.

No wonder the romantics' unconventional erotic style made good bourgeois anxious or, at the least, ambivalent. Lord Byron's private life pointedly contradicted the values by which the middle classes had been professing to live for centuries, values that preferred fidelity to promiscuity, self-denial to self-indulgence. The family magazines that sprang up across western Europe early in the century all preached the sanctity of hard work and unbending monogamy. Hence bourgeois everywhere recognized in romantic love, poised to invade the most sensitive areas of middle-class domesticity, an anarchic force that threat-

ened to subvert their time-honored marriage arrangements and social solidari-
ties. As the romantics gave their imagination free rein in highly visible sexual
entanglements, they offended all but the most liberated in the middle-class
public. Intent on anchoring erotic bliss in the permanence of lawful wedlock
and on keeping sexual pleasures strictly private, bourgeois could not be expected to grant their amorous appetites the space and the publicity that the
boldest among the romantics demanded for it.

For decades, then, the Victorian middle classes considered the morality of the
most exhibitionistic romantics an outrage far more than a guide. And yet they
found it somehow appealing as well. These strenuous Casanovas, male and
female, were not their kind, but. . . . Their response to Byron, surely the most
maligned, and probably the most envied, of lovers among the romantics, was
typical.* Yet to complicate matters in the way that students of the romantics
must if they want to do justice to their subject, Byron the arch-romantic was
not a romantic lover. He indulged his sexual appetites as he was pleased, or
driven, to do. His scattered comments add up to an anthology of cynicism. "I
do not believe in the existence of what is called Love," he told his confidante
Lady Melbourne in September 1812; five years later, he philosophized to his
friend Thomas Moore that constancy is but "that small change of Love, which
people exact so rigidly, receive in such counterfeit coin, and repay in baser
metal." Love is just a polite name we give to sexual hunger. Still, Byron was no
mere libertine. What he called his "besoin d'aimer" included gratifications less
fleeting than orgasm. As he told Moore in August 1820, soon after consummat-
ing his affair with the Italian countess Teresa Guiccioli, his last and most enduring liaison, "I verily believe that nor you, nor anyone of poetical temperament,
can avoid a strong passion of some kind. It is the poetry of life." Love, Byron
insisted, was the dominant impulse for making poetry—certainly for him:
"What should I have known or written, had I been a quiet, mercantile politician or a lord in waiting?"[16] His admirer Goethe would not have put it any
differently.

These glowing interludes were rare for Byron; he never shed his pessimistic
conviction that love cannot last—certainly cannot survive marriage. The By-
ronic hero he had invented and largely embodied, that alienated and adventurous voyager to romantic places, is fated to be unhappy. But at moments his

---

*Goethe, who became one of Byron's most energetic apologists, proved that a genius could live
down unorthodox behavior to end up as an icon of culture—provided he was not too unorthodox. He had defied the reigning code of Weimar, the tiny dukedom that was his home for half a
century, by taking a young mistress to act as housekeeper and mother of his children and not
marrying her until twenty years later, out of gratitude rather than love. But this violation of
decorum had been cushioned by Goethe's fame and generally unimpeachable respectability.

creator expected more from life than the melancholy that made him so irresistible. It was under the impress of this ephemeral hope, seasoned with pervasive gloom, that he recorded, in the third canto of *Don Juan,* the idyl of Juan and Haidée, the most charming segment in his great river of a poem. Haidée, seventeen, beautiful, auburn haired, and black eyed, discovers the stricken shipwrecked Don Juan and nurses him back to robust health. In the presence of benign nature, on the deserted beach, innocent, free of guilt, they make love, with no thought for the future. They feel that they will have to part, but Byron seems persuaded that this is probably just as well:

> There's doubtless something in domestic doings
>   Which forms, in fact, true love's antithesis;
> Romances paint at full length people's wooings,
>   But only give a bust of marriages;
> For no one cares for matrimonial cooings,
>   There's nothing wrong in a connubial kiss:
> Think you, if Laura had been Petrarch's wife,
> He would have written sonnets all his life?

For Byron love, the poetry of life, was doomed to be evanescent—hardly a sentiment for bourgeois to live by.

One may gauge the dimensions of Byron's notoriety by the fate of his unpublished memoirs. A few days after learning of Byron's death and angry, agonized wrangles, his closest friends decided to burn the manuscript. One of the handful who had read it, William Gifford of the *Quarterly Review,* said that its erotic episodes made it "fit only for a brothel" and would "doom Lord B to everlasting infamy if published." The dean of Westminster, Dr. Ireland, did not need to read the disputed document to refuse Byron burial in Westminster Abbey.[17] Yet Byron's public in Britain and abroad, much moved by word of his death, was not inclined to be censorious. The fury with which his intimates debated the best way of serving their friend's memory attests to their feeling of loss. And intelligent readers who had never met him responded as though a beloved friend had died.*

---

*Tennyson, then fifteen, groping for words, did his mourning on a solitary walk in the Lincolnshire countryside and inscribed the dread news on a rock: "Byron is dead." And Jane Welsh wrote her husband-to-be, Thomas Carlyle, "Byron is dead! I was told it all at once in a roomful of people. My God, if they had said that the sun or the moon had gone out of the heavens, it could not have struck me with the idea of a more awful and dreary blank in the creation." Quoted in Leslie A. Marchand, *Byron: A Biography,* 3 vols. continuously paginated (1957), III, 1248. Goethe, with whom Byron had been corresponding for some time, refused a publisher's invitation to write

Nor did the stories that followed Byron everywhere appear to have done the sales of his verses any harm. Byron struck a chord to which thousands responded no matter what busybodies might say. If anything, the gossip made him all the more interesting. Certainly the poetry-reading public did not desert him, or when it did, moral outrage was not the reason. The first two cantos of *Childe Harold's Pilgrimage,* published in 1812, made him famous overnight, and from then on, his poems formed one long parade of publishing triumphs. In 1818, John Murray offered Byron a thousand guineas for *Beppo,* his first work in the mock-heroic vein that he would perfect with *Don Juan.* And, issued in groups of cantos from 1819 on, *Don Juan* continued to sell and pay handsomely, despite—and because of—indignant denunciations. "The works of Lord Byron and Walter Scott," Goethe noted in 1822, two years before Byron's death, "are in the hands of all Germans, especially of the tender and the beautiful."[18] Decades later, Matthew Arnold attested to his lasting impress on his readers, observing a little sourly that Byron had borne, "with haughty scorn which mocked the smart," the "pageant of his bleeding heart." Not in vain: "thousands counted every groan, / And Europe made his woe her own."[19] With his life as with his poetry, Byron came to encompass for his middle-class readers romantic adventure, romantic triumph, and romantic loss—in a word, romantic love with all its manifest dangers and latent attractions.

Some of Byron's fellow romantics, we recall, led only marginally less unbourgeois lives. Novalis was at once in love with his dead fiancée and ready to conclude marriage with another young woman he adored. The wife of August Wilhelm Schlegel, the brilliant and attractive Caroline, had first come to his attention as the mother of an illegitimate child and later discarded her husband when the more interesting Schelling crossed her path. Wilhelm's younger brother, Friedrich, lived with Dorothea Veit before her divorce. Shelley at eighteen eloped with the sixteen-year-old Harriet Westbrook and, after he grew disenchanted with his marriage, eloped with Mary Godwin, whom he married after his first wife's suicide; nor did his second marriage keep him from entanglements with other women. Goethe kept falling in love with woman after woman right into his seventies.* Chateaubriand boasted some celebrated mistresses, including that legendary beauty Madame Récamier. Madame de Staël conducted her colorful love life virtually in public. Victor Hugo was a

---

about Byron after Byron's death because, he said, his pain was too deep to permit utterance that merely responded to some external impulse. Goethe to Josef Max, December 18, 1824, *Briefe von und an Goethe,* ed. Karl Robert Mandelkow, 6 vols. (1962–69; 3rd and 4th eds., 1988), IV, 131–32.

*See below, pp. 119–20.

sexual athlete who for decades simultaneously supported two households, sometimes three, and who in addition, as he rotated among his longer-term arrangements, engaged in literally countless sexual affairs. Schubert, who seems to have haunted obscure homosexual circles, was that rare romantic who preserved the secret of his sexual life inviolate. Adultery and promiscuity seemed as natural to most romantics as writing or painting or composing and, one suspects, almost as necessary to their fame.

Hence, driven by exacting moral imperatives, bourgeois could accept the doctrine of romantic love only after they had covered over the joys of erotic experience with silence or euphemisms, and after they had discarded Shelley's rejection of the "despotism" of wedlock in favor of that very institution. Even the most venturesome elements in the nineteenth-century bourgeoisie regarded marriage not as the nemesis of love but as its highest incarnation. "Only married life," wrote the German dramatist Friedrich Hebbel in his epic idyll *Mutter und Kind* in 1856, "makes a human being wholly human."[20] He spoke for the bourgeoisie: this was the theme on which popular romances in prose or verse, mainstays of middle-class reading by mid-century, played countless variations. Ordinary bourgeois could do very little with Novalis's metaphysical definition of love as the Amen of the universe or with the cynical identification of love with sexual prowess, much more with fictional lovers united after tantalizing travail—united, of course, in holy matrimony. For all these necessary concessions to moral conventions, though, bourgeois found the license romantics had granted to the melting inwardness of love hard to deny. Increasingly, they discovered their feelings by patterning them on the feelings, if not the adventures, of the most unbourgeois of poets.

The diffusion of romantic ways among the middle classes was fueled by impressive improvements in their standard of living. In earlier ages, the free time to read frivolous secular matter like novels or poems had been largely the preserve of the privileged classes. But fortunately for the romantic ideal of love, the benefits of industrialization were particularly striking in the technology of communication. Dazzling inventions modernizing the printing press, the production of paper, and the distribution of books made the pleasures of reading available to larger and larger circles. Until well after the French Revolution, books had been expensive, but these technical innovations drove prices down radically. What is more, by mid-century, a rapidly expanding network of lending libraries and public libraries was taking the curse off buying books for people with limited budgets. And, once again, for masses of readers whose personal libraries were confined to the Bible, volumes of sermons, and perhaps a few books on travel and self-improvement, there were the family maga-

zines—*Godey's Lady's Book* in the United States, the *Gartenlaube* in Germany—
which featured romantic stories, poems, and novels. At the same time, the
serious novelists, often far less popular than their adroit competitors, found new
readers by serializing their fictions in the *Revue des deux mondes* in France or the
Cornhill in Britain. These new channels gave the preoccupation with the self an
audience the romantics would have found astonishing.

Of course, the nineteenth century invented the emotion of love as little as it
invented the bourgeoisie. There are touching testimonies from letters, diaries,
funerary monuments that couples had centuries ago loved another sincerely,
passionately, often through a lifetime. What was new, and what gave the romantics much of their enduring effect even after their influence over the stage
and over fiction had waned, was their bold assertion that the play of emotions
was quite acceptable, indeed necessary, to one's full humanity. The rising tide
of printed words in the Victorian decades defending that claim intensified the
democratization of inwardness that the romantics had launched. While religious texts retained vast loyal audiences, more and more were reading for
pleasure to initiate themselves in a romantic aura. And most of these readers
cultivating their inmost selves were bourgeois.

To be sure, in popular fictions aimed at a new mass audience, the romantics'
later imitators offered a debased romanticism as they wrote of love, incapable
of rising to the subtleties or the riveting conflicts that had marked their models.
The old paraphernalia of romantic fiction—medieval castles, moonlit nights,
brooding heroes, and the rest—retained a certain vogue, but they had to compete with more up-to-date, less melancholy themes. The romantics' tales of
love had normally emphasized suffering rather than success. True, Schlegel's
Lucinde ends with the blissful pair bound to each other and sharing the joys of
parenthood. But Byron's Don Juan must part from his captivating Haidée;
Hazlitt's *Liber Amoris* ends with miserable separation, Constant's *Adolphe* with
the loneliness of the unheroic hero and the death of the sadly deceived heroine.
Heine's love poems are not about triumphs but about tribulations. In sharp
contrast, Victorian romances in prose or verse, as distinct from serious fiction,
found the happy ending virtually obligatory. In their works love—romantic
love—conquered all. Still, however impure the sources from which the Victorians absorbed romantic notions, they did absorb them.*

Necessarily, nineteenth-century romantic love in reality rather than fiction
conquered the Victorian bourgeoisie at varying rates of speed and not without
obstructions. In some pockets of obstinate conservatism, it did not conquer at
all. Italians, Germans, or Americans; Protestants, Catholics, or Jews; bourgeois

---

*For an analysis of fiction and the nineteenth-century bourgeois self, see below, pp. 222–76.

magnates, solid middle-class burghers, or small tradesmen—each had their own style of receiving, or resisting, romantic love as they wrestled with religious prescriptions, economic calculations, familial pressures, and cultural attitudes. Mixed motives prevailed; individual decisions varied in incalculable ways. Before 1800, in those days "averse to all romanticism" (as the novelist Johanna Schopenhauer recalled the time of her youth), the principals were usually not consulted or even informed about their parents' plans for them.[21] A century later, this sovereign way of disposing over the future of marriageable youth still found its supporters. As late as the 1880s, one prosperous businessman in Prague saw to it that his many daughters married in an orderly sequence, the older before the younger ones. Their "sentimental impulses" did not interest him. "As a merchant he wanted to see them well taken care of. He selected his sons-in-law according to profession and income. If the girl was in love with her intended, all the better! But it was possible without passion, too."[22]

This thoughtful autocrat was not out of place in late-nineteenth-century bourgeois culture—not yet. Down to the end of that century and beyond, rich and devout French families concluded alliances in which their children were little better than pawns; their daughters, educated by nuns who carefully screened the girls' reading and censored out all troubling sexual information, could not be expected to play an active role in the making of their future.[23] In much the same way, German-Jewish families, constricted in their opportunities for careers, kept alive their traditional scheme of arranged marriages. With them, the old ways only yielded reluctantly as young men, and a handful of women, made their way into the universities and discovered a new ideal: romantic self-determination.

In contrast, more liberal cultures, granting young men and women wide latitude in their courting, had smoothed the paths to romantic love even before the romantics began to write. As in so many other ways, the United States marked the future in this matter as well, setting a pattern of broad-mindedness still unknown in other countries and only tentatively, and unsuccessfully, proposed during the French Revolution. Liberalism did not imply libertinism: while Americans enjoyed considerable freedom in growing to like, and love, one another, and to build their life together on mutual affection, counsels of prudence still held sway over their minds. A proper American man rarely proposed marriage until he enjoyed an income steady enough, or prospects solid enough, to support a family. For her part, a proper American woman was unlikely to rush into the kind of attachment she had been taught to consider imprudent or premature. These young pioneers in modern love discovered that while parental consent was desirable, parents rarely insisted on it; there is persuasive evidence that inexperienced couples-to-be more often sought their parents' advice than the parents were ready to offer it. Concord between the generations worked mainly as emotional insurance. After all, normally brides were just out of their teens, if that, and moved directly from their parents' house to their new home.

Hence the love that Americans thought they ought to feel for one another before they plunged into permanent commitment was rarely the headlong, abandoned rush of overpowering passions they could read about in novels. Love, to them, must pass the test of time and gather proofs of compatibility. "Romantick extravagancies" were adolescent temptations to be outgrown, and romantic novels, those treacherous if irresistible guides to "extravagant and false views of life," must be distrusted.[24] Still, by mid-nineteenth century, even though reason continued to counsel circumspection and practical considerations remained a brake on passion, Americans had come to diagnose an inability to fall in love as a defect more troubling than the disposition to fall in love too easily.

Around these decades, young Englishmen and women of the middling orders had cleared similar space for the cultivation of emotional ties. They were permitted to see one another, even alone, far more freely than were their French or German contemporaries. Indeed, the French, the suppliers of so much romantic fiction, were exceptionally prudent about introducing the incalculable element of love into their marriage arrangements. In 1905, a well-informed English observer, Mrs. Betham-Edwards, put it bluntly: "The French fireside," in contrast with the English, which has witnessed much romance in courtship and marriage, "is strictly prosaic, wedlock being a partnership primarily arranged with deference to worldly circumstances." She saw nothing objectionable in this: "Where do we find closer unions, tenderer wives, more devoted husbands than in France?" The clannish nature of marriage was stronger there than in Mrs. Betham-Edwards's England: "In France wedlock is no mere individual, but a family matter, a kind of joint-stock affair. An Englishman marries a wife. A Frenchman takes not only his bride for better, for worse, for richer, for poorer, but her entire kith and kin." She conceded that a certain adroitness was required to make these *mariages de convenance* work: parents conspired to eliminate the ineligible and throw together young men and women who seemed suited to one another. That this calculated coupling was intended to enhance the prestige and income of both families went almost without saying.[25]

No doubt, like their counterparts on the Continent, the English and the Americans appreciated the value of money and the social advantages attaching to the "right" partner. They were likely to accept the terse counsel current in their time not to marry for money, but to go where the money is. It was only that the French, like many Germans, to say nothing of Russians or Italians, raised this cynical epigram into a policy. Elsewhere, too, romantic love had to do battle, but many good English and American bourgeois in love, rather like Julia in Byron's *Don Juan,* whispering they'd ne'er consent, consented.

Although the hold that romantic love secured over Victorian middle-class culture remained uncertain, this much was beyond doubt: wherever love was given its head, it virtually compelled subjectivity, ruminations on one's own state of mind and on one's self as perceived by the beloved. At their most wanton, romantic lovers, seeking to blend into a single being, found their identity by losing it.[26] This search for psychological merger—thinking the other's thoughts, literally feeling the other's pleasures and pains—was romantic regression driven to an extreme. That banal, earnest question, Do you love me?, with which lovers have always plagued their partners as they try to discover the other's true feelings, served inwardness just as well. The claim to one's partner's candor and sincerity imperiously pressed for total transparency. "I should have wanted her to read me"—*qu'elle me devinât*—says Constant's Adolphe, who, though himself incapable of real love, could brilliantly define it. To hold back anything, whether a serious criticism or a delicate moment of past history, is to betray the romantic ideal that enjoins lovers to be all in all to each other. "As soon as there is a secret between two hearts that love one another," to quote Adolphe once more, "as soon as one of them has been able to resolve to conceal one single thought from the other, the spell is broken, happiness destroyed."[27] The more perceptive among the romantics, including Constant, were perfectly aware that this wish to know was less a quest for information than a plea for reassurance; it is significant that lovers should obsessively repeat such inquisitions since the most categorical affirmation soon lost its effectiveness. To have one's merits certified by one's second self could only shore up the sense of inner worth.

Whether investigation or call for emotional support, to have this craving for access to another's innermost soul satisfied was a privilege attached to a lover's, and only a lover's, status. While strictly speaking these anxious researches violated privacy, Victorians preferred to take them as a guarantee of a larger, a shared privacy. Lovers must know everything. They recognized that lovers are notoriously antisocial, shutting out the world to concentrate their libido on each other, which may be, strictly speaking, themselves. Theirs was often a narcissism for two.

Lovers' unsatisfiable probing looks suspiciously like a worldly version of the anguished self-examinations that believers had for centuries undertaken to clarify the condition of their soul and their hope for salvation. But the ideology of romantic love was not simply a secular religion. It used sacred language for worldly purposes. Nineteenth-century lovers freely resorted to a blasphemous vocabulary to convey the exaltation of their emotions and to celebrate their beloved as touched with superhuman virtues and attractions. With all his extravagance, H., the haplessly infatuated protagonist of William Hazlitt's *Liber Amoris,* spoke for these romantic victims of love. He calls his beloved, the daughter of his boarding house keeper, "divine" and an "angel of light"; he sees her as "heavenly-soft, saint-like" before whom he, a "proud and happy slave," wants to "fall down and worship." The man who breathes her air "is like one of the Gods!" Had she not opened "the gates of Paradise" to him? But when his "adored," his "angel-wife," proves treacherous, he recognizes this vocabulary to be both trite and absurd: "What idle sounds the common phrases, *adorable creature, angel, divinity,* are!"[28] They were certainly common enough by the 1820s, when Hazlitt wrote this strange confessional love story, and they remained common in fiction and, often enough, in life.

The telling terms "magic" and, even more to the point, "enchantment" were no less familiar in amorous talk; they are reminders that in an age when old pious spells were failing, romantic love was stepping in to provide a surrogate. The romantic and post-romantic campaign to re-enchant the world was most active in the sphere of love. But romantic love did not in some mechanical fashion replace religious with amatory raptures; most Victorian couples in love wanted not only to sleep with each other but to attend church together.

What is more, there were Victorians who were brought back to God by the love of a good woman; the passionate young Protestant divine Charles Kingsley, who made himself famous with his crusade for a manly, muscular Christianity, is a striking example of divine cooperating with carnal love: adrift in skepticism and nagging doubt, he returned to the faith after meeting his sensual and pious future wife, Fanny Grenfell. Yet, while romantic love could not claim to have established itself among the nineteenth-century middle classes as a substitute for religion, it emerged as a usable secular ideology. The egotistical sublime was more visible among Victorians in love than among others, and it was the romantics they had to thank for this spur to inwardness. The romantics were the first in the century to provide the abiding concentration on the self with a theory and a path to general currency. They would not be the last.

➷ TWO ⟨

Exercises in Self-definition

Until the advent of psychoanalysis in the late 1890s, autobiographies served as the deepest soundings into the inner life the Victorians had at their disposal. The autobiography is, of course, an ancient form of self-definition. Any historical retrospect must go back at least to St. Augustine's *Confessions,* medieval clerics conducting devout investigations into the condition of their soul, Montaigne probing his inner life, which never ceased to fascinate him, Descartes boldly attempting to ground philosophy in the thinking self, scores of seventeenth-century Puritans and eighteenth-century Pietists solemnly compiling self-questioning balance sheets. But the nineteenth century spawned far more autobiographers, and far more readers for their work, than any of its predecessors. As early as the 1830s, in *Sartor Resartus,* that sensitive barometer of cultural strains, Thomas Carlyle had already called attention to "these Autobiographical times of ours."[1]

Many anxious Victorians, we know, diagnosed all this conspicuous introspection as a symptom rather than an achievement; Matthew Arnold was not alone in deploring "the dialogue of the mind with itself" as threatening to grow at once morbid and monotonous.[2] Whatever their verdict, contemporaries had no doubt that theirs was a notable age of reminiscences and confessions, of the private self on public view. With good reason: in country after country, scores of prominent writers and politicians, artists and military men rushed to record their lives for a receptive public and, they hoped, a grateful posterity. At least until the middle of the century, middle-class readers consumed mainly works of religious uplift, poetry, or, increasingly, novels. But across the Western world, editors and publishers profitably fostered the autobiographical impulse, catering to an apparently insatiable appetite for such fare.*

The Victorians took an exceptionally intense interest in self-revelation. In 1870, an English journalist, Robert Goodbrand, boasted about the novelty of contemporary inwardness and gave two recent autobiographers all the credit. "Until within the last hundred years there has been no idea of biography at all," he wrote. "It is a modern attainment, and Goethe and Rousseau have opened the double valves through which the world has arrived at it. These two great autobiographers had to come first, before men could learn how to look at their fellow-man."[3] This extravagant assertion disregarded ample instances from earlier centuries, but that precisely made it a representative self-appraisal.

Those who did not write autobiographies at least read them. When, in the mid-1830s, the aging Chateaubriand grew alarmed about his finances, a consortium of friends clubbed together to buy the rights to his autobiography in progress for the princely sum of 156,000 francs, and they did not expect to lose money on the arrangement. And in 1847, George Sand contracted to sell her Histoire de ma vie, still far from complete, for 130,000 francs.[4] These two, to be sure, were celebrities who could command high prices for their self-display, but lesser names found a substantial audience. The frankly egotistical sentence with which the English poet James Hogg launched his autobiography suggests a public preoccupation with self that betokened a new sensibility: "I like to write about myself; in fact there are few things which I like better."[5] This narcissistic pleasure lay at the heart of what, in the exploratory fragments he called "Mon coeur mis à nu," Baudelaire termed "the atomization and the centralization of the Self"—the Moi. "Everything is there."[6]

Everything? The historian must ask just how much autobiographies really contributed to insights into their authors' inner life. In 1811, in Dichtung und Wahrheit, Goethe had famously observed, "All my works are fragments of a great confession," and one must rank his autobiography highly among his array of self-disclosures. But how legible a fragment was it, and how truly penetrating? A century later, looking with the psychoanalyst Hanns Sachs at an imposing Goethe edition, Freud had his doubts. "All this," he commented sardoni-

---

*A splendid instance of how popular autobiographies of the famous could be in the Victorian age is Mark Twain's well-known venture into publishing with the memoirs of Ulysses S. Grant. The ex-president was dying of cancer and hoped to provide for his family. He did, and for Mark Twain's as well. "In May 1885," Justin Kaplan has written, Mark Twain "predicted—conservatively, as it turned out—a sale of 300,000 sets (600,000 books), a profit of $200,000 for his publishing house, and royalties to the Grant family of over $400,000." Mr. Clemens and Mark Twain: A Biography (1966), 277–78.

cally, "was used by him as a means of self-concealment."[7]

This is a playful and mordant caution against naive readings of all texts, including autobiographies. Freud's wariness has suited, indeed helped to create, the temper of the suspicion-prone twentieth century, more distrustful of surfaces even than the nineteenth century had been. We have been instructed to resist autobiographers' claims that they are, to speak with Baudelaire, showing their heart naked. We have been told that autobiographies, for all their parades of facts, all their boasts of authenticity, all their ostentatious unfolding of private secrets, are tendentious simplifications, artful constructs, prominent elements in the great game of self-fashioning—in short, nothing better than works of fiction.

Such distrust was not unknown to the Victorian years. In 1872, Samuel Smiles, who relied heavily on memoirs in his popular books of uplift, noted that "an autobiography may be true so far as it goes, but in communicating only part of the truth, it may convey an impression that is really false. It may be a disguise—sometimes it is an apology—exhibiting not so much what a man really was as what he would have liked to be."[8] Far from uncovering hidden realities of the inner life, Smiles and others feared that autobiographies threatened to be self-dramatizing resistances.

But the ostensible, earnestly proffered program of Victorian autobiographers, whether they were reticent or uninhibited, made grand claims to authenticity. Some of them, like Anthony Trollope, explicitly insisted that if in their autobiographies they did not publish the whole truth, they published nothing but the truth.* And Freud should have been the first to recognize that autobiographies cannot be dismissed as mere lies. After all, had he not boasted shortly after 1900, in his case history of Dora, that facing the alert, mortals can keep no secret: "If their lips are silent, they gossip with their fingertips; betrayal forces its way through every pore."[9] However hard Goethe or other autobiographers might try to conceal themselves behind words, their stratagems must sooner or later fail. It is the burden of these pages to show that the autobiographer's unconscious distortions or conscious deceptions are all part of the truth, the autobiographer's truth, never mere obstacles but, rather, guides to important intimate realities.[10]

This is not a recent post-Freudian insight. In the 1870s, Leslie Stephen in a spirited essay, one of the first Victorian treatments of the autobiography as a separate genre, reckoned it "a special felicity that an autobiography, alone of all books, may be more valuable in proportion to the amount of misrepresentation

*"But this I protest:—that nothing that I say shall be untrue." Trollope, An Autobiography (1883; World's Classics ed., 1953), 1 [ch. 1].

which it contains."[11] Surely it does matter whether a printed autobiography faithfully reproduces a past experience or invents, denies, or embroiders it. There is often no way of checking autobiographers' accounts; they are again and again the only witness to come forward. But even when internal evidence or the surviving testimony of contemporaries establish discrepancies between literal accuracy and fabricated tale, such discoveries are often more instructive than unabashed self-revelations. Fantasies, too, are realities begging to be interpreted. The same holds true of silences, those expressive mute witnesses, at times more meaningful than the most vehement assertion. It remains to read these witnesses to inwardness—skeptically but not cynically.

I. In Rousseau's Shadow

The widespread passion of Victorian bourgeois for self-revelation, whether that of another or one's own, controlled only by prudent reserve and a keen sense of privacy, accounts for the powerful prolonged resonance of Rousseau's *Confessions*. They took the book as yet another momentous legacy from the eighteenth century. A generation of French romantics, though some of them, including Stendhal, grew impatient with its excessively heated tone, were perceptibly in debt to Rousseau's autobiography.[1] Hazlitt, who singled out Rousseau as an acute observer and eloquent writer alike, praised the *Confessions* as "the best of all his works." Young Flaubert paid the book the ultimate tribute of writing an imitation in thinly disguised fiction. George Eliot's admiration was intense and constant, awed as she was by "the rushing mighty wind" of Rousseau's inspiration and "the fire of his genius."[2] All the labor of learning French, she suggested, would be worthwhile "if it resulted in nothing more than reading one book—Rousseau's Confessions." She told Waldo Emerson that it had "first awakened her to deep reflection," a comment Emerson found particularly interesting, since, he told Eliot, Carlyle had praised the same book for the same reason.[3]

There were nineteenth-century readers of Rousseau's *Confessions* who had reservations or were downright hostile, but all saw his unsparing disclosures as a looming presence. "That I, or any man, should tell everything of himself, I hold to be impossible," Trollope asserted in the opening paragraph of his *Autobiography,* published to mixed reviews in 1883, a year after his death. "Who can endure to own the doing of a mean thing?" Plainly, Trollope was addressing this rhetorical question to Rousseau, who had, everyone knew, owned doing many mean things. Rousseau's uncompromising confessional stance, then, at once fascinated and troubled his nineteenth-century successors. Decorous Victorians called for a more circumspect style of self-exploration than Rousseau's *Confessions* exemplified, a style to be pitted against all such unappetizing but interesting improprieties. Augustine Birrell, essayist and biographer, spoke for this dominant ambivalence when he denounced Rousseau's autobiography and at the same time attested to its power. The *Confessions,* he thought, "ought never to have been written; but written they were, and read they always will be."[4] Victorian autobiographers worked under Rousseau's long shadow, but a little resentfully.

One can see why. Rousseau seemed obsessed with publicizing unsavory incidents, chiefly sordid sexual scenes—his precocious, permanently damaging initiation into masochism, his unconventional affair with "maman," Madame de Warens, his calamitous visit to a Venetian courtesan who advised him to give up women and study mathematics. Such material struck the respectable as objectionable whether it was true or, even worse, had been invented. And not the respectable alone. In 1811, Shelley, no prude, judged the *Confessions* "either a disgrace to the confessor or a string of falsehoods, probably the latter." And in a splendid display of obtuseness, Thomas De Quincey, of all places in his *Confessions of an Opium-Eater,* which abounds with squalid revelations about his addiction and life of vagabondage, denounced the "spectacle of a human being obtruding on our notice his moral ulcers or scars." He thought "acts of gratuitous self-humiliation" typical of French or German literature "tainted with the spurious and defective sensibility of the French." De Quincey certainly had in mind Rousseau's *Confessions,* which, despite his own title, he was determined not to replicate. He found Rousseau's disclosures "revolting."[5]

Even the liberated George Sand, who recorded her admiration for Rousseau's *Confessions* in her autobiography, censured its accusations against others and himself as "wicked acts." It was in pointed contrast to such indiscretions that she proposed to write a *"history of my life (not confessions)."** And the sardonic Baudelaire, scarcely a censorious bourgeois, took an amused distance from Rousseau's strategies of self-justification: having "confessed himself to the universe not without a certain voluptuousness," he shrewdly observed, Rous-

---

*Sand: *Histoire de ma vie* (1854–55), in *Oeuvres autobiographiques,* ed. Georges Lubin, 2 vols. (1970–71), I, xvi. In the minds of severe critics, Rousseau's wickedness as an autobiographer was not confined to lack of restraint and sheer bad taste. They also denounced him as a liar. In 1858, in his own autobiography, *Histoire de mes idées* (1858), the liberal, vehemently anticlerical French historian Edgar Quinet declared himself shocked by Rousseau's admitted readiness to depart from literal veracity for the sake of making a useful, larger point. Unlike Rousseau, Quinet exclaimed, he would write his narrative "without any alien ornament, without embroidering any events, even more: without inventing anything." Unlike Rousseau, he would give himself "the pleasure of the truth." Pp. 14–18 passim.

seau had found it possible to trumpet his unexcelled virtuousness—unexcelled and unprecedented.[6]

For Rousseau flaunted his uniqueness. "I have conceived an enterprise that has no model whatever and that, once accomplished, will have no imitator." This is the famous opening sentence of his *Confessions,* setting its tone and staking its claim. While St. Augustine had started his autobiography with an invocation to the deity—"Great art Thou, O Lord"—Rousseau started with the first person singular, and insisted that no one before him had ever been, and no one after him would ever be, quite so honest about himself.[7] He would show himself in all the truth of his nature, dig deep beneath surfaces. He plainly believed that his self-display eminently deserved to be put on the record. Like other autobiographers, he found himself immensely interesting, and more than most, he could permit himself no doubt that the world would be as interested in him as he was. The Victorians proved him right.

Rousseau's ambitions reached beyond his desperate claim to the world's regard. "I know my heart," he wrote, "and understand mankind."[8] He thought himself blessed with powers of perceptiveness that surpassed, with their sheer intuitive grasp, all scholarly comprehension of human nature; he hoped to read within himself, like Hobbes before him, all mankind.[9] This unique stature was a grave responsibility to bear, one that exacted total honesty. The autobiographer must tell all, the bad as freely as the good, and tell it precisely as he had experienced it.

As a supreme exhibition of self, the *Confessions* was, as Rousseau's Victorian readers recognized, a thoroughly modern text. While its title and contrite passages hint at links to its remote ancestor, St. Augustine's *Confessions,* the differences between these landmarks in self-revelation are far more interesting than the resemblances. Unlike Augustine, Rousseau concluded the account of his life still searching, mired in misery and isolation. Unlike Augustine, too, Rousseau allowed the place of God to be usurped by Posterity.[10] Unlike Augustine, finally, Rousseau strenuously justified his misdeeds and accused his treacherous friends the philosophes of conspiring to drag him down to his pathetic state. For all of Rousseau's talk about God the merciful judge, his autobiography belongs in the company of such ungodly contemporaries as Benjamin Franklin and Edward Gibbon. Its nineteenth-century audience had every right to read the *Confessions* as a secular document for a secularizing age.

The nineteenth century, for its part, was rich in accomplished, highly appreciated self-revelations, from Goethe's *Dichtung und Wahrheit* to George Sand's *Histoire de ma vie,* from Fanny Lewald's vast, multivolume *Meine Lebensgeschichte* to John Stuart Mill's discreetly indiscreet *Autobiography*. Other masterpieces swelled the catalog: Stendhal's exuberant, stream-of-consciousness *Vie de*

Henry Brulard, Ernest Renan's suavely polished *Souvenirs d'enfance et de jeunesse,* Theodor Fontane's touching *Meine Kinderjahre.* Some autobiographies, like Edmund Gosse's *Father and Son,* became famous because they dissected with painful lucidity a self in conflict; others, like Werner von Siemens's dry, factual *Lebenserinnerungen,* clinging to the surfaces of his life as an inventor and railroad builder, became famous simply because their author was famous.[11]

In their lives and their writings, these much cited nineteenth-century autobiographers were scarcely average bourgeois. Some, Stendhal in the lead, in fact larded their confessions with open loathing for the middle classes.* Still, those major authors who memorably reminisced in print, most of them skilled in the writing trade, lent expressive voice to the bourgeois struggles for emotional transparency. It is their autobiographies that will necessarily hold the center of attention in these pages, because they reflect these struggles far more vividly than their imitators ever could. They were simply more professional in their style and, at best, more penetrating in their psychology than the more commonplace confessions, whose models and, in a sense, whose spokesmen they became.

The age, we have noted, was swamped with unremarkable self-revelations. Literally thousands wrote them, men and women with no claim to fame of any kind. They left their memoirs moldering in attics or buried in local archives, or asked a job printer to make an unpretentious book. These undistinguished autobiographers mused on their past for their own entertainment or the edification of their children, only yielding (they almost ritually insisted) to benign pressure from their inquisitive and loving family or importunate friends. Beguiling their retirement, good bourgeois—clergymen and merchants, engineers, impresarios, and hangers-on to high society or circles of power—reported on their childhood, their schooling, their army service, their business dealings, their dazzling moments with the great. They were more than ordinary folk only in putting pen to paper. And when they came to life's decisive moments of crisis, they sounded much like the autobiographies they admired. Anthony Trollope devoted a chapter to his mother in part from "filial duty." It was a motive that animated scores of obscure autobiographers in his time.[12]

Even the modest succumbed. In 1810, not long before his early death, the German travel writer and poet Johann Gottfried Seume opened *Mein Leben*

---

*"I have always and as if instinctually," wrote Stendhal in one of his fragmentary autobiographies, "(and thoroughly confirmed since by the Chambers) profoundly despised the bourgeoisie," though he immediately added, "All the same, I also sensed that it was only among bourgeois that energetic men could be found. . . ." *Vie de Henry Brulard* (published posthumously in 1890), in *Oeuvres intimes,* ed. V. Del Litto, 2 vols. (1981–82), II, 546–47 [ch. 2].

with an appealing disclaimer: "I know the awkwardness of an autobiography as well as anyone, and I do not consider myself important enough to have my life described at all." A few years before, he recalled, a reputable bookseller had offered him a considerable sum to write the "psychological history" of his education, and he had rejected the proposal. But now his friends, concerned over his failing health, had warned him that he would not escape a biographer. And so, lest he fall into the hands of a captious critic or, worse, a tasteless sycophant, he undertook to tell his own story after all.[13]

The century provided Seume with large company. As early as 1828, the minor Scottish poet David M. Moir published an amusing imaginary autobiography, *The Life of Mansie Wauch, Tailor in Dalkeith, Written by Himself,* in which he lampooned the popular fad of "committing to paper all the surprising occurrences and remarkable events that chanced to happen to them in the course of providence." Nor did he overlook the supposed reluctance of autobiographers to come forward, doing so only "urged by the elbowing on of not a few judicious friends."[14] A satire works only when there is much to satirize, and Moir's satire worked. Some eight decades later, in 1908, the French literary historian Edmond Biré, a writer of no particular eminence, opened *Mes Souvenirs* with a different humorous target: himself. "There was a time when to write one's memoirs one had to be an ambassador or cabinet minister, an army general or at least a member of the Académie française." That was the age of "grand memoirs." But now it is "the turn of the little ones. One has been nothing, one has done nothing, one has not been involved in any great event. That does not matter, one puts one's memories on paper."* He spoke for the tribe of obscure bourgeois self-explorers who had not been kept from writing their memoirs by the recognition that they had made no difference in history.

For the most part, these little-regarded middle-class autobiographies were sincere, at times halting accounts of external events behind which their author's self stood concealed—shadowy, almost inaccessible, but very much there. They were likely to be as rich in social observation as they were thin on introspection, and their disposition to scatter commonplace sentiments at critical moments makes them relatively predictable texts. Parents are paragons: mothers are models of selfless virtue, while fathers, often admired more than loved, are strong and commanding. And life's vicissitudes—sickness and death, religious certainties or doubts—call forth sententious comment.† Even the better educated

---

*Edmond Biré, "Preface," *Mes Souvenirs, 1846–1870* (1908), vii. One needs to read these disclaimers with some caution, since they are something of a pose. See below, pp. 114–23.

†To be sure, the autobiographers' facility with language, and with their inner experience, generally varied with their educational opportunities; a pastor or a rabbi was more at ease with

would inject emotion-laden matters like marriage into their manuscripts almost as an afterthought, as matter-of-factly as possible, recording the wealth of the father-in-law and the amount of the dowry before saying a few words about the wife who came with the fortune.[15]

Even though these unliterary bourgeois confessions provide only a slender harvest of explicit self-analysis, they retain their value as records of the inner life. It is true that the handful of celebrated autobiographies left their imprint on lesser self-portraits, presenting temptations to authors more or less unconsciously disposed to copy them. Thus, reminiscing on paper, impressionable amateurs unschooled in the business of authorship often looked less into themselves than into a book. Still, even if they did not recognize just what, and how much, they were confessing, their clichés and plagiarisms often enshrined an authentic feeling. Passions lurked beneath decorous or clumsy surfaces: however awkwardly stated, pages of piety toward one's parents, love for one's wife, struggles with one's faith could be authentic confessions. However derivative, autobiographers in the nineteenth century confronted their past as a unique story to be told, Werner von Siemens little less than Wolfgang von Goethe. Whether the feat of self-revelation was an obsessive act of reparation, a kind of therapy, or a harmless diversion, autobiographers found themselves confronted with choices of expressiveness or reserve for which the most admired model had no ready answers. Hence the least among memoirs could provide access to the naked heart of the nineteenth-century bourgeoisie. Even the memoirs of public figures, usually disappointing guides to the inner dimension, had their instructive moments.*

Plainly labeled autobiographies were only one kind of self-portrait that nineteenth-century bourgeois readers wanted, and bought. Carlyle's *Sartor Resartus* has been called many things: an unconventional novel, a political statement, a prophecy, an imaginative and undefinable jeu d'esprit. But it was also a semi-fictitious version of St. Augustine's *Confessions,* an autobiography that exhibited the author's religious travail and his hopes for serenity. Benjamin Constant's *Adolphe* was only the most confessional in an age of confessional fictions; Goethe's novels from *Werther* to *Wilhelm Meister,* as many of his readers were

---

words about the self than a small entrepreneur or government clerk might be. But the record shows some striking exceptions. Men and women with little schooling at times mustered an impressive eloquence as they talked of their loves and their anxieties.

*The autobiographies of political leaders must be read with a whole shaker of salt: Bismarck's *Gedanken und Erinnerungen,* for one, was a systematic effort at persuading readers to a favorable verdict on the author's actions during his decades of power. Yet, in its self-serving way, it, too, told some unsuspected truths.

well aware, drew freely on his emotional history.[16] Much nineteenth-century poetry and prose contained ample deposits of indiscretions, whether calculated or unintentional. It seems almost inescapable that Victorian literary critics should have been, almost without exception, biographical critics for whom writings were privileged clues to the writer. If some autobiographies of the time could have served as novels, a good many novels of the time served as autobiographies. Even programmatic paintings or musical compositions were often designed, and taken, to provide access to their makers' inner lives.* And these thinly veiled self-disclosures continued to flourish well after the romantic decades: though embroidered with literary license, Dickens's *David Copperfield* of 1850, the novel he called "my favourite child," visibly exploits experiences—or, better, affectively colored memories—of his childhood.

The informal essay from Charles Lamb to Saint-Beuve, prospering in an age of great periodicals, proved another copious treasure trove of hearts laid bare. Hazlitt's essays, Leslie Stephen wrote in the 1870s, "are autobiographical, sometimes even offensively." Although "shy with his friends," Stephen thought, Hazlitt "was the most unreserved of writers."[17] For his part, in a dialogue with his friends defending benevolence, Hazlitt playfully charged that they, principled egotists all, "would turn every thing into autobiography."[18] Plainly, undisguised self-reference was in the air. The thing existed before the name, folded into the capacious category known as "biography." But it is surely significant that while the precise date remains in dispute, the word "autobiography" was first used around 1800 and widely domesticated in several languages a few years later. The Victorians did not merely multiply instances of the genre but, as it were, liberated it to pursue its own career.[19]

Once isolated as a separate genre, the autobiography proved too protean for easy classification. In 1899, introducing Prince Kropotkin's *Memoirs of a Revolutionist,* the influential Danish critic and biographer Georg Brandes listed five distinct categories. For the most part, the confessions "we owe to great minds" belong to one of three types: " 'So far I went astray; thus I found the true path' (St. Augustine); or, 'So bad was I, but who dare consider himself better?' (Rousseau); or 'This is the way a genius has slowly been evolved from within and by favorable surroundings' (Goethe)." But Brandes quickly added two other types, both self-congratulatory, celebrating the writer's talents and triumphs or his way of overcoming undeserved obstacles. For Brandes, in short, autobiographies were exercises in apologetics, self-advertisement, and self-pity. But he was too intelligent not to see that his catalog was far from exhaustive.

*For painters, see below, pp. 277–309.

After all, the very autobiography he was introducing markedly differed from all the others in being neither self-centered nor self-serving.[20]

Brandes's failure to establish a reliable inventory of autobiographies must give joy to a nominalist. It may be facile to suggest that there were as many types of Victorian autobiography as there were examples of it, but the genre was almost by definition highly individualistic. Autobiographies could be entertaining or dull; some were neglected treasures, others chores to plow through. For every thoroughly enjoyable memoir like the spirited *Souvenirs* by the French portrait painter Elisabeth Vigée-Lebrun, written in the 1830s when she was in her eighties, there was the bulky *Autobiography* of Herbert Spencer, published in 1904, a work that only a historian of sociology can love. Autobiographies ranged from touching revelations to snobbish gossip about celebrities, from intimate disclosures of emotional traumas to bloodless résumés, from collections of telling anecdotes to self-exculpatory efforts at prettifying, or wholly concealing, unsavory conduct.

It is not as though autobiographers were professionally disingenuous; they would set out their intentions in the title, a self-conscious preface, or the opening sentence or paragraph, all highly sensitive indicators of revelations or reticences to come. "I have been so often asked by my musical and other friends to write my reminiscences that at last I have made up my mind to do so," thus the impresario Wilhelm Ganz starts his *Memories of a Musician*. The reader, duly warned in the next sentence of the author's "literary shortcomings," knows that on offer will be cheerful and superficial accounts of "many musical facts and events which have happened during my long career in England," concerts, meetings with famous artists, a few failures and a host of triumphs. This is shallow stuff, one anecdote chasing another. But, considering Ganz's unintrospective nature, his memoirs tell us, by telling us little, precisely as much as we want to know from him. Yet even this sort of gossipy reportage belongs to the history of nineteenth-century inwardness. The display of one's naked heart was not a universal fact of Victorian life but an ideal, and a highly controversial ideal at that.

The issue was so delicate because the Victorian reading public was of two minds on the question of frankness. The more forthright the self-portrait, the more interesting but, at the same time, the more problematic. Indiscretion sold, though at a price to the author no less than to the reader. Montaigne, the most uninhibited of self-probers who had laid open his convictions and prejudices, his political and literary opinions, his sexual tastes and his very digestion some three centuries before, had had few precursors and practically no successors—at least not until Rousseau's *Confessions*. This was the dilemma of nineteenth-century inwardness in print: saying too little was tedious and probably unrewarding; saying too much was unmannerly but somehow irresistible. Baring one's heart was proving to be a business commendable and dangerous alike.

2. Between Probes and Poses

In the fostering Victorian atmosphere, that perennial problem for all autobiographers, just what degree of self-exposure is proper, grew exceptionally acute. No single solution satisfied everyone. Hence exercises in exhibitionism jostled taciturn scraps of discreet reminiscences. To complicate matters, many presumed confessions failed to match their promised candor with authentic revelations. In 1825, in a burst of publicity seeking, an English lady of pleasure, Harriette Wilson, opened her four-volume *Memoirs,* advertised in the title as *Written by Herself,* with this teasing sentence: "I shall not say why and how I became, at the age of fifteen, the mistress of the Earl of Craven." But, disappointing the expectations she had aroused, she retailed whatever gossip she divulged in the most decorous tones, leaving virtually everything to the reader's imagination. In contrast, in 1886 and again in 1894, Wilhelm Busch, Germany's most beloved humorous versifier and illustrator, forced from himself two sparse articles about his early years; but, defying their brevity and defensive maneuvers, they ventilated some harrowing details about his emotionally starved youth.[1] In short, many nineteenth-century confessions confessed less, many of them more, than their authors planned, or proclaimed.

It is tempting, therefore, to accept Thomas Henry Huxley's dismissal of autobiographies as "essentially works of fiction"—a temptation to be resisted on the principle that all autobiographies are true.[2] But it is a powerful one. Even when an autobiographer's intended audience is only close family or a handful of intimate friends, the image that governs the work—journey or pilgrimage, climb to the heights or descent into the depths—unmasks it as a performance designed to amuse, to cajole, to appease. The autobiographer has decided, consciously or unconsciously, that he—or she—is different enough, guilty enough, in some sense important enough to warrant all this expenditure of time and energy to record past events, past encounters, past emotions. Not even the most colorless memoir of the most unspectacular career can escape the suspicion that it amounts to special pleading. No one can wonder that historians, despite all their professional respect for the past, will suspect the printed text before them of concealing unacknowledged, no doubt disagreeable, truths about the author.

The very decision to expose one's past to the scrutiny of others opens autobiographers to the charge of narcissism. As though to preempt that reproach, numbers of them took a certain emotional distance from their self-probing assignment. Darwin virtually blamed "a German editor" for suggesting that he write an account of his "mind and character," and noted that he had complied because he thought "the attempt would amuse me, and might possibly interest my children or their children." And he proposed to see himself from the chilling perspective of the grave: "I have attempted to write the following account of myself, as if I were a dead man in another world looking back at my own life." Nor had he found this difficult, "for life is nearly over with me. I have taken no pains about my style of writing."[3] It was as though he were disclaiming responsibility for his life—or at least for the revelations to come.

Other autobiographers went further, professing to dislike their preoccupation with self. Around mid-nineteenth century, George Sand, who had poured so much of her private experience into her fictions, described composing her formal autobiography as the most arduous of duties: "I know nothing more difficult than to define and to sum up oneself in person." After all, "when you get used to speaking about yourself, it is easy to start boasting, doubtless quite unintentionally, by a natural law of the human spirit which cannot help embellishing and elevating the object of its contemplation." In this "enthusiasm for yourself," the autobiographer forgets her failings and instead "identifies herself with the divinity, with the ideal she embraces," and "becomes Werther, or Manfred, or Faust, or Hamlet." In the 1870s, Madame d'Agoult, in her autobiography, which like her novels she published under the male pseudonym of Daniel Stern, echoed her more famous contemporary in her *Souvenirs:* "The pleasure of talking about oneself, so agreeable to many people, counts for nothing in the design I have formed to write my memoirs. With Pascal, I have always found the *self hateful*." Yet, curiously, this self-hatred did not keep her from setting down "the events and the feelings that have enlivened or troubled my intimate life."[4] Such heartfelt disclaimers were scarcely convincing. The very autobiographers who most loudly protested that they would prefer to remain silent spoke out.

A few of them left the impression that they spoke because they felt under some compulsion to do so. There were Victorian autobiographies that seemed therapeutic—one of them, Theodor Fontane's, in fact was ordered by a physician.* To look back was a way of coaxing the repressed to return to awareness. Stendhal, wandering across the landscape of his past as though he were practicing free association, hoped that the act of writing would enable him to discover fundamental truths about his character: "In the evening"—he marks the precise date, October 16, 1832, and notes that he is crowding fifty—"on returning

*See below, pp. 145–48.

from the ambassador's soirée quite bored, I said to myself, 'I ought to write my life; then perhaps when it is done in two or three years I should at last know what I have been, cheerful or sad, a witty man or a fool, a man of courage or fearful; and in sum happy or unhappy.' " He was cheered to see the process working for him: "I am making great discoveries about myself in writing these memoirs." All he now needs, he added, is an audience! In a similar vein, George Sand exclaimed to her publisher as she turned to her early years in *Histoire de ma vie* after discussing her ancestors, "It is almost a miracle how my childhood memories awaken to the degree that I come close to the period in which I shall speak about myself." She meant her religious language almost literally. "The dead are us, that is certain, there is a mysterious link through which our life nourishes itself from theirs."[5] Autobiographers less inclined to mystical intimations agreed that the mind turned in upon itself was likely to come up with unsuspected treasures.

Interesting as nineteenth-century readers found the ultimate motives of autobiographers, they subsumed them under the more general question of authenticity. In their age more than ever, they had to pick their way across minefields of assertions and admissions where nothing was quite what it was made out to be. Their explorations were bedeviled by discrepancies between published account and unpublished evidence, the testimony of contemporaries that contradicted the autobiographer, and the author's often maddeningly fragmentary or ambiguous reportage. Prudent self-protection, we know, can masquerade as ingenuous self-disclosure, but fortunately involuntary revelations can defeat the most strenuous evasive tactics. Apparent probes, in short, often turned out to be poses, often adopted not with an intent to deceive but in obedience to unknown impulsions.

Goethe's autobiography, *Aus meinem Leben. Dichtung und Wahrheit,* begun in 1809, when he was sixty, propels these complexities to center stage. The title and the more famous subtitle are a cunning mixture of promise and defense: "*Aus* meinem Leben"—*from* my life—hints that the author plans to be selective; the word *Dichtung,* which means *fiction* as much as *poetry,* that he plans to use the impressive literary resources at his command to embroider, perhaps invent additions to, the naked recital of facts. Indeed, at first glance Goethe's highly stylized account reads almost like a response to Rousseau's disheveled revelations. Although, like Rousseau, Goethe starts with his birth and tames the meandering stream of his life's experience by neatly organizing his text into symmetrical sections, there the closest resemblances cease. Unlike Rousseau, who brought his pathetic story down to the time of writing, 1765, when he was fifty-three, Goethe closed *Dichtung und Wahrheit* with his twenty-sixth year, in

William Sydney Mount, *The Power of Music* (1847). A segregated concert, illustrating the art of listening in humble surroundings.

The ten-year old Mozart playing his heart out while an aristocratic audience is enjoying lunch.

Fernand Khnopff, *En écoutant du Schumann* (1883). The emphasis has shifted from the performer to the rapt listener.

Friedrich von Hardenberg, better known as Novalis. The young much-admired German romantic.

Madame de Staël. Liberal politician and lover, influential interpreter of German romanticism to France.

Friedrich Schlegel. The most important theorist of German romanticism.

Dorothea Schlegel. Moses Mendelssohn's literary daughter, who left her Jewish husband to marry Protestant Friedrich Schlegel, and then converted with him to Roman Catholicism.

Percy Bysshe Shelley. Here shown —or imagined—as a wild-eyed poet.

George Gordon, Lord Byron. A dubious triumph of the engraver's art: he has made the irresistible Byron cross-eyed.

S.T. Coleridge. Poet, talker, controversial scholar.

William Wordsworth. The greatest of autobiographical poets.

VICTOR HUGO.

Victor Hugo. The most celebrated and long-lived of France's poets and novelists whose life was as romantic as his work.

Fritz Fleischer, *Der Tod Goethes*. The modest bed and tiny room in Goethe's luxurious mansion, where he died.

Hans Christian Andersen. The ugly
duckling as ugly duckling.

Theodor Fontane. Germany's
most interesting novelist between
Goethe and Thomas Mann.

Johann Joachim Winckelmann.
The autodidact who virtually invented art history.

Lord Nelson. Napoleon's English nemesis.

Edmund Gosse. The prolific litera-teur who wrote one masterpiece—*Father and Son*.

Leopold von Ranke. The great historian in all his beribboned and bemedaled glory.

John Lothrop Motley. With his dramatic and partisan histories of the early Dutch republic, a public great favorite.

1775, when he was making ready to settle—permanently, it emerged—in the duchy of Weimar. Rousseau wrote at a headlong pace, relying on flashes of memory and impassioned reconstructions of idylls and resentments; Goethe consulted eyewitnesses and volumes on recent history to refresh, and correct, his recollections of private and public events he had witnessed.

Most important, Rousseau treated discretion as the enemy, the refuge of hypocrites, while Goethe made discretion—or, perhaps better, a canny indiscretion—his governing principle. Reviewing *Dichtung und Wahrheit* in 1816, Sir Francis Palgrave handsomely acknowledged Goethe's attempts at baring his soul: "There is no doubt but that a person who writes his own life, must be allowed to put himself in the foreground: and it is his duty to reveal a great number of secrets respecting himself, of which he is the sole depositary. But Goethe makes no attempt to select such as are alone fit to be preserved. He strips himself stark-naked, and empties his pockets inside out into the bargain." Few who have read *Dichtung und Wahrheit* would wholeheartedly endorse this tribute to Goethe's frankness. In any event, Palgrave quickly backtracked to complain that Goethe was not really emptying his pockets very thoroughly: his "delineations of passion and character are almost always strained and unnatural."* How very different, we seem to hear, how much more satisfying, Rousseau's *Confessions*!

Palgrave's reservations were more to the point than his enthusiasm, especially when it came to Goethe's active erotic life. Far from stripping himself stark naked in *Dichtung und Wahrheit,* Goethe, even at the distance of four decades, refused to discuss why he should have broken with one particularly appealing young woman, give more than a hint why he retreated from a most plausible engagement, or confess the deeper meaning of his intimate attachment to his sister Cornelia. At most, he granted the reader partial access to his feelings of guilt and dismay, placing a veil of partial amnesia over these intriguing episodes.

Yet any attempt to pit *Dichtung und Wahrheit* against the *Confessions* as exemplars of incompatible attitudes must fail. Each was honest and devious in its own way; each at once constructed, and sincerely groped for, its author's past. There was more guile in Rousseau's guileless self-disclosures than he would have admitted. He documented his guilt but protested his innocence, retailed epi-

*[Sir Francis Palgrave], in *Edinburgh Review,* XXVI (June 1816), 314, 310. In 1909, in an important monograph on autobiography, Anna Robeson Burr repeated this reservation. She admired Rousseau's *Confessions* for being "permeated with emotion, an emotion expressed with the voice and accent of genius," while she denounced *Dichtung und Wahrheit* as "the weakest autobiography the world has ever had from so strong a hand. Enthusiasts over it are almost invariably to be found among those persons who think a sincere self-revelation pernicious and undesirable." *The Autobiography: A Critical and Comparative Study* (1909), 25–26, 68.

sodes that may never have happened and omitted others that certainly had. For his part Goethe, who controlled his self-disclosures with consummate craftsmanship, provided finely calculated doses of evidence for inner turmoil that breaks through the barriers of his stately pace and formal prose. Once readers have grown accustomed to his elevated diction, they find his intimate disclosures unrehearsed enough, deeply felt though delicately expressed. He leaves far more work for his readers than Rousseau would have thought necessary or desirable, but provides them with enough nourishment to invite inferences and provide access to jealously protected private domains. If *Dichtung und Wahrheit* teaches anything, it is that explicitness is not the only qualified, and often not the best, escort to the interior.

Goethe starts this fragment of his great confession guardedly, almost coyly, with a supposed letter from a friend—almost certainly written by himself—asking him to close the gap between his published writings and the "picture of the author and his talent." By parading this convenient external impulsion, Goethe instantly builds a wall of reserve between himself and the reader. Then, professing himself stimulated by this cordial request, he fills in the empty spaces on the map of his past and sets out to "depict humans in relation to the conditions of their time and to show in what way the whole resisted, in what way it favored him."[6]

Thus coolly launched, the contribution of *Dichtung und Wahrheit* to an understanding of its author's inner life promises to be anything but generous. But Goethe persistently shows himself as much concerned with the subjective as with the objective dimensions of his personal history. In chapter after chapter, he documents the subtle intertwining of his responses with realities, whether his narrow family circle or the greater world of his bustling native Frankfurt. When he describes the festive coronation of Emperor Joseph II, celebrated in his hometown in April 1864, he skillfully links his father expounding the historical significance of the colorful, arcane ceremonies to his adolescent puppy love for an elusive young woman named Gretchen, who is aching for explanations, which young Goethe happily supplies. And when he devotes substantial paragraphs to the history of German literature, he concentrates on his precursors' influence on him; in his most didactic mood, looking back from Olympian heights as the renowned poet and man of the world, he never slights the personal equation.

Goethe drew subtler connections still: between childhood and adult experience. He fondly recalled the puppet theater that his grandmother had given him when he was a little boy, and how the "unexpected spectacle" of the small, open wooden box had made "a very strong impression which resonated with great long-lasting effect." Proof of that resonance, Goethe's readers would be sure to know, was an early scene in his novel *Wilhelm Meisters Lehrjahre,* where the eponymous hero receives precisely such a gift, one that launches Wilhelm's passion for the theater.[7] Again, as an adult—a decade after *Dichtung und Wahrheit* breaks off, but in a crucial episode familiar to all of Goethe's audience—he revived long forgotten memories of the engravings of Rome that his father had hung up in his house to recall a trip to Italy he wanted never to forget. Every day, Goethe recalled, he saw those views of Rome—the Colosseum, St. Peter's Square, and much else—and these scenes had made "a deep impression" on him.[8] When, in 1786, he fled Weimar from his burdensome duties and a complicated amatory entanglement, he sought, and found, liberation in Rome, the city that must have haunted his imagination since infancy. Without sermonizing on this psychological truth, Goethe demonstrates in *Dichtung und Wahrheit* that the child is truly father to the man.

One does not need Goethe's autobiography to recognize him as the supreme poet of experience. A comparison of his letters, diaries, and recorded conversations with his poems, novels, and dramas supplies rich evidence for his gift of turning life into literature. But in *Dichtung und Wahrheit* he makes this disposition explicit. As a young man, he writes, he took a "direction from which I have been unable to deviate my whole life, namely to transform whatever pleased or tormented me, or preoccupied me in other ways, into a picture, a poem." He found this the most effective way of freeing himself from inner turmoil: he would correct his perceptions of external matters, often excessive in their coloring, by going over them in his mind; feeding his fantasy life with real experiences, he poured his infatuations into a literary mold. Thus, he confesses, certain senseless quarrels with Gretchen and guilt feelings over his conduct encouraged him to identify himself with her, and dramatize them in an early comedy, *Die Laune des Verliebten.*[9]

The amorous involvements that Goethe first went through and later immortalized in *Dichtung und Wahrheit*—the two are not quite identical—make his debt to experience most visible but, with his struggle to impose aesthetic form on distant and disturbing recollections, hard to read. In his attachments, as in other matters, Goethe the adult owed much to Goethe the child. "The first love, one says with justice," he observes, anticipating Freud by a century, "is the only one; for in the second, and through the second, the highest sense of love is already lost." Writing to a friend about his tense, long-lasting love for Charlotte von Stein in Weimar, he describes her as "by and by inheriting my mother, sister, and [other] beloved women."[10] Love was, for Goethe, an intricately varied and persistent set of variations on a single theme.

However emphatically Goethe insists in his autobiography on the connection between life and literature, it does not exhaust the truth about his proceedings as a poet. He could build substantial works on a very slender base; spinning out a small donnée, he translated experiences into poems or novels that occupied a peculiar domain at once factual and imaginative. He dramatized, he expanded, he played with or was diffident about his amorous experience; he was an artist, not a stenographer.

Still, Goethe was in love virtually all his life, with many different women, including, fatefully, his sister. He was in love so persistently, so intensely, so programmatically that he looks suspiciously like a man cultivating his passion to keep his muse fully occupied. Again and again, in his autobiography and in other texts, he testifies to his overwhelming need for this spur to creativity. "If I needed true documentation, feeling, or reflection for my poems," he noted, "I had to delve into my own bosom."[11] And what he found there, as he testifies over and over, were women who inspired him to song. "If I could only live without loving," he once exclaimed longingly to Charlotte von Stein. The point remains that he could not live—or, more precisely, could not make poetry—without it, and *Dichtung und Wahrheit* supplies ample, if subtle, clues to that truth about him.[12]

If Goethe's autobiography is more transparent than it at first appears, Hans Christian Andersen's first comprehensive autobiography, *Das Märchen meines Lebens ohne Dichtung,* of 1847, is less so. The title itself is deceptive, an exception to the rule that the autobiographer concludes a kind of contract with the reader with his title. Andersen's claim is extraordinary; calling his autobiography "the fairy tale of my life without fiction," he intimates that he aims to be more uninhibited than Goethe, who after all could not do without *Dichtung.* This is all the bolder particularly since Andersen longed, literally prayed, all his life to be a *Dichter* worthy of Goethe's company. In calling his life a fairy tale, Andersen is far from suggesting that he is inventing his past. Rather, he means to convey the impression that his life has been a succession of such marvelous triumphs that it resembled one of the stories—at least those with happy endings—that would make him a household name throughout the Western world by mid-century.

In the opening paragraph of *Das Märchen meines Lebens ohne Dichtung,* Andersen sustains the atmospheric metaphor of his title: "My life is a lovely fairy tale, so rich and happy. If, when I went out into the world poor and alone, I had met a powerful fairy godmother and she had said, 'Choose your career and your goal, and then, according to your mental development and the way it will rationally have to be in this world, I shall protect you and lead you!' my fate could not have been happier, could not have been guided better and more intelligently. My life's history will tell the world what it says to me: there is a loving God who leads all things for the best."[13] Cradled in God's affectionate arms, Andersen had risen from extreme want to fame and fortune, from a youth racked with deprivation and embittered by ridicule to astounding honors and universal favor and affection.

Andersen keeps up the resounding note of these introductory sentences through the body of his life's story; the sweet aroma of sentimental self-congratulation never lifts. He does acknowledge that he was born in poverty, suffering humiliating rejections in miserable schools and, later, when as an adolescent he tried to make his own way in Copenhagen. Yet, anything but apologetic about his harrowing first years, Andersen basks in them. He rede-scribes them as suffused with affection and underscores the distance he has traveled in his miracle-filled life. His unpromising beginnings did not destroy him, since those who mattered most to him, his parents, had swaddled him in incomparable devotion. As a young couple, living in a one-room house, they "loved each other infinitely." His father, he reports, was an independent-minded cobbler, "a very gifted man, an authentically poetic nature," whose hero was Napoleon; little Hans Christian possessed his "whole love." His mother was "a few years older, unacquainted with the world and life, with a heart full of love." Adoring their only child and spoiling it, Andersen tells us, his parents lived only for him.

So did his maternal grandmother, who came to visit the family every day. "I was her joy and her happiness." She brought him flowers and "loved me with all her soul." One dangerous incident—it reads like a screen memory—trans-mits his ostentatious sense of being lovable, barely concealing the fear that he is hateful. He had accompanied his mother to glean in the fields when a bailiff, well known as a coarse and brutal man, pursued them with "a terrible large whip." As the official was about to strike the boy, Andersen looked at him and exclaimed, "How can you beat me when God can see it!" The bailiff stopped, stroked little Hans Christian's cheek, asked his name and gave him money. His mother was not surprised at this display: my son, he has her saying, "is a remarkable child, all people think well of him, even that wicked fellow gave him money."[14] For Andersen, the family romance that accompanied him through life and informed many of his fairy tales embraced more than his family. Under his pen, his parents, whether the Andersens or such surrogates as rich and aristocratic admirers, were almost more than human.

Some of this fairy tale is even true. After some years of failure as a poet and playwright, Andersen was taken up by a succession of responsible, wealthy—and, of course, loving—patrons who recognized his talents and welcomed his presence beyond all realistic expectations. As Andersen continues with his life's *Märchen,* he drops the names of distinguished artists and writers, of noble hosts and royal admirers, on page after page. The actual roster was impressive enough: in his maturity—if that is the right word—Hans Christian Andersen, novelist and inventor of memorable modern fairy tales, grew into one of Europe's literary treasures. To his following, his best-known inventions—the little mermaid, the little match girl, the ugly duckling—were as real as any fictional characters the bourgeois century produced. But the character that mattered most in Andersen's autobiography was, naturally enough, Andersen himself: the ugly duckling who had become a beautiful swan.

Internal evidence by itself raises severe doubts whether Andersen's account of warming sunshine after freezing rain, and of happiness in all things, is an altogether candid emotional record. He recounts some terrifying memories— or fantasies: visiting his grandmother in the asylum for the aged and the insane where she works, he glimpses a naked madwoman who rushes at him, scream- ing, her arms outstretched. He records that his father went mad and died young, and that his mother infected him with some of her more frightening supersti- tions. Nor does he wholly suppress his intermittent schooling and his sufferings at the hands of obtuse, arbitrary masters. But far more central to his story are the fatherly patrons who smoothed his way to international stature. In 1829, when he was twenty-four, his odyssey as a pupil over, "life lay before me, the rays of the sun upon it."[15] All this relentless sunshine is dubious enough, but the testimony of his voluminous correspondence and the equally voluminous dia- ries he faithfully kept for decades show *Das Märchen meines Lebens ohne Dichtung* to be a work of almost naked wish fulfillment, a fiction disguised as a history without fiction. No autobiography documents better than Andersen's the risks of trusting an autobiographer's unsupported word.

The *Märchen* of Andersen's life is untrustworthy, to begin with, because it slides over some embarrassing details about his family, details that diligent re- searchers have uncovered. Contrary to his bland portrait, Andersen's mother was a far from innocent maiden: herself illegitimate, she had already borne an illegitimate daughter before meeting Andersen's father, and the two married just two months before Hans Christian was born. Nor does he tell his readers that his mother's sister ran a bordello in Copenhagen, or that his father enlisted in 1812 in the army of Denmark, then allied with France, not so much as a principled Bonapartist but largely because he had been well paid as a substi- tute.[16]

Telling as these attempts to erase blots on the family escutcheon may be, certain artless confessions that expose more than Andersen thought he was exposing are of still greater interest to the historian recording failures of self- concealment. As a small boy, in childish infatuation with storytelling and the theater, he had liked to sew doll's clothes with rags he had begged; a few years later, working in a textile mill, he found his fellow workers were making fun of his high singing voice, and joking that he must be a girl not a boy; from his earliest days on, and through much of his life, he wept at the slightest provocation; once, describing his naïveté, he calls himself "virginally foolish." His avid search for intimacy with other men, especially in the light of his lifelong infatuations with women who were unavailable to him smacks of an unending, desperate search for a sexual identity. His unsparing diaries testify that his erotic fantasies, for which he naturally found no place in his printed self-depictions, were of women and induced bouts of masturbation, which appears to have been his only path to gratification.

It seems most likely, then, that Andersen never reached the stage of adult sexual desire, whether open or repressed, but remained emotionally and erotically underdeveloped, forever a child. This conclusion is not interpretation but reportage; in his autobiography, Andersen calls himself a child more than once, especially around Christmastime.[17] He remained helplessly fixated on early fantasies, at once anxieties and wishes. So did his autobiography, an extreme instance where the need to pose, if largely unconsciously, had overwhelmed the effort to probe.

3. The Road from Damascus

In a century that saw the combat between atheistic science and Christian faith escalate, autobiographies provided deeply felt testimonies to the religious wars. By the end of Victoria's reign, secularism was far from secure; it was characteristic that a treatise like Andrew Dickson White's *History of the Warfare of Science with Theology in Christendom* should be popular reading around 1900. The modern intellect, driven by the triumphs of science and of scholarship, was turning its back on the consolations of religion, but believers had not been cowed into silence. In 1895, Emile Durkheim called his times, with some distaste, "these times of renascent mysticism."[1] The age was not only the age of Charles Darwin but also that of Cardinal Manning, not only of the assaults launched by French secularists against entrenched clerical privileges but also that of papal infallibility proclaimed in Rome. In the last quarter of the century, while socialists across Europe were ostentatiously discarding their inherited faith, Roman Catholic writers published religious novels—virtual autobiographies in disguise—that rehearsed their unease with the reality of hell or the divinely instituted need for human suffering. Bellicose unbelievers like Marx or Freud uneasily, often bitterly coexisted with defenders of the faith like the scholarly Protestant theologian Albrecht Ritschl in Germany or the Catholic apologist

Léon Bloy in France. In this atmosphere, no autobiographer could altogether sidestep the issue of religion—his religion.

Nineteenth-century reminiscences made few formal comments about technical theological issues but reflect them in deeply personal, often affecting ways. From the beginning of the age, the higher critics had thrown doubt on the unity, and hence the divine inspiration, of the Bible; in 1835, the German theologian David Friedrich Strauss had scandalized the faithful, and energized the skeptical, with his *Leben Jesu,* a learned biography of the Savior as a man. Skeptical philosophers kept alive the Enlightenment's campaign of tarring all belief with the brush of superstition; at the same time, the Oxford movement in England and social Catholicism on the Continent struggled to rescue Christianity, the first by combatting theological liberalism and the second by embracing it. Materialist philosophers like Ludwig Feuerbach did not write their polemics against supernaturalism in water, but among the most widely read, and among the most influential, self-diagnoses in the Victorian age was John Henry Newman's *Apologia pro vita sua,* a seductive memoir of his odyssey from the Anglican to the Roman Catholic Church. No wonder there was much anguished talk about a "crisis of faith" in Britain and elsewhere. The road from Damascus was crowded, the road to Damascus far less so; but in both directions it was noisy with confessions of faith secured, faith questioned, and faith lost.

Many autobiographies, Newman's among them, document—if such documentation is needed—that nineteenth-century bourgeois, whether believers or unbelievers, took matters of doctrine seriously. They register bruising battles as much within individuals as among them. Religious convictions were, to be sure, a grave private matter, but society had not relinquished its stake in them; defying the pressures of modern individualism, the Victorians lived embedded in a family, a neighborhood, a little world of schools and friendships. Their beliefs were virtually public property. That is why relatively frank statements about one's religious convictions were rarer in autobiographies intended for publication, where they could do much damage, than in those intended to remain in manuscript. In his voluminous reminiscences, the German-Jewish manufacturer Jacob Epstein spoke fondly of the influence his "pious" mother exerted on his childhood and no less fondly of his father's "independent way of thinking, free of any dogmatic belief." But he conceded that "this religious element disturbed my parents' marital peace."[2] That was precisely the reason why Darwin wrote and talked so little about religious matters: he was reluctant to stir up controversy and, even more, to hurt the feelings of his devout wife, Emma.

Yet, in the privacy of his autobiography, Darwin was explicit enough. He noted that while at Cambridge, as he prepared himself for a career in the church, he was still persuaded that every word of the Bible was literally true. In retrospect this struck him as comical: "Considering how fiercely I have been attacked by the orthodox, it seems ludicrous that I once intended to be a clergyman." But aboard the *Beagle,* enjoying extended leisure, he rethought his position and came to regard the Old Testament as a wholly untrustworthy history of the world. The more one knows of nature, he wrote, the less credible miracles appear to be, and Christian doctrines like eternal punishment for un-believers are simply "damnable." He never quite settled his religious position to his satisfaction. Late in life, he called himself a theist, and confessed to a tentative belief in the immortality of the soul. But then he admitted that the "religious sentiment" had never been strongly developed in him.[3]

The autobiographies of obscure bourgeois often charted far more intense, far more exhausting struggles with belief, and they differed from the recollections of the well educated and the facile mainly in a certain lack of literary sophistica-tion. But clumsy or adroit, hundreds felt the need to discuss their religious upbringing, religious convictions, religious travail. The memoirs of Jews living in German cities, a literate community that after 1800 slowly began to enter German society against formidable resistance, are crowded with these intimate themes. The more routine of these chronicles concentrated on events like Jewish holidays celebrated at home or encounters with anti-Semites and—surprisingly often—cordial gentiles at school and in business. Only the most sensitive of these Jewish autobiographers, registering their responses to shifting personal needs and cultural currents, dwelt affectingly on the perplexities that competing religious ideas or modern unbelief created for them.

Let one memoir, the privately printed *Erinnerungen* of Clara Geissmar, stand for many. Born in 1844 in the small town of Eppingen, in Baden, she recalled her Orthodox household and her unquestioning acceptance of age-old beliefs and rituals in fond detail, with a distance leavened by nostalgia. The seasonal feasts and the formal blessings, the family prayers and the ceremonial surround-ing circumcisions remained indelible into old age: "I had thoroughly tasted the joys and sufferings, the privations and the inner gratification that Judaism allots to the faithful." In her youthful orthodoxy, which, she said, warmed her heart, she had known somehow that "one belongs to a Whole, whose blessings only those can feel who do justice to all the laws and regulations with which it surrounds itself as with a fence." Then, at eighteen, she married a Jewish law-yer, worldly but faithful to the old practices, and her new life pushed her into unexpected friendships and new tensions she never quite resolved, including the tantalizing attractions of Protestant doctrine. "So much that was good and lovely forced itself upon me that it was almost too much for my spiritual capacity to digest. I had hours when I felt empty and unsatisfied. There was a little space in my heart that neither the love of my husband nor the finest passages from Shakespeare and Goethe could fill. I needed to belong to a religion."[4] Her husband wanted their children to receive a traditional Jewish education, but Clara Geissmar, her taste for Orthodox holidays now barely able to compete with Protestantism, thought to have her children baptized. And so, the earnest religious debate, with her husband and herself, went on, all artlessly rehearsed in her reminiscences.

Many autobiographers, famous or not, reported that they had spent painful years finding a satisfying place on the spectrum of belief. Darwin was fortunate: "Disbelief crept over me at a very slow rate," and "the rate was so slow that I felt no distress." But others suffered precisely because it took them so long to discard what they had been brought up to cherish. As Newman's friend R. W. Church, a well-informed Oxonian High Church divine, put it late in the nineteenth century, "The change of religion when it comes on a man gradually—when it is not welcomed from the first, but, on the contrary, long resisted, must always be a mysterious and perplexing process," as hard to understand "by the person most deeply interested, veiled and clouded to lookers-on." Newman himself acknowledged that he had found religious clarity only after "many years of intellectual unrest."[5] But his so-called novel *Loss and Gain,* a slightly touched-up account of his conversion, proves that his unrest had not been confined to the sphere of the intellect. And Newman was in large company. No wonder the autobiographical impulse found solid nourishment in this atmosphere of contest and crisis.

At times, solemn nineteenth-century memoirs recording religious gains and losses rise to the intensity of melodrama. Among the most poignant accounts of these wrestling matches with the sacred are the jottings of the minor French philosopher and psychologist Théodore Jouffroy, a follower of the influential eclectic philosopher Victor Cousin. His impassioned pages are unmatched in their meticulous dissection of psychological states at a moment of catastrophe. But they speak for others, since in confessing to an overpowering yearning for something to believe in, preferably a creed that a reasonable person could adopt without embarrassment, Jouffroy was voicing a widespread perplexity of the time. The hunt for a credible system of beliefs was a powerful motive force for many who had come to find supernatural religion primitive and incredible. The liberal French political thinker and novelist Benjamin Constant had already asserted some years before Jouffroy faced his crisis, "Man is not religious because he is timid; he is religious because he is man." Taking the same tack, Pierre Leroux, the radical editor and philosopher who had published Jouffroy, argued, "Man has a natural need of religion and of worship." In short, "he is religious because he is reasonable."[6] In fact, an impressive number of Victorian natural scientists and philosophers who rejected Christianity also rejected modern materialism as too narrow and too cold to be a home for them. Instead, they turned for support to spiritualism or an urbane natural religion. The prospect of a universe empty of the divine struck them as intolerable.

Jouffroy was the most eloquent of these honest seekers. In an autobiographical essay, he reconstructs the explosive encounter with his deepest self when he felt compelled to acknowledge his inability to continue as an orthodox Christian. Born in 1796 in the provinces, his marked intellectual gifts soon recognized, he was admitted to the renowned Ecole normale in Paris, and it was there, at twenty, that he had his flash of traumatic truth. As a sober young *normalien,* Jouffroy had been obsessively preoccupied with philosophy, and at first the faith of his fathers provided satisfactory answers to the inconvenient questions his ruminations were raising. The contours of his life, present and future, still seemed clear to him, tranquil and cloudless. But, he wrote, the age into which he had been born, buffeted by the winds of doubt, could not let this happiness last, but planted intelligent and tenacious objections to revealed religion.

Desperately, he held on to the certitudes of his youth: "The majesty, the antiquity, the authority of the faith I had been taught, all my memories, all my imagination, all my soul had risen up and rebelled against that invasion of an unbelief that wounded them deeply."[7] In vain: his heart, Jouffroy comments a little pathetically, could not stand up to his reason. The authority of Christianity once shaken, his newfound skepticism sent tremors through his mind. Significantly, this "melancholy revolution" had not taken place in the "daylight of his consciousness"; it was "an involuntary labor of which I was not an accomplice."[8] For some time after he had ceased to be a Christian, blindly resistant, he would not admit his changed state of mind even to himself.

But endowed with a sincere and meditative disposition—a self-appraisal the record bears out—and living in the "studious and solitary" atmosphere of the Ecole normale, he could not sustain this false position for long. During a terrifying night of self-analysis, he dredged his unconscious to bring his conflict to the surface. "I shall never forget the December evening when the veil keeping my unbelief from myself was torn. I can still hear my steps in that cramped and bare room where, long after bedtime, I used to walk back and forth; I can still see that moon, half veiled by clouds, at intervals lighting up the cold floor. The hours of night slipped away without my noticing it; I anxiously followed my thought, which descended layer by layer to the bottom of my consciousness; dissipating one after the other all the illusions which had until then obscured my vision, it increasingly clarified, from moment to moment, all twists and turns."

He felt like a shipwrecked sailor clinging to his ruined vessel. "Terrified by the unknown void in which I was about to float, I threw myself for the last time toward my childhood, my family, my country, everything that was dear and sacred to me: the inflexible current of my thought was stronger; it obliged me to leave everything: parents, family, recollections, beliefs. The examination proceeded all the more obstinately and severely to the degree that it approached the conclusion, and it stopped only after it had been reached. I knew then that at the bottom of myself there was nothing left standing." This was, Jouffroy concludes, a "horrible moment."[9]

His conquest of clarity did not lift Jouffroy's dismay. The frigid shower of victorious reason brought not refreshment but anguish. "When toward morning I threw myself on my bed, exhausted, I seemed to feel my first life, so smiling and so overflowing, extinguish itself, and another life opening behind me, somber and depopulated, in which I would henceforth live alone, alone with my fatal thought that had just exiled me and I was tempted to curse. The days that followed this discovery were the saddest of my life." He found his agitation literally indescribable. Although he took pride in his reasoning, he could not grow accustomed to agonizing doubt. Again and again, Jouffroy's inherited doctrines fought to regain lost territory, stirring up in the "cinders of its past beliefs sparks that seemed at intervals to relight its faith."[10] But once abandoned, Christianity could never recapture Jouffroy's allegiance.

Fortunately, he was happy to add, this loss did not extinguish his passion for philosophical issues, or throw him into the arms of a passive skepticism. Though an unbeliever, he detested unbelief, and this, he thought, gave his life its purpose. He would consecrate his whole existence to searching, by the light of unaided reason alone, for the solution to the questions his night of horror had left unanswered. In a penetrating characterization of himself and most others in his time, he described himself as "unable to tolerate the uncertainty concerning the enigma of human destiny."[11] Human weakness, he knew, requires belief. In 1825, as good as his word, he published a controversial analysis of a dead religion, "Come les dogmes finissent," in the organ of the rebellious French romantics, Le Globe. It was an obituary to Christianity, but not to faith itself. Skepticism, he argued once again, though a powerful solvent, cannot last. The cry for belief calls for an answer. Once a false faith has been set aside, a true faith must take its place. That alone can give peace.[12]

Everything in Jouffroy's harrowing self-examination rings true: the believer's agony, his obstinate unwillingness to give up what he had always taken for granted, his miserable surrender to the kind of rational argumentation to which he was professionally committed, his inability to live with the suspense of incertitude, and his eventual compromise with the urge to believe.[13] In an impressive display of fidelity to his own highest aspirations, Jouffroy the psychologist turned the instruments of his craft on himself to lay bare his heart.

He was engaged in a thoroughly romantic quest. The romantics, we recall, had attempted to resolve the predicament of unhappy unbelief in a variety of ways. While some had returned to traditional dogmas, more of them had carpentered together new, more "scientific" doctrines of their own. It was his joining this pursuit of certainty that made Jouffroy into a good romantic. And to judge by one of the most appealing among nineteenth-century autobiographies, Ernest Renan's *Souvenirs d'enfance et de jeunesse,* anguished bourgeois took the romantics' campaign to re-enchant their world into the second half of the century, decades after romanticism had been officially declared dead.

In that cunningly arranged feast of reminiscences, stories, maxims, and opinions published in 1883, when he was sixty, Renan professed allegiance to a "moral romanticism," a "romanticism of the soul and the imagination, the pure ideal." He had not read unorthodox romantic seekers after divine light for mere entertainment. In the seminary at Issy, where he was studying philosophy in preparation for the priesthood, he and his classmates devoured the writings of contemporary French doubters, mainly Cousin and Jouffroy. Naturally, his devout masters despised these heretics, but their very disapproval inspired the seminarians to read further. He was recalling the year 1842, the year of Jouffroy's death. "We were intoxicated with the beautiful pages of this despairing philosopher"—*ce désespéré de la philosophie.* Renan knew them by heart, and his memoirs show that he never quite got over his excited discipleship.

Appropriately enough, his years at three successive Catholic seminaries, first at Tréguier and then in Paris, occupy pride of place in Renan's *Souvenirs;* they are dominated by his loss of one faith and search for another, a search never quite concluded. "At bottom, I feel that my life is ever governed by a faith I no longer have."[14] His impressive career as a scholar bears him out: a master of Semitic languages, he published a vast history of early Christianity, beginning with a life of Jesus, and a little less vast history of the ancient Jews. Thus religion remained his principal preoccupation, at first as a postulant for the priesthood and later as France's most eminent orientalist. But he was not a timeserver: in 1862, appointed to the chair of Hebrew at the Collège de France, Renan dared to call Jesus, in his opening lecture, an "incomparable man," and was promptly dismissed from his professorship.

For all of Renan's spectacular intelligence, critical penetration, and scholarly virtuosity, his revolt against inherited beliefs and the clerical vocation for which his mother had destined him was a slow, agonizing affair.[15] It took years of inner turmoil before Renan was even remotely sure of himself, and, as his *Souvenirs* leave little doubt, serenity was never in his grasp. "For all my conscientious efforts in the opposite direction, I was predestined to be what I am, a romantic protesting against romanticism, a utopian preaching matter-of-fact politics, an idealist uselessly taking a good deal of pains to appear bourgeois, a tissue of contradictions." In short, "one of my halves must be busy with demolishing the other."[16]

While in his boyhood, Renan's destiny seemed almost self-evident, his clerical training, though on a high intellectual level, proved far from gratifying. Finally, at St. Sulpice, the last of the seminaries he attended, his burgeoning doubts grew into insurmountable rejection. The love of freedom came to him late, but it came. "I arrived at the point of emancipation that so many people reach without any mental effort only after having traversed all of German exegesis. I required six years of meditation and of frantic labor to see that my masters were not infallible."[17] And since he could not trust them to point the way to spiritual satisfaction, he had to find his own.

Sturdily facing down malicious rumors that his desertion had been driven by lust, he insisted that it had been philology alone that induced him to resign from the seminary.[18] He made his Hebrew into a chief weapon for the theological combat he was joining; it gave him access to the Old Testament in its original language. And, coupling his linguistic competence with the lessons he had absorbed from German critical scholarship, he became persuaded that the Bible was a far from unitary document. It was rife with contradictions and filled with legends. Isaiah could not have written the second half of the book named after him; Moses could not have written the Pentateuch.[19] Reluctantly, even grimly, he drew the consequences: a Roman Catholic at all consistent must concede that a single error in the sacred text would unmask it as a merely human document. But Renan, as desperate to believe as Jouffroy had been, did not seek transcendent reality in vain. "The greatest of simpletons," he wrote in one of his prefaces to the *Vie de Jésus,* "provided he practices the worship of the heart, is more enlightened about the reality of things than the materialist who believes he can explain everything by chance and the finite."[20] Having turned his back on one extreme, Catholic orthodoxy, Renan was unable to embrace the other orthodoxy, scientific naturalism.

In his quest for a faith purged of legends and superstitions, Renan belonged, as we have seen, to a small army of Victorian seekers. But his autobiographical style, at once grave and elegant, elegiacal and aphoristic, was all his own. Jouffroy had performed a single act of self-analysis in a single unsparing night; Renan performed a far more prolonged scrutiny during his later years.* Mod-

---

*He opens the preface to his *Souvenirs* with a charming metaphor, telling of an ancient popular Breton legend about the city of Is, which, untold centuries ago, had been swallowed up by the sea.

estly, he cautioned his readers that "everything one says of oneself is always poetry."* He warned that an autobiographer's vanity could operate subtly even in self-criticism.[21] But he did not really mean it. His experiences were true, for him, and he wanted to paint them as honestly as was within his power. In 1865, Renan visited Athens for the first time and climbed the Acropolis, only to be dazzled by a religious experience. He burst out into an extravagant prayer to the Greek miracle and to the "abyss," the only god, and for the first time in his life, he felt the need to return to his inner past, enjoying its presence like "a fresh, piercing breeze from far away."[22] Renan's encounter with the divine Greek abyss was an idiosyncratic interlude, a devout aesthetic moment. But his description of it, full of art no less than feeling, sheds a slant of light on the religious emotions of less articulate, more ordinary Victorians.

Among those nineteenth-century bourgeois tracing their road from Damascus, Edmund Gosse's *Father and Son* stands as the inescapable classic. From its publication in 1907, this history of a boy's struggle to free himself from his parents' fanaticism was hailed as a masterpiece—important, unique. What made it so important, though, was precisely that it was not unique, but mapped an itinerary that uncounted Victorians followed, and many put on paper, though not with Gosse's skill and penetration. This rare gem in the confessional literature provides a stunning contrast to the rest of Gosse's prolific output. In his long, eminently prosperous life—he died in 1928 at seventy-nine—Gosse took European literature from the early seventeenth to the late nineteenth century as his province. While few thought highly of his poetry, his essays and biographies secured him an appreciative public. And the world valued him, bestowing on him honorary degrees, prestigious titles, even a knighthood. And yet, although his writings on Scandinavian literature smoothed the reception of Ibsen and other northern moderns in Britain, upon his death Gosse's reputation drooped,

---

Yet, on stormy days, fishermen report, they glimpse the steeples of its churches, and on calm days, they hear the sound of its bells rising from the deep. "It often seems to me that I have a city of Is at the bottom of my heart which still sounds its obstinate bells to summon to divine services the faithful who no longer hear." Now that old age was pressing upon him, restful summers gave him the pleasure of gathering up those remote sounds. He was not writing a formal account of his life but recording the images that floated into his mind. *Souvenirs d'enfance et de jeunesse* (1883; introd. Henriette Psichari, 1973), 39.

*Ibid. It is true that Renan's autobiography displays the marks of re-vision. He changed some names and offered misleading accounts of the time when he first put down some of his memories, rather exaggerating the spontaneity of his responses. Moreover, he virtually omitted any references to his older sister, Henriette, who had been a second mother to him, but not from discretion: upon her death, in 1861, he had already devoted a touching memoir to her.

never to recover. He seemed too bland, too charming, too prissy—in a word, too Victorian—to suit the palate of a more astringent age. Only his autobiography remains, a solitary monument, the half-intended triumph of emotional candor over modest propriety.

Father and Son holds surprises, shaped as it was by unconscious pressures that the observant Gosse could not quite exorcise. Not that he did not try. Conscientiously advertising the autobiography as "the record of a struggle between two temperaments, two consciences and almost two epochs," he insisted that his narrative was "scrupulously true," designed to be a "document" recording educational and religious conditions that had disappeared, and as "a study of the development of moral and intellectual ideas during the progress of infancy."[23] One is forcibly reminded of John Stuart Mill's announced program for his autobiography, with its impersonal undertaking to illuminate current debates on education.

But these distancing devices do little to conceal the inner drama of Father and Son. And his announced choice of protagonists requires amendment. Philip Henry Gosse dominated his son's autobiography. But we soon learn that Gosse's father was on important issues a mere spokesman for his wife, Emily. "Until the hour of her death, she exercised, without suspecting it, a magnetic power over the will and nature of my Father. Both were strong, but my Mother was unquestionably the stronger of the two." Gosse ingenuously adds, "While it was with my Father that the long struggle which I have to narrate took place, behind my Father stood the ethereal memory of my Mother's will, guiding him, pressing him, holding him to the unswerving purpose which she had formed and defined."[24] Emily Gosse's influence over her husband, far from ceasing with her death, only mounted. The great duel that is the burden of this autobiography was really a triangle, but Gosse largely repressed his mother in its pages.[25]

The most spectacular force acting on the Gosse household was a piety that reached into every cranny of their lives. Edmund Gosse's parents had reasoned themselves into the extreme fundamentalism of the Calvinist Plymouth Brethren, his father leaving Methodism and his mother Anglicanism for sterner doctrines. The Brethren believed that their sect alone was saved; that every word of the Bible is true; that no clerical authority may intrude upon the search for guidance from the sacred book; that every decision grave or trivial, whether involving a child's education or the purchase of furniture, should be taken in the light that God has shed so graciously in his divinely inspired text. Having stripped themselves bare of Christian rituals, the Brethren celebrated only communion and admitted as full members only the converted.

When Edmund Gosse, dedicated from birth to the Lord, was about to turn ten, his father proposed him for membership in this select community. The solemn catechizing and the public baptism that followed, complete with total immersion, are a high point in *Father and Son*. His initiation made the boy feel terribly important, superior to lesser beings. "If I am to be loyal to the truth, I must record that some of the other little boys presently complained," Gosse recalled, that "I put out my tongue at them in mockery, during the services," just "to remind them that I now broke bread as one of the Saints and that they did not." The adult Gosse, looking back at his family's faith, was right to describe it as "a curious mixture of humbleness and arrogance."[26]

It was an austere faith, and the Gosses an austere couple. They filled their domestic life with prayer and banished all frivolous entertainment. At night, they discussed theology and translated scientific papers. They made no room for fiction, that seductive spreader of lies; young Gosse was kept from all story books. It is telling that this prohibition was the work of his mother, not of his father. After exercising her lively imagination as a child, she had come to damn literature for encouraging vanity and wickedness. Hence she felt compelled to deny her talent for storytelling—Gosse speculated that his mother might have become an accomplished novelist. Her adamantly enforced policy was, he comments, sounding positively Freudian, "a very painful instance of the repression of an instinct." Whatever the truth of this conjecture, his situation was "almost unique among the children of cultivated parents."[27] The adult Gosse's insatiable appetite for literature looks like a belated, and defiant, revenge on his parents as he made up for early deprivations.

While he thought his life at home rather strange, Gosse scrupulously noted that his parents were anything but gloomy. They joked almost as often as they prayed, happy with one another and in their work. Philip Gosse was an eminent naturalist, author of widely appreciated works on zoology, correspondent of Charles Darwin and other scientific luminaries; Emily Gosse found a gratifying career in writing popular religious tracts and accosting strangers she met on her travels to convert them—sometimes successfully. Then, in 1857, when Edmund Gosse was seven, two traumatic experiences tore the web of family contentment to shreds: a death and a failure. Emily Gosse died of cancer after suffering excruciating pain inflicted by an incompetent physician, reiterating on her death bed her son's dedication to the Lord: "What a weight, intolerable as the burden of Atlas," Edmund Gosse exclaimed half a century later, "to lay on the shoulders of a little fragile child!"[28]

And as his wife's death destroyed Philip Gosse's happiness, though not his submissive faith, his *Omphalos: An Attempt to Untie the Geological Knot* destroyed his reputation as a man of science. The book records a pathetic search for ways of reconciling the irreconcilable, symptomatic of the unremitting pressure to preserve cherished convictions no matter how incredible. As a scientist who delighted in fieldwork, Philip Gosse recognized the existence of fossils, which called for an extended process of creation; as a fundamentalist Christian, he insisted that God had, precisely as the Old Testament reports, created the world in six days. He was not alone in attempting to read geology the Book of Genesis in hand. But while other devout nineteenth-century researchers tried to rescue the phenomena by taking the biblical account as a metaphor—some spoke of the six "ages" of creation—Gosse disdained all such weak compromises: God must have planted fossils within the tight schedule the Bible provided. He seriously expected that his ingenious solution would end the war between scientists and believers then raging. But instead of appreciation, Gosse's grand reconciliation earned only ridicule, and an embarrassed silence. "Atheists and Christians alike looked at it, and laughed, and threw it away."[29]

At seven, Edmund Gosse was, of course, unprepared to grasp the meaning of his father's intellectual debacle. But the peculiar education he had been receiving in his isolated, endlessly verbal household had already planted seeds of skepticism in his young mind. Before he was six, he had developed "the consciousness of self, as a force and as a companion." And consciousness of self brought self-consciousness: he began to observe himself acting, talking, thinking. Significantly, that gift, at once glorious and dubious, came to him as he was beginning to make a distinction between his father and his God. To his dismay, he detected his father ignorant of a certain quite trivial fact. This "appalling discovery" gave him "a companion and a confidant"—himself—a sympathizer who had a secret from the world, even from his father, and thus endowed him with a sense of individuality.[30] This stirring moment stands as an event in the nineteenth-century search for self.

The rest of Father and Son traces the tortuous progress of Gosse's bid for inner freedom. He developed private superstitions before he was seven. A burgeoning casuist, he would baffle his parents with theological conundrums, and on one unforgettable day he practiced an elaborate act of idolatry by propping up a chair and praying to it—without the slightest sign of divine displeasure. He grew up among the saints, his father hovering over him, steadily worrying over his religious steadfastness. At ten, he was allowed to attend a day school, where he heard the name of Shakespeare for the first time, and then, after his father married again, to read Dickens. The distance between father and son widened after the boy went away to boarding school. He bought books with every penny he could save from his allowance, and indulged in a riot of writing poems and tragedies. The doctrines that had been drummed into him retained a certain authority over him until one day as he melodramatically, a little self-consciously, prayed for the appearance of the Lord, and the Lord did not come.

"From that moment forth my Father and I, though the fact was long success-fully concealed from him and even from myself, walked in opposite hemi-spheres of the soul, with 'the thick o' the world between us.' "[31]

Originally, Gosse had concluded his autobiography at this point. But at the urging of friends, he added an epilogue continuing his recital of the battle between father and son. Philip Gosse kept hectoring his son about the state of his soul even after Edmund had moved to London to take up a post as a humble cataloguer at the British Museum, putting him, in heartfelt, deeply wounding letters, through "the torment of a postal inquisition." These obsessive messages made Gosse weep with rage and desolation, and, at twenty-one, he had had enough. "No compromise, it is seen, was offered; no proposal of a truce would have been acceptable. It was a case of 'Everything or Nothing'; and thus desper-ately challenged, the young man's conscience threw off once for all the yoke of his 'dedication,' and, as respectfully as he could, without parade or remon-strance, he took a human being's privilege to fashion his inner life for him-self."[32]

Gosse's incomparable self-portrait is filled to bursting with tensions. It is not surprising that Gosse, usually so fluent, should find it difficult to write his autobiography and necessary to stylize his past. Some of his published memories contradict the evidence of his letters and the reminiscences of contemporaries. At points, *Father and Son* dramatized his experience as the son of Philip and Emily Gosse beyond the facts: he exaggerated his isolation as a boy and the abruptness of the break with his father.[33] His confessions abound with mov-ing—at times amusing—vignettes: his baptismal immersion, his helpless pres-ence at his mother's death bed. Yet *Father and Son* is also, quite naturally, considering its author's trade, a performance, a writer's book. It is saved from artificiality by the urgency Gosse brought to his theme. Yet his forthright search for the truth about his past did not protect him from reaching inconsistent verdicts. His father, Gosse assures the reader over and over, was generous and loving, a great man, a "unique and noble figure."[34] At the same time, he supplies copious evidence that Philip Gosse was a virtual sadist who made his son suffer keenly with his nagging inquisitor's efforts to shame him into reli-gious compliance.

In some measure, Gosse prepares his readers for such discrepancies. Human life, he tells them, is a complicated intermingling of discordant elements.* And

*He notes in the preface that, perhaps surprisingly, his history is going to be a mixture of solemnity and humor. "It is true that most funny books try to be funny throughout, while theology is scandalized if it awakens a single smile. But life is not constituted thus, and this book is nothing if it is not a genuine slice of life." *Father and Son: A Study of Two Temperaments* (1907; ed. Peter Abbs, 1983), 34.

people, we have good reason to know, *are* contradictory beings, Philip Gosse not least. But the incoherence of Edmund Gosse's judgments is rooted less in his father's conflict-ridden character than in his own. His autobiography is the product of an unresolved, probably unresolvable, not wholly conscious ambivalence. The epilogue of *Father and Son,* with its decisive declaration of independence, obscures the continued debate, at once tense and tender, conscious and unconscious. In the end, Edmund Gosse found it easier to lose his faith than to abandon his father.

This important subtext links *Father and Son* to untold numbers of other autobiographies in its time, including those altogether secular. And it helps to explain the popularity of the genre among nineteenth-century bourgeois readers. Theirs was a class that idealized the world of the family, waxed sentimental about its virtues, and worried over possible threats to its integrity. And theirs was, fittingly enough, the age in which Freud developed his theory of the Oedipus complex, that dramatic account of powerful mixed feelings linking and tearing apart parents and children, perhaps the most interesting discovery about the family and its strains that the century produced. And, in one way or another, this formidable and ubiquitous triangle was what autobiographers famous or obscure were writing about. When all is said, autobiographers are always sons—and daughters—longing to discover who they were and how they have come to be who they are. This pivotal theme provides much of the energy inherent in their reminiscences and, as we shall see, their most intractable problems with credibility.

4. Second Thoughts

It has become a platitude that an autobiography is necessarily the product of a double consciousness. An aged, or at least aging, autobiographer recalling the past confronts a younger self, and both, normally yoked into an uneasy truce, leave their mark on the printed reminiscence. Rousseau had already noted this duality. "In delivering myself over both to the memory of the impression received and to the present feeling," he wrote in an unpublished fragment of the *Confessions,* "I shall paint doubly the state of my soul, that is at the moment when the event happened to me and the moment when I describe it." This did not trouble him, nor did it much trouble his nineteenth-century successors.[1]

There were times, to be sure, when the pathos of the present broke through to bring the reader face to face with the author naked before the world at the moment of writing. The autobiography of the prolific and once very popular Scottish novelist and journalist Margaret Oliphant, published two years after her death in 1897, is awash with regret at having to write too much for money, and with mourning for her dead children. "And now," the book ends, "here I am all alone. I cannot write any more."[2] But these were rare interludes of direct communication. Most of the time, the autobiographer, even when caught at the writing desk, is too busy glancing backward to address the audience bluntly.

As the Victorians discovered, style could rescue much, but for many autobi-ographers in their day hindsight proved an uncertain dividend. The pressure of events intervening between the time remembered and the time of remem-brance threatened to color, more or less imperceptibly, the account of what actually happened long ago. Undetected second thoughts and shifting self-appraisals, the temptation of nostalgia and the impulse to make a case were likely sources of tendentious distortions, as autobiographers imposed current habits of mind on distant experiences. The greatest danger to dependability in autobiographical writings, Edmund Gosse noted in 1907, was that they may be "falsified by self-admiration and self-pity."[3]

In comparison, forgetfulness seemed far less of a hazard. "Houses, roads, avenues"—so runs the moving last phrase of Marcel Proust's *Du côté de chez Swann*—"are as fugitive, alas, as the years." No doubt, but nineteenth-century consumers of autobiography found that what was falsified in retrospect mat-tered more than what was lost. Many of the self-portraits then published offered striking instances of the present imposing itself on the past, self-serving fantasies on harsh realities. Friedrich Hebbel, that eminent German playwright, novelist, and essayist, revisited his youth in several autobiographical works, which, with their forced cheeriness, blatantly disregarded the somber testimony of his letters and diaries. In his self-portraits, he transfigured the "long winter" and the "misery" of his youth that "turned my soul to stone" into his parents' "friendly," roomy, and sunny house with a pretty garden attached. He im-proved out of all recognition his sense of himself as a "proletarian" with fanciful tales of life as a "little aristocrat" among the "lower orders." He covered over the recognition that his brutal and depressed father "actually hated" him and substituted a benign sketch of the elder Hebbel's "serious nature," a man who liked his household silent but loved to sing chorales and have his children fall in with him.[4]

Even more misleading than this defensive idealization was Hebbel's capitula-tion to a familiar autobiographer's snare: he was not reading his life so much as his fervently idolized Goethe's *Dichtung und Wahrheit*. "Whoever portrays his life," he wrote in his diary, "should, like Goethe, stress only the lovely, the beautiful, the soothing, and the conciliatory that can be discovered even in the darkest circumstances, and drop the rest."[5] Goethe was, we know, a convinced and skillful harmonizer who in his autobiography smoothed down the harsher edges of his early years, but never so assiduously, never so damaging to the emotional truth of his life, as his worshipful follower.

An autobiographer more famous than Hebbel, François René, vicomte de Chateaubriand, was quite as active in allowing his second thoughts to dominate his memories. Late in 1848, as the first installments of Chateaubriand's autobiography were being serialized shortly after the author's death, George Sand complained to her friend the novelist Hortense Allart, "I am reading the *Mémoires d'outre-tombe* and am losing patience with so many grand poses and draperies."[6] She would correct her own past in her *Histoire de ma vie* a few years later, but not in so self-centered a way as Chateaubriand. In 1850, Sainte-Beuve gave good reasons for Sand's scathing appraisal in one of his famous *causeries du lundi*. By then, enough of Chateaubriand's memoirs had appeared to invite a more conclusive verdict. They were, it turned out, a mélange of half-century-old materials, studious revisions, and recently added final reflections. In 1833, then sixty-five, Chateaubriand had explicitly noted in a "testamentary preface" that he had taken a serious stab at writing his life as early as 1811; apparently he had started thinking about it some eight years before that.[7] Subsequently, whenever the melodramatic upheavals in French political life gave him unwanted leave from public service and whenever he felt inspired to contemplate his past, he added to the initial texts—in 1817, in 1822, in 1826, more than once in the 1830s. Then, in the mid-1840s, he went over his vast manuscript once again. The result, Sainte-Beuve said bluntly, was "an immense disappointment."[8] There was simply too little past in it.

In Sainte-Beuve's exigent and sensitive assessment, the freshness and truthfulness of Chateaubriand's literary genius had manifested themselves most purely in his youthful writings, in *Atala* or in *René*. The latter struck Sainte-Beuve as Chateaubriand's only perfect work. Now, though the man who had written the *Mémoires d'outre-tombe* resembled that young romantic, there was "this difference, that in the interval more than one official personage has formed itself in him, as it were has been added to his nature." It was "in that inextricable combat between the natural man and these solemn personages, in this conflict between the two or three complicated natures in him," that one must seek the uneven quality and the disagreeable effect of this "motley work."[9]

It was, Sainte-Beuve thought, largely Chateaubriand's unreliable way with his splendid youthful productions that made for this unpalatable impression. The first part of the *Mémoires,* depicting the years of childhood and adolescence, showed "much the lightest touch and the purest, and I venture to say that it would appear even more so if he had not many times overloaded it as he grew older." From the mid-1830s on, Chateaubriand's style had visibly deteriorated; Sainte-Beuve conjectured that "certain pages bearing the date of 1822 received a coat of varnish in 1837." What ruined this autobiography, then, beyond Chateaubriand's mean-spiritedness, vindictiveness, and immense egotism, or his convenient amnesia about literary debts, was his tinkering with the truth of his life. After all, it was no secret that Chateaubriand had been, in Stendhal's words, "the king of *egotists.*" What mattered most was that "he has more or less substituted the sentiments he gave himself in the moment of writing for those he actually had at the moment he is recounting." He was speaking, Sainte-Beuve observed severely, "not in accord with what he had once seen and felt, but in accord with his feelings at the moment of editing."[10] Re-vision had spoiled vision.

The psychological devils guiding Chateaubriand's pen as he denigrated his enemies, forgot his masters, and "corrected" his past are not easy to sort out. But it seems plausible that the vanity Sainte-Beuve and others detected in this autobiographer, the need to have been right always, superior to others without exception, and possessed of the correct sentiments on all occasions, fed on a lifelong, unappeasable anxiety that he was in fact inferior and incapable of true feeling. The pose of superiority and of omniscience had become a necessity to him, and his distortions and outright lies were splendid clues to this unpalatable truth about Chateaubriand's character.

The double vision of Victorian autobiographies is so hard to interpret, and yet in the end so instructive, because they often reflected first thoughts driven underground. John Stuart Mill's *Autobiography* is probably the most telling exemplar of the genre. In any history of the heartfelt nineteenth-century quest for authentic self-portraiture, it must claim pride of place, with its lapses as much as with its triumphs. Mill was, of course, far from a representative member of his class: precocious, formidably intellectual, a cultural aristocrat, author of influential works on logic, political economy and social philosophy, feminist polemics, and, not to forget, a memorable self-scrutiny far beyond the reach of ordinary Victorians. But the historian of nineteenth-century bourgeois culture cannot afford to scant his *Autobiography,* published in 1873, shortly after his death. It was an inescapable classic of second thoughts in action.

It was also, with all of Mill's contempt for mediocrity, a bourgeois classic that celebrated and in great measure exemplified the ideals dominating middle-class culture: hard work, honorable dealings, moral seriousness, respect for careers open to talent. Still more characteristic for his time and class, Mill's *Autobiography* is an enlightening amalgam of reserve and frankness, enacting on the highest level the struggles of nineteenth-century bourgeois to preserve privacy while hesitantly yielding to the pressure for candor. Like Mill, most Victorians were confident that telling the truth and nothing but the truth did not require telling the whole truth. Thus lesser talents faced in their everyday lives and, if they ventured that far, in their written reminiscences, the ethical and literary conundrums that shaped his *Autobiography*.

Not surprisingly, the book is weighty with tight-lipped expository paragraphs and, even more significantly, with absences. Only Mill's letters, the testimony of friends, a tentative draft of the autobiography, and, perhaps most helpful, hints surviving in the published version turn his unacceptable, unconscious sentiments into more or less open secrets. As in other representatives of the genre, the opening of the *Autobiography* offers a taste of what is to come: "It seems proper that I should prefix to the following biographical sketch, some mention of the reasons which have made me think it desirable that I should leave behind me such a memorial of so uneventful a life as mine." The diction, formal, measured, and defensive, is telling: it virtually apologizes for pressing a quiet personal history on the public. Trollope writing the autobiography of "so insignificant a person as myself" a few years later must have gone to school to Mill.[11] The contrast with Rousseau's impulsive and boastful first page of the *Confessions* could not be more marked.

The list of reasons Mill adduces for recording his uneventful life is as neat as a proof in logic and almost as impersonal. But hardly convincing: he wants to leave a record of his "unusual and remarkable" upbringing in a time when education is being seriously studied, shed light on "an age of transition in opinions" by reflecting about his own experience, and acknowledge the debts that his "intellectual and moral development" owed to other persons, notably to his father, James Mill, and his wife, Helen.[12] One senses that there must have been more to Mill and to his motives than this. With himself as the uneasy target, these two personages add up to a tense triangle in Mill's mind. The aged Carlyle, a prophet now lonely and cranky from whom Mill had become estranged two decades before over Carlyle's inflammatory racism—a break Mill delicately passes over in the *Autobiography*—thought he had "never read a more uninteresting book," nor "a sillier." It was "a mournful psychical curiosity," the "Autobiography of a steam engine."[13] His dismissive epithets rank among Carlyle's most spectacular misjudgments. Mill's *Autobiography* pulsates with passions barely held in check.

Mill's reserve about his mother in a self-portrait in which his father looms as the protagonist is the most glaring instance of distorting self-control triumphing over clashing emotions. This, as one of its first reviewers perceptively complained as early as 1874, was a "singular omission."[14] In the published version, Mill drops a single hint about his mother: among the "disadvantages" under which his father, intent on pursuing his philosophical studies, had been forced to labor were the lack of a private income and "those which he brought upon himself by his marriage."[15] But in a draft for the *Autobiography* that did not survive his and his wife's editorial scrutiny, Mill poignantly laments that he had to make do without a "really warm hearted mother," who would have made his "father a totally different being" and "have made the children grow up loving & being loved." His mother was a drudge, kindly but ineffectual. "I thus grew up in the absence of love & in the presence of fear."[16] In the published version, Mill sacrificed this enlightening passage. Decorum won out over pain long felt and rage long suppressed. But that victory testifies, however subtly, to unfinished business.

It is notorious that Helen Taylor Mill wielded massive influence over her husband and that he extravagantly overestimated her intellectual prowess. The pages in the *Autobiography* in which he hails her as a prodigy are a pathetic illustration of judgment gone awry. Mill calls her "a person of the most eminent faculties, whose genius, as it grew and unfolded itself in thought, continually struck out truths far in advance of me," an idealization that amused Mill's detractors and embarrassed his admirers. Sir Leslie Stephen, not a harsh critic of Mill, thought it a "strained and exalted eulogy," an unconscious cover—since Helen Mill was only an echo of his own thoughts—for self-praise.[17] Perhaps, but, more than this, it reads like the mournful tribute of a man in search of a woman he could unconditionally adore as he could never adore his real mother.

The passage about his mother that Mill excised from his published autobiography is, if anything, still more instructive. It was intended as a crushing rebuke to a woman unequal to the task of catering to a brilliant, cold, in his philosophical way arrogant and cruel husband, and of caring for nine children, most of whom took their cue from their father's contempt for his wife. But deeper conflicts were at work: they reflect, guardedly, on his father. From the distance of decades, John Stuart Mill was undertaking a rescue mission by shifting at least part of the blame for his father's forbidding presence to the national character—and to his mother. "Personally I believe my father to have had much greater capacities of feeling than were ever developed in him. He resembled almost all Englishmen in being ashamed of the signs of feeling, & by the absence of demonstration, starving the feelings themselves. In an atmosphere of tenderness & affection he would have been tender & affectionate; but his ill assorted marriage & his asperities of temper disabled him from making such an atmosphere."[18] Had it been published, this apology would have made inordinate demands on the reader's ability to suspend disbelief: nothing seems more improbable than that James Mill, a martinet by inclination as much as on principle, would have become a tender father if his wife had possessed the intelligence of Mary Wollstonecraft or the wit of Jane Austen.

John Stuart Mill's filial charity, then, is a symptom rather than an explanation. James Mill, the pedagogue who inspired not love but fear, all too quick with censure and incapable of doling out praise, subjected his promising eldest son to a rigorous, exhausting intellectual training by imposing on him the most intractable readings under the strictest supervision. "I have no remembrance of the time when I began to learn Greek," Mill recalled.[19] He must have been three years old. By the time he was eight, he had started on Latin, read much of Plato, and begun to study arithmetic and tutor his younger siblings, two duties he hated. At twelve, he had read widely in Vergil and Horace, Sallust and Ovid and Cicero, to say nothing of Homer and Thucydides.

Despite this irrational rationalist routine, Mill apparently found that to criticize, let alone rebel against, his inhumanly exigent father was dangerous, even years after James Mill's death. The most frequently quoted pages in Mill's *Autobiography* document his anxiety, adding up to a devastating, though still oblique, confession of hostility toward his father. Denied children's books, the pleasures of poetry, and appreciation for his precocious scholarship, John Stuart Mill grew up starved for the warmth and playfulness he thought his mother had failed to awaken in his father. "For passionate emotions of all sorts," he judges, "and for everything which has been said or written in exaltation of them," James Mill "professed the greatest contempt. He regarded them as a form of madness." In this atmosphere, the young Mill became something of a "reasoning machine."[20]

At twenty, he paid the price: in the fall of 1826, he suffered a mental "crisis," a deepening spell of depression. Nothing, not a good night's sleep, not hard thinking, not even his favorite books, could shake it. The despair that overtook him was like the state "in which converts to Methodism usually are, when smitten by their first 'conviction of sin.'" Obscurely and intuitively, Mill thus linked his depression to feelings of guilt that made his life, and any imaginable achievement, appear worthless. "My father, to whom it would have been natural to me to have recourse in my practical difficulties, was the last person to whom, in such a case as this, I looked for help." Trained from boyhood to seek all solutions in philosophy, he found it especially humiliating that the utilitarian doctrines his father had imposed on him were powerless to alleviate his distress. He had studied for nothing.[21]

He kept working mechanically, finding no savor in any enterprise and, for months, no hope for relief. As the melancholy winter wore on, he contemplated suicide. But after half a year, rescue came from an unexpected quarter, another autobiography: the *Mémoires d'un père* of Jean François Marmontel, an eighteenth-century playwright and literary critic whose reminiscences enjoyed a certain vogue in Mill's time. The passage in Marmontel that roused Mill from a paralyzing sense of numbness "relates his father's death, the distressed position of the family, and the sudden inspiration by which he, then a mere boy, felt and made them feel that he would be everything to them—would supply the place of all that they had lost."[22] Marmontel's account depicting the suddenly matured son assuming the role of pater familias is far more melodramatic than Mill's temperate summary would suggest. Young Marmontel is away at school; hearing of his father's death, he rushes home, self-assured and dry-eyed—"I, who weep so easily"—to take command. He makes a little speech to his distraught mother and younger siblings, assuring them that they have a new father in him, ready to assume full responsibility: "You are no longer orphans." Exhausted by his performance, Marmontel then goes to bed—his father's bed—only to fall ill.[23]

Something in that episode moved Mill to tears—tears he welcomed. They signalized that he was "not a stock or a stone." From that moment, his burden of depression grew lighter, and, though he would suffer relapses, he was never again so miserable as he had been. He learned to soften the rigid contours of his father's philosophy, to accept the pleasures that listening to "delicious melodies" and reading poetry could give him.[24] Gradually Mill's "egotistical" and "in no way honourable distress" dissipated, and in the fall of 1828 he discovered Wordsworth, "an important event" in his life. This "medicine" completed the cure that the electrifying passage in Marmontel had begun. Wordsworth's poetry "expressed, not mere outward beauty, but states of feeling, and of thought coloured by feeling, under the excitement of beauty." Without turning into a romantic—Mill explicitly called his depression "very unromantic" and remained so after it had lifted—he was now cultivating his "inner life" as he never had before, and for which his father had not prepared him; that inner life which, he wrote to a friend in 1832, he now saw as "the chief part" of human existence.[25]

As some close readers have understood, Mill's crisis, to give it a name, was an oedipal revolt, long delayed but all the more explosive for that—he had found the burden of loving and hating his father heavier than he could bear. What gave his fortuitous, and fortunate, encounter with Marmontel's *Mémoires* its healing power was that it relieved his intolerable sense of isolation. Significantly, Mill saw the curative power of Wordsworth, "the poet of unpoetical natures," precisely in his common humanity; far from being the loftiest of poets, he had undergone, Mill was glad to report, "similar experience to mine."[26] Marmontel's masterful coping with his father's death licensed his ambivalence about the father to whom he owed everything, whom he openly admired, and, no doubt without knowing it, must have wanted to murder—if only in fantasy. His impressive later writings attest that Mill succeeded in integrating his rebellion into his thought: he complicated his father's utilitarian philosophy but never quite abandoned it. However radical the impact of his breakdown and its resolution, it never amounted to a conversion. Yet it was radical. And Mill rescued enough telling material into his published autobiography to permit the interpreter to gauge the depth of his guilt feelings and the poetic means of his deliverance.[27]

Mill's sober and superficially tranquil tone, then, was a defensive screen concealing persistent inner conflicts.* His almost comical devotion to his wife, which did not cease with her death, hints that for all his protestations, he never quite resolved the troubling legacy that his parents had imposed on him. More than a record of events in his past, his *Autobiography* was also an effort to exorcise it. In his hands, the self-probing enterprise became a form of self-analysis.

It was an incomplete self-portrait, not altogether satisfactory perhaps, but more indiscreet than Mill would have thought possible or desirable, more indiscreet than his fellow bourgeois would have welcomed had they given the book the attention it required. Ironically, most readers disliked Mill's *Autobiography* for precisely the opposite reason: its presumed coldness and distance. Carlyle's sour denunciation of the book as mere "logic-chopping" was only the extravagant expression of a widespread sentiment. "The *Autobiography*," thus Leslie Stephen summed up majority opinion at the end of the Victorian age, "though a very interesting, is to many readers far from an attractive, work; and its want of charm is, I think, significant of the weakness which is caricatured by the epithet 'reasoning machine.' " This is a curious verdict in view of Stephen's earlier, more sensitive appraisal: "Nothing could be clearer to readers of the autobiography," he wrote in his essay on the genre, than "that, so far from being a mere reasoning machine, Mill was a man of strong affections, and even feminine sensibility."[28] We may read this contradiction as a symptom of an uncertainty bedeviling the nineteenth-century bourgeoisie: a vacillation over just what constitutes appropriate self-revelation and authentic inwardness.

*That they involved mainly his father emerges from an obsessive preoccupation that Mill ingenuously discloses in the *Autobiography*. Even after he had begun to recover, he was, in his words, "seriously tormented" by ruminations he could not shake off, a symptom that Freud has recognized as springing from unacknowledged struggles between the ego and a harsh superego. Highly responsive to music, Mill worried over the "exhaustibility of musical combinations." Since he knew that the number of possible permutations of notes is limited, and since only a few of them are pleasing, he feared that the supply of new beautiful music must necessarily dry up. "There could not be room for a long succession of Mozarts and Webers to strike out, as these had done, entirely new and surpassingly rich veins of musical beauty." His recognition that at least this "anxiety" was not utterly selfish—that, in short, his concern for the well-being of his fellow mortals had not dried up—helped him to overcome this symptom. *Autobiography* (1873; ed. John J. Coss and Roger Howson, 1924), 102.

Mill's way of scanning his past from a later perspective and under his wife's alert eyes more or less unconsciously lowered the temperature and intensified the reticence of his self-portrayal. Other nineteenth-century autobiographers, though, deliberately exploited their double vision to improve rather than to mask their self-understanding. A rewarding representative of this school was Theodor Fontane, bringing to bear decades of practice as a reporter and novelist as he explored and re-explored the years of his childhood. He was dissecting his feelings not to distribute praise or blame but to find "clarity about a certain course of inner events." After all, he said firmly, "the *aesthetic* has its rights, too."[29] Born in 1819 in the provincial town of Neuruppin, less than forty miles from Berlin, in turn pharmacist, poet, journalist, war correspondent, travel writer, drama critic, and celebrant of his native Mark Brandenburg, he made himself the most interesting German novelist between Goethe and Thomas Mann. His incentive for looking back systematically, which he had long refused even to contemplate, was the frightening state of his health and his advanced age: he was seventy-two when, early in 1892, he undertook the opening volume of his life.

Meine Kinderjahre, a highly selective account, proved doubly therapeutic for Fontane. He had found writing *Effi Briest,* the novel that became his greatest critical triumph, unusually hard, and came down with some debilitating, intractable insomnia and a deep depression; his life was over, he told everyone, his creative spirit gone. Fontane's family feared for his sanity. His father had died at seventy-two, and he was obsessed with the fear that he, too, had now reached the end.[30] At this pathetic juncture, his physician proposed that he set aside his novel and start on an autobiography. The stratagem succeeded beyond expectations.[31] After rapidly completing the first draft around Christmas 1892, he thought that he had written himself back to health, only anxious—unnecessarily, it turned out—that the petty details he was recalling might alienate the public. But he was better and could return to the writing of *Effi Briest.*

Concentrating on his early life to relieve his depressive condition no doubt worked so well and so quickly because it permitted Fontane to settle his father's meaning for him once and for all. Louis Henri Fontane dominates Theodor Fontane's *Meine Kinderjahre* even more pervasively than James Mill dominates John Stuart Mill's *Autobiography.* But while casting up so intimate a balance sheet exacted a measure of self-disclosure, Fontane did not offer an unbuttoned self-portrait. Like other autobiographers from Goethe to Sand and beyond, he employed discreet disclaimers to shield him from perhaps excessive emotions. In its subtitle, he advertised the book to be an "autobiographical novel,"[32] and opened it with a drily factual account of his parents taking possession of a pharmacy. "On one of the last March days of 1819, a small chaise stopped in front of the Lion pharmacy in Neuruppin, and a young couple, with whose joint property the pharmacy had been bought shortly before, stepped down from the carriage and were received by the domestic personnel." They were his parents. The rest of the chapter is a brief account of Louis Henri and Emilie Fontane; the second chapter stays with them and with their Huguenot background. The boy Fontane appears only after this elaborate stage setting, and the aged Fontane protests that he has to offer only "the very little" he can still remember from that time.[33]

Fontane at work overlaying past events with current feelings is conspicuous everywhere. His generalizations about human nature, about happiness, about education mark *Meine Kinderjahre* as the fruit of ripe experience. And his authorial interventions leave no doubt that he is looking back from a very long distance. "It was only in my old days," he observes, speaking of his grandmother, "that her superiority became apparent to me." Remembering his father's refusal to buy medicine he badly needed for a persistent fever because the medication was a "luxury," he instantly draws the sting of his accusation by reporting "with cordial pleasure" and biblical diction that late in life, when his impecunious father had helped him "in a most cordial and touching way," without grand phrases. "And so it came to pass that he, who had failed a good deal in this and that, became in the end the founder of the modest happiness that this life has held for me."[34] Theodor Fontane is visibly looking back, commenting, judging, soothing.

The present has its own way of choosing what fragments from the past it wants to survive. Fontane reports that his father was the one to mete out corporal punishments either when he thought it justified or when his wife made him do it. "The former have left no great impression behind in my mind, but the latter, undertaken only on orders, pain me till this day." On a poignant festive day long ago that he never forgot, Fontane allowed his mother to poison his pleasure in Christmas; clumsily trying to amuse him, she presented him with a beautifully decorated leather whip. Was he wrong to get so upset by his mother's "well-meant but unsuitable" joke? "I do not think so. In any event, as I saw the matter sixty years ago, I still see it today."[35] A boy's grudge and an old man's verdict coincide.

Fontane's admiration for his fascinating father survived, was if anything strengthened by, his second thoughts. It inspired chapter 16 of *Meine Kinderjahre,* "Forty Years Later: An Intermezzo," the true climax of the autobiography. It recounts Fontane's last meeting with his father many years after the first volume of his autobiography ostensibly closes. Louis Henri Fontane was a kindly man, always prepared to entertain with historical anecdotes and stories from his life. He had enjoyed little formal education but, an avid reader of newspapers and periodicals, was a popular conversationalist who enjoyed the combat of verbal disputes. Fontane calls him *"ein Original"*—quite a character.[36]

Unfortunately, Louis Henri Fontane suffered the vices of his virtues; bored by mundane details, unbusinesslike, he could never turn himself into a successful pharmacist. And he gambled, passionately, self-destructively: "In the seven years from 1819 to 1826," his son reports, "he lost a small fortune." This addiction, piled on other eccentricities, soured his marriage: Emilie Fontane accused her husband of being too frivolous about his family obligations, too scatterbrained to prepare his children for practical life. A conventional and responsible bourgeoise intent on propriety and prosperity, she grew alienated from her husband's ways, and as young Fontane watched, his parents' life together grew into an increasingly embittered duel, particularly on his mother's part. After years of earnest and reproachful conversations, mainly about husbandly failings, the Fontanes separated. Reflecting on these traumatic years, though trying to be scrupulously fair to his mother, Fontane at seventy-two essentially took his father's side, as he had done at seventeen. He thought of him "in gratitude and love" as a good man, an inspired, if informal pedagogue.[37]

These sentiments mark the intermezzo injected into *Meine Kinderjahre*. He wrote it, Fontane tells his readers, to "complete the character sketch of my father as much as possible," to "round it off *upwards. For as he was at the end, that is how he really was*." During Theodor Fontane's childhood, his father had "stood in the midst of life and of errors." But in old age, these errors had dropped away from him. The more reduced his father's circumstances, the more generous and the more unassuming he became, unwilling to accuse anyone except himself. "He spent his last days *comme philosophe*."[38]

He spent them in a small village settlement, tolerating the company of an assiduous housekeeper he characterized to his son, justly enough, as stupid and weepy—spent them, in short, more or less alone. Once a year, Theodor Fontane would break his father's unvarying routine with a visit. In 1867, he made the annual pilgrimage once more. After an affectionate if stereotyped greeting—Fontane, ever precise, notes "a kiss on one another's left cheek"[39]—father and son launch the sort of conversation that intimates carry on, even after long interruptions: fragmentary, desultory, disjointed, leaping from the trivial to the portentous and back again. A quarter of a century after, Fontane epitomized it all, not suppressing the tedious parts. The father (as the son gently reminds him) tends to repetitiveness, dishing out old saws and old anecdotes about his war experiences or his unfading admiration for Napoleon's marshal Ney. At times, in his ruminative way, he turns to more serious subjects, especially his gambling, which he explains away as the shadow side of youthful innocence and relief from the daily routine. His wife, he freely admits, however severe with him, had been right all along—about everything. It is all familiar stuff, but Theodor Fontane refuses to despise it.

He also finds his father troubled by a new preoccupation: death waiting in the wings. Tenderly he tries to divert him from that "grisly" topic, but Louis Henri Fontane returns to it, with variations: "Everything marches off. . . . Well, it can't last forever." The two men share a companionable meal served by the housekeeper and then take a walk through the father's little domain. And on that stroll the son, sensitive to his father's needs, quotes one of his father's favorite couplets from a Schiller ballad. "Immediately he fondly tapped me on the shoulder, because he sensed that I had recited the two lines only to please him." Then they return for coffee, and it is time to say farewell. In a moved voice, the father hopes the son will come again. " 'I'll come again, quite soon.' He doffed his green cap and waved. And I did come again, soon. It was in the first days of October, and up on the mountain ridge," where the two had joked about Schiller, "he now rests from the joys and the troubles of life."[40] And then, as abruptly as he had left it, Fontane returns to an account of his childhood.

After two more short chapters, the book ends without fanfare, like a Mozart violin concerto, as the twelve-year-old leaves home to enter a *Gymnasium*. He brought to his school, Fontane tells us in the concluding paragraph, a strange medley of piecemeal knowledge—the conventional ability to read, write, and do arithmetic, and the historical anecdotes and the Schiller ballads his father had taught him. Fundamentally, he comments, he never would really get much beyond that. "True, a few gaps were plugged up, but everything remained accidental and unarranged, and the famous word 'patchwork' applied to me all my life and to an extreme degree."[41] Fontane ends as he began; a set of reminiscences about his childhood have served to introduce Fontane the man as much as Fontane the boy, with the artful artlessness of double consciousness in the service of an arduous voyage into the interior and the trophy of self-knowledge.

Nothing better exhibits the expressive possibilities open to the autobiographical impulse than the diversity of ways that nineteenth-century practitioners managed their double vision. The assertion of one's guileless transparency must always be suspect, but even that may claim a certain validity, as long as the author has somehow earned the reader's trust. Here is Mrs. Oliphant, aged fifty-seven, basking in the golden memory of love just before sixteen: "I recollect distinctly the first compliment, though not a compliment in the ordinary sense of the word, which gave me that bewildering happy sense of being able to touch somebody else's heart—which was half fun and infinitely amusing, yet something more. The speaker was a young Irishman, one of the young minis-

ters that came to our little church, at that time vacant. He had joined Frank"—
her older brother—"and me on a walk, and when we were passing and looking
at a very pretty cottage on the slope of the hill at Everton, embowered in
gardens and shrubberies, he suddenly looked at me and said, 'It would be
Elysium.' I laughed till I cried at this speech afterwards, though at the moment
demure and startled. But the little incident remains to me, as so many scenes in
my early life do, like a picture suffused with a soft, delightful light: the glow in
the young man's eyes; the lowered tone and little speech aside; the soft thrill of
meaning which was nothing and yet much. Perhaps if I were not a novelist
addicted to describing such scenes, I might not remember it after—how long?
Forty-one years. What a long time!"[42] It never seems to have occurred to Mrs.
Oliphant that her writer's trade might tempt her to invent or embroider unforgettable little incidents like this; to her mind, being a novelist only helped to
explain her sharp memory for such a scene. And the reader is likely to credit the
tale as a more or less literal transcription of a reality, long distant but still
reverberating.

But wariness must be the reader's rule, especially for a time in which, to
speak with Mrs. Oliphant, "the fashion for self-explanation" was powerful and
persistent.[43] An autobiography is a complex speech act, often a triumph over
anxiety, cajoling, apologizing, boasting, all in the name of narrating a dependable personal history. But, quite apart from other incentives for distortion, the
sheer passage of time often inflicted on the autobiographer a persona that hardened into a mask. If Goethe had decided to record his youth not at sixty but at
forty, he would probably have portrayed himself more heatedly, have written
without the armor of the cultural monument he was rapidly becoming.

The autobiographer's double vision, then, can be a trap for the credulous or
an opportunity for the observant. Chateaubriand revised and revised his *Mémoires,* erasing or prettifying episodes in his past for the sake of an idealized
self-portrait, to show himself more ethical, more generous, more grandiose
than his character and his life history warranted. His truth emerged from his
need for lies. Fontane, for his part, enlisted his vantage point, candidly displayed, to settle some unfinished business for himself. Other might have seen
his father differently, but what Fontane found, and conveyed to his audience,
was *his* truth. And that is what mattered most in autobiographies in an age that
hunted down the inner life all the way into its secret lair, matters far more than
the precise, verifiable recording of events in neat and perspicuous sequence. In
his essay on the subject, Sir Leslie Stephen spoke for his time when he announced confidently, "Nobody ever wrote a dull autobiography." He was
right, for the truth of autobiography, though not always obvious, was always
present, for all its discreet or insincere rhetoric—a self speaking to other selves.

⋟ THREE ⋞

Usable Pasts

The Victorians' sense of themselves was enriched and, with the passing decades, complicated by their sense of the past as they consumed biographies and histories in unprecedented numbers. Seldom a purely disinterested pursuit, their reading often amounted to the search for a usable past. But it will emerge that educated bourgeois learned to seek out studies that were better than mere aids to wish fulfillment. No doubt, they indulged in a good deal of idealization, whether crude or polished, and put pressure on biographers and historians to respond to powerful religious or political agendas. But what makes the impact of nineteenth-century biographies and histories on the inner life of the middle classes interesting is that authors and readers alike faced conflicting crosscurrents and dealt with them in sometimes unpredictable ways. The clashing claims of pride and truth were fought out in the marketplace of ideas—or, more mundanely put, the marketplace of publishing. It is striking that there was never unanimity about the definition of what was usable in the past.

That the age felt proud of its grip on the past makes biographies and histories particularly weighty witnesses to the bourgeois self-image. The educated knew, of course, that both genres had existed since the ancients. Many of them were still reading Thucydides and Plutarch, at times in the original. But they were disposed to carp at their precursors for having inadequately appreciated the distance that divides bygone days from their own time, for having skimped the vital differences that alone made earlier ages the subject of truly historical un-

derstanding. Professional practitioners, with the great Leopold von Ranke in
the lead, even found fault with the celebrated historians of the Enlightenment—Hume, Voltaire, Robertson, Gibbon—for seeing, and judging, distant
ages from their limited, self-satisfied perspective. Rather than practicing what
one might call retrospective sociology, Victorian biographers and historians
proposed to grasp the past in all its pastness. That they scarcely lived up to their
program does not reduce its relevance to the Victorians' self-understanding. On
the contrary, the very gap between profession and performance supplies clues
to their complicated inner experience.

Few biographers and historians openly succumbed to the demand that they
peddle superstition or self-serving partisanship.* Certainly the title "discipline" they liked to apply to their crafts suggestively hints at a commitment
to self-control, that prized nineteenth-century bourgeois trait. The disciplined reading of the record summoned up grand vistas of professional
probity, implied an unflagging ruthlessness in the cause of accuracy, in short,
of science. The ideal that these craftsmen professed invited them to sacrifice
quick satisfactions and cheap popularity in the service of that purer joy, the
well-grounded conviction that one had got the past right. Rather than joining conspiracies of silence or deception, they would correct, after collecting,
what their culture remembered, and ferret out what that culture had felt
compelled to repress. The sober restoration of distorted or unknown truths
about the past proved a most difficult assignment. But, more and more anticipating the stance of the cultural psychoanalyst digging into times gone by,
biographers and historians hoped they could bring to public consciousness
unwelcome news as much as grounds for self-satisfaction, the sins of the fathers together with their virtues. It speaks to deep divisions within the middle classes, and at the same time to the sturdy self-confidence of many among
them, that in the midst of calls for propaganda there developed a public ready
to tolerate, even welcome, biographies and histories that refused to cover the
blemishes on the face of the past.

---

*Interestingly enough, Freud thought biography a virtually impossible profession. In his
biographical-psychoanalytic study of Leonardo, he argued that biographers, "fixated" on
their subjects, are bound to idealize them. *Eine Kindheitserinnerung des Leonardo da Vinci*
(1910), in *Gesammelte Werke,* ed. Anna Freud et al., 18 vols. (1940–68), VIII, 202; *Leonardo da
Vinci and a Memory of his Childhood,* in *Standard Edition of the Complete Psychological Works,* tr.
and ed. James Strachey et al., 24 vols. (1953–74), XI, 130. When later his admirer Arnold
Zweig wanted to write his biography, Freud warned him off not on personal but on general
grounds.

1. The Biographic Appetite

Nineteenth-century readers were sensitive to living in a time of lives examined and lives told. At its beginning, Coleridge called it "emphatically the age of personality"; at its end, the English editor and essayist Charles Whibley, himself a biographer, denounced "the modern madness for biography." The collections of Samuel Johnson and Giorgio Vasari all the way back to Plutarch attest that biographies—of statesmen, painters, poets—antedate the nineteenth century. But in that century the pace quickened until, by the 1870s and 1880s, what Carlyle called the "Biographic appetite" became virtually insatiable.[1]

This is only mild hyperbole. The principal consumers of the burgeoning biographical literature, which profited, like other forms of reading, from the dramatic diffusion of leisure, remained a minority: the educated and the would-be educated. From the late 1840s on, Routledge in England and Hachette in France launched railway libraries that catered to travelers in need of quiet entertainment, but only a few of their offerings were Lives and Letters. Similarly, the free public libraries and circulating libraries springing up during these years recorded that the favorite fare remained religious tracts, tales of crime and adventure, travel guides, and, more and more, fiction cheap or—rarely—elevated. But biography kept pace. "Though for the last half-century pure fiction has been in the ascendant," R. C. Christie, a well-informed observer, wrote in 1884, "the popularity of biography, if not relatively yet absolutely, seems to be continually increasing."[2] He was testifying to the tastes of the upper and middling middle classes; when he wrote, the biographic appetite had been naturalized among the higher reaches of the Victorian bourgeois experience.

It grew at an uneven rate. Germans were slow to discard traditional panegyrics and continued to pour out eulogies to crowned heads and military commanders; surprisingly, the first substantial life of Goethe was not published until 1855, twenty-three years after his death, and its author was an Englishman, G. H. Lewes. But after mid-century the Germans, too, began to provide recruits for the new army of biographers. Like Frenchmen or Americans, they enlarged the catalog of worthies to be commemorated, and included good bourgeois—businessmen, engineers, even philosophers—and a few remarkable bohemians, notably artists and composers, among heroes deserving a Life and Letters of their own. In 1877, a German book club calling itself General Society for German Literature, added to its miscellaneous titles—poems, reminiscences, essays, and popular philosophy—a life of Alfred de Musset by Paul Lindau, editor, playwright, and literary journalist. It was, Lindau claimed, Musset's first authentic biography.

The invention of series was only a matter of time. In 1877, John Morley, a prolific biographer of English statesmen and French philosophes—Burke, Diderot, Voltaire, Rousseau, among others—inaugurated the English Men of Letters, with Macmillan, a prestigious publisher whom the general public could be expected to trust. His plan was to publish lives terse, well written, and as accurate as human fallibility could make them, an agenda scrupulously observed by his stable of authors that included esteemed professional writers like Edmund Gosse, Leslie Stephen, J. A. Froude, T. H. Huxley, and Henry James. For Morley, as for others in his time, biography must be both art and science. It was also, he hoped, an informal kind of education, a "useful contribution to knowledge, criticism, and reflection" that would bring "all these three good things within reach of an extensive, busy, and preoccupied world"—in short, those already cultivated and those aspiring to cultivation.[3]

His recipe soon spawned imitators at home and abroad. Harpers imported the English Men of Letters series to the United States. And in the 1880s, Macmillan, trading on its evident popularity, again followed Morley's advice and started Twelve English Statesmen. Once more, Morley enlisted resounding names: himself for Lord Chatham, Lord Rosebery for the younger Pitt. Publishers understood the commercial benefits accruing to series that could boast distinguished authors: each title, as it were, would draw strength from the others.

This was the principle, borrowed from Morley, on which the editor John T. Morse, Jr., persuaded the Boston publisher Houghton Mifflin to launch American Statesmen.[4] At first, his was a cozy arrangement: one Harvard man persuading other Harvard men—Theodore Roosevelt, Charles Francis Adams, Henry Cabot Lodge—to write short biographies on the English pattern. But the authority Morse's series established among reviewers and the public led him to look further and to ask outsiders like that well-known German-born American biographer and politician Carl Schurz to contribute a volume. Houghton Mifflin did not regret the project, which by the end added up to thirty-nine biographies. One of its best-selling titles, Lodge's *Alexander Hamilton,* had reached its fifteenth printing in 1887, five years after publication. For their part, the French, their relish for brief biographies whetted by the brilliant literary studies of Sainte-Beuve, started collections like Les Grands Écrivains Français, which early in the twentieth century reached some forty titles. Some of these were translated into English, and the series went on to masterly profiles like Gustave Lanson's *Voltaire,* published in 1910 and still worth consulting.[5]

The popularity of these series is proof that reading biographies had become a major indoor sport for the educated middle class: publishers, no philanthropists, captured distinctive reading publics by launching collections that would appeal to specialized interests. Statesmen, poets, novelists, all had their innings. In the late 1880s, Methuen and Company entered the market with English Leaders of Religion, which, the publisher promised, would be "free from party bias," underscoring the perception that objectivity, especially when wrapped in a small package, was a quality to be advertised.

Even though the short biography was a response to bulky Life and Letters, the age did not turn its back on those spacious productions. Biographers like Rudolf Haym, a distinguished literary historian, secured marked, if highly focused, recognition in Germany with his substantial lives of Herder, Hegel, and Schopenhauer. Nor did the American public balk at the ten volumes John G. Nicolay and John Hay took to tell the life of Lincoln. In fact, forbidding-looking, expansive lives could make their way in the market place: Morley's three-volume Life of William Ewart Gladstone, first published in 1903, sold more than thirty thousand sets in the year of publication; once cheaper editions reached the market, its sales totaled 130,000 copies in just ten years.*

The Danish critic Georg Brandes's triumphs as a biographer leave the same impression. Established from the late 1870s as the most compelling commentator on culture in Europe, Brandes wrote voluminous lives of Disraeli, Ferdinand Lassalle, Shakespeare, and others, all of them translated into several languages and highly praised for their encyclopedic learning and psychological sensitivity.[6] His was the inquisitive mood to which late in the century Lord Bryce, diplomat and political scientist, catered with some twenty biographical sketches of English politicians, historians, and novelists written to "analyse the character and powers of each of the persons described."[7] It was by then an almost commonplace assignment. While the most derisive among twentieth-century critics would scorn the Victorians' professed search for inner truths as a sham or a pathetic failure, these biographers thought they were digging below mere surfaces.[8]

In that benign climate, enterprising publishers produced a virtual explosion of biographical dictionaries that systematized, and often significantly enlarged, the information available about great men—and some great women, and not

---

*Morley, Recollections, 2 vols. (1917), II, 93. The proliferation of cheap editions shows how widespread the reading public for biography became, especially in the second half of the century. Macmillan first published Morley's Voltaire in 1872, and in a slightly smaller and less expensive edition in 1885. By 1909, this more accessible version had been reprinted ten times.

royalty alone. Such dictionaries built on a living tradition going back to the late Renaissance and, to name but the greatest, to the *Dictionnaire historique et critique,* edited late in the seventeenth century by Pierre Bayle, notorious for its author's conspicuous erudition and sly propaganda in behalf of religious skepticism. Pride of place belongs to the brothers Michaud, who between 1811 and 1828, seconded by a "society of men of letters and of scholars," brought out the fifty-two-volume *Biographie universelle, ancienne et moderne,* advertised as an "entirely new work" summing up the lives "public and private" of "men who had gained notice by their writings, their actions, their talents, their virtues, or their crimes." Introducing the concluding volume, the editors congratulated themselves on their independence, and scornfully observed that even before their work had been completed, it had been translated, copied, and imitated in all the languages of Europe, but that these "thefts and plagiarisms" had done nothing to damage their preeminence—and, one infers, their sales.[9]

This self-congratulatory and bellicose tone was prophetic of battles to come: competitors disputed the Michauds' originality to tout their own compendia, or shamelessly pirated complete articles from the *Biographie universelle.* For decades, French publishers sued and countersued one another, suggesting that there was a good deal of money in such projects. Yet profits were not the only motive for launching them. The sober and meticulous biographical dictionaries compiled in Germany and in Britain, eschewing plagiarism and shoddy work and deploying patient scholarship, required government subsidies or a publisher willing to lose money in the service of patriotism and prestige.[10]

When, after earnest prodding from academics and journalists, the Germans and the British joined an already crowded field of biographical dictionaries, they raised their tone, researched their entries, and controlled their biases. The Germans took the lead: the Historical Commission of the Royal Academy of Sciences in Munich, "at the suggestion and with the support" of Maximilian II of Bavaria, published the *Allgemeine deutsche Biographie.* The editors had planned for twenty volumes to be completed in a dozen years, but they needed a quarter century, from 1875 to 1900, and forty-five volumes. In the end, as they meticulously reported, they had secured 1,418 contributors and covered 23,273 lives. But they were not pedants: echoing the prevailing double appeal to *Wissenschaft* and literature, they expressed the hope that they had achieved a "high scientific value" and a certain "attractiveness of presentation."[11]

They had, but the British outdid all their rivals, even the Germans. In 1849, they had launched *Who's Who,* that record of distinction and tribute to personal vanity, concentrating on select worthies and soon imitated abroad; then, in

1897, the editors radically expanded the numbers listed to some 5,500 personages and the length of individual entries. For more tenacious readers, between
1885 and 1900 Leslie Stephen, that prolific essayist, biographer, and intellectual
historian, with his assistant Sidney Lee, superintended a sixty-three-volume
Dictionary of National Biography, with the aid of 653 contributors, who together
covered 29,120 lives in around thirty thousand pages, a monument to erudition
promptly followed up in 1901 with its first supplement.[12] Like Morley, Stephen
insisted on accuracy, felicity, and terseness—and got it. The *DNB* was a sign
that late in the age, biographies had become both scholarly and accessible,
worthy companions to other rich materials—encyclopedic national histories,
collections of documents—making the past ever more present.

As we shall soon see, at least some of these biographies had also become less
unctuous, more offensive to the worshipful, whether in religion or in politics.
A few bold biographers were showing the way, determined to reverse a course
that had to their mind corrupted the writing of lives for almost a century. In the
impressive company of novelists and playwrights, they meant to supplant a
literature of mindless celebration with a literature of stringent criticism. Unre-
spectful dramatists like Henrik Ibsen or George Bernard Shaw and realistic
novelists like Emile Zola were peering into crevices of psychological aberrations and social malfeasance that their predecessors had prudently left unexplored. In 1894, a rash German historian, Ludwig Quidde, wittily if not very
subtly called attention to the resemblances of Emperor Wilhelm II to the
megalomaniacal emperor Caligula. He was ahead of his time, certainly for
Germany: the satire ruined his career. Then, around the turn of the century,
with their revelations of unpalatable truths about the lives of hitherto sacrosanct
figures, muckrakers like Ida Tarbell and Lincoln Steffens in the United States,
matched by debunkers elsewhere, were tarnishing the names of politicians,
industrialists, and financiers. These were portents of an age of disenchanted
biography in the wings. Across Western civilization, the unmasking of presumably untouchable lives was beginning to prosper; biography was gradually
becoming an assault weapon on the recent past, deeply appreciated by progressive bourgeois even though—or perhaps because—the bourgeois deadly virtues
were the principal target.

But no generalization about Victorian biography can encompass its diversity
or deny its reach for inwardness. Even in the decades of the most determined
reticence, the most serious biographers displayed craftsmanship, vitality, bursts
of candor escaping from a fog of discretion, even a willingness and at times
ability to penetrate beneath the masks over their subject's mind. Nineteenth-
century anxiety over violating the rules of propriety, and skittishness about
sordid details in famous people's lives, was far from uniform across the decades

or across countries.* The evidence must remain scrappy and anecdotal, but there seems to have been a peak of squeamishness, a virtual conspiracy of silence, by biographers no less than by novelists, sometime around mid-century.

The reasons for this nervous desire to purge anything smacking of the libertine remain obscure, but most likely the revolutionary age bursting in 1848 upon Europe—all but Britain, and even that country showed symptoms of panic—alerted the devout and the powerful to the dangers of unconventionality. This was the time, precisely in 1857, that Flaubert and Baudelaire were haled before the French courts, the first for obscenity in *Madame Bovary,* the second for obscenity and blasphemy in *Les Fleurs du mal.* In 1841, in the preface to the third edition of *Oliver Twist,* Dickens had explicitly called Nancy a prostitute; in the edition of 1867, he deleted that graphic characterization.[13] Indeed, anxiety over wounding the sensibilities of young women waxed and waned, sometimes quite inconsistently in the same person: in the mid-1860s, Dickens could lampoon the very principles of propriety he had obeyed all his writing life. Some two decades later, despite its continuing influence, public prudishness was beginning to recede.† In short, just as the heavily worked, lavishly decorated, at times bizarre domestic furnishings that shone at the Great Exhibition of 1851 are no dependable guide to all of Victorian taste, so, as biographies reveal, the excesses of mid-Victorian blushing discretion were an extreme limit for the age, not its dominant feature.

2. Heroes and Antiheroes

The appetite for lives that marked Victorian culture enmeshed biographers in some fundamental conflicts. To what degree should they gratify, to what extent deny, their readers' need to adulate? This debate, often internal, remained inconclusive: readers themselves often seemed unaware how urgently they craved pure models, and how few flaws their portrait of the hero could safely accommodate. Biographers in tune with the larger public met it more than halfway, but some wrote Lives and Letters more demanding than this, and they, too, would make readers for themselves in the bourgeois century.‡

*The French, as we have had occasion to note and will have again, struck others as exceptionally candid. But, as we know, even France had its limits.

†For that power, see the American purity crusader Anthony Comstock, who, starting in the early 1870s, successfully campaigned against "smut" sent through the mails.

‡To illustrate the complexities: in 1830, Macaulay reviewed Thomas Moore's life of Byron and, referring to the public's condemnation of Byron's marital conduct, famously commented, "We

Beyond cavil, the classic nineteenth-century apology for the hero was Thomas Carlyle's *On Heroes, Hero-Worship, and the Heroic in History,* a course of six lectures he delivered in May 1840 and published in the following year. As a controversial biographer and historian, Carlyle could speak with a certain authority, and his book was widely reviewed and intensely discussed. Much as he disliked lecturing, this series was his greatest triumph on the platform, largely because he stated his case with refreshing clarity and because his thesis met the needs of his audience. He put it tersely on the opening page: "Universal History, the history of what man has accomplished in this world, is at bottom the History of the Great Men who have worked here." Later in the same lecture, he said it again, if anything more emphatically: "The History of the World is but the Biography of great men."[1] The hero is the savior of his time: nothing could be more categorical a statement of the Great Man theory of history, for which his earlier writings had been preparations and his later writings an extended commentary.[2]

Carlyle's calendar of great men was unconventional and raised some pious eyebrows. Not merely did he attribute to human agency what a good Christian should recognize as God's doing, but he singled out for benevolent attention idolators like Mahomet and pagan deities in Scandinavian mythology, to say nothing of that blasphemous, drunken, and sensual poet Robert Burns. But what made Carlyle's lectures symptomatic for his time was less whom he chose to praise than why he thought it necessary to praise them. In the course of his lectures, he insisted that "Hero-worship exists forever, and everywhere," even though contemporaries infatuated with notions of liberty and equality detested it. But this was a desperate wish masquerading as an established fact. For Carlyle feared that his was not a time for greatness. "Hero-worship, the thing I call Hero-Worship, professes to have gone out, and finally ceased." The age "denies the existence of great men, denies the desirability of great men." Truly, Carlyle told Emerson, he was living in a "scandalous" generation. In 1852, his lament descended to pathos: no heroes are being born, no heroism is visible anywhere; while "the genius of the world lies in wait for heroisms, and by seduction or compulsion unweariedly does its utmost to pervert them or extinguish them."[3]

---

know no spectacle so ridiculous as the British public in one of its periodic fits of morality." Yet, in the same essay, Macaulay mildly criticized Moore for being a little too indiscreet: "We will not say that we have not occasionally remarked in these two large quartos an anecdote which should have been omitted, a letter which should have been suppressed, a name which should have been concealed by asterisks. . . ." "Moore's Life of Byron" (1830), Macaulay, *Literary and Historical Essays Contributed to the "Edinburgh Review"* (1934), 161, 157.

Many in his scandalous generation, and the one following it, accepted Carlyle's diagnosis without necessarily endorsing his prescription. His perception, in Britain and elsewhere, pervaded his culture: unlike the Middle Ages, this was an unheroic age—in short, a thoroughly bourgeois age. The lasting legacy of romanticism, particularly popular novels and poems, only strengthened this diagnosis: romantic writers had fostered fantasies of intrepid adventurers and thrilling lovers who made the mundane realities of the century appear singularly uninspiring, and the craving for heroes all the more vivid. Thus, while there was no precise correspondence between the loss of faith and the adoption of surrogate earthly divinities, it remains true that as the hold of old creeds loosened, new doctrines sprang up to occupy their place, and a modern version of old-fashioned hero worship was prominent among them. Nineteenth-century nostalgia for ancient legendary giants bestriding the earth; the adulation of military leaders, concert singers, or piano virtuosos; the susceptibility to those pseudo-heroes, the demagogues—all were symptoms of an inner void waiting to be filled with idealized images. In *On Heroes,* thinking of Shakespeare, Carlyle suggested the psychological dynamics at work in this worship, dynamics that inevitably invaded the writing of biographies: "King Shakespeare" will outlast whatever empires British arms and British administrators may conquer. Wherever in the world there are English men and women, they will say to one another, " 'Yes, this Shakespeare is ours; we produced him, we speak and think by him; we are of one blood and kind with him.' "[4] In their fantasies, bourgeois, if they could not exactly identify themselves with the hero, could at least claim to possess him.

One powerful motive at work in the middle-class idolatry of cultural icons was the uncomfortable feeling that one's pacific, safe, unadventurous class was hopelessly unheroic. To be sure, Victorian hero worshipers did not have it all their own way. Especially after mid-century, idealizing biographies had to contend with a disrespectful antiheroic ideology. Its most brilliant manifestations, early instances of what a later generation would call debunking, were Thackeray's *Vanity Fair,* the Novel without a Hero, Honoré Daumier's irreverent lithographs making savage fun of classical myths and modern pseudo-heroes, Offenbach's equally irreverent send-ups of antique heroes and heroines in *La Belle Hélène* and *Orphée aux enfers,* to say nothing of his triumphant ridicule of military grandeur in *La Grande Duchesse de Gérolstein.* An age that cried out for heroes also cried out, though admittedly less noisily, for critics; searchers for the re-enchantment of the world were jeered by some amusing and effective disenchanters. And some of that healthy negativism found its way into biographies.

These assaults on heroism were largely for the sophisticated. On a more primitive level, the accent was almost invariably on the positive—the more grandiose, the better. The most egregious, and for decades most prosperous, instance of this literature is the life of Washington by Mason Locke ("Parson") Weems, book salesman, lecturer, moralist, preacher, businessman, plagiarist, sensitive detector of public tastes. His biography of the first president of the United States, a cynical commercial venture launched as a pamphlet shortly after Washington's death in 1799, gave a public thirsting for greatness the Father of his Country, the Unselfish and Devout Patriot, the Man Who Could Not Tell a Lie. Thanks to Weems, the legend of little George Washington's axe and the cherry tree entered American folklore. Weems wanted to make money by flamboyantly fostering hero worship, and he succeeded. In 1808, he turned the sixth edition of his biography into a full-fledged book, and before he died, in 1825, more than a score of editions, repeatedly revised and enlarged, had found their market, reaching with their modest price farmers and laborers as well as middle-class readers.

The secret of Weems's success lay in his ability to link his audiences to his—and their—idol with unashamed didacticism. Whatever Washington had been others could be, if on a more modest scale; earnestly Weems enjoined youth to take the first president as its model and to emulate him by walking in the path of virtue—sobriety, generosity, piety, courage, love of country. Elsewhere I have called the Victorian age an age of advice, and biographies had their part to play in a vast literature of printed sermons, medical treatises, handbooks on conduct, rags-to-riches novels, counsels to the lonely, the young, the masturbator, the aspiring merchant. Indeed, biographies resembled both the novels and the exhortations, but, unlike the first, they claimed to be true and, unlike the second, they enforced their message not with sweeping precepts but with concrete instances. After all, however pathetic their ending might be, however bedeviled their protagonists by misfortune, envious ill-wishers, or tragic failures, biographies were at heart supreme success stories. Victorian lives were many things, but a sizable contingent among them were advice proffered through examples.

Doing their pedagogic duty, then, biographers joined the troop of counselors taking the measure of the anxieties spawned in a rapidly changing time to address and perhaps to allay them. They importuned, they bullied, they pleaded, and the biographers among them told inspiring stories dripping with moral significance. Some texts in this avalanche inculcated piety, some thrift, some sexual abstinence, some all of these at once. Varied though their menu, these guides to a better life were as one in this: they aimed to mold character. It was on character that French and British, German and American, Belgian and Italian preceptors fastened: character—which is to say, good character—encompassed all the attributes essential to the good life: hard work, self-denial,

temperance, a sense of duty. Indeed character, many of these professional improvers agreed, mattered more than intellect.* Best of all, character could be
learned.

But the road to good character was pockmarked with traps and land mines.
Moralistic biographers of exemplary lives liked to dwell on obstacles overcome,
perplexities resolved, temptations resisted or learned from. Their story would
likely rise to a climax of historic triumphs—a decisive victory, a brilliant symphony, a humane reform—but it left little doubt that but for his genius, his
flawless nature, or his exemplary piety, the great man would probably have
failed. For behind their programmatic cheerful talk, the teachers of characters,
biographers and others, barely concealed a profound pessimism about human
nature. The inborn passions are unruly and imperious. Greed, sensuality, rage
are exigent and inexhaustible inner forces that must be brought to heel. To
tame them is to defy natural desires; hence it is an unending, unpredictable
struggle.

Biographies, then, presented themselves as vivid reports of that struggle and
supplied lessons how best to conclude it victoriously. One could not expect
ordinary readers to reenact in their own lives the exploits of a statesman or an
explorer, but they should be inspired to reach high. "Many a writer has conceived a noble ideal, cherished throughout years of earnest and successful toil,
owing to a perusal of Trevelyan's 'Macaulay,' " we read in the preface to a 1896
school edition of Robert Southey's perennially popular *Life of Nelson,* first
published in 1813. "Many a successful scholar has caught his first impulse from
the pages of Franklin's 'Autobiography' or Boswell's 'Life of Johnson.' " Thus
as the young reader absorbs the career of Nelson, his example "should set his
heart on fire with a burning wish, not, perhaps, to fight and die if need be for his
country's glory, but at least to do what thing soever it may be his duty to do,
with such zeal, such enthusiasm, and such determination as to wrest success, no
matter how adverse the circumstances may be, silence jealousy, and compel
admiration."[5] What Southey's *Nelson* could teach was, as expected, how a great
man rose above misfortune. Easy success was not half so interesting.

This preface was written when the streak of anxious didacticism was narrow-
ing and worshipfulness was coming under suspicion, but until the end of the
Victorian age, hero worship, though on the defensive, retained much of its hold

---

*"Character," wrote Samuel Smiles, "is one of the greatest motive powers in the world." And,
"although genius always commands admiration, character most secures respect. The former is
more the product of brain-power, the latter of heart-power, and in the long run it is the heart that
rules in life." Smiles knew his audience: few could even dream of being geniuses. *Character* (1871;
ed. 1872), 13–14.

on the public's imagination. The great celebrated by their biographers seemed to breathe purer air than ordinary mortals. "Even in his appearance," an English biographer of Friedrich Schiller observes, "there was an aspect of greatness as he walked through the streets with his firm military step," and "no one could talk with him without perceiving the loftiness of his aims." Similarly, Lord Dover, in his two-volume life of Frederick the Great, found one episode particularly worthy of caustic comment. When the Prussian king was buried, "his sword, which had won so many battles, was placed on his coffin, where it remained, till Napoleon came as a conqueror to Potsdam: he carried it away." This the author found most objectionable. "One hero should not surely thus have violated so interesting a relic of another."[6] To Dover's mind, the great, often defined with circular reasoning as those who had a major biography devoted to them, lived by standards that plain mortals could only admire from afar—or imitate as best they could.

It was customary to proclaim the exceptional stature of heroes with the organ tones of the preface, generally sustained through the text. "To follow a genius on his victorious spiritual journey," thus Heinrich Düntzer opened his life of Schiller in 1881, "ranks among the most elevating of purely human pleasures. The favorite poet of the German people, even more radiantly transfigured by his early departure"—Schiller had died in 1805, at forty-six—"exercises a particular power of attraction because he was compelled to battle against depressing circumstances, which at times threatened to pull him off course, even into the abyss. But over and over his genius pulled him back onto his path." The "ignoble touch of low circumstances" clung to him only temporarily. "A man," Düntzer philosophized in the accepted mode, "develops through vital energy in the struggle with his destiny, by which he grows, even becomes himself. To show this in its progress is the high assignment of every depiction of a significant human being."[7] While Düntzer emphatically distanced himself from rhetorical tricks and uncritical praise, he could not help treating Schiller as a virtually celestial being. As he lay dying, "lovely pictures fluttered about the soul of the exhausted man." His wife was ever near, and "he smiled at her with heavenly love." And the lesson was, once again, triumph over adversity: "Through activity and persistence Schiller had soared from the most straitened circumstances to a significant position without compromising his honor, and earned the love and gratitude of the German people," which will ever increase, "the more highly we learn to honor ideal poetry and genuine human value."[8] The character of an exceptional individual could purify the character of a whole nation, if that nation only appreciated its giants enough.

German biographers were by no means alone in waxing this lyrical. In 1894, M. A. Bardoux concluded his uncritical one-volume life of the eminent French politician and historian François Guizot with a fervent peroration, lauding Guizot's charming simplicity, eloquent conversation, good heart, unshakable patriotism, and serene soul. "So let us say it good and loud: the future will do more justice to him than his contemporaries. He has greatly honored our country, and his name is inscribed on the first page of our Golden Book."[9] Adulation was an international symptom.

Throughout the age, biographies and books of advice had been close allies. In the work of one of its most widely read advisers, Samuel Smiles, they blended into one. His most influential sermon on the virtues of independence, *Self-Help,* published in 1859, sold some 20,000 copies in the first twelve months and 150,000 in thirty years; its sequels, *Character* of 1871, *Thrift* of 1875, and *Duty* of 1887, were only marginally less popular.[10] All of them were essentially collections of anecdotes about great men, at times mini-biographies, designed to illustrate Smiles's fundamental argument: the resources needed for success in life lie within. It was with admirable sayings and stories of lives that Smiles exemplified these resources: hard work, self-reliance, mastery of the passions, rational control over one's disposition of time and expenditure of money, qualities that critics of the bourgeoisie would deride as fatal virtues.

A publicist like Smiles,·who saw the making of character and of history in such individualistic terms, was destined to the trade of biographer, and made a historic contribution to the craft by opening the pantheon to men previously thought unworthy of being remembered with a formal Life. He wrote highly regarded and substantial biographical sketches of British engineers and, in 1857, *The Life of George Stephenson, Railway Engineer,* which celebrated the eminent railroad pioneer with a kind of homily by other means. The illiterate son of a northern farmer painfully educating himself, the inspired tinkerer whom the urge to invent did not leave in peace, the doughty fighter against a foolish and reactionary society, the possessor of all the virtues, Stephenson was the epitome of self-help become flesh. Assessing in his customary way the character of his subject in the concluding chapter, Smiles found Stephenson concentrated on his work, amply endowed with common sense, cordial and never condescending with the men who worked for him and who all loved him, a devoted husband and father, generous, thrifty, patient, simple, modest, unassuming, persevering, energetic, and manly.* Smiles's Stephenson is an improbable human being, but he wrote about him in possession of most of the fact. And he kept the book to a single volume.

*Later biographers of Stephenson have complained that the sentimental Smiles idealized his subject and, in order to create a spotless hero, unduly minimized the share of his son Robert in the railroad revolution. See esp. L. T. C. Rolt, *George and Robert Stephenson: The Railway Revolution* (1960). But Smiles first secured George Stephenson a place in British history.

It was an intelligent decision. After all, the most characteristic, and later the most criticized, trait of Victorian biographies was their sheer size. "Those two fat volumes, with which it is our custom to commemorate the dead—who does not know them," Lytton Strachey famously asked in *Eminent Victorians,* that aggressive farewell to Victorianism, "with their ill-digested masses of material, their slipshod style, their tone of tedious panegyric, their lamentable lack of selection, of detachment, of design?"[11] But the Victorians, especially in the late decades of the century, did not need Strachey to tell them that to the biographer economy could be an asset and literary distinction a duty. It is significant that Southey, a poet before he was a biographer, should have dedicated his *Nelson* to John Wilson Croker because, as secretary of the Admiralty, Croker could appreciate its "historical accuracy" and, as a man of letters, recognize its "literary merits." Many decades later, in 1890, introducing his *Life of Honoré de Balzac,* a "small book" for a "great subject," Frederick Wedmore asserted, "A literary task, as I conceive it, is generally ill executed if, when it is done, the labour of omission, though chiefly concealed, is not found to have been its heaviest part."[12] Many Victorian biographers were more devoted to inclusion than to omission, but there were enough book-buying bourgeois, consulting their taste and their purse, who favored biographies short rather than long.

Yet, for all the Niagara of brief lives, the biographies most expressive of the Victorian style were massive indeed, more massive even than Strachey had charged. Pierre Lanfrey's Napoleon, Reinhold Koser's Frederick the Great, Carl Justi's Winckelmann, J. A. Froude's Carlyle each ran to three and even four volumes. Gustave Desnoiresterres took eight solid volumes to recount the life of Voltaire. But these painstaking explorations had little in common aside from their length. Some were extended panegyrics, whether political tributes or emotional surrenders, others struggled for independence from a haunting historic presence; some were little more than boring parades of trivial events and unedited documents, others exercises in elegant composition and felicitous paraphrase; some used a life to write a virtual history of an epoch, others were almost claustrophobic with their scanty sketches of the social or political background. The motives authors attributed to their subjects varied as much as their motives for devoting years of their life to a single human being.

One source for their devotion, though, aside from love or hatred, animated all these formidable publications: a search for safety in numbers—of pages rather than of statistics. And here the needs of many biographers met, once again, the needs of readers eager to trust the Life they were reading. Both welcomed the intimidating bulk of the century's most prominent biographies as a defense, more or less conscious, against bias—or the charge of bias. The Victorians recognized that a pure positivistic amassing of facts free of all interpretation is an impossibility. Quantity in itself—the piling up of letters, diary entries, or diplomatic dispatches—cannot guarantee objectivity: adulation or detestation can be loquacious as well as laconic. But impressed by the triumphs of contemporary science, that great treasure house of facts discovered, ordered, and interpreted, biographers were disposed to mobilize as much material as they could ferret out, in the hope that it would more or less speak for itself, or at least provide persuasive evidence that their opinions were well grounded. Francis Bacon, whom they fondly hailed (and rather misread) as the father of the modern scientific method, was their guide. As the typical maker of biographies liked to provide solid swatches of his subject's own words, so did his consumers enjoy basking in them. Theirs was, after all, an age of autobiographies, of often garrulous self-revelations in letters and diaries.* Extensive quotations brought them closer to, virtually into the presence of, the great man—at times, the great woman.

As we have noted, there is abundant evidence that in the long century from Napoleon to the First World War, the yearning for heroes abated among enough readers to permit biographers the distance they found essential as they worked to delineate a person rather than a statue. As historical and, with that, biographical scholarship grew more exigent, biographers retraced in a less reverent spirit lives told before and lifted veils their predecessors had left untouched. They grew, in short, not only more scientific but also more intimate and more censorious.

Three accounts of Lord Nelson may illustrate this progress. Robert Southey's *Life of Nelson,* though hailed as a classic soon after its appearance in 1813, treated its subject as a monument little less lofty than the Nelson column a grateful posterity would erect in Trafalgar Square in 1843. Southey conceded that his hero had been amorously involved with another man's wife, Lady Hamilton—that "unhappy attachment"—while he was still married. But, while his "acquaintance" with Emma Hamilton "ended in the destruction of Nelson's domestic happiness," the lady appears in passing only three or four times, as though she had played only a minor role in the sublime drama of Nelson's life.[13] Not surprisingly, Southey could discover but a single "blot" on Nelson's public character, his conduct in the Kingdom of the Two Sicilies in 1799, where he was partly responsible for the execution of Neapolitan Jacobins after they had honorably surrendered. But on this matter Southey is very severe: "A deplorable transaction! A stain upon the memory of Nelson, and the honour of England: To palliate would be in vain; to justify it would be wicked; there is no

---

*For letters and diaries, see below, pp. 310–46.

alternative for one who will not make himself a participator in guilt, but to record the disgraceful story with sorrow and with shame."[14] In the struggle between idealization and indignation, for once indignation won out.

Passionately patriotic, imbued with missionary zeal, a brilliant sailor beloved by all his men, a nemesis to corruption, pious and humane to a fault, except to Frenchmen and mutineers: this Nelson offered rich materials for a psychological profile. But Southey did not stop to analyze. Instead, he guided readers into uncritical esteem with anecdotes no less flattering, though more plausible, than the legend that Parson Weems had lavished on George Washington: the scrawny, sickly child destined to grow into the audacious warrior, the depressed young sailor rescued from thoughts of suicide by a mystic vision promising him a splendid future in his king's service, the dying conqueror aboard the *Victory* at Trafalgar asking his flag captain Hardy to kiss him. In Southey, Nelson's pedantry becomes a rigid sense of duty, insubordination a wise sticking to appropriate tactics, need for applause a laudable ambition. This titan, it seems, was always right, even when appearances were against him. The few warts that Southey allowed to show on his portrait only humanized the savior of his country.

Nelson was a proven hero; his magnificent share in checking Napoleon's designs on England remain beyond dispute, even if he was, as he had to be, only human. And in 1897, an authoritative student of naval history, Alfred Thayer Mahan, gave more space to the human Nelson, including his internal economy, than Southey would have thought desirable or even possible. In addition to buttressing his favorite thesis about the sway of sea power over history, Mahan saw room for a biography that would illuminate Nelson's "inner life as well as his external actions." What particularly interested Mahan was, in the spirit of Carlyle, Nelson's "inner history," his "underlying native character."[15] Unlike less inquisitive biographers, Mahan tried to discover the private springs of his subject's public actions. And in offering to study his man's inner life, he could be sure of the reading public's interest.

Although Mahan's self-imposed assignment called for comment on Nelson's erotic history, even he acquitted himself with a decency that later, more outspoken readers might note with a superior smile. The impact of Nelson's appetites on Nelson's conduct, though, did not escape him. Far from wishing to entertain readers with salacious gossip, he was persuaded that a candid inspection of Nelson's grand affair with Lady Hamilton would offer valuable clues to Nelson's character and activities as a sailor-statesman. It is well known that the sexual domain was treacherous, usually forbidden ground for Victorian biographers, one that many dodged and more faced grudgingly, but that a few invaded to tell as much of the truth as could safely be printed.

The space at Mahan's disposal allowed him to essay an extended, highly unflattering account of Emma Hamilton and her shady past without absolving Nelson himself of responsibility for the affair. Her success as a manipulator of men was impressive; it included charming her infatuated elderly husband, Sir William Hamilton, Britain's ambassador to the Kingdom of the Two Sicilies, and, still more important, her devoted lover Nelson, a man as needy, as susceptible to flattery, as he was gullible. Her conquest mattered because Nelson's thralldom not just broke up his marriage to a loving, docile wife but also, in foolish and insubordinate disregard of British interests, compromised the policies he adopted at Naples in the late 1790s—including his brutality toward the Jacobins noted before. Nelson's bold seamanship and stunning naval victories, Mahan concluded, made him the greatest of sailors, a titan who could have no successor. But he was a "sharer of our mortal weakness," that rare butterfly caught in the biographer's net: a real human being.[16]

This was going far, but by 1911, when David Hannay wrote a substantial entry on Nelson for the eleventh edition of the *Encyclopaedia Britannica,* he could go further. Hannay's Nelson remains a great man, but deeply flawed. "He loved being loved. . . . He had an insatiable appetite for praise. . . . He allowed [Lady Hamilton] to waste his money, to lead him about 'like a bear,' and to drag him into gambling, which he naturally hated. For her sake he offended old friends, and quarrelled with his wife in circumstances of vulgar brutality. . . . The intoxication produced on him by flattery . . . could not be too copious or gross for his taste."[17] Lytton Strachey would have been no more savage than this, if more feline.

A biographer's critical stance coupled with a readiness to explore the movements of his subject's mind could not end debates. With all the grasping at straws of scientific procedure, Victorian biographies remained susceptible to ideological distortion, none more than those of men—Caesar, Cromwell, Louis XIV—who had made history. It was probably inescapable that the masters of nations and events were peculiarly apt to serve the purpose of later generations, although this did not prevent brave efforts at an evenhanded treatment. But when political passions mastered them, they would employ the diagnosis of character as an instrument of adulation or aggression. This was not a deliberate policy but a failure in self-scrutiny. Yet, contrary to what one might expect, readers often judged the biographies of such historic figures less on the deeds they recorded than on the character they analyzed.

Unfortunately, most nineteenth-century biographers had only a homemade commonsensical psychology at their disposal and displayed a certain helplessness faced with the mind at work, including their own. This manifested itself in the haste with which they typically disposed of their subject's early years.* The scores of lives written for series like "American Statesmen" or "Les Grands Ecrivains français," and, for that matter, their more expansive cousins, galloped through the great personage's childhood with a virtually audible sigh of relief. Crude or subtle, short or long, no Victorian biography lingered over the growth of the hero.

True, biographers had learned too much from the romantics to disdain the formative influence of early years on later accomplishments. Living in an age perennially preoccupied with character, they thought much about the making of good and the checking of bad habits. Sainte-Beuve insisted that the biographer captures his subject's inner essence only by paying close attention to his family background, especially to his mother. Carlyle was not alone in affirming that the history of a person's childhood is an *"in*articulate but highly important history."[18] But not very much followed from such perceptions. When the connection between childhood and adult life was most conspicuous, biographers would give it a paragraph or two. In his *Lives of the Engineers,* Samuel Smiles found room for a few stereotyped anecdotes about his heroes' precocious "mechanical bias" or "strong inclination for mechanical pursuits" that foreshadowed their later careers.[19] But, as vulnerable as his fellows, he could do little more than state the fact, almost nothing to illuminate it.

This relative psychological innocence underlies many sweeping biographical generalizations. A rare biographer like Reinhold Koser in his authoritative four-volume *Geschichte Friedrichs des Grossen* might even recount a dream, but he would not, could not, interpret it. He and his fellow biographers rested content with time-honored commonplaces about heredity, national character, parental influence, religious teachings, and innate genius. Some Victorian Lives, intelligent, sensitive, and worldly, were probing, yet for the most part the light they shed on emotional depths was a personal flash of insight. Still, the springs of action were increasingly on their agenda.

Nineteenth-century lives of Napoleon Bonaparte may serve in evidence. They worked like a political Rorschach test, giving biographers and their readers ample opportunities to vent their feelings about the man who had redrawn the map, both physical and mental, of Europe. The clash of opinions about the

---

*Most biographers agreed with Lord Rosebery: "The details of the childhood of great men are apt to be petty and cloying. Hero-worship, extended to the bib and porringer, is more likely to repel than to attract." If Rosebery made room for a few such details in his brief life of the younger Pitt, that astonishing little scholar and no less astonishing youthful prime minister, it was because "they form the key to his career, which without them would be inexplicable." *Pitt* (1891), 5.

emperor's motives erupted even before his death on St. Helena, in 1821, as writers took sides determined less by his actions than by their politics. They made many Napoleons; inflexible French monarchists, grateful German Jews, doctrinaire liberals, romantic novelists took from his complex and contradictory history what they needed and constructed a figure that had little in common with the one that others had made for themselves. He *had* aped the Bourbons' court, ordered the killing of opponents, taken measures that chilled independent expression, exported the tolerant ideals of the French Revolution, preached—and embodied—the program of careers open to talent, established an enduring administrative machinery, sent the flower of French youth to their death. Grappling with this record, biographers had part of the truth, none all of it.

From the first, the making of the Napoleonic legend and the resistance to it were the work of poets, eyewitnesses, and pamphleteers. Enthusiasts recalling the days of grandeur, and literary men bored by the emperor's Bourbon successors, fed the legend. So did Napoleon himself, notoriously: the *Mémorial de Sainte Hélène,* which did so much to shape his image for posterity, consists largely of self-justifying monologues that the marquis Las Cases dutifully took down.* All of France's accomplishments were Napoleon's doing, all its failures the fault of hasty subordinates or treacherous enemies. He was a man of peace forced to war by perfidious Albion and, at the same time, the greatest military commander since Alexander the Great. In reply, the denigrators of Napoleon could only call him a liar and a murderer, and seek to document their charges.

While in the late 1820s, British romantics—William Hazlitt, John Lockhart, Sir Walter Scott himself—had turned the writing of biographies of Napoleon into a flourishing trade, the French long relied on memoirs and general histories of the age. It was not until 1867 that a massive life appeared: the first volumes of Pierre Lanfrey's *Histoire de Napoléon.* Using an introductory formula that was becoming almost obligatory among biographers, Lanfrey noted that while in the past, Bonapartists had deified and their opponents demonized the emperor, he felt himself free "alike from the preconceptions of hatred and the superstition of enthusiasm."[20] Adducing the sheer substantiality of his work, its ample documentation, and his cool attitude, he stationed himself among the scientists of memory. It was too large a claim: Lanfrey's hostility to Napoleon, the Nephew, shaped his unsparing judgment of the Uncle. He was detective, prosecuting attorney, and hanging judge in one. There was much in Napoleon I

---

*It is well known, and symptomatic, that Stendhal, that unreconstructed (if in the end slightly chastened) admirer of Napoleon, has Julien Sorel, the romantic hero of *Le Rouge et le noir,* treat this *Mémorial* as his Bible.

that Lanfrey, the unforgiving liberal, could not acknowledge, could not see. Yet he did capture much of the man. And for this biographer it was Napoleon's character that damned him beyond redemption. In a century that, as we have seen, was ever harping on character, this was a confidence-inspiring posture to take.

In volume after volume, Lanfrey offers plausible reasons for his detestation of Napoleon's very nature. To his mind, it never changed; some of the man's most repulsive traits may have been intensified by the temptations of absolute power or the tensions of critical moments, but they held no surprises. While Lanfrey had little to say about Napoleon's first years, the stuff of legend more than of truth, he thought he could confidently assert this much: the young Napoleon Bonaparte, imbued with Corsican patriotism, was serious and resolute, quarrelsome and gloomy, hardworking, stubborn, bitter, and imperious. Most characteristic was his restless appetite for action aided by a singular ability to disguise his real feelings and charm his audiences. Although he traded the desire to serve his native land for larger ambitions, all the traits he manifested in his youth he carried over into adult life. He remained the consummate actor who could profess comradely affection for the common folk, whom in fact he despised; debate novels with men of letters when it was only his own voice he wanted to hear; order opponents murdered while professing ignorance, or disapproval, of such crimes. One of history's signal manipulators, he never loved people but used them. It was a verdict that Napoleon's most spirited enemies, like Madame de Staël, would have endorsed.

Lanfrey's biography demonstrates what hardly requires demonstration: that the writing of lives is of necessity an unending and controversial enterprise. His Napoleon is, like Southey's Nelson, an outsize figure but, unlike him, a hero in reverse: a monumental villain. But it also demonstrates that the public for which this biography was written was interested in knowledge, or at least speculation, about the inner life of historic personages.

3. Conflicting Claims

The struggle of nineteenth-century biographers and their readers with the incompatible needs to know and to idealize was exacerbated by a closely related contest, that between privacy and candor. To a denigrator of Victorian biographers, to a Lytton Strachey, their practice of respecting a precinct sheltered from prying eyes was symptomatic of a larger cultural vice: hypocrisy—a conscious, self-serving deception concealing abysses of greed and sensuality. Such a hostile observer, though pleading for complexity, could never appreciate the biographers' dilemma, could never see them as anxious authors doing their best to navigate among conflicting claims. While Strachey and his friends accused biographers of their parents' and grandparents' generations of talking too much, their most pointed reproach was that they actually said too little, and read their torrents of words as a particularly canny form of evasive silence.

One rebel against the nineteenth century, Bertrand Russell, looking back in his *Autobiography,* was very severe with the "mist of Victorian sentiment" and "Victorian goody-goody priggery."[1] True enough, one need not look hard to find both sentimentality and priggishness in the Lives of the age, whether long or short. Only too often, Victorian biographers sought refuge from disturbing intimate facts, mainly erotic experience, by taking their stand on the surface, that platform so congenial to hero worship.

Privacy was no simple matter. A modern cultural habit, it acquired unprecedented prestige in the age of Victoria, only to decline thereafter. In earlier centuries, most of one's personal business had been more or less everyone's business. But by the French Revolution, respectable families had come to insist on carving out a place of their own. The reasons for the temporary, always incomplete triumph of privacy are hard to pin down, but they appear to be economic, social, and political. The new prosperity of the middling orders, with their commitment to domestic bliss, whether real, exaggerated, or downright fictitious, encouraged a measure of segregation of private from public life. This segregation was fostered by a growing tendency, especially in the bourgeoisie, to separate work from home. The family might be a prison, especially to young women, but the ideology that it was a sanctuary from the world was strong and widely accepted. And the emergence of a modern political public, which gradually acquired enough power to resist the invasion of personal life by the state, did its part. The conduct of elections by ballot, a device strenuously resisted but one that spread after mid-century, was a tribute to a citizen's right to veil his political choices.

The line that separated the private from the public sphere differed from group to group, family to family, person to person, issue to issue, and the inescapable border skirmishes did little to simplify things. There were secrets one confided only to one's mother, one's spouse, one's best friend, one's journal, oneself. And privacy was not a birthright but a conquest. Children encouraged to keep diaries had their naive confessions checked—which is to say, censored—by adults until they reached the age when they could lock away their cherished silent friend from all intruders, including their parents. And if respectable people thought some deeds, or desires, off limits to unauthorized strangers, why should biographers, themselves nearly all bourgeois, invade the carefully guarded terrain?

The heroism of this Victorian ideal as reflected in biographers' inhibitions has escaped its critics. To stop short at the bedroom door was to obey a demanding self-denying ordinance. It meant putting restraints on the natural curiosity about the secret life of others, originating in infancy and usually kept intact in adulthood. Humans are inveterate gossips, driven voyeurs. To resist the urges for forbidden knowledge was to do the work of civilization, which is in large part an unending battle against imperious desires. The assets and liabilities of the bourgeois cult of privacy, then, cannot be settled by name-calling.

Contemporaries were keenly aware and, for the most part, highly appreciative of the right to a private domain. "Behind every man's external life, which he leads in company," Walter Bagehot, that brilliant essayist, wrote in 1853, "there is another which he leads alone." We all "come down to dinner, but each has a room to himself."[2] The private room was a precise metaphor for a hiding place in which the individual was secure. In his *Autobiography,* Trollope made a plea for the right to ward off inquisitive outsiders. In telling his story, he warned, he did not intend to "give a record of my inner life." Indeed, "if the rustle of a woman's petticoat has ever stirred my blood; if a cup of wine has been a joy to me; if I have thought tobacco at midnight in pleasant company to be one of the elements of an earthly paradise; if now and again I have somewhat recklessly fluttered a £5 note over a card-table;—of what matter is that to any reader?"[3] His attitude was representative of his class and time.

Inevitably, this self-protectiveness raised barriers for biographers intent on digging deep. But whatever the anti-Victorians would later say, it was not necessarily hypocrisy, which is to mean one thing and to say another. At its best, privacy offered splendid support to the unfolding of the self. Once secured, this fortress gave a measure of freedom to the inner life; the more invulnerable the wall, in fact, the greater the freedom. Letters of middle-class married couples show again and again that within their refuge such couples could be very frank with one another, setting out their feelings, including their sexual desire, with ardor and a certain homely eloquence. Reasonably managed, the cultivation of privacy was an achievement for which bourgeois could take much credit.

But not credit alone. The middle-class men and women who crowded the consulting rooms of alienists or took a fashionable mind cure attest that the religion of reserve was often pushed beyond sensible limits. Insistence on a privileged inner space was shadowed by the risks of excessive repression. From the mid-Victorian era onward, rebels against tight-lipped bourgeois secrecy mongering objected that the respectable classes had guarded the sphere of privacy too intensely for the good of their mental health. There is doubtless some truth to the charge that prohibitions against the expression of urgent sexual or aggressive appetites could degenerate into campaigns against their very existence. And this led not to their atrophy but to their survival underground, forcing them to surface in the form of symptoms—of bad dreams, of psychosomatic ailments, of neuroses.

None of this was a secret to thoughtful bourgeois, who voiced uneasiness with reticence overdone decades before Freud would offer a psychoanalytic diagnosis of repressed middle-class culture. Calculated neglect of inner conflicts was not the announced ideal of nineteenth-century biographers. In a much quoted essay of 1832, Carlyle exclaimed over "how inexpressibly comfortable" it is "to know our fellow-creature; to see into him, understand his goings-forth, decipher the whole heart of his mystery." This, we shall see, was more than brave oratory. But Carlyle was aware that only too often fellow biographers shied away from such mysteries. "How delicate, decent is English Biography," he exclaimed, "bless its mealy mouth!"[4]

Especially around mid-century, this "decency" had its innings, and not in Britain alone. But in the late 1870s, introducing an English-language anthology of Sainte-Beuve's famous Monday columns, William Mathews returned to Carlyle as he praised Sainte-Beuve's ability "to penetrate to the core of every author, and pluck out 'the heart of the mystery,'—to live with him in his times, to feel with his feelings, and think his thoughts,—in short to be completely *en rapport* with him."[5] Mathews conceded that Sainte-Beuve's sensibility was exceptional, perhaps unique. But, if not his accomplishment, his program was widely shared. In 1885, half a century after Carlyle had savaged biographers for their prudishness, Gladstone, that faultless Victorian, again objected to it after reading the biography of George Eliot that her husband, J. W. Cross, had just published: "It is not a Life at all," he said. "It is a Reticence, in three volumes."[6] The question remains to what extent Victorian biographies could do without that form of censorship of vital information.

Obviously, nineteenth-century biographers were most vulnerable to the indictment of shamefaced suppression in the matter of their subject's erotic experience. Lady Hamilton was too conspicuous a figure in Nelson's life to be altogether dispensable. But Victorian biographers thought they could safely withhold many other loves, sometimes consummated and sometimes frustrated, from their audience. In 1857, in her much admired *Life of Charlotte Brontë,* a biography born of love and nourished by research, Elizabeth Gaskell skipped over Brontë's unrequited passion for her French teacher in Brussels, Monsieur Heger, a married man with a jealous wife. At the same time, she did not hesitate to denounce in the strongest language the woman, his employer's wife, who, she believed, had seduced Bramwell Brontë, Charlotte's brother, and thus shattered whatever health and sanity he had left. Threatened by a libel suit, she and

her publisher quickly expunged the offending passages in the third edition of
the same year. What remained was a disclaimer—"Of the causes of this deterio-
ration I cannot speak"—and some outspoken words about Bramwell's sponging, lying, alcoholism, and opium addiction.[7] This retreat was prudence rather
than prudery: Gaskell had some right to be uneasy about the reliability of her
informants. In any event, her mixture of candor and reserve in the first edition
was a fine instance of the selective reticence typical of so much Victorian
writing.

Much to the same effect, in the early 1870s John Forster, in a bulky, authoritative biography of Charles Dickens, gave no hint of his intimate friend's secre-
tive affair with the young actress Ellen Ternan. Even so, he felt authorized to
publish a short autobiographical statement that Dickens had written about what
he considered the most painful, most shameful episode in his young life: being
forced to work in a blacking warehouse while his father was in debtors' prison.
Again, in 1884, in an affectionate biography of his brother, Paul de Musset
managed to analyze Alfred de Musset's well-advertised emotional turmoil with
intimate particulars without mentioning the name of George Sand, although
Musset's youthful affair with her had been a formative and dramatic influence
on his life. Such choices depended on the biographer's sense of just how much
the public is entitled to, and how much he may assert the privilege of privacy.

These decisions were not wholly unpredictable. The Victorians always found
it easier to talk in print about aggressiveness than about erotic desire. Take the
best-known work by the German-born journalist and biographer Lady Blennerhasset: her voluble three-volume life of Madame de Staël. Her subject had
been, in her histrionic and literary way, a powerful political and cultural force.
It followed that the life of this "wonderful woman could be examined only
within the framework of current thoughts and events that surrounded her."
Hence Lady Blennerhasset slighted de Staël's love life, or circumscribed it so
fussily that all vitality oozed out of her heroine. For all her little disquisitions
about the passions, her Madame de Staël is a thinking machine, a political
animal pure and simple.

Unfortunately for this biographer, Madame de Staël's sexual and political
activities were an inextricable compound, each incomprehensible without the
other.[8] Her lovers included, among many others, Talleyrand and Constant; her
sexual appetites were ravenous and her conduct theatrical, featuring tantrums,
faintings, pleading letters, threats of suicide. Nor was all her eroticism necessarily ideological; witness her passionate, probably never consummated, friendship
with the enigmatic charmer Madame Recamier. And in her mid-forties she
allowed herself to become involved with a martial, handsome but not very
intelligent Genevan officer, Jean de Rocca, young enough to be her son, whom

she later secretly married. But for the rest, her drawing room and her bedroom, whether at Paris or at Coppet, were almost interchangeable. And all of this Lady Blennerhasset's *Frau von Staël. Ihre Freunde und ihre Bedeutung in Politik und Literatur* wrapped in muslin. She put "friend" where "lover" would be more precise. She is silent on the fact that none of de Staël's children were by her husband. She portrays her idealized heroine as asking for nothing more than a happy marriage. It reflects on Victorian tastes that Blennerhasset's biography was thought so necessary to an eager reading public that it was quickly translated from German into French and English. Plainly, late in the century many middle-class buyers of biographies were still content with blank spaces on the map of important minds.

And yet, a substantial part of the bourgeois public came to welcome biographies free of priggishness. In the hands of a skilled, sensitive, and forthright craftsman, civilized diction could illuminate secret passages. Let two impressive and illuminating nineteenth-century biographies, the German scholar Carl Justi's *Winckelmann und seine Zeitgenossen* and J. A. Froude's *Thomas Carlyle,* stand for many. Between 1866 and 1872, Justi published a magisterial three-volume biography of Johann Joachim Winckelmann, the autodidact who had virtually invented art history a century before. Like Byron about fifty years later, Winckelmann woke up one morning in 1755 and found himself famous. His pamphlet on Greek painting and sculpture, *Gedanken über die Nachahmung der griechischen Werke in der Malerei und Bildhauerkunst,* extolling the ancients as having reached the pinnacle of art, stands as a classic. And his sweeping masterpiece, the *Geschichte der Kunst des Altertums* of 1764, cemented his reputation. For many decades, Winckelmann set the agenda for perceiving historical periods, the taste for ancient sculpture, and the terms of controversies over originality and imitation. His quotable maxims acquired a life of their own: the monuments of Greek art, he wrote in a phrase interminably repeated through the nineteenth century, were characterized by "a noble simplicity and tranquil grandeur—*eine edle Einfalt und stille Grösse.*"

Those who made Winckelmann their cicerone add up to a parade of great names in German culture: Lessing, Herder, Schelling, August Wilhelm Schlegel, to say nothing of Goethe, who wrote a characteristically intelligent appreciation more than three decades after Winckelmann's death in 1768. When Justi published *Winckelmann,* the man's influence had not faded.

Justi found it an exacting task: Winckelmann was a difficult, unappealing subject. Born abjectly poor in 1717, in the provincial Prussian town of Stendal, the son of a cobbler, he was from his earliest youth possessed by a passion for classical learning. He labored to acquire an almost legendary erudition, working as a schoolteacher, then as a nobleman's librarian, longing for time to himself and for Italy. His supreme opportunity came in 1754. Though in tune with the Enlightenment's critique of revealed religion, this modern pagan converted to Catholicism for the sake of his mission. All the antique works of art he had seen so far had been poor copies or dim engravings. The papal nuncio in Saxony enticed this fanatical scholar by promising him secure employment in Rome, access to great libraries, acquaintance with prominent collectors, and the inspiring presence of ancient art. After long, bitter hesitation, Winckelmann decided that Rome was worth a mass. This was Justi's first test, and he passed it brilliantly. He described Winckelmann's defection at length and vigorously reproached the man he obviously admired. His proceeding had been undignified, his search for good reasons unconvincing. And yet he found a justification for Winckelmann's businesslike embrace of Romanism in his calling and supreme talent.[9] The noble end was worth the ignoble means.

Justi's treatment of the other awkward issue in Winckelmann's life, his sexual disposition, was no less probing. It stands at the beginning of a seismic shift when the unmentionable was slowly becoming the mentionable. As Justi was working on Winckelmann, homosexuality was scarcely a topic for polite conversation. Until nearly the end of the Victorian age, the love of men for men—the love of women for women many found virtually unthinkable—was almost literally the love that dared not speak its name.* True, there were many who knew about "buggery" in the navy or might gossip about a society lion forced to flee to more tolerant climes; the lower orders, at least those inclined to blood sports, had long derived pleasure from torturing a miserable sexual offender exposed, as he stood in the stocks, to public ridicule and filthy, at times lethal, missives. But sexual scandals involving more highly placed personages, like headmasters in English public schools or millionaire German manufacturers, were hushed up or fodder for the yellow press out of bounds for most middle-class readers.

One way of broaching the topic was to introduce the Greeks. Every schoolboy with a classical education—Winckelmann called Plato his "old friend"—knew that there had been a time, and a splendid civilization, when defined forms of homosexual attachments had been sanctioned, even codified. Significantly, Goethe had already called Winckelmann a Greek, and in an essay of 1867, filled with exquisite hints and suggestive passages from his writings, Walter Pater had echoed Goethe by calling Winckelmann "wholly Greek."†

---

*The term "homosexuality" was coined only in 1869 and did not enter general discourse until a quarter of a century later.

†Justi, *Winckelmann and seine Zeitgenossen*, 3 vols. (1866–72; 5th ed., ed. Walther Rehm, 1956), II, 87. As Pater slyly acknowledged, "That his affinity with Hellenism was not merely intellectual,

This was the atmosphere in which Justi wrote and to which he contributed. An aesthete whose every paragraph breathes the craftsman at work, a bookish academic more at home at his desk than at the lectern, and a lifelong bachelor, Justi seemed the ideal biographer for Winckelmann: a stylist entering the thoughts of another stylist, an unencumbered scholarly tourist free to let the Italian ambience work on him, a lonely searcher who could rehearse in himself the pains and pleasures of an isolated pioneer. The pains had outweighed the pleasures. All his life Winckelmann tried to break the cocoon of solitude by forging "lively, indeed at times passionate," intimacies, mainly with younger men. In enlightening pages on this "cult," Justi records Winckelmann's pathetic efforts to ingratiate himself with "sweet" friends. He professed perfect love for one pupil or one acquaintance after another, and timidly sought to awaken reciprocal feelings, afraid that he was too clumsy to be lovable. "The yearning, the desperation, the eagerness to make sacrifices, of which his letters give such numerous proofs," Justi comments, "seem to us like a flame into which sensuality has poured its oil." Winckelmann desired to " 'enjoy' his friends 'with body and spirit.' " That is why he refused to draw a distinction so familiar to others: "Friendship is love," Justi sums up Winckelmann's erotic ideology, "friendship without love is mere acquaintance."[10]

Such effusions were not just symptoms of a delayed adolescence: Winckelmann sought men to love all his life.[11] These "paroxysms of friendship" haunted him in Rome as they had in Germany.[12] Even his death stood under the sign of his erotic appetites, though when, at the end of the third volume, Justi reaches this appalling denouement, he flinches for once. Winckelmann was strangled and stabbed to death in an Italian inn for some gold coins he was showing off to a young lowlife who had taken his fancy. Justi, unable to face so gross a cause for his hero's untimely death, seeks out less unsavory causes leading Winckelmann to cultivate the company of a coarse, brutish fellow traveler.[13]

For all his disciplined candor, Justi was not a neutral reporter. Speaking virtually as a defense attorney, he made the obvious point that effusive friendships among men had been cultivated for centuries as an attempt to enlist an "aberration" in the service of the highest purposes. Was not friendship often

---

that the subtler threads of temperament were inwoven in it, is proved by his romantic, fervent friendships with young men. He had known, he says, many young men more beautiful than Guido's archangel." "Winckelmann: Et Ego in Arcadia Fui," first printed in the *Westminster Review* in 1867, then incorporated in *Studies in the History of the Renaissance* (1873; 2nd ed., 1877, Modern Library ed., n.d.), quotation at 159. For details see Peter Gay, *The Bourgeois Experience*, vol. II, *The Tender Passion* (1986), 198–254, esp. 239–41.

the only "asylum" available to the scholar's emotional life, the passion, in Voltaire's words, of the sage?[14] But Justi was too scrupulous to drown Winckelmann's sexual misery in generalizations. Winckelmann's exaltation of friendship was not just exceptionally intense. What was added "was a natural indifference to the other sex."[15] And the easier he found abstinence toward women, "the more susceptible his imaginative powers grew to manly beauty."[16]

This, of course, is why Justi felt pressed to dwell on Winckelmann's friendships: they are essential to an understanding of his enthusiasm for Greek art. The subjective dimension of his sophisticated periodization of ancient art, evocative descriptions of its masterpieces, and imaginative recounting of geographic, racial, and political ingredients in the unique stature of Greek culture lay near the surface of his work. Winckelmann, after all, had himself defined the cult of beauty as the quintessence of the Greek achievement, a definition, Justi reminded his readers, that "had only the human figure in mind."[17]

More, Winckelmann was convinced, and Justi duly reported, that a beautiful male body is the precondition for valuing great art, and that only men stirred by male comeliness possess the true sense of beauty. This far Justi was willing to go, but no further. In his late forties, Winckelmann had returned to the "sentimental overstimulation" that dominated his youth and seemed necessary to warm the "frosty temperature of the life of his heart." Puzzled by "the psychological problems that sink their roots deep into sensuality and its caprices," Justi declined to sound those depths. "We do not want to dig here after the dark roots."[18] He determined his own boundaries. But if "prudish" is a synonym for "Victorian," then Justi's *Winckelmann* is not a Victorian biography.

We have seen that at the heart of Victorian bourgeois culture there lay a conflict, as vivid in biographies as elsewhere, in which self-concealment and self-revelation struggled for supremacy. The defining reality for Victorian culture was not consensus but discussion, argument, discord. What, then, was the representative Victorian biography? The controversy surrounding Froude's life of Carlyle may provide clues to the answer. It is a familiar story, but it deserves to be told again, for it delineates the range within which the debate moved. Carlyle proved as consistent about others writing *his* life as he had been about writing the lives of others. When he felt the end near, he gave Froude, long his worshipful companion, permission to use all of his papers, including the most personal, for a biography. He did not want a biography, and hoped that Froude would burn materials he had confided to him. But if anyone was to write a life of him, it should be Froude, and he let Froude understand that the last thing he wanted was a compromise with uncomfortable truths.

Froude was an inspired choice. Pondering his four volumes in 1885, shortly after their appearance, Frederic Harrison, that respected positivist thinker and man of letters, exclaimed, "The greatest master of English prose within our generation entrusted the story of his life to one of the most skilful of living writers."[19] Froude had made his mark with a multivolume study of England in the century of the Reformation, and, like Justi a fine stylist, he saw no incompatibility between the demands of biographic art and biographic science. Readers had every right, Harrison implied, to expect a feast; but to him and to others Froude's life of Carlyle and edition of his correspondence proved a bitter meal. Had he betrayed his master with indiscretions baring Carlyle's private life? That was the question argued out, at time venomously, for a quarter of a century and more.[20]

Some of the reviewers insisted that Froude had venally traded on the public's appetite for gossip; others, no less firm, welcomed Froude's candor. But many betrayed a curious uncertainty. In 1882 and 1884, the *Saturday Review* filled the three articles it devoted to Froude's four volumes with regrets and reproaches. Why rehearse all of Carlyle's failings, all his nastiness, all the domestic anguish he had caused? Would not a small sample have been enough? Carlyle, wanting no biography, had been "recalled from his tomb by one who professes to have felt for him the love and veneration of a son, but who has performed by some marvellous perversion of judgment all that might have been looked for from his worst enemy." Froude "may almost be called the Iconoclast of his own idol." Yet, having discharged his duty to show moral outrage, the reviewer devoted most of his space to Carlyle's life and took Froude's word for his subject's abusiveness, irascibility, and his way of making his wife's existence a "long martyrdom."[21] Torn between indignation and admiration, the reviewer trusted the son who had betrayed his father.

Froude has always been called Carlyle's disciple, and so he was, but in a paradoxical way: his discipleship was yoked to a passion for unvarnished veracity. "I have no respect for idealizing biographies," he wrote in 1886, and the volumes on Carlyle prove that he meant it. But this incorruptibility was his way of appeasing the authority he adored by identifying his master's standards with his own; his shifting dependencies manifested themselves in displays of manly independence. The son of a cold, harsh, and demanding father who was openly disappointed in him, Froude had an inner history shadowed, it would seem, by the haunting need to win paternal approval and to defy it. As a student at Oxford in the mid-1830s, he swam in the wake of his brilliant elder brother Hurrell and came under the sway of that sweet persuader John Henry Newman, then just beginning his pilgrimage to Rome. But Froude fought his way clear, convincing himself that Protestantism was more credible, intellectually more respectable, than it appeared in the sermons of the High Church Oxonians. His road from Damascus was, as for many of his contemporaries, a time of torment. But in 1849 he at once achieved and recorded a drastic act of self-liberation with a heretical, blatantly confessional novel, *The Nemesis of Faith,* and resigned his Oxford fellowship.

His escape from devout high Anglicanism was eased by a new filial commitment. In the early 1840s, Froude came upon Carlyle and adopted his message without reserve. He exchanged one father for another.[22] Other admirers fell away as Carlyle's voice grew more strident and his pronouncements more reactionary, but Froude's loyalty remained unshaken. His Carlyle was the prophet thundering against the modern heresies of utilitarianism, optimism, and machine worship: the world sadly wanted heroes, since government should be in the hands of those fit to rule, not at the mercy of uninformed and fickle democratic opinion. What infatuated contemporaries called progress was an illusion, their display of liberal humanitarianism a sentimental sham. When Carlyle's embarrassing pronouncements called for apologetic skills, Froude would discover benign readings; he even attempted to rescue the racism of Carlyle's notorious article "The Nigger Question." Carlyle's tone, Froude admitted, was often savage, but, he insisted, the substance of his thought was unimpeachable.

That tone gave Froude much to worry about. Carlyle came to detest nearly everyone and called people names that betray spite and pleasure in verbal destructiveness. And Froude spared his readers none of Carlyle's vicious sallies.[23] Still, printing them all, he protested that Carlyle's verbal "ferocity" gave a false impression of him. "He was really the most tenderhearted of men. His savageness was but affection turned sour." Did he not disregard his principled objections to indiscriminate philanthropy by handing out shillings to beggars?[24] Speaking of Carlyle's letters, of which he said he had read thousands, Froude found "no sentence of his own which he could have wished unwritten."* This was, on Froude's own evidence, a partisan verdict, more revealing of his than of Carlyle's character: the disciple had overpowered the judge.

---

*Froude, *Thomas Carlyle: A History of the First Forty Years of His Life, 1795–1835,* 2 vols. (1882), II, 473. "This man, we read more than once, is a compound of 'frog and viper' "—I am giving Harrison's contemporary summary, as appalled at the venom of the author as at the indiscretions of his biographer—"that one is an inferior kind of Robespierre; Macaulay is a 'squat, low-browed,' 'commonplace' object; Wordsworth is a 'small, diluted man,' a 'contemptibility'; Coleridge, a 'weltering, ineffectual being'; Keats' poems are 'dead dog'; Keble, author of the *Christian Year,* is a 'little ape'; Cardinal Newman has 'not the intellect of a moderate-sized rabbit'; *Pickwick* is 'lowest trash'; Charles Lamb is a 'pitiful tomfool,' a 'despicable abortion'; the Saturday Reviewer is a 'dirty puppy'; Mill is a poor, frozen, mechanical being, a 'logic-chopping engine.' " Harrison, "Froude's Life of Carlyle" (1885), *The Choice of Books and Other Literary Pieces* (1886; ed. 1925), 187–88.

Yet, when he came to Carlyle's marriage, Froude discarded all alibis. His public Carlyle was insightful, courageous, much misunderstood, a Cassandra for a blind and ungrateful time; his private Carlyle was self-absorbed, unjust, something of a monster to his gifted, clever, long-suffering wife. It never occurred to Froude that there was a close link between these two Carlyles. But, for all his salvage attempts, Froude abandoned most of the reticence to which average Victorian readers were accustomed. Harrison spoke for such readers when he held up his hands in horror and defended himself against all this unwelcome information with a counterattack. He declared that he really wanted to hear nothing more of Carlyle's domestic failings. These leavings, which should have remained in the wastebasket where Froude found them, added nothing to the image of the sage that Victorians should continue to cherish. Disclosing unappetizing particulars about his hero's personal life, Froude had for many overstepped the edge of genteel Victorian discourse. In fact, Froude compounded his offense against discretion by publishing not merely his candid biography but the *Letters and Memorials* of Jane Welsh Carlyle, and Carlyle's *Reminiscences,* dominated by a long, guilt-ridden section on his wife that he had written in 1866, just after her death.

She left her husband bereft and remorseful, remorseful because, as he piously went through his wife's papers, he finally became aware how unhappy she had been—how unhappy he had made her. In Froude's anguished perception, she had served Carlyle when he was exigent; denied her physical pain while he moaned over minor ailments; slaved to make their home agreeable without a word of gratitude from him; endured his disregard of her justified jealousy against Lady Ashburton, with whom he had become infatuated in middle life; humored him as he sat ensconced in his study alone for hours, or retreated to his own room, unable to endure company and indulging in tantrums if a noise, no matter how slight, disturbed him; subjected her sprightly wit and marked intelligence to a man she thought a genius but who did not recognize until it was too late that she was in important respects his equal, perhaps his superior; and even taken physical abuse in silence. Froude, who beginning in 1861 was an intimate of the household, had come to suspect much of this, but it was not until a decade later, when Carlyle entrusted him with a mass of private papers, that the extent of Jane Carlyle's misery, and her husband's share in it, came to oppress him.

There was more. In early 1887, after swallowing starchy disapproval from shocked reviewers and furious abuse from the Carlyle family, Froude drafted an account of his relations with Carlyle to be published only in 1903. It shows an embattled biographer working through the conflicting claims of his time. He wrestles with himself, as he attends to rumors about the Carlyle household.

Carlyle had told him, refusing to elaborate, that the papers held a secret and that "without a knowledge of it no true biography of him was possible." It was a mystery of which Froude "would infinitely rather have remained in ignorance."[25] But faithful to Carlyle, he could not forget that his master had complained many years earlier of the "Damocles' sword of *Respectability*" that "hangs forever over the poor English Life-writer (as it does over poor English Life in general), and reduces him to the verge of paralysis."[26] Froude felt driven to sound the mystery lest he remain paralyzed.

But, having sounded it, he partially veiled his discovery. "The married life of Carlyle and Jane Welsh," he wrote in the biography, "was not happy in the roseate sense of happiness." Carlyle "did not find in his marriage the miraculous transformation of nature which he had promised himself. He remained lonely and dyspeptic." Froude's conclusion, though sober, was devastating. "Miss Welsh, it is probable, would have passed through life more pleasantly had she married someone in her own rank of life; Carlyle might have gone through it successfully with his mother or a sister to look after him."[27] These are grave hints, and Froude scattered others across the published text. He wondered at first whether the secret was that the Carlyles decided not to have children. But a statement from Geraldine Jewsbury, Jane Carlyle's closest friend and only confidante, gave him the light he needed and did not want. "Carlyle was one of those persons who ought never to have married." His "physical constitution" was at fault.[28]

In short, Froude came to believe that the Carlyles' childlessness resulted from the husband's sexual fiascos. It seems probable that Carlyle was impotent on his wedding night and may have remained so all his life.[29] If that was indeed Carlyle's secret, it would help to explain the separate bedrooms and much of his touchiness. It might explain, too, that the most intense of Jane Carlyle's sufferings sprang not from her husband's brutality, ingratitude, and selfishness but from a far more troubling failure. But on this matter not even Froude, the arch-Victorian servant of truth, was willing to be explicit.

The point is that he did not need to be. In 1903, responding quickly to the publication of Froude's private memorandum, *My Relations with Carlyle,* Alexander Carlyle and Sir James Crichton-Browne, a leading alienist, published an apoplectic rejoinder, *The Nemesis of Froude.* Froude may have overinterpreted the material at his disposal and underestimated Jane Carlyle's difficult side. But what matters here is the way the authors, attempting to discredit the most damaging of Froude's intimations, resort to the mixture of prissiness and indignation that the likes of Russell and Strachey would later denounce as typically Victorian.[30] Froude was not there to respond; he had died nine years before. Had he been alive to read it, he might have retreated a little from his more speculative inferences. But to one retort he would have been entitled: though still speaking for a minority in the respectable culture of his time, he was in his candor as good a Victorian as his more inhibited accusers.

For the historian of the Victorian bourgeoisie, the tempest unleashed by Froude's *Carlyle* exhibits just how troublesome reviewers found it to map the province of privacy. Struggling to legislate what the public ought to read in biographies, they shed much, if somewhat oblique, light on the wide spectrum of opinion of what in fact it did want to read.[31] Surpassed only by novels as a prod toward fantasies, biographies were particularly at home in the nineteenth-century bourgeois world because it was bourgeois wishes they showed as fulfilled. Lives and Letters continually emphasized that fame and fortune, grandeur in self-abnegation or public service, were the consequence of hard work and honest dealings, of talents schooled and opportunities taken. The display of greatness helped to relieve a reader's anxieties, notably those of isolation and ignorance.

The pain of isolation that a biography working in the reader's mind could assuage was not necessarily the pathos of an unappreciated and talented child or that of a penniless poet in a garret. More commonly it gratified the more abstract, less stressful yearning for a cultural or political or religious community; tracing the life and fortunes of a famous poet or prime minister, the biography could give readers the feeling that one of their own had been a great man. Those massive late-Victorian lives of Frederick the Great, Voltaire, Lincoln, or Gladstone were particularly apt to fulfill this role. That is what Carlyle had meant when he spoke of "King Shakespeare," who belonged to the whole English-speaking world.*

The making of, and the response to, Albert Bielschowsky's life of Goethe is an instructive instance of a producer and consumers happily met. While chauvinistic Germans had reservations about the cosmopolitan poet who had enjoyed chatting with the arch-enemy Napoleon and disdained the wave of patriotism that had washed over Germans during the Wars of Liberation, they could not keep Goethe from becoming something of a folk hero even before his death in 1832. The decades following had seen numerous editions of his writings, especially his poems and novels, pilgrimages to Weimar, and philosophical treatises. But strangely enough, when Oskar Beck, director of a prestigious publishing house in Munich, surveyed the scene in the 1880s, he could find only Lewes's Goethe biography of 1855 and Herman Grimm's lectures published in 1876; the first, for all its merits, out of date and the second, though a

*See above, p. 159.

literary pleasure, too allusive for the beginner. What he wanted was a popular biography, and in the early 1890s he found the author to gratify his dearest wish: to give the German people a life of Goethe that would be worthy of that great poet and be accessible to all the "educated—*Gebildeten.*"[32]

The poor health of Bielschowsky, a semiretired *Gymnasium* teacher, delayed the project. But the first volume of his smoothly written, emotionally satisfying *Goethe. Sein Leben und seine Werke* appeared in 1895; the second, posthumously a year after his death, in 1902. Only ten years later, his *Goethe* had already reached its twenty-fifth edition, and it remained a best-seller into the 1920s. In a letter to Oskar Beck of 1893, Bielschowsky had declared his hope that he might transmit to his readers something of Goethe's "divine mission," and produce an awareness that would make him into "that ferment for the German spiritual life that corresponds to his world-historical significance." In these very years, other substantial biographies of Goethe attest to a biographical appetite that specialists and editors had failed to satisfy. But Bielschowsky remained the biographer of choice, an inescapable presence in bourgeois bookcases. His pathetic touch outdid that of his competitors, as did his ability to digest the outpouring of documentary publications and monographic literature for readers both educated and ignorant. Bielschowsky's biography was soulful and dependable, an unbeatable combination.

Biographies could relieve another anxiety as well, that of ignorance. They were, for one thing, digestible introductions to history. As the editor of the American Statesman series, John T. Morse, Jr., recalled, he had intended it to present, once complete, "such a picture of the development of the country that the reader who had faithfully read all the volumes would have a full and fair view of the history of the United States told through the medium of the efforts of the men who had shaped our national career."[33] Nor was history the only subject that biographies could teach. Morley's English Men of Letters plainly aimed to tutor English-speaking readers about more than just the lives of Swift or Samuel Johnson; they were to instruct them also on just how to read their work. The typical tone in these volumes was unfailingly self-assured, a didactic, mildly hectoring manner employed by the educated to guide the half-educated, men and women who were, in Gosse's words, "groping their way through the darkness of the book-market."[34] It looks now as though these biographers were not democrats sharing their discoveries with their equals but cultural aristocrats imposing their conclusions on inferiors. But the impressive sales of these series strongly suggest that their audiences, far from feeling any condescension, welcomed the instruction. It brought them nearer to their idols.

This stress on anxiety should not overshadow the sheer pleasure of reading about other people's lives. It was not the promise of low gossip alone—we have

seen how strenuously Victorians resisted intimate disclosures about the famous
or how guilty they felt when they were compelled to enjoy them. Those
readers not particularly worried about their culture bought and read biographies
because they found the lives of past public figures quite simply interesting, even
though they, too, wanted virtue extolled and vice excoriated. And as the century went by, bourgeois readers recognized the fundamental fact of life that all
individuals, including those thought worthy of a biography, were only human
beings. Leslie Stephen, thinking of the *Dictionary of National Biography,* condemned biographies for being "too long and too idolatrous," and his successor,
Sidney Lee, coined the unofficial slogan of their ambitious enterprise: "No
flowers, by request."[35] Despite their reputation, the Victorians, especially the
late Victorians, could stand a good deal of reality. That their gift for realism was
in many instances quite incongruously accompanied by a blind contempt for
individuals, classes, and nations out of favor with them only documents that
they were as human as the lives about which they were reading.

4. The Price of Professionalism

Unlike biographers, whose relations with their Victorian audiences were relatively uncomplicated, historians working to define their professional identity
faced far greater tensions, with others and in themselves. It will turn out that,
participating in the nineteenth century's search for the self, they played an
ambiguous role as they wrote the autobiography of their culture.

Reminders of bygone days recent or remote were, of course, not confined to
print. They were everywhere and for everyone: statues, squares, national holidays, public speeches inculcating love of country—all gathered educated and
unlettered citizens into self-congratulatory communities. The Fourth of July
gave Americans annual opportunities to toast themselves as the most independent of peoples, the Fourteenth of July periodically revived French pride for
having dismantled the Old Regime. Yet, in their sense of the past, the middle
classes were necessarily better informed and more discriminating than their
more lowly compatriots. The bourgeoisie enjoyed ample opportunities to
make itself at home in history, and many took full advantage of them.*

But the sales figures for histories grew less impressive with the years. Reading

---

*Nor were bourgeois the only consumers of history. In Britain, after the Reform Act of 1867
widened the franchise beyond the prosperous middle classes and when the sweeping Education
Act of 1870 made the question of training the country's "future masters" acute, the public for
history texts grew at an exponential rate.

biographies proved a more undemanding and hence more enjoyable way of beguiling one's leisure, nourishing one's fantasies, or improving one's mind. Historians with marked literary talents and an agreeable message had once counted on a vast readership. By the mid-1870s, a quarter century after its first two volumes had appeared, Macaulay's *History of England* had sold some 300,-000 copies in editions expensive or cheap, legitimate or pirated.* Admittedly the appeal of Macaulay's masterpiece was almost proverbial. He had worked at it: in 1841, he declared, "I shall not be satisfied, unless I produce something which shall for a few days supersede the last fashionable novel on the tables of young ladies."[1] Other fluent writers, too, had piled up noteworthy numbers. John Lothrop Motley's three-volume *Rise of the Dutch Republic* of 1856, a hymn to a historic bid for freedom, sold some 30,000 sets a year.[2] And J. R. Green's *Short History of the English People,* published in 1874, and the longer, four-volume version he undertook immediately after, found literally hundreds of thousands of readers in Britain and the United States. "The book," wrote Lord Bryce, "was philosophical enough for scholars and popular enough for school-boys."† But these were the happy exceptions.

In fact, writing serious history was a hard way to make a living. Negotiating with Charles Scribner on completing the first volumes of his brilliant and exhaustive account of the Jefferson and Madison administrations, Henry Adams, counting on only a select public, grimly suggested that history has always been "the most aristocratic of all literary pursuits, because it obliges the historian to be rich as well as educated." He was right enough, certainly about himself: he sold no more than three thousand sets in a decade.[3] If historians continued to shape the Victorian mind, they did so largely by indirection: through lectures, loyal disciples, popular versions of technical texts, and the intellectual authority that influential men who read their work exerted over their culture. After all, even the volumes of the *Histoire de la France moderne* by Jules Michelet, much in the public eye, sold only a few thousand copies.

But periodicals spread the word. They reviewed interesting histories at length. They fed historical consciousness with pointed partisan articles. They

---

*Of that number, some 140,000 sets had been sold in Britain alone, profiting from the popularity of book clubs, while in 1848 and 1849 in the United States mainly pirated editions of the first two volumes had already sold some 60,000 copies. See George Otto Trevelyan, *The Life and Letters of Lord Macaulay* (1876; enlarged ed., 1908), 509, 516, 621–22.

†Bryce, in *Letters of John Richard Green,* ed. Leslie Stephen (1901), 385. Reflecting on Green's work, Bryce noted that "the conjunction of fine gifts for investigation with fine gifts for exposition is a rare conjunction, which cannot be prized too highly, for while it advances historical science, it brings historical methods, as well as historical facts, within the horizon of the ordinary reader." "John Richard Green," *Studies in Contemporary Biography* (1903), 167–68.

celebrated eminent historians with appreciative vignettes. The pages of monthlies or quarterlies and of journals devoted to education buzzed with controversies over the kind of past that should be transmitted to—or kept from—children, adolescents, and university students. The emotionally charged quarrels
about the appropriate measure of patriotism or place of religion in historical
study attest just how seriously Victorian bourgeois took the contents of history
books, and how incessantly they worried over their impact on the young.*
Their psychology of education was simple: histories, like biographies, form
their readers' character, probably for a lifetime; hence twigs must be bent in the
right direction. History, the nationalistic Prussian historian Johann Gustav
Droysen wrote, is a process that furthers self-knowledge; it is "humanity's
becoming aware and being aware of itself."[4] The claim was implicit but far-
reaching: the truths about the past that historians discover and impart furnish
their contemporaries' inner world.

Yet, as historians began to organize themselves into a profession with exacting standards, critics, some of them from their own ranks, began to indict them
for segregating themselves from the larger middle-class public. Were they not
willfully whittling down their audiences with tedious monographs and unread-
able syntheses? Were they not reduced to speaking only to one another? The
scientific ideal, to which most of them subscribed, proved far more costly to
them than its enthusiastic proponents had expected. Oddly enough, precisely
when the historians' professional self-awareness and self-confidence rose, their
influence seemed to be waning. By the turn of the century, this was the paradoxical position that historians had created for themselves in bourgeois culture.

One consequence of Victorian history making itself into a profession was its
emancipation from biography. In the early decades of the century, prominent
authors again and again defined history as biography on a larger, more crowded
canvas and found few to disagree with them. Carlyle's much quoted remark
"History is the essence of innumerable Biographies" and Emerson's "There is
properly no history, only biography" echoed a general conviction.[5] Certainly
the two disciplines long remained intertwined: even a highly self-conscious
craftsman like Ranke, whose overriding theme was the clash of the great powers in early modern times, inserted character sketches into his massive histories
of the popes and the Reformation, of England, France, and Prussia. Motley,
who, we know, was one of the most widely read historians in the century,
converted his painstaking account of the Dutch rebellion against Spanish over-
lordship into a duel between two outsized personalities, William of Orange and

*See below, pp. 213–21.

Philip II of Spain, and sprinkled his text with intimate profiles of lesser actors by the dozen.* Michelet spent a professional lifetime writing the collective biography of the French people. In 1856, reviewing the current state of his profession in the German states, Heinrich von Sybel, founder of the *Historische Zeitschrift,* described biography as a "branch of historical writing," one that, he was cheered to note, had recently blossomed into vigorous life.[6]

This near-identification of biography with history could not go unchallenged. Voices not easily ignored argued that any serious life of an epoch-making figure—Luther or Cromwell or Napoleon—must be a history of its time.[7] While the Carlyles and Motleys paraded their giants bestriding the past, rival conceptions of historical causation that minimized the power of individuals were emerging into prominence. Tocqueville's revisionist study of the impact of the Old Regime on the French Revolution, Marx's sardonic commentaries on recent events in France depicting the most powerful of personages as mere puppets gave pride of place to impersonal forces. In their thought, warring beliefs, inflexible institutions, developments in economic and social structures, the clash of classes were the true impulses to historical change. Even historians following neither Tocqueville nor Marx became persuaded of what John Morley called "the great historical principle that besides the prominent men of a generation there is a something at work underneath, a moving current on whose flood they are borne."[8] This conviction did not devalue biography but, as it were, put it in its proper place. In short, the exigencies of specialization left their impress on the study of the past. By century's end, only a few historians or biographers were poaching on the others' terrain. That this gave biography a distinct advantage over history in the competition for readers was another matter.

In gradually yielding to the pressures of the modern division of labor, late-nineteenth-century historians subjected their activities to academic rigor.[9] The wealthy dilettante survived into the second half of the century, but most luminaries of the profession held chairs in universities. Jared Sparks and Lord Acton, Leopold von Ranke and Jacob Burckhardt, Jules Michelet and F. W. Maitland, Fustel de Coulanges and Theodor Mommsen were all professors. In the early years, they were still responsible for vast stretches of the past; in 1839 Sparks, the first history professor in an American university, was appointed the McLean Professor of Ancient and Modern History at Harvard. By the end of the century, such required omniscience had become unthinkable: in 1892, bowing to new realities, Harvard established the first chair in economic history.

The craft was undergoing an epochal evolution. As late as the 1860s, history

*See below, pp. 195–99.

professors at the Sorbonne had still been required to lecture on ancient, medieval, and modern history in turn, but around this time the appointments to the Regius professorships in modern history at Oxford and Cambridge, founded in 1724 and long the booty of such dilettantes as Charles Kingsley, had begun to reward serious scholars. Thus the time-honored alliance between history and literature was exposed to severe strains. Historical associations sprang up in country after country, bringing journals with them; the *Historische Zeitschrift* was founded in 1859, the *Revue historique* in 1876, the *English Historical Review* in 1886, the *American Historical Review* in 1895. Historians' congresses and conferences, other devices spawned by the rush to professionalism, were not far behind. Only a few Cassandras warned that this meant the victory not of science but of pedantry.[10]

A telling episode of early 1903 lends color to this unexpected anxiety. In January, assuming his chair as Regius Professor of Modern History at Cambridge, J. B. Bury peppered his inaugural lecture with some aggressive assertions. "History," he said, "is not a branch of literature." While historical writings lend themselves to literary art, that is only their pleasing dress. In support, Bury offered the example of "the greatest living historian," Theodor Mommsen. He was of course aware, as were his listeners, that Mommsen had just received the Nobel Prize in literature, and that made him all the more useful to Bury. "The reputation of Mommsen as a great man of letters depends on his Roman History; but his greatness as a historian is to be sought far less in that dazzling work than in the *Corpus* and the *Staatsrecht* and the *Chronicles*," imperishable monuments to Mommsen's supreme scholarly diligence and reconstructive gifts. And Bury famously concluded that while history "may supply material for literary art or philosophical speculation, she is herself simply a science, no less and no more."[11]

Among Bury's listeners was the historian George Macaulay Trevelyan, then in his mid-twenties, later to become the best-selling and most influential historian in his country. As the son of George Otto Trevelyan and the great-nephew of Thomas Babington Macaulay, he was related to two historians known for their literary touch. Infuriated by what he thought Bury's disparagement of good writing and, with that, of the two luminaries in his family, he dashed off a tart rejoinder. Ten years later, he revised that riposte, excised Bury's name, and offered an energetic plea for history as an art. He reminded fellow historians that Clio is, after all, a muse, an ancient truth that his generation had forgotten. "If, as we have so often been told with such glee, the days of 'literary history' have gone never to return," he warned, "the world is left the poorer." By despising the muse, historians had thrown away the authority they had once commanded.[12] Novelists and playwrights had always enjoyed marked influence; now they easily outdistanced historians as teachers to their culture.

Trevelyan acknowledged that the shift from amateur to professional had produced solid gains for his craft. But he saw the new scientific historians all too ready to discard felicitousness with their narrow focus, their dry-as-dust footnotes, and their statistics. These were ill-conceived, in fact damaging, remedies for the imagined perils of literature. "How indeed could history be a 'science'?"[13] Trevelyan's target was unmistakable: the professor who had dared to reduce his craft to a science, nothing less and nothing more.

The matter of style was worth addressing. For centuries, historians had been in thrall to theology, recording for the faithful, often in ungainly prose, the lives of saints and monarchs, tracing the divinely appointed course of empires, and rescuing sacred documents for posterity. But the Enlightenment had made written history a conscious literary pursuit. The philosophic eighteenth-century masters had all written elegant histories that secured them responsive audiences. Their vocal critics, mainly good Christians appalled at the impieties that unbelievers like Hume, Voltaire, and Gibbon were propagating in their histories, conceded that they wrote well—too well.

The philosophes' stylishness survived into the nineteenth century, to the time that historians were beginning to yearn for the accolades that scientists alone seemed to be garnering. For decades, they were confident that they could reconcile the competing demands of style and accuracy. In 1828, years before he began thinking about writing a history of England, Macaulay laid it down in his characteristic positive tones that "a perfect historian must possess an imagination sufficiently powerful to make his narrative affecting and picturesque. Yet he must control it so absolutely as to content himself with the materials which he finds, and to refrain from supplying deficiencies by additions of his own."[14] This, then, was the man who would write history to compete with novels; for him, the only difference between a history and a novel was that a history is true. But both were literary products.

Ranke, too, saw no conflict between loyalty to science and loyalty to literature.* While studying with him in Berlin, Burckhardt expressed doubts that his master had resolved the issue quite so successfully; had he not "sacrificed a great deal of the truth, a very great deal," to his "splendid" gift of presentation?[15] Ranke himself, though, never felt any need to choose between matter and manner. "The task of the historian," he wrote in his history of France, "is at once literary and learned; history is both art and science. It must fulfill all the demands of criticism and learning as well as, say, a philological work, but at the same time offer the educated spirit the same pleasure as the most accomplished

*See below, pp. 198–210.

literary production."[16] Only the earnest debates among historians about the fundamental nature of their craft show that realizing this dual program would not be quite so easy.

The turning point for the kind of attitude thought appropriate for historical work, shifting from emotional self-display to clinical self-concealment, came some time after mid-century. Before then, practitioners had typically shown traces of romanticism in their presentation of themselves, treating history as a magnificent, colorful epic calling for literary skills and moral judgments. But it was a sign of changing times after the 1850s that the self-referential first-person singular, which historians had displayed with pride, came to be modestly relegated to prefaces. In 1848, Macaulay could still open the first volume of his vast *History of England* with himself: "I propose to write the history of England from the accession of King James the Second down to a time which is within the memory of men still living." Four decades later, Henry Adams opened his still vaster *History of the United States during the Administrations of Thomas Jefferson and James Madison* in a sharply contrasting style: "According to the census of 1800, the United States of America contained 5,308,483 persons." The enormous historical literature of the Victorian age abounded in crosscurrents, but the drift was unmistakable—toward science, in rhetoric if not always in substance. The bourgeois who made up nearly all their readers were both gainers and losers.

By the time that Trevelyan issued his protest, he thought that the alliance of literature and science had virtually broken down. Still, to aim his shafts at Bury was to shadowbox: he had picked the wrong antagonist. Scattering his quotable pronunciamentos, Bury had no doubt sacrificed sensible advocacy to dramatic effects, but he was no compiler of rebarbative treatises. A scholar's scholar with proverbial energy, catholic curiosity, and an enviable talent for languages, Bury was at ease in the remotest reaches of ancient Greece and Byzantium as well as the sweep of Western thought through the ages. He had edited Euripides and Gibbon's *Decline and Fall of the Roman Empire*—classic achievements. But he had also demonstrated a talent for popularization: his *History of Greece,* first published in 1900 and several times revised, shows him a pleasing preceptor to the common reader. And Trevelyan's polemical response was no less excessive than Bury's provocations as he denounced those colleagues who arrogantly disdained a public thirsting for enjoyable narrative, uplifting instruction, and sheer information. He did admit, after all, sounding much like Macaulay, that history has an "element" of both science and art.[17] Undercutting his pessimism about current conditions in his craft, he even acknowledged that a concordat between literary and scientific historians might still be a possibility.

But, as Jacob Burckhardt, one of the ornaments of the profession, discovered, style could do much to secure a popular response but not everything. He

yielded to no one in his self-assurance that he was doing reliable history, but in
1842, early in his career, he pledged that he would never slight his literary
obligations: "I have made a vow to myself to write in a readable style all my life
long."[18] His classic *Kultur der Renaissance in Italien* proves that he kept the
promise he had made to himself. Yet, a profoundly original work that has
enjoyed a stunning posthumous fame, his masterpiece long failed to interest the
public. The early reception of the book was chilling. Few periodicals reviewed
it, few historians read it.* Published in late 1860 by a friend of Burckhardt's, it
had sold only 200 copies by early 1862, and the printing of 750 copies was not
exhausted for several years. In 1868, when a new publisher called for a second
edition, it had been out of print for some time. The book made its way very
gradually, with translations into Italian, English, and French by 1885.

Why the delay? The central theme of Burckhardt's cultural history was a
radical change of mind: he saw the Renaissance, with its discovery of history, of
antiquity, and of modern man, as the mother of his own age—in view of
Burckhardt's detestation of contemporary vulgarity and restlessness, an ambiguous compliment. A sympathetic reading of his *Renaissance in Italien,* then, would
have forced nineteenth-century readers to take a close look at their own inner
world with all its incoherences and complexities. But for decades the relevance
of the book to the Victorians' own ways of thinking remained obscure. Considering its flair and its colorful, often melodramatic passages, this neglect looks
suspiciously like a more or less unconscious defense against self-scrutiny. In one
of his gloomiest prognostications, Burckhardt once warned against the advent
of the "terrible simplifiers." He had meant demagogues, but the phrase works
as a critique of middle-brow bourgeois preferring their easily digestible Macaulay to their more demanding Burckhardt: Victorians could be hard on sophisticated mind readers who told them more about themselves than they wanted
to know. As late as 1911, fourteen years after his death, the eleventh edition of
the *Encyclopaedia Britannica* gave Burckhardt a perfunctory and inaccurate half
column—one seventh of the space it devoted to Ranke—and identified him as
a "Swiss writer on art."[19]

None of this should be taken to suggest that history lost all access to the inner
life of the bourgeois public. Quite the contrary; to hear some Victorians tell it,
their century had invented historical consciousness. This claim was an instance

---

*Three or four art historians graciously thanked Burckhardt for the copy he had sent them and
engaged, a little reluctantly, with his ideas. Wilhelm Dilthey, at the start of a distinguished career as
an intellectual historian and philosopher of history, found the book worth his attention, if open to
severe reservations. In 1869, Hippolyte Taine called it admirable. That was about all.

of self-infatuation to which confident ages are susceptible: the sense of distance from the past, of its sheer otherness, goes back to the early Renaissance. Yet judging from the outpouring of histories, even if they lost the popularity contest with biographies, one may concede that the nineteenth century was preeminently the historical century. Taught in schools, read by people who counted, invoked in debates and legal opinions to buttress an argument, history was on many tongues and in more minds.

A professional habit, identification, threw an inviting bridge between nineteenth-century writers of history and its readers. Identification is a many-layered mental act all the more elusive because it is in part unconscious. Its first primitive stirrings emerge very early in life, and it branches out with the passage of time into a rich menu of thoughts and feelings. At its most reasonable, identification is empathy, a recognition and acceptance of past states of mind in their own context. More strenuously, it may rise to an indiscriminate embrace and, at its most intense, to a total merger with the other. Whatever its level, for readers identification was an emotional response; for historians, a carefully honed attitude. To discover the past, then, historians enlisted precisely the quality that most conspicuously sets the science of history apart from the natural sciences—the identity of the scientist with his materials. This very intimacy opened the door to prized insights. Consumers of historical works, even if they only observed it, profited from this cultivated inwardness: it assured them that under expert guidance they were being offered not disguised discussions of present-day affairs but true history.

There were times when these identifications rose to dramatic intensity. One day, at the height of his career as a distinguished historian of ancient Greece and medieval France, Fustel de Coulanges uttered a heartfelt caution to ward off the impending cheers of his students as he approached the end of one of his famous lectures. "Do not applaud me," he implored them. "I am not the one who is speaking to you; it is history that is speaking through me."[20] Evidently Fustel was penetrated by the sense that Clio had appointed him as her chosen spokesman. This sublime repudiation of presumptuousness looks suspiciously like covert boasting, but, far from arrogance, it was an acquired stance of higher humility. It will emerge that nineteenth-century historians thought that in the right hands, engagement with the present could be turned into a key to secure entry to the past.* They were even more confident that their identification with the past was not a flaw to be corrected but, with all its risks, a splendid precondition for historical insight; they hoped for nothing less than a dazzled sense of entering historic moments or historic personages. This desired presence

*See below, pp. 212–13.

in the past became part of their hard-won identity as professional historians.

Fustel's plea was a culmination, not a beginning. For at least two generations, historians had fostered the feeling that they possessed the past; the most sensitive and histrionic among them acted as though the past possessed them. Augustin Thierry furnishes one graphic early instance. In 1827, in his *Lettres sur l'histoire de France,* eulogizing the bourgeois of medieval Laon, he wondered whether—which is to say, hoped that—readers would share his fellow feeling for the "obscure names of these outlaws of the twelfth century" he had just recited. "I cannot keep myself from rereading them and pronouncing them several times as if they should reveal to me the secret of what the men who bore them felt and desired seven hundred years ago."[21] Thus a magical surrender to the past might restore a long-vanished inner world to life, for historians and their readers alike.

Not all historians identified themselves quite so fiercely with the sweep of the past. But all of them defended their craft as a privileged transmitter of human experience to generation after generation. They exercised their imagination, free and disciplined at the same time, to stretch their lives into far-away centuries. Small things reminded them of large ones. "I am no sooner in the streets," Macaulay said in 1831, already an accomplished essayist, "than I am in Greece, in Rome, in the midst of the French Revolution. Precision in dates, the day or hour in which a man was born or died, becomes absolutely necessary. A slight fact, a sentence, a word, are of importance in my romance. Pepys' Diary formed almost inexhaustible food for my fancy. I seem to know every inch of Whitehall," and he meant the Whitehall not of the early nineteenth but of the late seventeenth century.[22]

Around the same time, in a more mystical vein, Jules Michelet, for whom the writing of history was a feast of rhetorical self-indulgence, worked this vein as well. Contemplating the French Revolution, he engaged in a gripping dialogue with himself. "I interrogate myself about my teaching, about my history and its all-powerful interpreter, the spirit of the Revolution." Not content with being a mere listener, he appointed himself Clio's ventriloquist: "Living spirit of France, where shall I seize you if not within myself?" In his diary, he spoke a little despairingly about the "impossible ideal of identification," but, vibrating to importunate echoes from bygone times, he labored heroically to attain that ideal as he became in turn the Spirit of the Revolution, the People, his beloved France.[23]

With his feverish, almost hypnotic prose, Michelet more visibly than most of his colleagues tried to transmit his identification with the past to a general public. Literary histories, in sharp distinction to the monographs that Trevelyan feared but like the biographies they so closely resembled, solicited their readers to take heroes and heroines as their models or, at the most extravagant, to usurp their place. In heady moments, readers of history were Luther nailing the ninety-five theses to the church door at Wittenberg or Napoleon routing the Allies at Austerlitz. More modestly, they could turn themselves into humbler actors on the historical stage, reexperiencing the past as imagined eyewitnesses as they crossed the moat with other brave assailants to conquer the Bastille or joined a crowd to weep at King Charles I's martyrdom. To *be* the historic figure, to be *like* the historic figure, to *love* the historic figure: these were the ways that well-written nineteenth-century histories could make their audiences feel. For the most part, of course, presuming the reader to be sane, these fantasies were playful enough. Mundane reality intervened to restore distance. But the temporary adoption of a historic role remained enjoyable at the same time that it supplied information or confirmed opinions.

Discriminating readers, though, soon discovered that identification could be a trap no less than an opportunity. Motley is a splendid instance of this fortunate failure—fortunate, that is to say, for sales. He wrote his *Rise of the Dutch Republic* vividly aware and not a little proud of his identification with the Dutch past. An independently wealthy and well-connected Boston Brahmin, he went to Europe in 1851 with two novels and a handful of essays to his credit, traveling from archive to archive. During four years of intensive reading and drafting, he steeped himself in the past of the country he so extravagantly admired. Occupied "ten hours a day," he wrote in May 1852 from Dresden, he consorted "with folks who lived three centuries ago."[24]

By the time he reached Brussels in the late fall of 1853, Motley's rapport had grown more intimate still. The magnificent Grande Place, dominated by the Hôtel de Ville, gripped him with thrilling associations. "I haunt this place because it is my scene, my theatre. Here were enacted so many deep tragedies, so many stately dramas, and even so many farces, which have been familiar to me so long, that I have got to imagine myself invested with a kind of property in the place." True, "with the present generation I am not familiar. *En revanche* the dead men of the place are my intimate friends," so that "any ghost that ever flits by night across the moonlit square is at once hailed by me as a man and a brother. I call him by his Christian name at once." In short, he was burying himself "in the past ages," imagining himself "really a contemporary of the fellows" he was writing about.[25] Living with the intrepid Dutch rebels who had defied the might of Spain was a heartening experience. Then, and all his life, Motley longed for his "beloved sixteenth century."[26]

Unwittingly, though, Motley documents the risks of identification as much as its promise. When, writing the third volume of the sequel, the *History of the United Netherlands,* he reached the Spanish king's death in 1598, he savored the moment with unholy joy. "I had the pleasure of killing Philip II. a few weeks

ago," he wrote his daughter Lily, "and didn't I serve him out in his obituary."[27]
Motley used his pen, in short, as a dagger to revenge himself on the enemies of
reason, progress, and humanity. Not surprisingly, his history dwells on carnage
with a righteous indignation that looks like disguised, no doubt unconscious,
pleasure. The blood lust of the Spanish regents and commanders, their sadism
masquerading as severity, the inhumanity of the Spanish troops carrying out
their masters' instructions and in chilling episodes of rapine and murder exceed-
ing them, supply Motley with some of his most lovingly sculpted pages. Identification could serve aggression no less than insight.

His aggressive identifications emerge most pointedly in his character
sketches. Motley confronted William of Orange with Philip II of Spain as the
incarnations of conflicting principles. He was not just rehearsing a rhetorical
device; Motley designed his set pieces, once much admired, to make larger
points, delineating his protagonists with broad strokes down to trivial, though
in his judgment revealing, details of appearance. Did not features speak of the
inner person? Sketching Margaret of Parma, Philip's half sister and from 1559
regent of the Spanish Netherlands, Motley took care to mention her virile
appearance, including "the famous mustache upon her upper lip."[28] This was
intended not as a casual sneer but as a clue to character, somehow emblematic
of the Machiavellian deviousness she had learned from the Jesuits.

Motley's Philip II was no better. The antithesis of his hero, William the
Silent—accomplished linguist, delightful companion, eloquent speaker, discreet listener, unsurpassed leader—the Spanish king's mind was "incredibly
small," his talents "very much below mediocrity." A slave to protocol, he was
"prolix with his pen, not from affluence, but from paucity of ideas," a man
"grossly licentious" whose "chief amusement" was "to issue forth at night
disguised, that he might indulge himself in the common haunts of vice."[29]
Worst of all, he was a bigot brimming with rancorous hostility to the heretic, a
fiend of operatic dimensions. We have observed Motley before this: as we saw
just a moment ago, he hounded Philip II with implacable hatred. No one can
legitimately deny Motley's right to be called a diligent, even exhaustive scholar.
But much of his popularity rested on his ability to allay all doubts about just
who were the heroes and who the villains in his tale. Like popular novelists of
Victorian times, historians who simplified the complicated and did so skillfully
could count on the gratitude of the reading public, a gratitude attesting to the
boundaries that average bourgeois taste was reluctant to cross.* Motley's more
discriminating fellows mustered more nuanced responses to human nature than

*For the popular novelists, see below, pp. 225–37.

this, but they were rarely to be found among the best-sellers of their day.

Motley shared his grand simplicities with other successful historians. Reread-ing Macaulay's *History of England,* John Morley protested: "This," he sternly confided to his diary, "is not the way in which things happen." Such amateur-ish line drawings betrayed a supreme failure of insight: "Macaulay, great though he was, did not find his way to the indwelling man of many of his figures."[30] If Macaulay was open to this criticism, Motley was far more so. A man with a message and a mission, he did not divorce his self from his conclusions, and his moralizing drove him to expand his identification from the past to the present. He saw history as a duel between good and evil: between freedom and slavery, reason and superstition, the modern and the medieval world. And he was convinced that the historian who recognizes this essential truth about the past must give his all in the war for virtue, and make a difference to his readers' political understanding: "If ten people in the world hate despotism a little more and love civil and religious liberty a little better in consequence of what I have written, I shall be satisfied."*

Nor did his commitment to freedom exhaust Motley's political agenda. Un-fortunately, he believed, virtue was not yet secure. The Dutch revolt had been the opening act in a history play still on the boards: the Glorious Revolution had constituted its second act and the American Revolution the third, but the denouement was still in doubt. For Motley, an impassioned abolitionist, the American Civil War was a "sacred conflict." Hence William of Orange was the spiritual ancestor of George Washington and, what is more, of Abraham Lin-coln: Motley's letters of the Civil War period attest to his conviction that what the Dutch statesman had begun, the American president must complete.[31] It is ironic: Motley was a considerable scholar and a satisfying stylist, but the suspi-cion will not down that his political agenda, which opened him to the criticism of his peers, was precisely the quality that commended him to the mass of his readers.† After all, the most conspicuous drawback of scientific histories was

---

*Motley to Christina Forbes, January 4, 1854, *John Lothrop Motley and His Family: Further Letters and Records,* ed. Susan St. John Mildmay (1910), 42. "All I care for," he writes in the same letter, hard at work on his masterpiece, "if my book does ever get into print, is that it may do some good as a picture of the most diabolical tyranny, which was ever permitted to be exercised, and of a free commonwealth which was absolutely forced into existence and self-defence."

†Motley's work encountered expert objections from the start; the vogue for *The Rise of the Dutch Republic* exhibited popular appetites more than professional endorsement. His vision of the past impelled Motley's contemporary Robert Fruin, most highly respected among Dutch histori-ans specializing in the "Eighty Years War," to publish a devastating, though courteous, pamphlet-length refutation. And William Prescott, the seasoned student of sixteenth-century Spain, even

that they rejected identifications. It took a specialized taste not to yawn at a study of coal production in Upper Silesia or of railroad management in the suburbs of Paris. Only colleagues could love a historical monograph.

5. Ranke

For the student of Victorian history writing, Ranke is a monument to pause over. He was the most admired, most quoted, most imitated professional historian of the century. Even his critics acknowledged his unmatched authority.[1] Nor was he the property of the historical craft alone: Ranke was a national treasure. Thousands who never read a line of his fifty-odd volumes knew his name and, roughly, what he stood for: objectivity. He lived in a glare of publicity: in his ninety years he collected scores of honorary degrees, memberships in learned associations across the Western world, decorations from royal houses, sumptuous celebrations of birthdays and anniversaries, honorary citizenship of his adopted city, Berlin. A formal portrait shows him decked out with important medals.

Ranke's conservatism, idealization of the state, and anxiety over the socialist menace placed him solidly among the bulk of the German *Bürgertum;* abroad, where his politics were largely irrelevant, his professional ideal, whether correctly understood or not, was hailed as exemplary. When, in 1895, the American Historical Association took note of his hundredth birthday, Professor Edward G. Bourne of Yale, the secretary reported, "gave an appreciative account of the critical methods of Leopold von Ranke who had such a profound influence upon modern students of history."[2] Foreign orators, even in France, had been saying the same thing for some years.

At home with princes, Ranke was, to be sure, no ordinary bourgeois. Yet his suave subservience to those who counted—King Maximilian II of Bavaria, King Friedrich Wilhelm IV of Prussia, well-placed aristocrats who could grant him access to archives or a leave for yet another research trip abroad—was not flattery for the sake of social status but for service to Clio. Though Leopold *von* Ranke from 1865, he incorporated, and never abandoned, the bourgeois virtues of diligence, purposefulness, accuracy, the primacy of work.

Quite as much to the point, Ranke's theory and practice of history illuminate

---

though he shared Motley's hostility to Roman Catholicism, objected that he had "laid it on Philip rather hard," and made William of Orange his idol: "You are looking through a pair of Dutch spectacles." Prescott to Motley, April 28, 1856, *The Correspondence of John Lothrop Motley, D. L. C.,* ed. George William Curtis, 2 vols. (1889), I, 192.

the issues that characterized, often troubled, the nineteenth-century pilgrimage to the past: the involvement with earlier ages facing the pressure of current politics, the tug of war between national and cosmopolitan perspectives, the strains between style and substance, all tensions that Ranke worked, more successfully than many, to resolve. He scattered clues to his mind in his books, supplemented by halting poems and letters eloquent with emotion. His impact on the inner life of his readers is harder to assess; Ranke's doctoral students, some of them to grow into eminent historians in their own right, carried the master's word to universities at home and abroad. He was, as Bourne put it, a teacher of teachers.[3]

Granted, his histories of England, France, and Prussia in the early modern period, though brilliantly written and cunningly dramatic, never could rival the sales of a Macaulay or a Motley. Still, they found their readers: his *Reformation,* first published in six volumes from 1839 to 1847, reached its eighth edition in 1909. And his best-selling history of the popes made him almost literally a household word: *Die römischen Päpste in den letzten vier Jahrhunderten* had gone into eight editions by 1885, the year before Ranke's death, and was widely translated: there were no fewer than five English versions of the *Popes,* and each went into printing after printing.

Ranke's program envisioned, and his procedure largely enacted, a delicate mixture of engagement and detachment. He controlled his identifications, absorbing the feelings, the values, the beliefs of distant ages, with scholarly and critical reserve. "Every epoch is immediate to God," thus his famous dictum, "and its value in no way depends on what it has produced, but in its existence itself, in its own self."[4] Rounded out with his equally famous stipulation that he was limiting himself to saying "only how it had really been," this is the supreme slogan of the historicist school he founded, the school that stresses the import of seeing the past not as it appears through the eyes of the present but as it appeared to itself.

Ranke's historicism, then, mixed ambition with modesty. His declaration that he was *only* undertaking to discover historical actuality, seeing it as close to God as his own time, was less a claim than a disclaimer. He proposed to enter the past humbly, hat in hand, that he might faithfully transmit the messages he had learned to decipher. This empathy required him to strip away current interests and private preferences to confront early modern France or England burdened with as little baggage as possible. Whether the past under the scholar's gaze proved different from the present or similar to it, working historians must sacrifice their identity. They must remain "remote from all contemporary politics."[5] Once he spoke of *Selbstauslöschung*—self-obliteration.

This self-denying prescription raised respectful questions among Ranke's peers. As we have seen, Thierry with his twelfth-century outlaws or Sybel with his modern Prussians did not think that their political commitments had kept them from identifying themselves with the past. But, unable to topple Ranke from his pedestal, the vast majority of his colleagues remained awestruck at his gifts and his productivity. He was not quite the lonely pioneer his acolytes made him out to be, but he remained the conquistador who had opened a new world.[6] Even Lord Acton, the stern conscience of his profession, canonized Ranke as "the representative of the age which instituted the modern study of History. He taught it to be critical, to be colourless, and to be new. We meet him at every step, and he has done more for us than any other man." Acton meant "colorless" as a compliment. "He decided effectually to repress the poet, the patriot, the religious or political partisan, to sustain no cause, to banish himself from his books, and to write nothing that would gratify his own feelings or disclose his private convictions."[7]

Lacking false shame, Ranke would have welcomed this accolade; he never doubted that he had succeeded in banishing himself from his books. No one would know, he once boasted, whether he had written the history of the modern papacy for or against it. What cynics might take as a source of subjective judgments was, for Ranke, the principal ground of scientific precision. He saw the impartial and impassioned investigation of the past as a religious duty; precisely his self-imposed calling as a secular priest made his devout invasion of earlier centuries so productive. He was bearing witness.

Ranke's theology of history was Lutheranism by other means. Born in 1795 in a small Thuringian town to devout parents who had expected him to enter the ministry, he deviated first into classical philology and then into the study of history. He sought God in the traces he had planted in human affairs across the centuries.[8] Steeped in the German romantics, Ranke discovered God not through special providences but in the rise of empires, the clashes of nations, the careers of great men. The documented past was for Ranke "an eternal living and moving, a singing and rejoicing in God's plenty, a blessed having, holding, certainty." Teaching was "a remembering, a legend of God from the present and from time."[9] Thus reinterpreting Lutheranism and romanticism, Ranke retained his respect for the inwardness of great figures and for his responses to them. Crucial for his conversion to history was his discovery that he found it "more beautiful" than Sir Walter Scott's novels. A universal favorite with historians of the age and the young Ranke, Scott served him as a ladder to the real thing, the historical truth.[10]

None of this makes Ranke a covert unbeliever. "God dwells, lives, is manifest in all history," he told his devout brother Heinrich in a well-known letter of 1820. "Every act gives witness of him, every moment preaches his name, but most of all, I think, in the great connections of history. There he stands, like a holy hieroglyphic." This glimpse of God's sacred writing virtually compelled him to take up history. "I still hope for a life that is childlike"—a wish that, we have seen, pervades nineteenth-century German culture—"secure, active, without doubt," he wrote later that year.[11] These were more than youthful outpourings. "I cannot get rid of my old theological tendencies," he told his brother Heinrich in 1833. Nor did he ever get rid of them altogether: he continued to muse on his craft with the religious vocabulary natural to him from childhood. "I still think," he noted in the late 1830s, "ignorance, too, is original sin." In contrast, "blessedness would consist in full insight."[12] That this blessedness included God's mercy to him was no argument against it. If being an instrument in such hands involved tangible rewards, Ranke accepted them as a sign that the divinity was taking care of its devoted interpreter.*

Some of Ranke's most authoritative readers found this brand of devotion not very devout. Lord Acton judged him "ignorant of the power of religious senti-ments" and "unable to give them their due place in the lives of others."[13] This is a startling charge against a self-proclaimed servant of God, startling but reveal-ing: it suggests that, even in the most professional historian, identifications are likely to be imperfect and may clash with one another. Ranke's familiar com-merce with the past, wholehearted as it was, stopped short at the edge of his horizon. That is what Acton meant when he diagnosed Ranke's concentration on the sixteenth to the eighteenth century, the age of state making, as showing his inability to enter into the religious mind of the Middle Ages. Ranke "is a fair weather historian, of rise and progress, not of decline and fall."[14]

This telling critique reaches a principal source of Ranke's power over the German public, whether dreaming, before 1871, of a unified country or, after that date, basking in it: his tacit timeliness lent its sentiments scholarly support.

---

*This sounds self-serving, but Ranke was apparently perfectly sincere. His career was a parade of triumphs: his first book had secured him an appointment at the University of Berlin in 1825, translated into a professor's chair only eleven years later. By that time, he had spent more than three years abroad, doing archival research. From then on, his massive histories brought him international acclaim. But he persistently professed resignation before God's decrees. To accept the pleasing dividends of divine favor was not hubris. "What would providence be if it did not care for the individual too!" he wrote his brother Ferdinand in 1843. "That we are thought by an eternal thought, not transitory like the falling leaf of autumn, that we belong to the essence of things—that is the sum of all religion." Ranke to Ferdinand Ranke, July 10 [1843], *Neue Briefe,* ed. Bernhard Hoeft and Hans Herzfeld (1949), 299. As a very famous, very old man looking back on his worldly success, he observed that Prince Metternich had earned "immortal merit" by granting him access to the Austrian archives. "Diktat vom November 1885," *Sämmtliche Werke,* 54 vols. in 42 (2nd and 3rd eds., 1868–90), LIII–LIV, 63.

No wonder that Ranke gave Acton abundant reasons for concern. "Great nations and states," Ranke wrote in his *Französische Geschichte,* "have a double vocation, a national and a world-historical one."[15] Though they struggle for survival under the compendious umbrella of universal history, to which Ranke devoted his last years, the great powers remain the most distinct expression of the divine scheme for humanity. That is why the age of their emergence was Ranke's emotional home. His assertion that every epoch is immediate to God could not conceal distinct preferences: some epochs seemed more immediate to God than others. Ranke's eye for power reduced his perception of the shaping role of economic forces and internal social strains; his celebrated doctrine that foreign affairs have primacy over domestic affairs is typical of him. It endorsed success. In Ranke's historical creed, the first shall be first.

Ranke made this point of view easy on himself by visualizing great states as compound persons, much like Hobbes's Leviathan. In a much quoted dialogue on politics published in 1836, he asserted that a state is never merely a subdivision of some general categories but a living entity, "an individual." States are "original creations of the human mind—I might say, thoughts of God."[16] In this Rankean scheme, conflict is inescapable, even desirable; good comes of evil; enemies are valuable sparring partners to keep a nation's energies at high pitch. Years before Darwin, Ranke advocated a kind of historical Darwinism: liberals, socialists, democrats, and other modern troublemakers are essential for historic struggles but scarcely equipped to rule. Ranke, in short, made room for suffering in his historical world, but not for tragedy. All will be well, order will prevail. Would God otherwise think the great states as his thoughts? The Mensheviks of history, the losers, played their part for Ranke largely as foils.

But though patriots could use Ranke as an agent for German self-satisfaction, he was no simple apologist for past victors and present power holders. If power stood at one pole of his professional credo, service stood at the other and it was not necessarily service *to* power. Unable to rise above, or to reconcile, his complex identifications—good German, tough-minded conservative, exemplary historicist with a vision that transcended the individual nation-state—kept him from achieving his ideal of speaking for history unhampered by the blinkers of unconscious wishes and conscious predilections. It is arguable that he might have done the past even more justice than he did if his German peers had helped him trace the boundaries of his insights. Instead, they carped at him for not being political enough: the criticism he got he could not use, and the criticism he could have used he did not get. Still, he remained a fanatic for the truth about the past as he labored to make himself the passive receptacle of its essential message.

A privileged instrument for securing authentic identifications with the past, one that Ranke pioneered and employed as deftly as anyone, was the search for documents. "Everything hangs together," he declared in his history of England, "the critical study of authentic sources, an unbiased understanding, an objective narration—the aim is to bring the whole truth to life."[17] For him as for others, scholarship was a defense against the grip of emotions on judgment. As we have observed before, the philosophers and poets have long known that we see what we seek, but nineteenth-century historians thought that they had discovered a sure antidote to this professional malady: the study of unmediated testimony.* One might try to dismantle the screens obscuring the past through a critical reading of one's colleagues' work and cultivating one's trained superego. But the specific against arbitrariness and partisanship by which historians of the age set the greatest store was the document. Only the gems that archives yield, Ranke insisted, would permit historians to "return to the most pristine communications," allow them to attain "pure perception."[18]

Ranke was explicit about the therapeutic function of primary sources: "Every age and its dominant direction makes history its own, and transfers its ideas to it. Praise and blame are dealt out accordingly. And that drags along until we can hardly recognize the thing itself. Then nothing can help but a return to the most pristine reports." Autopsy—seeing for oneself—was the watchword. Let so ravenous a reader as Edward Gibbon depend on printed materials; Ranke would comb libraries and attics to gratify what he affectionately described as his "archival curiosity." Despising the lamentable "materialism" and the "emptiness" of Enlightenment historians, Ranke underscored his distance from his predecessors by pointing with visible pride to his own explorations. In the prefaces to his major histories, each of them a substantial multivolume publication, he enumerated the repositories he had conquered. Again and again, he had been the first to unlock the gates. "The archive here," he wrote his brother Ferdinand from Berlin in 1836, after the authorities had permitted him to consult holdings in royal ministries, "is still wholly virgin. I am longing for the moment when I gain admittance to her, to make her my declaration of love, whether she is pretty or not."[19]

The metaphor playfully hints at the emotional sources of Ranke's lust for the unprinted and the unseen; his was a consuming gluttony of the mind. In the preface to the first volume of his *Deutsche Geschichte im Zeitalter der Reformation* of 1839, a favorite with the discriminating Burckhardt, he listed holdings in

---

*Bacon had already noted that "numberless" are the ways, "and sometimes imperceptible, in which the affections colour and infect the understanding."

Frankfurt, Berlin, Dresden, Weimar, Dessau, Vienna, Venice, Rome, and Florence, and detailed the plunder they yielded. "I see the time approaching," he concluded buoyantly, "when we will no longer found modern history on reports, not even on those of contemporary historians, except in so far as they possessed some original knowledge, let alone on still more derivative treatments, but on the narratives of eyewitnesses and the most authentic, most immediate documents."[20] He was never in favor of writing an eleventh book out of ten others.

Credulity was not one of Ranke's flaws; he knew the risks that material, even dating from distant times, holds for the investigator. It may be a forgery; it is often contaminated by interpolations; it may, self-serving or servile, tell an incomplete and one-sided story.[21] All the more reason to consult and, if possible, exhaust all the sources. The first law was access, and Ranke, as we know, deployed his academic, aristocratic, and diplomatic connections to secure entry to jealously guarded bundles of correspondence, secret dispatches of envoys, or forgotten pamphlets.

None of Ranke's letters breathe a purer visceral pleasure than those announcing one discovery after another. Documents were his booty, "hitherto wholly neglected sources for modern history" his obsession.[22] The gleaming word "treasures—*Schätze*" punctuated the bulletins he sent home to his family, his friends, his superiors recording his finds.[23] Even while he was making plans for a rare visit to his brothers in the provinces, he inquired whether a local aristocrat might not have some interesting papers: "Just a fleeting thought! But once I am with you, I might as well take a look, too."[24] As he relished the confidential memoranda that Venice's ambassadors had sent home from across European capitals, candid and well-informed reports that historians had left unexplored, he grandly called himself the Columbus of the *relazioni*.[25]

This appetite for direct experience of what had been inspired other voyagers to the past trailing in the wake of Ranke's caravel. Especially after mid-century, readers of history could count on ritual prefaces virtually guaranteeing that what followed rested on hard-won original materials. Macaulay reassured his audience that once he had in the two opening chapters rushed across English history at great speed and with few footnotes, he would "carefully indicate the sources" of his information, and it appears that this tireless traveler across the English landscape and collector of out-of-the-way tidbits drew on far more evidence for his *History of England* than his predecessors had ever done.

When Macaulay made his pledge around mid-century, his attitude was becoming representative of the profession. Fustel de Coulanges was speaking as a good Rankean when he held that only the "conscientious and critical study of

original texts" would permit his profession to achieve "truly scientific certainty."[26] The aesthete Burckhardt, as he became certain of his vocation, found
himself growing "quite prosaic in the investigation of past times." In 1860,
sending a friend his just-published *Renaissance in Italien,* he told him, "One
word of praise I would like to hear from you, namely that the author has
energetically resisted many opportunities to let his imagination roam freely and
has firmly held fast to the testimony of the sources."[27] One public result of such
scholarly covetousness was that it quieted serious readers' skepticism. Diligently
tracing, fairly digesting, and scrupulously weighing documents was the corrective action that the historian's reality principle could take against his pleasure
principle.

We can surprise the impact of archival research on historical knowledge in
Tocqueville's preface to *L'Ancien Régime et la Révolution.* The more closely he
studied authentic documents to "strike to the heart" of eighteenth-century
France, he reports, the more he became persuaded of "innumerable resemblances between the France of that period and nineteenth-century France."
The revolutionaries, so insistent that they had made everything new, had in fact
taken over far more from their detested predecessors than they knew. Tocqueville arrived at this unexpected insight, radically different from the view of
other historians, he insisted, by studying the *cahiers* of grievances, that "swan
song" of the Old Regime, drawn up in early 1789 for the Estates General, the
frank and revealing manuscripts of the interior ministry, and the records left by
the intendancy of Tours. Tocqueville's self-advertisement implied a reproach
against his competitors: less deeply immersed in the past than he, they had
missed some fundamental truths about Old Regime France.

Yet, by and large, his fellow historians were diligent enough. In the preface
to his *Römische Geschichte,* Mommsen, whose mastery and scrupulousness no
one dared question, cautioned his readers that the evidence for the earliest
centuries of Rome was so fragmentary that much must remain conjectural even
after the most strenuous efforts—an implicit invitation to trust to his guidance
in periods where the material was more complete and more perspicuous. Parkman, for his part, repeatedly took the trouble in his seven-volume *France and
England in North America* to emphasize that his work was "founded on original
documents" alone. In the preface to *Montcalm and Wolfe,* published in 1884, we
read that "a very large amount of unpublished material has been used in its
preparation, consisting for the most part of documents copied from the archives
and libraries of France and England," followed by an exhaustive accounting.
The "statements of secondary writers," he wrote in *A Half-Century of Conflict* of
1892, "have been accepted only when found to conform to the evidence of
contemporaries, whose writings have been sifted and collated with the greatest

care."[28] Like other American historians, Parkman had absorbed the lessons of Ranke well.

To what effect all this straining for empathy, all this grubbing in dusty repositories? A study of the nineteenth century's inner life cannot evade the question just how its historians perceived human nature as they worked to enter and appropriate the past. We have seen that the responses to historical writings, ranging from entertainment to chauvinism, were refreshingly varied but hardly mysterious. In contrast, the historians' way with past minds is more elusive, largely because they so rarely reflected about it systematically. They were no doubt committed to sounding the hidden life of their subjects. In the 1850s, Mommsen took satisfaction in having laid bare the "innermost characteristic feature" of that epochal figure Julius Caesar.* And Burckhardt proposed the study of "wishes and presuppositions" to permit the historian to reach the heart of the past.[29] But the technical resources at their command were scanty enough; theirs were the means available to dilettantes. "National character, the genius of a people," wrote the great English medievalist F. W. Maitland a little quizzically in 1901, "is a wonder-working spirit which stands at the beck and call of every historian."[30]

Historians started being psychologists when Thucydides probed the irrational behavior of the Athenians during the plague that struck their city, or their drive to power. True, during the more than thousand years of undisputed Christian dominance, chroniclers had left the field of human nature largely uncultivated. Devout historians would have thought it impious to guess at the designs of God beyond recognizing his hand in the careers of great movements and the lives of great men. The religious drama written and directed by providence in which men and women were models of piety or of wickedness, or repentant sinners struggling to find salvation, left no room for secular psycho-

---

*Mommsen, *Römische Geschichte,* 3 vols. (1856; 2nd ed., 1856), III, 442. Mommsen's own character sketches remain controversial. His admiration for Caesar—though not for Caesarism— was proverbial. Caesar was the only creative genius Rome ever produced. Endowed with a character as firm and flexible as steel, with stunning oratorical and literary gifts, military and diplomatic skills, patience and decisiveness, clarity of purpose and long-range vision, he could best athletes, and outdo all others with his unrivaled memory. A thoroughgoing realist, he knew what Rome needed and was the man to supply it. Not without a certain vanity, he concealed his balding pate beneath a laurel wreath and triumphantly pursued amorous adventures all his life. Yet this incomparable statesman, living in a cruel, vindictive, and self-serving time, was generous to his enemies and, in his own way, a good son and husband. Mommsen found the core of Caesar's being in the propitious interaction of two, only apparently incompatible, traits: passion and sobriety. "It goes without saying that Caesar was a passionate man, for without passion there is no genius, but his passion was never more powerful than he." See ibid., 444–47 passim.

logical investigations. But the historians of the Enlightenment, making their home in a universe without miracles, had once again read minds to uncover the mixed motives driving monarchs, statesmen, military and religious leaders, martyrs and mobs, sometimes—witness Gibbon—with stunning finesse. They had dusted off ancient models, notably Thucydides and Tacitus, to make their diagnoses, yet another eighteenth-century legacy the nineteenth century would adopt.[31] While the discipline of psychology was becoming increasingly available, it did not figure among the auxiliary disciplines that Victorian historians chose to deploy.

Hence the German cultural historian Karl Lamprecht, who toward the end of the century declared social psychology the essential foundation of historical understanding, was an embattled maverick. And Hippolyte Taine, whose historical world was far more mental than physical? Man, he wrote, savoring the oxymoron, is a "spiritual machine," and this meant, he flatly asserted, that history is simply applied psychology. Persuaded, much like Balzac, that a *faculté maîtresse* shapes every individual's life, Taine offered historians a heady agenda. The "mass of faculties and feelings" that constitute the inner man had generated a "new subject matter" for historical investigation; interpreting "past sensations" had given the historical discipline, Taine proudly noted, a second birth in his time.* But Taine was a philosopher, psychologist, and literary critic who had come to writing the history of modern France late, under the impress of his country's disastrous defeat of 1870, and he had no disciples. Far more typical of the professional mood was Leslie Stephen's comfortable dictum: "A little analysis of motive may be necessary here and there: when, for example, your hero has put his hand in somebody's pocket and you have to demonstrate that his conduct was due to sheer absence of mind. But you must always remember that a single concrete fact, or a saying into which a man has put his whole soul, is worth pages of psychological analysis."[32]

Predictably, then, historians did not present a united front on the matter of mind. Ranke and his school persisted in holding that identifications and archive hounding were the royal road to good history. But as the scientific ideology gained converts in the profession, the notion that the past is subject to ascertainable laws grew more popular and generated some extravagant claims. When, late in the 1850s, H. T. Buckle sought to establish the laws that had governed

---

*Taine, "Introduction," *Histoire de la littérature anglaise,* 5 vols. (1864), I, xi–xxii passim. "When you observe the visible man, what do you look for?" he asked. "The invisible man. Those words that enter your ears, those gestures, those motions of the head, those garments, those visible actions and deeds of every sort are merely expressions for you; something expresses itself: a soul. There is an inner man concealed beneath the outer man, and the second simply reveals the first." Ibid., xi.

the course of the past, he encountered spirited resistance, but mainly because his generalizations seemed too rigid and too sweeping. In 1862, Fustel de Cou-langes could say in his inaugural lecture at Strasbourg, without meeting any protest, "History is, and ought to be, a science." And his countryman Taine, the most extreme of positivists, was secure in his faith that humans, as part of nature, obey physical laws and hence are proper material for a natural science of history. Perhaps only his English counterpart Buckle and his dour American admirer Henry Adams were quite so extravagant in their obsession with scien-tific determinism.* Hence in 1867 it was no longer eccentric for John Morley to announce that "the business of the scientific historian is to discover the laws" of historical causation, "a process for which a precise and strictly scientific method has been laid down."[33] Frederick York Powell, Regius Professor of Modern History at Oxford around the turn of the century, put the case tersely: "The method of history is not different from the method of physical sciences."[34] Bury's inaugural lecture at Cambridge might be offensive to the lovers of the muse Clio, but it was no innovation.[35]

This brave materialist talk, though, far outdistanced the faith of most histori-ans in the science of memory. Many, we know, recognized that if the histori-ans' craft is indeed a science, it is a very peculiar one, and the Rankeans took full advantage of the fact. Unlike chemists or geologists, historical scholars find themselves and their subject matter to be of the same clay; historians are humans studying other humans. This makes the distance necessary to scientific detach-ment virtually impossible to sustain and the results of investigations starkly different, perhaps in kind, from the laws that are the business of the natural scientist. Indeed, critics complained that heedless scientific historians misdiag-nosed the nature of their discipline and boasted about their methods with an insouciance that betrayed a lamentable ignorance of how natural scientists actu-ally work. A potent slogan seemed to have usurped the place of thoughtful reflection.

Yet it proved, oddly enough, a hidden strength of the historians that precise definitions were not of burning interest to them. A few philosophy-minded practitioners apart, they were reluctant to raise knotty questions of method, let alone epistemology. Rather, as hardworking artisans, they saved historiograph-ical musings for introductory handbooks, reminiscent moments, or festive oc-casions. Ranke, for one, was given to improvising as he introduced historio-graphical reflections into his lectures and prefaces. The overwhelming impulse among historians, as they dug in the archives or wrote at their desks, was to

---

*Taine notoriously believed that "vice and virtue are products like vitriol and sugar." "Intro-duction," *Histoire de la littérature anglaise,* 5 vols. (1864), I, xi.

disregard philosophy, even their own: the common sense they cultivated was rarely free of a certain philistinism. The main point was to get the past right. Francis Parkman mirrored this dominant attitude when he wrote a little defiantly in 1877, "It will, I think be clear to an impartial reader that [my] story is told, not in the interest of any race or nationality, but simply in that of historical truth."[36] How indisputable the truths that historians might discover was a more intractable question. The answer depended not so much on the existence of the past—this, unlike some modern critics, they took for granted—as on the degree of its interpreters' inner freedom from the pressures assailing them from society and themselves.

We have observed that Ranke, the teacher of teachers, saw no conflict between history as art and history as science. He certainly did not object to unearthing facts, or to discovering regular patterns in the past. But like nineteenth-century biographers who trusted the testimony of letters and diary entries to provide the most reliable access to their subject, Ranke never doubted, we saw, that direct testimony uncontaminated by secondary accounts was the best guarantee of authenticity. The historian seizes the past by confronting, absorbing, and interpreting its survivals. For Ranke, the key term was "understanding," which meant working through material as he aimed at a secure interpretation.[37] He spoke of "comprehending its essence" as his goal.[38] In the end, for all but the most infatuated scientist among historians, the success or failure of the attempt to understand the mind of the past remained an individual issue, depending far less on esoteric methodology than on such unfathomable qualities as good sense, worldly experience, and mature wisdom. In 1877, when he was eighty-three and, though his eyesight was dimming, still working hard, Ranke noted in his diary that "a historian must grow old, not solely because of the immeasurable extent of his studies necessitated by insight into historical developments, but also because of the changes of circumstances that occur in a long life."[39]

But old or young, Ranke in his work developed a consistent view of the mind in history. It is telling that he should include "personal motivations" among the elements he thought necessary to "a completely true history."[40] It is just as telling that his psychology was, conveniently for his historical vision, a social psychology. Visualizing states as individuals, he thought of individuals, though each the sole center of experience, as in large measure social products. In a striking metaphor, he likened persons to trees that draw their strength less from their soil than from their surroundings, from "air and light, wind and weather."[41] It is only when the individual, no matter how great, is in tune with the drift of his age that he can make history. Ranke's lovingly detailed character sketches of world-historical personages like Luther, Richelieu, and Frederick the Great offer no exceptions to this rule. They are, in his pages, marvels of energy, will power, and single-mindedness. But, to make history, they must appear on the scene at the right moment. The way for them must have been prepared, and, Ranke believed, the world at once fosters and tests them in times of crisis, for those are the times that develop great personalities. "It is only in a storm that the helmsman proves himself."[42]

In the running commentaries on human nature at work that punctuate his recital of events, Ranke fleshed out this sketch, all with the intention of underscoring his view that it is the interplay of large-scale situations and personal responses, of long-range tendencies and moments of opportunity, that makes history. Thus baldly stated, Ranke's psychology sounds banal. But it was a gigantic step away from Carlyle's sense of history as the sum of innumerable biographies, and toward a truly historical psychology. Historians who could do nothing with Ranke's unchanging devotion to a God who thinks the world, an undogmatic Christian faith that underpins every line he wrote, could still work with his psychological perceptions. It was, until after the turn of the century, all they had.

6. Agendas High and Low

The reasons why Victorians read history are anything but mysterious. Secondary school children did because they were told to read it that they might purify their character. Adults could make it serve as a model of conduct for statesmen, a source of gratifying feelings of superiority over lesser nations, a nostalgic evocation of ancestral glories, or proof that one's country had progressed, was progressing, and was bound to progress further. Few nineteenth-century English readers could resist Macaulay's invidious comparisons between their country's condition in the seventeenth century and that in the early Victorian years, all in their own favor.

What is more, and far from negligible, historians could entertain with stylistic felicities: the pointed epigram, the witty observation, the dramatic paragraph, the cunningly told episode lending suspense to a tale whose outcome the reader already knew. The historian as artist could tell stories and paint pictures, and many nineteenth-century historians were artists. Only the hard of heart could withhold the tribute of a tear to the closing sentence of *The Rise of the Dutch Republic*. Motley's hero, William the Silent, has just been assassinated, and the people mourn his passing. Astutely borrowing a contemporary report, Motley concludes, "As long as he lived, he was the guiding-star of a brave nation, and when he died the little children cried in the streets."[1]

Historians could give the nineteenth-century public what it wanted all the more readily because the insidious smuggling of current concerns into presumably objective accounts of the past flourished precisely at the time that the ideal of identification, advertised as a protection against present-mindedness, was riding high. Not that historians intentionally deceived their readers; it was only that too many of them failed to recognize how their blinkers were distorting their judgment because they did not sufficiently distrust them.

The most pressing temptation to partisanship was, of course, politics, including religious politics, for writers and readers of history alike. Historians made their versions of the past palatable by claiming that their own political activities—and many historians were exceedingly active—in no way impaired their impartiality. During the Bourbon Restoration, the French liberal Augustin Thierry, perhaps the most consistent champion of the bourgeoisie the profession produced during the century, rejected the suggestion that partisanship might compromise his search for historical truth. He was only one French historian among many who saw no danger in the kind of "new history" he was writing, allowing him to "paint the men of other ages with the physiognomy of their time, but speak the language of my own." The history of France, which he thought badly in need of reform, presented itself to him "under two aspects, the one scientific and the other political." Doing "science united with patriotism" was the assignment to which he had long devoted his best energies, with no fear of discrediting his findings. Solemnly he declared that devotion to reliable knowledge was more important than material pleasures, more than riches, more than good health itself.[2] His allies, gifted and tendentious historians like François Guizot and Auguste Mignet, as involved in French politics as Thierry, enthusiastically agreed.

So did their equally patriotic counterparts elsewhere. Heinrich von Sybel, an avid advocate of Prussia's preeminent role in German unification and no less avid an admirer of Bismarck, rested secure in the conviction that he had done his duty as a historian. Had he not declared his *Historische Zeitschrift* to be devoted to true method and to science? In the preface to his massive account of the establishment of the German Empire in 1871, he asserted that although at no time had he attempted to deny his "Prussian and National-Liberal convictions," he hoped that the reader would not fail to recognize that he had "striven to acknowledge all the mistakes and blunders" made by his own camp "without palliation." To cap his unapologetic apology, he added that he had "judged the conduct of adversaries justly; to derive, in other words, the motives of their action not from stupidity or wickedness, but to comprehend their entire attitude from historical presuppositions."[3]

Such pronouncements sound naive, even disingenuous. But the ideological

historians should not be dismissed as simply self-deluded. Few of them dis-
counted the roadblocks in the path of scientific history. They hardly expected
an American to speak well of George III, a Roman Catholic to find good words
for Martin Luther, a partisan of the French Revolution to praise the Old Regime. Competent and conscientious historians, they knew, might be hiding
what Lord Acton called "the cloven hoof of party preference."[4] But challenged
on their own ground, they would defend their opinions as justified by unimpeachable evidence, by documents diligently gathered and skeptically read.
Had they detected a prejudice in themselves, they liked to believe, they would
have abandoned their conclusions with no hesitation. Could they, as scientists,
do less?

But if their scientific stature was more hope than reality, even so, in the right
hands, controlled by the right constraints, engagement, even political engagement, could serve as a clue rather than an obstacle to historical insight. Biases,
built-in preferences, early experiences could generate understanding by allowing the historian to see what others, less impassioned, had not seen. "The events
of the last fifty years," wrote Thierry in 1840, "have taught us to understand the
revolutions of the Middle Ages."[5] This was the rather unexpected aid to discovery Gibbon had had in mind when, thinking of his military service, he
recalled that "the captain of the Hampshire grenadiers (the reader may smile)
has not been useless to the historian of the Roman Empire."[6] There was no
need for the reader to smile. Again and again, historians proved that political
vistas were one way of wresting truth from wishes.

Lord Acton had this benefit in mind when he insisted that partisan historians
of the French Revolution had broken through to new perceptions with their
gladiatorial posture. "No man feels the grandeur of the Revolution till he reads
Michelet," he told his students in the 1890s, "or the horror of it without
reading Taine."[7] He summed up the case with customary forthrightness:
"Don't let us utter too much evil of party writers, for we owe them much. If
not honest, they are helpful, as the advocates aid the judge; and they would not
have done so well from the mere inspiration of disinterested veracity. We might
wait long if we watched for the man who knows the whole truth and has the
courage to speak it, who is careful of other interests besides his own, and labours
to satisfy opponents, who can be liberal towards those who have erred, who
have sinned, who have failed, and deal evenly with friend or foe—assuming
that it would be possible for an honest historian to have a friend."[8]

Eduard Bernstein's discovery of the Diggers, that small and interesting clan of
seventeenth-century English communists, is a case in point. A German Social
Democrat in political exile in London in the 1890s, scratching out a scant living
with journalism, Bernstein was enlisted to write a volume in an ambitious

collective history recording the precursors of modern socialism. His assignment: the decades of the English Civil War. At the time that Bernstein was doing his research, the period was prominent on the agenda of English historians. Sober professionals like C. H. Firth and S. R. Gardiner were doing first-rate work editing documents and writing histories as nonpartisan as humanly possible. Nor had they overlooked radical, ideological strands in the heated civil-war debates, giving the Levelers' radical political demands substantial space. But the Diggers had been quite literally invisible until Bernstein found them, and he found them because, looking through Marxist spectacles, he was looking for them.[9]

The perils of such tunnel vision, acute but narrow, are manifest; historians blinded by tendentious fantasies may detect in the past what is only in their minds, or vastly overstate the significance of their discoveries. But this is precisely where discipline—which is to say, self-discipline—had to do its work.[10] We know that humans are in some measure social constructs, partly made up of the multiple identifications that generate class loyalties and social prejudices, attitudes toward work and play, moral and sexual choices, all imports from intrusive, virtually irresistible external impulsions.* The work nineteenth-century historians knew they had to do, then, was to look into themselves, to recognize their preferences, and to overcome or, at best, to tame and utilize them.

This was hard, often ungrateful work. Whatever their private convictions, historians were exposed to indignant moralists, anxious believers, noisy politicians, zealous chauvinists—all pushing them toward idealization and oversimplification. In search of a usable past, Clio's suitors were persistent and importunate. This exposed historians to demands that they relax their strict vocational superego. To be sure, as we have seen, most historians would have scorned any hint that they could ever betray the cause of truth for any incentive whatever. They were by no means so sure about their rivals; in the verbal duels they fought on the lecture platform or in the reviews, they were pleased to discover incorrigible partiality in their adversaries. The ideologist was always the other.†
As they had ever been, then, historians in the nineteenth century, too, were

---

*This is not the newly found insight of a post-Freudian age. "The impressions that the youthful soul receives have their effects on all of the life that follows," wrote Ranke, "and they are not produced by accident. The events of the time, the traditions of family, the ambitions of ancestors, a secret sense of one's own powers, fill the soul with designs and expectations and fantasies and give it a direction that runs through all of life." Quoted in Eugen Guglia, *Leopold von Rankes Leben und Werke* (1893), 5.

†In defense of his great-uncle much attacked for his Whiggish bias, G. M. Trevelyan struck back by observing that "Mommsen and Treitschke, at whose German shrines we have been instructed to sacrifice the traditions of English history, were partisans, the one of Roman, the other

under siege to make themselves into flattering mirrors of their time rather than
unclouded telescopes trained on bygone days. Jacob Burckhardt once said that
history is a record of what one age finds interesting in another. Put more
cynically, it looks as though historians might more likely find interesting what
the age thought flattering in itself.

This should occasion no surprise. Historians were inextricably woven into
the fabric of their culture. Sharing most of their society's dominant perspectives
and many of its prejudices, they found that temptations to act as the slaves rather
than the masters of their audience stemmed not simply from corruptibility but
from something stronger: their own mind-set. "Each age," wrote Frederick
Jackson Turner in 1891, "tries to form its own conception of the past. Each age
writes the history of the past anew with reference to the conditions uppermost
in its own time."[11] Self-serving and, it seemed, self-evident presuppositions—
the inherent superiority of the Anglo-Saxon race, the Manifest Destiny of the
American people, the mission of Russia to the world—proved a far greater
threat to objectivity than venality or timeserving.

Wrestling with their readers and themselves, historians were susceptible,
then, to psychological dispositions, political imperatives, religious doctrines.*
In 1895, launching his monumental collaborative work, the *Cambridge Modern
History,* a tribute to the conviction that history is "a progressive science," Lord
Acton urged his contributors to write their chapters so dispassionately that their
Waterloo would silence disputes by satisfying French and English, German and
Dutch readers alike. In retrospect, and to some even at the time, this reads like a
utopian demand. Not that historians stopped trying for impartiality. A profession working in the critical spirit inherited from the Enlightenment was not
innocent of self-criticism. In the aphorisms Ranke scattered in private notes,
letters, and published writings, he repeatedly worried that present-day concerns
might obscure the face of history. He did not exempt himself from the threat;
the "running current," he wrote his son Otto in 1873, "tries to dominate the

---

of Prussian Caesarism, more blind and bitter than Macaulay was of middle-class Parliamentary
government." "Clio, a Muse," *Clio, a Muse and Other Essays, Literary and Pedestrian* (1913), 44.

*As the late Richard Hofstadter has summed up the case, "The historians of the nineteenth
century worked under the pressure of two internal tensions: on one side there was the constant
demand of society—whether through the nation-state, the church, or some special group or class
interest—for memory mixed with myth, for the historical tale that would strengthen group
loyalties or confirm national pride; and against this there were the demands of critical method,
and even, after a time, the goal of writing 'scientific' history." Hofstadter was, of course, speaking of American historians in this text, but he could easily have generalized his analysis to their
colleagues across the Western world. *The Progressive Historians: Turner, Beard, Parrington* (1968),
3–4.

past and force it into its course."[12] This is what Lord Acton meant when he warned against the "cloven hoof." And that is why he suggested that historians study the masters of their discipline and their letters; this might enable them to detect and disarm their own prejudices.[13]

Of course, if they would not look into themselves, their colleagues were only too pleased to do it for them in reviews and polemics.[14] "Of centennial sermons and Fourth-of-July orations, whether professedly such or in the guise of history, there are more than enough," wrote the iconoclastic American historian Richard Hildreth in 1849, introducing his history of the United States. "It is due to our fathers and ourselves, it is due to truth and philosophy, to present for once on the historic stage, the founders of our American nation unbedaubed with patriotic rouge, wrapped up in no fine-spun cloaks of excuses and apology."[15] Hildreth was an outsider, but he was not alone.

Best-selling works of history offer instructive instances of the excuses and apologies much of the reading public wanted from its historians, and how the struggle against partisanship played itself out in the Victorian decades. A source equally enlightening, especially about bourgeois habits of mind, was the readings assigned to pupils in secondary schools. For the most part, these institutions—the *Gymnasium* in Germany, the *lycée* in France, the public school in England—were, and long remained, privileged havens for the prosperous middle class; their classical curriculum set them apart from the rudimentary education that even improved primary schools made available to the children of the poor. Collectively, school texts mirror the fantasies of respectable parents imagining what they wanted their children to believe, and to become. They embodied fantasies forcefully advocated and angrily defended, for in the century after the upheavals of the French Revolution and the Napoleonic age, with the dramatic increase in literacy and the troubling birth of mass politics, educational questions were more intimately linked to larger public issues than ever before. Granted, compared to Greek and Latin, and religion, instruction in history took up a relatively minor space in the curriculum. But the kind of history that the young were supposed to absorb tells much about the bourgeoisie's self-image, or at least its wishes.

The nineteenth century was, as everyone knows, an age of nationalism, a potent symptom of the craving for self-esteem and an agenda that appealed to diverse circles of readers. Ernest Renan's magnanimous vision of a nation as a plebiscite daily renewed faded, especially late in the century, before aggressive chauvinistic declamations. At the same time, the century witnessed envenomed quarrels over how many should be educated and how much; and, perhaps most visibly, religious conflicts that pitted Protestants against Catholics, liberal Jews against the Orthodox, secularists against the devout. To make the turmoil over education fiercer still, by mid-century the clamor for technological literacy roiled the prestigious secondary schools obstinately clinging to their classical program. Inevitably, these sensitive issues blended into one another and were thrashed out in the political arena. Just as inevitably, the history syllabus reflected, and in some measure shaped, public debates.

But it was not all politics. Everywhere schoolmasters, in tune with their times, wanted to form good citizens, but their definitions of good citizenship varied greatly, and history instruction varied with them. In France, an interminable reiteration of the glorious national past stood at the core of the history syllabus. But there were schools in other countries where the jingoistic tone was far more muted. Take Rugby under Dr. Arnold, that charismatic and imaginative headmaster from 1827 to his untimely death in 1842.[16] Though at Rugby, as in other public—which is to say, private—schools in England and elsewhere, Greek and Latin overshadowed all else, history was taught every year, from the first form to the sixth. In fact, Dr. Arnold yoked the history of recent times to that of antiquity, assigning liberal doses of Herodotus, Thucydides, Xenophon, Livy. He wanted pupils to take these survivals from distant ages not as a holiday from contemporary issues but as historians supremely wise, supremely relevant, indeed supremely modern. "The history of Greece and Rome," he contended, "is not an idle inquiry about remote ages and forgotten institutions, but a living picture of things present, fitted not so much for the curiosity of the scholar, as for the instruction of the statesman and the citizen."[17] Thus broadly conceived, history at Rugby was to provide training in character second only to the teachings of religion.

Nor were the history textbooks prescribed at Rugby particularly self-absorbed. Two of them, Guizot's *Histoire de la Révolution de l'Angleterre,* an account of the English Civil War, and Mignet's liberal *Histoire de la Révolution française,* taught French as much as history. English texts included Mrs. Markham's adroit, chatty *History of England,* political history decked out with colorful anecdotes, appropriate for the first two forms; excerpts from Henry Hallam's far more demanding *History of Europe during the Middle Ages* and from William Russell's stodgy but exhaustive *History of Modern Europe.*[18] Though each had its distinct point of view—Hallam, for one, was a conservative Whig—and all took the excellence of England for granted, they were comparatively light on self-congratulation. So was Dr. Arnold. As he came to occupy himself with the victims of industrialization in his country, his politics grew increasingly radical; a nineteenth-century Dr. Johnson, he objected to "that feeling of pride and selfishness" which, "under the name of patriotism, has so long tried to pass itself off for a virtue." He held, firmly, that "exclusive patriotism should be cast off" as "one of the follies and selfishness of our uncultivated nature."[19] Ethics and Christianity were better teachers than national arrogance.

Rugby was exceptional only in the consistency of its generous perspectives. The lessons that history books were designed to impart to pupils in nineteenth-century England mirrored an impressive range of views and caused the unending controversies that, we have seen more than once, were a hallmark of bourgeois culture.[20] Still, from the 1870s, as the great powers were intensifying their imperialistic ventures and racist slogans became acceptable weapons in the chauvinist armory, rhetoric grew more heated even in Britain, and complaisant textbook writers followed editorialists and politicians in making claims to national superiority. Not that those beating the drums for their country openly called for mendacious texts: to their minds the unique blessings of English culture, English arms, the English race were so self-evident that a truthful history could only endorse the most grandiose insularity.

No doubt, Dr. Arnold would have detested so self-satisfied an ideology. But even at the crest of the jingoist wave during the Boer War, English schoolbooks rarely neglected the moral and religious dimensions of patriotism. If some exploited what they called true love of country as a convenient alibi for colonizing "inferior" peoples, many believed that Britain must assume responsibility for its own greatness. Educators deplored the denigration of foreigners as immoral, even counterproductive; some dared to call it un-English. In history teaching in Britain, the passion for forming good character served as a brake on national megalomania.

Not even German pedagogues, often held up by envious foreigners as men unashamed to teach love of country, escaped such debates. Yet German historians easily outdid the British in stridency. Witness the histrionic historian and demagogue Heinrich von Treitschke; his influential writings on recent German history, grating in tone and nationalistic in message, and his militant lectures on politics lent a ruthless Teutonism the prestige of an eminent professorial chair at the University of Berlin. Mommsen thought that by calling Treitschke "the poet of Prussian history," he had discredited the man and his work.[21] Far from it; Treitschke spoke for a powerful current of thought.

Indeed, *Am deutschen Wesen soll die Welt genesen*—the world shall be healed by the Germans' essential nature—grew into a widely mouthed slogan after the founding of the German Empire in 1871.[22] Superpatriotic historians, and not Treitschke alone, sounded defensive in their aggressiveness, as though, citizens of a newly minted empire, they had something to prove to foreigners and to themselves. Before 1871, of course, the hope for a united Germany had been a cherished, fervent dream as nationalists did verbal battle with particularists, with loyal Saxons or Bavarians. But once Bismarck had made Germany, though individual states kept control of the schools, nationalism found a political home. Against this reality, the remnants of the cosmopolitan ideals of the eighteenth century and the neoclassical humanism of the early nineteenth had a hard stand. Bitter quarrels over related issues, notably over the respective roles of science and of classics in the secondary schools, complicated the situation. But that did not make the anti-chauvinist stance any easier.

Indeed, once Wilhelm II ascended the throne in 1888, these conflicts grew more and more one-sided. Naturally, even before, the teaching of history had not remained insulated from stirring current events, and Bismarck's astounding success in state building prodded writers of history textbooks to offer uncritical support to the glorious present, which to their minds called for tireless emphasis on the need for national unity as against parochial attachments and for measures to combat the subversive socialists, men who, sad to say, hated their country. As cosmopolitans on principle, a handful of historians sympathetic to older ideals and even Social Democrats deserted this consensus, while unrepentant liberals who had not been bought off by Bismarck's strokes of genius objected to the kind of history instruction that, they thought, amounted to little more than indoctrination.

The most persistent and articulate spokesman for classical, humanistic education was Oskar Jäger, himself a director of a *Gymnasium* in Cologne. In speeches, articles, and pamphlets, he reiterated his vision of the historian as a student of all humanity, and of his professional obligation to follow the truth alone. "Humanity," he wrote in 1895, "is an ethical whole," and the "highest law" of historical instruction is to offer "only *what* really happened"; in short, an effort at "complete objectivity" is essential. Jäger had no use for educators who "loudly din patriotism into pupils' ears" day after day and who want to replace ancient literature by modern, indeed contemporary, history.[23]

The decreasing numbers and isolated position of these dissenters should have reassured the conservative camp, but it continued to worry that, far from getting too many lessons in German pride, pupils got too few. The cause enlisted the young emperor Wilhelm II, by his position the most influential partisan for conformist, German-centered history instruction. He was keen that schools increase their offerings in German literature and, along with that, in German history.[24] In 1890, two years after his accession, in a provocative address to a national school conference, he exclaimed, "We ought to educate national young Germans and not young Greeks and Romans." The war against unpatriotic subversion had been virtually won.

Hence, while some countercurrents survived, they were to little purpose. The pressures of a modern German empire—for a more adaptable curriculum that would make room for natural science, and the demands of an expansive state intent on cementing its subjects' loyalties—were too strong. True, in 1893, at the first congress of German historians, after a lively debate, a sizable majority passed a resolution insisting that history in the schools not serve as a "preparation for participating in the tasks of public life" by "systematically supporting a certain point of view." But even those who deprecated the emperor's attempt to politicize history in the schools and voted for this brave defense of professional autonomy took care to leave no doubt that they, too, were good Germans. Authentic history, they argued, would with its very veracity inculcate devotion to the fatherland and strengthen readiness for public service.[25] Even Jäger made his home in this camp: the two-volume *Deutsche Geschichte* he published in 1909 and 1910, near the end of his life, is the bulky confession of an octogenarian nationalist. His narrative is filled with pride and anxiety—pride in the German people, anxiety over the socialist menace and the damage that the country's unprecedented prosperity might do to unselfish love of country. If a lifelong champion of the classical curriculum and the independence of historical study could write in this vein, the image of German history that his triumphant opponents displayed in their texts can be easily imagined.

The event that added fuel to patriotic German history writing, the Franco-Prussian War, also gave chauvinism its innings in France, naturally for opposite reasons. The boastfulness of the first was matched in intensity by the fury of the second. In France, the struggle over education had occupied public figures, the legislature, and the press for decades, from the time of the Revolution to the victory of the secularists after 1900, and beyond. All parties agreed that children should read history so that they might learn to love France, but which France were they supposed to love? The stakes were high and straightforward. While priests and nuns, highly visible as dispensers of charity and physicians of souls, continued to guide the religious instruction offered in the schools and, naturally, to dominate the schools run by Christian brotherhoods, the state had a decisive role to play. To control the state machinery was to control the schools, and to control the schools was to control the future. The issue was particularly acute for French bourgeois, who monopolized the *lycées,* where history was taken seriously.

From the days of Napoleon I, the French government had a potent voice in the organization of the school system, the status of teachers, the character of the curriculum. At moments politically fraught when the church saw a good chance of tightening its grip on pupils, clerics would loose a veritable avalanche of pamphlets fulminating against the threat of atheism in secular schools and trumpeting the virtues of what they called the "free schools"—their own. One such propaganda wave began to sweep over the country in 1848, when even far from devout liberal bourgeois, frightened by revolutionary upheavals, began to appreciate the utility of the piety and social conformity that clerics taught so well. Another wave came in defense against the eminent anticlerical historian Victor Duruy, a versatile writer of texts from antiquity to modern times, whom Napoleon III appointed minister of education in 1863. An energetic reformer, Duruy left his traces all over the schools in the tense six years he held office. He did much for the lay teachers in the state system, improved the badly neglected education of girls, and, revamping the curriculum of the primary schools, was the first to introduce history as a compulsory subject.

History was much on Duruy's mind, and he dared to include contemporary affairs, that politically sensitive matter, in the syllabus. Necessarily his history program reflected his complex political positions, at once liberal and Bonapartist, cosmopolitan and nationalistic, progressive and anti-socialist, unequivocal only in his hostility to France's Bourbon past.[26] Yet, although there was an unbridgeable gulf between the kind of history instruction that Duruy developed and one that a devout minister of education would have imposed on French pupils, both would have been intent on forming patriotic Frenchmen. The issue which France pupils should love remained contentious, but that they should love France was beyond cavil. Ernest Lavisse, one of Duruy's protégés, a prolific, timeserving, politically powerful historian, editor, and author of terse, readable textbooks for the young, put the issue succinctly: if the pupil does not grow into "a citizen imbued with his duties and a soldier who loves his rifle, the teacher will have wasted his time."[27]

This sounds like advocacy of history as sheer propaganda; the schoolteacher as recruiting sergeant. Lavisse was too professional a historian, too committed to winning the respect of his peers, to remain content with that role. But he was speaking to a France smarting under its humiliation at the hands of the Prussian troops and its loss of territories. What is more, he and a small army of his compatriots were convinced that their beloved country had been defeated not just by smarter generalship and superior weapons but by high morale inculcated in the history lessons that German soldiers had absorbed in school. France must imitate its enemy at least in this: it must turn history education into civic education. As Gabriel Monod, editor of the *Revue historique,* wrote in 1876, in its first issue: the "painful events" of the recent past have "given us the duty of reawakening in the nation's soul its self-awareness through the thoroughgoing knowledge of its history."[28] That Lavisse, like Monod and other allies, insisted on the scientific character of his writings, actually did meritorious scholarly work, and seems to have believed his own sermons only made them all the more problematic.

A nagging question remains. What lasting deposits of conviction, what incentives to public action, did histories written in the age leave in the Victorians' minds? As we have seen, books, whether for pupils or adults, were only one source of character formation. Sermons, editorials, gossip, festivals, family traditions, class attitudes were no less formative, at times pointing in directions quite incompatible with the official version of national history. The Marxist parties emerging in industrial societies offered their supporters, numbers of them left-wing bourgeois and sympathetic intellectuals, competing identities as they extolled international working-class solidarity at the expense of patriotism. What is more, the ideal of serving Clio rather than the state, fortified by solid scholarship, produced works relatively free of political or religious ideology.

Yet for the majority the simplistic versions of the past they had been fed in school or, later, by tendentious orators and journalists were the only history they knew, the only lenses through which to read the past most relevant to them and to discover their own place in it. One thinks of August 4, 1914, and the days following: overage merchants volunteering for active service, dignified professors returning honorary degrees awarded by universities in the camp of the Other, sophisticated men of letters recapturing the passionate solidarity with their compatriots they had disdained for years. This torrent of enthusiasm for one's side and hatred for the enemy that flooded Europe with the coming of war strongly suggests that in a moment of crisis the demanding Rankean ideal stood helpless before the power of regressive, primitive emotions. But, though this instantaneous rethinking—or, better, refeeling—of history may seem abrupt in retrospect, the ground had been well prepared, and it had been a popular, increasingly common strand in the historical literature that had prepared it.

➢ FOUR ➢

The Truths of Fiction

1. Toward the Terrible Core

In the course of the nineteenth century, fiction, ever more acceptable to the bourgeoisie, increasingly touched the inner life of its readers. Around 1800, many especially among the pious had still disdained the novel, that recently invented genre, as a frivolous, probably corrupting diversion. With delicious irony, Jane Austen has a character in *Northanger Abbey,* itself a novel of course, admit in some embarrassment that she is reading "only a novel."[1] At the same time, so dignified a man of letters as Goethe did not disdain writing novels; and by the early 1830s, Sir Walter Scott had made the novel respectable, even fashionable. A decade or so later, the time of Dickens and Flaubert, Balzac and Thackeray, makers of imaginative prose could claim a prestige that their most eminent eighteenth-century forebears had claimed in vain.* In 1849, commenting on his novel *Coningsby,* published five years earlier, Disraeli observed that while he had not originally thought to make his advocacy of modern Toryism into a novel, "after reflection, he resolved to avail himself of a method which, in the temper of the times, offered the best chance of influencing opinion."[2]

A handful of militant Victorian authors and critics, professing the doctrine of

---

*It is perhaps necessary to observe that what follows is neither literary criticism nor literary history. My estimate of the fictions I shall be examining is no doubt plain enough, but what interests me here is solely how, and how much, novels and stories participated in the great voyage to the interior that is the theme of this volume.

literature for literature's sake, did in fact proclaim the novel a pure work of art; the majority, more in tune with their didactic times, advertised it as an instrument for moral improvement, cultural criticism, even philosophical or religious meditation. Thackeray came to liken his profession to that of the parson. The house of fiction, to paraphrase Henry James, had many windows. So did the apologies for writing and reading novels, ever more elevated and at war with one another.

Novelists took no little pride in exhibiting their psychological acumen. Even Karl May, that supreme German manufacturer of daydreams, whom we shall meet again, called himself a psychologist.* And the best of them seriously sought to realize Fielding's program for *Tom Jones,* the probing of human nature.[3] In a much quoted metaphor, Stendhal likened the novel to a mirror traveling along a highway. To be sure, it was a distorting, often obscure mirror, but, for all that, it distilled enough truths about nineteenth-century minds at work to make it an indispensable witness to the bourgeoisie's inner life. Nathaniel Hawthorne spoke for the more ambitious in his calling when he described himself as "burrowing, to his utmost ability, into the depths of our common nature, for the purposes of psychological romance," thus hoping to "reach the terrible core of man's being." Some two decades later, in 1865, Leo Tolstoy, dazzled by a newly acquired grandiose self-definition, confided to his diary that he was raising the sights of *War and Peace* to attempt "a psychological history of the romance of Alexander and Napoleon."[4] This was a memorable moment in the career of nineteenth-century fiction.

Nowadays, such sweeping aspirations must face the objection that the novel, after all, occupies a domain of its own. Does not this most self-conscious of genres, even as handled by strict realists, manipulate its personages like so many puppets? Just before the First World War, the Russian formalists, most uncompromising of literary theorists, insisted that novelists' psychological investigations only serve their narrative experiments rather than the narrative serving their psychology.[5] Eccentric eighteenth-century novelists like Laurence Sterne, or equally eccentric nineteenth-century advocates of art for art's sake like Stéphane Mallarmé or Oscar Wilde, came to be hailed as prophets of the radical dispensation that literature at its purest is enchantment and never reportage, let alone analysis. The motives that animate and the conflicts that plague fictional characters exist only in so far as their maker has chosen to disclose them; what they were like before they entered the story or after they left it is none of the reader's business.† How, then, can historians presume to scrutinize the

*See below, pp. 237–40.

†True, in 1913, close upon the end of the time span that this book covers, George Bernard

thoughts and doings of imaginary characters as clues to the self-exploration of
the bourgeoisie?

But it was only after the Victorian age that the radical separation of art and
life grew into a commanding fashion. Before that, a few doctrinaire aesthetes
like Théophile Gautier and Walter Pater apart, virtually everyone believed that
fictional characters must be as real as possible. Novels and stories must draw on
reality and function not just to beautify but to explain it. In his prefaces, his
reviews, and his invented surrogates, Henry James tirelessly repeated that life
alone, fully grasped and fully told, is the novelist's true subject. In the same vein,
Anton Chekhov announced it his supreme task "to paint life in its true aspects."[6] For once, these two masters, exceptional in their gifts as in their views,
were at one with the mediocre majority.

Even those Victorians, then, who did not think it the purpose of literature to
improve its readers' character insisted on the novelist's duty to be fundamentally
truthful. In short, novelists and their publics shared the largely unspoken expectation that fictional personages will behave like human beings. Even the heroes
of adventure tales or the heroines of romances ought to display recognizable
conduct and plausible motives. This was, as will appear, rather self-deceptive.
In the best-sellers of the age, the attraction of their protagonists lay precisely in
the fact that they spoke and acted as no humans have ever spoken and acted.
But, with all their implausible psychology, as objects of blissful identification or
of gratifying loathing, these two-dimensional figures throw much needed light
on the fantasy life of nineteenth-century readers and on their very human
needs.

On the other hand, the consumers of more taxing fiction could ask for, and
often got, characters endowed with unmistakable psychological coherence. Sophisticated readers reckoned an unmotivated or incomprehensible course of
conduct a literary flaw, a failure of analytic empathy, or an unwarranted yielding to the cheap tricks of melodrama. Whatever psychological dimensions a
novelist left unexplored must be, like the dark side of the moon, somehow "in
character." And so, whatever their intentions or their audiences' capacities,
writers of more demanding fiction made human nature their study.

While these authors could be opaque in their motives and at times in their
prose, they supported, in fact frequently generated, pressing fantasies among
their audiences and helped to shape identities both individual and collective.

Shaw provided a postscript for his play *Pygmalion* that reported on the fate of Professor 'Iggins,
Eliza, and Freddy after the final curtain falls. She will marry Freddy and, with the help of their
fatherly friend Professor 'Iggins, open a flower shop. But this was a typical Shavian defiance,
flouting the principle that fiction and biography are radically different enterprises.

Although by definition uncommon personages, novelists were firmly enmeshed in their society, and revealed in their writings more than private idiosyncrasies; the wide market they created proves that they were not writing for themselves or for one another alone. No doubt, many readers' responses were stereotyped. Like others before and after them, docile Victorians bowed to the dictates of fashion, drifted with the tides of taste, and shared predictable social prejudices. Their culture sent signals that the most truculent among them could not entirely ignore. Yet, whether its reception was original or derivative, fiction created communities of producers and consumers, and probed the middle classes' naked heart.

Though attuned to more elevated rewards, devotees of strenuous fare, being only human, were not innocent of primitive desires, and called on their favorite authors to satisfy them. They were rarely altogether disappointed. After all, the most severe, most self-aware literary artists of the age had a touch of the entertainer in them as they resorted to heroic rescues, criminal mischief, abrupt reversals of fortunes. They could provide conventional thrills and equally conventional happy endings while posing—and some of the time really acting—as moral censors, social critics, sensitive readers of minds. It will emerge, then, that in the Victorian age, the frontier between facile entertainment and serious fiction was anything but clear-cut. It is only that in its appeal to raw emotions the best-selling fiction of the nineteenth century was shamelessly direct, far more single-minded in its agenda than novels harboring more dignified literary aspirations.

From the early nineteenth century on, the regressive seductions of fiction were often initiated by shrewd editors and publishers. By mid-century, in all the industrial countries, daily newspapers, periodical magazines, book peddlers, cheap editions flooding bookstores or railroad stalls, and, ever more lending libraries catered to an apparently insatiable appetite for the excitement of visiting the golden realms of the imagination. The playfulness of storytelling was seldom wholly spontaneous, seldom free of commercial stratagems: authors and their promoters had fully acquired the arts of publicity and aimed fictions, with astonishing precision and growing effectiveness, at specifically targeted audiences.

For one, female readers with some time on their hands and money in their pockets became the preferred prey of the publishing industry.[7] For another, so did adolescents hungry for models to emulate, and consumers of newspapers, whether male or female, commanding just enough leisure to absorb the day's dose of fiction. Supplying a well-aimed avalanche of novels had become a lively cottage industry. And yet, the wholesale production of best-sellers was never simply a purely calculated enterprise. In the work of nineteenth-century imaginative writers, the producers' were likely to meet the consumers' daydreams. Unconscious spoke to unconscious.

No doubt, the average middle-class reader, that statistical invention, did not care, or could not manage, to follow the subtleties of Benjamin Constant or Anton Chekhov, let alone Henry James or Marcel Proust. The history of bestsellers shows that the bulk of Victorian readership wanted little more from novels than escape and perhaps a touch of moral improvement. With growing literacy and stirring advances in the manufacture and distribution of printed matter, that readership broadened out beyond the bourgeoisie. Novels became cheap, in both senses. Yet bourgeois, however divided by levels of education or of polish, remained the principal consumers of fiction, enriching their inner lives, restoring their inner resources, or evading their inner problems as they increasingly replaced religious uplift with agreeable fiction.

Historians of nineteenth-century reading publics—and the plural is a useful deterrent against plausible oversimplifications—have generated elaborate schemes to discriminate each layer of the book-consuming population from the others. The Victorians were content with drawing a fairly gross distinction between ordinary citizens limited to an unassuming menu and rare spirits seeking out more sublime gratifications.* In 1847, in a sociological appraisal characteristic of his time, the well-known German poet, playwright, literary theorist, and political liberal Robert Prutz judged that it was remarkable enough if middle-class readers like small merchants and bureaucrats reached for a book to find their entertainment and recreation there. Imprisoned in their shops or at their desks, they could hardly be expected to read fiction calling for a level of education they did not possess. "If instead they reach for the compact nourishment of light literature, a literature requiring no prerequisites other than curiosity and boredom—what can be more natural?" The true cultivation that serious literature called for was, in Prutz's view, confined to a vanishingly small minority of the middle-class public.[8]

But this simple scheme could not accommodate the diversity of nineteenth-century reading habits. As already noted, writers and readers alike broke through the boundary segregating frivolous from serious literature. Some gifted novelists, Charles Dickens being only the most famous, straddled the line,

---

*They also identified a third reading public, one that was of great concern to them, and persuaded it that legislation or voluntary efforts were needed to improve uncultivated minds: the barely literate poor who got their fiction from crude broadsides, chapbooks, cheap thrillers they could buy in weekly installments. But that important public is, of course, beyond the confines of this study of the bourgeoisie.

defying any attempts at an authoritative diagnosis, and middle-brow periodicals did their share to confuse categories further.* The English *Graphic* and the German *Gartenlaube,* impressively popular family periodicals not known for their exacting tastes, gave house room to distinguished novelists: the one to Henry James, the other to Theodor Fontane. For their part, civilized readers took holidays from their austere diet by amusing themselves with a slight love story. Again, not all readers read a book in the same way: an Englishman warned off a scandalous French import like Flaubert's *Madame Bovary* might try the novel to supply himself with sexual titillation.

What is more, different stages of life obviously make for different tastes: the tale of adventure that helps an adolescent to define his manhood may no longer be so necessary two or three decades later. And in the long, rapidly changing Victorian decades, the very passage of years moved the barriers separating popular from more difficult fiction: the appropriate sentiment of one decade became the mawkish sentimentality of another.† Some constituencies for fiction remained relatively stable; others shifted with the sea changes that moved taste toward an outspoken realism in the later years of Victoria. But early or late, easy or hard, direct or indirect, low or high, the fiction of the age, as of other ages, ultimately derived its energies from fantasies, whether sexual or aggressive, disguised, organized, and orchestrated by craftsmanship.

At first glance, the pleasures of reading for the middle-class public seem hard to define; they appear to be as diverse as its incomes or its tastes. Those pleasures, Freud wrote in a pioneering paper on the psychology of literary production and consumption, "probably flow together from many sources." The "fantasies, castles in the air, and day dreams" that imaginative writers borrow and transform, far from "rigid or unalterable," cling to "life's shifting impressions of existence, change with every variation in the human situation."[9] Freud was touching on one of the joys of fiction. Though its allure was primitive at heart, the guises that fictional characters could assume were almost unlimited; they had more uniforms in their wardrobe than Germany's emperor Wilhelm II. The nineteenth-century novel, in other words, justified its reputation as the most protean of genres. Yet this much seems undeniable: the emotional roots of fiction, readily accessible, amount to the wish fulfillment of daydreams.

---

*For Dickens, see below, pp. 262–76.
†For a famous instance, the death of Little Nell, see below pp. 265–66.

2. Regression to Polarities

In sharp contrast with the fiction canonical in the century, popular literature gratified the emotional needs of its readers with little embarrassment. It offered escape from a drab present to colorful worlds far away or long ago; the vicarious enjoyment of hair-raising adventures without their risks; the relish of seeing justice dealt out to brutes deserving their fate; the satisfaction of belonging to a community of patriotic fellow readers, to say nothing of secretly sharing in the spectacle of erotic conquests. In 1909, near the close of his career as a prolific spawner of pot boilers, travel stories, and pretentious allegories, Karl May diagnosed his kind of fiction as a psychological salve for those "shoved aside" by society. It offered a way back to the enchantment of which a cruel world had robbed them. "At least they want to read that the happiness for which they long in vain really exists. Life offers them only labor, toil, and trouble, nothing more." For them, all "faith is gone, trust in God has vanished." But perhaps, they desperately ask, there is happiness somewhere? "Then comes the book peddler. He says, 'Yes, there still is happiness. . . . I bring it to you. Here: read!' "[1]

May was limiting his analysis to the disadvantaged and the disinherited, but his notion that fiction is a factory of compensatory daydreams had wider applications. Reduced to a common denominator, however guileful their devices and circuitous their route, novels generated fantasies of identification with manly heroes or melting heroines and of sweet revenge on hateful villains. That readers' mental gymnastics were partly unconscious only made them the more compelling—and instructive: the century's publishing successes testify mainly to the mind-set of their readers. Their contribution to an understanding of the inner life of the Victorian middling orders, in other words, is largely that it permits historians to draw inferences about a public addicted to this fare.

The Victorians had some inkling of this. Thoughtful literati and artists recognized that every act of reading, anything but a purely passive reception, is a highly subjective encounter, a kind of collusion profitable to both sides. In mid-century, the prominent German playwright and literary theorist Otto Ludwig explored the reader's share in some sensible verses. Just as "a painting is completed only by the viewer," so a book needs to "find the proper reader, who / In reading it completes it." In short, every reader makes the book he is reading his own in a deeply personal way.[2] And some active readers literally changed the books they were imbibing in installments by persuading the author to bring them closer to their dreams: only the best-known of these was Dickens's rewriting the ending of *Great Expectations,* at the request of his friend the novelist Bulwer-Lytton, to permit at least the possibility of a happy ending for the protagonists.

Recalling his impassioned youthful engagement with books and magazines at the turn of the century, the brilliant and original left-wing German political artist George Grosz aptly illustrates the way that readers cooperate with writers to generate their unique inner experience. He declared himself lastingly grateful to the tales of derring-do that had rescued him from the tawdry realities of his proletarian existence. "It seemed as though our unconscious dreams were lent more reality when our thoughts, nourished by popular articles and drawings, floated along—far away, high above the sooty backyards" of his native Berlin.[3] His literary debauches allowed Grosz to forget his confining and disheartening world, dominated by factories and office buildings. In time, in these daydreams, fiction and life became interchangeable, as he identified himself with his heroes and actively participated in the stories he swallowed. Grosz spoke for the experience of millions of readers. Ludwig had already remarked that readers got out of fiction largely what they put into it as they let novelists do the work of embodying their fantasies for them.

As we have noted, the daydreams that the fiction industry served up for the delectation of the reading masses shared one overriding quality: the characters in popular novels were walking and talking clichés, stock figures that could be moved with little loss from one tale to another. And authors took good care to establish their creatures' role in the unfolding melodrama without delay, and without appeal. A hero was a hero from his first appearance, a villain a villain quite as swiftly; the heroine was beautiful, pure, energetic, talented—an astonishing number of them were gifted musicians who could make strong men weep with their playing—in short, infinitely worth winning. The fashionable device of having the forces of evil gradually unmasked did not work against the identification of the good and the bad: the revelations were designed to astonish the world but rarely the reader, who had been let into the secret all along.

This is not to deny that the most interesting among the caterers of fantasies had appealing gifts. They showed a feel for pacing or for racy dialogue and an instinct for sustaining suspense. They knew how to arouse the question that anyone, even the discriminating reader, will ask of fiction: What happened next? And the most adroit best-selling fabulists invented striking characters who departed from the banal flawlessness the marketplace liked to see and normally got. Consider the remarkable best-seller *Les Trois Mousquetaires* by Alexandre Dumas, serialized in the Parisian daily *Le Siècle* from 1844 to 1845. In that sprawling historical romance set in the France of Richelieu, parasitical on published seventeenth-century memoirs and the labors of a diligent hidden collaborator, Dumas introduced no fewer than four imperfect heroes, and took his panting readers with him. D'Artagnan, to whom the three musketeers learn to defer as they acknowledge his superior good sense, is impetuous, almost comically jealous of his honor, and none too scrupulous in his love affairs; the powerfully built Porthos is vain, boastful, and addicted to gambling; Aramis suffers, for all his military valor and loyalty, from an obsessive hankering for the priesthood; Athos is a man carrying a dark secret.[4]

These marked characteristics secured Dumas's leading men a certain individuality and lent their author a humorous distance that set off their noble conduct and intimidating accomplishments in riding, fighting, lovemaking, and sustaining their ruinously expensive mode of life. A closer reading, though, reveals that these genial touches did not make the musketeers and their dashing friend into believable human beings. Their apparent complexity is an ingenious sham that cannot mask Dumas's intention to make the quartet into the reader's favorites from the start and to remain so. And his villains highlight the heroes' virtues. Richelieu, in love with power, commands a troop of unscrupulous minions; the most formidable of them, the ferocious—and superbly beautiful— Milady, is exposed as a professional seducer and cold-blooded poisoner. Her capture, trial, and conviction near the end, somberly staged by the four heroes, has been foreshadowed and made inescapable by these stark contrasts. And her execution is an exercise in poetic justice: she is beheaded by a man whom, too, she had almost fatally wronged.

This was the stuff of fairy tales. Did not the Grimm brothers, the masters of this dying folk literature, begin more than one *Märchen* with the promise that they will tell of a time when wishing still made a difference? The resemblance of popular novels to the fairy tale is nothing less than striking; in fantasy, grown-up readers returned, as it were, to childhood, emotionally revisiting stories they had heard long ago. They were only too content to see enforced once again the rigid, predictable conventions that had given them so much pleasure. The fictions the Victorians swallowed settled accounts with a comforting air of finality, freely utilized miraculous coincidences, and caressed sadistic scenes— just as fairy tales had done. In the Grimms' "Die zwölf Brüder," the wicked stepmother is sentenced to die in a barrel filled with boiling oil and poisonous snakes; in their "Aschenputtel," the malevolent sisters who had snubbed and tormented Cinderella have their eyes pecked out by doves.[5] Evoking much the same wishes, Rodolphe, the hero-avenger who dominates Eugène Sue's *Les Mystères de Paris,* condemns an unrepentant thief and murderer to be blinded; the Apaches in Karl May's *Winnetou, der rote Gentleman,* after putting a cowardly white man who has murdered one of their own through some exquisite tortures, shoot him to death.[6] Popular Victorian fiction took good care to gratify aggressive needs that develop early and generally survive only underground.

Erotic wishes, too, so charmingly and quickly accommodated in *Märchen,* found themselves realized in modern fiction. In fairy tales for children, the young king falls in love at first sight with the despised and pure beauty who will, after ritual trials, reign as his queen; in fairy tales for adults, this master plot would be spun out and larded with space-consuming complications, but with the same denouement. To call popular nineteenth-century novels fairy tales, then, is not to resort to an idle metaphor: there were ogres in them and witches, enchanted princes and princesses kissed into life, fairy godmothers and godfathers who made dreams come true. There were mysterious castles, impossible rescues, lost children and lost parents marvelously restored, endings that did violence to the limited possibilities we call nature.

This defining quality of light Victorian fiction has become something of a commonplace among twentieth-century literary critics, but nineteenth-century writers had anticipated them.* Some openly associated their fictions with fairy tales and scattered reminiscences of *Märchen* to enlist their readers' nostalgia. The realists who from mid-century on aggressively campaigned against the reign of magic in fiction could never root out that middle-class taste.† Dickens, we shall see, was aware, and proud, of his dependence on fairy tales, and lesser writers took the same tack. Sir Arthur Conan Doyle likened the puzzles starring Sherlock Holmes to fairy tales. And in 1910, two years before his death, Karl May insisted that his purpose in writing had been to "tell

---

*The atmosphere was set by the Grimm brothers and their disciples, who expended untold hours in gathering up fairy tales to rescue them from oblivion for the sake of adults quite as much as for that of children. It is telling, too, that German romantics should have invented their own *Märchen,* stories for grown-ups in order to rediscover their national past—and themselves. As the royal road back to the innocence, the transparency, of childhood, fairy tales were for them a splendid way of reversing what they called the depoeticization of the world, one way of reconquering the lost realm of mystery.

†It was this taste that Thackeray lampooned in the preface to *The History of Pendennis: His Fortunes and Misfortunes, His Friends and His Greatest Enemy* (1848–50): "Perhaps the lovers of 'excitement' may care to know that this book began with a very precise plan, which was entirely put aside. Ladies and gentlemen, you were to have been treated, and the writer's and the publisher's pocket benefited, by the recital of the most active horrors. What more exciting than a ruffian (with many admirable virtues) in St. Giles's visited constantly by a young lady from Belgravia? What more stirring than the contrasts of society? the mixture of slang and fashionable language? the escapes, the battles, the murders? . . . The 'exciting' plan was laid aside (with a very honourable forbearance on the part of the publishers) because, on attempting it, I found that I failed from want of experience of my subject; and never having been intimate with any convict in my life, and the manners of ruffians and gaol-birds being quite unfamiliar to me, the idea of entering into competition with M. Eugène Sue was abandoned." *The Works of William Makepeace Thackeray,* Centenary Biographical Edition, ed. Lady Ritchie, 26 vols. (1910–11), III, liv.

parables and fairy tales in which the truth lies deeply concealed." Readers took
their cue from the writers: in 1895, the year of its publication in the United
States, the *Atlantic Monthly* called George du Maurier's *Trilby,* a run-away best-
seller about hypnotism and its occult powers, a "nineteenth century fairy tale
for grown men and women."[7] In popular novels of the time, as in the Grimms'
collections, all was polarity.

It is of cardinal importance for the act of reading that the earliest human
experiences are severely polarized. The infant's desires and dissatisfactions, its
mother's presence or absence, its dawning ability to distinguish between male
and female, its acts of love and hate permitted or forbidden, shape its perception
of a world divided between antagonistic forces, pictured in the harsh outlines of
a crude woodcut. Contrasts are combats. And this is the world that popular
fiction once again opened up to its consumers, recapturing a simplicity in
which nothing had been nuanced, no motive had been mixed, and no wickedness gone unpunished. In truth, the facts of children's lives can never be so
purely blessed, shadowed as they are by anxiety over the loss of love and the
strains of growth. Early education, we know, forces reluctant retreats from
dreams of unlimited power when, trained to conformity, the child submits to
schedules and rules of conduct. But escapist fiction was not interested in these
truths. Far from pointing back to authentic memories, it reawakened primitive
fantasies, long buried but never extirpated and easily revived. Popular fiction
restored lost omnipotence.

This artfully reconstructed imaginative world put a premium on authorial
ingenuity. If all outcomes are foreordained from the start, the problem of
keeping the reader reading beyond the first chapter becomes acute. The solution was, of course, the interesting complication; novelists embroidered fantasies with enticing grace notes. Their imaginative uncertainties were bearable
tortures that made the triumphant resolution all the sweeter. Authors took care
to depict the enemy as resourceful and—especially at the end of an installment—apparently unsurmountable. At times they invented villains who seem
charitable and devout but are evil incarnate behind their social mask. The
notary Ferrand, the most devilish among many human devils in Sue's *Les Mystères de Paris,* enjoys the reputation of being a solid citizen until the truth about
his murderous and voluptuary nature begins to dawn. And when necessary,
authors mobilized the most improbable excuses to keep hero and heroine apart
for a time.

One efficient, impressively flexible stratagem, always good for a few chapters
swarming with wrathful manly scowls and bitter feminine sobs, was the apparently fatal, but in the end reparable, misunderstanding: a lover misreads an

awkward word, an ambiguous gesture, an apparently damaging document, and feels that all is over. Shakespeare had not disdained this device in his comedies, and Victorian writers turned to it with an enthusiasm that no repetition could dim. "Do you regret the years that are past, Bert? Are you sorry that it is only now that we understand each other?"[8] Tantalizing questions like these populated the concluding chapter of nineteenth-century novels by the score.

Significantly, popular fiction enlisted poetic justice, the wish to restore balance to a world thrown out of joint by wicked deeds, in its depiction of gratifying primitive revenge. This literary formula, too, had been borrowed from more exacting literature and democratized. Offering a cheerful version in the *Mikado,* W. S. Gilbert lightheartedly defined poetic justice as punishment that fits the crime: the billiard shark is sentenced to play his game on a cloth untrue, with a twisted cue and elliptical billiard balls. Novelists for their part did not treat this kind of retribution as amusing at all. In *Les Mystères de Paris,* the wicked are hoisted by their own petard. Those who live by the knife are killed by the knife, and Ferrand, that criminal satyr, falls victim to a secret agent of Rodolphe's, a carnal, seductive beauty who literally drives her victim mad.[9] One characteristic story, drawn from America's most widely read women's magazine, *Godey's Lady's Book,* as different from Sue's most notorious novel as can be, attests to the range of such retaliation: in Mrs. C. Lee Hentz's "The Parlour Serpent," a perverse and destructive gossip who enjoys breaking up lovers or happy homes is visited with an accident to her jaw that leaves her hideously disfigured and all but speechless. In fiction as in its rare embodiment in life, dealing out poetic justice proved a highly respectable alibi for aggression, particularly among righteous bourgeois, always in search of good reasons for hitting out.[10]

Behind the appeal of light fiction, then, there lurked that fairly predictable thing—human nature. The novels that readers stood in line to buy or borrow were historical romances, tales of adventure, and, inevitably, love stories. Yet these types blended together in rich, uneven mixtures. The self-segregation among nineteenth-century readers—adventures for men and love stories for women—was no more absolute than the distinctions among the genres. Historical novels, which after Sir Walter Scott became international favorites, were political statements, educational aids, costume pieces. But virtually all of these stagy excursions into a glamorized past boasted protagonists who were also at home in stories of adventure and of love.

For their part, adventure tales, in which a manly protagonist tests his mettle against the cruel tricks of nature and of fiendish rogues, piled up crises that stretched the hero's endurance, shrewdness, and sheer physical prowess to the

limit. And such tales, too, proffered more or less delicate erotic tidbits to stimulate, or embody, readers' desires. Finally Victorian love stories, probably the
most sought-after mirrors and makers of fantasies, decorated the winding paths
of their plots with melodramatic stopping points. Take *Goldelse,* the novel that
launched E. Marlitt's career as Germany's best-loved entertainer of female readers, first published serially in 1866 in the *Gartenlaube.* The ravishing and spirited
heroine, though "girlish" and anxious, is abruptly "overcome by magnificent
courage" as she frustrates the assault of an assassin aiming his pistol at the man
she loves.[11] Such episodes claimed their place in the most domestic fare: the
lovable waif rescued for respectability, and marriage, by the intervention of a
fatherly (but not too fatherly) prince charming, the cripple made whole by a
miracle-working (and eligible) healer, the scheming interloper exposed for
claiming a fortune that rightfully belongs to others. The recipes for pot-boiling
novels added up to variations on a handful of themes, all of them serving
regressive pressures. They differed from each other chiefly in the props they
featured—and in their temperature. The histrionic moments that added spice to
love stories and historical novels were, of course, the daily diet for tales of
adventure.

The emotional dividends attached to love stories require little analysis. Late
in the century, Rudolf von Gottschall, a respected historian of German literature, hinted at a general explanation in judging Marlitt's novels to be new
editions of Cinderella. A young woman of middle-class background, gifted,
independent minded, of course beautiful and often poor but happy, finds love
with a man higher in the social scale—an educated bourgeois or, if he happens
to be an aristocrat, one democratic in his sentiments. Victorian novelists explored this motif tirelessly and tiresomely: an orphan, miserable and mistreated
in her childhood, grows into a sensible beauty that a vigorous, bearded professor finds worthy of an honorable proposal; the daughter of a penniless but
honest forester wins the heart and hand of the local squire. The dreams that
most of these tales told were middle-class dreams.

These heroines were not so passive as their fairy-tale counterparts who did
little but shine as brightly as the sun; they usually managed to train their men to
piety and domesticity as long as they performed their pedagogic task without
damaging the hero's sense of manly superiority. At times, the education went
the other way. Heroines, most of them already perfect, were rarely compelled
to make themselves over; but in much didactic fiction, especially stories in
women's magazines, spoiled but at heart sound young women discover that
they must put affection before pride, lasting goods before meretricious tinsel.
Normally the lessons were mild: in one typical instance, Dorothy, an ambitious
but appealing heroine who has been searching for a vocation, learns from the

man who conquers her that her "Vocation" is to be his wife.[12] In such fiction, rebellions against accepted clichés about the respective place of men and women are reserved for characters who come to a bad end. In their message, the love stories read by the thousands were conservative forces in bourgeois culture, limping after developments in real life.

The psychological rewards of adventure tales, though they at times invaded the preserve of social criticism, were no more complicated. While James Fenimore Cooper's leather stocking tales, avidly read in Europe, set the pattern, the French perfected the vogue in the newspapers. The basic facts are familiar. In 1836, the Parisian entrepreneur Emile de Girardin launched the daily *La Presse* and undercut his competitors by offering the paper at an annual subscription price of forty rather than the customary eighty francs. Armand Duracq promptly imitated his former employer with *Le Siècle,* and so, sniffing ready cash, did other publishers. And to capture the attention of the wider reading public these mass newspapers were serving—and creating—they began to run novels in the feuilleton space previously given over to a miscellany of cultural news. Periodicals like the *Revue des deux mondes* had been serializing novels for several years, but now fiction was transformed into a frequent feature. The scheme worked beyond its inventors' fondest hopes; circulation soared, and novelists ground out fictions as demand grew urgent.

It was with Eugène Sue's *Les Mystères de Paris,* launched on June 1, 1842, for a fifteen-and-a-half-month run in the *Journal des débats,* that the *roman-feuilleton* came into its own. Sue had already published several novels with some success, but he now enthralled the French, and soon not the French alone, from uneducated laborers to appreciative fellow authors. Opening up new horizons for fiction with forays into the Parisian underworld and its argot, the book became an extraordinary publishing triumph and, in its lurid way, probably the most influential. It spawned legends from the very outset. The French legislature, it was reported, did not get down to business until the deputies had read the latest installment, and in Théophile Gautier's much quoted witticism, the dying delayed their exit from the world until they found out how the novel ended. It was turned into a play, translated into a dozen languages and run in scores of newspapers and periodicals across Europe, earnestly dissected at astounding length by literary critics, and imitated over and over.

Naturally there were dissenting voices. Balzac, himself a prolific writer of serial fiction, was jealous. More generously, George Sand, who had wept copiously over the affecting fate of Fleur-de-Marie, the most hapless of protagonists in *Les Mystères,* admitted to mixed feelings: the story of that young prostitute pure in heart, seemed to her at once "trivial and sublime." And Thackeray, who summarized the earlier parts of the swollen and involuted plot for his English readers, pointed to the most vulnerable aspects of the genre that Sue had so evidently mastered: it was unashamedly a business proposition. Sue, he wrote, not without a tinge of envy at the sums the man commanded, was the shrewdest among France's "literary merchants," a "quack, but one of the cleverest quacks now quacking."[13] Other critics like V. C. Belinsky in Russia and Edgar Allan Poe in the United States agreed that *Les Mystères* was not literature but commerce—if commerce well done.*

The hold of *Les Mystères de Paris* on the reading public and the writing profession is easy to explain. In hectic, breathless short paragraphs sustained through hundreds of pages, Sue recounts the adventures of the mysterious prince Rodolphe of Gérolstein, alternating between the slums of Paris and the salons of his court. The story meanders at will—soon, as Sue responded to an avalanche of letters, in part at his readers' will: *Les Mystères de Paris* is one of the first Victorian novels reshaped by audience responses. Scenes shift arbitrarily and characters presumed murdered reemerge alive and well at inconvenient moments. This much was beyond revision: Rodolphe is on a mission to do good and avenge evil to atone for an oedipal crime he did not commit. Some seventeen years earlier, in thrall to a widow as lovely as she is treacherous, he had raised a dagger to his disapproving father and would have killed him if a devoted attendant had not stayed his hand. In his pilgrimage, Rodolphe encounters an outlandish assortment of personages, most of them—excepting Ferrand—plainly on one side of the moral ledger or the other: a quack who hires himself out as a poisoner; assassins who enjoy their work; young lovers in desperate straits; ruffians who, overcome by Rodolphe's strength and generosity, become his willing slaves and serve him unto death. Virtually all are outsized characters; none of them are human. Despite the parade of motives—Rodolphe's guilt feelings, Fleur-de-Marie's determination to escape the trade that has been forced on her—these characters have no recognizable inner life.

Rodolphe, the heart of the novel, least of all. Yet he became the pattern for many an adored nineteenth-century fictional hero: a charismatic being beyond the reach of sober reality. His physical powers, like his guile, are unsurpassed;

---

*In *Die Heilige Familie, oder Kritik der kritischen Kritik. Gegen Bruno Bauer & Consorten* (1845), Karl Marx delivered a sharp critique of a long appreciation of *Les Mystères de Paris* by Franz Zychlin von Zychlinski, to argue that Sue's supposedly radical social criticism in the novel was not radical at all. And while Flaubert seems to have let *Les Mystères* pass by without comment, he did come upon Sue's early novel *Arthur* (1838), and wrote that it was enough to make him vomit. But, then, lots of things made Flaubert want to vomit. "One must read that," he added, "to take pity on money, success, and the public." Flaubert to Louis Bouilhet, September 14, 1850, *Correspondance,* ed. Jean Bruneau, 3 vols. so far (1973–), I, 709.

his resources both intellectual and financial are inexhaustible. Some of Rodolphe's clones, to be sure, would master the world without his endless supply
of gold but made up for it with a prowess matching that of their model.
Rodolphe is the pitiless judge who punishes all crimes, the omnipotent rescuer
who rights all wrongs, in short the dreamt-of father, more divine than human,
though human enough to wander among lesser folk and feel the pangs of love.
Many of the protagonists dominating adventure fiction from then on, like
Dumas's count of Monte Cristo, were reincarnations, or recognizable relatives,
of this superman. With all its intricate plot and assemblage of unconventional
characters, Sue's greatest hit is little more than the old battle of day against
night, attesting once again to the fundamental urge behind popular fiction, the
polarized vision of the world.

Among the modern bards for whom polarity was king, Karl May, the most
widely read storyteller Germany produced in the century, must claim a prominent place. Not even Eugène Sue can attest more eloquently to the responses of
readers than this much beloved and much derided figure; no author's obsessions
were better in tune with the appetites of the reading public. May's life was
almost as implausible as the fictions he gave out as fact. Before he died, in 1912,
some two million copies of his books had been sold. That he professed, quite
ignorantly, to be an adept in contemporary psychology, a discipline whose
increasing importance he proclaimed, only raises the value of his testimony. As
we saw, May advertised his life's purpose to tell parables and fairy tales that
conceal deep truths. In his self-serving, defensive, unintentionally indiscreet
autobiography of 1910, he claimed that in order to fulfill his grand design, "I
myself, my own ego, had to become a fairy tale."[14] This is an unwitting hint at
the mystifications May imposed on his legions of credulous adorers with self-
aggrandizing tall tales. Life is not like fiction; poetic justice is only too rare: the
penalty May was doomed to pay for youthful transgressions and lifelong mendacity far outdistanced the offenses with which he may justly be charged.
    Karl Friedrich May was born in 1842 in the Saxon hamlet of Ernstthal, the
son of an irresponsible, often unemployed weaver and a "martyr" of a mother,
a gentle and hardworking midwife.[15] Ill-nourished and sickly, he grew up in
dire want lightened by occasional windfalls. The shaping episode of his early life
seems to have been being blinded by a childhood disease and restored to sight
only at five, a condition to which he attributed his luxuriant inner life, lovingly
nourished by a storytelling grandmother. He wanted, he recalled, to grow up to
be like her, and in a way, at once profitably and pathetically, he did.
    Poverty and blindness were not young Karl May's only antagonists. He and
his siblings were abused by a father who, in his words, had two natures: reason-

able when sober, quarrelsome and ferocious when drunk; he liked to beat his
children with a specially treated birch rod until he was exhausted—a repeated
trauma that left its mark on May's later fictions with their sadistic beating
scenes, recorded in unappetizing detail, as blood flows and skin is torn.[16] Yet
the boy's talent was irrepressible, and as a student in a teachers' seminary, he
stood on the threshold of a modest career.

Then a rash of increasingly bizarre misdemeanors derailed May's hopes. He
was dismissed from the seminary for stealing a few candles, presumably taken to
bring home for Christmas, but allowed to resume his studies elsewhere, only to
be accused of a graver theft. After serving time, he went on a spree as a confidence man that documents the wealth of his boasted imagination, though not
his good sense or psychological stability. To defraud the simple, he appeared in
small Saxonian towns and villages, using a variety of prestigious aliases—including, significantly, that of an ophthalmologist. The harvest of his thieveries and
impersonations was slim; they look like the guilt-ridden attention-provoking
exploits of a grown-up little boy taking responsibility, and seeking punishment,
for his father's rages. Whatever the inner dynamics, in 1874 May landed in the
penitentiary for four years.

This prison term broke May's self-destructive cycle: he learned to write and
to consult works of reference, both with demonic efficiency. This allowed him
to scratch out a meager living with ill-paid stories for periodicals, rehearsals for
more rewarding work, and then imprudently to sell himself to an exploitative
publisher specializing in trashy installment novels. Between 1882 and 1887, he
fabricated five of these *Kolportageromane,* each well over two thousand pages
long, a logorrhea whose very existence would come to haunt him. For these
swollen concoctions, May devised wooden puppets, crude plots, and garrulous,
unnatural dialogue whose only virtue—for him—was that it ate up page after
page.

Then ambition struck. May discarded his slave-driving publisher and began
to spill out the travel tales that by the 1890s made him a national treasure. His
adventure tales took the narrator, a transparent stand-in for their apparently
much traveled author, to three continents. In the Near East, he was called Kara
Ben Nemsi—Karl, son of the Germans; in the United States, he was Old
Shatterhand. These self-advertising fantasies sealed his fame and made his fortune. The most treasured among them, a stroke of genius, was *Winnetou, der rote
Gentleman* of 1893, a trilogy featuring the narrator's treasured friend, the brave
and lamented chief of the Apaches. May had first introduced this paragon in the
late 1870s; elevating him to epic stature, he created a mythical figure who sells
books in Germany to this day.

But prosperity lured May into hazardous fabulations: like failure earlier, success activated a self-punishing need to be discovered with purloined loot in his hand. He had himself photographed in western garb complete with a rifle reported to possess legendary precision and power, and gave out the picture as a memento of real voyages and his uncanny way with a gun. He claimed that he had made all the far-ranging safaris and enjoyed all the exotic friendships he had so racily depicted in his best-sellers: "I really am Old Shatterhand or Kara Ben Nemsi and have experienced what I recount." He strenuously objected to his novels' being called novels—they were reports. He decked himself out with a bogus title, the "Dr." so beloved of Germans, presumably awarded by a French university. He developed for his fans circumstantial life histories of his imaginary heroes complete with vital statistics. And in a notorious letter, he claimed that he spoke and wrote all the major European and Asian languages, and dozens of esoteric dialects.*

This rickety house of cards had to collapse sooner or later. May had become, to borrow his language, his own fairy tale, in a world in which a mass press avid for sensational revelations would not let such self-dramatizations go unchallenged. Around the turn of the century, a publisher exploited May's name by republishing his appalling installment novels of the 1880s, books he had hoped to erase from his mind; soon after, journalists garnered fleeting fame by exposing his criminal record and piously charging him with all sorts of moral failings. The lawsuits in which May sought to clear his name made his last years a hell; a few partial court victories over a slanderer who had called him a born criminal were a meager consolation. None of Karl May's tales had had so pitiful, so sordid an ending.

His life offers fascinating glimpses into a public's need for heroes to believe in. It mattered to his vast audience that May, risen from working-class tribulations to affluent middle-class respectability, encouraged imaginative identifications by giving himself the attributes of fabulous omnicompetence: he was the bourgeois as hero inviting his readers to be heroic like himself, in their easy chairs. What is so astonishing is not that May, confidence man to the last, was exposed, but that he was trusted for so long, and by so many. He was, of course, a deft and by the early 1890s an experienced storyteller; he skillfully deployed deadly dangers and changes of picturesque scenery, villains allowed to escape to be villainous another day, mysterious treasures beckoning in the distance, and

*"I speak and write: French, English, Italian, Spanish, Greek, Latin, Hebrew, Romanian, 6 dialects of Arabic, Persian, 2 Kurdish dialects, 6 Chinese dialects, Malaysian, Namaqua, a few Sunda-idioms, Swahili, Hindustanic, Turkish, and the Indian languages of the Sioux, Apaches, Comanches, Snakes, Utahs, Kiowas, in addition to the Ketshumanu 3 South American dialect. Lapp I will not count among them." November 2, 1894. Hans Wollschläger, *Karl May. Grundriss eines gebrochenen Lebens* (1965; ed. 1976), 82–91, quotation at 91.

other stigmata of the adventure tale. The record of May's protagonists, so obviously himself, was, in a word, perfect. He could outshoot a company of trained riflemen; ride longer and faster than hardy cowboys; swim like a fish; stun the sturdiest adversary with a single blow; detect a trail underfoot and interpret the language of broken twigs more surely than the most experienced scout; master an obscure oriental dialect more rapidly than a professional linguist; force open doors that the toughest of his comrades had failed to unlock. And he possessed not only the strength of Ajax and the nobility of Achilles but also the cunning of Odysseus, needed to prevail against ingenious enemies.

Nor was this all. May's hero was the consummate Boy Scout: he did not smoke or drink or swear; a sane and strong Don Quixote, he cordially condescended to his eccentric Sancho Panzas, who provided some humor and served him loyally; he would plead, with Christian forbearance, for the life of the most vicious killer. In fact, as students of May's work have observed, his heroes rarely needed to snuff out a life: others performed the executions for him, or had his enemies conveniently drown or fall off mountains.[17] It was predictable that Winnetou, "Scharlie's" blood brother, would die with his adherence to Christ on his lips. That May larded this conventional fare with a mildly progressive message—the whites who rob Indians of their land or who call them savages are worse than the most illiterate tribe—did not lessen his impact on his bourgeois readers.

The appeal of May's fairy tales on adolescent boys should be obvious. What is remarkable is the persistence of that appeal to adults, often unreconstructed aficionados. May himself did not like being called a writer for youth; he was writing for all the people. There is some justice to his demurrer, in the perverse sense that May's grown-up readers, like other consumers of popular fiction, happily regressed to the polarities that had early been their key to the world. It was the child in them that made them reach for their tattered copy of *Winnetou,* confirming Freud's observation that no one likes to give up a pleasure once enjoyed.

3. Immediacy

In his most beloved novels, Karl May ingratiated himself with his public by employing a first-person narrator. The stratagem permits authors to establish a complicitous alliance with their audience by securing it immediate access to the protagonist's mind. "It is desirable," wrote Dickens in *The Chimes,* a Christmas story told in the first person, "that a story-teller and a story-reader should establish a mutual understanding as soon as possible."[1] In such fiction, the speaker represents novelist, narrator, and protagonist all in one, engaged, as it were, in informal, if one-sided, conversation with the reader. Unlike the ubiquitous anonymous narrator who knows everything, ranges across the entire domain the novel encompasses, and freely delves into his characters' most private thoughts, the first-person voice has something homely about it. The narrator who reports the unfolding tale from his own perspective is offering to share the kind of confidences one expects from a close friend in a confessional mood.

As the name of Dickens suggests, Karl May was in large company, many of them his betters. From Benjamin Constant to Arthur Schnitzler, Gottfried Keller to Jens Peter Jacobsen, nineteenth-century writers of the most varied schools and the greatest distinction resorted to such a speaker. Feodor Dostoevsky cast most of his first tales and some of his later work in the first person. Henry James returned to the convention over and over.* Hawthorne's *Blithedale Romance*, Dickens's *David Copperfield*, Charlotte Brontë's *Jane Eyre*, Tolstoy's trilogy *Childhood, Boyhood,* and *Youth* are told in the first person—the list is almost endless. Ingenious technicians played with a narrator unreliable or self-deluded; if so, he became a test of the reader's acuity. But he—at times she—was always voluble and forthcoming, and that mattered. A few, like Tolstoy experimenting with the first-person gambit in *Childhood,* complained that the genre was confining.[2] Still, it is instructive how attractive the first-person novel, establishing intimacy at a moment's notice, proved to be in the self-conscious nineteenth century.

No wonder that opening sentences in the finest fictions written before the First World War have become memorable. "Call me Ishmael," and "My father was a merchant," and "For a long time I used to go to bed early" evoke Herman Melville's *Moby-Dick,* Adalbert Stifter's *Nachsommer,* and Proust's *A la Recherche du temps perdu,* the last perhaps the most searching first-person novel ever written. Like so many invitations, these sentences promise privileged access to the inner life of a significant fictional figure that will pervade the reader's consciousness for some time and, at best, remain a permanent possession.

The first-person novel, anything but stereotyped, assumed as many forms as literary ingenuity could invent. Some novelists reduced their narrator to a passive transmitter of documents; others eked out their eyewitness tale with a revealing letter that has conveniently come to hand. At times, as in Dostoevsky's *The Possessed,* the narrator is a marginal figure, largely confined to

---

*Perhaps most brilliantly in *The Aspern Papers,* a novella notable for, among other things, its strict adherence to the rules of probability: Henry James's narrator tells only what he has himself experienced; when he describes sentiments to which he has no direct access, he scrupulously makes clear that he is reporting what he conjectures is going on in other minds.

reporting, and briefly commenting on, the action. Often enough, the narrator—or, rather, his creator—cheats a little, recording not only what he saw or
heard, or was told, but also what went on in the minds of characters who had no
opportunity to reveal their workings to him. Most readers facing these flagrant
violations of the narrator's tacit contract with them suspended their disbelief,
thus underscoring the fact that the device is a convention open to manipulation.
The first version of Gottfried Keller's classic, *Der grüne Heinrich,* had the hero
tell his own story, only to be replaced by a third-person novel in its second,
canonical incarnation. Artificial or not, though, as we have seen, first-person
novels gave authors welcome opportunities to practice depth psychology.

It is a commonplace, and true enough, that a good number of these literary
inventions were barely disguised confessions. But while these first-person fictions obviously contained at least some, often momentous self-disclosures,
whether conscious memories or unconscious deposits, it does not follow that a
first-person novel must be simply an autobiography in another form. It is true
by definition that a writer writes only what it is possible for him to write: his
work, published and unpublished, attests to this uninstructive proposition. But
a sensitive and disciplined novelist trying to infiltrate hidden domains was not
confined to digging into himself; he could recruit his technical facility and
imaginative powers to sound the inner lives of personages very different from
his own.[3]

Anton Chekhov, among the most thoughtful of nineteenth-century story-
tellers, put the case with his customary sense for complexity. "Do not invent
sufferings that you never experienced," he lectured his eldest brother, Alexander, who was trying his hand at writing fiction, "and do not paint pictures you
never saw." This was a plea less for self-absorption than for visual precision,
sincere reporting, and emotional authenticity. Chekhov never equated fiction
with confession. On the contrary, his critique of subjectivity in storytelling and
his attendant praise of objectivity asked that writers forgo sententious, moralizing authorial glosses and let their characters speak for themselves. "One needs
only to be more honest, to throw oneself overboard everywhere," he told his
brother, "not to obtrude oneself into the hero of one's own novel, to renounce
oneself for at least half an hour."[4] A good writer, Chekhov was saying, profits
from the paradox that his very detachment, his ability to suppress sobs at the
sight of his characters' misfortunes, will secure him the access to the naked heart
he craves.

Again and again, Chekhov, among the least doctrinaire of writers, rejected
the notion that imagined characters are merely faithful shadows of, or privileged
spokesmen for, the author's mental life. In October 1889, he warned his close
friend Alexei Suvorin, the influential editor who had been the first to take his

talent seriously, "If someone serves you coffee, don't try to look for beer in it." Chekhov was explaining, and defending, his just-published controversial tale "A Boring Story," whose narrator is a talkative, slowly dying elderly academic. "If I present you with the professor's ideas, have confidence in me and don't look for Chekhovian ideas in them."[5] He had, he wrote, made up the story. But not out of whole cloth—Chekhov possessed, and believed that other writers needed, the gift of empathy in its literal sense: a knack for suffering with his inventions and truthfully reporting their sufferings.*

Resisting all demands from his liberal and radical friends that he take sides in the political debates roiling the Russian intelligentsia and enlist his fictions under the banner of reform, he fiercely concentrated on showing his cast of characters grappling with life. If they spouted radical commonplaces or homely folk wisdom, it did not follow that Chekhov was arguing a case; he was making them say what it was natural for them to say. "In my opinion," he told Suvorin in a famous letter of May 1888, a virtual manifesto outlining his credo, "it is not the writer's job to solve such problems as God, pessimism, etc.; his job is merely to record who, under what conditions, said or thought what about God or pessimism. The artist is not meant to be a judge of his characters and what they say; his only job is to be an impartial witness." Indeed, "drawing conclusions is up to the jury, that is, the readers." The writer's task is not to pose as an all-knowing psychologist but to admit that in life, as he has one of his characters say in the story "Lights," one cannot figure anything out. "Only fools and charlatans know and understand everything."[6] What impressed him particularly about *Anna Karenina* was that Tolstoy had not pretended to resolve anything. Chekhov was being overly modest: his very refusal to claim unobstructed insights into human nature freed him to understand the inner life in ways a psychologist would have had reason to envy.

A glance at the flood of incomparable stories that Chekhov poured out from the mid-1880s on shows that he carried out his ambitiously unassuming program. His narrators include an educated sportsman witnessing peasants committing adultery, a young eccentric forever professing his innocence of various offenses he is charged with, a prosperous, insufferable, rather sadistic landowner who enjoys tormenting his wife. Even when he does not use a visible narrator, Chekhov manages to enter the consciousness of the most disparate individuals:

*Responding to the suggestion that he write a story about a seventeen-year-old boy who commits suicide, Chekhov begged off: it would prove very painful and very difficult. "To handle a figure like that, an author has to be capable of suffering, while all our contemporary authors can do is whine and snivel." Chekhov to Dmitry Grigorovich, January 12, 1888, *Letters of Chekhov*, tr. Henry Heim in collaboration with Simon Karlinsky, sel. and ed. by Karlinsky (1973), 92.

in two particularly impressive tours de force, he tells stories from the perspective of little boys, the one nine and the other just two years and eight months old.[7] Despite all of Chekhov's disdain for literary tricks and acrobatic verbal pirouettes, these tales, whether told in the first person or not, are virtuoso pieces, but in the service of stripping away pretensions and sentimentality. They prove that art and analysis need not be adversaries.

Among Chekhov's enemies to the truths of fiction, lofty philosophizing ranked high, alongside tendentious pressures to support good causes. The only ideology he cheerfully embraced in his work was to see it as a massive protest against lying.[8] That is why the later Tolstoy, the writer whom he never ceased to prize, troubled Chekhov with his fervent self-made theology, vegetarian passions, and diatribes against lust. Turning stories into tracts was, to Chekhov's mind, sabotage against the writer's vocation. Reading the afterword to the *Kreutzer Sonata,* that controversial novella in which Tolstoy damns all sexual intercourse, including marital relations not devoted to procreation, Chekhov exploded. "To hell with the philosophy of the great men of this world!" he exclaimed to Suvorin. He found the novella, however stimulating and beautifully written, almost defiantly ignorant on medical issues—on which, of course, Chekhov the physician was an expert.[9]

But long before Tolstoy had discovered his mission as a prophet to the world, leading him to repudiate the literary masterpieces that Chekhov, like many others, thought unsurpassed, he had demonstrated impressive psychological acumen in his fiction. His first novel, *Childhood,* published in 1852 when he was twenty-four, is an apprentice work of genius. The novel, as students of Tolstoy have noted, is deeply in debt to Sterne and to Dickens, but in succeeding drafts Tolstoy tried to purge external influences to let his own voice come forth all the more audibly. He constructed *Childhood,* and then *Boyhood* and *Youth,* as a fictional autobiography. The stress was on "fictional"; when Nikolai Nekrasov, publishing the novel in his prestigious literary journal, *The Contemporary,* changed its title to *A History of My Childhood,* Tolstoy furiously objected. He was voicing more than authorial vanity. "Who," he asked rhetorically, "is interested in the history of *my* childhood?"[10] Yet, as will emerge, the novel was largely just that: the history of Tolstoy's childhood. It stands as an early exercise in Tolstoy's lifelong effort to examine himself as unsparingly as humanly possible, a counterpart to the diary he had been keeping from the age of nineteen.*

Still, *Childhood* is fiction that subjected memories of early years, and stories he had been told about them to the aesthetic pressures of literature. He invented or reshaped important moments. Thus he has the ten-year-old narrator, intelli-

---

*See below, p. 338.

Jacob Burckhardt. The discoverer
(some critics have said, inventor, in
vain) of the Renaissance.

Karl May. A photograph taken two
years before his death, still natty
and composed. But note the shaky
signature speaking of pervasive
anxiety.

Karl May. Das Waldröschen oder
die Verfolgung rund um die Erde.

Max Beerbohm. A witty comment
on James's two styles.

Fyodor Dostoevsky. Looking like
the author of his disturbing novels.

Jean-Francois Millet, *The Angelus* (1859). One of the most widely admired paintings of the Victorian age, fought over by the United States and France, and reproduced innumerable times on innumerable materials.

Arnold Böcklin, *Toteninsel.* The only rival of Millet's *Angelus,* a treasure for bourgeois walls.

James Ensor, *Autoportrait* (1884). Ensor's last conventional self-portrait.

Albrecht Dürer, *Selbstbildnis* (1500). Probably the most famous self-portrait by a German artist, evoking innumerable ecstatic comments.

Rembrandt, *Self-Portrait* (1631). One of at least seventy-five attempts to fix his face on canvas, paper, and the etching plate.

Rembrandt, *Self-Portrait*. This version, and the following one are, we might say, nineteenth-century Rembrandts.

Rembrandt, *Self-Portrait*.

Caspar David Friedrich, *Selbstbildnis* (1810).

Caspar David Friedrich *Wanderer am Abgrund vor nebliger Berg-Landschaft (The Wanderer above the Mist.)*

Alfred Rethel, *Auch ein Totentanz*. One instance of the masterly modern adaptation of the late-medieval cycle, the Dance of Death.

Max Klinger, *Auf den Schiene* *Vom Tode*. From yet another cyc on death.

Berthe Morisot, *Julie Manet*. Morisot's charming only child, a pleasure to paint, and an obsessive subject for her mother.

gently observant of himself and his little world, experience his mother's death—the novel's centerpiece, to which we shall return—although in real life she had died when Tolstoy was not quite two. The mother in *Childhood* is largely the mother of his yearning fantasies. Yet there is truth in such literary liberties, truth contained in their fidelity to psychological realities. If Tolstoy really did feel the first-person genre to be limiting, this novel, a marked critical success, shows that it did not compromise his control over his material.

Tolstoy places the narrator, his age and social station and his talent for precise perceptions, with the opening sentence. "On the 12th of August 18——, exactly three days after my tenth birthday, for which I had received such wonderful presents, Karl Ivanych," his tutor, "woke me at seven in the morning by hitting at a fly just over my head with a flap made of sugar-bag paper fastened to a stick."[11] It is the profusion of such details, whether physical or mental, that makes *Childhood* a superb document of Victorian self-awareness.

The narrator, we soon discover, extends his pitiless roving eye to observations of the inner world. As his beloved Sonya laughs at him till the tears come as she watches him trying to pull his hand away from his doting grandmother, he wonders whether she is seriously mocking him and is relieved that she is not. "I realized that her laughter was too full and too natural to be sarcastic."[12] The novel is filled with such shards of memory, fragmentary jagged pieces for the portrait Tolstoy is sculpting before the reader's eyes. It is characteristic of the book, and psychologically right, that its chapters are discrete episodes in the narrator's young life held together by his selective recall. Like so many pictures at an exhibition, they are individual gems thematically related.

Tolstoy makes *Childhood* into a feast of perceptiveness with the young narrator's complicated, often ambivalent responses to incidents trivial and portentous. His capacity to register contradictory feelings in himself—helped along, as we shall see, by the adult author leading the boy's pen—is more impressive still. They rise to subtleties wholly inaccessible to the manufacturers of popular fiction. The narrator, annoyed at himself and his tutor, "wanted to laugh and cry at the same time." Thinking that he must do without his beloved mother for a while as his father plans to take him along to Moscow, "I felt very very sorry to leave mamma, and at the same time pleased at the idea we were now really big boys." He is painfully aware that his feelings are infected with self-centeredness. Watching his mother wave at the departing carriage, he "continued to cry and the thought that my tears were a proof of my sensitiveness pleased and consoled me." He candidly acknowledges that a child's grief can rarely withstand competing emotions: "And the tears rushed to my eyes again; but it was not for long."[13]

The climax of *Childhood*, which gathers up these strands of mixed feelings into one supreme crisis, is the death of the narrator's mother. Notified of her mortal illness, he and his father rush home only to find her unconscious and dying. The narrator sits by her lifeless body, mourning but conscious of every detail in the room—the dim light, the noises, the smells. Through it all, he remains intent on impressing his family and the servants with his unexampled grief, starting to weep when he fears that they may think him indifferent. During the funeral, he never sheds his selfishness: "I despised myself for not experiencing sorrow to the exclusion of everything else, and tried to conceal all other feelings: this made my grief insincere and unnatural." He experiences the joys of mild masochism: "I felt a kind of enjoyment in knowing that I was unhappy and I tried to stimulate my sense of unhappiness, and this interest in myself did more than anything else to stifle real sorrow in me." He weeps copiously, but notices in the midst of all the solemnity—a superb touch—that his jacket is too tight under his arms. Just as he observes himself, he observes others and judges them quite as severely. Few of the mourners are pure in heart, except for his mother's old nurse and a pretty five-year-old girl who keeps screaming as she is held up to the body, which has begun to smell oppressively. No wonder he envies his father, pale, barely able to contain his tears, making all the right public gestures, for giving such a splendid performance: "I don't know why, I did not like him being able to show himself off so effectively at that moment."[14]

What complicates the reader's responses to *Childhood,* without reducing its searching perceptions, is its pervasive double consciousness. The novel resembles autobiographies with their second thoughts alternating between the immediacy of youth and the distance of age.* Thus Tolstoy's narrative voice in *Childhood* belongs to a boy recording his experiences in all their naive freshness and to an adult, necessarily far wiser. "Much water has flowed under the bridge since then," the narrator muses at one point, "many memories of the past have lost their meaning for me and become dim recollections." Vivid directness alternates with melancholic nostalgia. "So many memories of the past arise," we read, "when one tries to recall the features of somebody we love that one sees those features dimly through the memories, as though through tears. They are the tears of imagination." We seem to hear Proust's voice in the wings.[15]

But precisely who is speaking in *Childhood* is not always clear. When the tutor, feeling slighted by his employer, takes revenge by dictating to his pupils a German sentence decrying ingratitude and setting a history lesson, "his face was not so morose as it had been: it was now eloquent of the gratification a man feels who has worthily avenged an insult."[16] It is hardly likely that someone the

*See above, pp. 136–49.

narrator's age would have read so precisely, let alone articulated so eloquently, the fleeting facial expressions of another. Again, the narrator recalls, "I had noticed that many girls had a way of twitching their shoulders to bring a low-necked frock that had slipped back into its proper place."[17] Is this an observation of a youngster tremulously on the verge of puberty or a later gloss? The dominant voice in *Childhood* is the voice of a precocious boy; the hand is the hand of the adult Tolstoy.

First-person revelations of inner states were an international phenomenon. But since French authors enjoyed wider latitude than contemporaries elsewhere to admit the public to their emotional travail, they proved particularly skilled at translating intimate experience into literary art. Perhaps the most compelling French exemplar of autobiography-into-fiction until Proust's masterpiece half a century later was Eugène Fromentin's *Dominique,* published in 1863. The novel was reminiscent of some splendid models: Benjamin Constant's *Adolphe* of 1816, a minor classic of self-analysis revealing the pathos of an egotistical, even cruel, but uncommonly lucid lover; Sainte-Beuve's *Volupté,* published in 1834, which blurred the boundaries between fact and fiction by solemnly asserting that it was not a novel at all, but "the analysis of an inclination, a passion, even a vice"; and, in 1836, Alfred de Musset's *Confessions d'un enfant du siècle,* in which the author's unmistakable surrogate, the narrator, interweaves the history of Musset's political disillusionment with a relatively faithful transcription of a tempestuous love affair with George Sand. But *Dominique,* though in a familiar confessional tradition, was a much admired text on its own, proof that public self-laceration could serve not only to analyze inner turmoil but to exorcise it.

When Fromentin published *Dominique,* he was already an accomplished academic painter of exotic landscapes and a highly regarded travel writer. The principal narrator in his only work of fiction, a middle-aged, socially conscious and apparently happily married country squire, recollects in tranquillity a doomed love affair of long ago.[18] He had reconciled himself to himself, "which is the greatest victory we can win over the impossible."[19] In real life, Fromentin had been infatuated with a woman three years his senior—since they had been childhood playmates, she was always the older woman for him—who had married someone else, then become his mistress, and died young. Long after her death, she remained lodged in Fromentin's memory as the love of his life once enjoyed and now forever unattainable. In *Dominique,* Fromentin has the narrator's amour marry someone else, although she loves him alone. To free him from his hopeless attachment—as a dutiful wife, she is unlikely to cuckold her husband—she undertakes to meet him often, and alone. The prescription, worse than the disease, fails, as it must, and the two doomed lovers part forever.

This story is of little importance, a mere framework for a minute psychological investigation. With all the subtlety at his command, Fromentin probes the narrator's emotional roller coaster, his desires and frustrations, his moments of exaltation and of shame, many borrowed from his own carefully guarded past. Early in the century, Stendhal had observed in his fragmentary autobiography, *La Vie de Henry Brulard,* that "one could write, making use of the third person, *he* did, *he* said. But then how to account for the inner movements of the soul?"[20] It will emerge that many novelists accounted for these movements very creditably in the third person as well.

4. The Strains of Complexity

Major novelists shared certain literary devices with popular favorites, but plainly what separated them from the Dumases of the age was far more significant: they dug deeper and (almost without exception) earned less. If purveyors of best-sellers could not—or would not—invent authentic selves, the preeminent Victorian novelists pursued human nature into its lair. And they paid a price for it. In 1855, Nathaniel Hawthorne bitterly complained to William Ticknor, his publisher and good friend, that while his searching tales were finding a few thousand readers at best—his *Scarlet Letter* had sold about five thousand copies six months after publication—a "d——d mob of scribbling women" was selling its trash "by the 100,000."[1] His was a voice from the angry and disheartened camp of high literature.

To be sure, some novelists who would secure a place in the canon enjoyed a following and even a modicum of financial rewards. Tolstoy, soon after making his name in cultivated circles with *Childhood,* became a popular favorite as well. But popularity was a relative term. Speaking of Tolstoy's *Boyhood,* a correspondent told him in 1855 that the book "had what is called an effect, that is people in Petersburg are all talking about it." Unfortunately, "all Petersburg" signified only the cultivated few who read the literary monthlies. They appreciated Tolstoy largely for the right reasons, for his "delicate analysis of the psychological processes" and for his subtlety in describing "the various inner movements of the soul."[2] But the sales of his books reached six figures only after the triumphs of *War and Peace* and *Anna Karenina,* and then mainly for the simple children's stories he had written in the early 1870s. His collected works, steadily enlarged from the mid-1880s on, sold in sets of 5,000 or more, until the fourteenth edition, of 1897, could boast a printing of 16,000.[3] These totals stamp Tolstoy a successful author. Yet, considering the millions of readers that an

Eugène Sue or a Karl May, to say nothing of Harriet Beecher Stowe, could command, these were sobering numbers.

George Eliot's publishing history described a comparable if more convoluted trajectory. After a slow start as a novelist, Eliot fought her way to the exclusive summit of leading English writers and saw herself compared, often favorably, to Dickens and Thackeray. The fears of her live-in critic, G. H. Lewes, that she might lack the necessary dramatic talent were shown to be groundless by the response to *Adam Bede*. By May 1859, three months after publication, 3,000 copies had been sold, and by the end of the year, sales stood at 16,000. Welcoming this tangible stamp of approval, Lewes drew the characteristic nineteenth-century distinction between popular entertainment and serious writing that has dominated the study of literature since his day. *Adam Bede*, he wrote, had enjoyed "greater success than any novel since Scott (except Dickens)," and specified his claim: "I do not mean has *sold* more—for *Uncle Tom's Cabin* and *Les mystères de Paris* surpass all novels in sales." Fortunately, he added, at rare moments the gulf could be bridged: "In its *influence*, and in obtaining the suffrages of the highest and wisest as well as of the ordinary novel reader, nothing equals *Adam Bede*."[4] Nor did most of Eliot's later novels equal—and only *Middlemarch*, more than a decade later, surpassed—that first success. True, *The Mill on the Floss* of 1860 sold 6,000 copies in seven weeks after publication; and a year later *Silas Marner*, some 8,000 copies within a year, both respectable and financially gratifying totals. But publishers who invested heavily in Eliot on the strength of these sales—Blackwood £5,000 for *Felix Holt* and George Smith £7,000 for *Romola*—lived to regret the liberality of their advance.[5]

Eliot's bid for a wide readership was shadowed by the fact that she was controversial and thought difficult. That she injected philosophizing into her fictions, and that her religion of humanity sounded suspiciously like atheism, only strengthened the public's reserve. As long as her evocations of English country life and unsentimental, though warmhearted, character sketches could be ticketed "Dutch realism," her novels raised few hackles. But Eliot's recognition that humans can be torn apart by the conflicting demands of passion and reason, and that sexual urges exercise potent pressure on the self-denying demands of bourgeois culture, made her most liberal-minded readers uneasy.

Indeed, her analyses of that arcane but potent drive alienated the public that bought novels at railroad stalls or borrowed them from lending libraries, even though—or perhaps precisely because—they in no way resembled the licentiousness of French novels. The most sensitive of her many reviewers tried to make peace with Eliot's ability to see humans as complex beings, pushed and pulled by mixed, often hidden, motives. But the erotic domain was another matter. Discussing *The Mill on the Floss*, the *Saturday Review*, alarmed at Maggie

Tulliver's scandalous infatuation with Stephen Guest, declared the author's candor open to criticism. "There are emotions over which we ought to throw a veil."[6] This judgment no doubt owed something to English prudery; French novelists had been investigating sexuality for decades and been roundly denounced for it in more reticent bourgeois cultures. Whatever her reasons, Eliot seemed to be joining the French by shining light into the dark crevices in the human soul that respectable people should know were off limits—especially if she insisted on burdening her readers with unhappy or ambiguous endings.

She was undeterred. "There is a great deal of unmapped country within us," Eliot announced in *Daniel Deronda,* her last novel, and "men, like planets, have both a visible and an invisible history."[7] A whole program lies revealed in these maxims. Unmapped country must be mapped; invisible histories must be made visible. Eliot's exploration of the links that bind heredity and circumstances to character invited a profound redefinition and, with that, expansion of the domain of experience that the truthful writer of fiction may rightfully claim. It was this kind of intrepid, often tactless exploration of the naked heart that principally distinguished the major novelists of the age from their more commonplace and commercially minded competitors.

Two masters, Feodor Dostoevsky and Henry James, may serve to demonstrate this controversial achievement. As students of human nature, they seemed to have little in common as they stalked their prey in markedly divergent ways, demonstrating that there is more than one road to the secrets of the mind. Whatever their differences, neither of them neglected the clashes of their protagonists with the external world and with one another. Dostoevsky, from the beginning of his career burdened with a political-religious agenda—though its contents radically shifted—pitted the despised and rejected against arrogant plutocrats, skeptics and atheists against true believers, hapless individuals against an arbitrary and corrupt state apparatus. And for James, too, the world and the Other defined his characters' opportunities and boundaries. Yet James's devils, like Dostoevsky's, did their work largely within, only in a more civilized manner.

Dostoevsky possessed what Henry James called the imagination of disaster in barely controlled abundance. This is not the place to retell his life in detail, but some biographical markers are indispensable, for he acquired his apocalyptic vision honestly and his extremism came naturally to him. He was born in 1821 into a family at once loving and anxiety-provoking. His mother seems to have been the perfect housewife, dutiful and tender, if spirited; his father, a physician attached to a Moscow hospital for the poor, was more problematic. Dr. Dostoevsky was the traditional domestic autocrat, but for all that an affectionate husband and father—when he could manage it. He was susceptible to depressions and a suspiciousness amounting to paranoia. Frustrating young Feodor's wish to be a writer, he enrolled him in the Academy of Engineers. No intellectual desert, the academy gave Dostoevsky access to Russian and foreign literary classics. But it was not what he wanted in life.

Dostoevsky's fiction has been interpreted through the lenses of two harrowing traumas that struck him ten years apart, in 1839 and 1849. There is much to that reading, but even before, he wandered in the mists of high-pitched romantic fantasies and inner religious strife.[8] The most nightmarish imaginings of E. T. A. Hoffmann and Victor Hugo worked on him like oppressive realities.[9] So did his anguish at godless humanity, decades before he turned himself into a reactionary social and religious prophet.[10] To study the meaning of man and of life became his announced vocation.

Then, in June 1839, his father died suddenly, ostensibly from an apoplectic stroke, yet the rumor that he had been suffocated by his serfs quickly gained currency. True or not, the point is that Dostoevsky believed it.[11] The death wishes he seems to have harbored had become reality, and his guilt feelings apparently intensified by awareness that he had been sponging on his father, whom he had kept asking for money even after the elder Dostoevsky had been suffering grave financial reverses. Had he been murdered because anguish had driven him to bear down hard on his serfs?

But literature beckoned, and in 1845 Dostoevsky published his first novel, *Poor Folk,* to enthusiastic applause; Belinsky, the most authoritative critic of the day, greeted him as a splendid new talent. His seductive, unanticipated status as the pet of Moscow's literati proved short-lived; Dostoevsky dropped from favor as rapidly as he had risen, as his disillusioned admirers pronounced his second novel, *The Double,* a sad letdown. But Dostoevsky kept writing. He also began to frequent radical political coteries, at the worst possible time to cultivate such connections: the government of Nicholas I was intent on stamping out all, even slight signs of, subversion. In April 1849, Dostoevsky was arrested and in December, upon the czar's orders, subjected to a diabolical charade. Though his actual sentence was four years of penal servitude, he was put through all the preparatory stages of an execution—the solemn reading of the sentence, the priest's ministrations—and awaited the lethal shot that never came. He was, as he later said, born again. In shackles, he was transported to a penal colony in Siberia, where he lived in overcrowded, stinking conditions, his career in tatters. The epileptic attacks to which he had been subject for some years grew worse. Considering what he had lived through before he was thirty, the melodramatic personages and events that crowd his novels read like portraits drawn from life.

Dostoevsky returned to St. Petersburg only in 1859, after a ten years' exile. He was writing again, drawing freely on his appalling decade, exquisitely suffering both in body and in mind. He restlessly traveled through Europe, learning to despise it and the Russian Westernizers who took it as their model; edited literary journals that failed or were forced to close; endured a bizarre love affair and married unhappily; continued to be devastated by periodic epileptic fits. For several years, until he conquered the addiction with the aid of his supportive second wife, he was fatally attracted to the gambling salons in European spas, never content to leave the tables until he had lost everything. Yet, through it all, he wrote a quartet of masterpieces, from *Crime and Punishment,* published in 1866, to *The Brothers Karamazov,* serialized in 1879 and 1880. A year later he died, a renowned but contested figure.

Contested largely because his admirers and detractors had long since divided more vehemently over Dostoevsky's political-religious dogmas than over his psychological intuitions.[12]* They hailed—or denigrated—him as an evangelist, a mystic, a prophet; they analyzed him as a seer or a sadist.[13] He had traded in the political radicalism of his youth for a ferocious hatred of all revolutionaries, socialists, atheists, Roman Catholics, and Westernizers, and preached the gospel of orthodox Christianity and of holy Russia, both honored with a mission to the world, a mission that an army of Satans in human form was plotting to abort.

Dostoevsky's crusading zeal pervaded his novels; all bear a religious-political message debated, and acted out, by extravagant protagonists. Raskolnikov, the antihero of *Crime and Punishment,* stands as a caution for those who think they can do without God; as a would-be Napoleon, he commits two murders largely to demonstrate that the masters of men are exempt from the religious and ethical constraints that, in his arrogant view, reduce ordinary humans into herd animals. The hero of *The Idiot,* Myshkin, "a truly good man," retains his innocence amid an unsavory swarm of sensualists and schemers who in their greed, their lust, their cynicism have denied Christ. The charismatic, severely disoriented Stavrogin, who towers over *The Possessed,* Dostoevsky's free translation of contemporary nihilist activities into feverish fiction, is on a quest after experience at all costs; a leader of others who cannot lead himself and who has the sexual violation of a ten-year-old girl on his fragile conscience, he ends up

---

*"Political-religious" is an ungainly adjective, but it is to the point. In late October 1838, Dostoevsky wrote to his brother Mikhail, "The poet, in a transport of inspiration, makes out God, con[sequently], he fulfills the purpose of philosophy. Con[sequently], poetic rapture is the rapture of philosophy. . . . Con[sequently], philosophy is that same poetry, only in the highest degree!" Dostoevsky, *Complete Letters,* ed. and tr. David Lowe and Ronald Meyer, 5 vols. (1988–91), I, 440.

hanging himself. The brothers Karamazov box the compass of religious and moral attitudes: the saintly Alyosha; the clumsy and irresponsible Dmitri; the clever and unstable rationalist Ivan.*

These great sinners and sufferers act with a supporting cast of marginal characters that include precocious masochists; neurotic, self-destructive young women; elderly society ladies making fools of themselves over shallow poets; fanatics bent on forcing the world into their crazy schemes; affected liberals who mouth the clichés of Western philosophy; unscrupulous manipulators and boorish bureaucrats; sex-crazed libertines who will stop at nothing. All experience sudden bursts of love and hatred, the overpowering need to sin and lust for atonement. And they all talk endlessly to each other and themselves, about religion and politics and their innermost feelings. Dostoevsky was, to paraphrase a remark by his admirer Nietzsche, writing with a hammer. His fiction is one long confrontation: with society, with lovers, with political enemies, with God, above all with oneself. Catastrophe lurks everywhere; Dostoevsky's characters are given to bruising self-laceration, manic declamations, attacks of delirium, and, at defining moments, violence.

Dostoevsky's hysterics and psychotics were no mere ideological puppets and had all too much to say to students of the mind. Freud once observed that neurotics, driving normal behavior to extremes, teach valuable lessons about the mental life of less disturbed persons. Something like this held true of Dostoevsky's characters.[14] He regarded his creations as real persons rather than outlandish monsters; in a much quoted letter, he insisted that what most people call fantastic, he thought the essence of the truth, and declared himself a "realist in a higher sense," that is, a writer who portrayed "all the depth of the human soul."[15] His was the realism of George Eliot at its most extreme, as though he were displaying his characters flayed, the carapace of civilization brutally stripped away. Raskolnikov and the others seem to be acting out in broad daylight what belongs only to the night. Desires and terrors generally repressed, emotions that normally emerge, if at all, as peculiar acts or neurotic symptoms, manifest themselves before readers at once unnerved and seduced by their uncanny relevance. It is only natural that in his major novels, murder is the climax; Dostoevsky's madmen and madwomen find killing inevitable, almost commonplace. To them, the wish is father to the act.

What makes his realism so convincing is that Dostoevsky's most fanatical characters can be shaken by ambivalence. Their will, the beast within, or their conscience, that hidden angel, subverts their doctrines. Stavrogin, the center of

---

*It is Ivan, of course, who recounts the famous fable of the Grand Inquisitor, in which Christ returns to the world and is rejected by it once again, in the name of Christianity.

energy in *The Possessed,* speaks for them all. "I'm still capable of wishing to do a good deed and taking pleasure in doing so," he says in the last letter he writes before his suicide, "but at the same time I wish to do evil and also take pleasure in that."[16] And the unrepentant Raskolnikov, to the end unable to see his double murder as a crime, thirsts for punishment and turns himself in to assuage the terrible feeling of emptiness that haunts him. Even the sly, mean-spirited, repellent murderer and suicide Smerdyakov, the villain in *The Brothers Karamazov,* leaves a note generously absolving everyone else from responsibility.

The text that most visibly encapsulates the tensions tormenting Dostoevsky's characters is *The Double,* that early disappointment. As late as 1877, he called the tale, though he admitted that it had failed as a drama, the most serious idea he had ever contributed to literature.[17] In the light of his most celebrated novels, that seems quite excessive, for the novella is no masterpiece. Dostoevsky too plainly loathed his protagonist, failed to discipline his narrative, and could never make up his mind just what the double represents. But as a clue to his psychological preoccupations as both a writer and a sufferer, it is immensely serviceable. Golyadkin is a minor bureaucrat, vain, stupid, something of a dandy. His self-image fluctuates perilously between self-importance and self-hatred. This "hero," as Dostoevsky sarcastically calls him, aspires to the hand of his chief's daughter. When he crashes her birthday party, he is unceremoniously ejected, and at midnight, as he wanders the streets of St. Petersburg, his double manifests itself. At times subservient and at times taunting, the "younger Golyadkin" continues to persecute him and drives him into open insanity.

The theme of the double had, of course, been in the air since the romantics. Dostoevsky had encountered it in Hoffmann's tales and in the stories of the admired Gogol. And his later work testifies to its importance to him; Ivan Karamazov's conversation with the devil is only the most spectacular heir to Golyadkin's predicament. And these doubles, at times a stern superego and at times the embodiment of the lowest impulses, dramatize the rift that their creator uncovered at the core of the human soul. Nietzsche, himself no mean psychologist, called Dostoevsky the only psychologist from whom he had anything to learn.[18] It was an extravagant tribute, but not undeserved.

Unlike Dostoevsky, who penetrated to his characters' naked heart by placing them into appalling situations, Henry James got inside *his* characters largely by staging cultivated encounters supported by paragraphs of pointed analysis. And as he got older, James grew more rather than less experimental in search of the right mood, the right word, the right diagnosis. I said earlier that in populating their fictions with human beings instead of cardboard images, the serious novelists of the Victorian age paid a price—none a heavier one than James.

In most of his tales, James's characters live in the rarefied atmosphere of elegant houses, vast horizons, refined conversations, and knotty entanglements. Even the poor swim in the ambiance of the rich. But they act out conflicts fundamental to all humans; their high visibility only permits all the closer analysis. What looks like snobbery in Henry James was in reality his well-earned conviction that he was blessed with insights into the human situation denied more commonplace authors.

Unlike Dostoevsky, Henry James never had to contend with parental obstructions to his literary vocation. Born in New York in 1843 to a cultivated and talkative family, he was swamped in combative discourse at home from his boyhood on. His older brother, William, was to become the most famous of the five young Jameses; his younger sister, Alice, frail and high-strung, the most beloved. It was a household in which Dickens and Shakespeare were read aloud, one that Emerson and Thackeray visited. Before 1875, when he decided to settle abroad to savor the richer cultural texture he craved—London won out over Paris after a year—Henry James had already visited Europe several times. He had been writing reviews and short stories for a decade, and from 1870 on, he began to turn out novels. His self-assigned task from the beginning and never abandoned was "splendid and supreme creation."[19]

But before his death in 1916, those who conceded that he had reached his high-flying goal were the select few. Of his sustained fiction, only *Daisy Miller,* a charming novella about a young American woman conquering and dying in Europe, succeeded in the marketplace: over 20,000 copies were sold upon its publication in 1878. James considered himself lucky if his novels found five or six thousand buyers. And the trio of novels he published between 1902 and 1904—*The Ambassadors, The Wings of the Dove,* and *The Golden Bowl*—books on which his posthumous fame largely rests, ran not only into commercial but into critical resistance. Yet James's skirmishes with the reading public, though exacerbated by his final novels, antedated his difficult late style.* In 1892, working out a story, "Owen Wingrave," he noted significantly that since he was writing it for the *Graphic,* that middle-brow London weekly, he "mustn't

---

*Two novels of the 1880s on which he had pinned great hopes, *The Bostonians* and *The Princess Casamassima,* both eminently readable, sold only around 13,000 copies in Britain and the United States together. Some readers were apparently offended by these texts, but more thought them simply boring. In 1888, in a much quoted lament, he told his friend William Dean Howells, one of a select handful who valued him to the full, "I am still staggering a good deal under the mysterious and (to me) inexplicable injury wrought—apparently—upon my situation by my two last novels, the *Bostonians* and the *Princess,* from which I expected so much and derived so little. They have reduced the desire, and the demand, for my production to zero." James to Howells, January 2, 1888, Henry James, *Letters,* ed. Leon Edel, 4 vols. (1974–84), III, 209.

make it 'psychological'—they understand that no more than a donkey understands a violin."[20] The book-buying and magazine-reading public refused to
follow James in his expeditions into the maze that is the human mind.

Far from blind to the vagaries of the marketplace, James faced them with
sturdy professionalism. He worked "for fame's sake, and art's, and fortune's."
And, though he had some money of his own, fortune was never far from
James's mind, as he lamented his "uninterrupted need of making money on the
spot."[21] He shrewdly sold stories and novels separately to English and American
publishers. He fitted the length, at times even the manner, of his stories to the
requirements editors thought prudent. He filled his notebooks, the laboratory
in which he recorded ideas for stories and germs of plots, with little pep talks
attesting to the survival of his ambition in a sordid "age of advertisement and
newspaperism." In 1882, he propped himself up with, "I shall have been a
failure unless I do something *great!*" and nine years later he told himself, "Try
everything, do everything, render everything—be an artist, be distinguished, to
the last."[22] He wanted to sell without selling out. But there were those greedy
editors, those mediocre reviewers, those undiscriminating readers!

His century, James feared, was given over to that worst of all social offenses,
vulgarity, and vulgar was precisely what James thought himself least capable of
being.[23] One of his most poignant, most autobiographical tales, "The Next
Time," tells the story of a serious novelist who diligently tries to commit
best-sellers but finds that everything he touches turns into a masterpiece. For
James, whatever allowances he was willing to make for the public's taste, it was
a hard lot to be condemned to greatness.

The reserved, often obtuse reception of his work, then, reflects far less on
James than on the reading public; it was a failure of the bourgeois imagination
before one of its most searching psychologists. There is something paradoxical
about this response, for James was impeached not for being too penetrating but
for being not penetrating enough. Even professional reviewers mistook subtlety
for frigidity. In 1881, summing up his career to this point, James described
himself as "one who has the passion of observation and whose business is the
study of human life."[24] It was the year of *The Portrait of a Lady,* his most serious
bid for literary stature so far. But James's detractors—and he had many—rarely
gave him credit for the passion he claimed for himself. They charged that the
petit point meticulousness to which he increasingly resorted was getting in the
way of his narrative drive. They hinted at effeminacy. They dismissed him as
cold and bloodless. James, wrote Oscar Wilde in 1899, "will never arrive at
passion, I fear."[25]

For once, Wilde, that scorner of philistine opinion, was echoing the prosaic majority. Arnold Bennett, like Wilde, thought highly of James's technical skills yet insisted that he was "tremendously lacking in emotional power."[26] Even William James, though affectionate and empathetic—but, Henry James thought, tone deaf to the resonances of subtle fiction—complained about the labyrinthine indirections of his younger brother's late novels. Henry James shared Wordsworth's fate: he was perhaps parodied more often and more maliciously than any other novelist. Inevitably rejection and ridicule had their consequences. When H. M. Alden, the long-term editor of *Harper's Magazine,* reviewed the manuscript of *The Ambassadors* for his publisher—it was, James thought, the finest thing he had ever done—he spoke for a consensus: "The scenario is interesting, but it does not promise a popular novel. The tissues of it are too subtly fine for general appreciation. It is subjective, fold within fold of a complex mental web, in which the reader is lost if his much-wearied attention falters." And he advised the publisher to reject the novel. "We ought to do better."*

Such readings are not beyond explanation, but they remain desperately shallow. One could *not* do better—except commercially. Alert readers could find his fiction abounding in action, provided they redefined action to include the inward motions of the soul. The tensions pulsating through his work could escape only readers in search of easy gratification; he wielded the instrument of suspense adroitly, even diabolically. The manner in which he postponed the resolution of *The Wings of the Dove* to its breathless final paragraphs is typical of him.† But even on the ordinary definition of action, James's work hardly lacked excitement. He staged betrayals, painful separations and reversals of roles, divorces and dark mysteries, painful or welcome deaths and, occasionally, a suicide. He delivered moments of recognition that would send shock waves through the reader prepared for James's touch. And he was, as we have seen, a great hand at triangles—one man between two women, one woman between two men, an artist between art and money or, entering dangerous territory, a daughter between her father and a suitor.

*Quoted in *The Notebooks of Henry James,* ed. F. O. Mattiessen and Kenneth B. Murdock (1947), 372. The editors call this verdict "a masterpiece of incomprehension." So, no doubt, it is. But Alden was right to predict that *The Ambassadors* would not be popular, and too subtle for the general reading public.

†He wrote novellas, like the famous *Turn of the Screw* or *The Altar of the Dead,* that are not resolved until literally the last word. "Dramatise it, dramatise it!" he told himself more than once, and his ambition to be a successful playwright—he felt his disappointment over the failures of his plays more poignantly than his disappointment over the small readership for his novels—attests to the seriousness of that call. See his comment, "The dramatic form seems to me the most beautiful thing possible; the misery of the thing is that the baseness of the English-speaking stage affords no setting for it." Undated entry, between November and December 1882, *Notebooks,* 44.

James's massive *The Princess Casamassima,* published in 1886, exemplifies his way with action at once manifest and concealed. A bald summary makes the novel sound like sheer melodrama, but James enriched it with what he had learned about the seamy side of London life during long nocturnal ambles, and with his brilliant study of the conflicts besetting the protagonist. Hyacinth Robinson is a bookbinder, intelligent and sensitive, with a romantic history as the illegitimate son of an English aristocrat and a French seamstress who has killed her seducer. Early exposed and solemnly committed to nihilist doctrines, Hyacinth is taken up by a jaded American heiress, the Princess Casamassima, who introduces him to the glories of culture and the charms of polite society, stark antitheses to his revolutionary ideology. Increasingly skeptical about the first and fascinated by the second, Robinson is almost literally torn apart by the clash of his politics with his aesthetic discoveries. Ordered to assassinate a duke as a political gesture, he turns the gun on himself.

Is Hyacinth hero or dupe? Impatient readers, as usual in the majority, did not want to bother with such questions. They wanted to get on with the story and be plainly told whose side they were supposed to take. Almost defiantly, James refused to simplify his characters by smoothing away conflicting motives. The drama that held his attention was the pressure of moral scruples or artistic obligations on the blandishments of affluence, the temptations of love, the anxieties of respectability, the burdens of memory, as he inched toward the core of human nature.

Yet, with all his gift for unmasking, Henry James was a cunning rather than an ostentatious psychologist. His starting point was almost always a situation; the geometry of his tale literally came first. But the themes to which he repeatedly returned were variations on his own experience, deeply felt and deftly translated into his unmistakable prose: the American innocent invading a supercivilized, often corrupt Europe; the artist confronting a vulgar society; the victim assailed by uncanny terrors internal or external; or, more private still, the hero caught in the toils of strained family relations. The plots he started with were banal enough, for the most part twisted amorous entanglements burdened with the secrets that destroy relationships: an undisclosed infidelity, a hidden love, an illegitimate child. But what mattered was James's way with his raw materials as each revision sharpened his literary detective work. His moves toward psychological truths were not without their risks: James feared at times that they might interfere with the imperatives of dramatic action.* To make his

---

*"The weakness of the whole story," he noted, at work on *The Portrait of a Lady,* "is that it is too exclusively psychological—that it depends to[o] little on incident." Undated entry [probably 1880], *Notebooks,* 15.

"puppets" real—and interesting—it was necessary to reconcile psychology with incident. James's notebook amply attest that he could move from notion to story only after he could *see* his characters. He found the experience of having them appear before his mental eye indispensable to his acts of creation.

This is another way of saying that James felt obliged to invent believable human beings. His unvarying ideal was nature. It did not commit him to the flat-footed realistic doctrine that fiction ought to be a copy of life: he was a novelist, not a mere reporter. But fiction must *capture* life. When he distrusted one of his intricate plots, he labored to make it "strongly dramatic and natural." At times, as with *The Portrait of a Lady,* he found its convolutions supremely difficult to make "natural." But once he "honestly" believed on reflection that they did rest on nature, he proceeded with the writing. When he devised a plot that struck him as thin and artificial somehow, he gave it his most particular care.[27] But if he could not overcome the technical difficulties of turning shadowy outlines into living people, he dropped the story altogether. "Art," he insisted, "deals with what we see, it must first contribute full-handed that ingredient; it plucks its material, otherwise expressed, in the garden of life—which material elsewhere grown is stale and uneatable."[28]

Tellingly, when James found fault with fellow writers, his most solemn reproach was that they had failed to infuse their characters with living human truth. Though he had loved Dickens since he was a little boy, in 1865, a fledgling reviewer, he thought *Our Mutual Friend* sadly wanting because its characters were "lifeless, forced, mechanical." Dickens had "created nothing but figure. He has added nothing to our understanding of human character." Perhaps worst of all, the book bore the stigmata of composition: "Seldom, we reflected, have we read a book so intensely *written,* so little seen, known, or felt."[29]

This carping dismissal antedates James's late style by a quarter century, a style in which his fiction, too, would be intensely *written*—but, he would insist, not at the expense of inner integrity. In those novels, James's search for ever finer shadings of motivation propelled him to invent dialogue that peeled away layer upon layer of conventionality and concealment and made comprehension dawn after tantalizing delays. These conversations, punctuated with slight misunderstandings that only lead to greater lucidity, were sparring matches that could rise to deadly duels. And, much as James liked to dramatize his characters' minds in action—his experimental novel *The Awkward Age* of 1899 is virtually all dialogue—he supplemented these mannered confrontations with authorial interventions that add up to little psychological treatises, all in the service of life seen, known, and felt.

While the decision to excise the artificial and the forced from his work demonstrates James's self-discipline in the name of nature, his skittish treatment of the sexual urge hints at a certain nervousness over aspects of life that were troubling to him. James closed the bedroom door on his lovers and refused to explore the hidden erotic roots of his characters' intimacy. It is interesting to watch him, particularly in his late fiction, aestheticizing the sensual element with adjectives like "charming" and "beautiful" as if to sublimate grosser needs. But this evasiveness was not simply a furtive escape from his own repressed, inconclusive sexuality. James's fellow Victorians in the English-speaking world were no more candid; and with an interesting mixture of envy and censoriousness, he commented on the latitude open to his French contemporaries. He skirted the edges of the permissible, almost but not quite ready to affront "the prejudices of the Anglo-Saxon reader."[30] As a self-employed author seeking outlets in respectable markets, he recognized the dangers of transgressing the boundaries they had set up. Yet, especially after the turn of the century, he increasingly allowed the forbidden topic to pulsate through his novels, though still discreetly.

Consider *The Wings of the Dove,* published in 1902. Kate Croy, a beautiful, self-possessed, and impecunious woman in her early twenties, visits her father and offers to share his poverty. Her rich, socially ambitious aunt Maud has put before Kate the choice of living with her and having nothing to do with Lionel Croy—whom she detests, not unjustly, as an irresponsible, self-absorbed manipulator—or keeping in touch with him and giving up her prospects for social and, eventually, marital preferment. Cruelly and cynically, Lionel Croy rejects his daughter's overtures, evidently hoping for some crumbs from the tables of the rich if Kate keeps her strategic post in high society. Unwisely, Kate falls in love with a journalist, Merton Densher, and engages herself to him—secretly, since Aunt Maud has great plans for her niece, which certainly exclude a penniless scribbler, however prepossessing.

Enter Millie Theale, a likable American millionairess who, though apparently perfectly healthy, is suffering from an obscure, probably fatal ailment.* Encouraged by her sage physician, she decides to live as intensely as she can while her strength lasts. A tour of European sights is one way; gaining Kate Croy's friendship is another. Then she discovers the manly allure of Merton Densher. Millie Theale's mysterious ill health raises this imbroglio above conventional triangles; her love, as she desperately grasps at life through romantic passion, complicates it further. For Kate Croy, with the connivance of Aunt

---

*Pondered for years, James's portrait of gallant Millie was a monument to his cherished cousin Minny Temple, who had died of tuberculosis three decades before and whom he had never forgotten.

Maud, hatches a scheme of which her fiancé forms the half-reluctant center-piece: the couple will reveal to Millie that Merton Densher loves Kate Croy but suppress the crucial fact that Kate Croy loves Morton Densher. The hope is, of course, that the invalid heiress, aglow with her first and last love and all alone in the world, will leave her immense wealth to the one man in her life. Active for once, Densher, who usually follows Kate's lead, consents on condition that, as an earnest of her devotion, she will come to his rooms to consummate their engagement. Kate agrees, and the intrigue runs its course.

The conversation of Merton Densher and Kate Croy that leads up to her promise to sleep with him swarms with sexual intimations. So, even more, do Densher's fantasies the morning after. "What had come to pass within his walls lingered there as an obsession importunate to all his senses; it lived again, as a cluster of pleasant memories, at every hour and in every object; it made every-thing but itself irrelevant and tasteless."[31] James is silent on Kate Croy's memo-ries of her "surrender," but her pleasure in her lover's physical touch leaves little doubt that it must have been delightful to her.

Soon Millie, near death, learns the truth about the deception the pair have practiced on her, heroically defies her disillusionment, and leaves Densher a fortune. It is the rigors of conscience that spoil Merton and Kate's triumph. Densher refuses to accept the legacy and presents Kate Croy with an agonizing alternative: take the money or take him. Her dilemma makes for a gripping last page. She suggests that Densher is in love with Millie's memory. When he demurs, she protests: " 'I could be in your place; and you're one for whom it will do. Her memory's your love. You *want* no other.' He heard her out in stillness, watching her face but not moving. Then he only said: 'I'll marry you, mind you, in an hour.' 'As we were?' 'As we were.' But she turned to the door, and her headshake was now the end. 'We shall never be again as we were.' "[32]

The question lingers, how real is Kate Croy? Steely in her handsome self-presentation, keeping her aim once glimpsed firmly in view, she is anything but vulgar. Nor is she simply mercenary; if she were, she would never have permit-ted her emotions to overcome her calculations and chosen Merton Densher, the man without prospects. Even her great conspiracy has a touch of disinterest-edness in it—or so she can make herself believe. Why not have her doomed friend enjoy the company of an attractive man for the little time she has left? It is a rationalization, a superb alibi for avarice, but, with her warm feelings for Millie, it has a certain plausibility.

Kate Croy's hunger for money, so powerful that she basely betrays her charming American friend, then, leaves that question mark. But James has planted the answer in a psychological tour de force, the opening chapters, in which she offers to choose her father over her aunt.[33] She sees him, with his shabbiness and self-serving mendacity, as an example to avoid at all cost, just as she sees her grievance-collecting older sister, no less exploitative, as a dire warning.* But her family visits arouse feelings far deeper than the fear of want. Though she remains calm and tearless, Kate takes Lionel Croy's lack of response to her offer as a supreme rejection, no doubt the last of many, as a narcissistic insult hard to overcome or forgive. Kate's determination to master so cold and indifferent a world with every means at her command, including energy, intelligence, and beauty, reads like the revenge of an unloved child. Merton Densher, trying to force Kate Croy to choose between love and money, cannot in the end save her. The need never to fall back into her old shabbiness has become second nature. She will never be again as she was with Densher, because she will always be what she had become on her own.

In short, though he leaves a slight ambiguity hanging over the ending, James would not compromise with the psychological truth of his characters by supplying a happy ending. It has taken readers decades since *The Wings of the Dove* was published to see it for what it was: a stunning performance of literary psychology. Few writers in his time could even approximate James's piling up insight after insight into the intricacies of human nature. But he was, for decades, writing for the happy few. The sales of this novel speak eloquently to the refusal of the general book-buying public to follow James's expedition into the interior: in Britain and the United States, fewer than seven thousand copies were sold. This was not the sort of fiction that even sensitive bourgeois were disposed to admire during James's lifetime.

5. Dickens

Charles Dickens, the representative writer for the century, deserves a chapter of his own. For he was more agile in crossing boundaries than any other of its novelists: entertainer and moralist, buffoon and tragedian in one. When he died in June 1870, at the age of fifty-eight, the whole world went into mourning— or so it appeared to his bereft contemporaries.† Naturally, at home expressions

---

*See *The Wings of the Dove* (1902; New York ed., 1908; ed. John Bayley with notes by Patricia Crick, 1986), 97. [bk. 2, ch. 1]. In speaking of that sister's "greasy children, her impossible claims, her odious visitors," and her selfish speculation that Kate, banking on her good looks, should marry money so that she—the elder—may share in the wealth, James is being at his most direct and uses the simplest possible vocabulary.

†"Before the news of it even reached the remoter parts of England," wrote John Forster, Dickens's longtime friend and first biographer, "it had been flashed across Europe, was known in the distant continents of India, Australia, and America; and not in English-speaking communities

of sorrow were all the more heartfelt. Luke Fildes, who had illustrated Dickens's last, unfinished novel, *The Mystery of Edwin Drood,* famously captured the sense of loss in picturing Dickens's empty armchair and writing desk surrounded by his favorite creations: Mr. Pecksniff, Sam Weller and Mr. Pickwick, Oliver Twist asking for more, and others in that inimitable crew. Her Majesty Queen Victoria sent an affecting telegram of condolence, and crowds filed past Dickens's open grave for days. His wish for a quiet country burial ignored, he was entombed at Westminster Abbey as became a national treasure.

This unprecedented outpouring of sorrow for a novelist speaks to Dickens's range. He seemed to have something for every reader everywhere. Few makers of fiction had ventured into so many neighborhoods, from London slums to pretentious mansions, cathedral towns to industrial cities, opium dens to fishing villages. His cast of characters embraced pimps and prostitutes, merchants active and retired, old rich and newly rich, heiresses and charity boys, beautiful young women from diverse social ranks, servants, scavengers, lawyers, idlers, clerks, nurses, sailors, taxidermists, bureaucrats, executioners, evangelical divines, uncharitable philanthropists, confidence men, schoolteachers, labor leaders, innkeepers, and a host of lesser folk, spear carriers in his teeming operatic dramas. A Dickens novel gives the busy impression of a rococo palace: leaving not an inch of his fictive canvas undecorated, he would endow a waiter, a domestic servant, even a fly, destined for a fleeting appearance, with memorable individuality. Some exacting critics denied him the depths of understanding granted only a handful of novelists. In 1865, reviewing the last novel Dickens completed, *Our Mutual Friend,* Henry James called him, a little cruelly, "the greatest of superficial novelists."[1] But even if he was deficient in psychological acuity—we shall return to the question—Dickens met the needs of his vast reading publics by making himself available to each on its own level.

The conviction that Dickens was the universal storyteller of the Victorian century, delighting all ages and all tastes, from peers to lowly clerks and beyond them to the common people, emerged early.[2] No doubt, the monthly installments of his novels cut an imposing swath: the *Pickwick Papers,* which made him famous, gathered more and more purchasers as successive numbers poured out, until they totaled some 40,000. By 1870, more than a million copies of that quixotic comedy had been sold. Yet the core of his most faithful support was occupied by the proper middle classes. As the perceptive Mrs. Oliphant, herself a prolific and popular novelist, observed in 1855: notwithstanding Dickens's eloquent sympathies for the poor, he was "perhaps more distinctly than any

only, but in every country of the civilised earth, had awakened grief and sympathy." *The Life of Charles Dickens,* 3 vols. (1872–74; ed. Andrew Lang, 2 vols., n.d.), II, 513 [bk. 12, ch. 2].

other author of the time, a *class* writer, the historian and representative of one circle in the many ranks of our social scale."[3] That circle was the bourgeoisie. In Dickens's time, it was already very large and waxing in numbers, confidence, influence, and subtle internal gradations. And Dickens was its novelist—a potent ingredient in the Victorian bourgeois experience and one of its most cherished expressions.

His publics wanted many things from fiction, and Dickens provided them all: humor, pathos, suspense, uplift, satire. He touched masses of readers with a vocabulary rich in resonances from the Bible. He virtually patented quaint, at times monomaniacal eccentrics. He devised intricate plots requiring clever detective work for their unraveling. He enriched the literature of first-person novels, notably with *David Copperfield* and *Great Expectations*. He contributed, in the same two works, to the tradition of the bildungsroman, which traces the formative years of a hero as he encounters, and is schooled by, travel, work, and the instructive mistakes of an apprentice heart.

In short, Dickens steeped his fictions in an atmosphere of magical realism— often more magical than realistic: he furnished his imaginative world with benevolent godfathers and godmothers waving their wands to rescue hapless heroes and heroines from danger and neglect by battling monsters who would stop at nothing, not even murder. His celebrated grotesques—Sairey Gamp, Mr. Micawber, Quilp—would have been at home in the Grimms' collections; the easy familiarity with which his characters identify themselves as figures in fairy tales is telling. Speaking of his celebrated Christmas books, John Forster recalled that "no one was more intensely fond than Dickens of old nursery tales, and he had a secret delight in feeling that he was only giving them a higher form."[4] This was a delight his readers shared.

It seems only fitting that Dickens should have established a virtual corner on Christmas: he had already hailed the holiday in his youthful *Sketches by Boz* as a magical feast of reconciliation and expressed the wish that it might last all the year through. Bringing his affection for the holiday to vivid life, he lingered in *The Pickwick Papers* over a jolly Christmas celebration larded with good will and kisses under the mistletoe. And in rapid succession he published five immensely popular tributes, beginning with *A Christmas Carol* of 1843. They were succeeded by his no less popular periodicals *Household Words* and *All the Year Round,* whose special Christmas numbers, dwarfing all the others, sold as many as a quarter million copies. There were those for whom the Christmas stories struck false notes; Thackeray and others privately found Dickens's seasonal optimism concerning human goodness rather too sticky for their tastes. But these sardonic spirits knew that it was pointless to criticize, let alone ridicule, his effusions: the general reading public blessed Dickens for taking the part of decency and charitableness.

Dickens welcomed these practical and emotional accolades. Speaking in Boston at a banquet given for him in February 1842, he solemnly declared his "earnest and true desire to contribute, as far as in me lies, to the common stock of healthful cheerfulness and enjoyment."[5] But his readers' expectations reached higher than so humble a program, and it is their affectionate and loyal admiration that makes Dickens so instructive to the historian of bourgeois inner life. Whatever captious critics would say, most readers—and many reviewers—trusted him as a student of human motives. They praised him for being a good observer, putting living creatures into his fiction, keeping faith with experience. All his books, G. H. Lewes wrote, "are volumes of human nature" endowed with a "deep and subtle philosophy."[6] None of these professional readers seemed to be disturbed by Dickens's oddities; they thought him entitled to exaggerate traits in the service of a larger truthfulness.

In fact, those who in the 1850s grew testy with Dickens objected not to his psychology but to his forays into social and political criticism. They disliked seeing Dickens invading terrain unfamiliar to him—the court system, the bureaucracy—and derided his satire as uninformed, unfair, or anachronistic. His famous "Circumlocution Office" in *Little Dorrit* struck them as a witty invention but too remote from the reality of government administration to hit home. If only he had stayed with the delightful storytelling of his early novels! "We appeal from the author of *Bleak House* and *Little Dorrit* to the author of *Pickwick,* the *Old Curiosity Shop,* and the better parts of *Chuzzlewit,*" groaned one critic in 1857. "Not in humour only are you dear to us, but in tragedy also, and in pathos we own your power."[7]

But with the passage of years, not all of Dickens's readers remained infatuated with his pathos. One generation's sublimity became another generation's kitsch. The change of heart was dramatized in the response to the death of Little Nell. This long-drawn-out episode in Victorian cultural history has been deservedly explored. Dickens's *Old Curiosity Shop* is now ranked among his minor efforts, but at the time it was as great a favorite as *Pickwick;* its last weekly numbers sold up to 100,000 copies. Late in 1840 and early 1841, as the novel wound toward its end, and its heroine, the good orphan Little Nell, appeared increasingly endangered, strong men dissolved in tears and readers pleaded with Dickens to spare her life.

Waxing sentimental at his own sentimentality, Dickens rejoiced in the interest the world had taken "in favour of that little heroine of mine." He acknowledged letters from two continents, from great cities and camps in the remote wilderness.* Apparently, his pages on Nell's death made the losses others had suffered somehow easier to bear. His most susceptible admirers begged Dickens to introduce similar pathetic scenes into his fiction, and he obliged by giving them the demise of little Paul in *Dombey and Son* and of Jo, the illiterate crossing sweeper, in *Bleak House*. Scenes like Nell's death tweaked the heartstrings of thousands.

To judge from Dickens's letters, they tweaked his own. As usual, he lived among his creations in *The Old Curiosity Shop* as though they were human beings, but more intensely than ever. The "child" pursued him at night, he reported in November 1840. "It makes me very melancholy," he told John Forster the following January, "to think that all these people are lost to me for ever, and I feel as if I never could become attached to any new set of characters." He found the sad logic of his story, of which Forster had persuaded him, as hard to endure as it was necessary to enforce. In March, his travail over, he confessed that his "Nellicide" had pained him deeply.[8] The emotions that some among his closest friends displayed, and shared with him, only legitimated this enjoyable self-torment. Forster, moved almost—but not quite—beyond words, called Nell a "literary masterpiece" and experienced her death as "a kind of discipline of feeling and emotion which would do me lasting good."[9] He was in large company. The elderly Lord Jeffrey, editor, essayist, judge, who wept freely over lachrymose scenes in fiction, told his "dear, dear Dickens" he had fallen in love with him over "Nelly," that "sweet and touching" young woman, and thought her as good a literary inspiration as Shakespeare's Cordelia.[10]

This was heady stuff. But the death of Little Nell also aroused some adverse responses that only grew noisier with succeeding decades. That the religious press should object to the secular quality of Dickens's denouement belongs to the debate over his undenominational, anti-evangelical religiosity; it is of greater moment for an appraisal of Dickens's way with the inner life that some detractors derided his Nellicide as a cheap literary trick. Understandably enough, the obituaries of Dickens that filled British newspapers and periodicals three decades later uncritically saluted his pathos as tender and truthful.[11] But more astringent voices made themselves heard. In 1869, one reviewer called Nell, like Tiny Tim in *A Christmas Carol*, "exceedingly tiresome" and Dickens's pathos "unnatural and unlovely."[12]

---

*He had got letters, he told an American audience, "in England, from the dwellers in log-houses among the morasses, and swamps, and densest forests, and deepest solitudes of the Far West. Many a sturdy hand, hard with the axe and spade, and browned by the summer's sun, has taken up the pen, and written to me a little history of domestic joy or sorrow." Speech in Boston, February 1, 1842, *The Speeches of Dickens,* ed. K. J. Fielding (1960), 20.

That epithet, "unnatural," cuts to the heart of the matter of Dickens the psychologist. Discerning literary men looking back over his career composed variations on it. "Most critical readers," wrote G. H. Lewes in 1872, judge Nell to be "maudlin and unreal." And the following year William Dean Howells asked rhetorically, recalling Lord Jeffrey weeping over little Nell and Paul Dombey, "Does any peer of the realm now shed tears for their fate?" Oscar Wilde's wicked quip, "One must have a heart of stone to read the death of Little Nell without laughing,"[13] was obviously meant to be provocative. But it documented a seismic shift in middle-class sensibilities whose timid beginnings can be traced to the time Dickens wrote *The Old Curiosity Shop*.

The most crushing critique of Dickens's way with human nature came from Anthony Trollope in his posthumous *Autobiography,* all the more devastating for Trollope's acknowledgment that the familiarity of Dickens's books across the country, the canonization of his characters as household names, and the outpouring of grief at his death all confirmed his preeminence. "There is no withstanding such testimony as this." After all, "the primary object of a novelist is to please; and this man's novels have been found more pleasant than those of any other writer." And yet, ranking the leading English novelists like so many prizefighters, Trollope placed Dickens third, behind Thackeray and George Eliot. Mindful that he was defying prevailing sentiments, he denied Dickens's celebrated originals the stature of human beings. And he applied his dissatisfaction to all of Dickens's inventions: "Nor are any of the characters human which Dickens has portrayed."[14] Forster's report that *The Old Curiosity Shop,* "more than any other of his works," made "the bond between himself and his readers one of personal attachment" was accurate enough, but it was not the whole story.[15] As Dickens tightened his grip on middle-class, middle-brow book buyers, he increasingly put off fastidious readers.

This division among Dickens's following must complicate any attempt to fix him firmly on the Victorian map of self-understanding. The derisive adjectives that grave literary critics expended on Dickens—maudlin, sentimental, unnatural, more than a little vulgar—are too searing to be ignored. And these indictments were not twentieth-century discoveries, though recent critics would elaborate on them. In 1858, Walter Bagehot, as shrewd on literature as on politics, never shy about airing his opinions, complained about Dickens's "great, we might say complete, inability to make a love-story." Unable to invent convincing dialogue for his couples or describe his heroines acceptably, he "pours out painful sentiments as if he wished the abundance should make up for the inferior quality."[16] And in the 1860s, in his famous *Histoire de la littérature anglaise,* Hippolyte Taine imagined the proper, Protestant English public forcing Dickens to be moralistic about love instead of truthful, to make his lovers uninteresting and his young women suitable companions for sheltered girls.

To sum up the charges: Dickens is a remarkably uneven writer. He has unlimited amounts of energy but no taste. He reaches for the sublime only to start gushing. His apostrophes—to the reader, the powerful, the world—are embarrassing. When he invokes "GOD," that benign, Christmassy philanthropist, he becomes offensive to the devout and distasteful to the unbeliever. His famous humor has sadistic touches. His male leads are stiff and unconvincing. Worse: his women have no bodies, and float across his pages as awkward mixtures of child and angel. One can hardly imagine them having sexual intercourse, even though they somehow end up with children. Only Estella in *Great Expectations* has any spirit, and she is compounded of arrogance and viciousness. When Dickens has his lovers kiss, he grows coy beyond endurance. All of which raises the uncomfortable question whether a writer at once so prissy and so histrionic can have anything revealing to say about the inner life—except perhaps to disclose, by inadvertence, what his audiences, grasping at his fictions like so many drugs, were trying to escape.

But—and here the complication emerges—even those who found serious fault with Dickens's psychology kept on reading and rereading his novels, apparently with genuine profit. And the avalanche of critical attention, of reprints and collected editions, attests that his place in the canon was never in question. What is more, the list of major writers whom Dickens influenced is long: Dostoevsky, Proust, Shaw, Kafka. Tolstoy flatly called him "the greatest novel writer of the 19th century."[17] Mere success in his unassuming assignment to cheer up respectable families cannot sufficiently explain his lifetime triumphs and his enduring reputation. The fact is that he consistently exceeded his modest aims, and his sophisticated admirers did not read him just for escape; lesser novelists would have served such shallow purposes equally well, if not better.

One of Freud's much quoted letters may point the way out of this dilemma. Sophocles' *Oedipus Rex* had held its "gripping power" across the centuries, he wrote in October 1897, because it confronted "a compulsion that everyone acknowledges because he has sensed its existence in himself. Everyone in the audience was once in germ and in fantasy such an Oedipus."[18] In other words, a truly memorable rather than momentarily diverting work of fiction, one that transcends primitive wish fulfillment, must merge the seductions of literary felicities—wit, style, suspense—with the deft handling of universal inner experiences. And this fusion was the true source of Dickens's power.

Admittedly, facing the encounter of cultural constraints and personal audacity involved in every act of original writing, Dickens was, for all his open aggressions, mealy-mouthed conventionality itself. He made wicked fun of prudes who do not want to see a blush brought to the cheeks of a young person, but in his own work he followed that very precept and was thanked for it. Not even his slum denizens, or his prostitutes, invite impure thoughts. What is more, his affirmations were often disguised denials. By making his freaks appear to have stepped directly out of a fairy-tale world, he minimized their ominous reality. By permitting the exigencies of a plot to override the coherence that obedience to the rules of human nature would demand, he stepped away from the insightfulness he had displayed elsewhere.*

Such departures from verisimilitude, though, did not loosen Dickens's grasp on pathology. One thinks of "The History of a Self-Tormentor," that odd chapter interpolated in *Little Dorrit,* or one of Dickens's last stories, "George Silverman's Explanation." He cast both in the first person and made both voices unreliable narrators, letting readers draw conclusions at variance from those the speakers wanted to convey. The first is a persuasively motivated self-justification of a young misfit with just a hint of tastes for her own sex; she is the picture of rage and frustration whose paranoid reading of others reinterprets the kindnesses they show her as sly acts of aggression. The second, no less plausible, shows the permanent effects of the narrator's mother indoctrinating her son in the belief that he is a "worldly little devil"; as he grows up, he startles and infuriates his little world with obsessive schemes to appear selfless. His rewards are irony itself; scattering self-destructive renunciations, he discovers that others only interpret them as worldliness in disguise. And the twisted mind of the killer—it is worth noting that there are almost as many murderers in Dickens as in Dostoevsky—was one of Dickens's most intensely felt preoccupations.[19]

Dickens's psychological astuteness was not confined to isolated studies in the neuroses. Major themes governing his novels tackle that intimate storm center, the family, and its forbidden secrets. He made unforgettable literature from painful childhood memories and from half-understood, half-repressed emotions: revisiting his ineffectual sponging father and, he thought, callous mother, and that beloved angel his sister-in-law Mary Hogarth, who died at seventeen and whose memory he virtually worshiped. Readers have noticed, justly enough, that Dickens liked to portray presumably unerotic family ties ripening

---

*Thus some of Dickens's characters prove immune to the evil experiences of childhood, which, he firmly believed, immutably shape the adult. To give but two examples from *Little Dorrit:* Arthur Clennam, the incarnation of decency and disinterestedness, has survived intact the unloving, destructive treatment his mother—or, rather, the woman who raised him pretending to be his mother—meted out to him. And the woman he will marry, Little Dorrit, has escaped quite unscathed the dismal prison world into which she was born.

from fraternal love into legitimate sexual union. Only a writer who understood—or at least strongly sensed—the workings of ambivalence and the strains
of the incest taboo could have invented the love story of Agnes Wickfield and
David Copperfield, of Amy Dorrit and Arthur Clennam, of Florence Dombey
and Walter Gay.

Quite as impressively, he has his characters searching for father or mother,
stumbling through life to find the truth about their origins that will give them
peace. Arthur Clennam's stubborn "I want to know" runs like a leitmotiv
through much of Dickens's work. He is describing the family romance in
action, lending it poignant turns. Oliver Twist, the little nobody, the despised
charity boy, learns the story of his parents at long last and ends up the adopted
son of a truly benevolent man; Esther Summerson, in *Bleak House,* discovers
that Lady Dedlock is her mother; and in a stunning reversal, proud Estella in
Great Expectations is revealed as the daughter of two convicts. One striking
variant of that romance is to have the father alive, and his child, scorned,
shunned, or exploited, groping for a flicker of goodness beneath the icy surface.
Florence, daughter of the rich, stern Mr. Dombey, who begins by disliking and
ends up hating her, finds that spark in the end; so does Amy Dorrit, ever
forgiving, as she detects virtues in her father he never really possessed.

Exploring such fraught entanglements, Dickens invariably places the child at
center stage. His admirers claimed, and his detractors acknowledged, that his
sensitivity to the psychological processes of growth was exceptionally acute.
One of his discoveries, never formally analyzed but effectively dramatized, is
the tendency of children to take the sins of their parents upon themselves, to
bear a burden of guilt that is not theirs. Esther Summerson, raised by a forbidding, vindictive godmother filled with evangelical wrath, feels her illegitimacy,
steadily thrown up to her, as somehow her own fault; it makes her, she mistak-
enly believes, unworthy and unattractive. George Silverman, accepting his
mother's cruel verdict that he is a diabolical worldling, can never escape a
shadow not of his making.

In these ventures into his characters' emotional life, Dickens did not evade
the triangle we have learned to call the oedipal situation. The Oedipus complex
is more than a simple confrontation in which the son wants the father out of the
way to have his mother to himself. It is, to begin with, just as significant an
experience for a daughter. What is more, it is mired in mixed feelings. Little
Hans, one of Freud's published cases, illustrates the proposition that the oedipal
child can reject the parent it longs for and long for the parent it rejects. The
Oedipus complex is the name for powerful, usually ambivalent passions that
little aggressive lovers—or loving aggressors—must learn to sort out. It was in
David Copperfield that Dickens worked out the family drama most consistently.

With its tantalizing autobiographical admixtures, the claim of *David Copper-field* as a key text for the study of Dickens is undisputed. In 1869, half a dozen novels and twenty years after its first serialization, Dickens famously singled it out as his "favourite child." While many preferred (and prefer) *Bleak House,* readers on many levels of cultivation—including Tolstoy—agreed that *David Copperfield* was his masterpiece.[20] And it was an explicit bourgeois masterpiece, whose eponymous hero exhibits and extols the vaunted middle-class virtues: determination, hard work, self-reliance, honest dealings, commitment to do-mestic love. Significantly, Matthew Arnold appreciated the "charming and instructive" *David Copperfield* as an "all-containing treasure house" that re-vealed both the severe and the lighter side of "English middle-class civilisa-tion."[21] And these revelations included the bourgeois mind at work.

Its unique stature has been supported by nonliterary reasons, which have lent *David Copperfield* a certain gratuitous, gossipy interest: its autobiographical reve-lations real and imagined. But, however intimately involved Dickens's past in the making of this favorite child, the stress on biographical traces at the expense of its literary qualities slights Dickens's ability to transform raw facts and buried fantasies into imaginative prose and into a convincing fictional portrait. John Forster, better informed than anyone else about the parallels between this novel and its author's life, energetically warned against identifying David Copperfield with Charles Dickens. So did the author himself. "I really think I have done it ingeniously," he wrote Forster in July 1849, as publication was in its early stages, "and with a complicated interweaving of truth and fiction."[22] Certainly Dickens's emotional engagement did not preclude him from mustering the kind of distance an author needs to see his creations not just passionately but clearly. Just as Goethe's Faust was not Goethe, though there was much Goethe in him, Dickens's David Copperfield was not Charles Dickens.

Preeminent among his tales of a young man growing up and, after he has traversed mine fields of error and blindness, disciplining his heart and finding his vocation and his happiness, *David Copperfield* is an oedipal bildungsroman.[23] Dickens's *Great Expectations* is its only rival. David's father, twice his mother's age, mercifully died before David was born, and his life begins in a delightful haze of an erotic monopoly, with seductive caresses and total happiness. This idyll is destroyed by an interloper, the sinister Mr. Murdstone, tight-lipped, unbending, self-righteous, something of a sadist. By marrying this improbable suitor, the unworldly, innocently vain Clara Copperfield constructs an oedipal triangle disastrous for mother and son alike. The bad father can only hate, and try to destroy, the resentful son. Mr. Murdstone beats David with all his strength for his failures at lessons, only redoubling his efforts as David bites him—there is plenty of aggression in the novel—and the boy is sent away to the kind of school that Dickens liked to pillory, run by mercenary and corrupt ignoramuses. There David falls in love with Steerforth—no other term will do—a charming, masterful, well-to-do bully who takes the forlorn David under his wing. But he is torn from this problematic haven when his mother dies and Murdstone apprentices him to a warehouse, where David, in an agony of humiliation and distress, among rough urchins, cleans and labels wine bottles until he runs away to an aunt he has never seen.

Nowhere in *David Copperfield* do life and art intersect more poignantly than in this episode. Not long before starting on the novel, Dickens had begun to draft an autobiographical memoir that he set aside once the figure of David claimed his attention, as though fiction could serve as a substitute for his confession. Just before Dickens's twelfth birthday, his father, John, who had persistent difficulties living within his income, had been arrested for debt and spent some months in debtor's prison. To make this time of shame even worse for his sensitive and precocious son, all during this time the young Dickens worked at a blacking warehouse, labeling pots. "No words can express the secret agony of my soul as I sunk into this companionship," he recalled in his autobiographical fragment, a sentence he incorporated word for word into *David Copperfield*.[24] And he borrowed his father for the novel, incorporating his traits, even his droll tricks of speech, in that immortal clown the improvident Mr. Micawber, maker of sententious sayings, an exasperating and appealing man given to vaulting hopes and limitless despair.

But now pure fiction took the pen. Quickly winning over his singular aunt, David Copperfield begins to enjoy all the advantages: decent clothes, regular meals, unvarying affection, a good education. He engages himself as a lawyer's clerk, and then becomes a writer, but not before he has fallen in love with, and married, his employer's daughter Dora. Sweet, pretty, utterly impractical and immature, she is a second edition of Clara Copperfield, a sure indication that David's oedipal education is far from complete, as he regresses to his first love. David's affectionate aunt persistently, and pointedly, calls Dora a child, and so does Dora herself. It is not until well after she dies of a miscarriage—a calamity that Dickens mentions so delicately that the reader can easily miss it—that David may finally grow up. Bereft, he goes on a long trip to the Continent on a voyage of self-discovery. Dora, as it were, had to die in him as well as in real life before he could accept the burdens of maturity. He returns to marry Agnes Wickfield, his angel, a young woman he has known and, much to her disciplined, silent regret, treated as a sister, since they were children together.

Virtually all other families in the novel, serving as a chorus in the story of David's Oedipus complex traversed and transcended, are conveniently incomplete as well. Triangles have been reduced to couples, recalling David's enviable infantile constellation: the child's death wishes have been realized.[25] David's first wife, Dora, lives happily with her widowed father; when he dies shortly before she marries David, she will not be consoled. David's second wife, Agnes, too, has lived alone with *her* father, a tightly bonded pair. David's formidable aunt, Betsey Trotwood, who is a mature and acerbic version of his mother, is also, as it were, oedipally available: married to—and separated from—a shadowy ne'er-do-well, she becomes, except for her loyalty to the mad Mr. Dick, David's almost exclusive emotional property. There is more: the mother of David's beloved Steerforth is a widow, and she loves her son with a proprietary love that recalls primitive pre-oedipal bonds between mother and son. Even the principal villain, Uriah Heep, Mr. Wickfield's "umble" clerk, who entraps his employer and lusts after his daughter, basks in such a love: his father lives in his widow's and his son's memory as the maker of "umble" homilies, and presents no obstacles to the mutual affection of this revolting but devoted pair.

As *David Copperfield* is the supreme test of Dickens's psychological powers, Agnes Wickfield is the supreme challenge to any such claims. She had a bad press almost from the outset.* Nineteenth-century critics accused Dickens of failing to endow her with individuality. Even the adoring Forster preferred Dora, "the loving little child-wife," to the "angel wife, Agnes," with her "too unfailing wisdom and self-sacrificing goodness." And R. H. Hutton, that highly respected man of letters, brusquely placed her in the company of other Dickensian saintly heroines, and denounced her as a "detestable" female who "insists on pointing upwards."[26]

This monitory gesture must be the most awkward moment in *David Copperfield,* the one hardest to explain away. As Dora lies dying in an upstairs bedroom, she begs to see her beloved Agnes, alone. She wishes, we learn only later, to will her husband to the one woman who really deserves him. When Agnes rejoins David, who is waiting downstairs, all is over, and she raises her hand, solemnly, toward heaven. A year later, when David Copperfield returns from a long continental voyage of mourning and renewal, he reminds Agnes of that gesture, linking it to her inestimable gift of "ever leading me to something better; ever directing me to higher things." Not enough: on the last page, as David Copperfield looks back at his life and old faces fade away, only one remains, "shining on me like a Heavenly light"—Agnes. "O Agnes, O my soul," the novel closes on this apostrophe, "so may thy face be by me when I

*It has not got much better since. George Orwell's dismissal of Agnes in an appreciative essay on Dickens is perhaps the best known. He calls her "the most disagreeable of his heroines, the real legless angel of Victorian romance." "Charles Dickens" (1940), *The Collected Essays, Journalism and Letters of George Orwell,* ed. Sonia Orwell and Ian Angus, 4 vols. (1968), I, 459.

close my life indeed; so may I, when realities are melting from me, like the shadows which I now dismiss, still find thee near me, pointing upward!"[27] The burden this places on poor Agnes—and on the reader's forbearance—is formidable. One can imagine what Jane Austen would have made of that concluding paragraph.

But the evidence that the narrator provides about Agnes's life history invites a more nuanced verdict. For David, Agnes is an icon, a superhuman superego pointing him toward finer, purer goals. He certainly refers to her as an angel often enough. But that is his problem, not hers. From all we are allowed to know about her, she has shown herself competent in her domestic and her professional roles, busy and efficient as she keeps house for her lonely father and, later, as she runs a small school. There is still more to know about Agnes than this. Ever since she was a little girl, she had mothered her widowed father, who loved her, as he concedes years later, with a "diseased love." It was an infatuation even more neurotic than he recognized, a species of sadism masquerading as a consuming paternal fondness. As Agnes was made only too aware, her mother had died just after childbirth, and her very presence persistently reminded her father of the adored wife he had lost. She could not help reading her father's affection for her, then, as the severest of reproaches: to put it bluntly, he was accusing Agnes of having killed his paragon of a wife simply by being born.[28] And Agnes, as children will, had internalized the slander and taken her mother's death, and her father's insatiable grief, on her shoulders. Her exemplary serenity, her patience and fortitude are symptoms; they amount to an extreme passivity in the erotic sphere of love, including her quite unsisterly feelings for David.

It is arguable that Agnes would have been entitled to reflect that a man who could become besotted with so flighty and immature a creature as Dora was not yet ready for her, and that waiting for David was the soundest policy. That would in any event have been appropriate conduct for her time and station: respectable nineteenth-century society decried as forward a woman who took the initiative in courtship; the code prescribed that David should make the first move. But this purposeful inactivity was not an invariable rule in Victorian life or, for that matter, in its fiction, even the fiction of Dickens: he has Florence Dombey, in the novel that just preceded *David Copperfield,* ask Walter Gay to marry her. "If you will take me for your wife, Walter," says this irreproachable Dickensian heroine, "I will love you dearly."[29] Dickens must have known, or sensed, that Agnes's character is shot through with inhibitions.

Not that she fails to struggle with her conflicts. Just before David Copperfield finally makes his declaration to Agnes Wickfield, he asks her whether she is attached to anyone, and, in a brilliantly observed scene, Dickens has her lose control. She breaks down and cries; she begs him to let her go away; she tells him she is unwell and will write to him. But, precisely as she labors to keep her secret inviolable, she gives him clues enough to let him understand that the man she has loved all her life is, of course, David himself. Eros has won at last.

Her long-maintained goodness and her reserve, then, read like defenses against an ever renewed inner hurt. Being very good, almost beyond human possibilities, was a way of denying that she was very bad. In a long self-lacerating tirade, an uncharacteristic outburst she visits on David while she is still his "sister," she cries out, "I almost feel as if I had been papa's enemy, instead of his loving child." She professes herself grimly informed just how much he has given up for her sake, "and how his anxious thoughts of me have shadowed his life, and weakened his strength and energy." Weeping bitterly, she wishes she could make restitution. "If I could ever set this right! If I could ever work out his restoration, as I have so innocently been the cause of his decline."[30] Half a century before Freud, Dickens knew that the most innocent can damn themselves as the most guilty. *David Copperfield* is full of such insights.

But not on the surface. Dickens's insights into the depths of the mind have to be teased out, for his richly decorated texts—funny, melodramatic, often hysterical—cover them perhaps as much as they display them. He was far from thoughtless: the rigorous schemes he developed for his novels testify to rational control over his fictions. But he was scarcely a patient, let alone a systematic, thinker; his reading was haphazard rather than deep. His philosophy—if so pretentious a term is at all appropriate—was a private, undogmatic Christianity that seems to have owed much to Unitarianism; he was committed to life and to the curative powers of love, and hated forces like doctrinaire evangelicalism, which, he thought, threatened to constrict life and love alike. What he was fortunate to possess was unequaled vitality, an observant eye, and brilliant intuitions.

In fact, the very tensions that exacting readers detected in his fiction endeared him to his bourgeois loyalists all the more. What later critics would deplore as Dickens's unresolved struggles between his gift for drama and his self-intoxicated sermonizing, his craving for candor subverted by his prudence, his many admirers welcomed as striking the proper balance between literature and morality, expressiveness and reserve. With these crucial compromises, Dickens showed himself, as so often, the archetypal mid-century bourgeois. He was a good bourgeois, too, in his respect for that much disputed, though cardinal, Victorian ideal, privacy—of his characters no less than of his readers. And, one must add, the privacy of his own life: his increasingly unhappy marriage, the education of his children, his restless trips abroad with chosen intimates, his failing health were matters that Dickens liked to confine to a circle of intimates, and at times to no one but the devoted Forster. The publicity attending the separation from his wife was a rare lapse; the secrecy with which he conducted his affair with Ellen Ternan, far more characteristic for the age.

In the battles over the proper range of the inward domain, the novel had a strategic role to play. A public airing of private affairs, fiction stood on both sides of the struggle at the same time. One significant part of its mission was to trespass on that most personal precinct, the passions; another, not to trespass too far, or too indelicately. In the novel, at least—always excepting the French, of course—the bedroom was a sanctuary where one was born or died or slept, nothing else. But few readers asked novelists to pretend that the essential urges they could only circumscribe did not exist. One cannot repeat too often that many Victorian bourgeois proved in their diaries, their intimate correspondence, and their private conduct that it is a gross misreading of their experience to think they did not know, or did not practice, or did not enjoy what they did not discuss. It was Dickens's genius to understand these attitudes, to share them and translate them into memorable characters in which his vast readership could see itself—and escape from itself.

FIVE

Images of the Mind

In tune with their taste for affecting music, romantic love, intimate self-revelations, probing histories, and confessional novels, Victorian bourgeois found a willing ally in the pictorial arts as they penetrated the veils of the inner world. We remember that Carlyle had called his age "these Autobiographical times of ours" and noted its "Biographic appetite," two closely related expressions of the same impulse. Nineteenth-century painters translated this preoccupation with the self, whether their own or another's, onto canvas, paper, and the etcher's plate. Doubtless the self-portrait was the artists' most conspicuous contribution to self-examination, but it will emerge that it was only one of several possible roads to the interior. In short, the share of nineteenth-century artists in the cause of self-discovery had a complicated history; an account of how their work entered the intimate bourgeois experience, like that of other expressive gestures, must attend to both producers and consumers. The pages that follow will necessarily navigate between the two.

Frequently makers and viewers of pictures were at odds, their relations tense, even hostile. It is true that, embracing stylistic traditions with which middle-class lovers of art were comfortable, the majority of artists aimed to gratify reigning tastes. The family periodicals that had swamped the civilized world around mid-century were filled with reproductions of undemanding, anecdotal paintings intended to raise an amused smile or a sympathetic sigh. But the individualists among artists usually outran those tastes. Buoyed up by the romantics' ideal of the creative genius who scorns passing fashions, painters striving for originality showed little regard for a public they denigrated as philistine and materialistic. Hence the nineteenth-century bourgeois public, it will appear, absorbed art in a variety of interesting and unpredictable ways.

I. Ego

On August 3, 1913, on vacation in the Tyrolean resort of St. Ulrich, the German Postimpressionist Lovis Corinth painted a remarkable self-portrait. In the course of an extended and very productive career—he was born in 1858—Corinth had looked into the mirror many times. For years, he would paint himself on July 21, his birthday, and the catalogue raisonné of his paintings lists no fewer than forty-two self-portraits in oils; those in other media—drawings, etchings, lithographs—must add up to as many more.[1] Like his strapping nudes and vigorous portraits, many of these self-portraits exhibit an engaging vitality, at times a brutal erotic energy. But some of them certify that his exhibitions of manly cheer were covers for darker moods. He had been hounded by recurrent depressions and thoughts of suicide from his youth and suffered a debilitating stroke in 1911, two years before he painted himself at St. Ulrich.[2]

Corinth's fine self-accounting of 1913 testifies to the tension between appearance and reality. With its bright blue summery background and meticulous recording of the precise date and place, it looks almost like a picture postcard. The painter is dressed in a jaunty hunter green jacket boldly checked in the local fashion, topped off by a stripe of brilliant white shirt, and wearing a Tyrolean hat complete with feather. But his glowering face makes this glimpse of Corinth downright ominous; his scowl painfully contrasts with the mechanical cheerfulness of his tourist's attire. His brows are knitted, his lips compressed under a bushy graying mustache; the high red slapped onto his cheeks savors not of a tan but of a feverish flush. Most striking of all, his eyes betray stress, almost fear. It is this strain between protective garb and patent misery that first arrests the attention. Even more arresting, on a level with the brim of his hat, Corinth has inscribed a laconic legend: "Ego."

The word, to be sure, might stand as a casual greeting. Seven years later, Corinth in fact varied this verbal touch with a self-portrait inscribed, "Ich, 62 Jahre." But the painter who put that charged little word on his canvas had some loftier disclosures on his mind. The artist on vacation, he seems to say, takes his brushes with him. Corinth's landscapes and portraits from the same year and the same resort attest that he was on a working holiday. While in this self-portrait he grasps brushes and palette stiffly, just for show, his posture underscores their emblematic quality, serving as reminders of Corinth's exalted and exacting vocation. But there is more to this painting than self-advertisement: Corinth has also taken his ego with him, with all its anguish. Anxiety peers through his bluff exterior.

The self-portraits he did after that catastrophe continued to record, frankly, his appearance and, with their loose, tremulous brushwork, the struggle to restore his formidable painterly powers. Anything but mementos of resignation, they are brave, sad canvases; nothing astonished Corinth more than the public's view of him as a man who easily, glibly affirms life. But, then, Corinth fed this widespread misreading of his inner experience with self-portraits in which he posed as a lusty gourmet, a medieval knight, an aggressive lover. Much of the time, he hid his suffering soul in his wrestler's body. But at times, especially in his later years, he abandoned disguises for confessions and attested to the pain in his naked heart. It was a revelation he was asking his viewers to perceive, perhaps to share.

By the time Corinth did the revealing self-portrait of 1913, he could look back on a tradition some five hundred years old. Starting with experiments in the Renaissance, the genre was to entice the most luminous names in art: Jan van Eyck, Albrecht Dürer, Leonardo da Vinci, Peter Paul Rubens, Rembrandt van Rijn, Nicholas Poussin, Diego Velázquez.* In the latter half of the seventeenth century, Cosimo Medici III began to collect artists' self-portraits in the Uffizi, and around 1800, his Florentine gallery already housed well over two hundred specimens. After that, the tempo of artistic self-examination greatly accelerated and its claims to cultural significance intensified: the nineteenth century put its unmistakable mark on self-portraiture.

History-minded to the core, then, the Victorians appealed to their artistic legacy, but, though resorting to earlier painters as their guides, they added an earnestness of their own and transformed the genre forever. They knew, of course, that great precursors, notably Dürer and Rembrandt, had painted, drawn, and etched themselves often and insightfully.† The eighteenth century, too, had anticipated them. We have a dozen portraits of Reynolds by Reynolds. Anton Raphael Mengs, the best-known of German painters, recorded his appearance at least fifteen times from promising youth to maturity to the

---

*Around the time that Lorenzo Ghiberti carved his head on a bronze door of the Baptistery in Florence, Leon Battista Alberti cast his feature in two bronze reliefs. In their time, smuggling one's features into one's work was becoming something of an artist's game. Since little dependable documentation has survived, one can only conjecture that group portraits and sculptures conceal more sly representations of the artist than we shall ever know. These hidden Renaissance self-portraits did not publicly affirm, let alone glorify, the self to the world. Alberti cast his medals in the antique style, saluting the reemergence of the classical manner rather than the artist's ego.

†For these two artists, see below, pp. 301–9.

decay of age.* And that prodigy the German face painter Anton Graff, who did his last self-portrait in 1813, the year of his death at seventy-seven, established some sort of record with more than eight hundred sitters, 1,600 canvases, and at least eighty self-portraits to his credit. Interestingly enough, contemporaries praised Graff less for his industry or mimetic skills than for his psychological acuity.[3] Following in this path, nineteenth-century European and American artists freely tested their skills before the mirror; a list of painters who did not do their self-portrait would probably be shorter than a list of those who did. The painter painting himself is a distinctly modern type of aesthetic exhibitionist, and nineteenth-century artists took to this open self-exploration with a will. But while Graff regarded himself simply as one of his many sitters, the Victorians, to hear them talk, aimed to strike through the façade of outward show. It was a matter less of copiousness than of intention. They would improve on literal fidelity and sound their mind to its core.

Hence Gustave Courbet was saying nothing unconventional when he told his patron Alfred Bruyas in 1854, "I have done a good many self-portraits in my life, as my attitude gradually changed. One could say I have written my autobiography."[4] Three decades of vigorous output prove that this was not an empty boast; Courbet charted his progress as a political and artistic rebel by doing more than half a dozen striking self-portraits, as a pipe-smoking youth, a wounded man, a painter in his studio, a cellist, a political prisoner. He wrote his life as he was best equipped to do: with the brush. But he wrote it also with pictures not labeled as self-portraits: the claims of nineteenth-century artists to provide access to their mind were nothing if not far-reaching. Indeed, many Victorian painters implied, even if few of them insisted, that their self-portraits should not be read as a distinct genre; they wanted all of their works—still lifes, landscapes, portraits, genre scenes—to be taken as fragments of their great confession. As Francisco Goya's biographer V. Carderera put it in 1835, "an artist's productions are usually the most vivid reflections of his soul."[5] Caspar David Friedrich, the most interesting German painter of the early nineteenth century, had already set the tone: "Every picture," he wrote around 1830, with his own work very much in mind, "is more or less a character study of the one who painted it, just as generally the inner spiritual and moral human being expresses himself in every action."[6]

*Mengs, who secured a European reputation with grandiloquent frescoes on religious and mythological subjects, left a moving record. His early self-portraits show a handsome, confident youth obviously proud of his looks; at the height of his career, he preened as the carefully groomed man of the world. But in his last years—he died in 1779, at fifty-one—he portrayed himself as aging and ailing. A lesser Rembrandt, he left his last self-portraits bare of all accessories to concentrate on his appearance and, beneath that appearance, his inner being.

Courbet's much debated "real allegory," exhibited in 1855, underscores the ease with which an iconoclast could set aside traditional categories and show himself by showing others. On a gigantic canvas, the bearded artist displays himself in his handsome "Assyrian profile" at the center painting a landscape, with a still life of studio props at his left and a score of bystanders, some watching him and others engaged with one another: a female model covering her nakedness with a sheet as she watches Courbet painting, a beggar, a priest, a Jew he remembered from London, a pair of lovers, a little boy admiring Courbet at work, art lovers, friends like Baudelaire and Pierre Joseph Proudhon. The title Courbet gave this self-portrait complete with a slice of autobiography, *L'Atelier du peintre: Allégorie réelle déterminant une phase de sept années de ma vie artistique,* is more puzzling than illuminating. Though in a letter to Bruyas he carefully identified the personages, he just as carefully refused to spell out his meaning. "You'll have to understand it as best you can," he wrote, providing art historians with employment for more than a century.[7] But whatever Courbet intended his real allegory to say, it documents that the boundaries between self-portraiture and other self-revelations were vanishing. The romantic vision of art as an expressive vehicle survived into the decades of realism and beyond.

By mid-century, the idea had become commonplace that artists were diggers into their hidden being who paraded their inner history before an audience that, they hoped, would be touched by their candid confessions. It is telling that painters now known mainly to specialists made as much of their introspective acumen as did their more celebrated brethren. Around 1872, Barthélemy Menn did a *Self-Portrait in a Straw Hat,* showing himself soberly dressed and fit, sporting a trim gray beard, his eyes shaded by a large hat. A Genevan by birth, well traveled and well schooled, the student of Dominique Ingres, friend of Camille Corot, and teacher of Ferdinand Hodler, Menn carved out a sensible, productive career as a professor of painting. Modern Swiss artists owe much to his instruction and his landscapes. In his late fifties, he turned to the mirror and eulogized his canvas as the epitome of his life's experience, as his "testament" and "passport," which defined his relatively modest position in the world of art. The picture was his "autobiography."[8] In the solemn game of aesthetic self-revelation, formal self-portrait or not, a brash subversive like Courbet and a good bourgeois like Menn could join hands as they explored their psyches and took their often reluctant public with them.

Motives for doing a self-portrait are rarely as obvious as they appear to be. Some schools like the French Impressionists and the English Pre-Raphaelites painted themselves rarely, though they sometimes portrayed one another; in contrast, the Postimpressionists—Van Gogh, Gauguin, Cézanne—did scores of self-portraits. Poverty, diffidence, pride in one's looks, preoccupation with the outside world all played their part. One artist—van Gogh comes to mind—wants to present friends or patrons with a personal remembrance. Another, like Corot, leaves a token of his appearance for his parents as he departs for a long stay in Italy. A third, for instance Edouard Vuillard, explores his appearance to experiment with a new style. A fourth—and here the list is long—shows off his craftsman's ingenuity by capturing extravagant or evanescent facial expressions. A fifth, whether narcissist or masochist, finds himself—or herself—so rewarding, so repellent, or so interesting that the temptation to do a self-portrait proves simply irresistible: those of Max Liebermann speak of self-love and those of Egon Schiele of self-hatred, while Berthe Morisot's are exercises in resolute self-understanding.

In short, professional pressures, aesthetic notions, character traits, the lust for fame or revenge enter into the making of self-portraits, providing ample opportunities to present the painter as a respectable artist, a perceptive psychologist, or a self-styled philosopher—or all of these together. Simplicity is suspect. In late 1889, van Gogh told his brother Theo that he was working on two self-portraits "for want of another model" and "because it is more than time I did a little figure work."[9] But this is too ingenuous to be the whole truth: the evidence suggests that van Gogh chose himself as a model for reasons more interesting than these. His self-portraits were desperate efforts—unsuccessful efforts, it turned out—to master the destructive forces at work within.

However private their origins, self-portraits possess a cultural dimension; they disclose more than a single self. They ape or affront prevailing mores; they perpetuate or challenge artistic fashions. Even those done in defiance of dominant styles from a posture of self-sought isolation are saturated with contemporary values and conflicts. As acts of pictorial speech, they are a mute communication that presupposes an audience, however select; it is a message from the painter's to the viewer's ego. Self-portraiture is play with appearances, with accessories, with modes of presentation, but play that obeys rules and employs a vocabulary that with rare exceptions others have made. Self-proclaimed outsiders like Paul Gauguin aching to exhibit their individuality as offensively as possible were still working on the shadow side of the culture they despised. It is a tribute to the relative openness—or, critics would say, the unprincipled character—of nineteenth-century society that so many self-portraits ventured beyond the pale of bourgeois respectability, only to be praised for their daring later.

Among types of self-portraiture, probably the most predictable of poses is the painter painting himself in the act of painting. This moment of self-assertion goes back to Dürer and found dazzling expression in the seventeenth century, with Velázquez and Rembrandt.* And beginning with Dürer, the painter posing in his professional capacity confronted some fascinating complications. Unless the artist reverses what he sees, the image he transcribes from the mirror—the only prop available before the invention of photography—is a mirror image; the right becomes the left. Trickier still, the hand holding the brush is notoriously hard to represent convincingly.[10] It is disturbing, too, as art historians have not failed to observe, that the painter working to capture his physiognomy must struggle with an expression that may not be habitual; his customary intense stare is generated by the stiff posture that attentive self-observation imposes. We can reasonably assume that not all self-portraitists were so depressed as their frowning renditions intimate. But, precisely by compelling the artist to master such technical predicaments, self-portraits stand as so many trophies celebrating daunting technical difficulties overcome. These tributes to a craft—and, more emphatically still, to the craftsman—are integral to the great modern search for the self, an affirmation of inner worth no less compelling when it is accompanied by acknowledgment of neurotic turmoil. Whether the average lover of art appreciated it or not, these pictures seemed to be saying that the artist deserves respect because he is an artist.†

---

*One of the most splendid representatives of the genre is, of course, Velázquez's celebrated, intricate *Las Meninas,* in which the artist shows himself brush in hand in front of an oversized canvas, at work on a portrait of the Infanta Margarita and her ladies, as the king and queen, cleverly shown in a small mirror on the back wall, look on. Students of Velázquez agree that he was in this canvas asserting nothing less than the dignity of his profession.

†Through the centuries, never more frequently than in the nineteenth, artists made these little triumphs explicit. In 1484, the young Dürer had noted on his first self-portrait that he had drawn it "from myself in the mirror." More than four centuries later, in 1892, the German painter Max Slevogt displayed similar virtuosity; posing the artist Nelly von Seidlitz before a mirror, he shows her profile in it and has captured himself at the easel in the back of the same mirror, working on this very canvas. Again, early in the twentieth century, Schiele exhibited his nervous draftsmanship with a self-portrait in which the viewer must infer the mirror that, subtly in control though invisible, stands between the nude model seen from the rear and her frontal reflection, accompanied by the seated artist feverishly sketching the intricate composition he has posed. In such exercises, painters exhibit their control over their noblest accessory, the mirror, with a manual dexterity and intellectual mastery far superior to those of the ordinary craftsman. Such virtuosity, too, showed the self at work. Painters also engaged in acts of mutual congratulation, painting another painter in the act of painting. The Impressionists, we know, particularly enjoyed these well-deserved mutual advertisements. Manet paints Claude Monet painting in his floating studio; Monet paints Manet painting in Monet's garden; Auguste Renoir paints Monet painting in his garden at Argenteuil. Henri Fantin-Latour, master of homages, collects a group of admiring artists around Manet in a studio at Batignolles, including Renoir, Jean Frédéric Bazille, and Monet.

And he deserves respect for reasons quite apart from professional status. Painters reached for the rank of philosopher by expanding the definition of self-revelation to embrace genres other than self-portraits. By offering themselves as witnesses and spurs to introspection, these artists helped to subvert the neoclassical hierarchies that had long ranked paintings by their subject matter. They came to reinterpret landscape especially, hitherto assigned a humble position, as sublime evidence for Nature's works and gave landscape paintings new prestige and prosperity. They had some splendid seventeenth-century models to admire, and earnestly tried to emulate Jacob van Ruisdael, Peter Paul Rubens, Nicolas Poussin, or Claude Lorrain. Even *plein air* painting had been tried before. But the powerful guardians of art who organized the great exhibitions continued to prefer and conservative critics continued to commend the historical, the monumental, the moralistic, and, for lighter moments, the anecdotal. Yet there were signs of breakup everywhere: in Britain landscape artists from Richard Parkes Bonington to Frederick Jackson Turner, in France the Barbizon school, in the United States the Hudson River painters, in the new kingdom of Italy the Macchiaioli, took themselves out of doors. More: many of them insisted that their trees, lakes, and mountains were laden with profound philosophical significance. They labored to put landscape on the map of meaningful art.

Romantics or not, articulate or not, these painters were imbued with the religion of Nature. Some among the best of them, uncomfortable with theology or metaphysics, were content with lovingly depicting reality and limited the demands they made on their public. John Constable's aphorism "Painting is another word for feeling" has been much quoted, but the feeling he meant was essentially the ability to make visible the abiding affection for the scenes he had known from his youth, the lovely hills and valleys, sunlight and shade and clouds.[11] Landscape, he once said, was his mistress, but mistress in the sense of master: he took the close, never-ending study of nature to be his life's vocation. Yet, with all his modesty, he too paid the price of going his own way. "So few among the buyers and sellers of pictures possess any knowledge," said Constable in 1836, near the end of his life; knowledge, he meant, derived from the serious pursuit of nature.[12] He spoke for the more adventurous of his fellows. True, he was elevated into a national treasure—but after his death.

Camille Corot, far less vocal about his approach to painting than Constable but like him in his unremitting quest for fidelity to nature, was only marginally better served. In his last years—he died in 1875, at the age of seventy-nine— French painters gratefully dubbed him the father of modern landscape, and collectors paid extravagant prices for his canvases. But he had been painting for a quarter of a century, until he was around fifty, before his work—the classical cityscapes of ancient Rome and the misty outdoor scenes glimpsed through feathery trees—found appreciation in a wider audience.

Unlike Constable and Corot, with their earnest but unpretentious program, other painters preached the gospel of "a higher style of landscape." It was Louis Noble, in his 1853 biography of the American landscapist Thomas Cole, who was responsible for this resonant phrase. In grandiose cycles like *The Voyage of Life* or *The Course of Empire,* Cole exhibited his conviction that his "mission" as a painter was "great and serious"; with his ambitious themes, vast horizons, and outsized canvases, he hoped to transcend the "dead imitation of things" that he might "impress a sentiment or enforce a truth."[13] For some time, Cole's renderings of landscapes, whether imaginary or real, complete with portentous messages, secured him a celebrity few American artists could rival. But his fame was evanescent and its fading preordained. It would seem that the devout pictorial pantheism of the metaphysician-painters, for the most part exacting no confessional commitments, was programmed for popularity. To capture on canvas the worship of Nature—a sentiment quite different from the sensual pleasure in the outdoors—seemed to promise easy access to bourgeois sensibilities. Those who painted in that faith were offering the picture-buying public an aesthetic-religious experience for which country walks, lyrical poems, old Dutch paintings should have prepared them. Yet the history of nineteenth-century landscape painters down to the Impressionists documents the travail in store for those defying the historic rank order.

Caspar David Friedrich, whose importance as artist and witness to his time has only recently been appreciated outside Germany, is most instructive in this regard. That dubious compliment "metaphysician with the brush" was first applied to him, and he fully deserved it.[14] But, for decades after his death in 1840, art critics dismissed him, art historians forgot him, collectors passed him by, museums stored their Friedrichs in their reserve holdings. It was only after 1900 that he was rediscovered, and then, significantly enough, as a pawn in an internecine struggle among German bourgeois: the cultivated *Bürger* who came to value him played the Friedrich card as they contrasted his "healthy" inwardness with the "materialism" and "superficiality" of Wilhelminian culture.[15] What makes this revival astonishing is not that it occurred but that it was so long in coming: in his religiosity and his inwardness, Friedrich was characteristic of his time, his class, and his culture. It was just that he was too demanding, not obvious enough, about his message.

Friedrich himself never questioned his vocation as a confessional artist. In the course of his long career, he did some ten identifiable self-portraits, mainly drawings. But virtually all of his paintings served as proof of his contention that every picture is essentially a self-portrait. Nor was Friedrich isolated in this way of approaching his calling: his emotional commitment to an oceanic identification with Nature was a staple conviction among his fellow romantics.

Still, his painted autobiographies gave the wider public a daunting assignment. In 1815, describing one of his symbolic landscapes, he told a fellow artist, "It has no church, no tree, no plant, not a blade of grass. On the naked, stony seashore there stands, straight upright, a cross which is, for those who see it that way, a consolation, for those who do not see it that way, a cross." The aspirations of nineteenth-century art as self-revelation are packed into this sentence, and its conundrums no less. Friedrich's disclosures were programmatic; in a stream of letters, poems, and aphorisms, he reiterated, and exemplified, his ambition to record his innermost thoughts and sentiments. "The painter," he said, "should not paint only what he sees in front of him but also what he sees within himself. But if he sees nothing within himself, then he should also stop painting what he sees in front of him."[16] These comments seem redundant: few could doubt that Friedrich's true subject matter was his inner self, or that his oeuvre amounted to a single-minded exercise in religious autobiography.

Friedrich had started to paint before 1800, while Novalis was still alive and Hölderlin had not yet descended into madness. For four decades, he transcribed German romantic theology into paintings, significantly indebted to the aesthetic religiosity of Schleiermacher, Tieck, and Schelling and even the difficult Hegel. Anything but an original thinker, he took from their writings the devout attitudes he had already detected in himself. As a painting metaphysician, Friedrich set out to fight the romantics' battles to reclaim the world for faith, reassert the creative powers of the imagination, and exhibit the centrality of the humble self. In conflict with his "shallow" age, he demanded that "what our forefathers believed and did in childlike simplicity, that too we should believe and do with purified knowledge." His canvases of mountains in the mist, blasted trees in a field, a monk looking out to an empty sea from a deserted shore, two men facing away from the viewer to gaze at the moon—all testified to the hand of the divinity. So did his innumerable sketches of leaves and branches, drawn with a precision that document his supreme allegiance to Nature; they were declarations of faith in the God who had made it. A painting, Friedrich insisted, must be a "free, spiritual replica of Nature"; it must be felt, not just copied.[17]

Hence technique, though Friedrich excelled in it, was never enough. When he commended another artist for being "more poet than painter," he was describing his own aesthetic ideal. It was only logical that he should acknowledge his private self as his true teacher. "Whoever has spirit—*Geist*—himself," he wrote, "does not copy others." The "artist's feeling is his law. Pure sentiment can never be contrary to Nature, is always according to Nature." Since his remarks on fellow painters were usually scornful, even mean-spirited, it is noteworthy that one of his rare words of praise for another artist was that he had a "pure, childlike soul." In the approved romantic manner, Friedrich likened science to an adult, art to a child, and that comparison was, we must remember, a tribute to art.[18]

At times of exaltation, Friedrich felt his self melting into his work. By 1810, he hoped he had "brushed my thoughts into canvas."[19] But while the inner truths he meant to convey baffled many, the sensitive ones professed to have no trouble reading his "hieroglyphics of omnipotent Nature." Yet his landscapes, he insisted, were esoteric, allegories all of them. Many of them he animated—if that is the right word—with solitary figures looking into the distance, a harbor with departing vessels, a desolate winter landscape, a dizzying abyss, a nocturnal cemetery, vast empty mountainscapes. They seem to invite viewers into the painting to share the artist's awe before the heavenly spectacle he has conjured up. Taking his vocation with lofty seriousness, Friedrich saw art as an "intercessor between Nature and humans."*

Accordingly some of Friedrich's first interpreters, followed by credulous successors, treated his paintings like transparent dreams to which a straightforward catalog of symbols would provide the key. A cross stands for faith, a rock for stability, a flag for patriotism, a shipwreck for death. But such mechanical proceedings, devised to elevate Friedrich, actually trivialized him. The contours of his piety remain unclear, and he would have wanted it that way. He did not think it his task to lead others to his highly personal version of Lutheranism. As a seer, he had invited others to see. That, he believed, should have been enough, but for decades it was not.

The public response to the Barbizon painters echoes Friedrich's experience. As their master Corot had done, their undisputed leader, Théodore Rousseau, accompanied by Charles François Daubigny, Constant Troyon, Jean François Millet, and others set up their studios in the village of Barbizon and their easels in the Fontainebleau woods to face, and paint, Nature directly. Their intensity was that of missionaries as they tried to convey their feeling for the literally marvelous out-of-doors in the hope of reaching and moving the art-buying public's hearts. "All art," Millet exclaimed, "is a language, a language designed

---

*Describing two early Friedrich landscapes, the portrait painter Gerhard von Kügelgen interpreted them in a way that Friedrich could only have applauded: "It is *life* and *death* that the painter has here wanted to express with summer and winter." The weather, the figures, the trees in each of these pictures stand as "silent symbols." To be sure, Kügelgen had a moment of hesitation, leaving himself an escape route with the little word "probably." But he rejected this evasion in view of the evidence and struck out the qualifier. Enclosure in a letter from Gerhard von Kügelgen to Karl August Böttiger, probably 1808, *Caspar David Friedrich—Unbekannte Dokumente seines Lebens,* ed. Karl-Ludwig Hoch (1985), 31.

to express one's thoughts."[20] And Rousseau interpreted those thoughts as he rhapsodized over hearing the trees and the stones speak to him in the silence of the forests. But for years few appreciated their message. Apart from Corot, who was well off, and Millet, who became a public icon, the men of Barbizon were long rejected by collectors and by the juries of the French Salon, spending decades in penury before the art establishment honored a few of them, now aging, and before they could sell their landscapes at decent prices.*

These histories of nineteenth-century metaphysicians with the brush suggest that most respectable consumers of art needed time to absorb the self-revelations of modern artists. To the tradition-bound, these confessions were no better than narcissistic performances addressed to only a few fellow artists. But in a century of radical changes, taste in art, too, changed and made the new claims of artists comprehensible, even palatable, to the bourgeois, museum-going public.

2. Icons to Dream By

Just as there was more than one reason why artists bared their hearts in paintings, drawings, and etchings, so there was more than one reason why bourgeois viewers responded to them. The more cultivated among the middle classes solemnly believed that art mattered. The Victorian century was a time of amateur artists; fostering a talent for sketching and copying masterpieces in museums formed part of much middle-class upbringing, and applying it served many a traveler. This exposure gave most educated some sense of the messages that professional artists were seeking to convey. Growing segments of the bourgeois public, whether passive spectator or munificent patron, learned to appreciate artists, provided they did not depart too radically from accepted styles.

Differences in bourgeois tastes rested in significant measure on differences in income. The Victorian middle classes were riven by economic and social divisions ranging from the *grande* to the *petite bourgeoisie,* the *Bildungsbürgertum* to the *Kleinbürgertum,* and naturally one's place in these hierarchies helped to determine the choice of art to hang on one's walls. The banker in Paris, the manufacturer in Liverpool, the rentier in Cologne, the magnate's wife in Chicago could collect originals, while less affluent bourgeois had to be content with copies or, far more frequently, with reproductions. But the *kind* of art work the buyer liked was not wholly predictable. The conviction that art had something more meaningful to impart than visual attractiveness or ostentatious expenditure

*For Millet, see below, pp. 290–93.

complicated choices and at least partly transcended economic or social status.

The advice literature that untold thousands of aspiring Victorian bourgeois found so indispensable took account of these realities. "No cultivated person will tolerate worthless paintings in ostentatious frames," Constanze von Franken said sternly in her manual laying down the law for the middling German *Bürgertum* late in the century. "If you can afford good oil paintings, they will become the loveliest ornament in your home, a refreshment for your and others' eyes. If good oil paintings are too expensive for you, then prefer beautiful photographs, steel engravings, and similar reproductions of famous paintings that you can nowadays acquire in rare perfection and at small expense to poor paintings or worthless chromolithographs."[1] By her time, the modern art industry, already highly developed, made masterpieces easily available. In 1874, *Die Gartenlaube,* the secular Bible of German middle-brow culture, exclaimed over the techniques that had made this possible: "Recently, among the arts of reproduction, the woodcut, copper and steel engraving, the typography of painting in the form of chromolithograph and photography have taken an ever higher rank, because they have made accessible to large masses the rarest and most expensive treasures of all times and all climes." Studiously ignoring the anxious resentment of painters over that insidious newly invented rival— photography—the *Gartenlaube* hoped that the promise of accurate color reproductions would soon become reality: "We can hardly imagine a lovelier triumph in the domain of art and the beautification of life."[2]

In this atmosphere, professional advisers stood ready to grant individual preferences generous leeway, but kept lifted the monitory finger enjoining discrimination: "The furnishing of a sitting room can be left to the taste and the imagination of the lady of the house, and varied in accord with one's wealth," a French manual on domestic economy observed in 1885. The pictures should be "paintings or engravings in a gilt frame." And the authors instructed their readers that "good taste" should reign with the choice of art no less than with the silverware or the wallpaper.[3] It was such counsel to the educated and the educable that served to free tastes for art from the dictates of income levels. Nor did bourgeois rich or poor establish a universally favored type of painting; portraits, landscapes, genre pieces religious and secular found partisans across financial and national boundaries, preferences shifting with the tides of sensibility.

Another distinction, of particular relevance to this study, was the ability, and the willingness, of art lovers to probe beneath surfaces. Many evidently could not, or would not, forsake entertainment for self-scrutiny. The popular canvases reproduced in family magazines attest to that: stag at bay, bibulous monks smiling over a glass of wine, kittens playing with a ball of wool, babies reaching up to their mother's cheek, a highly colored Savior blessing the multitudes were designed, as we have seen, to produce a chuckle or a sentimental tear rather than deep emotion, let alone introspection. Kitsch was a defense against inwardness. But at times what ended as kitsch had started as art; the vagaries of popularity were many. A look at two artists who throve in the marketplace, Jean François Millet and Arnold Böcklin, should illuminate the situation.

Millet was the one member of the Barbizon school to flourish intermittently in his lifetime and even more impressively after his death in 1875. The painter famous for making inarticulate men and women working the land into the centerpieces of his landscapes came to Barbizon in 1849 penniless, quickly made friends with his equally destitute fellow painters, and stayed. The enthusiasts who reviewed his pictures favorably, and later wrote the monographs and the biographies, have liked to dwell on the pathos of Millet's career: his canvases turned away by Salon juries that thought them low, his hungry family anxiously awaiting news that he had sold another of his unconventional canvases, his life embittered by philistines misconstruing his intentions. There is some truth to this portrait in black: Millet did have paintings rejected by the Salon, did have a live-in companion and many children to feed, did have to worry about money. And yet, to trumpet Millet's misery at the expense of his successes is to give excessive credence to the testimony of antibourgeois ideologues, whether nostalgic celebrants of rural innocence or radical spokesmen for the literary-political avant-garde. At war with the bourgeoisie, they were busy maligning what they called the obtuseness and the vulgarity of respectable—which is to say, middle-class—gallerygoers.

It was a typical move for this aggressive troop that when Millet exhibited *Le Vanneur* at the Salon of 1848, Théophile Gautier hailed this rendition of a sturdy peasant winnowing as a "painting that has everything it needs to make the clean-shaven bourgeois' flesh creep." Reviewing the salons in the 1850s and 1860s, the brilliant, outspoken art critic Théophile Thoré hailed Millet as a rare glimpse of hope for French art in a decadent time, even though—rather because—the bourgeoisie detested him.[4] Actually many of Millet's submissions were exhibited in the Salon, generous friends and shrewd dealers kept him in funds, and, in the 1860s, he watched prices for his paintings at auction rise fourfold. And art critics, a vocal, contentious, increasingly flourishing tribe in mid-century Paris, took him seriously enough to debate the merits of his work. In 1867, Millet was even awarded the coveted *Légion d'honneur,* an unexpected tribute to a painter of peasants. But, not content with all this, his closest friend and first biographer, Alfred Sensier, made Millet palatable to rich and pious collectors by overdramatizing his early poverty and conveniently overlooking the fact that he was not married to the woman with whom he had nine children.

True, Millet was born a peasant, raised as a peasant, and, though well read in classical and modern literature, never disclaimed his peasant youth in a Norman village. On the contrary, drawing strength from his heritage, he could portray without condescension and, he hoped, without idealization the country folk he knew so well. Analyzing his *Paysanne revenant du puits* for Thoré, he insisted that he had "as always avoided, with a sort of horror, whatever could tend toward sentimentality."[5] He showed peasants sowing, gleaning, spinning, herding sheep, cutting wood, gathering faggots, their faces bronzed with outdoor labor and their backs bent with endless toil, their hands coarse and their eyes vacant. After early excursions into portraits, self-portraits, and nudes, he made peasants into virtually his only subject and his only ideology—peasants as towering manifestations of Nature. What his admirers made of them is an astonishing and enlightening story.

It can best be told by a glance at the history of the *Angelus,* completed in 1859. Millet was used to criticism and controversy: his *Les Glaneuses* of 1857 struck some reviewers as a revolutionary manifesto, while others offered *L'Homme à la houe,* completed five years later, as evidence of Millet's taste for "ignoble" models or "extreme" political opinions.* These were strong adjectives, and Millet's man with a hoe did elicit strong responses, but a far larger public, on two continents, persisted in calling Millet, as an American pamphleteer did in 1889, the painter of the *Angelus*.

Two peasants are standing in a plowed field with farm implements at their feet. The woman is bathed in light, her head bowed and her hands folded in prayer; the man facing her stands with his back to the sun, his hands fingering his hat. They are observing the sacred moment when the bell of the village church, visible in the background, tolls the Angelus, that daily devotion reminding the faithful of the Incarnation. Whatever the painter's private designs, this picture was soon securely lodged in the bourgeoisie's mental economy and, once cheap reproductions became available, even that of poor households. In expensively produced, heavily illustrated volumes on Millet's work published in the 1890s, the *Angelus* usually served as the frontispiece or decorated the title

---

*The poet Edwin Markham minced no words about that much debated peasant leaning on his hoe in a frequently recited poem of 1899, seeing him as brutal and mindless, a message of supreme pessimism: "Bowed by the weight of centuries he leans / Upon his hoe and gazes on the ground / The emptiness of ages in his face / And on his back the burden of the world. / Who loosened and let down this brutal jaw? / Whose was the hand that slanted back this brow? / Whose breath blew out the light within this brain?"

page. Poets wrote verses on it for the newspapers. Reasonably priced engravings and even cheaper etchings and chromolithographs secured its circulation
among the untold thousands who normally did not buy paintings; entrepre-
neurs toured it around major American cities, while manufacturers imprinted it
on commonplace items of domestic use: napkins, towels, wall plaques, medals,
lamps, china, salt boxes.[6]

The attention lavished on the *Angelus* and its sales history support one's sense
of an artifact out of control, with a life of its own. Commissioned by an American who never claimed it, Millet sold the painting for a pathetic 1,000 francs,
but, with repeated changes of hands, its price rapidly rose. At the end of the
1860s, Durand-Ruel, Millet's dealer, bought it for 30,000 francs, only to dis-
pose of it soon after with a healthy profit. The escalation, once launched,
proved unstoppable: in 1881, the painting fetched 160,000 and before long
climbed to 300,000 francs. Then the Americans began to bid for it, and, when
the French were unable to raise the funds, the American Art Association acquired the *Angelus* for a total of 580,650 francs. The press in the United States
and in France turned the competition into a sensational story; in the end,
French patriotism won out over French frugality. The *Angelus* was returned to
its home country for the princely sum of 800,000 francs, and in 1909 it came to
rest in the Louvre. National pride had proved expensive.

It was not publicity alone that made the *Angelus* a treasured feast for the eyes
and souls of the many. The heated disputes over the painting, the speeches in
the Chamber of Deputies, the letters to the editor, the pronouncements of
museum directors could only stimulate interest, but for its fervent admirers, its
essential secret was the lesson they read into it. Often effusive, rarely temperate,
the students of Millet's work were hardly responsible for the career of the
Angelus. They liked to quote his wish to "make the trivial serve the expression
of the sublime," and they respected his disclaimers: whatever tendentious spirits
might say, Millet's heroic peasants were not a protest against social injustice, not
an attack on the Second Empire, not a profession of sectarian faith. Had he not
emphasized more than once that he was not a socialist, not a revolutionary?
Appreciating the monumentality of his figures, essayists and biographers concentrated on Millet's way of elevating realistic depictions of the rural poor to
universal, symbolic significance.[7]

But Millet's more infatuated admirers came closer to the heart of his popularity. They called him a realist with a poet's soul, or (as the most excited had it)
better than a realist; "his truth," wrote one, "is of a much higher order," that of
a "seer" who ennobles what he touches. They pictured Millet taking the public
into his confidence, letting others see and feel what he himself had seen and felt.
This electric charge leaping from the spirit of a master to that of multitudes

went beyond mundane anecdotes about peasants laboring or at rest: his "pains-taking scrutiny of Nature" had allowed "a great religious and mystic emana-tion" to rise from his splendid canvases. In the United States, which took the *Angelus* to its heart, writers called him an "apostle of the peasants" and "the evangelist of the fields." Whether reactionaries celebrating his abiding commit-ment to the soil or radicals reading his bent figures as a call to social action, they saw him embodying a sacred cause. In the *Angelus,* wrote the Reverend George McDermot, a Catholic devotee, "one sees, as in a kind of ecstasy, lines like rays of grace connecting the peasants in the fields with the light of life beyond the grave." What kept Millet's peasants from being mere brutes, said another Cath-olic admirer, was "that voice from the sky."[8]

This was pure projection. We know that in painting the *Angelus,* Millet had relived a moment of nostalgia: he had painted it, he wrote a friend, recalling his grandmother working in the fields stopping every day to say the Angelus. For Millet's worshipers this was not enough; they took the *Angelus* not as a tribute to one godly peasant but as a reverent statement to the world. Quite unwit-tingly Millet, not a practicing Catholic, had touched a nerve, the nerve that Friedrich's paintings had not been blunt enough to set vibrating: the longing for a life cured of its godlessness. The heart of its appeal lay in its hint at an easy religiosity. "The world is disenchanted," wrote the German art historian Albert Dresdner in 1904; "it is imperative to teach it to recognize and honor the divinity and the divine once again."[9] It says much about the inner needs of the Victorians that Dresdner should have issued this call in an essay on Millet.

Arnold Böcklin is Millet's most formidable rival for the title of quintessential artist to the bourgeoisie. His paintings traveled less well than Millet's; the cachet they acquired after a slow start was concentrated in the German-speaking world, where his sensibility seemed peculiarly at home. Yet he, too, repays study because he captured the middle-class imagination like few other painters of his century. Born in Basel in 1827, he led a wandering life for years. He studied in Düsseldorf, returned to Basel more than once, settled in Zurich and Munich and at last in Italy, where he died in 1901. Italy gave him sun and rest, paintable scenes and a sense of home, even though he truculently identified himself as the most German of painters, an identification that patriotic Germans confirmed and saluted. At first, critics and connoisseurs carped at what they denounced as Böcklin's celebration of ugliness and his self-made pantheon of gods and satyrs. But gradually he conquered an ardent following prepared for mythmaking by Wagner, bored with the realists, unreceptive to the new French imports, and open to Böcklin's rugged eroticism. It was the moods that Böcklin created with his subjects that made him, after a time, irresistible. "First they ridiculed him," the crusading journalist Maximilian Harden recalled in a lyrical retrospect, "then they deified him."[10]

The language is only marginally too strong. Before the end of the century, when Böcklin's popularity was riding high, the respected literary essayist Franz Servaes went so far as to place him into the company of Goethe and Beethoven in a great German trinity. The capacity of civilized nineteenth-century bourgeois culture to integrate avant-garde subverters is an impressive thing to watch. In art as in literature, middle-class consumers of art managed to transform their fiercest challengers into icons.[11]

In his early years, Böcklin had specialized in brooding landscapes, though his reputation as a major German artist would rest on his fanciful canvases of vigorous pagan creatures like centaurs and mermaids, nymphs and the god Pan, disporting themselves in untamed woods or foaming waves. His reputation began to decline after his death, but not among his determined and vocal admirers. When Böcklin died, Harden wrote, choosing his words carefully, "one wept for the poet"—poet, not painter. After all, was it not the *Dichter* Böcklin who had given the world a new mythology and dreams of a new, youthful, beautiful life?[12] All his work, not only his self-portraits, emphatically testified to a search for renewal in art through renewal of the self. Whatever Böcklin had absorbed in his stays abroad, Fritz von Ostini, one of his first and most doting biographers, observed in 1904, "the true home of his art was in himself." His immensely strong artistic personality sprang from the fact that "everything he was came from his own self."[13]

It was characteristic for an artist drawing out of himself alone that Böcklin's self-portrait should be among his most emphatic gestures. Doubtless the best-known and most instructive of these was his *Selbstportrait mit dem fiedelnden Tod* of 1872. Böcklin shows himself palette in hand and loaded brush at the ready, listening intently to a grinning skeleton playing a spectral violin as it whispers into his ear. The juxtaposition is dramatic in the extreme: death stands as a subversive comment on the full-bearded artist's robust virility. Some two years later, he depicted himself alert and challenging: he stands somewhat aggressively—which is to say, defensively—with crossed arms, positioning his half figure before marble columns and laurels, symbols of fame and immortality. A few years later, he reiterated this self-idealization by placing the same emblems of greatness into the background once again.[14] One of his early biographers, Franz Hermann Meissner, breathlessly discovered that, as late as 1893, the gray-haired Böcklin still appeared on canvas "lion-like, with the self-confidence of a giant."[15] In seven self-portraits, stretching from 1861 to 1894, Böcklin posed in diverse attitudes: with his supportive wife or standing alone erect, elegantly attired, before a large easel. One of these self-presentations shows him holding a wineglass in a confident display of vitality; it reads less like the projection of a personality than the transmission of pointed testimony that, whatever fiddling death might intimate, in the midst of life he was still surrounded by life.

Understandably, the most sensational of his self-portraits aroused conjectures from the start; most chose to read it as a piece of autobiography. Some, turning gossip into adoration, saw the painting as "a melancholy sign" that the "suffering artist," just recovered from a serious illness, had "already looked into the beyond" and plainly heard the "ringing of the spheres."[16] Such grandiose surmises were reduced to irrelevance by reliable evidence that fiddling death had been a later addition. But that did not inhibit soulful scrutinies of Böcklin's meaning that say more about the emotional needs of the art-consuming public than about the aesthetic intentions of the painter.[17]

The most controversial and most influential product of Böcklin's inwardness, though, was not a formal self-portrait at all but a seascape, the famous *Toteninsel*. Like *Selbstportrait mit dem fiedelden Tod,* this painting, too, evoked death. Commissioned in 1879 by a young widow who wanted a "picture to dream by" and completed the following year, it proved so appealing that in the next few years Böcklin painted four more versions. Before long, this painting (definitively named *Isle of the Dead* in 1883 by the art dealer Fritz Gurlitt, who was beginning to find Böcklin profitable) became a favorite topic of conversation. A boat with a figure draped in white standing by a covered coffin is quietly approaching an island from whose rocky surface springs a ruined castle, made all the more desolate by a stand of blackish cypresses. The mood is melancholy, perhaps world-weary but suitably vague, a painting open to many fantasies, none of them cheerful. That there was no identifiable model for the scene—an Etruscan grave site, an Italian islet, a compound of the painter's imagination and memories were all candidates—only added to its hypnotic seductions. Freud was much like other conventional bourgeois who, knowing his Böcklins, dreamt about them.[18]

Faced with this inscrutable work, viewers projected into the *Toteninsel* whatever profundities occurred to them. Who was that figure standing in the boat? "A guardian angel affectionately accompanying a hero torn from happy creativity?" one writer asked. "The priest of a remote, forgotten religion? A mourning woman following her dearest without asking after the goal of the voyage?" Some thought it an elegy on dying antiquity; others preferred to see it as a portrait of solitude in stone. Knowledgeable art lovers compared each version with the others, but all impressed them with their "sense of solitude, wildness, and forlornness." As early as 1888, the essayist Otto von Leixner predicted that in the distant future, "feeling hearts will stand before that *Toteninsel* with admiration."[19]

The marvels of modern printing spread its fame. Before long, the *Toteninsel* etched, engraved, photolithographed became a standard decoration in middle-class German drawing rooms, lending a whiff of exoticism and mystery to sedentary, unadventurous lives. "Between 1885 and 1900," the naturalistic playwright and novelist Max Halbe recalled, "no good middle-class household could be without reproductions of Böcklin's paintings," with the *Toteninsel* the undisputed favorite.[20] Buttressing its towering stature, Sergei Rachmaninoff wrote a symphonic poem on the picture, and Max Reger included it among four of Böcklin's paintings that inspired him to composition. Not long after the painter's death, Odol, proudly extolling itself as *"demonstrably"* the "best mouthwash in the world," featured Böcklin's deserted castle in an advertising campaign, while another German firm enlisted a fat Böcklin merman sporting in the waves to sell sparkling wine. This says much about Böcklin's appeal: advertisers, anything but sentimentalists, knew that everyone from the mouth-wash-buying to the champagne-buying public would recognize the allusion. Von Ostini was exaggerating only mildly, then, when he claimed that Böcklin had become the most popular artist of his time. "Soon there will not be a single household of cultivated people in which there are no reproductions of his works. The prices of his pictures have reached the very first place among art dealers." In fact, he added, "authentic snobs" were already starting to grumble about him.[21]

Certainly a main reason for this enviable prominence was the philosophical freight that weighed down Böcklin's oeuvre. In 1905, the fiercely opinionated art historian and critic Julius Meier-Graefe, committed to Manet and Monet, launched a powerful assault on this bourgeois favorite. But he was promptly rebuked by the faithful, who ridiculed his "apparent profundity" and dismissed him as a "fanatical admirer and adorer" of Impressionism.[22] For some years, most educated German burghers held fast to the conviction that Böcklin was among the most intuitive, most inward of their compatriots, a poet of the brush who captured on canvas unearthly echoes for the edification of all. In the year that Meier-Graefe sought to puncture this consensus, one critic inserted a chapter titled "Böcklin as Educator"—provocatively echoing Julius Langbehn's *Rembrandt as Educator* of 1890, of which more below—into a pretentious study on art and religion; another called Böcklin a hero, "one of the eternals" who stands "in an age that has turned away from idealism as the lonely one high above the human race."[23] Böcklin was credited with a vision denied the more superficial painters of impressions, though precisely what that vision might be remained obscure.

Böcklin supplied abundant fuel for this wordy puzzlement, which only kept the pot of publicity boiling in agreeable ways. In 1888 alone, he painted a *Vita*

Somnium Breve that compressed the battle between life and death, delight and depression, with figures embodying the generations, and the *Lebensinsel,* a self-conscious counterpart to the *Toteninsel,* showing cheerful clumps of trees and dancing, festively dressed men and women, celebrating life, as swans, mermaids, and mermen animate the waters below. Once Böcklin, whose sayings more than one Boswell thought worth recording, wondered, "Why write about pictures? They speak for themselves."[24] Not *his* pictures: a painter like Böcklin lived off commentary. Granted, the literary and anecdotal implications of his paintings were fairly obvious on their own. But their inner meaning was another matter. That his commentators searching for it could never agree with one another, except to believe that it was profound, only shows that his mass of devoted supporters, most of them bourgeois proud of their cultivation, felt compelled to ferret out depths even where there were no depths worth sounding. Looking at these images, which touched so many minds, viewers responded more to their own inner needs than to the artists' message.

3. Teutonic Mirrors

A self-portrait, whether overt or concealed, is the most individualistic of acts, but it cannot escape history. And their history predisposed Germans, in an age given to self-exploration, to turn inward more radically than did other nations. We recall Schiller, musing on the advent of a century awash in murder and war, counseling a friend to flee from the pressures of life to the holy quietness of the heart, to the freedom that exists only in the "realm of dreams."* In contrast, however limited their opportunities, early-nineteenth-century Britons and Frenchmen, to say nothing of democratic Americans, were trading their status of subject for that of citizen. They were participating in an experiment to create a political public from which Germans were largely debarred. But it was possible to convert impotence into grandiosity. The Germans' claim to superior inwardness was their way of translating political frustration into a political program. Though they were not alone in searching the heart, inhabiting the realm of dreams gave German metaphysician-painters unequaled opportunities. A sizable contingent of German artists reached for the mantle of sage. Not content with parading their dignity as painters and their sensitivity as psychologists, they presented their work as touching on fundamental wishes and anxieties.

The German romantics had shown the way. When Friedrich Schlegel asked the true artist to put "*poetry* into painting," he had in mind the imaginative

*See above, p. 63.

reconstruction of reality through the felicitous choice of color and harmonious composition.[1] More venturesome compatriots claimed to transcend such modest aspirations to endow their art with the "poetry" of important ideas. Early in the century, the Nazarenes, those intensely pious young Germans who did most of their religious painting in Italy, chose the resounding name of Lukasbund to recall St. Luke, the apostle who had painted the Virgin. Franz Pforr, the most fluent among them, reminded them that their calling was literally sacred.* As though to underscore this sentiment, Friedrich Overbeck, with Pforr the Nazarenes' dominant spirit, painted himself holding a Bible.[2]

Resort to Scriptures was only one way to reach beyond decoration or superficial precision. That highly literary artist Philipp Otto Runge devised, though he did not live to complete, a cycle called *The Times of Day,* in which he disposed allegorical figures, mainly children, floating in a vast vista, the whole to symbolize a mysterious eclectic cult. Others, as we have seen, loaded a weight of significance on landscapes or anecdotes that these usually innocuous genres had rarely been asked to bear.

Revising the moralistic tradition of northern secular art, notably the rude reminder that in the midst of life we are surrounded by death, German artists modernized time-honored symbols—the skull, the soap bubble, the hour glass—as concrete reminders of ineluctable mortality. It was in this mood that Caspar David Friedrich would ponder death. "The question has often been put to me, Why do you so often choose death, transience, and the grave as themes for your painting?" he noted in a short poem, and replied, "If ever we want to live eternally, we must often surrender ourselves to death."[3] We seem to be hearing the voice of Novalis echoing through the century.

There is something natural, then, about that self-portrait Arnold Böcklin painted in 1872. Evidently romantic intimations of death retained their appeal. Indeed, by the time Böcklin began to paint himself, the public stood ready to be moved by such displays, even if the artist himself remained cool. In 1875, three years later, Hans Thoma, one of Germany's most popular painters, who did at least ten self-portraits, painted himself beset by the same uninvited visitor. He was then thirty-six. Ghastly death hovers behind his right shoulder, whispering

*"I should like to ask someone who wants to devote himself to art what one asks someone who wants to become a monk: if you can make and keep the vow of poverty, chastity, and obedience, then enter. Poverty? Where is the artist rich in the true sense of the word? Chastity in word and work is a principal requirement of his pure occupation, and obedient he must be to art in all things—it commands him to do this and to stop doing that. He must obey and obey gladly, for what can replace the pleasure that art gives him?" Ludwig Grote, *Joseph Sutter und der nazarenische Gedanke* (1972), 46.

to Thoma, who, brush poised, stares into the distance while a slightly insipid cupid—death's great adversary, Eros—floats above his left, bow in hand, ready to fight for the party of life. The message of Thoma's Böcklinesque self-portrait that pits two elemental forces against each other was more hopeful than Böcklin's bleak encounter, in which death looks to be in command. Whatever his point, Thoma must have relished making it, since he returned to it more than once: twice in the late 1870s he painted himself and his wife as a pair of lovers engaged in intimate conversation, blissfully unaware that just over their heads a stout-hearted little winged Eros is about to launch his arrow at skeletal death.

Death, it seems, was often on Thoma's mind, certainly on his canvases. In 1871, he had already done *Der Tod und das Mädchen,* a landscape recalling Schubert: a peasant girl gathering wild flowers is being stalked from a respectful distance by a fully dressed skeleton, scythe over its shoulder. Two years later, in a rendition of the same scene, Thoma has a young woman picking flowers while the Enemy, hideous with his weapon the scythe, hovers close. Death has caught up with youth. Uncanonical death even invaded Thoma's vision of paradise: in two canvases dating from the 1880s and 1890s, he has a lovely naked Eve grasping at the fatal apple as a skeleton stands watch.

Thoma, like Böcklin, started out as a landscape painter and never abandoned nature to populate his fields and rivers with peasants, goddesses, and biblical figures. For years, he had his canvases rejected as too unconventional but was later elevated into the ranks of an archetypal German artist. In an extravagant appreciation, Otto Julius Bierbaum, novelist, essayist, satirist, his habitual light-hearted tone all gone, called Thoma "a poet" whose paintings "do not merely translate a piece of reality into art but, beyond that, also amount to a representation of poetic feelings." And of more than this: "Thoma's art is religious, without any relationship to a particular confession." The art historian Henry Thode, Thoma's most persistent and influential publicity agent, agreed: his paintings speak "an unadorned, distinct, soulful language," expressing "the essence" of the painter.[4] Soulfulness, essence—these were what distinguished Thoma's truly native work from the cosmopolitan self-portraiture of foreigners or of German Impressionists who revealed no national identity in their art.

Their favorite's unmistakable national attributes were the quality that Thoma's partisans liked to stress, a reminder that an artist's heart could beat for many causes, including patriotic pride.* The "shallow" French Impressionists

---

*What applies to Thoma also applies to Böcklin. Conveniently forgetting Böcklin's Swiss origins and Italian residence, one admirer called him a "thorough German" who had "steadily forged new links between nature and the human soul." He had looked upon his world, said

who were making inroads among collectors gave patriots a particular stake in praising *Innerlichkeit,* which they liked to think their countrymen had invented, or at least perfected. In an age of materialism, selfishness, and greed, authentic German artists had the noble and unenviable task of keeping alive the flame of emotional depth endangered by a "scientificized generation."[5] Thode saw Thoma as a reincarnation of German fifteenth- and sixteenth-century masters; inspired by Richard Wagner among other exemplary Teutons, he had shown himself "a poet"—a German poet.*

The heartfelt tributes to national art issued by German critics and painters leave the impression that, in pitting life against death, Thoma was drawing on a rooted, still vital cultural habit. In fact, through the long nineteenth century, lesser-known German painters did self-portraits with skeletons, or just a skull, as their companion. Evidently, Cézanne, who occasionally posed skulls on a table, was nothing compared to this. It was as though to proclaim this tribal continuity that Böcklin had modeled his self-portrait with fiddling death after a portrait in Munich, *Sir Bryan Tuke,* ascribed to Hans Holbein the Younger.[6] Nor should it surprise anyone that the dance of death, that pointed late-medieval and early-modern morality cycle, had found a particular welcome in German art: Holbein's series of graphic woodcuts showing death pitilessly dragging peasants and priests, burghers and magistrates away from their occupations had been reproduced uncounted times in inexpensive little books. It was certainly familiar to most nineteenth-century Germans.

It became more familiar still through Alfred Rethel's brilliantly executed cycle of wood engravings *Auch ein Totentanz,* begun in 1848. Rethel, who died in 1859, at forty-three, in depression and madness, had earned a reputation as a painter of ambitious historical murals. But it was his modern version of Holbein's allegory that made him famous; the cycle, wrote Josef Ponten in 1911 in a substantial monograph, "became a piece of the people's soul, just like folk songs

---

another, whether a flower or a stone, with love. "And that is German, sounding like something out of old fairy tales." Karl Woermann, *Von deutscher Kunst. Betrachtungen und Folgerungen* (1907; 2nd ed., 1925), 92; Gustav Floerke, *Arnold Böcklin und seine Kunst. Aufzeichnungen* (1901; 3rd ed., 1921), 17, 140.

*Unable to resist these patriotic accolades, Thoma was as proud of his German roots as he was of his compatriots. "As Germans we are happy," he said at sixty, "if we can find in our art traces of what we regard as our very own, and art can well be an answer to the question, What is German?" For Thoma, the answer was, in a word, feeling: "For us Germans, art will never be for long a matter of display and luxury—we will ever again have to try to make it a matter of the heart," for the foundations of great German art had been laid "from within." Otto Julius Bierbaum, *Hans Thoma,* in *Deutsche Meister. Schwind, Klinger, Thoma* (n.d.), separately paginated, 63.

for which we seek no author." Rethel's self-portraits, done mainly during the 1830s, exhibit a good-looking, gifted young artist with a drooping mustache, and reveal nothing of the turmoil within. His art spoke of it all the more loudly. "From the outset," Ponten judged, "Rethel had been the heroic singer of death. Death was the real hero he served," as he painted and engraved "death in all its faces," above all in his masterpiece, the modern-medieval dance of death.[7]

Inspired by what he condemned as the excesses of democratic demagogues during the revolutionary days of 1848, Rethel has death, a skeleton barely covering its nakedness with a variety of appropriate attire, devastate German towns and villages. It rides toward modern Cologne as peasant women flee in panic; incites mobs to violence with inflammatory speeches; seduces the gullible with talk of liberty, equality, and fraternity; comes as a friend to liberate the aged from the burden of living. Then, toward the end of the century, in 1889, the eccentric painter, sculptor, and etcher Max Klinger, committed to astonishing the public, gave the dance of death uncompromising modern dress. In this cycle, one art historian suggested, Klinger "showed himself an authentic German artist," with "high spiritual grandeur." Death in the shape of a naked skeleton haunts nurseries, highways, and railroad ties. "We flee the form of death, not death," Klinger inscribed in the last number of his painful *Der Tod als Heiland,* death as the Savior, "for the goal of our highest wishes is death."[8]

There are signs that Klinger, at least, took this solemnity with a touch of self-deprecating humor; in 1880, in a shocking drawing, *Der Tod am See,* he has a skeleton leaning on its scythe pissing into the sea, a homely scene that subverts its grim associations. At all events, late in the bourgeois century, the belated romantic infatuation with death had evidently conquered a sizable middle-class public. In 1896, at a time when these artists were enjoying great acclaim, Lovis Corinth enlarged the corpus in a half-length self-portrait, particularly chilling in its matter-of-factness. The painter, sturdy, tanned, in shirtsleeves and tie, stands before studio windows that look out upon a sun-drenched industrial cityscape; but next to him he has placed a skeleton hanging from an iron hook.

This pervasive cultural attitude accounts for some remarkable acts of kidnapping the past that educated Germans undertook in the nineteenth century. Ostentatiously honoring Dürer and Rembrandt, they conflated the history of art with the demands of politics. Novelists, professors, journalists, and politicians subjected these masters to ideological agendas with imaginative evocations, reverential lives, and pious festivals. Like Wagner's Music of the Future, though more unwittingly, the self-portraits of Dürer and Rembrandt entered middle-class awareness and were forged into weapons in cultural politics.

Nothing in the century documents more dramatically than these curious transactions the intimate commerce between personal and social life, intimacy and
publicity.*

The nineteenth-century German reception of Dürer was not a sudden erup-
tion of sentiment. In the late 1790s, the young romantic enthusiast Wilhelm
Heinrich Wackenroder, who literally adored art, brooded on "the forgotten
bones of our old Albrecht Dürer" in a Nürnberg cemetery, and proclaimed that
they made him "glad to be a German." That in truth Dürer had long been well
remembered, that visitors to his tomb were dissolving in tears and scholars
anatomizing his art, did not modify Wackenroder's elegiac message: inconvenient facts were no obstacle to his cloudy inward vision. But, though a patriot,
he was not a chauvinist. Like his contemporaries, he saw Raphael, greatest of all
painters, as a worthy companion to Dürer. "Are Rome and Germany not on
the same earth?" he asked rhetorically. "It should be possible for more than one
love to coexist in the breast of man." After all, the Alps are not impassable![9]

In 1811, illustrating this genial cosmopolitanism, the Nazarene Franz Pforr
drew Dürer and Raphael companionably kneeling, their hands folded in devotion, before Art enthroned like a Virgin Mary with the sun a halo behind her
lovely head. But then, as calls for German unification grew increasingly strident, Raphael receded from the awareness of the public, and Dürer came to
stand preeminent, alone. German mythmakers could scarcely deny that Dürer
had visited Italy twice, but they asserted that he had gone south to teach, not to
learn.†

Even before his death in 1528, Dürer had enjoyed an international reputation, for his character no less than his versatility as painter, etcher, engraver,
designer, autobiographer, theorist of art. His devotees transfigured him into the
model of the good German: hardworking, pious, manly, moved by beauty but
uncorrupted by sensuality. With the emergence of a self-conscious Germanic
art and literature just before the dawn of the nineteenth century, and with its
spread during the heyday of romanticism, regard for Dürer reached the highest
possible pitch. To revive Dürer was to make claims for the nation into which he
had been born, and for his "childlike German heart."[10] As we have noted, to be
a grown-up child was becoming an asset. Did it not rescue into adult life a time

---

*It is essential to remember for what follows that Dürer and Rembrandt enjoyed exceptionally
wide recognition because both were masters in the graphic arts, which circulated more easily than
paintings.

†Yet the old cosmopolitan spirit, long manifested in the yearning of Germans for Italy—its
classical monuments, memorable history, warming sunlight, and sexual freedom—died hard. In
1815, the Nazarenes holding a Dürer festival toasted the master and the future of German art
without turning their convivial get-together into an occasion for denigrating foreigners.

of lovable transparency? In children, the naked heart had not yet been covered over by cant or conventionality. One can see why Dürer's worshipers canonized him. He was a German among Germans. No wonder lovers of higher things paired him with Bach.

Dürer's stature was guaranteed by his self-portraits. Across four decades, he had drawn and painted himself in a variety of poses and attires, including, in an arresting knee-length drawing, no attire at all. He presented himself as dandified bridegroom, self-conscious craftsman, sickly patient, and, in an affecting late drawing, the Man of Sorrows complete with the instruments of the Passion. But it was the powerful frontal view of 1500 that became canonical in nineteenth-century Germany, extravagantly admired and endlessly reproduced. This half-length symmetrical self-portrait, in which Dürer, fashionably attired, stares wide-eyed at the viewer, must be the best-known self-portrait in the history of German art. Friedrich Matthisson, poet, educator, and traveler, who saw it in Nürnberg in 1794, helped to consolidate a forming consensus. Dürer had immortalized "an authentic robust German physiognomy, full of manliness and probity."*

Writing to Goethe some seventeen years later, Bettina von Arnim, liberal publicist and collector of the eminent, matched this response. The self-portrait of 1500 showed him wise, serious, competent, she said, and documented the triumph of inwardness. Goethe had been saying much the same thing for years. Others viewing this self-portrait celebrated the seriousness in Dürer's eyes, his piety, great soul and poetry, noble seriousness, religious profundity, steadfastness and uprightness. It is hardly necessary to add that these pilgrims to Dürer saw such traits as German to the core, *Innerlichkeit* at its purest. Dürer's works, wrote Gustav Friedrich Waagen, connoisseur and pioneering art historian, in 1862, are "the true mirror of a noble, pure, truthful, genuinely German spirit."[11]

This veneration had been growing among the German middling orders for some decades. In 1828, the organizers of the Dürer tercentenary, all the while

---

* *"Eine ächt deutsche Kernphysiognomie, voll Mannsinn und Biederkeit."* Matthisson, *Erinnerungen*, pt. 1 (1810), 410. Some art historians have argued that the self-portrait was designed to recall the Savior. Thus, in his classic *Die Kunst Albrecht Dürers* of 1905, the Swiss art historian Heinrich Wölfflin found "something Christlike" in the painting. More than thirty-five years earlier, the English etcher and writer William B. Scott had already found Dürer's self-portrait showing "a face of perfect manly beauty, both in form and expression, indeed, resembling the ideal head attributed to the founder of Christianity." *Albert Durer [sic]* (1869), 62. And in 1870 Mrs. Charles Heaton commented that the idea was already well known: it "has often been remarked" that this self-portrait bears "resemblance" to "the traditional portraits of Christ." *The History of the Life of Albrecht Dürer of Nürnberg* (1870; 2nd ed., 1881), 63n.

professing pure artistic piety, tried to show how resurrecting an old artist would produce a new German art. At the commemoration in Berlin, speakers took a truculant patriotic line: "We borrow neither the name of Raphael nor that of any other among his contemporaries to honor him." Italy had no worthy rival to pit against Dürer. Yet, generally, the spirit of the festival remained pacific; political fantasies about a united Germany were outdone by Dürer's subjectivity as displayed in his self-portraits. "Who has transfigured the inner life of the spirit in the human face as well as you?" solemnly asked Konrad Levezow in the cantata he had written for the occasion; who has captured "the gentle tremor of the pious heart, the divine and serene tranquillity of the soul at peace?" But the future lay in a more bellicose direction. The claims to depths denied inferior nations acquired political even more than aesthetic resonance. Interestingly enough, Felix Mendelssohn, who had composed the music for the cantata, was criticized for being "soft and tender."[12] The Germany to come, Dürer's Germany, called for sterner, manlier tones.[13]

Fellow artists and art historians were no less worshipful. And once in place, the rhetoric on Dürer rarely dropped below this breathless level. In 1866, Herman Grimm, a learned and widely read biographer, prescribed how to visit Dürer's house: with pious devotion. Dürer had transcended the status of artist to become a national icon. Those who do not know him, Grimm maintained, do not really know a significant part of German history. "But those who do know him—for them, whenever Dürer is mentioned, his name must have a sound as if someone were saying: Germany, Fatherland."[14] It was in large measure his self-portraits that had made him an exemplar for his culture. "The feeling for Nature," which Grimm judged to be Dürer's distinctive quality, "emerges most plainly in the portraits in which Dürer depicts himself." Grimm had a point about Dürer's self-portraits, but his piety, which was doing duty for tough-minded biographical criticism, required a sustained suspension of disbelief: the publication of Dürer's papers in 1828 had revealed an artist raunchy in his letters and participating—perhaps only vicariously—in the whoring and other dissipations in which his intimate friend Pirckheimer liked to indulge.[15]

Scholarly nineteenth-century biographers, German or foreign, did nothing to subvert this idolatry. "The self-portrait plays a role in Dürer's activity more than in that of any other master of the Renaissance," wrote Moriz Thausing in 1876, in a solid life advertised as scientific. Perhaps the pleasure Dürer took in himself was part of the "raised self-awareness of the age," but, though not alone, he was more emphatically self-aware than others in the Renaissance. "The disposition to self-exploration, to the deepening of his own being, always alive in Dürer, also led him to the meticulous observation of his external appearance. With pleasure, and frequently, he made his own face the subject of his study." Thausing spoke for a consensus: the most meaningful among Dürer's voyages to the interior was, of course, that of 1500. "It is through this painting that Dürer principally survives in the perception of posterity. Who does not know him, that magnificent man!" He was "worthy of veneration," wrote Grimm, "part of the German character." In the right circumstances, the naked heart had ideological implications. In 1869, just before unification, Cosima Wagner summed up the Dürer religion: "Surely," she noted in her diary, "such a son has never been born to a romanic nation!"[16] To her mind, as to that of others, Germans had patented inwardness.

Nineteenth-century German patriots boasting about their superior *Innerlich-keit* had at least the shadow of an alibi for appropriating Dürer three centuries after his death. He was, after all, one of their own. But to congratulate them-selves on Rembrandt the German was to claim a much more implausible tro-phy; Georg Brandes, the great Danish critic, called it an annexation.[17] It was far more specific, far more aggressive than Eugène Fromentin's observation in his classic study of Netherlandish art, *Les Maîtres d'autrefois* of 1876, that Rem-brandt, "whose domain is the domain of ideas," was "the least Dutch among Dutch painters."[18] Obviously, Rembrandt was not a German at all. Yet his celebrated parade of self-portraits belongs in any discussion of modern German self-perception. Just as Germans could call Shakespeare, after the triumphant Tieck and Schlegel translations, *"unser* Shakespeare" only half in jest, they tried to lend Rembrandt, especially near the end of the century, the stature of a homegrown example for Germans: *"unser* Rembrandt."

What that age saw in Rembrandt is more significant for the historian of nineteenth-century culture than what he saw in himself. In 1906, echoing his compatriots, the art critic Georg Fuchs asserted in a collection of aesthetic "confessions" that Rembrandt was "a spiritual phenomenon," a "prodigious" and "immeasurably momentous event," who had left works comparable to Beethoven's last quartets.[19] Few Germans would have dared to patronize Rem-brandt as Fromentin had done, for his "mania for posing before a mirror and painting himself." Unlike Rubens in his heroic self-portraits, Fromentin thought, Rembrandt preferred to be "alone, in a small circumference, his eyes looking into his own, for himself and for the rare gratification of getting a crisp light or a rarer half-tint, working at the round surfaces of his large face."[20] In contrast, Rembrandt's German devotees detected in his self-portraits disclo-sures far more profound than an appetite for sensual gratification. But, then, what could one expect? Fromentin was only a Frenchman.

The modern museumgoer is likely to take as demonstrated that, more than all other painters in the history of art, Rembrandt van Rijn was the prince of psychologists. He had explored his face scores of times with unwearied patience and unsurpassed honesty, capturing the telltale marks that the decades had engraved on his cheeks and forehead. And he had done so, many believed, as much for posterity as for himself.[21] Compared with this intense self-exploration, even van Gogh, though obsessed with his face, must pale. From about 1800, art lovers read Rembrandt's pictorial autobiography as a moving record of a heroic private odyssey, an incomparable artistic revelation.

The inconvenient fact remains that Rembrandt left virtually no documentary evidence about his intentions as he defied current practice by spending untold hours before the mirror.[22] That he departed from the Dutch way with art is beyond question. He was an individualist who lived and borrowed money and painted much as he liked. But his first biographers almost wholly ignored the very canvases that the nineteenth century found so arresting; only one of them, Arnold Houbraken, in his brief life of Rembrandt, so much as mentions a self-portrait.

Still, the testimonies of his face that Rembrandt had left behind, their un-precedented number and rich diversity, invited speculation. Some of his self-portraits indulge in humorous play or caress exotic textures; others depict the fashionable painter at work or, in the witty manner of the day, challenge great forerunners like Titian; still others experiment with facial expressions or, charged with erotic energy, immortalize a bacchanalian moment. Even more than these, Rembrandt's late self-portraits, for the most part stripped of all accessories or narrative incident, appeared to Victorian viewers, and not just Germans, as highly self-conscious psychological studies, the culmination of a lifelong quest for self-understanding. To them the silence of the painter, or of those who knew him, was no refutation; if he had in fact been unaware of any program other than objective self-representation, this could only mean, by definition, that he had unconsciously made more insightful soundings than he knew. To the important Dutch art historian Carel Vosmaer, Rembrandt was "the painter of life and of the human soul," necessarily including his own.[23] Whether this view of the self-portraits was the projection of nineteenth-century museumgoers or a true effort at self-definition on the painter's part, Rembrandt the self-portraitist served the Victorian passion for inwardness to perfection.[24]

Among the first Germans to value Rembrandt highly and rank him with acknowledged past masters was the young Goethe, in a typically original move.[25] But his summary linking of Rembrandt with Raphael and Rubens as a true saint of art was only a pallid foretaste of the Rembrandt cult that became almost obligatory decades later. Living off Goethe's prestige, Germans put Rembrandt into the pantheon of idealized ancestors and linked this act of homage to the fading of the fraternal appreciation of Italian beauty. In 1860, when the novelist Gustav Freytag learned that his fellow author Wilhelm Raabe was planning a trip south, he protested strenuously: "What is it that German artists are steadily seeking in Italy? They should go to the Netherlands instead. *There* is the Promised Land of German art."[26]

Meanwhile, self-portraitists like Wilhelm Busch and Arnold Böcklin were offering Rembrandt the supreme tribute of imitation. Franz von Lenbach, the best-known and best-paid portrait painter in imperial Germany, proved an even more assiduous disciple. His somber emperors, statesmen, and society lions owe a palpable debt to Rembrandt's chiaroscuro. So do Lenbach's self-portraits: his frowning, light-drenched face emerges from a bleak, virtually undifferentiated background. And Lovis Corinth venerated Rembrandt all his life. After his death in 1925, his widow found a revealing note: "Life description or biography: the painter would call it a self-portrait created through words. I already have a whole lot of self-portraits behind me, a few biographies too—the remarkable thing is, all turn out differently, even though the innermost character always shows itself. See Rembrandt."[27]

See Rembrandt: it was into this hothouse, quasi-religious aura that the extremist pamphleteer Julius Langbehn, "a German," exploded with a pernicious anonymous polemic, *Rembrandt als Erzieher*. Its title page was decorated with a poor reproduction of Rembrandt's jaunty self-portrait of 1639. Though reviews of the book mixed marked reserve with astonished respect, it became an immediate and long-lasting, much discussed best-seller. Langbehn's cranky diagnoses, rhetorical overkill, and woolly-minded proposals for German regeneration became oppressively obvious, but their absurdities were drowned out by what his enthusiasts took to be timely cultural criticism.[28]

Langbehn's thesis is only too easy to summarize. German culture stands in mortal danger of losing "modesty, solitude, calm, individualism, aristocratism, art," all the qualities for which it had once been justly esteemed, as it whored after the false gods of greed, materialism, shallowness, rationalism, and citified haste. It was against the enemies of pure Aryan Germanness—money-makers, journalists, Francophiles, dry specialized philosophers, assimilated Jews who had betrayed their venerable tradition—that Langbehn pitted Rembrandt, the greatest of Lower Germans. He must become, in the provocative word of Langbehn's title, their educator. "Music and uprightness, barbarism and piety, childlikeness, and independence are the most prominent traits of the German character; in doing justice to them in the realm of art, Rembrandt shows himself by preference an authentic German." That romantic worship of childlike innocence—*Kindersinn*—as a distinctive German trait enjoyed an ominous revival at Langbehn's hands. Rembrandt's "inwardness goes far" and makes

him a reliable guide out of the morass. As "an authentic Aryan," he will "educate Germans into human beings." Animated by the quiet and mighty breath of
Rembrandt's spirit, characteristic Germanic qualities will reawaken.[29] And the
educated reading public, nervous about a perceived threat of decadence in an
age of mass literacy, the worship of modern science, and the baneful triumph of
Mammon, took Langbehn to its heart.

Langbehn was exploiting Rembrandt as a convenient stalking horse. His
muscular rhetoric, bad history, and dubious etymologies matter less to the study
of nineteenth-century inwardness—which, we have seen from the outset,
could be a menace as much as a blessing—than his electing Rembrandt as his
ideal educator. Rembrandt was the counterpart to Martin Luther, the hero who
had put the German people on its feet. Plainly, as Rembrandt shows, self-
knowledge is the first step toward eliminating the blight of mediocrity. "He
dives into the deep and brings back pearls." His ability, shared by Luther and
Bismarck, to speak to the lowest of the low without condescension, his healthy
appetite and good humor, his love of life, powerful even if he painted darkly,
emerge in all his work. And it is in his self-portraits, his complete autobiography, that Germans will see their mission most plainly.[30]

However eccentric Langbehn's abduction of Rembrandt, it caught the German imagination. In 1904, the far from unsophisticated Albert Dresdner
warmed up an appraisal of the German character that had become a tired, but
evidently not too tired, commonplace by then: "The author of *Rembrandt als
Erzieher* has championed the idea, with warmth and truth, that German rebirth
must start from the Germans' childlike nature." The modern world has grown
so sophisticated, so alienated from its roots, "that it is high time we let ourselves
be educated once again by the child, which is nearest to nature."[31] Dresdner,
and for that matter Langbehn, never dreamt what men this child would produce.

Langbehn's plea for the restoration of German *Innerlichkeit,* then, was one to
which even skeptics responded sympathetically. It was, after all, not new. As
early as 1824, the young German artist Ludwig Richter, to become literally a
household name for his cozy illustrations, had written into his Roman diary,
"My aspiration should be profundity and simplicity," and linked this agenda to
his national loyalties: "Always to live according to the *old, German* way, in strict
righteousness, and to remain pure in trade and commerce." In 1828, on the
occasion of the Dürer tercentenary, Richter, still a student, celebrated all alone
by piously turning over the pages of Dürer's cycle *The Life of Mary,* "looking
attentively at the eternally young, everlasting blossoms of his spirit with a feeling of bliss."[32]

This was a representative attitude. We have seen that German painters took their work seriously and saw themselves as active in a culture in which the cold shower of self-critical analysis, let alone humor, was exceedingly rare. So rare, in fact, that foreign observers, like a few unillusioned Germans, were disposed to comment on it. In 1820, Sir Charles Eastlake, art critic, painter, later director of London's National Gallery, put it bluntly: "The English have the matter and the Germans have the mind of art."[33] Soon after, Heinrich Heine comically lamented that while the British own the sea and the French the land, the Germans lay claim to the sky. Rembrandt might not really be a German, but there was much, it seemed, he had to teach Germans—in Dürer's company. In the mid-1880s, in *Jenseits von Gut und Böse,* Nietzsche identified this spirit as the hallmark of the German soul, complex, labyrinthine, virtually undefinable, but "loving the clouds and everything that is unclear, becoming, dawning, moist, and draped."[34] To such a soul, self-portraits were expressive gestures opening unplumbed reserves of noble and mysterious inner worlds.

It would be manifestly unjust to make this subjectivity a German monopoly; not all nineteenth-century mirrors were of Teutonic manufacture. One need only think of the skeletons that dominated the work of the Belgian James Ensor, including his macabre self-portraits, to recognize the claims of artists to be privileged students of their own soul and, by extension, of their viewer's, as a widespread phenomenon in the Victorian decades. But, as would surprise no one who recalls the shaping attitudes of German romantics, it was German artists who proffered such claims with the greatest panache and who explored their *Innerlichkeit* with a consistency and a desperate earnestness that makes them ideal witnesses to how far the champions of inwardness were ready to go— without in the long run losing their bourgeois public in the process.

≫ SIX ≪

The Common Touch

In the Victorian century, bourgeois turned letters and diaries into repositories for glimpses into their innermost life in unprecedented numbers and with unmatched intensity. These communications to others and to oneself could, to be sure, serve as exercises in self-protection and self-concealment. But, though intended for a carefully selected audience, they became favorite agents of self-scrutiny and, with that, of self-revelation. They attest just where bourgeois drew the line at baring their heart. It will emerge that they were far more frankly confessional than their critics have liked to imagine.

There is extensive evidence that a goodly proportion of these literally innumerable documents must have been flat in tone and stingy with self-perception.* But the age generated striking, at times unpredictable, variations in the quality of these private bulletins. It seems plausible to suppose that major writers would write memorable letters, but there was no guarantee of that: Anthony Trollope's letters were as matter-of-fact, even dull, as Gustave Flaubert's or Henry James's letters were passionate and brilliant. In general, the societies earliest to be won over to the ideal of marriage for love and to prize feeling above calculation allowed writers to express themselves more openly on the page than did societies keeping up the time-hallowed custom of erotic reserve and practical alliances. Beyond such distinct cultural habits, status and

---

*Nothing would obviously be easier than to replace many times over the passages I shall be quoting in the pages that follow and still make the same points. I have chosen my exemplars after sampling a far larger population.

gender divided letter writers and diary keepers into diverse populations. The educated had more words and better models to help them gain access to their inner life—and, naturally, to veil it—than did petty bourgeois, whose personal messages, to themselves or others, were often touching in their inarticulateness. Inescapably men would record experiences different from those of women: they could write about work and business and politics, arenas of action in the world foreclosed for most women, largely confined as they were to domesticity.

Still, it will emerge that the cliché about the male as a reasoning and the female as an emotional being did not govern Victorian letters and diaries. The confidential, confessional style, available to bourgeois of all persuasions, to Protestants, Catholics, and Jews as to unbelievers, flourished among men as much as among women. Romanticism propagandizing in behalf of mutual love as the only acceptable ground for permanent commitments and for the unbuttoned outpouring of emotions was, after all, an international phenomenon with lasting consequences, encouraging its heirs not to stint their confessions—all the while remaining, of course, within proper limits.

Obviously it is impossible fully to sort out the untold millions of letters and diaries the Victorians produced; doubtless those destroyed or moldering in attics unread greatly outnumber the thousands that have come down to us. It would be hasty to assume that only the best educated left papers to archives and libraries; many documents humble enough in expression, even spelling, have found their way into public depositories. Nor can we assume that the most intimate, most candid revelations were natural casualties. The ravages of time, the inevitable losses that moving house entails, a certain degree of self-censorship of diarists purging their own entries or recipients rendering passages of letters illegible were no less significant for keeping private material from the future than the interventions of family members or friends anxious to protect the writer's good name. All played cruel games with an inquisitive posterity. But enough letters and enough diaries markedly differing from one another, including those their contemporaries would have regarded as scandalous, have survived to justify the historian's confidence that his sample is relatively representative of bourgeois sentiments.

I. The Spirit of the Letter

The letter has a long history. Plato wrote memorable letters, as did Cicero and St. Paul. But their epistles differed radically from their modern counterparts. Not that they lacked feeling, but they were social documents far more than

personal communications, addressed to an interested public, at times to generations to come. Cicero cast his letters in a style less self-conscious than that of his
orations and philosophical treatises, praising their "informality—*neglegentia*"
and their "language of conversation."[1] But he meant to publish them just the
same. Again, the moving love letters between Héloïse and Abelard that have
survived are part homily, part classical allusion, and were most probably revised
for a larger audience after the fact. Until recent times, no letter, except for a
secret diplomatic dispatch, could have borne the writer's entreaty, so familiar to
the nineteenth century, not to show it to anyone or, better, to burn it.

Even the celebrated letters that Madame de Sévigné sent her far-away daughter late in the seventeenth century make at best a partial exception. First published in the 1720s and reissued in scholarly editions a hundred years later, they
were exceptionally candid, lively, intelligent, various, observant—and personal.
But, as Madame de Sévigné well knew, although intended for her daughter, her
letters were copied and shown about, serving the fortunate few as a handwritten
gossipy gazette. Nor were the confidences proffered by the most distinguished
correspondents of the eighteenth century—Lord Chesterfield, Horace Walpole, Voltaire—a match for the intense inwardness of many a nineteenth-
century letter writer. Far from being spontaneous messages, they conformed to
sophisticated recipes; dressing up their writer's emotions with balanced sentences and forensic logic, and above all with wit, they prove that in letters
stylishness may be the nemesis of authentic intimacy.

The tide turned with the mid-eighteenth-century cult of sensibility later
canonized by the romantics: the nineteenth century learned much from the
confessions by mail that their parents' generation had begun to write. In fiction
as in correspondence, middle-class culture was experimenting with softer, more
humane, at times lachrymose attitudes. It was this spirit that the immensely
popular epistolary novels of the day, from Richardson to Rousseau and
Goethe, at once exhibited and promoted, and that inevitably fostered the taste
for more forthcoming, less formulaic exchanges. Across Europe, the molders of
manners moved to replace the formal style with written speech. In 1751, Christoph Gellert, academic, playwright, novelist, famous for his versified fables,
published a widely appreciated menu of specimen letters exemplifying the gospel of naturalness and disdain for affectation, and this was to become the standard recipe for letter writing and not in Germany alone.[2]

Not without resistance. In 1788, Adolph Freiherr von Knigge, who made
himself into the authoritative pundit on German middle-class manners, warned
his readers to subject their letter writing to severe curbs, limit the circle of their
correspondents, and, above all, exercise caution; an imprudent, inexpungeable
word could do untold damage. But, even though Gellert's examples did not

perfectly carry out his precepts, the trend was running against Knigge, most spectacularly in the torrent of letters that the young Goethe lavished on his beloved sister and a few other confidants. He had studied with Gellert at the University of Leipzig and showed what his professor's doctrine could mean if pushed to extremes. Writing at great heat, injecting French or English phrases as the mood took him, liberally resorting to exclamation points, incomplete sentences, broken phrases, and wild ejaculations of affection or despair, he shared his self. For Goethe, given to impulsive self-disclosure, *Die Leiden des jungen Werther,* the novel that made him famous, was a continuation of his letter writing in a different medium.

While other correspondents failed to equal Goethe's unforgettable utterances, they imitated his fervor and received credit for it among the Victorians. In 1891, in a substantial history of the German letter, Georg Steinhausen devoted much of his space to the eighteenth century, "the century of the letter." He detected a veritable "cult of the letter" that matched the cult of friendship, and offered in evidence a bouquet of emotional tributes by Goethe's contemporaries to the powers of the written word. One defined the letter as the "language of the heart"; another as a "copy of the soul." Lessing put the program tersely: "Write as you speak," he told his sister, "and you will be writing beautifully." By the onset of the nineteenth century, such counsel had attained the stature of a commonplace: "I have now attained the true art of letter-writing," Jane Austen wrote her sister Cassandra in January 1801, "which we are always told is to express on paper exactly what one would say to the same person by word of mouth. I have been talking to you almost as fast as I could the whole of this letter."[3]

Austen was deftly summarizing—and exemplifying—a relaxed and sincere style that the romantics were pushing beyond conventionality and that, directly and indirectly, would enter respectable bourgeois culture in the years ahead. One did not need to be a romantic to compose emotional and self-revealing letters, but, as their collected correspondence attests, the romantics wrote that way almost on principle. "The true letter," declared Novalis, "is by its nature poetic," which is to say, a revelation of self.[4] Accordingly, Byron regaled friends and lovers with brilliant missives, in turn amusing and melancholic, always frank and rarely sentimental, and infused them with demonic speed by the free use of dashes. Intoxicated with words, he would string them together for sheer oral gratification without ever neglecting his self-imposed obligation to be the observant reporter. He captured his exhilarating epistolary habits when he told Mary Shelley, "I am not a cautious letter-writer and generally say what comes uppermost at the moment"—the romantic agenda for letter writing in a sentence.[5]

Byron, to be sure, was a lord, but a middle-class romantic like Keats was no more reticent, if far less scatological, though the letters to his fiancée, Fanny Brawne, written when he was aware he was dying, breathe the torments of sexual frustration. But before then, the pleasures of investing his deepest self in letters to those he loved blended smoothly with Keats's cherished vocation, the writing of poetry. He would insert verses he had just composed, still warm as it were, as though he literally could not wait to involve others in his innermost feelings the best way he knew. So did, in their more prosaic way, the Schlegel brothers, who corresponded with one another freely, often testily, and did not spare the other their own secret turmoil. Achim von Arnim and his wife, Bettina, born Brentano, those German arch-romantics, exchanged cordial erotic messages: "When I get back," he wrote her, "nothing shall stop me from diving straightways under your blanket.—Amen, amen, may it happen!" Her reply, only marginally more inhibited: "Ah, I wish I hung on your neck and could look only upon you until death." He remained her "dear, silken body"; she to be kissed "a thousand times." This rush of feeling coexisted with more mundane but no less intimate messages: "For God's sake," she reminded him, "buy yourself a pair of suspenders and bring the children some apples."[6]

Among French romantics, it was Stendhal who mastered this manner better than anyone else. A consummate setter of the scene, he would invite his correspondents into his presence for a private chat: "Paris, December 26, 1829," he started a letter to his friend Prosper Mérimée, "at five o'clock in the evening, without a candle." It was to Mérimée, too, that he confided the real story behind the façade of his novella *Armance:* the hero is impotent and is giving his adoring, uncomplaining wife "two or three ecstasies every night by hand."[7]

This is not the sort of news that most bourgeois liked to exchange, even though, once their privacy was secure, some of them came close. After Harriet Beecher Stowe had been away on one of her long stays at spas, her husband, Calvin Stowe, reminded her in a longing letter that it had been "almost 18 months since I have had a wife to sleep with me." (Separation was the couple's only means of contraception.) "It is enough to kill any man, especially such a man as I am." He tempered, or complicated, his plea by adding, "When I get desperate, & cannot stand it any longer, I get dear, good kind hearted Br[other] Stagg to come and sleep with me, and he puts his arms round me & hugs me to my heart's content."[8] Neither Calvin Stowe, an ordained minister, nor his wife, soon to become her country's most effective abolitionist, was a romantic, but the heritage of romanticism resonates in this pathetic cry of a frustrated lover.

What made Victorian letter writing distinctive, then, was less style than mass. Their time welcomed, and bought, handsomely decorated volumes of letters and, as we have seen, found expansive, though often doctored, excerpts embedded in biographies. Publishers expected profits from bouquets of courtship letters, collections chattily documenting two centuries of cultural habits, or the most interesting letters of the famous.[9] We have seen it before: the age was adept at spreading among the many what had been the privilege of the few. When the well-known English editor and art critic Philip Gilbert Hamerton characterized his time as "this age of communication," he was expressing a widespread and perfectly just conviction.[10] The principal agent in democratizing written testimonials to the self was technology, an unforeseen but efficient ally of the romantics' mission to put feelings on the map. The improvement in roads, the rapid spread of the railroad network with its astonishing speed and dependable schedules, transformed the mails out of all recognition. So did that humble innovation the postage stamp.

Its history is well known but deserves retelling: in 1837, the year of Queen Victoria's accession, that professional, self-assured, and exceedingly difficult reformer Sir Rowland Hill proposed in a famous pamphlet, *Post Office Reform: Its Importance and Practicability,* a radical reorganization of the traffic in letters. At the time he wrote, the British mails were mired in a confusion of regulations, massive inconveniences, and extortionate rates. Before the reform, "a 'single' letter," Rowland Hill's daughter recalled in an adoring biography of her father, "had to be written on a single sheet of paper, whose use probably gave rise to the practice of that now obsolete 'cross' writing which often made an epistle all but illegible, to which in those days of dear postage recourse was unavoidable." Indeed, "if a second sheet, or even the smallest piece of paper, were added to the first, the postage was doubled."[11] When Hill wrote, the price of a letter was regulated not only by numbers of sheets but by weight, distance, and local rates, and averaged, including local mail, more than six pence. Distance aggravated expense: for example, the charge for a single letter between London and Edinburgh or Glasgow was 1s. 3½d., a tidy sum unthinkable for the poor and hard for most of their "betters." To say nothing of the "lower orders," who were virtually cut off from their families, wrote Harriet Martineau, biographer, historian, political economist, unexcelled popularizer of pressing current issues; "there were few families in the wide middle class who did not feel the cost of postage a heavy item in their expenditure; and if the young people sent letters home only once a fortnight the amount at the year's end was a rather serious matter."[12]

To make matters worse, traffic in letters was far from secure, exposed as it was to loss, pilferage, smuggling, and inordinate delays. Need spawned fraud: many communicated by sending franked newspapers in which words were picked out to make a message. The ancient privilege of franking, which allowed peers, members of Parliament, officers, and favorite friends to send letters free of charge, had survived into the nineteenth century and widened the gap between those who could easily afford to write letters and those who could not. Opponents of the practice vehemently denounced it, and high charges in general, as a tax on knowledge; it was also a tax on sociability, putting a premium on self-expression. Since, for the most part, postage had to be paid by the recipients, letter carriers had to find them and collect the money due—a time-consuming and irritating procedure. "Mismanagement, waste, and fraud," Hill's daughter summed up the situation, were virtually inescapable.[13] Analyzing it coolly, Hill made two proposals, staggering in their simplicity: all letters should be prepaid, and the post office should establish a uniform rate: a penny for letters weighing half an ounce or less.

Despite its rationality, so frequently a source of bureaucratic sabotage, Hill's penny post became a reality in 1840. The official figures for England and Wales chart the arresting results: in 1839, just before the reform, the number of letters delivered stood at some 76 million. In the following year it doubled, only to explode after that: 347 million in 1850, 564 million in 1860, 3.5 billion in 1914. Letter writing, in short, had become a major occupation among the literate: if in 1839 the average Britisher wrote three letters a year, by just before the outbreak of the First World War that figure had grown to seventy-five.[14] To put flesh on these statistical bones: as Hill had promised in his pamphlet, the modern way with the mails introduced sizable segments of the public to the habit of letter writing and encouraged the educated to write frequently and regularly. He had wanted to benefit the whole of the population, whether rich or poor, including the "middle classes," which would obtain "relief from oppressive and irritating demands which they pay grudgingly."[15] Those who could command enough leisure, incorporated doing their correspondence into their daily routine. Looking back in 1866, Gladstone placed "the introduction of cheap postage for letters, documents, patterns, and printed matter, and the abolition of all taxes on printed matter, in the catalogue of free trade legislation," all "great measures" that formed part of "the great code of industrial emancipation."[16] The word "emancipation" is striking: Gladstone knew no higher praise.

Other countries promptly followed Hill's lead. In the summer of 1845, a young American, Catherine Huntington, who had been sending flirtatious letters to her cousin Joseph Huntington in Connecticut, wrote to him, "How does the P. O. reformation suit you: For my part I can render my heartfelt thanks to the first mover of this reform. Maybe the letters will come pouring in upon you in such multitudes that you'll wish for the old rates of postage."[17] She was alluding to an act of March that repealed an onerous, expensive system and substituted a far simpler one. Before this legislation, letters had cost anywhere

from six to twenty-five cents and even more, the postage varying with numerous zones across the states and territories and with the number of sheets; the act
divided postage into five cents for letters sent less than 300 miles and twice as
much for longer distances, and as in Britain weight in half-ounce increments
helped to determine the charges. Two years later, the U.S. post office issued the
first adhesive stamps, and by 1855 all letters had to be prepaid. A new era of
communication had begun. Again the figures tell the story: in the decisive
decade between 1845 to 1855, the number of letters mailed in the United States
more than tripled, from roughly 40 million to 132 million. Joseph Huntington
was obviously not the only one to have letters pouring in on him. The postcard,
introduced in the Austro-Hungarian Empire in 1869 and in Britain the year
after, did not increase the intimacy of the mails but its frequency. It was soon
followed by the cheerful picture postcard, a tribute to the rise of pleasure travel
among those of middling income. One way or the other, people felt entitled to
hear from those on holiday. By 1897, a German compiler of sample letters could
in the opening sentence of his book state without fear of contradiction that "it
should be impossible to find anyone in the wide world of civilized nations who
is not daily confronted with the necessity to make a written communication."[18]
He could not have written this sixty years earlier.

For decades, especially in rural areas, the mail reached its destination not by
the railroad alone but also by riders on horseback or by coach. With the multi-
plication of opportunities for confidential, often romantic communications—
the enormous, steadily growing bulk of business and governmental mail is not
part of this study—popular artists added the post to their repertory, thus en-
hancing its mystique. They painted and etched the mailman struggling against a
snowstorm, the post coach speeding along the highway scattering all before it,
and, best of all, the blushing young woman waiting for a love letter. Even
before these reforms, bourgeois cherished the "fine idea," as one of Joseph
Huntington's friends wrote him in 1843, "that, although separated from each
other by any distance, thoughts and sentiments may be freely exchanged."[19]
Once the Hill era had taken hold, this freedom grew exponentially and the
thoughts and sentiments more unconstrained.

Writing and receiving letters, then, and indeed postcards, came to enjoy a
high priority in the emotional economy of the Victorians. Far more than ever
before, correspondence spawned, and sustained, the desire for reciprocity; even
a letter that did not explicitly beg for a reply was an implicit demand for
conversation at a distance. This obvious metaphor was, as we have seen, at least
as old as Cicero and would be freely bandied about among the Victorians. It had
reached Russia by 1819, in an essay on letter writing by N. I. Grech, which
repeated the old saying once again: "*Letters,* in the exact sense of the word, are

conversations or talks with those who are absent."[20] Unnumbered millions must have felt like Joseph Selden Huntington, Jr., a freshman at Yale in 1886, who confided to his diary virtually every day that each morning his first act was to walk to the post office and look for his mail.[21] Especially men and women in love transfigured the mailman into an almost mythical messenger, the bringer of happiness or misery. In country after country, it became the custom, more honored in the observance than in the breach, for couples in love, and even more for those engaged, to write one another daily.

The letters exchanged by some nineteenth-century German-Jewish couples are particularly illuminating. They attest to the spread of romantic conventions and the emergence of an international style for love letters among groups long kept isolated from the mainstream of Victorian culture. Decades before Jews were granted full legal equality in the German states, at a time when many of them were still forbidden to settle in certain cities or practice certain professions, they poured out their affection in language wholly indistinguishable from that of their often antagonistic hosts. They wrote middle-class letters typical in every respect; if it were not for the names of the correspondents and an occasional reference to religious matters, one would be unable to conjecture about their origins. "You, my precious, were today, as usual, my first thought," wrote the young rabbi Meyer Keyserling to his adored Bertha Philippson, on February 4, 1861, from Berlin, where he was doing research for a biography of Moses Mendelssohn. "Around 7:30 the mailman knocked with your precious letter."[22]

Giving was as exciting as getting. The next morning, Keyserling greeted the woman he was soon to marry: "Good morning, my heart!" All he had in mind was to "write down a morning greeting with a newly fastened pen. I so much like to occupy myself with you before I start with my work!" The mailman had not yet arrived, and Keyserling was not expecting to hear from his fiancée this day. "But tomorrow morning! You can believe me how blissful your letters make me, I read them over and over until the latest is replaced by a later one." He noted, and evidently it meant much to him, that his mother, too, had kept and reread his last letter until a new one arrived. "She loved me as I love you."[23] Her response, probably tactful, has not survived.

Couples who could not keep the demanding schedule of a daily letter steadily exhorted one another to write soon, and tried to extract promises for more assiduous epistolary attention. "Most tenderly loved Adolph," wrote Nanny Herzberg to her fiancé, Adolph Koritzer, a fur trader in Leipzig, in May 1856. " 'An upright man keeps his word!' Even though I am not an upright man and only a girl, whether upright or not I do not know, still I want to keep my word, since I once promised you to reply right after receipt of your letter."[24] A bundle of forty-nine letters between May 15 and December 23, 1856, attests that she, though only a girl, was indeed as good as her word.

For all the striking cultural disparities and appropriate differences in forms of expression, then, love letters were at heart all alike. This can be documented with lovers writing in societies in which arranged marriages were the rule. Among strictly observant eastern European Jewish families, where the young couple-to-be often did not even meet until the wedding ceremony and correspondence between the betrothed required special permission, Eros found the way. To be sure, only those who conveniently disregard the massive evidence for parental arbitrariness, women's forced passivity, and marital misery can possibly throw the sheen of sentiment over such dealings. But on rare occasions two young people whom their families had brought together would fall in love literally at first sight, doubtless well prepared by their fantasies.

One remarkable instance, as eloquent as it is exceptional, is the love letter that Chonon Wengeroff, the son of a rich merchant in Konotop, Ukraine, wrote to his bride, Pauline, in July 1849. He had spoken with her only two or three times. It was a letter—the first, she recalled decades later, she had ever received—she preserved with all others for half a century. "Deeply loved and cherished Peschinke, may you live, be healthy, my only soul! We have reached Sluzk. You are surely at home, I am already 275 versts from you. Only yesterday I was next to you, and I heard your sweet, dear talk! O how happy I was. . . . Now all I see is that after the two hours my father wants to spend here, I'll have to travel on and with every minute, every second, I'm farther and farther away from you, my dear Pessinju. My dear, only soul Pessunja, you can imagine how I felt when I got into the carriage to start the trip, and two seconds later I couldn't see you any more! I could fill pages with how I felt after that, but I'm afraid that you will be uneasy; only you can understand, my angel, only this can be my consolation that I'll read your dear handwriting, in which I can read your feelings for me. Oh, that will give me new birth!" And more for another page.[25]

In short, a letter was a token, *the* token, of true affection, proof that the other was ready to set aside valuable time to visualizing, and addressing, the loved one. Letters could express deep emotions especially between proper couples because they took it for granted—or, often, the more venturesome of the two would urge the other to practice taking it for granted—that neither would hold back anything, whether the most painful experiences or the most carefully guarded confidences. Letters were surrogates for a longed-for physical presence. "You ask me, beloved woman, whether I read your letters *several times,*" Ulrich Levysohn assured his fiancée, Clara Herrmann, in 1876, the year of their marriage. "My child, every evening, when I come home, I open the letter

cabinet and read them in bed over and over again."[26] Reading her letters in bed
was not a complete substitute for having her in bed, but it would have to do
until marriage. And when one partner was remiss in fulfilling the unwritten
contract of intimacy and frequency, the other would send a reminder, usually
affectionate, at times tart.

Silence generated anger or anxiety. "My dear good Emilie! I just wrote you
the day before yesterday and expectantly look forward to more frequent letters,
I already told you, my dear, that you should write to me more often even if I fall
behind a little because business matters kept me from it." Thus Marcus Pflaum,
a merchant in Munich, gently reproaching his fiancée, Emilie Hoeter, in Karls-
ruhe, on June 11, 1833. The next day—as usual his letter of the eleventh had
traveled quickly—the dear good Emilie launched a reproach of her own. "Although I had been quite angry at you," she wrote, "still, I will not revenge
myself and therefore already reply to your *long awaited letter* today. Yes, my dear
Marcus, I was quite embarrassed this time, for I had thought I would receive
one as early as Sunday, and so I remained in this embarrassing situation until
Wednesday. You must not do this to me any more, I think you really could
devote a bit of time to me." And, though saying that she would not revenge
herself, she did so by giving details of a sudden illness in the family that had
greatly worried her. But her fiancé was too wily to let her reprimand rest on his
shoulders. He had only given way to impatience, he told her, because he so
admired her letters for their style and wit that he wanted more of them.[27] Such
duels were skirmishes, normally settled before they did much damage.

The appetite for abandoning customary discretion was oddly nourished by
that modern invention—the ideal of privacy. That, too, like so much else in the
bourgeois nineteenth century, was problematic; the boundaries beyond which
no one might go were uncertain, especially within the family where the need of
growing boys and girls to establish their private space clashed with the parents'
authority to invade their children's domain. Thus, to give but one instance, in
1849, Richard Cary Morse, an American newspaper publisher and ordained
minister, wrote his wife that he expected their daughter Elizabeth to be upset
by his practice of breaking the seal of letters addressed to her. She ought to
know, though, that "I recognize the sacredness of a seal & the seal of her letters
no less than others, & where there is reason to believe that secrecy should be
regarded [I] should not feel at liberty to break the seal; nor indeed in any case, if
she forbids. But I take it for granted that she has all confidence in me, & that her
secrets, if I should discover them are safe in her father's keeping. Yet children
can never know the interest their parents take in them. We regard our children
as part of ourselves."[28] This was no doubt obtuse; but the family battle over

Elizabeth Morse's right to her privacy was symptomatic of a larger and, to many, painful shift: the increasing claim of adolescents, in defiance of time-honored parental authority, to their own feelings. And the generational struggle this entailed was frequently carried out by mail.

Even those who circumvented the sacredness of the post professed to respect privacy. When in a constitutional state government officials opened letters not addressed to them, they cloaked their actions in deepest secrecy; detected in their snooping, they took the high ground that public duty supersedes the ideal of the inviolable mails: they had been pursuing criminals or protecting national security. In 1844, it was revealed that the Home Office had opened the political correspondence of Giuseppe Mazzini, then in exile in England, and com-municated its contents to the authorities in Italy, a betrayal that cost a couple of idealistic Venetian conspirators their life. Such shabby treatment outraged many who shared Mazzini's scorn for what he called this "un-English activity." Members asked indignant questions in the House of Commons, ministers felt under pressure to tell lies in their defense, Macaulay denounced turning "the Post Office into an engine of the police" as "utterly abhorrent to the public feeling." And Carlyle was moved, in a letter to the *Times,* to lay down the charter of the right to privacy in correspondence: "It is a question vital to us that sealed letters in an English post-office be, as we all fancied they were, respected as things sacred." He called opening mail "a practice near of kin to picking men's pockets, and to other still viler and far fataler forms of scoundrel-ism."[29] But scoundrelism or necessary policy, it did not touch ordinary letter writers, who could pour out their hearts without fear that the state had any interest in their affairs.

For middle-class men and women, then, the threat of having their personal exchanges exposed came not from the police or some official but from prying families. Stratagems to escape unwelcome attentions, so imaginatively depicted in novels, were a realistic necessity: lovers enlisted discreet confidantes, leased a post office box, learned shorthand to keep their amorous exchanges from in-truders, folded scraps of intimate messages into innocuous letters that could safely be shown to one's family. Not surprisingly, the embarrassments caused by love letters piously preserved and inopportunely discovered haunted lovers in actuality as it animated writers in need of a dramatic plot device. In his best-known novel, *Effi Briest,* which turns on the husband's finding incriminating love letters in his wife's desk, Theodor Fontane was imitating life.

In turn, Victorian letter writers were steadily importuned to imitate books and sacrifice homespun improvisation for genteel address. At the upper end of the scale, the educated could draw on exemplars like the letters of Madame de Sévigné: the grandmother of Proust's Marcel was only one among many cul-

tivated nineteenth-century French readers to cherish them. Others might polish their skills by consulting volumes of letters by Alexander Pope or Voltaire,
usually bowdlerized, or collections of near-contemporaries—Byron or Balzac
or Goethe's correspondence with Schiller. But among anxious moralists, the
choice of such models raised difficulties of its own. Some much quoted letter
writers, it seemed, were unworthy tempters: in 1852, H. Hastings Weld cautioned the readers of *Godey's Lady's Book* against the published correspondence
of Horace Walpole, "read with avidity and widely circulated." Its vicious tendency was "enough to ruin the character of the correspondence of an age.
Flippant, gossiping, and mendacious, their evil characteristics are easily imitated; and, without the wit of the author, may affect his audacious disregard of
truth and of the rights of others."[30] Prudence, that bourgeois virtue, was a shield
against all sorts of temptations—cynicism, gambling, promiscuity.

    In the lower reaches of the social scale, correspondents relatively inept with
the pen—and this seems to have constituted the majority of petty bourgeois—
had at their disposal a sizable literature of manuals to relieve their verbal clumsi-
ness. For centuries, that "unpretending but useful form-book, the 'Letter-
writer,' " as an American author, R. Turner, called it in 1835, had served as the
scribe for those who would be more literary than they were. It strove above all
for versatility, with letters to the woman one loved, the suitor one rejected, the
adolescent one counseled, the nobleman one petitioned, the employer one
solicited, the customer one cajoled, the duel one declined, and more. The very
title of Turner's vademecum, typical in an age of long titles, conveys a sense of
the audience in view: *The Parlour-Letter-Writer and Secretary's Assistant: Consisting of Original Letters on Every Occurrence in Life, Written in a Concise and Familiar
Style, and Adapted to Both Sexes, to Which Are Added, Complimentary Cards, Wills,
Bonds etc.*[31] While Turner went in for bulk, scores of such manuals, in a score of
languages, were slim volumes easily slipped into one's pocket or purse, over-
grown pamphlets that printed only draft letters for plausible occasions and
without commentary. In a world avid for self-improvement, the demand for all
these educators was apparently inexhaustible.

    There was a market, too, for more encyclopedic guides in which letter
writing formed the centerpiece surrounded by other signposts to civility. Consider Otto Friedrich Rammler's encyclopedic *Deutscher Reichs-Universal-Briefsteller oder Musterbuch*. First published in Leipzig in 1834, it was regularly revised
and enlarged. In 1892, in the preface to the sixty-second edition, the publisher
proudly called the volume a "book for the people—*Volksbuch*," and pointed to
the qualities that had distinguished it through the years: "Scientific and practical!"[32] By 1907, Rammler had reached its seventy-third edition, with over
310,000 copies sold. Its full title was even longer and ranged even more widely

than Turner's, including as it did a menu of topics, from vocabulary to foreign phrases, formulas for wills to rudimentary lessons in arithmetic, the language of flowers to warnings against unsafe and unhealthy products poisoning a greedy and undiscriminating age. Shrewdly, authors of such compendia recognized that those who turned to them for help in letter writing were lamentably ignorant about the world and commendably eager to improve their acquaintance with it. If these books disclose anything about the bourgeoisie's naked heart, it is that much anxiety lay at its core.

Necessarily these lowly, though often pretentious, guidebooks adjusted their lessons from country to country or decade to decade. But early or late, all were in agreement that a letter must, above all, shun affectation. The "fashionable world" has laid it down, Turner advised his readers, "that *letters should be easy and natural,*" since they are, after all, *"a conversation between absent persons."* This was also the view of the anonymous American editor of *The Letter Writer's Own Book,* published in Philadelphia in 1846: "Letters are the copies of conversation," he wrote, and waxed enthusiastic about the possibilities of the genre: "Letters are the life of trade, the fuel of love, the pleasure of friendship, the food of the politician, and the entertainment of the curious." Rammler told his German readers much the same thing. "Naturalness must be the character of a letter"; especially letters to one's family, friends, and lovers should contain "the pure and unadulterated expression of the *language of the heart.*"[33]

Yet these authors, like their many competitors, were caught in a conflict they could not resolve, and did not even notice. Preaching freedom, they called for discipline. Exuberance of sentiment, especially in love, was a precious but heedless quality that needed to be curbed. Thus, for all their protests, in the advice givers' scheme of things naturalness confronted, and was bound to be defeated by, artifice. Turner counseled his readers to study the art of letter writing with care to master clarity, length, consistency, purity, neatness, and simplicity. Anonymous of Philadelphia took the same tack: it is necessary to acquire the rules and the decorum of letter writing by spending months of constant attention to them. And Rammler insisted that even the most familiar communications must not offend decency. In short, these cicerones to written conversation wanted their readers at the same time to be spontaneous and to resist spontaneity.

In fact, pure spontaneity was not always valued. In 1834, Joseph Huntington got this note: "Dear Friend. These lines are wrote in a hurry and are not verry good read this letter and tear it up do not let anyboddy se it it is wrote so bad." And there were letter writers for whom spontaneity was impossible. In August 1888, Marcel Proust, then a seventeen-year-old schoolboy at the Lycée Condorcet, wrote his friend Robert Dreyfus hurriedly, "Forgive my handwriting, my style, my spelling. I don't dare reread myself when I write in a rush! I know very well that one shouldn't write in a rush. But I have so much to say. It comes surging like a wave."[34] One can believe him: nineteenth-century schools trained pupils in penmanship, so that a rapid and legible handwriting was far from rare. But it is well known that Proust was the most assiduous of flatterers; no one was better attuned to what he perceived to be the wishes of his correspondents, no one better equipped to gratify the other's need. Breakneck speed, like informal diction, was no guarantee that the pose of self-revelation was as spontaneous as it looked. The mind, after all, is quicker than the pen.

Although in the books of advice self-control triumphed over impulse every time, the samples these letter writers devised were often remarkably imaginative. *The Ladies' and Gentleman's Model Letter-Writer,* published in London in 1871, contains in addition to the obvious subjects, a letter applying "for a ticket of admission, as an indoor patient to an hospital, for a sick child," and one from "a dressmaker to a lady, excusing herself from coming at the appointed time." An earlier manual from Philadelphia dating from 1854, *The Universal Letter-Writer; or, Complete Art of Polite Correspondence,* reached higher still, with a letter "From a Daughter to her Father, wherein she dutifully expostulates against a match he had proposed to her, with a gentleman much older than herself," and one "From a Merchant's Widow, to a Lady, a distant Relation, in behalf of her two Orphans."[35] Yet even these models, probably taken from real situations, were almost as stilted as more ordinary fare. Nor could they be otherwise, since no personal feeling had inspired the prototypes they were prodding aspiring bourgeois to imitate. Efforts to organize feelings in acceptable flowing diction, they sounded as though transcribed from cheap novels.

Let one exemplar stand for thousands, a woman's letter to her lover invented by Otto Friedrich Rammler or one of his editors: "Dear Karl! What would I not give if, on the anniversary of your birth the wings of my love carried me to you! It's only a thought, but a thought that fills me with bliss. Fortunate me who can call you hers! No, dearest Karl, it is no dream, no illusion, that I have in you all that the world can have for me; no, this rapturous conviction fills my heart with the liveliest joy and presses me to offer you my fondest felicitations for your health and happiness. Accept, too, the gift that accompanies these lines. My hands have made it for you. True, it's very little, but you know, my dear Karl, how limited my time is, and I know you: the small is worth just as much to you as if I could have given you something large. I pray God for your well-being, you dearest of my heart. May it be possible for you to come back soon. This is the wish of, Your Luise."[36] It was the kind of letter that might appeal to a bourgeoise who had an engraving of Millet's *Angelus* on her wall.

To patronize aids to refined self-expression is all too easy. The conflicts that marked these handbooks were largely unconscious, symptoms of the endemic warfare between the urge for utterance and the need for self-command, which has always haunted humans and had become particularly acute in an age when the demands and the instruments for translating inner freedom into public discourse had grown insistent. The letter writers reflected the struggle between desire and anxiety that could tear bourgeois apart. Yet this said, it is plain that they could not substitute for an authentic voice on paper, however awkwardly phrased.

Disregarding such advice, whether explicit or implicit, whether the samples available to them in novels, letter writers, or the published letters of the great, unknown numbers of middling bourgeois conducted their correspondence without consulting anyone but themselves. While they often struggled with words and resorted to platitudes that carried the strong feelings they were unable to verbalize, their formulations could be graceful and their awareness of complexity impressive. But cliché-ridden or articulate, tremulous or confident, their letters tackled subjects that sample books would have considered taboo, and tried to resolve issues beyond the reach of Rammler or the anonymous of Philadelphia. They wrote about the pleasures of the marriage bed, the anguish and rewards of pregnancy, the torments of religious uncertainty; they mastered the art of lying to their parents, indoctrinating their children, exciting their spouses. Being forced back on their own resources virtually guaranteed the authenticity of their self-revelations—or the intensity of their self-concealment.

Victorian letter writers doled out their disclosures with a fine feeling for appropriateness, reserving their most candid communications for their confi-dantes—their spouse, their sister, their best friend. At times, the passion for secrecy transgressed the bounds of sensible prudence, but, in general, letter writers bestowed confidences on the deserving. One respectable middle-class woman reports to her sister a painful miscarriage she just suffered and offers to share whatever contraceptive information her physician has promised to give her. Another equally respectable middle-class husband sends his wife perverse dreams as evidence that he longs for her. A third tantalizes her husband, who is away serving in the army, by picturing for him how fresh she smells after her bath. A fourth, learning from the reserved young woman he loves that she reciprocates his affection, informs her that he has just vaulted over his sofa in sheer exuberance. In fact, when it came to writing about sexual pleasures antici-pated or recalled, the more liberated Victorian couples could be almost as uninhibited as the romantics had been.[37]

To be sure, as we have seen, many Victorians found it inappropriate to put their erotic desires on paper. But those who did—and they were not just rare, extremist exceptions—offer suggestive clues to the salient role that sexual satisfaction, whether in reality or as hope, played in the lives of respectable women little less than of men. Even fairly inexplicit love letters, proffering epistolary kisses and recalling delightful embraces, hint at erotic appetites with their sentimental effusions and romantic flourishes. Letters, then, seemed ideally suited to the disclosure of deep feelings in the courtship dance; lovers, it seemed, found it easier to send their sentiments by mail than to express them in person. In 1862, a hopeful American suitor put the case plainly to the young lady with whom he was taken: "We men are so bold upon paper."[38] One has the feeling that paper was indeed the only place where erotic boldness was permitted. Fiancées who begged their beloved man to come to their arms; fiancés who closed their letters with sending thousands of kisses had never gone further, if this far, in reality.[39] Letters were a safe way of breaching the barriers of bourgeois reticence.

Salient as this fantasized courage might be, the theme that dominated the nineteenth-century personal letter was health, mainly the writer's health, seldom perfect and normally compromised by complaints described with clinical details and in a matter-of-fact tone that speaks of resignation. Illnesses were, after all, so prevalent and physicians so helpless. Many of these ailments, we can see now, were psychosomatic: fainting spells, bouts of inexplicable fatigue and lassitude, stomachaches and digestive disorders with no organic basis, at times vanishing as suddenly as they had appeared. Others were deadly enough, and when cholera epidemics struck, as they did intermittently through the nineteenth century, letter writers saw it as their duty to warn family and friends against the cities, whether at home or abroad, where the infection raged.

News about the health of family and friends was a natural pendant to such shards of medical autobiography. Anxiety about others was almost as pressing as anxiety about oneself. Thus, in December 1856, Nanny Herzberg reassured her fiancé, who had clearly worried over some recent intimations about her state of health, "Today I am completely *healthy*. I tell you this on my *word of honor*."[40] Letter writers punctuated such reports with news about deaths in the family or among their acquaintances; they did not need to be pious to recognize the fragility and brevity of life.

Naturally letters also abounded in accounts just how the writer was faring in trade or on the job, particulars about the children at school, plans for visits, and whatever else exercised a correspondent's little world. But they were not all amorous expression, health bulletins, or businesslike communiqués. Apprehension, indignation, even rage, frequently tamed by familial affection, found their voice by mail. That all too common domestic drama, the conflict of generations, notably the struggle between father and son, played itself out in duels with the pen; the combatants deployed whatever weapons they could mobilize in this psychological warfare: threats, reproaches, cajolery, alibis, blackmail, even silence—letters not written could be as eloquent as letters mailed. These missives, too, were fragments of autobiography: reproaching others for their subversive or impious sentiments was a way of disclosing one's own feelings.

A telling instance of such oedipal battles is the tense correspondence that the young Austrian Hermann Bahr, on the verge of launching a career as a journalist, drama critic, novelist, and playwright, carried on with his father, Erich. In 1883, a student at the University of Vienna, he had publicly orated in behalf of "the most sacred cause," the cause of a greater German republic, and laid himself open to expulsion from the university by the skittish Hapsburg authorities. It would be cowardly to deny his convictions, Hermann told his father, and adroitly blamed him: "Why did you bring me up to be an honorable human being?" In response, his father urged him to remain politically neutral, at least until he had his degree; deploying time-honored tactics, he conveniently recalled his sickly wife, his irresponsible younger son, and the difficulties in making a decent living: "And so I enter upon my fiftieth year—I strongly hope not to have to enter upon any more of them!"[41] We have seen it before: self-pity could be an effective form of epistolary aggression.

The Bahrs' altercation dragged on for years. The son kept insisting on his German patriotism and the urgent need for revolutionary economic reforms, all the while lamenting his financial dependence; the father praised the Hapsburg empire, scolded his disobedient boy, monitored his studies—Hermann Bahr had transferred to the University of Berlin—and sent money. The son's utopian notions and slowness in getting his doctorate aroused the father's scornful disappointment, and brought repeated reminders that they were directly contributing to his own ill health. "The principal cause of my ailment, which is called neuralgic, is the nerves and they don't improve when you have children and a profession that constantly provide new excitement." He had no use for his son's publications. "I want to know just one thing," he wrote after reading Hermann's first novel, "what good are such mental productions to humanity?"[42] And sent more money.

Religion was, if anything, more explosive a subject for censorious letter writers than politics. We recall the "postal inquisition" to which Philip Gosse subjected his son Edmund, away in London, persecuting him with alarm over the young man's soul and prospects for an eternity in hell. This issue, too, animated the correspondence between Selden Huntington, a Connecticut merchant and land speculator, and his son Joseph from 1833, when the boy was thirteen, at boarding school, to 1846, the year of the father's death. "I hope you will remember with thankfulness your Maker," Selden Huntington wrote Joseph in November 1833. "Do *not* fail to pray to God that you may have faith in Christ." In March of the following year, Joseph's mother weighed in with the same admonition: "Above all, my son, let me entreat you to 'Remember your Creator in the days of your youth.' " In March 1835, the father was back on the lecture platform: "Hope you will be diligent in your studies & never forget for a moment your duty to the being who made you & preserves you & continues your life." In the same year, Joseph's cousin Sybil reminded him that "we have but a short time to stay on the earth & a great preparation to make for those scenes which we shall have to pass through after we enter the Dark Valley of the Shadow of Death."[43] Frightening a sinner into religiosity was a legitimate tactic for Victorian letter writers.

But young Huntington's mother and cousin played at best supporting roles to his father in these admonitory assaults. "Our business is to do as we think our Saviour would direct us if he was here." This in October 1835, and so it went on. In 1838: "God is always befriending us—we owe him our constant adoration & praise." Then, three years later, the elder Huntington took the familiar, he hoped guilt-inducing road to his son's hard secular heart: "I had been declining in health ever since I was at Windsor & could attribute it to no other cause than my solicitude about your welfare. I considered you in a very dangerous state, for with such views of God & his Providence as you seemed to have no good can be expected." He had solid reason to be apprehensive. His mother had already scolded him in 1836 for his lack of concern for his "never-dying soul," but Joseph refused to be persuaded. "I think some times if religion would comfort me any," he told his father in 1842, "I should like to have it but I dont see how it can, as you say it does."[44] To judge from the father's continuing exhortations, there is no record that his son ever did see it. Perhaps that was in part because Joseph Huntington knew that, for all his pious hectoring, his father was not one to preach: in a quarrel, he had laid violent hands on his wife, and the couple were separated in the late 1830s. But this is not to suggest that his letters to his obstinate boy were not wholly sincere.

Obviously enough, letter writing is virtually never an altogether solitary act. Except for the narcissist writing in effect to himself, the other is always there, a photograph on the desk, a faded flower pressed between the pages of a book, an image in the mind, waiting to be informed, corrected, pleased—above all, pleased. As we have seen, the nineteenth-century literature on letter writing, modernizing Cicero, made into a truism the truth that letter writing is a kind of conversation. But how truly unrehearsed?

This question raises difficult problems of interpretation. What price sincerity? Once a letter writer has acquired sufficient practice and knowledge of the world, pleasing formulas become second nature, so automatic as to require no reflection, no hesitation. Yet this does not mean that a practiced presentation must be an act of hypocrisy, mere playing with emotion. Nor does it necessarily leave the writer's mind opaque: the urges to compliment and cajole—or to be complimented and cajoled—are facts of mental life as open to study as any other. That old half-serious question, How do I know who I am until I read what I have written? contains an important truth: writing letters may become an exercise in self-definition. Hence any form they take, natural or affected, may become fragments of a great confession.

These are subtle matters. But, significantly, the Victorians took little note of such intricacies. By mid-century, letter writing had become a cultural impera-tive for the middle classes, and correspondents took it for granted that a letter not obviously formulaic would give its recipient a glimmer of the very soul of the sender. Barbey D'Aurevilly, novelist and essayist, perhaps put it best in 1876, in a review of *La Correspondance de Balzac*. These letters, he asserted, gave the world more of Balzac the man and writer than pictorial representations could ever do. They were "infinitely better than a portrait, even if done by a Michelangelo or a Raphael of the pen. Here is flesh and blood, head and heart, soul and life of a man who was, in literary art, the most dazzling and the most profound, was at once a Raphael and a Michelangelo."[45] He was putting into words the inarticulate assumptions of ordinary bourgeois. If the published work was the writer booted and spurred, private letters were the man—and woman—in dressing gown and slippers, talking freely.

This sense of things helps to explain a puzzling nineteenth-century habit that has made historians of the age grateful beneficiaries. For centuries, people had kept letters, whether hidden in a desk drawer or a receptacle designed for the purpose. But in the Victorian age, recipients went further. They underscored their demands to keep their letters *"secret, secret, secret."*[46] And they preserved letters they had been earnestly enjoined to destroy. Letters, written by hand and hence all the more eloquent witnesses of their author, seemed an essential part of an important living being. It is as though even people not superstitious obscurely felt that to burn a letter was to do the sender some unspecified harm or to deprive oneself of a cherished gift: the presence of an absent one. It followed that it was unacceptable to leave testimony of oneself entrusted to unworthy hands. The Victorians took for granted that when a couple broke off their engagement, gifts—a ring, a book, a photograph—would be returned. So, too, were the letters they had exchanged. One was almost literally getting one's own back, the self fixed on a handwritten page safe once again.

2. The Discreet Best Friend

A letter, we have sufficiently seen, even an unanswered letter, is a dialogue real or fancied. So, in the nineteenth century, were thousands of diaries and journals.* That banal address "Dear Diary," so popular in that age, conjures up a gushing teenager caught up in the travails of puberty and has been subjected to smiling condescension. But it supplies a telling clue to the Victorians' inner life: the strongly felt need for self-expression to a confidante, even if it had to be a fictitious companion or a split-off part of oneself in the guise of solemn listener. Great diarists of earlier centuries—Samuel Pepys or John Evelyn or James Boswell—had given room to their feelings of piety, of love, of remorse, without inventing an independent personage for the purpose. In contrast, ordinary Victorian keepers of these literally self-centered documents explicitly treated them like a discreet best friend. They lent their diaries human qualities, whether visualizing them as a male or female comrade, apologized to them for neglecting them, and affectionately apostrophized them for their faithful support. When Victorian diarists had filled one volume to go on to the next, they would sadly, sincerely, say farewell.

This posture, brimming over with sensibility, became common, even commonplace. "O my *cahier*," exclaimed the French poet Maurice de Guérin in 1834, "you are to me not a pile of paper, not unfeeling or lifeless; no, you live, you have a soul, intelligence, love, goodness, compassion, patience, charity, and pure, constant sympathy. You are for me what I have not found among humans, a tender and devoted being that is attached to a weak and sickly soul," one that gave him what he craved and had not found: love.[1] De Guérin, pious, tormented, haunted by ill health, was not a bourgeois but the scion of a noble if impecunious house, but bourgeois diarists sounded much like him. As with letters, plainly the late-eighteenth-century cult of emotional expressiveness and the romantics' impassioned involvement with self left their mark on Victorian diaries and journals. Receptacles of innermost sentiments, they were elevated to the status of an authentic alter ego.

It has been suggested, with some justice, that the diary is particularly at home

---

*Speaking literally, the distinction between a diary and a journal is a simple one: the first is a daily (or almost daily) terse record; the second, more intermittent, with more substantial entries. A sizable number of bourgeois, of course, kept both. In fact, the boundaries between the two genres were fluid: some diarists spent a good deal of time each day with their silent best friend; and the psychological springs of diary or journal keeping were scarcely distinct. Hence, in the following pages I shall use the two terms interchangeably.

in a bourgeois environment, especially among the prosperous. The classic age for launching one, apart from the childish jottings of seven- or eight-year-olds following parents' prompting, was early adolescence—a space between childhood and adulthood first really carved out in the eighteenth century and more highly developed in the nineteenth. Some, like Nietzsche, were precocious. "At last," he wrote in 1856, when he was twelve, in the first of many ventures into autobiography, "my decision has been taken to write a diary in which one transmits to one's memory everything that moves the heart cheerfully or sadly, to remember years later the life and doings of this time and especially *mine*. May this resolution not be made to falter, although significant obstacles stand in its way."[2] Others started rather late. The first entry in the diary of the American architect Theodate Pope Riddle, a pioneer in her profession then largely closed to women, is dated January 31, 1886, just two days before she turned nineteen: "Uncle Jud gave me some good advice. He suggested my keeping a diary, saying that by so doing I could train my mind to grasp hard topics better." She would not remain on the formal level of self-pedagogy as she recorded her episodes of depressions and her happiness at seeing her designs realized.[3]

Most diarists, though, did not wait until they were adults; there was something about the awakening and turmoil of puberty most congenial to engaging in literally self-serving self-examination. Consider the diary of Julie Manet, daughter of Berthe Morisot and niece of Edouard Manet. "I have often had a mind to keep a journal, I expect to start now," she begins her intimate record, a gem to which we shall return. She appears a little astonished that she had not done so before: "It seems to me this is a little late, but the more I wait, the later it will be, and anyhow I am only fourteen years old"—actually almost fifteen. Her gentle self-reproach implies that many others had started at a younger age.[4]

The silent conversation that diarists carried on benefited from another modern cultural phenomenon that we have discussed before: privacy. They could write as freely as they did because they hoped that their diary, locked in the drawer of a desk or ingeniously concealed, was assured inviolability. In short, again like letters, diaries could flower as confessions only if the writer could feel sure that only the invited would read them. The self-confident or self-promoting few who aspired to lasting fame—politicians, generals, artists—might, as it were, glance over their shoulder as they fashioned entries that biographers should find worthy of attention and later generations worthy of admiration. In 1835, the German playwright Friedrich Hebbel launched his journal, which he would expand into a copious multivolume affair through the decades, with a flamboyant leap of faith: "I am starting this booklet not just as a favor to my future biographer, although with my prospects for immortality I can be sure I shall have one. It shall be a notebook of my heart, which, true to the tones my heart sets, will preserve them for my delight in future years."[5] In trying to attenuate in the second sentence the vaulting lust for fame of the first, a characteristic tactic, Hebbel was protesting too much: whatever pleasure he might someday derive from his journals, he was, he knew, writing for posterity.

It is remarkable how many of these records are repositories for great ambition, indeed its engine. Consider the diary of Marie Bashkirtseff, which, published after her early death of tuberculosis at twenty-four, enjoyed an international vogue among the late Victorians. "Yes," she noted on the first page, "it is clear that I have the desire, if not the hope, to *remain* on this earth in some form or other. If I do not die young, I hope to remain as a great artist; but if I should die young, I should like to have my diary published—it cannot be anything but interesting."[6] The popular French novelist Jules Renard echoed this sentiment in his posthumously published journal on the first of day of 1897: "Today, since dawn, I have been busily thinking of writing, as a New Year's present, a book whose title pleases me: *'The Habits, Tastes, Ideas of a Man of Thirty.'* I am sure this will be a beautiful and a good book, and that it will make me famous."[7] In an access of candor, as frequent in diarists as contradictions, he quickly noted that he was actually thirty-three. But he thought he could be, in the diary he was inaugurating, fascinating and truthful at once.

Most diarists had more limited aspirations. "It's well this diary is intended for my eyes alone," wrote G. L. Reed, a thoughtful Pennsylvania farmer, in 1849, "as some queer passages would excite the risible faculties of the most sober-minded; or, if they should fall into the hands of some of my gossip-loving friends, would afford them many subjects of mirth." Others confirmed that their confidences were meant to be secret, and possible only because they were secret. Melchior Meyr, a minor German poet and playwright, who liked to formulate philosophical aphorisms about the decay of culture in his time, noted in his journal in 1861, "Here I pour out my heart when it is overly oppressed; for certain things one can tell no one."[8] No one except this silent friend—which indeed often spoke of the unspeakable.

The Victorian fashion for compiling confidential daily or intermittent autobiographical jottings was anything but an innovative form of inwardness. By 1812, when the London bookbinder John Letts started selling bound volumes suitable for keeping these intimate notations, they were already familiar and the repertory of inducements for private communings virtually complete. The devout had been taking their religious temperature for several centuries; social climbers had long preened themselves with the great personage they had been privileged to meet and what he—or she—had said to them; nineteenth-century travel diaries could call on an impressive ancestry; even before the romantics, professional writers had exhibited their sensitive responses to the world by jotting down potentially usable incidents, ideas, and impressions. What set the nineteenth-century keeper of a diary or a journal apart was, as it had been with letters, quantity more than intent.

Enterprising manufacturers stood ready to accommodate the humblest of record keepers. By 1839, Thomas Letts, who had joined his father's business, had vastly expanded its range and its sales. Offering some twenty-eight varieties, all the way from the generous folio volume with room for prolonged effusions to the diminutive pocket calendar that exacted economy of expression, Letts & Co. numbered its customers in the hundreds of thousands.[9] In a New Year's "sermon" for 1862, "On Letts's Diary," Thackeray paid tribute to the firm with his patented mixture of sardonic humor and sententious moralizing: he trusted his readers would not have to repeat in their diary for 1862 the bad habits that honesty had compelled them to enter during the year just past, and that sad news like the loss of friends through death or quarrels would not recur. "How queer to read are some of the entries in the journal!" Dinners eaten, jokes told, bills paid, pantomimes watched, anniversaries remembered, kindnesses done, tears shed, it had room for them all. "Ah me! Every person who turns this page over has his own little diary, in paper or ruled in his memory tablets, and in which are set down the transactions of the now dying year."[10] When Victorian parents encouraged their children, teachers their pupils, moralists their readers to report on themselves in privacy, they found the materials ready to hand. In a word, this kind of self-exposure became a recognizable ingredient in the bourgeois experience.

In recent years, when the diary and the journal have received sustained scholarly attention and been richly anthologized, it has become plainer than ever that the motives for giving a written account of oneself have varied immensely. The degree of introspection varied with them. Taking oneself as a subject might amount to little more than cataloging the mundane—the price of food, encounters with a neighbor, letters received—from sheer habit or defense against boredom, itemizing sexual conquests as needed reassurance that one's virility was up to par, compiling maxims to be quarried later, collecting evidence for future self-exculpation, and, often enough, simply keeping in touch with one's inner states.[11] Numerous diaries were exercises in delicacy and denial. "One day so closely resembles another in its occupations and pursuits," wrote Fanny Anne Burney Wood in late August 1835, "that I have nothing to record in my Journal," an entry interesting because it was written on her honeymoon, though she did immediately add, "I continue to be very happy at this quietest of all quiet places." Not that Fanny Wood lacked feeling, but that some feelings were too intimate even for her journal; two weeks earlier, on her wedding day, she had openly dwelled on her *"very, very* painful" parting from her family.[12]

Diaries were many things, then. They could work as therapy, self-prescribed or indeed recommended by a physician. In 1902, a doctor suggested to Theodore Dreiser, living hand to mouth with few prospects, sick and depressed after the failure of his first novel, *Sister Carrie,* that he keep a medical diary. Taking the advice and soon going beyond it, Dreiser proceeded to string together the details of his life in a single flat tone of voice, whether he was noting when he had eaten lunch, how much he had got for an article, or what woman he had seduced.[13]

Others took to making records of the self to capture the passing scene and fix their experiences in the amber of the written word. The urge thus to relive one's life could become irrepressible. But, as apologetic admissions of laziness disclose, diary keeping required self-discipline; all too many diarists let days and months go by without resorting to their friend and then ruefully returned to it. In 1839, the distinguished American entomologist Asa Fitch offered concrete reasons for returning to a practice he had abandoned. "Have resolved to resume my journal. Having lately had an interview with my dearest & most esteemed earthly friend, G. F. Horton, & been thus led to review some of the times we have spent together, by reference to my old diaries, the value of these records is brought with redoubled force to my mind." His resolution made, he thought back two weeks to keep a shocking event alive in his memory. Visiting Mrs. Sutherland, the local tavern keeper, he discovered that a rich and insinuating "ninny" had seduced Joan, the daughter of the house, "virtuous, high-minded, esteemed, & vivacious," got her pregnant, tried to talk her into an abortion, and then deserted her. "Alas! what a withering thunder stroke has blasted the happiness of this family." Riding home, Fitch thought of "poor Joan"; with a bleeding heart, he wrote a little poem, which he inserted, not without some pride, in his journal.[14]

In September of the same year, Fitch devoted a long entry to another scandal. He had just visited a man infected with venereal disease and reported, "A worthy, moral man, in easy circumstances, coming home from Warrensburg one evening 2 yrs. ago, somewhat intoxicated, went into the house of her whose house is the way to hell, going down to the chambers of death. In a short time syphilis made its appearance, & his wife too received the same disease." But, though disapproving and searching for biblical precepts, Fitch was not pharisaical: "Poor fellow, he is to be pitied." Though medical treatment had freed the sufferer of symptoms, he continued to be "perpetually tormented with the idea that the virus is still lurking in his system," and had in consequence turned exceedingly religious. "How mysterious," Fitch exclaims, himself devout, "are the ways of Providence."[15] What could be a more appropriate repository than his diary for Fitch to work out his highly personal response: a mixture of pious indignation and humane sympathy?

To prevent one's past from slipping into oblivion and to keep returning to it was agreeable enough to provide significant narcissistic dividends and delightful regressive sentiments. In 1822, the young German poet and novelist Wilhelm Waiblinger, who kept extravagant remembrances of his feelings, adventures, and friendships with poets alive in his diary, wrote, "To read in my diaries is an infinite bliss to me. Then I am cradled in the sweetest coziness." A third of a century later, in early January 1856, Macaulay, after reviewing his journal dating three and four years back, took the same view: "No kind of reading is so delightful, so fascinating, as this minute history of a man's self." Oscar Wilde was expressing a deep truth with his expected wit in *The Importance of Being Earnest,* when he has the Honorable Gwendolyn Fairfax say to Miss Cecily Cardew, "I never travel without my diary. One should always have something sensational to read on the train." Rather more soberly, G. L. Reed noted on December 20, 1848, "Having frequently felt the want of something to recall to memory the events of past days and to record the everyday incidents of life for future benefit and amusement, I have commenced this diary. In it I intend to make a correct and true record of my most important acts and thoughts, so that I may see them and weigh them hereafter." What Reed recorded and weighed before the end of the year was the weather, his opinion of a sermon, his expectation of being married soon, the stirring political events of the revolutionary year just past—and the recent American elections. Reed did not approve of the winning candidate, Zachary Taylor: "Again has this great nation elected a Chief Magistrate, and I regret that her choice has fallen upon one who has no other apparent qualification than that of a hero," affording a glimpse into a sensible, politically mature mind.[16]

Matter-of-fact though his tone, Reed did not censor more fervent emotions. Shortly before his marriage, he asked himself why he had moved into a ramshackle house, abandoning his loving parents and an adolescent sister who could use his guidance, and answered the question he had posed to himself: "I have left home, parents, and sister for one whom I love better than all else besides, one who has promised to share this house with me, who has promised to make it a home. Can she make it so? Hope and love tell me she will. Can I make her happy? Will I always love her as I do now? Heaven grant that I may. In the ardor of youthful love it is easy to promise, but many a youthful pair have set out in life with as bright hopes and prospects, who drank deeply of the cup of disappointment"—a potion, it appears, he did not have to drink.[17]

Another powerful prompter was hateful solitude. In May 1889, Alice James, the brilliant, invalid sister of William and Henry James, started her diary explicitly to relieve her overpowering sense of isolation: "I think that if I can get into the habit of writing a little about what happens, or rather doesn't happen, I may lose a little of the sense of loneliness and desolation which abides with me. My circumstances allowing of nothing but the ejaculation of one-syllabled reflections, a written monologue by that most interesting being, *myself,* may have its yet to be discovered consolations." It might, she added, provide "an outlet to that geyser of emotions, sensations, speculations and reflections which ferments perpetually within my poor old carcass for its sins; so here goes, my first Journal!"[18] A late starter, she was forty.

She had been anticipated by that most obsessive and garrulous of nineteenth-century diarists, the Genevan academic and critic Henri-Frédéric Amiel. In September 1864, in the seventeenth year of his addiction, he asked himself, "For what reason keep up this journal?" In response, that lifelong bachelor who seems to have lived in order to keep a diary—its 16,840 closely written and carefully counted pages must make it the longest of the century—dramatized his longing to escape his exile from life and at the same time his inability to muster the required energy: "Because I am alone. It is my dialogue, my society, my companion, my confidant. It is also my consolation, my memory, my scapegoat, my echo, the reservoir of my intimate experiences, my psychological itinerary, my protection against the mildew of thought, my excuse for living, almost the only useful thing I can leave behind."[19] It is certainly the only part of Amiel's writings that later decades have found worth reading.

The self-examinations of diary keepers suggest that Amiel's list, though long, is still not exhaustive. Many diaries, to be sure, are eloquent only in what they omit, as they tersely list business dealings, the daily routine on a farm, household chores, and little else. One uncommon housewife's journal protesting against her domestic slavery and her unhelpful lord and master is like an isolated flash of lightning affording an exceptional, highly informative glimpse into resentments that must have been endemic but that women for the most part kept out of sight and even out of consciousness.* But most reports, even reticent ones, are of

---

*In the first volume in this series, I quoted from the fragmentary diary—only the pages for 1880 have survived—of an anonymous housewife in Haddam, Connecticut, who is sardonic about the monotony of her domestic labors, "chained" to her "cell," and condemned to "wretched, wearisome days." Standing at the wash tub gave her just one more example of her "romantic life." Her husband was of little or no help: "The figure-head looked on while the slaves labored." She was articulating what thousands must have felt. Vol. 11, box 1, Diaries, Miscellaneous, Yale, Manuscripts and Archives. See Peter Gay, *The Bourgeois Experience,* vol. I, *Education of the Senses* (1984), 172–73.

more than casual interest. There were those who kept diaries or journals to anchor in their memory extraordinary, at times traumatic experiences, like service in the Franco-Prussian or the American Civil War. Others established a zone of privacy for two and exchanged their diary with the person who meant the most to them—Richard Wagner and his lover Mathilde Wesendonck, Leo Tolstoy and his wife, Sophia, were only the most famous among these secret sharers—as a sign of trust and proof of love or as a weapon in their prolonged marital duel. Still others wanted to preserve their daily lives for their children, or earnestly claimed that they wanted to monitor the development of their character to learn how to control their untamed will.*

To complicate matters further, frequently diarists rethought the purpose of their entries as they matured. An instance: the extensive and eloquent jottings of Emily Shore, daughter of an Anglican cleric, who was doomed to die of tuberculosis at the age of nineteen, a fate she accepted as she prayerfully placed herself into God's hands. Cerebral, ambitious, voracious for knowledge, almost stoical in the face of doom, she could at the ripe age of eighteen look back on poems, plays, histories of her composition, and set herself a schedule of self-instruction that would have impressed a John Stuart Mill: geography, history, drawing, starting on Italian, keeping up her French, Latin, and Greek, with German in the offing. Poignantly aware of her ill health—the last entries show her aware that she is dying—she had begun her diary before she turned twelve, and allowed her friends to see it. But after a time, she wrote in July 1838, the year before her death, it "altered its character," becoming "a valuable index of my mind," written impulsively at times, thoughtfully at others. "I have poured out my feelings into these later pages"; hence "I have written much that I would show only to a very few, and much that I would on no account submit to any human eye."[20] Her innermost self was nobody's business but her own.

Interestingly enough, Emily Shore's first entry was a matter-of-fact catalog of persons and places: "Our family consists of papa, mamma, and five children," and then proceeds in this vein for half a dozen paragraphs or more, confuting the conventional wisdom that the opening statements of a diary set its tone.

---

*For the first, see Elizabeth Gaskell: "To my dear little Marianne I shall 'dedicate' this book, which, if I should not live to give it to her myself, will I trust be reserved for her as a token of her Mother's love and extreme anxiety in the formation of her little daughter's character. . . . I wish that I could give her the slightest idea of the love and the hope that is bound up in her." *My Diary: The Early Years of My Daughter Marianne* (1923), 5; for the second, Leo Tolstoy: "I have never kept a diary before, because I could never see the benefit of it. But now that I am concerned with the development of my own faculties, I shall be able to judge from a diary the progress of that development." Tolstoy, April 7 [1847]. *Tolstoy's Diaries,* ed. and tr. R. F. Christian, 2 vols. (1985), I, 4.

There is no hint here of the ruminations on religion, on her sins—invisible to anyone else—and on death that would loom so large over later pages.[21] Again: "We left England on the 13 September two days after [my sister] Georgina's marriage," thus Beatrice Potter—more famous under her married name, Beatrice Webb—abruptly starts a journal she kept devotedly and quarried decades later for her autobiography. "I only enjoyed our passage pretty well, the people not being anything particular." She was on her way to New York, at fifteen.[22]

The great majority of diarists, on the other hand, launched themselves on the uncertain seas of self-accounting without troubling themselves with preambles, but anticipated in their overture the melodies that would dominate the rest. "A letter from Guldberg." This is Hans Christian Andersen in September 1825, at twenty catching up on his neglected education. "My God! My God! how good you are, I have not deserved this—I have a friend, a father, oh God, how I love him!"[23] All the pathos, all the excessive emotional investment we have come to expect from the great fabulist, lies open to the reader in this starting entry. For his part, Tolstoy at nineteen, a late starter, is all candor, far more revealing than Beatrice Potter, who soon after her unemotional beginning would shift from external events to analyze her moods and her passions: "It's now six days since I entered the clinic, and for six days now I have been almost satisfied with myself. *Les petits causes produisent des grands effets.* I caught gonorrhoea where one usually catches it of course."[24] Evidently Tolstoy was prepared to strip naked from the outset. He saw no point in pretending to himself. Nor did Marie Bashkirtseff, who launched her diary with an aggressive rhetorical question: "Why lie and pose?"[25]

Precisely what did telling the truth in private converse amount to? A studious, talented, and articulate young American, Rachel Van Dyke, claimed in 1810, after favorably comparing her diary with that of a friend, "To read my journal, I may almost say that with a few exceptions you read my heart—but his is merely a register of time." She was then twenty. Marie Bashkirtseff, too, who, we know, intended her diary to establish her posthumous celebrity, reiterated her resolute commitment to truth. "At first I wrote for a long time, without any thought of being read and now, precisely because I hope to be read, I am thoroughly honest. If this book is not the *exact, absolute, strict truth,* it has no right to exist. Not only do I say all the time what I think, but also I have never dreamt for a moment to conceal whatever could make me appear ridiculous or be unflattering to me.—Besides, I find myself too wonderful to find fault with myself.—In short, my kindly readers, you can be sure that I am exposing myself in these pages."[26] This was a brave, not very common attempt to yoke two apparently incompatible pursuits: personal candor and literary distinction.

No wonder some diarists were skeptical that they could really afford to search themselves without reserve even when they had no thought of later publication. Some of them were ashamed of what they denigrated, in attacks of self-laceration, as their record of triviality or wickedness—but wrote down that self-appraisal nonetheless; some were afraid that their confessions would fall into the hands of others—and made that part of the record, too. It was this anxiety over unwanted publicity that, Emily Shore believed, had "cramped" her urge to speak openly. A piece by the well-known English Dissenting minister and essayist John Foster on writing an autobiography had set her to thinking about herself once more, and to worry that her diary might, "some future day, when I am in my grave, be read by some individual." The consequence? "I have by no means confessed myself in my journal; I have not opened my whole heart." And so, "the *secret chamber of the heart,* of which Foster speaks so strikingly, does not find in my pen the key to unlock it."[27] Her scrupulousness was no doubt nice beyond the average. But even diarists not torn between their programs and their fears raised, and still raise, uncomfortable questions just how close nineteenth-century diaries and journals could come to their ideal of perfect transparency.

One particularly instructive serial autobiography, the diary of Julie Manet, may serve as a witness both to its possibilities and to its limitations in nineteenth-century bourgeois culture. True, she was not a commonplace bourgeoise. As we have noted, she was related to two major painters: Berthe Morisot and Edouard Manet. Her father, Eugène Manet, too, was involved in the arts as a well-to-do, cultivated patron. Affectionately educated largely at home, she boasted such paternal friends as Auguste Renoir and Stéphane Mallarmé. The Impressionists came to her house and shared holidays with her. Even the misogynist Edgar Degas admitted to being fond of her. Intelligent, alert, and attractive, Julie Manet had all the advantages as she developed her talents in the spirited atmosphere of her family—her gift for observation, her expressive way with words, her emerging independence of mind. Well before she started her diary, at fourteen, she was painting by her mother's side. And it can only have boosted her burgeoning sense of self that her mother painted her, repeatedly, almost obsessively, concentrating on her daughter as though she wanted no other subject. Yet her life, sheltered and surrounded by love, was thoroughly middle-class, with no hint of preciosity, arrogant exclusiveness, or bohemian raffishness. She lived enclosed within a proper family intent upon the conventions expected of its class, read the right books, spent time with her cousins, stayed at resorts frequented by affluent bourgeois. What makes Julie Manet so valuable to the historian is that her auspicious start gave her the words and fostered her desire to explore her innermost feelings while exhibiting at the same time the self-imposed limits of such virginal explorations.

Much of her diary, which she faithfully kept, with a few significant interruptions, from August 1893 to late December 1899, when she was about to marry, stays on the surfaces of daily routine: family picnics, painting outdoors with her mother, a visit to a studio, an evening at the opera. But from the start, Julie Manet endowed these workaday experiences with vividness and precision. Watching fellow guests in a hotel, she allows herself slightly malicious comments on their appearance, and speculates that the way they carry themselves may be a clue to their hidden character. And, though refreshingly impolite about others in the privacy of her diary, she does not spare herself. In October 1897, almost nineteen, she is dismayed rather than exhilarated by the realization that she has been making progress in her painting, her manner of dressing—and her diary entries: "When I think of the things that I've said, that I've written since I started this journal, I find that I was pretty childish, pretty stupid, and it seems to me that I'm still pretty idiotic. And it's always this way: I don't notice grotesque and stupid things until afterwards, so I will be that way all my life, which is a little saddening."[28]

Fortunately she has much to enjoy. There are holidays with her cherished cousins and friends in lovely, varied French landscapes. There is music—she was almost as fond of her violin as of her paint brushes—especially Wagner's. Listening to the first act of *Tristan and Isolde,* she feels herself overcome by this "music of supernatural beauty" with its "harmonic fluid" and its "atmosphere like that of beautiful painting." As the daughter and niece of great artists and herself something of a painter, she likes to deploy metaphors drawn from a favorite sister art when she tries to convey how deeply music stirs her soul. Gluck's *Iphigenie* is "a beautiful design with pure lines." It seems to her, as it must have to countless other civilized young diarists, that "no art can elevate you as much, no art speaks to the soul so much as music." And, of course, there is painting, that of others and her own: in January 1898, visiting Renoir's studio, she pronounces his latest work to be "ravishing": since "this winter he has done things more delicious than ever." As for her own work, there are times when she "thinks nothing but painting," declares herself "crazy about painting," and spends as much time at the easel as she can muster.[29]

Then there is Ernest Rouart, the man she will marry. Like the well-brought-up bourgeoise she is, Julie Manet is fastidious about her choice and decorous about her erotic urges, but insistent on her independence as well. When someone tells her that she has a duty to marry and have children, she demurs: "Does this duty extend to the point of marrying someone who displeases you just to populate France?" The man worthy of her must share her interests as well as speak to her passion. Late in 1898, as she watches her cousin Jeanne being taken in to dinner by Paul Valéry and herself on Ernest's arm, she confides to her diary, "I have a flash of joy; it seems to me there is a chance that this first encounter could continue further." With unaccustomed boldness, she adds, "I ask myself if on that charming evening we aren't on the arm of the one with whom we will thus travel through life." Then, almost as though afraid of her daring, she quickly subverts her fantasy: "Nothing is less certain."[30] Such things must take time.

In fact, nothing was more certain. By November 14, 1899, analyzing herself on her twenty-first birthday, she shyly confesses, "I no longer hesitate to tell myself he is the one I want." She is relieved to see how much his character resembles hers: both of them, she believes, are outwardly cool and inwardly passionate, and protests that "it is the very excess" of her "restrained passion" and the fear of being considered sentimental "that engender coldness in me." Yet the essential compatibility of the pair is coming to their rescue, spreading over them both "a balm of unutterable sweetness. Ah, it is a dream of love I am mapping out, a love of the spirit, a love of two souls!" It is a love guaranteed not only by their carefully husbanded and well-matched appetites but also by admiration for the same painters and the same composers. "It seems to me," she concludes, back to bourgeois self-protective correctness, "that I will exchange many ideas, share his tastes."[31]

Though cheerful in the main, Julie Manet's diary is pervaded by a strain of melancholy, elicited by mourning. Her father had died in the spring of 1892, the year before she started her diary; her mother, after she had nursed Julie through a severe attack of influenza in January 1895, caught pneumonia and died two months later. Julie Manet records her anguish and her prayers; unlike her parents, who were thoroughly irreligious, she took her Catholicism seriously, responding to communion and trusting in God. On March 1, 1895, watching her mother's excruciating sufferings—in terrible pain, Berthe Morisot had trouble breathing and swallowing, let alone talking—she damned her helplessness. The family, including her cousins, were rallying round, the physician was attentive, but what could she do? "I would do just anything to have Maman recover quickly, it is so painful to see her so ill. It is hard for me not to cry, and besides I can't be of service, I don't know how to take care of her, and they want me to sleep at night. How sad it all is, O my God, heal Maman."[32]

Julie Manet's sorrow is exquisite and expressive. Her next entry, shadowed by grief, dates from April 17, after a break of seven weeks. "Oh! pain, since I wrote, I have lost Maman, on Saturday, March 2, she died at 10:30, I cannot say how great my misery, how profound my sadness. I am now an orphan, in three years my parents have left me." She wants to remember the details of her mother's last days: Berthe Morisot did not want her daughter admitted to the sickroom, lest she retain too sad a memory of her mother's wasted looks, but she did see her on her last morning looking to her daughter as beautiful as ever. "Oh never, never would I have believed so distressing a thing." If it were only nothing more than a nightmare! "O my God, help me to bear this loss." There had been a deep silence in the sickroom, then voices; she was made to go to sleep knowing the truth and not believing it. "Oh! when I recall the anguish of that day, it seems to me my heart would break."[33]

Life went on; so did her mourning. The next entry in Julie Manet's journal, after a long silence, dates from July 20 and is pursued by thoughts of her loss. On her way to Britanny, she remembers that she made a very similar, most enjoyable trip a year before—with her mother. "With every pretty landscape, I tell myself, 'How well Maman would have painted that.'" Whenever sadness overcomes her, it is because she is remembering her parents. Too self-observant and too honest to trick herself into believing that put-on cheerfulness is the real thing, she writes at eighteen, "At certain moments lugubrious visions enter your mind, then one is alone to cry, one cannot always speak of one's sadness"—except, of course, to the diary—"even when one abandons oneself to gaiety; but that gaiety is superficial, one's heart of hearts is plunged more and more into gloom, then I see again that day, the day after April 13, 1892, when I wept in the carriage with mother, I could not believe that Papa was dead."[34]

Such memories are prompted almost daily by a web of indelible associations. Painting, an art she "adores" and that gives her "great pleasure," is precious to her because "it is connected with those I loved and who are no more." At an exhibition of her mother's work, luxuriating in its "glory," she recalls the time and place where each picture was painted and exclaims, "O Maman, inspire me!" Reading the posthumous diary of Marie Bashkirtseff, she finds it intriguing, except for the gossip and Bashkirtseff's "boring" admiration for "bad painters." But the point is that her reading reminds her of her parents, who had vehemently debated Bashkirtseff in her presence. Her confidence in her good sense is not in abeyance; she feels sure that she, "a young girl," is better placed even than her parents to understand the Bashkirtseff diary. But what dominates her reflections is not her self-assertion but her unassuageable need: on the same day, she praises Renoir for giving sound moral advice to the younger generation, and mildly criticizes Mallarmé for doing too little of that. "People say the young don't profit from the advice of older men; I find that a mistake; in any case, if one does not seem to profit from it, one thinks about it a good deal and men of merit should always give direction to the young."[35] She is speaking of what she wants most, and will never get back. That, with all her love of life, is the principal theme of her diary. It is fitting that once she committed herself to adult life and completed the work of mourning through marriage to Ernest Rouart, she never wrote in it again.

It would be naive to suppose that nineteenth-century diarists, including one so artless as Julie Manet, could unlock, in Emily Shore's words, every secret chamber of the heart. Like other humans, the Victorians deployed defensive stratagems to drive unacceptable wishes into inaccessible hiding places; when they did reach the surface of awareness (and were duly recorded), they came disguised and distorted as inexplicable feelings or strange dreams, and were left uninterpreted. Diarists could not read the language of their unconscious. What is more, the bourgeois cult of reserve and reticence kept even some conscious feelings from the trusted companion and comforter of their solitary moments. The censorship that inhabits—and inhibits—everyone was particularly assiduous among the genteel Victorians. Yet, in regulating access to their confessions, these diarists could, as it were, privately publish hidden emotions for the few, or the one, who in their judgment deserved their confidences; often enough, we know, the only worthy recipient was their discreet silent friend, the diary itself. Thus human nature and Victorian middle-class culture conspired to establish a measure of transparency and at the same time to frustrate its full realization. True, there were respectable bourgeois or bourgeoises who reported their sexual longings and sexual pleasures to paper in explicit detail, but, as before and after them, they remained exceptions.*

This is not a criticism of the Victorians. The cultural consequences of respect for privacy brought rewards that no charges of cant and hypocrisy, or even their reality, can discredit. "Adam made fig leaves necessary for the mind, as well as for the body," noted the poet Elizabeth Barrett on the opening page of her diary of 1831, compressing into one sentence the contribution of partial repression to the very possibility for civilization.[36] For most Victorians, the fig leaves were large and solidly kept in place, but not for all. There are indications that for every dry account that eschewed introspection there was one that reveled in it. Nor was deep probing reserved to adolescent girls, married women, or the upper bourgeoisie. Certainly, as we have observed, skilled writers and those comfortably enjoying leisure and a literary education were more disposed than their less fortunate fellows to keep polished what a German romantic once called the mirror of their imagination. But a small army of middling and petty bourgeois also compiled penetrating private records.

It is worth repeating, then, that any sweeping generalization about the motives for diary writing is bound to fail before their bewildering diversity. Some

*For one striking instance, see the pocket diary, extensive journal, and private correspondence of Mabel Loomis Todd, recording her sexual experiences with her husband, even showing entries for her orgasms, and intimate details of her affair with Austin Dickinson. I have given an analysis of this wellborn American bourgeoise and her unbuttoned record in *The Bourgeois Experience,* vol. I, *Education of the Senses* (1984), 71–108.

diarists wanted their journal to function as a kind of auxiliary superego that
would prompt them to see themselves as they really were. "I will write,"
insisted Elizabeth Barrett, "I must write—& the oftener wrong I know myself
to be, the less wrong I shall be in one thing—the less *vain* I shall be." Gladstone,
too, employed his great diary, a mixture of curt, dry entries on pamphlets read
or politicians visited and guilt-ridden meditations, to monitor what he called
"the delusions of Selflove."[37] But others—one thinks of Marie Bashkirtseff—
wanted to use their diary for precisely the opposite purpose: to establish their
lofty claims on the world. Prominent among reasons for undertaking a diary
were family custom, peer pressures, teachers' assignments, the sheer pleasure in
the passing parade or far-flung travels, the hope for solace from catastrophies or
tremulous fear of one's threatened demise, the need to investigate one's chances
for salvation or to relieve oneself of guilt feelings, the desire to know oneself
better—or several of these together. The reasons for nineteenth-century diaries
were as varied as their form.

And self-creation, self-invention? That enterprise, too, belongs in the repertory of motives, for a number of diarists reported on themselves to find, and
securely establish, what seemed to them so elusive: their identity. Lending the
vagaries of their inner life a certain objective status by writing them down
should help to make them what they were. In 1824, Eugène Delacroix mused
in his journal, to become almost as famous as his paintings: "I have just hastily
reread all the preceding; I deplore the gaps." He was then twenty-six and had
started a journal two years before, after several futile resolves. He wanted to be,
he wrote, honest with himself—whoever that was. "It seems to me that I am
still master of the days I have written down, although they are past. But the ones
this paper does not mention are as though they have never been." Gloomily he
asked himself, "Into what darkness have I been plunged? Must it turn out that
with my human weakness a wretched and fragile piece of paper will be the only
memorial to my life that remains to me?" In his predicament, he hoped that the
regular occupation of keeping a diary would "bring order to the rest of life." By
bringing back the past, he thought he would lead—in the best sense of the
term—a double life.[38]

But humans are never simply the creatures of words, not even of their own.
They may screen themselves, at times quite unawares, behind a false self. But
the most fanciful of constructions cannot escape from the pressures of the
diarist's past inner history. Diaries, precisely like their more coherent cousins,
autobiographies, are all true, the evasive and mendacious ones no less than the
others. They all testify, ingenuously or indirectly, to desires and anxieties, to
pleasures and traumas, to inner discord discovered, at times fought out, pen in
hand. Julie Manet's recognition that there was a conflict between her restrained

demeanor and her explosive desires, Emily Shore's frankness about her inability to be frank, Friedrich Hebbel's contradictory hopes for fame and for privacy, G. L. Reed's effort to understand his novel emotional situation as a married man, and countless similar entries are reliable signs that even those Victorian bourgeois who did not write a formal autobiography found themselves interesting.

Judging oneself to be interesting was a private decision that nineteenth-century bourgeois made into a cultural trait. Not without uneasiness: to be interesting bore the risks of deserting the conventional consensus, and thus of isolation. What more welcome, then, than a diary, that discreet, utterly uncritical vessel for grandiose fantasies, masochistic self-reproaches, and secret longings for love! Indeed, what is astonishing about Victorian stabs at self-analysis is not how much they concealed but how little—and how many of them there were. Quite apart from the introspective nuggets the historian can dig out from their pages, their sheer number supplements all the other impressive testimony we have reviewed—the democratization of romantic love, the fashion for autobiography, biography, history, and imaginative fiction, the claims of art and music as aids to introspection—to show just how deeply the century was infatuated with the more or less naked heart.

For the Victorian bourgeoisie, flooded by torrential, deep-running currents of change, this love affair was beset with uncertainties. We have seen that they had at their disposal two drastically divergent attitudes toward their inner life: defensive discretion or bold exploration—often enough, something of both. The appeal of the conservative mental style, the urge to keep things as they are, is profoundly embedded in human nature. It sustains the comforting feeling that one may trust the directional signs culture has put up, that the trajectory of one's past virtually promises that the future will hold few surprises about one's place in the world or one's essential loyalties. But the nineteenth century, committed to innovation, offered challenges, at once exhilarating and unsettling, to established habits. It experienced dramatic movement in virtually all areas of life.

Movement is indeed the staple of the history books that deal with the nineteenth century.* The list is long: movement from country to city, continent to continent, horse wagons to railroad carriages, cozy specialty shops to palatial department stores, slow and occasional communications to rapid and frequent

---

*Beyond doubt, classes other than the bourgeoisie were exposed to the same risks, as Irish immigrants to the English industrial regions or Jews leaving an inhospitable eastern Europe by the millions can attest. But the point of this study, concentrating as it does on the bourgeoisie, is that it, too, faced all these hazards.

correspondence, arranged marriages to love matches, and, probably most traumatic, religious certainty to religious doubt. The Victorians were compelled to
cope with epochal discoveries in science, dazzling achievements in technology,
to say nothing of the modernization of politics and fierce debates over the
claims of nationalism. In a century racing into the unknown, many bourgeois
had good reason to be anxious about the stability of their self. Rationality had
never registered more spectacular accomplishments, and yet irrationality in
many guises flourished as it had not for many decades. In 1904, in a single issue
of that high-brow German periodical *Hochland,* one writer cataloged the triumphs of technology while another agonized over the revival of regressive
mysticism.[39]

We must not take these stressful mixed signals lightly. They amounted to far
more than worries about just how to cope with unaccustomed tasks in unaccustomed settings. Rather, they raised questions about basic self-definitions;
uprootedness, whether mental or physical, could induce moments of crisis or a
lifelong sense of dislocation. Since time out of mind, men had decried the new
as an impious departure from ancient verities. But the Enlightenment's heady
program for a science of man and society, and the philosophes' confidence that
the rewards of knowledge would outweigh its risks, had begun to usurp the
prestige once attached to the familiar.

Thus in the nineteenth century, building on the eighteenth century's progressive agenda, novelty proved subversive of crippling prejudices on the one
hand and the soothing security of routine on the other. That modern doctrine
individualism, a legacy from the Renaissance that persistently widened its conquests among the Victorians, was a road to personal freedom and psychological
isolation alike. The almost hysterical insistence of nineteenth-century bourgeois on the sacredness of the family was a symptom masquerading as an ideal: it
attests to the sense of cherished presuppositions in danger. In short, the Victorian middle-class self paid the price of progress. At the very least, it was haunted
by hesitations and confusions. The prevailing assault on tradition did not help to
anchor identity as securely as optimists had hoped. But this made the travail of
the bourgeois naked heart all the more poignant.

Notes

Bibliographical Essay

Acknowledgments

Index

NOTES

Introduction

1. See editor's note in Baudelaire, *Oeuvres complètes*, ed. Y. G. Le Dantec, rev. Claude Pichois (1961), 1722.

2. Kant: *Anthropologie in pragmatischer Hinsicht* (1798; 2nd ed., 1800), in *Werke*, ed. Wilhelm Weischedel, 6 vols. (1956–64), VI, 408 [pt. 1, bk. 1]; Mill: "Bentham" (1838), *Dissertations and Discussions Political, Philosophical, and Historical*, in *Collected Works of John Stuart Mill*, ed. J. M. Robson et al., 33 vols. (1963–91), X (1969), 92; Wordsworth: quoted in Jerome Hamilton Buckley, *The Turning Key: Autobiography and the Subjective Impulse since 1800* (1984), 1.

3. Turgenev, *On the Eve* (1859; tr. Gilbert Gardiner, 1950), 197.

4. For details, see Peter Gay, *The Bourgeois Experience*, vol. II, *The Tender Passion* (1986), 330–51; and vol. III, *The Cultivation of Hatred* (1993), 491–513.

5. Emerson, "The American Scholar: An Oration Delivered before the Phi Beta Kappa Society, at Cambridge, August 31, 1837," *Selected Essays*, ed. Larzer Ziff (1982), 101.

6. Poe: Daniel Hoffman, *Poe, Poe, Poe . . .* (1972), 2; Thackeray: *The History of Pendennis: His Fortunes and Misfortunes, His Friends and His Greatest Enemy* (1848–50), in *The Works of William Makepeace Thackeray*, Centenary Biographical Edition, ed. Lady Ritchie, 26 vols. (1910–11), III, 401 [ch. 31].

7. Goethe: *Bedeutende Fördernis durch ein einziges geistreiches Wort* (1823), in *Werke, Kommentare und Register*, ed. Erich Trunz et al., 14 vols. (1948–72; 7th to 14th ed., 1982), XIII, 38; Goethe to Lavater, October 4, 1782, *Briefe von und an Goethe*, ed. Karl Robert Mandelkow, 6 vols. (1962–69; 3rd and 4th eds., 1988), I, 408; Disraeli: Robert Blake, *Disraeli* (1967; ed. 1968), 36.

8. Ribot: Anna Robeson Burr, *The Autobiography: A Critical and Comparative Study* (1909), 145; Emerson: Buckley, *Turning Key*, 4.

9. Laurence Sterne: *Tristram Shandy* (1759–67; World's Classics ed., 1903), 479 [bk. 7, ch. 33]; Goethe: *Wilhelm Meisters Lehrjahre* (1795–96), *Werke*, VII, 411 [bk. 6].

10. The following three paragraphs summarize a longer effort at definition in Peter Gay, *The Bourgeois Experience*, vol. I, *Education of the Senses* (1984), General Introduction.

BOURGEOIS EXPERIENCES, IV:
The Art of Listening

1. See Mount, *Rustic Dance after a Sleigh Ride* (1830), *Dancing on the Barn Floor* (1831), *Self Portrait with Flute* (1828), *Dance of the Haymakers* (1845), reproduced in color in Martha V. Pike, "Catching the Tune: Music and William Sidney Mount," *Catching the Tune: Music and William Sidney Mount,* ed. Janice Gray Armstrong (1984), 12, 10, 15.

2. Peter G. Buckley, "The Place to Make an Artist Work," ibid., 34. A few American paintings testify to racially mixed musical groups; note Thomas Hicks, *The Musicale, Barber Shop, Trenton Falls, N. Y.* (1866, in the North Carolina Museum of Art, Raleigh), in which half a dozen women and one man listen to a small orchestra that contains both black and white musicians.

3. De Quincey: Grevel Lindop, *The Opium-Eater: A Life of Thomas De Quincey* (1981), 47; Hunt: Ian Jack, *English Literature, 1815–1832* (1963), 409.

4. Gluck: James H. Johnson, "Musical Experience and the Formation of a French Musical Public," *Journal of Modern History,* LXIV (June 1992), 216–26; Lapécède: *Poétique de la musique,* 2 vols. (1785), I, 8–9, ibid., 221.

5. Dr. Charles Burney, "Essay on Musical Criticism," *A General History of Music from the Earliest Ages to the Present Period (1789),* 4 vols. (1776–89; 2-vol. ed., ed. Frank Mercer, 1935), II, 7 [prefacing bk. 3].

6. Lahalle, *Essai sur la musique, ses fonctions dans les moeurs, et sa véritable expression* (1825), 2–3, 1.

7. Thus toward the end of the eighteenth century, Gottfried, Freiherr van Swieten, who held impressive concerts in his Vienna mansion several times a year, taught his guests manners: "If it chanced that a whispered conversation began, His Excellency, who was in the habit of sitting in the first row of seats, would rise solemnly, draw himself up to his full height, turn to the culprits, fix a long and solemn gaze upon them, and slowly resume his chair. It was effective, always." *Thayer's Life of Beethoven,* rev. and ed. Elliot Forbes (1964; rev. ed. 1967), 157.

8. See ibid., 155.

9. De La Morlière: *Angola. Histoire indienne,* 2 vols. (1746), I, 69, quoted in Johnson, "Musical Experience," 201; Stendhal: *Life of Rossini* (1824; tr. and ed. Richard N. Coe, 1970), 178.

10. Brightly lit opera house: P. D. Olivero, *Interno del Teatro Regio di Torino* (ca. 1740); ten-year-old Mozart: M. Ollivier, *Mozart al piano* (ca. 1766), both in [Giampiero Tintori], *Vedere la musica* (1985), 137–39, 132–33.

11. Wolfgang Amadeus Mozart to Leopold Mozart, April 8, 1781, *Briefe und Aufzeichnungen. Gesamtausgabe,* ed. Wilhelm A. Bauer and Otto Erich Deutsch, 7 vols. (1962–75), III, 103.

12. Stendhal, *Life of Rossini,* 53, 491.

13. D'Alembert: *Discours préliminaire de l'Encyclopédie* (1751; ed. 1763; ed. F. Picavet, 1929), 49; Burney: "Essay on Musical Criticism," *General History,* II, 7; Sulzer: Carl Dahlhaus, *The Idea of Absolute Music* (1978; tr. Roger Lustig, 1989), 3. In mid-nineteenth century, in his novel *Der grüne Heinrich,* Gottfried Keller has the hero come upon "a few volumes" of Sulzer's work, and observes, "This book must have enjoyed a powerful circulation in its time, since one finds it in almost all old bookcases, and it haunts every auction and can be had for very little money." Pt. 1, ch. 20.

14. Eduard Hanslick, *Geschichte des Concertwesens in Wien,* 2 vols. (1869–70), I, 42.

15. Rossini: Herbert Weinstock, *Rossini: A Biography* (1968), 27 (*Ciro* was called an "oratorio," but it was really an opera with a sacred subject that made it eligible to be performed during Lent);

Blessington: *The Magic Lantern; or, Sketches of Scenes in the Metropolis* (1822), 59.

16. See Hoffmann, *Kreisleriana,* no. 3, "Gedanken über den hohen Wert der Musik" (1812), *Werke,* ed. Herbert Kraft and Manfred Wacker, 4 vols. (1967), I, 31–36.

17. Ibid., 35.

18. Berlioz, *Mémoires de Hector Berlioz comprenant ses voyages en Italie, en Allemagne, en Russie et en Angleterre (1803–1865),* 2 vols. (1870; 2nd ed., 1881), I, 27 [ch. 5].

19. "Wiener Scizzen," *Signale für die musikalische Welt,* ed. Bartholf Senff, XVIII, 9 (January 26, 1860), 76.

20. Goethe to Franz Ludwig Albrecht v. Hendrich, March 21, 1803, *Briefe von und an Goethe,* ed. Karl Robert Mandelkow, 6 vols. (1962–69; 3rd and 4th eds., 1988) II, 446–47.

21. *Das "Museum." Einhundertfünfzig Jahre Frankfurter Konzertleben, 1808–1958,* ed. Hildegard Weber (1958), 107.

22. Frankfurt: ibid., 111; New York: Howard Shanet, *Philharmonic: A History of New York's Orchestra* (1975), 90.

23. John H. Mueller, *The American Symphony Orchestra: A Social History of Musical Taste* (1951), 354–55.

24. Letters to *Algemeen Handelsblad* (Amsterdam), November 7 and 21, 1888. (I owe this material, with illuminating comments, to Peter de Bach. Personal communication, June 27, 1992.)

25. E. Kossak, "Die italienische Oper," *Signale,* XVIII, 15 (March 8, 1860), 162–63.

26. *American,* November 30, 1825, quoted in Karen E. Ahlquist, "Opera, Theatre, and Audience in Antebellum New York," Ph.D. diss., University of Michigan, 2 vols. in 1, continuously paginated (1991), I, 96.

27. London audience: Robert Elkin, *Royal Philharmonic: The Annals of the Royal Philharmonic Society* (1946), 20; Carnegie Hall: Richard Schickel, *The World of Carnegie Hall* (1960), 46.

28. Chicago concert: *Musical Courier,* January 1, 1896, quoted in Schickel, *Carnegie Hall,* 354; Metropolitan Opera Board: Irving Kolodin, *The Story of the Metropolitan Opera, 1883–1950: A Candid History* (1953), 56.

29. Jacques Offenbach, *Offenbach en Amérique. Notes d'un musicien en voyage* (ca. 1876), 237–38 (drawn from letters home).

30. See Lawrence W. Levine, *Highbrow/Lowbrow: The Emergence of Cultural Hierarchy in America* (1988), 95.

31. In psychoanalytic language, one might call silent listening a triumph of the secondary over the primary process—a civilized response that overrides instinctual urges.

32. Stendhal, *Life of Rossini,* 15. See Heinz Kohut and Siegmund Levarie, "On the Enjoyment of Listening to Music," *Psychoanalytic Quarterly,* XIX (1950), 75.

33. Arthur Schopenhauer, *Die Welt als Wille und Vorstellung,* 2 vols. (1818; ed. 1924), I, 259, 262, 263, 263 [bk. 3, par. 52].

34. Wackenroder: *Phantasien über die Kunst für Freunde der Kunst* (1799), in *Schriften,* ed. Ernesto Grassi with Walter Hess (1968), 158–59; Schelling: René Wellek, *A History of Modern Criticism, 1750–1950,* vol. II, *The Romantic Age* (1955), 369, 370.

35. The category of "secular religion" is by no means self-evident, but with the charms of music it is justified.

36. Elssler: Levine, *Highbrow/Lowbrow,* 109; Germania Music Society: ibid., 110–11;

37. Robert W. Gutman, *Richard Wagner: The Man, His Mind, and His Music* (1968), 252.

38. Hans Richter to Wilhelm Ganz, 1903, quoted in Ganz, *Memories of a Musician: Reminiscences of Seventy Years of Musical Life* (1913), 333.

39. Robert Schumann, in his famous review of Berlioz's *Symphonie fantastique,* wrote, "Berlioz can hardly have dissected the head of a handsome murderer with greater repugnance than I feel at dissecting his first movement." "Symphonie von H. Berlioz" (1835), *Gesammelte Schriften,* ed. Paul Bekker (1922), 101.

40. See Berlioz, *Mémoires,* 2 [ch. 2], 20 [ch. 4], and numerous other instances; Stendhal, *Life of Rossini,* 72–73 and passim.

41. Rellstab, *Aus meinem Leben,* 2 vols. in 1 (1861), II, 254.

42. Hoffmann, *"Sinfonie . . .* composée et dediée etc., par *Louis van Beethoven," Allgemeine musikalische Zeitung,* XII (July 4 and 11, 1810), *Werke,* ed. Georg Ellinger, 15 vols. (1912–20), XIII, 41–42.

43. Ibid.

44. Stendhal, *The Present State of Music in France and Italy,* quoted in Arthur Ware Locke, *Music and the Romantic Movement in France* (1920), 90.

45. Lahalle, *Essai sur la musique,* 39, 78, 83.

46. Berlioz, "Biographie de Beethoven," *Le Correspondant* (1829). See Locke, *Music and the Romantic Movement,* 77.

47. As reported by Comtesse d'Agoult, *Mémoires, 1833–1854,* ed. M. David Ollivier (1927), 92. See Claude Laforêt [pseud. for Flavien Bonnet-Roy], *La Vie musicale au temps romantique (salons, théâtres et concerts)* (1929), 207. Rousseau had anticipated this attitude by half a century. In his posthumous and uncompleted *Essai sur l'origine des langues,* he wrote, "Music can paint sleep, the stillness of night, loneliness, even silence. The composer does not present such scenes directly, but rouses in our souls the same impressions we receive from the real scenes."

48. Antoine Fontaney, *Journal intime* (for 1830 to 1836) (1925), 83 and 108, quoted in Léon Guichard, *La Musique et les lettres au temps du romantisme* (1955), 103n.

49. Liszt: Alessandra Comini, *The Changing Image of Beethoven: A Study in Mythmaking* (1987), 213; Hallé: Michael Kennedy, *The Hallé Tradition: A Century of Music* (1960), 8–9, 22; Ingres: ibid., 10.

50. Grünfeld to Gutmann, February 27, 1892, Gutmanniana, manuscript division, Bayerische Staatsbibliothek, Munich.

51. Comini, *Changing Image of Beethoven,* 213.

52. The term "absolute music" was first extensively used at mid-century by Richard Wagner, and with disparaging intent. But it has come to mean the kind of music that Hoffmann and his fellow romantics raised above all other kinds. See Dahlhaus, *Idea of Absolute Music.*

53. See Desiderius Monsonyi, "Die irrationalen Grundlagen der Musik," *Imago,* XXI (1935), 225–26.

54. *"Sinfonie,"* 43. Hoffmann had been anticipated by the German aesthetician, poet, and performer Christian Friedrich Schubart, who, in an essay of the 1770s on musical genius, had already pointed out that while all musical geniuses are self-taught, "nevertheless, no musical genius can reach perfection without cultivation and training. Art must perfect what Nature sketched in the raw." Quoted in Edward E. Lowinsky, "Musical Genius—Evolution and Origins of a Concept," *Musical Quarterly,* XXX (1964), 326.

55. See Alma-Tadema's interesting *A Reading from Homer* and, even more interesting, *The Favourite Poet,* which shows a lovely seated young woman reading aloud to another young beauty, stretched out on an upholstered window seat in a pose of dreamy languor. In this painting, quasi-religious attentiveness shades into erotic fantasizing. A canvas by Alexander Johnston, *Family Devotions,* in which a young man earnestly reads from Scriptures to his family, from grandparents

to infant, underscores that readings from sacred texts naturally required the most devoted attention.

56. Only Stendhal surpassed him, as he haunted opera houses and concert halls and wrote—or, better, compiled—biographies of major modern composers.

57. See Daniel Maclise's drawing of Paganini playing (ca. 1831).

58. This painting has been exhaustively analyzed in Comini, *Changing Image of Beethoven*, 207–17, which I have followed closely.

59. As a well-known English writer on music, H. R. Haweis, put it in the 1870s, "The emotional force in women is usually stronger, and always more delicate, than in men. Their constitutions are like those fine violins which vibrate to the lightest touch. Women are the great listeners, not only to eloquence, but also to music." *Music and Morals* (1871), 112.

60. "Applause," *Encyclopaedia Britannica*, 3 vols. (1768–71; 11th ed., 29 vols., 1910–11), II, 223. "Baireuth" *(sic!)*.

61. Elisabet von Herzogenberg to Adolf and Irene Hildebrand, August 7, 1889, *Adolf von Hildebrand und seine Welt. Briefe und Erinnerungen*, ed. Max Kalbeck, 2 vols. (1907), II, 177. For a more detailed treatment, see Peter Gay, *The Bourgeois Experience*, vol. II, *The Tender Passion* (1986), 267–69.

62. Nietzsche, *Nietzsche contra Wagner* (1888), in *Werke*, ed. Karl Schlechta, 3 vols. (1966; 6th ed., 1969), II, 1054; "Vermischte Meinungen und Sprüche" (1886), *Menschliches, Allzumenschliches*, ibid., I, 802.

63. Ludwig II to Richard Wagner, October 7, 1865, quoted in Lore Lucas, *Die Festspiel-Idee Richard Wagners* (1972), 86.

64. Cosima Wagner to Houston Stewart Chamberlain, October 23, 1888, *Cosima Wagner und Houston Stewart Chamberlain im Briefwechsel, 1888–1901* (1934) 30.

ONE: The Re-enchantment of the World

1. Kierkegaard, journal, March 1836, *The Journals of Søren Kierkegaard*, sel., ed., and tr. Alexander Dru (1938), 25.

2. Coleridge to Southey, November 13, 1795, *Collected Letters of Samuel Taylor Coleridge*, ed. Earl Leslie Griggs, 6 vols. (1956–71), I, 165.

3. Novalis: *Werke, Tagebücher und Briefe Friedrich von Hardenbergs*, ed. Hans-Joachim Mähl and Richard Samuel, 2 vols. (1978), II, 334; Hegel: *Vorlesungen über die Aesthetik*, in *Vollständige Ausgabe durch einen Verein von Freunden des Verewigten*, ed. Ph. Marheineke et al., 18 vols. in 20 (1832–45), X, 122–23 [pt. 2, ch. 3, sec. 2].

4. Delécluze, in Roger Fayolle, "Introduction," Stendhal, *Racine et Shakespeare. Etudes sur le romanticisme* (1970), 40.

5. This was Novalis's judgment of Friedrich Schlegel's *Athenäum* fragments. Novalis to Friedrich Schlegel, December 26, 1797, *Werke*, I, 652.

6. Coleridge, *Biographia Literaria; or, Biographical Sketches of My Literary Life and Opinions*, 2 vols. (1815), in *The Collected Works of Samuel Taylor Coleridge*, ed. Kathleen Coburn et al., 16 vols. (1969–92), VII, 69 [ch. 4].

7. For Michelet on Géricault, see Marcel Brion, *Art of the Romantic Era* (1966), 152.

8. Constant: J. Christopher Herold, *Mistress to an Age: A Life of Madame de Staël* (1958), 300–301; Stendhal: *Racine et Shakespeare*, 154.

9. Hazlitt's review of Schlegel's *Lectures on Dramatic Literature* (1816), printed as "Schlegel on the Drama," *The Complete Works of William Hazlitt*, ed. P. P. Howe, 21 vols. (1930–34), XVI, 57.

10. Victor Hugo: André Maurois, *Olympio, ou la vie de Victor Hugo* (1954), 144; Bulwer-Lytton: *England and the English* (1833; ed. Standish Meacham, 1970), 300 [bk. 4, ch. 4]. It is well known that Byron denied that classicism and romanticism were in any way distinguished while he lived in England.

11. Louis-Simon Auger, "Discours" opening the session of the Académie française on April 24, 1824. See Stendhal, *Racine et Shakespeare*, 237.

1. The Imagination Unleashed

1. Friedrich Schlegel: to Georg Reimer, March 16, 1805, *Briefe von und an Friedrich und Dorothea Schlegel*, ed. Josef Körner (1926), 58; Coleridge: *Anima Poetae: From the Unpublished Note-books of Samuel Taylor Coleridge*, ed. Ernest Hartley Coleridge (1895), 128; Wordsworth: *The Convention of Cintra* (1808), in *Prose Works*, ed. Alexander B. Grosart, 3 vols. (1876), I, 161–62; August Wilhelm Schlegel: Eckart Klessmann, *Die deutsche Romantik* (1979), 79; Novalis: *Die Christenheit oder Europa* (written 1799, publ. 1826), in *Werke, Tagebücher und Briefe Friedrich von Hardenbergs*, ed. Hans-Joachim Mähl and Richard Samuel, 2 vols. (1978), II, 741; Philipp Otto Runge: undated letter (ca. 1801 or 1802), *Hinterlassene Schriften*, ed. by his older brother, 2 vols. (1840–41), II, 179.

2. Friedrich Schlegel to August Wilhelm Schlegel, October 31, 1797, *Friedrich Schlegels Briefe an seinen Bruder August Wilhelm*, ed. Oskar Walzel (1890), 299.

3. See "Kritik der philosophischen Systeme," *Friedrich Schlegels philosophische Vorlesungen aus den Jahren 1804–1806*, in *Kritische Friedrich-Schlegel Ausgabe*, ed. Ernst Behler et al., 35 vols. so far (1958–), XIII, 327–84 passim.

4. It is a tribute to the diversity of romanticisms that the romantics did not reach a consensus even on the value of originality. In 1826, Alphonse de Lamartine alerted Victor Hugo after reading his recently published *Odes et ballades*: "Do not try for originality! . . . It is a *jeu d'esprit* and not what you need." See André Maurois, *Olympio, ou la vie de Victor Hugo* (1954), 138.

5. Wordsworth, *The Prelude* (version of 1805), XIII, lines 189–92.

6. Addison: *The Spectator*, no. 421 (July 3, 1712), ed. Donald F. Bond, 5 vols. (1965), III, 578–79; Kant: *Kritik der Urtheilskraft* (1790), in *Kants Werke*, ed. G. Hartenstein, 8 vols. (1867–68), V, 317–18 [par. 46]; Keats to Benjamin Bailey, November 22, 1817, *The Letters of John Keats, 1814–1821*, ed. Hyder Edward Rollins, 2 vols. (1958), I, 185.

7. Coleridge, *Notebooks*, ed. Kathleen Coburn, 4 vols. (1957–90), II, 2375; *The Statesman's Manual* (1816), in *The Collected Works of Samuel Taylor Coleridge*, ed. Kathleen Coburn et al., 16 vols. (1969–92), VI, 23.

8. Trublet: "De la poésie et des poètes," quoted in Margaret Gilman, *The Idea of Poetry in France from Houdar de La Motte to Baudelaire* (1958), 1; de Gérando: Alan Bewell, *Wordsworth and the Enlightenment* (1989), 43.

9. Hölderlin: *Hyperion, oder Der Eremit in Griechenland* (1797–99), in *Sämtliche Werke und Briefe*, ed. Günther Mieth, 2 vols. (1970), I, 584 [vol. 1, bk. 1]; 628 [vol. 1, bk. 2]; Schlegel: *Lucinde* (1799), in *Kritische Ausgabe*, V, 30.

10. Macaulay: "Milton" (1825), *Literary and Historical Essays Contributed to the "Edinburgh Review,"* 2 vols. in 1 (1934), I, 15; Peacock: "The Four Ages of Poetry" (1820), *Memoirs of Shelley and Other Essays & Reviews*, ed. Howard Mills (1970), 129–30.

11. Shelley, *A Defence of Poetry* (written 1821; publ. 1840; ed. Albert S. Cook, 1891), 36.

12. William Blake, "Annotations to Sir Joshua Reynolds's Discourses," *Complete Writings, with*

Variant Readings, ed. Geoffrey Keynes (1957; 2nd ed., 1966), 476–77, 456, 470.

13. In 1819, Blake reported a hallucination in which the poet Cowper had appeared to him, informing him that he, Blake, was as mad as everyone, "mad as a refuge from unbelief—from Bacon, Newton, and Locke." Charles Rosen, "The Mad Poets," *New York Review of Books,* XXXIX, no. 17 (October 22, 1992), 35.

14. Blake, as Marilyn Butler has observed, changed his mind on important issues. *Romantics, Rebels, and Reactionaries: English Literature and Its Background, 1760–1830* (1982), 39–53. Incidentally, Goethe in his most romantic manner has Faust informing Gretchen, "Feeling is all." But that was not a declaration of a romantic principle in which Goethe believed: he was lending Faust seductive language to distract the pious Gretchen from his shocking lack of Christian faith.

15. "meanest faculty": Thomas De Quincey, "On the Knocking at the Gate in 'Macbeth' " (1823), *Selected Writings of Thomas De Quincey,* ed. Philip Van Doren Stern (1949), 1090; "Reason is feasted": Coleridge to his brother George, March 31, 1791, *Collected Letters of Samuel Taylor Coleridge,* ed. Earl Leslie Griggs, 6 vols. (1956–71), I, 7; "Association": Coleridge to Thomas Poole, March 16, 1801, ibid., II, 706; "puerilities": I. A. Richards, *Coleridge on Imagination* (1934; 2nd ed., 1950), 51n; "Rapture": Coleridge to Thomas Poole, October 16, 1797, *Collected Letters,* I, 354–55.

16. Heine reminded his readers in his brilliant and malicious account of the German romantic school that *Lucinde* was virtually "the only original creation that Fr. Schlegel has left behind." *Die romantische Schule* (1835), in *Sämtliche Schriften,* ed. Klaus Briegleb, 6 vols. (1968–76), III, 408.

17. France: "Reise nach Frankreich" (written 1802, published 1803 in *Europa,* a periodical edited by Friedrich Schlegel), *Studien zur Geschichte und Politik,* ed. Ernst Behler (1966), in *Kritische Ausgabe,* VII, 70; Shakespeare: "Gespräch über die Poesie: Brief über den Roman," ibid., II, 335; "dangerous asset": *Philosophie des Lebens* (1827), first lecture, ibid., X, 21.

18. Friedrich Schlegel, *Philosophie des Lebens,* ibid., X, 19.

19. Friedrich Schlegel, "Reise nach Frankreich," ibid., VII, 65.

20. August Wilhelm Schlegel, *Vorlesungen über schöne Litteratur und Kunst,* ed. J. Minor, 3 vols. (1884), I, 292.

21. August Wilhelm Schlegel, *Über dramatische Kunst und Litteratur,* 3 vols. (1817), III, 48.

22. Taking a walk with Coleridge in 1819, Keats was impressed: "In those two Miles he broached a thousand things. . . . Nightingales, Poetry—on Poetical sensation—Metaphysics— Different general and species of Dreams—Nightmare—a dream accompanied by a sense of touch—single and double touch—A dream related. . . . Monsters—the Kraken—Mermaids— southey believes in them—southey's belief too much diluted—A Ghost story—Good morning." Keats added, "I heard his voice as he came towards me, I heard it as it moved away—I had heard it all the interval." See Ian Jack, *English Literature, 1815–1832* (1963), 4.

23. Coleridge to Thelwall, November 19, 1796, *Collected Letters,* I, 181.

24. *Biographia Literaria; or, Biographical Sketches of My Literary Life and Opinions,* 2 vols. (1815), in *Collected Works,* VII, 81 [ch. 4]. See also 24 [ch. 1], 31–32, 38–39 [ch. 2].

25. Ibid., 304–5 [ch. 13].

26. See ibid., 82 [ch. 4], 168 [ch. 10]

27. Shelley, *Defence of Poetry,* 5, 11–12, 5, 2, 13–14, 38, 46.

2. The Self in Politics

1. Hugo, preface to *Lucrèce Borgia* (1833), in *Oeuvres complètes,* ed. Jacques Seebacher et al., 15 vols. (1985–90), VIII, 972.

2. See Peter Gay, *The Bourgeois Experience,* vol. III, *The Cultivation of Hatred* (1993), 219–35.

3. Stephen Gill, *William Wordsworth: A Life* (1990), 84–85.

4. Hazlitt, "Lecture VIII: On the Living Poets," *Lectures on the English Poets* (1818), in *The Complete Works of William Hazlitt,* ed. P. P. Howe, 21 vols. (1930–34), V, 161–62.

5. Ibid., 163.

6. Chateaubriand: *Mémoires d'outre-tombe* (1849–50; ed. Maurice Levaillant and Georges Moulinier, 2 vols., 1951, 3rd ed., 1957), I, 109 [bk. 4, ch. 1]; de Musset: ("Il est tombé sur nous, cet édifice immense / Que de tes larges mains tu sapais nuit et jour"), *Rolla* (1835), in *Oeuvres de Alfred de Musset. Poésies, 1833–1852* (1876), 19. The French were, of course, not Voltaire's only detractors. In 1798, Novalis called him, in the privacy of a notebook, "one of the greatest minus-poets who ever lived," and thought it a pity that "his world was a Parisian salon. With less personal and national vanity he would have been much more." *Werke, Tagebücher und Briefe Friedrich von Hardenbergs,* ed. Hans-Joachim Mähl and Richard Samuel, 2 vols. (1978), II, 326.

7. "Where does so much mad agitation come from?" the Parisian magistrate Pierre Gerbier, renowned for his rhetorical skills, asked in June 1789, and answered his own question: "From a crowd of minor clerks and lawyers, from unknown writers, starving scribblers, who go about rabblerousing in clubs and cafés. These are the hotheads that have forged the weapons with which the masses are armed today." See Robert Darnton, *The Literary Underground of the Old Regime* (1982), 1.

8. Known as the "doctrinaires," this middle-of-the-road party stood "between the ultra-royalists who wanted the king without the charter, and the liberals who wanted the charter without the king." Pierre Trahard, *Le Romantisme défini par "Le Globe"* (1924), 1.

9. André Maurois, *Olympio, ou la vie de Victor Hugo* (1954), 277.

10. H. R. Haweis, *Music and Morals* (1871), 297.

11. Sainte-Beuve, "Victor Hugo en 1831" (1835), *Portraits contemporains,* 5 vols. (1870–89), I, 409.

12. Hugo, preface to *Hernani,* signed March 9, 1830, in *Oeuvres complètes,* VIII, 539–40.

13. For a discussion of this tract in shape of a novella, see Gay, *Cultivation of Hatred,* 178–80.

14. "Deeply rooted in absolutism, German burghers dreamt no dreams of revolution; they were satisfied with pushing for reforms but not for the abolition of the authoritarian state." Hajo Holborn, "Der deutsche Idealismus in sozialgeschichtlicher Beleuchtung," *Historische Zeitschrift,* CLXXIV (1959), 366. This paragraph is indebted to Holborn's brilliant article (pp. 359–84).

15. Friedrich Schlegel, *Ideen* (1800), no. 106, *Kritische Friedrich-Schlegel Ausgabe,* ed. Ernst Behler et al., 35 vols. so far (1958–), II, 266.

16. Friedrich Schlegel, "Signatur des Zeitalters" (a series of articles published from 1820 to 1823), ibid., VII, 534.

17. Friedrich Schlegel, *Ideen,* no. 41, ibid., II, 259.

18. At least that is what he told Prince Metternich in the dedication of his remarkable *Geschichte der alten und neuen Literatur.*

19. Gentz: to Johann Phillip Freiherr von Wessenberg, May 18, 1816, in Ernst Behler, *Friedrich Schlegel in Selbstzeugnissen und Bilddokumenten* (1966), 129; Friedrich Schlegel: to August Wilhelm Schlegel, January 21, 1828, *Friedrich Schlegels Briefe an seinen Bruder August Wilhelm,* ed. Oskar F. Walzel (1890), 654.

20. Friedrich to August Wilhelm Schlegel, February 17, 1798, ibid., 351.

21. Behler, *Schlegel,* 124–25.

22. Friedrich Schlegel, "Signatur des Zeitalters," *Kritische Ausgabe,* VII, 538.

23. Ibid., 534–46 passim.

24. Ibid., 540.

25. Coleridge to George Coleridge, ca. March 12, 1798, *Collected Letters,* ed. Earl Leslie Griggs, 6 vols. (1956–71), I, 238; Coleridge to Thomas Poole (March 23, 1801), ibid., II, 709; Coleridge, "Lay Sermon" (1817), *The Collected Works of Samuel Taylor Coleridge,* ed. Kathleen Coburn et al., 16 vols. (1969–92), VI, 215n.

26. Hazlitt, *Lectures on the English Poets,* in *Works,* V, 166–67.

27. Byron to Francis Hodgson, March 5, 1812, *Byron's Letters and Journals,* ed. Leslie A. Marchand, 12 vols. (1973–82), II, 105.

28. J. S. Mill to John Sterling, October 20–22, 1831, *Collected Works of John Stuart Mill,* ed. J. M. Robson et al., 33 vols. (1963–91), vol. XII, *The Earlier Letters* (pt. 1), 80–81.

29. Wordsworth to Dorothy Wordsworth, September 6 [and 16], 1790, *The Letters of William and Dorothy Wordsworth,* ed. Ernest De Selincourt, rev. Chester L. Shaver et al., 7 vols. (1967–88), I, 36.

30. *Prelude,* VI, lines 364–67.

31. *Prelude* (1805), IX, lines 511–24.

32. Ibid., X, line 637.

33. *The Debate on the French Revolution, 1789–1800,* ed. Alfred Cobban (1950), 42.

34. Wordsworth, *Prelude,* XI, lines 211–14. Coleridge's shift away from the Revolution was quite as slow and as regretful. See his *France: An Ode* of February 1798, in which Coleridge vividly describes his disillusionment with a revolution for which he had such great hopes.

35. David V. Erdman, "The Dawn of Universal Patriotism: William Wordsworth among the British in Revolutionary France," in *The Age of William Wordsworth: Critical Essays on the Romantic Tradition,* ed. Kenneth R. Johnston and Gene W. Ruoff (1987), 3.

36. Wordsworth to his family, April 1, 1833, *Letters of William and Dorothy Wordsworth,* V, 601; Wordsworth to Lord Lonsdale, February 24, 1832, ibid., 500–501.

37. Mary Shelley: journal, September 18, 1814, *Mary Shelley's Journal,* ed. Frederick L. Jones (1947), 15; Browning: "The Lost Leader" (1845), lines 1–2.

38. Hazlitt, "silence of thought": "Character of Mr. Wordsworth's New Poem, *The Excursion,*" *The Examiner,* August 21, 28, October 2, 1814, *Works,* XIX, 10–11; "all that others were": "On Shakespeare and Milton," *Lectures on the English Poets,* ibid., V, 47. Wordsworth's friends dismissed this view as mere spite, but whatever the biographical background to Hazlitt's judgment, it seems appropriate enough, if perhaps too strongly stated.

39. Walter Bagehot, one of the shrewdest readers the mid-Victorian age produced, thought that "in the most exciting parts of Wordsworth . . . you always feel, you never forget, that what you have before you is the excitement of a recluse. There is nothing of the stir of life; nothing of the brawl of the world." "Wordsworth, Tennyson, and Browning; or, The Pure, Ornate, and Grotesque Art in English Poetry" (1864), *Literary Studies (Miscellaneous Essays),* ed. Richard Holt Hutton, 2 vols. (1879; 2nd ed., 3 vols., 1902–05), II, 345.

40. Keats to Richard Woodhouse, October 27, 1818, *The Letters of John Keats,* ed. Maurice Buxton Forman, 2 vols. (1931; 4th ed., 1952), I, 226.

3. Heart Religion

1. Macaulay, review of Thomas Moore, *Letters, Journals and other Prose Writings of Lord Byron; with Notices of his Life,* in *Edinburgh Review* (June 1831), *Literary and Historical Essays,* 2 vols. in 1 (1934), I, 186.

2. Manzoni, quoted in Archibald Colquhoun, "Alessandro Manzoni," in Manzoni, *The Betrothed, "I Promessi Sposi": A Tale of XVIIth Century Milan* (1825–26; 3rd ed., 1840–42; tr. Colquhoun, 1951), 590.

3. "You must know," Schleiermacher added, apostrophizing the reader, that "the imagination is the highest and most original thing in man; you must know that it is your imagination that creates the world for you." *Über die Religion. Reden an die Gebildeten unter ihren Verächtern,* in Friedrich Daniel Ernst Schleiermacher, *Kritische Gesamtausgabe,* ed. Hans-Joachim Birkner et al., 1st division, *Schriften und Entwürfe,* vol. II, *Schriften aus der Berliner Zeit, 1796–1799,* ed. Günter Meckenstock (1984), 245 [second speech].

4. Friedrich Schlegel, "Signatur des Zeitalters" (1820–23), *Kritische Friedrich-Schlegel Ausgabe,* ed. Ernst Behler et al., 35 vols. so far (1958–), VII, 484.

5. It seems virtually inescapable for anyone writing about Bilderdijk (1756–1831) to avoid the adjective "eccentric." Thus the eminent Dutch historian Pieter Geyl calls him "that great counter-revolutionary eccentric," whose twelve-volume history of his country, the *Geschiedenis des Vaderlands,* was nothing better than "one protracted pamphlet, and one of unprecedented virulence." Yet, for all his "pathological bitterness," that "dynamic personality exercised, not a wide, but a profound influence." *History of the Low Countries: Episodes and Problems* (1964), 150.

6. Willem Bilderdijk, *De Ondergang der eerste Wereld* (1809; publ. 1820; English tr., 1858), quoted in Nicholas A. Rupke, "Romanticism in The Netherlands," *Romanticism in National Context,* ed. Roy Porter and Mikuláš Teich (1988), 198.

7. See Pierre Reboul, "Introduction," Chateaubriand, *Le Génie du Christianisme* (1802; 2-vol. ed., 1966), I, 11.

8. "it's delicious": Madame Hamelin, *Souvenirs,* quoted ibid.; "music and color": Maurois, *Olympio, ou la vie de Victor Hugo* (1954), 78.

9. See Reboul, "Introduction," *Génie du Christianisme,* I, 16.

10. Chateaubriand, preface to 1st ed. (1802), ibid., II, 398.

11. Reboul, "Introduction," ibid., I, 16.

12. In 1910, an anonymous author in the *Encyclopaedia Britannica* shrewdly listed the ingredients that had gone into Chateaubriand's aesthetic Christianity: "His naturally poetical temperament was fostered in childhood by picturesque influences, the mysterious reserve of his morose father, the ardent piety of his mother, the traditions of his ancient family, the legends and antiquated customs of the sequestered Breton district, above all, the vagueness and solemnity of the neighbouring ocean," to say nothing of "his closest friend," his "sister Lucile, a passionate-hearted girl, divided between her devotion to him and to religion." "Chateaubriand, François René, Vicomte de (1768–1848)," *Encyclopaedia Britannica,* 3 vols. (1768–71; 11th ed., 29 vols., 1910–11), V, 960.

13. Chateaubriand, *Génie du Christianisme,* I, 365 [pt. 2, bk. 5, ch. 3]. See also ch. 4.

14. Hölderlin, undated fragment (late 1798 or early 1799) usually called "Über Religion," *Sämtliche Werke und Briefe,* ed. Günter Mieth, 2 vols. (1970), I, 864.

15. Hölderlin: *Hyperion* (1797–99), ibid., 657 [vol. 1, bk. 2]; Novalis: "Das allgemeine Brouillon (Materialien zur Enzyklopädistik)" (1798–99), *Werke, Tagebücher und Briefe Friedrich von Hardenbergs,* ed. Hans-Joachim Mähl and Richard Samuel, 2 vols. (1978), II, 480.

16. Friedrich Schlegel to Novalis, December 17, 1798, *Kritische Ausgabe,* XXIV, 215.

17. "Moments of enthusiasm": Novalis, "Journal," May 1797, *Werke,* I, 463.

18. Novalis, "Life beginning of death": *Blüthenstaubfragment* no. 14, ibid., II, 231; "self-killing": [Fragmentblatt], ibid., 223; "stirrings": journal, ibid., I, 456; "fantasies": ibid., 457; "lasciviousness": ibid., 462; "much lasciviousness": ibid., 463.

19. Novalis, "Absolute love," "absolute will," "absolute feeling": [Fragmentblatt], ibid., II, 223.

20. Novalis, "Hinunter zu der süssen Braut, / Zu Jesus dem Geliebten. . . . / Ein Traum bricht unsre Banden los / Und senkt uns in des Vaters Schooß." *Hymnen an die Nacht,* ibid., I, 177.

21. Novalis, *Blüthenstaubfragment* no. 16, ibid. II, 233.

22. Schleiermacher, *Über die Religion,* in *Kritische Gesamtausgabe,* 1st division, vol. II, 196, 211 (2) [first speech; second speech].

23. Ibid., 221 [second speech].

24. Ibid.

25. Ibid., 224, 231 [second speech].

26. Ibid., 232, 228 (2), 237, 247 [second speech].

27. Coleridge, Appendix C, *The Statesman's Manual,* in *The Collected Works of Samuel Taylor Coleridge,* ed. Kathleen Coburn et al., 16 vols. (1969–92), VI, 70.

28. Heine, *Zur Geschichte der Religion und Philosophie in Deutschland* (1843; 2nd ed., 1852), in *Sämtliche Schriften,* ed. Klaus Briegleb et al., 6 vols. (1968–76), III, 571.

29. Goethe to Karl Ludwig von Knebel, November 11, 1785, *Briefe von und an Goethe,* ed. Karl Robert Mandelkow, 6 vols. (1962–69; 3rd and 4th eds., 1988), I, 459; and Goethe to Friedrich Heinrich Jacobi, June 9, 1785, ibid., 475.

30. Schleiermacher said of Spinoza, "He was penetrated by the high World Spirit, the Infinite was his beginning and end, the Universe his sole and eternal love; in holy innocence and deep humility he mirrored himself in the eternal world and saw how He, too, was its most engaging mirror; full of religion was He and full of the Holy Spirit; and therefore He stands, alone and unrivaled, master of his art, but lofty above the profane guild, without disciples and without the rights of citizenship." *Reden über die Religion,* in *Kritische Gesamtausgabe,* 1st division, vol. II, 213 [second speech].

31. Goethe, "Was kann der Mensch im Leben mehr gewinnen, / Als dass sich Gott-Natur ihm offenbare?" "Im ernsten Beinhaus war's" (1826), in *Werke, Kommentare und Register,* ed. Erich Trunz et al., 14 vols. (1948–60; 6th to 12th ed., 1981–86), I, 367.

32. Goethe, "Religion und Christentum," *Maximen und Reflexionen,* ibid., XII, 372.

33. Goethe to Lavater, November 14, 1781, *Briefe,* I, 375.

34. He was trying, he wrote, to "trace the multifarious, particular manifestations of the magnificent world garden to one general, simple principle." Karl Viëtor, *Goethe the Thinker* (1950), 31.

35. "Newton as mathematician has so great a reputation that the clumsiest of errors—namely, that the clear, pure, eternally unalloyed light is made up of dark lights—has persisted to this day." "Erkenntnis und Wissenschaft," *Maximen und Reflexionen,* in *Goethes Werke,* XII, 457.

36. Goethe, "Einleitung," *Zur Farbenlehre,* ibid., XIII, 329. The "ethical character," he wrote in 1798, "is quite inseparable from the scientific effects" of his theory of colors. Goethe to Schiller, February 14, 1798, *Briefe,* II, 330.

37. Goethe, "So kann man sagen, daß wir schon bei jedem aufmerksamen Blick in die Welt theorisieren." "Vorwort," *Zur Farbenlehre,* in *Goethes Werke,* XIII, 317.

38. Goethe, "Wär nicht das Auge sonnenhaft, / Wie könnten wir das Licht erblicken? / Lebt nicht in uns des Gottes eigne Kraft, / Wie könnt uns Göttliches entzücken?" "Einleitung," ibid., 324. On himself as a pantheist, see one of his maxims: "As researchers into Nature, we are pantheists; as poets, polytheists; ethically, monotheists." "Religion und Christentum," *Maximen und Reflexionen,* ibid., XII, 372.

39. An early version of "Dejection," in a letter to from Coleridge to William Sotheby, July 19,

1802, *Collected Letters,* ed. Earl Leslie Griggs, 6 vols. (1956–71), II, 817.

40. Mill, *Autobiography* (1873; ed. John J. Coss and Roger Howson, 1924), 104, 103.

41. Wordsworth, *Prelude* (1805), XII, lines 50–52.

4. The Bourgeois Egotistical Sublime

1. Stendhal, *De l'amour* (1822; ed. Henri Martineau, 1938), 63.

2. Shelley, "perception": note to *Queen Mab* (1813), in *The Complete Poetical Works of Percy Bysshe Shelley,* ed. Thomas Hutchinson (1929), 796 (italics mine); "nature of love": "Fragment of an Essay on Friendship" (ca. 1822), in *Shelley on Love: An Anthology,* ed. Richard Holmes (1980), 19; for pursuing the phantom of love, see ibid., 38.

3. Shelley, "love withers . . . unreserve . . . usurpation," "present system," "prostitution": *Complete Poetical Works,* 796–98 passim.

4. Shelley, "We are born": "Essay on Love" (ca. 1815), in *Shelley on Love,* 71; "the act itself": "A Discourse on the Manners of the Ancient Greeks Relative to the Subject of Love" (1818), ibid., 109.

5. I have treated the prehistory to nineteenth-century ideas of love, and those ideas themselves, extensively in *The Bourgeois Experience,* vol. II, *The Tender Passion* (1986). These pages concentrate on the relationship of the ideology of romantic love to a wider bourgeois culture.

6. Diderot to Sophie Volland, August 29, 1762, *Correspondance,* ed. Georges Roth, 16 vols. (1955–70), IV, 120. It is instructive to see how emphatically Rousseau's *La Nouvelle Héloïse,* possibly the most widely read novel the century produced, kept love and marriage separated. Julie adores, sleeps with, and is impregnated by Saint-Preux, but marries a rich older man, the baron de Wolmar, for whom she feels high esteem, nothing more; secretly she will yearn for her first and only love until her death.

7. Schlegel, Athaeneum fragments 34, 268, *Kritische Friedrich-Schlegel Ausgabe,* ed. Ernst Behler et al., 35 vols. so far (1958–), II, 170, 210.

8. Nor did he believe, as Novalis did at least experimentally, that "rape is the greatest pleasure." See Friedrich Schlegel, *Theorie der Weiblichkeit,* a collection of texts, ed. Winfried Menninghaus (1983), 160, 169.

9. Friedrich Schlegel, *Lucinde* (1799), in *Kritische Ausgabe,* V, 11.

10. In Ernst Behler, *Friedrich Schlegel in Selbstzeugnissen und Bilddokumenten* (1966), 16.

11. Schlegel, *Lucinde,* in *Kritische Ausgabe,* V, 7.

12. Friedrich Schlegel to Novalis, October 20, [17]98, ibid., XXIV, 183. Heine complained that the novel's protagonists were nothing better than abstractions, "a mixture of sensuality and wit." Heine, *Die romantische Schule* (1835), in *Sämtliche Schriften,* ed. Klaus Briegleb et al., 6 vols. (1968–76), III, 408.

13. Anon. [Schleiermacher], *Vertraute Briefe über Friedrich Schlegels "Lucinde"* (1800; ed. 1907), 15.

14. See Leslie A. Marchand, *Byron: A Biography,* 3 vols. continuously paginated (1957), II, 602n. Compare Friedrich Schlegel's tart observation that the grotesque novels of Jean Paul were "the only romantic product of our unromantic age"—another overstatement exaggerating the gulf between the romantics and the middle-class public. "Brief über den Roman; Gespräch über die Poesie" (1800), *Kritische Ausgabe,* II, 30.

15. Writing to some English friends from Italy in early 1819, Byron listed his sexual conquests for the year past that reads like a version of Leporello's catalog aria: some twenty-three names,

"cum multis aliis." He added, not to slight his record, "I have had them all & thrice as many to boot since 1817." Byron to John Cam Hobhouse and Douglas Kinnaird, January 19, 1819, *Byron's Letters and Journals,* ed. Leslie A. Marchand, 12 vols. (1973–82), VI, 92. See Gay, *Tender Passion,* 59.

16. Byron to Lady Melbourne, September 13, 1812, *Letters,* II, 194; Byron to Thomas Moore, November 17, 1816, ibid., V, 131; Byron to [Douglas Kinnaird], November 27, 1816, ibid., V, 135; Byron to Moore, August 31, 1820, ibid., VII, 170.

17. Marchand, *Byron,* III, 1246, 1256.

18. Goethe to Knebel, December 14, 1822, *Briefe von und an Goethe,* ed. Karl Robert Mandelkow, 6 vols. (1962–69; 3rd and 4th eds., 1988), IV, 55.

19. Arnold, *Stanzas from the Grand Chartreuse* (1855), lines 134–38.

20. Hebbel, *Mutter und Kind.* See Hayo Matthiesen, "Friedrich Hebbel," in *Genie und Geld. Vom Auskommen deutscher Schriftsteller,* ed. Karl Corino (1987), 253.

21. Johanna Schopenhauer, *Jugendleben und Wanderbilder,* 2 vols. in one (1839), I, 254.

22. Hermine Hanel, *Die Geschichte meiner Jugend* (1930), 40.

23. Flaubert's Emma Bovary provides a harrowing, not implausible, fictional instance of what might happen to a susceptible young woman with free access to the seductions of romantic novels.

24. See Ellen K. Rothman, *Hands and Hearts: A History of Courtship in America* (1984), 39–40. This paragraph is indebted to that excellent monograph.

25. Betham-Edwards, *Home Life in France* (1905), 266, 57, 77; see also 78–80.

26. That is what Friedrich Schlegel meant when he argued that "real marriage"—which is to say, romantic marriage—amounts to "several persons becoming just one." In that ideal, the beloved other must grow into the familiar self, in exalted moments a self miraculously identical with one's own. *"Just like you,"* exclaims Julius, the protagonist of his novel, "is a greater word than all superlatives." *Lucinde,* in *Kritische Ausgabe,* V, 64.

27. Constant, *Adolphe* (1816; 4th ed., 1828; ed. Gustave Rudler, 1941), 46, 43 [ch. 5].

28. Hazlitt, *Liber Amoris; or, The New Pygmalion* (1823; facs. ed. with introduction by Gerald Lahey, 1980), 8 (2), 12, 41, 20, 66, 75, 90, 107.

TWO: Exercises in Self-definition

1. Carlyle, *Sartor Resartus* (1833–34; ed. Kerry McSweeney and Peter Sabor, 1987), 73.

2. "Preface," *Poems* (1853), in *The Poetical Works of Matthew Arnold,* ed. Chauncey Brewster Tinker and H. F. Lowry (1950), xvii–xviii.

3. Goodbrand: "A Suggestion for a New Kind of Biography," *Contemporary Review* (1870), 20.

4. "No feature of the literature of the early nineteenth century is more striking than the prominence of the element of autobiography.... For those of the writers of our period"—1815 to 1832—"who lived well into the Victorian age, particularly, it was to become very much of a 'financial sacrifice' to refrain from some sort of autobiography." Ian Jack, *English Literature, 1815–1832* (1963), 363–64, 365. Jack is speaking of England alone, but the same development can be documented for other countries.

5. Hogg, *The Private Memoirs and Confessions of a Justified Sinner, Written by Himself* (1824; ed. T. E. Welby, 1924), 1.

6. Baudelaire, "Mon coeur mis à nu," *Oeuvres complètes,* ed. Y. G. Le Dantec, rev. Claude Pichois (1961), 1271.

7. Hanns Sachs, *Freud: Master and Friend* (1945), 103.

N O T E S   (pp. 105–8)

8. Smiles, *Character* (1871; ed. 1872), 283.

9. Freud, "Dora," *Gesammelte Werke,* ed. Anna Freud et al., 18 vols. (1940–68), V, 240; *Standard Edition of the Complete Psychological Works,* tr. and ed. James Strachey et al., 24 vols. (1953–74), VII, 77–78.

10. "Autobiography in one sense is always true, since the author, whatever his intentions or unconscious self-deceptions, presents—in the very tone and emphasis with which he talks of himself—some of the materials we need to assess his actual personality." Jerome Hamilton Buckley, *The Turning Key: Autobiography and the Subjective Impulse since 1800* (1984), 41.

11. Leslie Stephen, "Autobiography," *Hours in a Library,* 3 vols. (1874–79; ed. 1892), III, 237.

1. In Rousseau's Shadow

1. See Stendhal to Félix Faure, October 2, 1812, *The Private Diaries of Stendhal,* ed. and tr. Robert Sage (1954), 484.

2. Hazlitt: "On the Character of Rousseau," *The Round Table* (1817), in *The Complete Works of William Hazlitt,* ed. P. P. Howe, 21 vols. (1930–34), IV, 90; George Eliot to Sara Sophia Hennell, February 9, 1849, *The George Eliot Letters,* ed. Gordon S. Haight, 9 vols. (1954–78), I, 277.

3. See Gordon S. Haight, *George Eliot: A Biography* (1968), 65.

4. Anna Robeson Burr, *The Autobiography: A Critical and Comparative Study* (1909), 45.

5. Shelley: to Thomas Jefferson Hogg, May 14, 1811, *The Letters of Percy Bysshe Shelley,* ed. Frederick L. Jones, 2 vols. (1964), I, 84; De Quincey: *Confessions of an English Opium-Eater* (1821; first book publication 1822; ed. Alethea Hayter, 1971), 29.

6. Baudelaire, "Les Paradis artificiels. Opium et haschisch" (1860), *Oeuvres complètes,* ed. Y. G. Le Dantec, rev. Claude Pichois (1961), 381.

7. In one of his drafts to the *Confessions,* Rousseau alludes in passing to Montaigne and to Montaigne's contemporary the speculative natural philosopher Cardano, whose posthumous *De vita propria* had once enjoyed something of a reputation. But he insists—not without doing some injustice—that neither of these widely read autobiographers had anything to teach him. In the rejected preface, he made virtually the same claim: "Here is the only portrait of a man, painted exactly after nature and in all its truth, that exists and will probably ever exist." Rousseau, *Oeuvres complètes,* ed..Bernard Gagnebin, Robert Osmont, and Marcel Raymond, 4 vols. (1959–69), I, 3. Rousseau put Montaigne "at the head of those false sincere men who want to deceive by telling the truth." And Cardano, for his part, was "so mad that one can derive no instruction from his reveries." Rousseau, "Ebauches des *Confessions,*" ibid., I, 1150.

8. *Confessions,* ibid., 5 [bk. 1]. Here Rousseau links his *Confessions* to Hobbes, who believed in the power of introspection as an instrument of wider insight: reading in himself would enable him to read all of humanity.

9. "Whence could the painter and apologist of human nature, today so defamed and maligned, have taken his model, if not from his own heart?" Rousseau would ask in another autobiographical work. Surely none of his contemporaries could even remotely approach him in self-knowledge. "I am not made like anyone I have met; I dare to think that I am not made like anyone now alive." *Rousseau, juge de Jean-Jacques,* ibid., 936 [3rd dialogue].

10. In a prefatory note he did not publish, in a tone that would have been impossible to Augustine, Rousseau implored his readers of the future "not to deprive the honor of my memory of the only certain monument to my character that has not been mutilated by my enemies." Rousseau, *Oeuvres complètes,* I, 3.

11. In 1916, twenty-four years after its publication, it was in its tenth printing.

12. Trollope, *An Autobiography* (1883; World's Classics ed., 1953), 17 [ch. 2].

13. *Mein Leben* (posthumously published in 1813), in *Seumes Werke,* ed. Anneliese and Karl-Heinz Klingenberg, 2 vols. (1965), I, 35.

14. *The Life of Mansie Wauch, Tailor in Dalkeith, Written by Himself* (1828), v.

15. For one instance, see the manuscript autobiography of Hermann Elias Weigert, "Meine Lebensgeschichte bis 1895, verbunden mit der meines Bruders, Kommerzienrat Salomon Weigert" (written ca. 1895), Leo Baeck Institute, New York, partially printed in *Jüdisches Leben in Deutschland. Selbstzeugnisse zur Sozialgeschichte, 1780–1871,* ed. Monika Richarz (1976), 317–34, esp. 331.

16. "Goethe's Life, it seems," wrote an anonymous reviewer in 1816 on the published segments of Goethe's autobiography, "must be considered as having, in many instances, furnished the matter for his works of imagination, whilst in them we are to seek for a poetical view of his life and sentiments." [Sir Francis Palgrave], in *Edinburgh Review,* XXVI (June 1816), 312.

17. Leslie Stephen, "William Hazlitt," *Hours in a Library,* 3 vols. (1874–79; ed. 1892), II, 69, 73.

18. Hazlitt, "Self-Love and Benevolence" (1828), *Complete Works,* XX, 178.

19. In 1797, an anonymous reviewer in the *Monthly Review* termed the name "pedantic"; in 1809 Southey, it appears, still hyphenated the word: "auto-biography." See Ian Jack, *English Literature, 1815–1832* (1963), 365; Jerome Hamilton Buckley, *The Turning Key: Autobiography and the Subjective Impulse since 1800* (1984), 19.

20. Georg Brandes, "Introduction" to Peter Kropotkin, *Memoirs of a Revolutionist* (1899; ed. 1930), vii.

2. Between Probes and Poses

1. Wilson: *The Memoirs of Harriette Wilson, Written by Herself,* 4 vols. (1825; ed. E. Nash, 2 vols., 1909), I, 1; Busch: "Was mich betrifft" (1886), in *Wilhelm Busch Gesamtausgabe,* ed. Friedrich Bohne, 4 vols. (1958), IV, 147–57. In 1894, Busch allowed himself another autobiographical sketch, no more intimate than the first: "Von mir über mich," ibid., 205–11. For Busch, see Peter Gay, *The Bourgeois Experience,* vol. III, *The Cultivation of Hatred* (1993), 408–23.

2. From a letter to Mr. Engel with which Huxley prefaced his terse and distant "autobiography." Charles Darwin, Thomas Henry Huxley, *Autobiographies,* ed. Gavin de Beer (1974), 100.

3. Darwin, *Autobiography,* ibid., 8.

4. Sand: *Histoire de ma vie* (1850–51), in *Oeuvres autobiographiques,* ed. Georges Lubin, 2 vols. (1970–71), I, 3, 6; Daniel Stern [Madame d'Agoult]: *Mes Souvenirs, 1806–1833* (1877), iii.

5. Stendhal (Henri Bayle): *Vie de Henry Brulard* (published posthumously in 1890), in *Oeuvres intimes,* ed. V. Del Litto, 2 vols. (1981–82), II, 534 [ch. 1], 833 [ch. 32]; Sand: to Pierre Jules Hetzel, February 1 [1848], *Correspondance,* ed. Georges Lubin, 25 vols. (1964–91), VIII, 264.

6. Goethe, *Aus meinem Leben. Dichtung und Wahrheit* (1811–32), in *Werke, Kommentare und Register,* ed. Erich Trunz et al., 14 vols. (1948–60; 6th to 12th ed., 1981–86) IX, 7–9 [preface].

7. Ibid., 15, 14 [pt. 1, bk. 1].

8. Ibid., 14 [pt. 1, bk. 1].

9. Ibid., 283, 285 [pt. 2, bk. 7].

10. Goethe to Johann Caspar Lavater, ca. September 20, 1780, *Briefe von und an Goethe,* ed. Karl Robert Mandelkow, 6 vols. (1962–69; 3rd and 4th eds., 1988), I, 324.

11. *Dichtung und Wahrheit,* in *Goethes Werke,* IX, 282 [pt. 2, bk. 7]. In a late letter, to the king of

Bavaria, he reiterated the point he had made before: the gift of poetry is peculiar as it "compels its possessor to reveal himself. Poetic utterances are involuntary confessions in which our interior opens itself up." Goethe to Ludwig I, April 14, 1829, *Briefe,* IV, 326. On March 14, 1830, he told his faithful Eckermann that during the wars of liberation from Napoleon in 1813, he had not written bellicose anti-French ballads, because "I did not make poetry of what I did not love, of what did not closely impinge upon me, or give me a hard time. . . . I made love poems only when I loved. How could I have written songs of hate without hating?" Johann Peter Eckermann, *Gespräche mit Goethe in den letzten Jahren seines Lebens,* 3 vols. (1837–48; 1-vol. ed., ed. Ernst Beutler, 1948 [vol. 24 of the Artemis ed. of Goethe's works and conversations]), 733.

12. Goethe to Frau von Stein, July 16 and 17, 1776, *Briefe,* I, 222.

13. Andersen, *Das Märchen meines Lebens ohne Dichtung* (tr. from Danish, but the first publication, of 1847, was in German, and this is what I shall be quoting here), 9.

14. Ibid., 9, 9, 9, 12, 13, 14, 17.

15. Ibid., 67.

16. These biographical details are well summarized in Elias Bredsdorff, *Hans Christian Andersen: The Story of His Life and Work, 1805–75* (1975), 15–17, 21–22.

17. See *Das Märchen meines Lebens,* 183.

3. The Road from Damascus

1. *Les Règles de la méthode sociologique* (1895), preface to 1st ed. A decade earlier, Frederic W. H. Myers, an English essayist and student of psychic phenomena, observed that "whether or no this modern age be in its actual practice manifesting an increased regard for morals and religion, there seems at least to be no doubt that those subjects occupy now a larger space in its thoughts than has been the case since the Reformation." "Ernest Renan," in *Essays Modern* (1883; 2nd ed., 1885), 201.

2. Jacob Epstein, "Erinnerungen" (written between 1909 and 1918), in *Jüdisches Leben in Deutschland. Selbstzeugnisse zur Sozialgeschichte, 1780–1871,* ed. Monika Richarz (1976), 259–60.

3. Darwin, *Autobiography* (1887), in Charles Darwin, Thomas Henry Huxley, *Autobiographies,* ed. Gavin de Beer (1974), 31, 49–50, 53.

4. Clara Geissmar, *Erinnerungen* (privately printed in 1913, two years after her death), in *Jüdisches Leben in Deutschland,* 452–61, quotation at 458.

5. Darwin: *Autobiography,* 50; R. W. Church: *The Oxford Movement: Twelve Years, 1833–1845* (posthumously published, 1891; ed. Geoffrey Best, 1970), 183; John Henry Cardinal Newman: *Apologia pro vita sua: Being a History of His Religious Opinions* (1864; ed. 1890; ed. David J. DeLaura, 1968), 19.

6. Both in D. G. Charlton, *Secular Religions in France, 1815–1870* (1963), 28, 30.

7. Théodore Jouffroy, "De l'organisation des sciences philosophiques," *Nouveaux mélanges philosophiques,* ed. Ph. Damiron (1842), 112, 113.

8. Ibid., 113.

9. Ibid., 113–15.

10. Ibid., 115.

11. Ibid., 116.

12. Théodore Jouffroy, "Comme les dogmes finissent" (written in 1823, published in 1825), *Le Cahier vert. Comment les dogmes finissent. Lettres inédites,* ed. Pierre Poux (1923), 67.

13. The ability to tolerate ambiguity and uncertainty is a rare gift, a sign of psychological

maturity that is granted to a few courageous skeptics like Hume or Freud. It is essential to what I have called the "liberal temper." *The Bourgeois Experience,* vol. III, *The Cultivation of Hatred* (1993), 526.

14. Ernest Renan, *Souvenirs d'enfance et de jeunesse* (1883; introd. Henriette Psichari, 1973), 81, 86, 157, 53.

15. "The greatest torment with which a man who has fought his way through to a life of reflection must pay for his exceptional position," Renan once wrote, "is to see himself excluded from a large religious family to which the best souls in the world belong, and to be regarded as a corrupt man by beings with whom he would most want to live in spiritual harmony. One must be very sure of oneself not to be shaken, when the women and children fold their hands and say to you, 'Oh believe as we do!' " *Etudes d'histoire religieuse,* quoted in German in Georg Brandes, "Ernest Renan," in *Moderne Geister. Literarische Bildnisse aus dem neunzehnten Jahrhundert* (1882), 165.

16. Renan, *Souvenirs,* 80.

17. Ibid., 55.

18. Ibid., 85. The point was important to Renan: he insisted, here and elsewhere, that the temptations of the flesh had had nothing whatever to do with his decision. See esp. ibid., 84–85.

19. Ibid., 174, 177.

20. Renan, *Vie de Jésus* (1863; 13th ed., 1928), xxxi.

21. See *Souvenirs,* 211.

22. Ibid., 79, 73.

23. Edmund Gosse, *Father and Son: A Study of Two Temperaments* (1907; ed. Peter Abbs, 1983), 35 [ch. 1]; ibid., 33 [preface].

24. Ibid., 42 [ch. 1].

25. In the biography he wrote of his father, Edmund Gosse suggests that his mother's power would have softened his father's "opposition to the new ideas," notably Darwinism. She exercised, he writes, "an influence over him which was on the whole opposed to the stern and fanatic tendency of his own native temperament." *The Life of Philip Henry Gosse, F.R.S.* (1890), 273, 272. It seems far more probable that after his wife's death, Philip Gosse grew more stern and fanatical not as liberated from his wife's influence but to fulfill what he thought her program.

26. Gosse, *Father and Son,* 161, 43 [chs. 8, 1].

27. Ibid., 49 [ch. 2].

28. Ibid., 81 [ch. 3].

29. Ibid., 105 [ch. 5]. See Gosse, *Life of Philip Henry Gosse,* 279.

30. Gosse, *Father and Son,* 56, 58 [ch. 2].

31. Ibid., 235 [ch. 12].

32. Ibid., 236, 251 [epilogue].

33. The authoritative biography by Ann Thwaite, *Edmund Gosse: A Literary Landscape, 1849–1928* (1985), documents these contradictions, esp. 23–24.

34. Gosse, *Father and Son,* 236 [epilogue].

4. Second Thoughts

1. "My style," he went on, "uneven and natural, at times rapid and at times diffuse, at times wise and at times mad, at times grave and at times cheerful, will itself make part of my history." "Ebauches des *Confessions,"* *Oeuvres complètes,* ed. Bernard Gagnebin, Robert Osmont, and Marcel Raymond, 4 vols. (1959–69), I, 1154.

2. *The Autobiography and Letters of Mrs. M. O. W. Oliphant,* arranged and ed. Mrs. Harry Coghill (1899), 150.

3. Edmund Gosse, *Father and Son: A Study of Two Temperaments* (1907; ed. Peter Abbs, 1983), 33 [preface].

4. These transformations have been exhaustively documented in Ingrid Aichinger, *Künstlerische Selbstdarstellung. Goethes "Dichtung und Wahrheit" und die Autobiographie der Folgezeit* (1977), 62–77.

5. Hebbel, diary, late March 1842, *Friedrich Hebbels Tagebücher,* ed. Karl Pörnbacher, 3 vols. (1984), I, 483.

6. Sand to Hortense Allart, December 18, 1848, *Correspondance,* ed. Georges Lubin, 25 vols. (1964–91), VIII, 735–36.

7. See Chateaubriand, *Mémoires d'outre-tombe* (1849–50; ed. Maurice Levaillant and Georges Moulinier, 2 vols., 1951; 3rd ed., 1957), I, 1044, ix, xiii.

8. Sainte-Beuve, *"Mémoires d'outre-tombe* par M. de Chateaubriand," March 18, 1850, *Causeries du lundi,* 15 vols. (1850–70, many reprintings), I, 433.

9. Ibid., 435–36. It is worth noting that Sainte-Beuve did not have to rely on his intuition alone to make this charge. In 1802, after making a pilgrimage to the fountain at Vaucluse, forever associated with Petrarch and his Laura, Chateaubriand wrote in a private letter, "Laura the prude and Petrarch the wit have spoiled the fountain for me." But recounting this visit in the *Mémoires,* he waxes lyrical, professing himself to have been charmed by the "immortal melancholy" of Vaucluse. See ibid., 446–47. For the objectionable text see *Mémoires d'outre-tombe,* I, 481.

10. Sainte-Beuve: "Chateaubriand," *Lundis,* I, 437; Stendhal: *La vie de Henry Brulard* (posthumously published in 1890; ed. Henri Martineau, 2 vols., 1949), I, 15 [ch. 1].

11. John Stuart Mill, *Autobiography* (1873; ed. John J. Coss and Roger Howson, 1924), 1; Trollope, *An Autobiography* (1883; World's Classics ed., 1953), 1.

12. Mill, *Autobiography,* 1.

13. Thomas Carlyle to John Carlyle, November 5, 1873, cited in James Anthony Froude, *Thomas Carlyle: A History of His Life in London, 1834–1881,* 2 vols. (1884; ed. 1890), II, 449. Another reader, R. H. Hutton, the influential editor of the *Spectator,* thought the *Autobiography* revealed "a certain poverty of nature" and "a monotonous joylessness," marred by self-importance, egotism, and a "dry and abstract style." See Jerome Hamilton Buckley, *The Turning Key: Autobiography and the Subjective Impulse since 1800* (1984), 42.

14. S. E. Henshaw, "John Stuart Mill and Mrs. Taylor," *Overland Monthly* [San Francisco] (December 1874), 516–27, in *John Stuart Mill: Critical Assessments,* ed. John Cunningham Ward, 4 vols. (1987), I, 15.

15. Mill, *Autobiography,* 2.

16. *The Early Draft of John Stuart Mill's "Autobiography,"* ed. Jack Stillinger (1961), 184.

17. See Mill, *Autobiography,* 172; Leslie Stephen, "Autobiography," *Hours in a Library,* 3 vols. (1874–79; ed. 1892), III, 263.

18. *Early Draft of Mill's "Autobiography",* 183.

19. Mill, *Autobiography,* 3.

20. Ibid., 34, 76.

21. Ibid., 93, 94, 95.

22. Ibid., 99.

23. Marmontel, *Mémoires d'un père pour servir à l'instruction de ses enfants* (1804; ed. 1857), 49–51.

24. Mill, *Autobiography,* 99, 101. While he did not pursue the matter in the *Autobiography,* Mill's

letters give occasional evidence of later states of depression. Thus on April 15, 1829, two and a half years after the onset of his "crisis," he wrote to his friend John Sterling that "among the very various states of mind, some of them extremely painful ones," there had been "something distinctly approximating to misanthropy." *Collected Works of John Stuart Mill*, ed. J. M. Robson et al., 33 vols. (1963–91), vol. XII, *The Earlier Letters of John Stuart Mill, 1812–1848*, ed. Francis E. Mineka, 2 vols. (1963), I, 29.

25. See Mill, *Autobiography*, 102, 103; Mill to John Sterling, May 24, 1832, *Earlier Letters*, I, 99.
26. Mill, *Autobiography*, 105.
27. Thus "his father's 'authority & indignation' " is "rewritten as 'displeasure'; and the fact that he 'often mockingly caricatured' Mill's bad reading" is "discarded, along with mention of the futile 'short sharp contest[s]' between them over differences in opinion" and "his father's 'asperities of temper.' " Stillinger, *Early Draft of Mill's "Autobiography,"* 13. Stillinger cites numerous other changes, most of them small, all of them in the same direction.
28. Carlyle: Froude, *Thomas Carlyle: A History of His Life in London, 1834–1881*, 2 vols. (1884), II, 449; Leslie Stephen: *The English Utilitarians*, vol. III, *John Stuart Mill* (1900; ed. 1912), 69–70; Stephen, "Autobiography," *Hours in a Library*, III, 259.
29. Fontane, *Meine Kinderjahre* (1893; ed. Jutta Neuendorff-Fürstenau, with Kurt Schreinert, 1971; 2nd ed., 1972), 116, 117n [ch. 12].
30. See Helmuth Nürnberger, *Theodor Fontane in Selbstzeugnissen und Bilddokumenten* (1968), 147.
31. After only a few weeks, Fontane confided to a friend, "The enterprise is making me very happy." Fontane to Georg Friedlaender, November 1, 1892, *Briefe an Georg Friedlaender*, ed. Kurt Schreinert (1954), 195.
32. In the preface he exclaimed, "For possible doubters let it be a novel!" Fontane, *Meine Kinderjahre*, 8 [ch. 1].
33. Ibid., 9, 25 [chs. 1, 2].
34. Ibid., 40 [ch. 4].
35. Ibid., 15–16, 40, 140, 171 [chs. 1, 4, 14, 17].
36. Ibid., 140 [ch. 14].
37. Ibid., 21, 157 [chs. 2, 16].
38. Ibid., 157 [ch. 17].
39. Ibid., 159 [ch. 17].
40. Ibid., 160, 162, 165, 168 [ch. 17].
41. Ibid., 185 [ch. 18].
42. Mrs. Oliphant, *Autobiography*, 15.
43. Ibid., 4.

THREE: Usable Pasts

1. The Biographic Appetite

1. Coleridge: "A Prefatory Observation on Modern Biography," *The Friend*, no. 21 (January 25, 1810), *The Collected Works of Samuel Taylor Coleridge*, ed. Kathleen Coburn et al., 16 vols. (1969–92), IV, pt. 2, 286; Whibley: "The Limits of Biography," *Nineteenth Century*, XVI (March 1897), 433; Carlyle: "Biography," review of Croker's edition of Boswell's *Life of Johnson* (1832), in

[*Works*], Centennial Memorial Edition, 26 vols. (ca. 1892), XVI, 387.

2. [Christie], "Art. VIII.—1. *Biographie Universelle, Ancienne et Moderne,* Nouvelle édition . . . ," *Quarterly Review,* CLVII (January 1884), 187.

3. John, Viscount Morley, *Recollections,* 2 vols. (1917), I, 92.

4. He recalled that his idea for American Statesmen had been inspired by reading a volume in Morley's English Men of Letters. See John T. Morse, Jr., "Incidents Connected with the American Statesmen Series," *Proceedings of the Massachusetts Historical Society,* LXIV (October 1930–June 1932), 371.

5. Thus Albert Sorel's life of Madame de Staël (1890) was done into English in 1891, translated by Fanny Hale Gardiner. Earlier, Henry James noted that the French "do their duty by their great men" with "a liberal tribute of criticism, commentary, annotation, biographical analysis," but found few French examples "of that class of literature to which Boswell's 'Johnson' and Lockhart's 'Scott' belong." "Honoré de Balzac," *French Poets and Novelists* (1878; ed. 1884), 66.

6. Thus British reviewers singled out the English edition of *William Shakespeare* not only for Brandes's intimate knowledge of English literature and English history but also for his display of an exceptional gift for insight into character.

7. Bryce, *Studies in Contemporary Biography* (1903), viii.

8. It says more about Virginia Woolf than about her father, Leslie Stephen, an indefatigable biographer, that she could rudely condemn her father's efforts at psychological analysis: "Give him life, a character, and he is so crude, so elementary, so conventional, that a child with a box of coloured chalks is as able a portrait painter as he." This verdict is significant only for its mixture of hyperbole and misjudgment, and interesting mainly as a specimen of the post-Victorian assault on Victorianism. "A Sketch of the Past" (a fragment written between 1939 and 1940), *Moments of Being: Unpublished Autobiographical Writings,* ed. Jeanne Schulkind (1976), 126.

9. *Biographie universelle, ancienne et moderne, ou histoire, par ordre alphabétique, de la vie publique et privée de tous les hommes qui se sont fait remarquer par leurs écrits, leurs actions, leurs talents, leurs vertus ou leurs crimes,* ed. "par une société de gens de lettres et de savants," 52 vols. (1811–28), LII, v, x.

10. The English publisher George Smith poured the profits he had made from the English concession of Apollinaris—"The Queen of Table Waters," of German origin—into the *Dictionary of National Biography.* See Victoria Glendinning, *Anthony Trollope* (1992), 337, 337n.

11. Rochus Wilhelm, Freiherr von Liliencron, and Franz Xaver von Wegele, "Vorrede," *Allgemeine deutsche Biographie,* 45 vols. (1875–1900), XXXXV, v.

12. See David Cannadine, "The Dictionary of National Biography" (1981), *The Pleasures of the Past* (1989), 275–84, esp. 275; and Ira Nadel, *Biography: Fiction, Fact, Form* (1984), 45–60.

13. See, for this and other persuasive evidence of change, Kathleen Tillotson, *Novels of the Eighteen-forties* (1954), 66–67 and 67n.

2. Heroes and Antiheroes

1. Carlyle, *On Heroes, Hero-Worship, & the Heroic in History* (1841; ed. Michael K. Goldberg et al., 1993), 3, 26 [lecture 1].

2. Defenders of Carlyle like to quote a sentence from his 1830 essay on history: "History is the essence of innumerable Biographies." But there are enough texts in Carlyle, both in *On Heroes* and elsewhere, that he committed himself uncompromisingly to the need for worshiping the great who have shaped and changed the world.

3. Ibid., 175 (lecture 6); 12 (lecture 1); Carlyle to Ralph Waldo Emerson, February 3, 1835, *The*

Correspondence of Emerson and Carlyle, ed. Joseph Slater (1964), 114; "The Opera" (1852), in [*Works*], Centennial Memorial Edition, 26 vols. (ca. 1892), XVIII, 345.

4. Carlyle, *On Heroes,* 97 [lecture 3].

5. Edwin L. Miller, "Preface," *Robert Southey's Life of Nelson* (1896), v–vi.

6. James Sime: *Schiller* (1882), 1; Lord Dover: *The Life of Frederick the Second, King of Prussia,* 2 vols. (1832), II, 468.

7. Düntzer, *Schillers Leben* (1881), v, vi.

8. Ibid., 538, 539. In 1864—to give a particularly lyrical instance—G. H. Pertz published the first volume of a multivolume biography of the Prussian field marshal Count Neithardt von Gneisenau, one of the principal architects of the Wars of Liberation against Napoleon: "In the circle of heroes," Pertz begins, "at whose head King Friedrich Wilhelm III rescued his country from deepest distress, ennobled and elevated his death-defying people to the greatest effort, and liberated Prussia, Germany, Europe from ignominious servitude, there emerged at the same level with their leader, the minister vom Stein, the great figures of General Scharnhorst, Prince Blücher, and Field Marshal Count Gneisenau. Equal in highest honor, in unlimited devotion to king and fatherland, they battled for greatness by each other's side, each in his calling, unenvious, and with their comrades carried off the highest prize of victory." G. H. Pertz, *Das Leben des Feldmarschalls Grafen Neithardt von Gneisenau,* 3 vols. (1864–69), I, iii.

9. A. Bardoux, *Guizot,* Les Grands Ecrivains français (1894), 222.

10. See Asa Briggs, "Samuel Smiles and the Gospel of Work," *Victorian People: A Reassessment of Persons and Themes, 1851–67* (1955), 118.

11. Strachey, "Preface," *Eminent Victorians* (1918), viii.

12. Wedmore, "Note," *Life of Honoré de Balzac* (1890), 5.

13. Southey, *The Life of Nelson* (1813; ed. Edwin L. Miller, 1896), 56, 55–56, 169.

14. Ibid., 170. Southey's editor of 1896 does find it possible to "defend Nelson" on the ground that he regarded the revolutionaries as traitors. Ibid., 170–71n.

15. A. T. Mahan, *The Life of Nelson: The Embodiment of the Sea Power of Great Britain* (1897; 2nd ed., 1899), x, 2.

16. See ibid., 317–33, 445–49, quotation at 742. No Edwardian could have been more ungallant than Mahan, the late Victorian, as he details Emma Hamilton's impoverished childhood and unsavory youth in London: "utterly inexperienced, and with scarcely any moral standards . . . she was speedily ruined, fell so far, in fact, that even with all her attractions it seemed doubtful whether any man would own himself responsible for her condition, or befriend her." Ibid., 319. Mahan is no less scathing about the men who rescued her and whom she, with her loveless skills and lovely face and figure, later enslaved.

17. D[avid] H[annay], "Nelson," *Encyclopaedia Britannica,* 3 vols. (1768–71; 11th ed., 29 vols., 1910–11), XIX, 355a.

18. Carlyle, *Life of John Sterling* (1851), in [*Works*], XX, 12.

19. "mechanical": life of James Brindley, in Smiles, *Selections from the Lives of the Engineers* (original full ed., 1859), ed. Thomas Parke Hughes (1966), 35; "inclination": life of John Rennie, ibid., 186.

20. Lanfrey, *Histoire de Napoléon,* 5 vols. (1869–75), I, 2.

3. Conflicting Claims

1. *The Autobiography of Bertrand Russell, 1872–1914* (1951), 15–16.

2. Bagehot, "Shakespeare—the Man" (1853), *Literary Studies*, ed. R. H. Hutton, 2 vols. (1879; 3-vol. ed., 1910), I, 63–64.

3. Trollope, *An Autobiography* (1883; World's Classics ed., 1953), 314–15 [ch. 20].

4. See James Anthony Froude: "Preface," *Thomas Carlyle: A History of the First Forty Years of His Life, 1795–1835*, 2 vols. (1882), I, v–xvi; Carlyle: "Sir Walter Scott" (1838) [review of John Lockhart, *Memoirs of the Life of Sir Walter Scott*], in [*Works*], Centennial Memorial Edition, 26 vols. (ca. 1892), XVII, 407.

5. William Mathews, *C. A. Sainte-Beuve, Monday-Chats, Selected and Translated from the "Causeries du Lundi," with an Introductory Essay on the Life and Writings of Sainte-Beuve* (1877), xlii.

6. E. F. Benson reports that Gladstone said this to his—Benson's—mother. *As We Were* (1930), 97.

7. Gaskell, *The Life of Charlotte Brontë* (1857; World's Classics ed., 1919), 224.

8. In his fine biography of Madame de Staël, J. Christopher Herold appropriately singles out her "love-and-politics complex." For her, politics "was always intensely personal, a 'matter of proper names,' as she put it. Exaltation for such abstract causes as freedom, justice, or virtue required a hero who personified them or, at the least, friends with whom the exaltation could be shared." *Mistress to an Age: A Life of Madame de Staël* (1958), 99.

9. "It was the drive of his spiritual nature toward an activity appropriate to it." Justi, *Winckelmann und seine Zeitgenossen*, 3 vols. (1866–72; 5th ed., ed. Walther Rehm, 1956), I, 372.

10. Ibid., 148–60, quotations at 149, 148, 157.

11. Every breach left a scar, and there were times when Winckelmann lost faith in the idea of friendship. "In vain: he needed that state of fond excitement far too much; he seized the first possible opportunity to fasten his ideal to a worthier object, and then again and again believed for a moment that now he had found the friend he had long yearned for, while all the earlier ones had been found to weigh too little in the balance." Ibid., 155.

12. Ibid., III, 78.

13. Ibid., 481–92.

14. See ibid., I, 156–57.

15. Ibid., 157. Justi, though, cannot forbear mentioning at least one extenuating circumstance to explain this indifference: "it may have been linked to the sense of having mastered social formalities only incompletely." Ibid.

16. Ibid.

17. Ibid., III, 194.

18. Ibid., 76.

19. Harrison, "Froude's Life of Carlyle" (1885), *The Choice of Books and Other Literary Pieces* (1886; ed. 1925), 175.

20. The debate was confused but not sidetracked by a squabble between Froude and Carlyle's favorite niece, who had taken loving care of her uncle during his last years, over the rights to Carlyle's papers. It produced an acrimonious literature, which we may here set aside. What matters is Froude's way with Carlyle's private life.

21. [Anon.], "Thomas Carlyle," *Saturday Review*, LVI (November 8, 1884), 598; and "Thomas Carlyle. First Notice," ibid., LIII (April 22, 1882), 500. Among the large harvest of reviews, perhaps most noteworthy are G. S. Venables, "Carlyle's Life in London," *Fortnightly Review*, XLII

(1884), 594–608 (favorable); and [anon.], "Biography," *Cornhill Magazine,* XLVII (January–June 1883), 601–7 (scathing).

22. As psychoanalytic critics have rightly hinted, Froude seems to have been engaged in a lifelong set of repetitions on oedipal themes. In one of his last essays, "Froude" (1930), Lytton Strachey, by that time deeply influenced by Freud (largely as transmitted to him by his brother James and sister-in-law Alix Strachey), already made that point. But it is valid even so. "From the time I became acquainted with his writings," Froude observed four decades later, he had looked on Carlyle as his "own guide and master," and preferred to err with him than to be right with someone else. Froude, *Thomas Carlyle: A History of His Life in London, 1834–1881,* 2 vols. (1884; ed. 1890), II, 195.

23. Harrison, "Froude's Life of Carlyle," 187–88.

24. Froude, *Carlyle: Life in London,* II, 32.

25. Froude, *My Relations with Carlyle* (1903), 19, 20.

26. Carlyle, "Sir Walter Scott," [*Works*], XVII, 407.

27. Ibid., 364, 365, 367.

28. Froude, *My Relations with Carlyle,* 21, 23.

29. One recent biographer who accepts this account is Fred Kaplan, in his *Thomas Carlyle: A Biography* (1983), 118–19.

30. "Delicacy forbids that we should here discuss Froude's mystery or Miss Jewsbury's communication," they write. Yet having said that, they insist that "there is no truth in them. The evidence of their falsity," mainly lack of corroboration, "is absolutely conclusive. The use made of them by Froude and his representatives must be regarded as deplorable and a stain on English literature." After all, "all readers of Carlyle must allow that his writings are characterised by splendid virility, and that he was every inch a man." Thus literary diagnosis took the place of psychological inquiry. *"My Relations with Carlyle,"* they conclude, "is a kind of literary garbage." Alexander Carlyle and Sir James Crichton-Browne, *The Nemesis of Froude: A Rejoinder to James Anthony Froude's "My Relations with Carlyle"* (1903), 67–68, 129.

31. "The motives which prompt one man to write the life of another," wrote an anonymous critic of Froude's *Carlyle* in 1883, "may be divided, roughly speaking, into three. The primary object of a biographer may be either the amusement of the public for the sake of the money to be got by it, or the erection of a suitable monument to some one whom he loved or venerated, or the effect to be produced upon mankind by a great or wise man, and a truthful narrative of the motives and opinions by which his career was regulated"—or a combination of the three. [Anon.], "Biography," *Cornhill Magazine,* XLVII (January–June 1883), 601.

32. See *Verlagskatalog der C. H. Beckschen Verlagsbuchhandlung. Oskar Beck in München, 1763–1913* (1913), 127.

33. Morse, "Incidents Connected with the American Statesmen Series," *Proceedings of the Massachusetts Historical Society,* LXIV (October 1930–June 1932), 373. By its very nature, this attitude invited a view of the past that gave the individual considerable leverage over his world. This theory of history was getting rather old-fashioned late in the nineteenth century; still, it looked beyond a single life to a larger canvas.

34. Gosse in 1891, quoted in John L. Kijinski, "John Morley's 'English Men of Letters' Series and the Politics of Reading," *Victorian Studies,* XXXIV (Winter 1991), 209.

35. Stephen: Sidney Lee, *Principles of Biography* (1911), 38; Lee: *Dictionary of National Biography, Supplement, 1901–1911,* 3 vols. (1912), I, 27.

4. The Price of Professionalism

1. George Otto Trevelyan, *The Life and Letters of Lord Macaulay* (1876; enlarged ed., 1908), 621.

2. Motley's four-volume continuation, *The United Netherlands* (1860), like its long coda, the two-volume *Life and Death of John Barneveld* (1874), though less spectacular, remained great favorites in the Netherlands as much as in English-speaking countries.

3. Henry Adams to Charles Scribner, August 1, 1888, *The Letters of Henry Adams,* ed. J. C. Levenson et al., 6 vols. (1982–88), III, 131.

4. Droysen, *Grundriss der Historik* (1858; 3rd ed., 1882), in *Historik,* ed. Peter Leyh, vol. I (1977), 444 [par. 83].

5. Carlyle: "On History" (1830), in [*Works*], Centennial Memorial Edition, 26 vols. (ca. 1892), XVI, 62. He liked the aphorism well enough to use it again in his review of Croker's edition of Boswell's *Life of Johnson,* where he slyly quotes himself as an unnamed writer ("Boswell's Life of Johnson" [1832], ibid., 421); Emerson: "History" (1841), *Selected Essays,* ed. Larzer Ziff (1982), 153. In a series of lectures delivered in Dublin, the Irish savant W. Torrens McCullagh defined "history" as "the biography of a people." *The Use and Study of History* (1842), 68.

6. See Friedrich Sengle, *Biedermeierzeit. Deutsche Literatur im Spannungsfeld zwischen Restauration und Revolution, 1815–1848,* vol. II, *Die Formenwelt* (1972), 306.

7. "When I was young," Arnaldo Momigliano has written, "scholars wrote history and gentlemen wrote biography. But were they gentlemen? Scholars were beginning to wonder." *The Development of Greek Biography* (1971), 1; and see ibid., 1–7.

8. Morley, *Voltaire* (1872; printing of 1909), 307–8.

9. See Peter Gay, *The Bourgeois Experience,* vol. III, *The Cultivation of Hatred* (1993), 484–91.

10. See ibid., 485–86.

11. John Bagnell Bury, "The Science of History" (1903), *Selected Essays of J. B. Bury,* ed. Harold Temperley (1930), 9, 22. For the episode discussed in these paragraphs, see David Cannadine, *G. M. Trevelyan: A Life in History* (1992), 213–15.

12. George Macaulay Trevelyan, "Clio, a Muse," *Clio, a Muse and Other Essays, Literary and Pedestrian* (1913), 54–55.

13. Ibid., 9.

14. Macaulay, "History," *Edinburgh Review,* IIIL (1828), 332.

15. Burckhardt to Heinrich Schreiber, October 2, 1842, *Briefe,* ed. Max Burckhardt, 10 vols. (1949–86), I, 217.

16. Ranke, *Französische Geschichte vornehmlich im sechzehnten und siebzehnten Jahrhundert* (1852–61), in *Sämmtliche Werke,* 54 vols. in 42 (2nd and 3rd eds., 1868–90), XII, 5. Note that Ranke somewhat revised his histories as they were incorporated into his collected works. I shall be quoting from these throughout.

17. Trevelyan, "Clio, a Muse," 30.

18. Jacob Burckhardt to Gottfried Kinkel, March 21, 1842, *Briefe,* I, 197.

19. W[illiam] A[ugustus] B[revoort] C[oolidge], "Burckhardt, Jakob," *Encyclopaedia Britannica,* 3 vols. (1768–71; 11th ed., 29 vols., 1910–11), IV, 809.

20. Gabriel Monod, "M. Fustel de Coulanges," *Revue historique,* XLI (1889), 279. Whether this episode took place at the University of Strasbourg, the Ecole Normale, or the Sorbonne our informant does not say.

21. Thierry, "Lettre XVII," *Lettres sur l'histoire de France, pour servir d'introduction à l'étude de cette histoire* (1827; ed. 1834), 496 (I owe this reference to Lionel Gossman, *Between History and Literature* [1990], 88).

22. Margaret Macaulay's journal, March 30, 1831, quoted in Sir Charles Firth, *A Commentary on Macaulay's History of England* (1938), 276.

23. Michelet: Preface of 1869, *Histoire de la Révolution française*, 7 vols. (1847–53; ed. Gérard Walter, 2 vols., 1939), I, 1; "impossible ideal": Gossman, *Between History and Literature*, 161.

24. Motley to his father, May 18, 1852, *The Correspondence of John Lothrop Motley, D. L. C.*, ed. George William Curtis, 2 vols. (1889), I, 142.

25. Motley to Oliver Wendell Holmes, November 20, 1853, ibid., 162; Motley to Christina Forbes, January 4, 1854, *John Lothrop Motley and His Family: Further Letters and Records*, ed. Susan St. John Mildmay (1910), 41–42.

26. Motley to his daughter Lily, January 18, 1865, *Motley and His Family*, 229. A candid progress report he sent his friend Oliver Wendell Holmes on November 20, 1853, as symptomatic a self-description as we have of any historian identifying himself with his subject, remains worth quoting. Motley had found so much material in Brussels that he felt compelled to "penelopise" his manuscript, "pull to pieces and stitch away again." His picturesque despair stood for his profound pleasure in the overpowering presence of the past. "This reading of dead letters," he mildly ironized his obsession, was "not without its amusement in a mouldy sort of way." Nothing could surpass reading authentic texts "of such fellows as William of Orange, Count Egmont, Alexander Farnese, Philip the Second, Cardinal Granvelle, and the rest of them." *Correspondence*, I, 163.

27. Motley to his daughter Lily, January 18, 1865, *Motley and His Family*, 230.

28. Motley, *The Rise of the Dutch Republic*, 3 vols. (1856), I, 130–33 [pt. 1, ch. 2]; 202 [pt. 2, ch. 1].

29. Ibid., 142 [pt. 1, ch. 2]; 145 [pt. 1, ch. 2].

30. Morley, *Recollections*, 2 vols. (1917), II, 133; I, 118.

31. Motley to T. Hughes, February 9, [18]63, *Motley and His Family*, 152–53. Lincoln embodied "singularly well the healthy American mind." Motley to his mother, June 30, 1862, *Correspondence*, II, 80. The "Netherland nation during sixteen centuries" has ever been marked "by one prevailing characteristic, one master passion—the love of liberty, the instinct of self-government." In contrast, its foreign enemies, often its masters, have pitilessly labored to undermine "the bulwarks raised, age after age, against the despotic principle. The combat is ever renewed. Liberty, often crushed, rises again and again from her native earth with redoubled energy." The animating cause of the Dutch revolt was, to Motley's mind, simplicity itself: the Inquisition. "It is almost puerile to look further or deeper, when such a source of convulsion lies at the very outset of any investigation." Motley, "Historical Introduction," *Rise of the Dutch Republic*, I, 90–91; ibid., 321 [pt. 2, ch. 3].

5. Ranke

1. Reviewing Sarah Austin's English translation of Ranke's *The Ecclesiastical and Political History of the Popes of Rome during the Sixteenth and Seventeenth Centuries*, 3 vols. (1840), Macaulay spoke for the profession when he called it an "excellent book," written "in an admirable spirit, equally remote from levity and bigotry, serious and earnest, yet tolerant and impartial." "Von Ranke" (1840), *Literary and Historical Essays Contributed to the "Edinburgh Review"* 2 vols. in one (1934), II, 475.

2. Theodore von Laue, *Leopold Ranke: The Formative Years* (1950), 1.

3. Bourne, "Leopold von Ranke," *Sewanee Review,* V (August 1896), 15.

4. Ranke, first of the lectures delivered in 1854 to King Maximilian of Bavaria, *Weltgeschichte,* 9 vols. (1881–88), IX, pt. 2, p. 2.

5. Ranke to Christian Günther Graf von Bernstorff, January 30, 1825, *Neue Briefe,* ed. Bernhard Hoeft and Hans Herzfeld (1949), 60.

6. Late in the eighteenth century, the Göttingen school and, early in the nineteenth, the great Roman historian Barthold Georg Niebuhr had anticipated some of Ranke's most cherished techniques, discrediting long-held legends and applying sophisticated methods to elusive materials.

7. Acton: "Inaugural Lecture on the Study of History" (1895), *Essays in the Liberal Interpretation of History,* ed. William H. McNeill (1967), 335–36. Burckhardt, the most independent-minded of Ranke's contemporaries, made sure everyone knew that he had studied with Ranke in Berlin; Herbert Baxter Adams, the historian most instrumental in importing Ranke's seminar to American universities, called him "the father of scientific history." Burckhardt: Felix Gilbert, *History: Politics or Culture? Reflections on Ranke and Burckhardt* (1990), 94–95; Adams: Georg G. Iggers, *The German Conception of History: The National Tradition of Historical Thought from Herder to the Present* (1968), 63.

8. His first biographer, Eugen Guglia, insisted that Ranke "always held fast to the dogmas on which the Christian faith, the Catholic like the Protestant, mainly rests, such as the incarnation of Christ and his work of salvation." *Leopold von Rankes Leben und Werk* (1893), 48. This badly misreads the character of Ranke's piety.

9. Ranke to Heinrich Ranke, December 23, 1820, *Neue Briefe,* 18.

10. See Ranke, "Diktat vom November 1885," *Sämmtliche Werke,* 54 vols. in 42 (2nd and 3rd eds., 1868–90), LIII–LIV, 61.

11. Ranke to Heinrich Ranke, end of March 1820, *Das Briefwerk,* ed. Walther Peter Fuchs (1949), 18; Ranke to the same, December 23, 1820, *Neue Briefe,* 19.

12. "Theological tendencies": Ranke to Heinrich Ranke, January 13 [18]33, *Neue Briefe,* 176; "insight": diary entry after 1836, *Tagebücher,* ed. Walther Peter Fuchs (1964), 127. God remained under Ranke's pen all his life. "The writer, the teacher, is powerful only insofar as he tells the truth." Unlike Shelley, who had elevated the poet to the role of unacknowledged legislator of the world, Ranke believed that the historian could claim such an eminence only if he included God in his calculations. "He governs, too, insofar as the world accepts his opinions. But it will not accept these if they eschew the truth, if they are arbitrary, not grounded in God, that is, the divine on earth." Diary entry, December 21, 1850, *Tagebücher,* 132–33.

13. Lord Acton, draft written before 1864, quoted in Herbert Butterfield, "Appendix VII: Acton on Ranke," *Man on His Past: The Study of the History of Historical Scholarship* (1955), 221.

14. Ibid., 223. With an avalanche of succulent metaphors, Acton argued that Ranke's history was "all plums and no suet. It is all garnish, and no beef. He is a great historical decorator, and avoids whatever is dull or unpleasant, whatever cannot be told in a lively way, or cannot help to his end. He is an epicure and likes only tit-bits." Ibid., 222. Interestingly enough, Friedrich Nietzsche called Ranke, a little sarcastically, "that born classic *advocatus* of every *causa fortior,* that cleverest of all clever 'advocates of reality—*Tatsächlichen.*' " *Zur Genealogie der Moral. Eine Streitschrift* (1887), in *Werke,* ed. Karl Schlechta, 3 vols. (1966; 6th ed., 1969), II, 879.

15. Ranke, *Französische Geschichte vornehmlich im sechzehnten und siebzehnten Jahrhundert* (1852–61), in *Sämmtliche Werke,* VIII, 5.

16. Ranke, "Politisches Gespräch" (1836), ibid., IL–L, 329.

17. Ranke, *Englische Geschichte vornehmlich im siebzehnten Jahrhundert* (1859–68), ibid., XXI–XXII, 113.

18. Diary entry from the 1840s, *Tagebücher*, 241.

19. "pristine reports": Ranke, *Sämmtliche Werke*, LIII–LIV, 569; "archival curiosity": Ranke to Ferdinand Ranke, August 11, 1839, *Neue Briefe*, 168; "emptiness": the same to the same, May 16, 1856, ibid., 371; "pretty or not": the same to the same, November 11, 1836, ibid., 230.

20. Ranke, "Vorrede," *Deutsche Geschichte im Zeitalter der Reformation* (1839–47), in *Sämmtliche Werke*, I, ix–x.

21. See Ranke to Georg Friedrich von Guaita, March 19, 1837, *Neue Briefe*, 236. Guaita, mayor of Frankfurt am Main, had permitted Ranke to take some valuable papers with him to Berlin, and Ranke noted that in comparing these documents with those he had been allowed to see in Berlin, he had been able to see two sides to the story.

22. See Ranke to Karl Freiherr von Stein zum Altenstein, July 26, 1827, ibid., 95.

23. For one instance, see Ranke to Karl Freiherr von Stein zum Altenstein, January 17, 1828, ibid., 101; for another, Ranke to Friedrich Perthes, October 12, 1828, ibid., 109.

24. See Ranke to his brother Heinrich Ranke, June 24, 1837, ibid., 213–15, quotation at 214.

25. See Ranke to Friedrich Perthes, October 12, 1828, ibid., 109; Ranke to Karl Freiherr von Stein zum Altenstein, October 1, 1829, ibid., 129; and von Laue, *Leopold Ranke*, 34.

26. This characterization of Fustel's scientific ideal is Gabriel Monod's, offered in an obituary he wrote in the professional review he had founded. "M. Fustel de Coulanges," *Revue historique*, XLI (1889), 279.

27. Burckhardt to Emanuel Geibel, October 10, 1863, *Briefe*, ed. Max Burckhardt, 10 vols. (1949–86), IV, 137; Burckhardt to Heinrich Schreiber, August 1, 1860, ibid., IV, 53.

28. Mommsen: *Römische Geschichte*, 3 vols. (1856; 2nd ed., 1856), I, v–vi; Parkman: "Preface," *Montcalm and Wolfe* (1884), in *France and England in North America*, 2 vols. (1983), II, 843; "Preface," *A Half-Century of Conflict* (1892), ibid., 337.

29. Burckhardt, "Einleitung" (written 1872), *Griechische Kulturgeschichte* (posthumously published in 4 vols., ed. Jacob Oeri, 1898–1902; ed. Felix Stähelin and Samuel Merian, 1930–31; ed. 1977), I, 5.

30. Maitland, "English Law and the Renaissance" (1901), *Selected Historical Essays*, ed. Helen M. Cam (1957), 143.

31. As for Thucydides: "Of what historian . . . do you say that he best knew the art of telling things as they really happened? Bare chronicles apart, I suppose Thucydides," wrote John Morley into his diary on May 9, 1905. What Thucydides did was "to envelop things of the occasion in the general reflections suggested by them on human nature, and the course of human events to which they belong." *Recollections*, 2 vols. (1917), II, 133–34. As for Tacitus: Macaulay in his *History of England* quoted one of his tart aphorisms without attribution; in an age of classical learning, he did not need to identify his source. Speaking of the average country parson conducting a "petty war" against Dissenters in the England of 1685, Macaulay noted that "he too often hated them for the wrong which he had done them," an unmistakable borrowing from Tacitus' observation in *Agricola*: "It is characteristic of human nature to hate the one you have injured." See *The History of England from the Accession of James II*, 4 vols. (1848–61; 5-vol. ed., n.d.), I, 304–45 [ch. 3].

32. Leslie Stephen, "Biography," *National Review* (1893), 181.

33. Morley, "Mr. Froude on the Science of History," *Fortnightly Review*, n.s., II (1867), 324, quoted in Jeffrey Paul von Arx, *Progress and Pessimism: Religion, Politics, and History in Late Nine-*

teenth Century Britain (1985), 228. In 1881, the French historian Charles Seignobos called for a "scientific synthesis," which to his mind pedantic German fact grubbing could never achieve. A decade later, in a pioneering history of historical scholarship in the United States, J. Franklin Jameson cozily referred to his discipline as "our science."

34. Richard Hofstadter, *The Progressive Historians: Turner, Beard, Parrington* (1968; ed. 1970), 178.

35. The Germans, of course, had an easier time of it, since *Wissenschaft,* loosely translated as "science," does not necessarily appropriate the methods of physics or chemistry. In 1894, the philosopher Wilhelm Windelband summed up his thinking in a famous address on history and natural science. Rejecting current classifications, he noted that while it is logical to segregate philosophy and mathematics from the "sciences of experience," the real difficulties emerge with attempts to differentiate among the latter. Psychology, the empirical science of mind, explodes any convenient dichotomy. In its aims psychology is a human science; in its methods it is modeled on those of the natural sciences. Windelband's solution was elegant in its lucidity. A *Wissenschaft* is either "nomothetic," aiming at universal abstractions, or "idiographic," aiming at individual perceptions, and history, the science of past events, belongs in the second camp. That is why the "historical discipline" has such close affinities to "belles lettres." True: a few infatuated system builders apart, nineteenth-century historians were not interested in establishing general laws. Rather, they worked to offer a reliable account of the Battle of Waterloo, the conflict between Cicero and Caesar, the rise of the Dutch Republic. But they did generalize, whether sensibly or not, especially on human nature at work, and Windelband, not enamored enough of his definitions to disdain the lessons of practice, appreciated their frame of mind. In fact, he went so far as to assert that "the idiographic sciences need general propositions at every step of the way, propositions they can reasonably take only from the nomothetic disciplines." Both sciences, he concluded, "require for their foundation an experience purified in science, schooled in criticism, and tested in practice." See esp. Windelband, "Geschichte und Naturwissenschaft" (1894), in *Präludien. Aufsätze und Reden zur Philosophie und ihrer Geschichte,* 2 vols. (1883; 8th ed., 1921), II, 136–60.

36. Parkman, "Preface," *Count Frontenac and New France under Louis XIV* (1877), in *France and England in North America,* II, 10.

37. The late Thomas Nipperdey has defined Ranke's ideal of objectivity as an "interpretative shaping—*deutende Verarbeitung,"* a "critically understanding interpretation also of connections—*die kritisch verstehende Interpretation auch der Zusammenhänge."* "Zum Problem der Objektivität bei Ranke," *Leopold von Ranke und die moderne Geschichtswissenschaft,* ed. Wolfgang J. Mommsen (1988), 219.

38. Ranke, "Ueber die Restauration in Frankreich" (1832), *Sämmtliche Werke,* IL–L, 9. See Wolfgang Hardtwig, "Die Verwissenschaftlichung der Geschichtsschreibung zwischen Aufklärung und Historismus" (1982), *Geschichtskultur und Wissenschaft* (1990), 85. As Wilhelm Dilthey, the influential philosopher of the social sciences, who had learned much from Ranke, observed in the 1880s, "When Ranke once remarked he wished to obliterate his self in order to see things as they had been, this beautifully and vigorously expresses the deep longing of the true historian for objective reality." *Einleitung in die Geisteswissenschaften. Versuch einer Grundlegung für das Studium der Gesellschaft und der Geschichte* (1883), 94.

39. Ranke, diary entry, January 1877, *Sämmtliche Werke,* LIII–LIV, 613.

40. "Tagebuchblätter. Allgemeine Bemerkungen, 1831–49," ibid., 569.

41. See Ranke, "Geburtstagsansprache" on the occasion of his ninetieth birthday, December 21, 1885, *Abhandlungen und Versuche. Neue Versuche,* ibid., LI–LII, 592.

42. *Die römischen Päpste in den letzten vier Jahrhunderten* (1834–36), ibid., XXXVII, 64. And see "Einleitung," *Geschichte Wallensteins* (1869), ibid., XXIII, vii–viii.

6. Agendas High and Low

1. Motley, *The Rise of the Dutch Republic,* 3 vols. (1856; ed. 1906), III, 456.

2. Augustin Thierry, "Preface," *Dix ans d'études historiques* (1834), in *Oeuvres d'Aug. Thierry* (1839), 554, 551, 557.

3. Heinrich von Sybel, *Die Begründung des deutschen Reiches durch Wilhelm I,* 7 vols. (1890–94; complete popular ed., 1913), I, x–xi. In his great *Römische Geschichte,* Theodor Mommsen, a political animal to his bones, used modern terms like "Junkers" without yielding an inch to his claims to objectivity.

4. Acton, *Lectures on the French Revolution,* ed. John Neville Figgis and Reginald Vere Laurence (1910), 372.

5. Lionel Gossman, *Between History and Literature* (1990), 96.

6. Gibbon, *Autobiography* (posthumously ed. Lord Sheffield, 1827; rev. ed., Dero A. Saunders, 1961), 134.

7. Lord Acton, *Lectures on the French Revolution,* 360.

8. Lord Acton, "Appendix," ibid., 373.

9. His fellow historians Firth and Gardiner proved to be generous laborers in the seventeenth-century vineyard rather than envious competitors. Both congratulated Bernstein on his discovery. See Peter Gay, *The Dilemma of Democratic Socialism: Eduard Bernstein's Challenge to Marx* (1952), 64–67.

10. For a development of this theme, see Peter Gay, *Style in History* (1974).

11. See Richard Hofstadter, *The Progressive Historians: Turner, Beard, Parrington* (1968), 84.

12. Acton: Letter to Contributors to the Cambridge Modern History, March 12, 1898, *Essays in the Liberal Interpretation of History,* ed. William H. McNeill (1967), 398–99; Leopold von Ranke: to his son Otto, May 25, 1873, in "Erinnerungen an Leopold von Ranke mit bisher ungedruckten Aufzeichnungen desselben," *Gartenlaube,* LI (1895), 874, cited in *Leopold von Ranke: The Secret of World History,* ed. Roger Wines (1981), 259.

13. See Herbert Butterfield, *Man on His Past: The Study of the History of Historical Scholarship* (1955), 63–64.

14. To resort to technical language once more: a psychoanalyst would here speak of these public agencies as so many auxiliary superegos, those internal agents severe with unexamined premises as the source of faulty judgments.

15. Hildreth, *History of the United States,* 6 vols. (1849–52), I, iii.

16. Dr. Arnold was, of course, immortalized in Thomas Hughes's *Tom Brown's Schooldays* and the reminiscences of his adoring pupils.

17. "Preface to the Third Volume of the Edition of Thucydides" (1835), *The Miscellaneous Works of Thomas Arnold, D. D.,* ed. A. P. Stanley (1845; 2nd ed., 1858), 399. "There is, in fact, an ancient and a modern period in the history of every people," he wrote, "the ancient differing, and the modern in many essential points agreeing with that in which we now live. . . . Thucydides and Xenophon, the orators of Athens, and the philosophers, speak a wisdom more applicable to us politically than the wisdom of even our own countrymen who lived in the middle ages." "On the Social Progress of States" (1830), the first appendix to the first volume of his edition of Thucydides, ibid., 108–9.

18. "Markham" was the pseudonym of Elizabeth Penrose. The full title of her greatest success is *A History of England from the First Invasion by the Romans to the End of the Reign of George III* (1823), highly popular and often reprinted.

19. Arnold, "On the Social Progress of States," *Miscellaneous Works*, 111.

20. See Valerie E. Chancellor, *History for Their Masters: Opinion in the English History Textbook, 1800–1914* (1970).

21. Albert Wucher, *Theodor Mommsen. Geschichtsschreibung und Politik* (1956), 204n.

22. As has been properly pointed out, the slogan is a slightly misquoted pair of lines from a poem of 1861, *Deutschlands Beruf,* printed in 1871, by Emanuel Geibel.

23. Oskar Jäger, *Didaktik und Methodik des Geschichtsunterrichts* (1895; 2nd ed., 1905), 3–4; "Patriotismus und Nationalerziehung" (1894), *Erlebtes und Erstrebtes. Reden und Aufsätze* (1907), 101–2. It is worth noting that despite the striking resemblance of this phrasing with Ranke's famous formulations—and Jäger quotes Ranke—he disapproves of what he considers to be Ranke's hidden subjectivity.

24. Determined opponents were in important respects really, literally, conservatives: they wanted to keep the classical curriculum of the *Gymnasium* from being watered down with admixtures of more German literature and modern subjects.

25. See "Vermischtes," *Historische Zeitschrift,* LXXI (1893), 392–94.

26. For an appreciation of Duruy's amalgam of views, see R. D. Anderson, *Education in France, 1848–1870* (1975), 178–80.

27. Lavisse, *L'Enseignement de l'histoire à l'école primaire* (1912), 32, quoted in William R. Keylor, *Academy and Community: The Foundation of the French Historical Profession* (1975), 93.

28. Monod, "Introduction. Du progrès des études historiques en France depuis le XVIe siècle," *Revue historique* I, 1 (January 1876), 38.

FOUR: The Truths of Fiction

1. Toward the Terrible Core

1. Jane Austen, *Northanger Abbey* (1818; ed. Anne Henry Ehrenpreis, 1972; ed. 1985), 58 [ch. 5].

2. Benjamin Disraeli, preface, *Coningsby; or, The New Generation* (1844; 5th ed., 1849).

3. See Fielding, *The History of Tom Jones, a Foundling* (1749; Modern Library ed., n.d.), 2 [bk. 1, ch. 1] Nineteenth-century literary characters, like Isabel Archer, one of Henry James's most appealing invention, too, were "interested in human nature." *The Portrait of a Lady* (1881; ed. 1908; Penguin Classic, ed. Geoffrey Moore, 1986), 118 [ch. 7].

4. Hawthorne: Frederick Crews, *The Sins of the Fathers: Hawthorne's Psychological Themes* (1966), 10–11; Tolstoy: Diary entry, March 17, 1865, *Tolstoy's Diaries,* ed. and tr. R. F. Christian, 2 vols. (1985), I, 182.

5. The more extreme among the Russian formalists suggested that "Tolstoj's passion for minute psychological analysis, for ruthless introspection and discursiveness, was fundamentally a matter of his struggle for a new narrative manner." Victor Erlich, *Russian Formalism: History—Doctrine* (1955; 3rd ed., 1981), 196. In his well-known Clark Lectures of 1927, E. M. Forster aptly summarized this view without endorsing it: "A novel is a work of art, with its own laws, which are not those of daily life . . . a character is real when it lives in accordance with such laws." *Aspects of the Novel* (1927; ed. 1949), 61.

6. Chekhov to A. N. Pleshcheyev, April 9, 1889, Anton Chekhov, *Letters on the Short Story, the Drama, and Other Literary Topics,* sel. and ed. Louis S. Friedland (1924), 15. This was one of his two goals; the other was to "show how far this life falls short of the ideal life." Ibid.

7. In her characteristic *Aus dem Leben meiner alten Freundin* of 1878, Wilhelmine Heimburg, a producer of predictable sentimental tales that subscribers to the German family weekly *Die Gartenlaube* found irresistible, apostrophized her "friendly female readers—*freundliche Leserinnen.*" Heimburg (pseud. Bertha Behrens), *Aus dem Leben meiner alten Freundin* (1878; ed. 1975), 7 [opening page].

8. See Rudolf Schenda, *Volk ohne Buch. Studien zur Sozialgeschichte der populären Lesestoffe, 1770–1910* (1970), 459–60, quotation at 460.

9. Freud, "Der Dichter und das Phantasieren" (1908), *Gesammelte Werke,* ed. Anna Freud et al., 2nd ed., 19 vols. (1952–87), VII, 223, 217; "Creative Writers and Day-Dreaming," *Standard Edition of the Complete Psychological Works of Sigmund Freud,* tr. and ed. James Strachey et al., 24 vols. (1953–74), IX, 153, 147.

2. Regression to Polarities

1. Fritz Langer (pseud. Karl May), "Die Schund- und Giftliteratur und Karl May, ihr unerbittlicher Gegner," *Augsburger Postzeitung,* July 20, 1909, quoted in Jochen Schulte-Sasse, "Karl Mays Amerika-Exotik und deutsche Wirklichkeit. Zur sozialpsychologischen Funktion von Trivialliteratur im wilhelminischen Deutschland," in *Karl May,* ed. Helmut Schmiedt (1983), 117.

2. Otto Ludwig, *Gesammelte Schriften,* ed. Adolf Stern, 6 vols. (1891), III, 168.

3. Grosz, *Ein kleines Ja und ein grosses Nein* (1946; ed. 1955), 12.

4. These defining characteristics resemble the salient traits that Dickens had a few years earlier, in *The Pickwick Papers,* attached to the club members who accompany Mr. Pickwick as he travels in search of human nature: the susceptible Tupman, the poetic Snodgrass, the sporting Winkle.

5. Brüder Grimm, *Kinder und Hausmärchen,* no. 9, "Die zwölf Brüder" (2 vols., 1811–14; 1-vol. 16th ed., 1879), 42; no. 21, "Aschenputtel," ibid., 99.

6. Eugène Sue: *Les Mystères de Paris,* 10 vols. (1842–43), pt. 1, vol. I, 318–46 [ch. 21]; Karl May: *Winnetou, der rote Gentleman* (3 vols., 1893; 1-vol. ed., ed. Roland Schmid, 1960), 255–62.

7. Doyle: see John Bayley, "The Fangs of Fiction," *Times Literary Supplement,* no. 4728 (November 12, 1993), 6; May: *Mein Leben und Streben* (1910), 137; du Maurier's *Trilby:* see Avis Berman, "George du Maurier's *Trilby* Whipped Up a Worldwide Storm." *Smithsonian,* XXIV, 9 (December 1993), 120.

8. Maggie Symington, *Working to Win: A Story for Girls* (3rd ed., n.d.), 444 [ch. 40].

9. This recalls the chapter in *Les Mystères de Paris* that caused some controversy over Rodolphe's order to have a repellent murderer's eyes put out—some thought the punishment excessive, or simply too horrible.

10. Hentz, "The Parlour Serpent," *Godey's Lady's Book,* XXII (January 1841), 26–34. See Peter Gay, *The Bourgeois Experience,* vol. III, *The Cultivation of Hatred* (1993), 309–19. For the idea of an alibi for aggression (a term used quite neutrally), see ibid., 35–127.

11. E. Marlitt (pseud. Eugenie John), *Goldelse* (1867; ed. Michael Koser, 1974), 158–59 [ch. 13].

12. Evelyn Everett-Green, *Dorothy's Vocation* (new ed., 1892), 244 [ch. 17].

13. Sand: to Eugène Sue, ca. April 20, 1843, *Correspondance,* ed. Georges Lubin, 25 vols. (1964–91), VI, 109; Thackeray: [anon.], "Art. XV.—*Les Mystères de Paris. (The Mysteries of Paris).* Par Eugène Sue, 6 vols. Paris 1843," repr. in Helga Grubitzsch, ed., *Materialien zur Kritik des*

Feuilleton-Romans. "Die Geheimnisse von Paris" von Eugène Sue (1977), 240–41, 243.

14. May, *Mein Leben und Streben,* 138.

15. Ibid., 9.

16. On this point see Arno Schmidt, *Sitara und der Weg dorthin. Eine Studie über Wesen, Werk & Wirkung Karl Mays* (1963; repr. 1985), 174–84.

17. See Volker Klotz, "Durch die Wüste und so weiter" (1962; slightly rev. 1982), in *Karl May,* ed. Schmiedt, 90–91.

3. Immediacy

1. Dickens, *The Chimes: A Goblin Story of Some Bells That Rang an Old Year Out and a New Year In* (1845; ed. n.d.), 1.

2. See Tolstoy to Nikolai Nekrasov, September 15, 1852, *Tolstoy's Letters,* sel., ed., and tr. R. F. Christian, 2 vols. (1978), I, 31.

3. As the psychoanalyst Ernst Kris once wrote, in a paper on Shakespeare, "Clinical analysis of creative artists suggests that the life experience of the artist is sometimes only in a limited sense the source of his vision; that his power to imagine conflicts may by far transcend the range of his own experience; or, to put it more accurately, that at least some artists possess the particular gift to generalize from whatever their own experience has been. . . . Some great artists seem to be equally close to several of their characters, and may feel many of them as parts of themselves. The artist has created a world and not indulged in a daydream." "Prince Hal's Conflict," *Psychoanalytic Explorations in Art* (1952; ed. 1964), 288.

4. Chekhov to Alexander Chekhov, April 6, 1886, Chekhov, *Letters on the Short Story, the Drama, and Other Literary Topics,* sel. and ed. Louis S. Friedland (1924), 70; the same to the same, April 1883, ibid., 59.

5. Chekhov to Alexei Suvorin, October 17, 1889, *Letters of Anton Chekhov,* tr. Michael Henry Heim in collaboration with Simon Karlinsky, sel. and ed. by Karlinsky (1973), 149.

6. Chekhov to Suvorin, May 30, 1888, ibid., 104; Chekhov to I. L. Shcheglov, June 9, 1888, *Letters,* ed. Friedland, 8.

7. The Chekhov stories mentioned in this paragraph: sportsman: "Agafya" (1886); eccentric young man: "My Life: A Provincial's Story" (1896); sadistic landowner: "My Wife" (1892); nine-year-old: "The Steppe" (1888); two-year-old: "Grisha" (1886).

8. See Chekhov to Alexei Pleshcheyev, October 9, 1888, *Letters,* ed. Karlinsky, 112.

9. Chekhov to Suvorin, September 8, 1891, ibid., 203.

10. Tolstoy to Nikolai Nekrasov, November 27, 1852, *Tolstoy's Letters,* I, 35.

11. Tolstoy, *Childhood* (1852; tr. Rosemary Edmonds, 1964), 13 [ch. 1].

12. Ibid., 77 [ch. 21].

13. Ibid., 52 [ch. 14].

14. Ibid., 85–96 [chs. 25–27], quotation at 94. For an excellent discussion of this scene, see John Bayley, *Tolstoy and the Novel* (1966; ed. 1968), 83–85.

15. Tolstoy, *Childhood,* 44, 17–18 [chs. 12, 2].

16. Ibid., 25 [ch. 4].

17. Ibid., 13, 37 [chs. 1, 9].

18. The organization of *Dominique* shows once again the infinite flexibility of the novel. It has two narrators: the frame narrator (I shall call him) and the central narrator. The first meets the second, M. Dominique, describes him and his relationship to him in vivid detail, and then listens

to the recital that M. Dominique imposes on his avid listener, to close with some relevant remarks and further conversations between the two.

19. Fromentin, *Dominique* (1863; ed. Daniel Leuwers, 1972), 3 [ch. 1].

20. Stendhal (Henri Bayle), *Vie de Henry Brulard* (published posthumously in 1890), in *Oeuvres intimes,* ed. V. del Lillo, 2 vols. (1981–82), II, 534 [ch. 1].

4. The Strains of Complexity

1. Hawthorne to William Ticknor, January 19, 1855, *The Centenary Edition of the Works of Nathaniel Hawthorne,* ed. William Charvat et al., 20 vols. (1962–88), XVII, 304. See Peter Gay, *The Bourgeois Experience,* vol. III, *The Cultivation of Hatred* (1993), 335.

2. "Your *Boyhood*": Letter to Tolstoy, February 17, 1855, *Tolstoy: The Critical Heritage,* ed. A. V. Knowles (1978), 48; "delicate analysis": anon. [N. G. Chernyshevsky], review of *Childhood, Boyhood,* and *The Military Tales,* in *The Contemporary,* 1856, ibid., 60; "inner movements": V. P. Botkin to A. A. Fet, February 14, 1865, ibid. 89.

3. See ibid., 8–9.

4. G. H. Lewes to Charles Lee Lewes, March 17, 1860, *The George Eliot Letters,* ed. Gordon S. Haight, 9 vols. (1954–78), III, 275.

5. See David Carroll, "Introduction," *George Eliot: The Critical Heritage* (1971), 12, 16, 18–19, 27.

6. Anon., review of *The Mill on the Floss,* in *Saturday Review,* IX (April 14, 1860), 471.

7. Eliot, *Daniel Deronda* (1876; ed. Barbara Hardy, 1967), 321, 202 [chs. 24, 16].

8. On August 9, 1838, he wrote his brother Mikhail, "I have a project: to become insane. Let people rave, let them be treated. . . ." Fyodor Dostoevsky, *Complete Letters,* ed. and tr. David Lowe and Ronald Meyer, 5 vols. (1988–91), I, 41.

9. *Le Dernier Jour d'un condamné,* Hugo's powerful, somber first-person novella about a criminal about to be guillotined, originally published in 1828 and revised in 1830, was a portentous presence for Dostoevsky.

10. In the letter of August 1838 already quoted (see n. 8 above), he told his brother Mikhail, "It seems to me that our world is a purgatory of heavenly Spirits bedimmed by sinful thoughts." *Complete Letters,* I, 39.

11. Some doubts have recently been thrown on the generally accepted account, but, as I note in the text, what matters psychologically is that Dostoevsky thought the rumor to be true. See Joseph Frank, *Dostoevsky: The Seeds of Revolt, 1821–1849* (1976), 85–90, esp. 86–87 n.

12. Irving Howe has aptly generalized this attitude: "In nineteenth-century Russia the usual categories of discourse tend to break down. Politics, religion, literature, philosophy—these do not fall into neat departments of the mind. Pressed together by the Tsarist censorship, ideas acquire an extraordinary concentration; the novel, which in the West is generally regarded as a means of portraying human behavior, acquires the tone and manner of prophetic passion. . . . And that is why, in dealing with the Russian novel, one is obliged to take religion as a branch of politics and politics as a form of religion." *Politics and the Novel* (1957), 51.

13. His psychological extremism was the target of comment early on. "No thanks for these new tellers of fairy tales!" the writer and philanthropist Prince Vladimir Fjodorovich Odoyevsky exclaimed after reading *The Double.* "Instead of writing something useful, agreeable, and heartwarming, they only sniff around in the most secret secrets in the world and drag everything into the light of day." Quoted in introduction, *Der Doppelgänger. Frühe Romane und Erzählungen,* in Dostoevsky,

Sämtliche Werke, 10 vols., ed. and tr. E. K. Rahsin (1952; ed. 1977–80), I, 1.

14. Chekhov, with his horror of overstatement, had his reservations about them; he thought Dostoevsky an important writer but indiscreet and pretentious. See Chekhov to Suvorin, March 5, 1889, *Letters on the Short Story, the Drama, and Other Literary Topics,* sel. and ed. Louis S. Friedland (1924), 234.

15. Dostoevsky to Strachov, February 26 [March 10], 1869, cited in Donald Fanger, *Dostoevsky and Romantic Realism: A Study of Dostoevsky in Relation to Balzac, Dickens, and Gogol* (1965), 215.

16. Dostoevsky, *The Possessed* (1871; tr. Michael R. Katz, ed. 1992), 754 ["Conclusion"].

17. Dostoevsky, *Diary of a Writer* (November 1877), tr. and ed. Boris Brasol, 2 vols. (1954), II, 883.

18. Nietzsche, *Götzen-Dämmerung. Oder wie man mit einem Hammer philosophiert* (1889), in *Werke,* ed. Karl Schlechta, 3 vols. (1966; 6th ed., 1969), III, 467.

19. Entry for February 14, 1895, *The Notebooks of Henry James,* ed. F. O. Matthiessen and Kenneth B. Murdock (1947), 187.

20. Entry for May 8, 1892, *Notebooks,* 119–20.

21. Entry for May 12, 1889, ibid., 99; undated entry [end of 1881, early 1882], ibid., 37.

22. Entry for February 3, 1894, ibid., 148; undated entry [probably end of 1882], ibid., 45; entry for July 13, 1891, ibid., 106.

23. A little treatise could be written on James's use of the words "vulgar" or "vulgarity." It crowds his diary entries, his letters, and his novels as the cardinal sin of cardinal sins.

24. Entry for November 25, 1881, *Notebooks,* 28.

25. Oscar Wilde to Robert Ross [?January 12, 1899], *The Letters of Oscar Wilde,* ed. Rupert Hart-Davis (1962), 776.

26. Bennett: Jacob Tonson [pseud.], *New Age,* n.s., VII (October 1910), 614, quoted in *Henry James: The Critical Heritage,* ed. Roger Gard (1968), 489.

27. Contemplating "Lady Barberina," for example, he found that he must make her marriage to a poor but handsome Protestant minister "seem natural and possible." Entry for May 17, 1883, *Notebooks,* 50; and see ibid., 6, 17, 50, 59.

28. "Preface," *The Ambassadors* (1903; New York ed., 1909; Norton Critical Edition, ed. S. P. Rosenbaum, 1964), 4.

29. Henry James, review of Dickens, *Our Mutual Friend,* (1865), *The Nation,* December 21, 1865, in *The Critical Muse: Selected Literary Criticism,* ed. Roger Gard (1987), 50, 53, 50.

30. Entry for March 11, 1888, *Notebooks,* 88.

31. *The Wings of the Dove* (1902; New York ed., 1908; ed. John Bayley with notes by Patricia Crick, 1986), 399 [bk. 9, ch. 1].

32. Ibid., 508–9 [bk. 10, ch. 6].

33. James came to criticize these pages as too long-drawn-out, but for once his second thoughts were inferior to his first.

5. Dickens

1. Henry James, *"Our Mutual Friend,* by Charles Dickens" (1865), in *The Critical Muse: Selected Literary Criticism,* ed. Roger Gard (1987), 52.

2. In 1837, near the beginning of a meteoric career, when Dickens had the *Sketches by Boz,* the triumphant *Pickwick Papers,* and *Oliver Twist* to his credit, G. H. Lewes established the pattern: Dickens, he wrote, delighted "the young and old, the grave and gay, the witty, the intellectual, the

moralist, and the thoughtless of both sexes in the reading circles, from the peer and judge to the merchant's clerk," and beyond that, "the common people, both in town and country." [G. H. Lewes], review of *Sketches by Boz, The Pickwick Papers,* and *Oliver Twist,* in *National Magazine and Monthly Critic,* I (1837), 445, in *Dickens: The Critical Heritage,* ed. Philip Collins (1971), 64.

3. [Margaret Oliphant], "Charles Dickens," *Blackwood's Edinburgh Magazine,* LXXVII (April 1855), 451.

4. Forster, *The Life of Charles Dickens,* 3 vols. (1872–74; ed. Andrew Lang, 2 vols., n.d.), I, 347. Little David Copperfield wonders, after his widowed mother has married the dreadful Murdstone and he has been sent off with his beloved nurse Peggotty, whether she might not have been "employed to lose me like the boy in the fairy tale." *David Copperfield* (1849–50; ed. Trevor Blount, 1966), 76 [ch. 2]. Such reminiscences are frequent in his work.

5. Dickens, speech in Boston, February 1, 1842, *The Speeches of Dickens,* ed. K. J. Fielding (1960), 19.

6. "good observer": [Forster], review of *Sketches by Boz,* in *Examiner,* XXVIII (February 1836), 132; "faithful to actual experience": [anon.], "Some Thoughts on Arch-Waggery, and in especial, on the Genius of 'Boz,' " *Court Magazine and Monthly Critic,* X (April 1837), 187. Two years later, another reviewer, Richard Ford, reinforced this growing consensus, though not without certain reservations: "he deals truly with human nature." [Ford], review of *Oliver Twist,* in *Quarterly Review,* LXIV (June 1839), 91. John Forster praised Dickens's work as early as 1837, even before the two men had met, for showing "real life and human nature": [Forster], review of *Pickwick Papers,* no. XV, in *Examiner* (July 2, 1837), 422. Others quite early, though praising Dickens for presenting "living creatures," criticized the improbability of his plots. See [anon.], "Boz's *Oliver Twist,*" *Spectator,* XI (November 24, 1838), 1115.

7. [E. B. Hamley], "Remonstrance with Dickens," *Blackwood's Edinburgh Magazine,* LXXXI (April 1857), 503.

8. "pursued by the child": Dickens to John Forster, November 3, 1840, *The Letters of Charles Dickens,* Pilgrim Edition, vol. II, *1840–1841,* ed. Madeline House and Graham Storey (1969), 144; "melancholy": Dickens to the same, January [17?], 1841, ibid., 188; "Nellicide": Dickens to Richard Monckton Milnes, March 10, 1841, ibid., 228.

9. Forster to Dickens, January 16, 1841, ibid., 187n. Another of Dickens's intimates, the actor and theater manager William Macready, told him that he was so affected by this "beautiful fiction" that he "could not weep for some time." Macready to Dickens, January 22, 1841, ibid., 192n. (Macready was mourning the recent death of a daughter of his own.)

10. See George H. Ford, *Dickens and His Readers: Aspects of Novel Criticism since 1836* (1955; ed. 1965), 56–59; Jeffrey to Dickens, January 31, 1847, and March 16 or 17, 1841, quoted in Forster, *Life of Dickens,* II, 41–42 n; I, 168.

11. "Who has not laughed at Mr Pickwick and Sam Weller; or cried over Little Nell and Paul Dombey," asked a journalist in London on June 10, 1870. [Anon.], "The Death of Mr Charles Dickens," *Daily News,* June 10, 1870, p. 5, in *Dickens, Critical Heritage,* 504.

12. George Stott, "Charles Dickens," *Contemporary Review,* X (January 1869), 221.

13. Lewes: "Dickens in Relation to Criticism" (review of John Forster, *Life of Dickens,* vol. I), in *Fortnightly Review,* n.s., XI (February 1872), 154; [Howells]: review of Forster, *Life of Dickens,* vol. II, in *Atlantic Monthly,* XXXI (February 1873), 238; Wilde: in conversation with Ada Leverson, quoted in Richard Ellmann, *Oscar Wilde* (1988), 469.

14. Trollope, *An Autobiography* (1883; World's Classics ed., 1953), 212–13 [ch. 13].

15. Forster, *Life of Dickens,* I, 133–34.

16. Bagehot, "Charles Dickens" (1858), in *Literary Studies,* 3 vols. (1895; ed. 1910), II, 154–55.

17. Tolstoy to James Ley, January 21 [February 3], 1904 (in English), *Tolstoy's Letters,* sel., ed., and tr. R. F. Christian, 2 vols. (1978), II, 637.

18. Freud to Fliess, October 15, 1897, *Sigmund Freuds Briefe an Wilhelm Fliess, 1887–1904,* ed. Jeffrey Moussaieff Masson, German edition Michael Schröter (1986), 291.

19. "George Silverman's Explanation" (1868), *Charles Dickens: Selected Short Fiction,* ed. Deborah A. Thomas (1976), 380. And consider, among other murderers, described in melodramatic, at times psychologically astute detail, Bill Sikes in *Oliver Twist* (1838), Jonas Chuzzlewit in *Martin Chuzzlewit* (1843), to say nothing of John Jasper in the posthumous *Edwin Drood* (1870).

20. "If you sift the world's prose literature, Dickens will remain," Tolstoy wrote. "Sift Dickens, *David Copperfield* will remain; sift *David Copperfield,* the description of the storm at sea will remain." *Dickens, Critical Heritage,* 242.

21. Arnold, "The Incompatibles," *Nineteenth Century,* IX (June 1881), 1035–39 passim. See also Peter Gay, *The Bourgeois Experience,* vol. II, *The Tender Passion* (1986), 148.

22. Dickens to Forster, July 10, 1849, *Letters,* vol. V, *1847–1849,* ed. Graham Storey and K. J. Fielding (1981), 569.

23. See esp. Fred Kaplan, *Dickens: A Biography* (1988), 250–56.

24. Forster, *Life of Dickens,* I, 26; *David Copperfield,* 210 [ch. 11].

25. George H. Ford compiled a similar list, but instead of the oedipal pairing stresses Dickens's preoccupation with orphans. See Ford, "Introduction" to *David Copperfield,* repr. in *The Dickens Critics,* ed. Ford and Lauriat Lane, Jr. (1961), 352–58. Certainly in Victorian England, as in other countries, many families were indeed incomplete. But obviously the point I am making in the text is quite different.

26. Forster: *Life of Dickens,* II, 133; [Hutton]: "Mr. Dickens's Moral Services to Literature," *Spectator,* XLII, pt. 1 (April 17, 1869), 475.

27. *David Copperfield,* 838–39, 916, 950 [chs. 53, 60, 64].

28. Strictly speaking, Agnes had company in the murder: her mother's stern father, who had repudiated his daughter for marrying Wickfield and broken her heart. But one can hardly expect a small child to make such fine distinctions.

29. *Dealings with the Firm Dombey and Son, Wholesale, Retail, and for Exportation* (1848; ed. H. W. Garrod, 1950), 713 [ch. 50].

30. *David Copperfield,* 429–30 [ch. 25].

FIVE: Images of the Mind

1. Ego

1. See Lovis Corinth, *Selbstbiographie* (1926), 167, and Charlotte Berend-Corinth, *Die Gemälde von Lovis Corinth. Werkkatalog* (1958), 181.

2. Charlotte Berend-Corinth, his pupil, model, loyal wife, and inconsolable widow, confirms that her husband's self-portraits were "very serious and critical encounters with his own ego." Charlotte Berend-Corinth, quoted in Joachim Heusinger von Waldegg, "Tradition and Actualität. Über Corinths Selbstbildnisse und einige andere Motive," *Lovis Corinth, 1858–1925,* catalog ed. Zdenek Felix (1985), 60. She was given to melodramatic overstatement, but her account is amply documented not only in Corinth's autobiography but also in canvases in which he seems to be barely in control of some suppressed fury.

3. A reviewer of his work in the *Augsburger Allgemeine Zeitung* thought that Graff painted "not the body but the spirit," and his father-in-law, the aesthetician Johann Georg Sulzer, noted that Graff's subjects could "hardly bear the sharp and sensitive glances he threw at them, since each seemed to penetrate to the interior of the soul." See Ekhart Berckenhagen, *Anton Graff. Leben und Werk,* a catalogue raisonné (1967), 16.

4. Courbet to Alfred Bruyas, May 3, 1854, in *Letters of Gustave Courbet,* ed. and tr. Petra ten-Doesschate Chu (1992), 122.

5. "Biografia de D. Francisco Goya, pintor," *El Artista,* II (1835), 253–55, quoted in Enriqueta Harris, *Goya* (1969), 27.

6. "Äusserung bei Betrachtung einer Sammlung von Gemälden von größtenteils noch lebenden und unlängst verstorbenen Künstlern" (ca. 1830), *Caspar David Friedrich in Briefen und Bekenntnissen,* ed. Sigrid Hinz (1968; 2nd ed., 1984), 101.

7. Courbet to Bruyas, November–December 1854, *Letters,* 131–33, quotations at 132.

8. Manuel Gasser, *Self-portraits: From the Fifteenth Century to the Present Day* (1961; tr. Angus Malcolm, 1963), 148–51, illustration at 149, quotation at 151.

9. Vincent van Gogh to his brother Théodore, September 1889, *The Complete Letters of Vincent van Gogh,* 3 vols. (1958), III, 201.

10. One need only recall Edouard Manet's self-portrait with its fuzzy active hand to appreciate the difficulty.

11. See Basil Taylor, *Constable: Paintings, Drawings and Watercolors* (1973), 42. In his letters and lectures, the openly religious comments are rare. Thus he said of Poussin, whose penetrating and studious gaze he valued, "His landscape is full of religious & moral feeling, & shows how much of his own nature God has implanted in the mind of man." Ibid., 228.

12. Constable, *John Constable's Discourses,* ed. R. B. Beckett (1970), 57.

13. Louis L. Noble, *The Life and Works of Thomas Cole* (1852; ed. Eliot S. Vesell, 1964), 59; Cole to Daniel Wadsworth, *The Correspondence of Thomas Cole and Daniel Wadsworth,* ed. J. Bard McNulty (1983), 71. Both are quoted in Franklin Kelly, "A Passion for Landscape: The Paintings of Frederic Edwin Church," in Kelly, with Stephen Jay Gould, James Anthony Ryan, and Debora Rindge, *Frederic Edwin Church* (1989), 34.

14. "*Metaphysikus* with the brush." See Joseph Leo Koerner, *Caspar David Friedrich and the Subject of Landscape* (1990), 95.

15. See (though ideologically oversimplified) Klaus Wolbert, "III A, 'Deutsche Innerlichkeit.' Die Wiederentdeckung im deutschen Imperialismus," *Caspar David Friedrich und die deutsche Nachwelt,* ed. Werner Hofmann (1974), 34–55.

16. Caspar David Friedrich to Louise Seidler, May 9 (1815), *Friedrich in Briefen und Bekenntnissen,* 27.

17. "Äusserung," ibid., 88, 90.

18. Unpublished segment from "Äusserung," ibid., 118; ibid., 88, 89.

19. Caspar David Friedrich to Friedrich August Köthe, August 18, 1810, *Caspar David Friedrich—Unbekannte Dokumente seines Lebens,* ed. Karl-Ludwig Hoch (1985), 40.

20. Millet to Théodore Pelloquet, June 2, 1863, quoted in Jean Bouret, *The Barbizon School and 19th Century French Landscape Painting* (1972; tr. 1973), 14.

2. Icons to Dream By

1. Franken, *Handbuch des guten Tones und der feinen Sitten* (23rd improved ed., 1900; ed. 1977), 50.

2. H. Beta, "Moderne Kunstindustrie," *Gartenlaube*, XXII (1874), 521.

3. Mme G. Schéfer and Mme Sophie Amis, *Travaux manuels et économie domestique à l'usage des jeunes filles* (1885), 20–22.

4. Gautier: Robert L. Herbert et al., *Jean-François Millet* (1976), 73; Thoré: see [Théophile Thoré], *Salons de W. Bürger, 1861 à 1868*, 2 vols. (1870), I, 3–6, 35–36 (Salon de 1861); 369–70, 382–83, ibid. (Salon de 1863).

5. Millet to Thoré, February 18, 1862, quoted in Herbert, *Jean-François Millet*, 196.

6. "L'Alcove de l'Angelus," *Prosopopées*, V, 9 (November 1982), an "erratic" publication of the Académie de Muséologue Evocatoire, ed. Jennifer Gough-Cooper and Jacques Caumont.

7. See esp. anon. [E. Bénézit-Constant], *Le Livre d'or de J.-F. Millet par un ancien ami* (n.d.; 1891), 147, 153.

8. "Apostle" and "evangelist": Wesley Reid Davis, "The Angelus," *Brooklyn Daily Eagle*, November 18, 1889, quoted in Laura L. Meixner, "Popular Criticism of Jean-François Millet in Nineteenth-Century America," *Art Bulletin*, LXV, 1 (March 1983), 94; "rays of grace": Rev. George McDermot, "Markham: Mischievous Pessimist," *Catholic World*, LXIX (1889), 692, ibid., 104; "sky": Edward A. Steiner, "The Woman of the Angelus," *Woman's Home Companion*, XXVI (1889), 4, ibid.

9. See Léonce Bénédite, introduction, *The Drawings of Jean François Millet with Fifty Facsimile Reproductions of the Master's Work* (1906), 35–36; Albert Dresdner, *Der Weg der Kunst* (1904), 81.

10. Servaes: see "Böcklin," *Praeludien. Ein Essaybuch* (1899), 235; Harden: "Böcklin," *Köpfe*, 4 vols. (1910–24; 12th ed., 1910), I, 328. "Böcklin owes his final 'Beautify-Your-Home' success," Hugo von Tschudi wrote in 1889, "simply to the poetic motifs of his pictures." Tschudi, "Die Werke Arnold Böcklins (16. Januar 1901) in der kgl. Nationalgalerie zu Berlin," *Die Kunst*, V (1902), 204.

11. The next and concluding volume of this series on the bourgeois experience will take up what has been called—far too simply—the great civil war between the presumably rebellious avant-garde and the presumably conventional middle classes. It is a complicated and a fascinating story.

12. Harden, "Böcklin," 316.

13. Von Ostini, *Arnold Böcklin* (1904), 3.

14. See Franz Zelger, *Arnold Böcklin. Die Toteninsel. Selbstheroisierung und Abgesang der abendländischen Kultur* (1991), 20–21, 42–43.

15. Meissner, *Arnold Böcklin* (1899), 110.

16. Ibid., 62.

17. See Margot Bryner-Beader, *Arnold Böcklins Stellung zum Portrait* (1952), 10, 65–66; Ludwig Justi, *Von Runge bis Thoma* (1932), 166.

18. See Freud, *The Interpretation of Dreams*, in *The Standard Edition of the Complete Psychological Works*, tr. and ed. James Strachey et al., 24 vols. (1953–74), IV, 166.

19. "Elegy": Meissner, *Arnold Böcklin*, 91; "solitude": Heinrich Wölfflin, "Arnold Böcklin," *Kleine Schriften* (1946), 116; "forlornness": *Arnold Böcklin. Aus den Tagebüchern von Otto Lasius (1884–1889)*, ed. Maria Lina Lasius (1903), 86; "admiration": Leixner, "Landschaftsmalerei," *Kunstwart*, III (1888–89), 51.

20. Jürgen Wissmann, *Arnold Böcklin und das Nachleben seiner Malerei. Studien zur Kunst der Jahrhundertwende* (1968), passim.

21. Ostini had championed Böcklin for years, and celebrated him in the 1890s with a long, well-illustrated article, neglecting neither the *Selbstportrait mit dem fiedelden Tod* nor the *Toteninsel,* in the popular German monthly *Velhagen & Klasings Monatshefte.* "We stand at the beginning of an era that will idolize Arnold Böcklin—more: that will understand him." *Böcklin,* 1.

22. See Henry Thode, *Böcklin und Thoma. Acht Vorträge über neudeutsche Malerei* (1905), 3.

23. Johannes Mankopft, *Kunst und Religion,* quoted in Kenworth Moffett, *Meier-Graefe as Art Critic* (1973), 54; Hans Rosenhagen, *Würdigungen* (1902), ibid., 81.

24. Gustav Floerke, *Arnold Böcklin und seine Kunst. Aufzeichnungen* (1901; 3rd ed., 1921), 164.

3. Teutonic Mirrors

1. Friedrich Schlegel, "Allgemeine Grundsätze über die Malerkunst" (1803), *Schriften und Fragmente. Ein Gesamtbild seines Geistes,* ed. Ernst Behler (1956), 140.

2. As a sign of the cosmopolitanism of the group on which I have commented, Overbeck has right next to the title page of Scriptures a drawing of a young woman in classical garb.

3. Friedrich: "Aphorismen über Kunst und Leben," *Caspar David Friedrich in Briefen und Bekenntnissen,* ed. Sigrid Hinz (1968; 2nd ed., 1984), 84.

4. Otto Julius Bierbaum, *Hans Thoma* (1904), 6, 38; Henry Thode, *Thoma. Des Meisters Gemälde in 874 Abbildungen* (1909), XV, LI.

5. Gustav Floerke, *Arnold Böcklin und seine Kunst. Aufzeichnungen* (1901; 3rd ed., 1921), 80.

6. Interestingly enough, in this portrait, just as in Böcklin's self-portrait with fiddling death, the skeleton seems to have been a later addition. See Karl Voll, *Führer durch die Alte Pinakothek* (1908), 96.

7. Ponten, *Alfred Rethel. Des Meisters Werke in 300 Abbildungen* (1911), XLVIII, XLVII.

8. Max Schmid, *Klinger* (1899; 2nd ed., 1901), 89, 92.

9. Wackenroder: *Herzergiessungen eines kunstliebenden Klosterbruders* (1797), in *Sämtliche Schriften* (1968), 48, 47. At the turn of the century, August Wilhelm Schlegel endorsed this generous vision. One should appreciate German excellence, "not merely because it is German, but far more because it is excellent." "Fragment 178," *Athenäum,* I, 2 (1798), 46.

10. The Catholic romantic Otto Heinrich Graf von Loeben, writing to Friedrich de la Motte Fouqué, November 27, 1812, spoke for more than reactionary Germans. See *Dürer und die Nachwelt. Urkunden, Briefe, Dichtungen und wissenschaftliche Betrachtungen aus vier Jahrhunderten,* ed. Heinz Lüdecke and Susanne Heiland (1955), 165. And see Herman Grimm in 1866, in an essay that reads like a eulogy: although Dürer had long been a favorite among his compatriots, his deserved fame, which "raises him so high, and embraces the man as a whole," was of "relatively recent date." *Albrecht Dürer* (1866), 6.

11. Triumph of inwardness: "The nature of the inner man may secure the upper hand against the unreliability, the accidents of the outer man." Bettina von Arnim to Goethe, June 16, 1809, *Briefe von und an Goethe,* ed. Karl Robert Mandelkow, 6 vols. (1962–69; 3rd and 4th eds., 1988), II, 13; "genuinely German spirit": Waagen, *Handbuch der Geschichte der Malerei,* vol. I, *Die deutschen und niederländischen Malerschulen* (1862), 201. "And Dürer's own picture with his abundance of black, long, much curled, fine locks!" exclaimed the poet August Graf von Platen, known for poetic effusions even in his prose, in his diary in 1820. "What a genius in these traits! How great a seriousness in these eyes, in which piety and high soul and poetry are paired!" Diary entry, March

27, 1820, *Die Tagebücher des Grafen August von Platen,* ed. Georg von Laubmann and Ludwig von Scheffler, 2 vols. (1896–1900), II, 382. Five year later, Max Procop von Freyberg-Eisenberg, historian, politician, and archivist, experienced the same painting with the same emotions. "In Dürer's expression there is something melancholy, infinitely deep and significant, penetrating and earnest at work." His "expression of steadfastness and genuineness of mind and feeling, of the strictest fidelity and uprightness and an unshakable reliability necessarily win our whole heart." "Dritter Kunst-Abend. Albrecht Dürer," *Orpheus, eine Zeitschrift in zwanglosen Heften,* no. 4 (1825), ibid., 181–82.

12. No worthy rival: Ernst Heinrich Tölken, professor of art at Berlin University, festive speech on April 18, 1828, in Berlin's Singakademie, *Dürer und die Nachwelt,* 209; cantata: ("Wer hat des Geistes inn'res Leben / Im Menschenangesicht verklärt wie du? / Des frommen Herzens leises Beben, / Des Seelenfriedens göttlich heitre Ruh?"), ibid., 212; Mendelssohn: ibid., 209.

13. When, in 1840, at carnival time, the artists of Munich—the city where Dürer's best-known self-portrait had finally settled—held a masked parade, they made no room for Italy. Rather, they depicted two aspects of German life during the Reformation, one of them embodied by Dürer, representing "peaceful and middle-class life." Predictably the artist in the role of the painter, with his long locks, vividly reminded the public of the 1500 self-portrait. Rudolf Marggraff, "Gedenk-buch," ibid., 213–14. For the same sort of hero worship from an Englishwoman (she even calls Dürer, in the most purple Carlylean prose, a hero), see the substantial biography by Mrs. Charles Heaton, *The History of the Life of Albrecht Dürer of Nürmberg* (1870; 2nd ed., 1881).

14. Grimm, *Dürer,* 5, 46, 21–22. The painter Hans Thoma singled out Dürer for revealing his vocation to him in a blinding flash. He had experienced a veritable conversion to art: "Awakened by Dürer, I saw that every blade of grass, every stone is full of expression, and that for painting there is nothing insignificant in nature. Only open your eyes, and everything is beautiful." Bier-baum, *Thoma,* 14.

15. See Jane Campbell Hutchinson, *Albrecht Dürer: A Biography* (1990), 197.

16. Moriz Thausing: *Dürer. Geschichte seines Lebens und seiner Kunst* (1876), 355, 140, 355; Grimm: *Dürer,* 38; Cosima Wagner: diary, February 11, 1869, *Die Tagebücher,* ed. Martin Gregor-Dellin and Dietrich Mack, 2 vols. (1976), I, 54.

17. Speaking of Julius Langbehn, the anonymous author of *Rembrandt als Erzieher* (1890), Brandes writes, "For the author, Rembrandt, as a Dutchman, is a lower German, and is, so to speak, spiritually annexed." "Rembrandt als Erzieher," *Freie Bühne,* I (May 7, 1890), 391.

18. Fromentin, *Les Maîtres d'autrefois* (1876; 9th ed., 1898), 413, 408.

19. Georg Fuchs, "Rembrandt und die Geburt der neuen malerischen Form," *Deutsche Form* (1906; 2nd ed., 1907), v, 48.

20. Fromentin, *Les Maîtres d'autrefois,* 398. It would be unjust to confine such rhapsodies to Germans. In 1863, the prolific and ubiquitous French writer Arsène Houssaye, to give but one instance, compared Rembrandt to Shakespeare: he was a "philosophical painter" and "a somber, strange, daring, bizarre, romantic poet." Théophile Gautier, Arsène Houssaye, and Paul de Saint-Victor, *Les Dieux et les demi-dieux de la peinture* (1893), 243, 260.

21. One of his devotees, John W. Mollett, contemplating Rembrandt's "splendid" late self-portrait in Rouen, saw it as "Rembrandt's farewell! His face is wrinkled across and across by time and care, but it is no gloomy misanthrope crushed by evil fortune whom we see, but the man who opposed to all fortunes the talisman of Labour, and thus paints the secret of his life in his final portrait of himself, in the midst of his work, scorning destiny." *Rembrandt* (1879), 76–77. This

book by an Englishman working in France was derived, as the author admits, from Carel Vos-maer's famous Rembrandt biography of 1868. Since the precise corpus of authentic Rembrandts remains a matter of lively controversy to this day—as I write, the Rembrandt Research Project is still reevaluating pictures attributed to the master—the exact number of his self-portraits in oils, etchings, and drawings must remain uncertain. But seventy-five is a minimum.

22. "Virtually," because we have one statement recording his intention to capture "die meeste ende die naetureelste beweechgelickheyt." This may mean (and the debate continues to rage) that he wanted either to capture, with "beweechgelickheyt," inward emotion or outward motion. Those who opt for the former can build a certain case in behalf of Rembrandt's conscious desire to render inner life visible on the etcher's plate or on canvas.

23. Vosmaer, *Rembrandt Harmens van Rijn. Sa vie et ses oeuvres* (1868), 396.

24. The French, too, as we have seen, joined the club of Rembrandt worshipers. "All the sentiments of humanity, all the actions and all ages of life, all the passions of the heart, all the conditions of the soul," wrote the critic Charles Blanc, "are expressed by Rembrandt in decisive, profound, brilliant, inimitable, and indelible strokes: delicate love and brutal love, paternal and maternal tenderness, the games and the gluttony of children, the passion of the hunt, the voluptu-ous idleness of contemplatives. . . ." *L'Oeuvre complet de Rembrandt* (1877), 2–3.

25. Goethe: "Aus Goethes Brieftasche" (1776), *Werke, Kommentare und Register,* ed. Erich Trunz et al., 14 vols. (1948–60; 6th to 12th ed., 1981–86), XII, 25. "After Rembrandt died," the popular art historian Adolf Rosenberg observed in 1911, his "sun seems to have almost set; during the eighteenth century, he was not highly esteemed." Indeed, "to mention his name by the side of Raphael would have appeared to be high treason." *Lenbach* (1911), 6. (Rosenberg was scarcely consistent. In an earlier monograph virtually identical with the text from which I have just quoted, he wrote, "Rembrandt's sun still illuminated the whole eighteenth century. Then it set com-pletely, as the French and the English made a quite opposed pictorial style fashionable." *Lenbach* [1898], 8.)

26. Freytag: A. Krüger, *Der junge Raabe* (1911), 54. Two decades later, in 1882, Alfred Licht-wark, connoisseur and art historian soon to be appointed director of Hamburg's Kunsthalle, confided to his mother, a cherished correspondent, that he was finding Rembrandt even more rewarding than Dürer. "Life has never been so powerfully seized by anyone before him and after him, at least not by a painter. Shakespeare is the only one to compare with him." Lichtwark to his mother, end of January 1882, *Alfred Lichtwarks Briefe an seine Familie, 1875–1913,* ed. Carl Schellen-berg (1972), 238.

27. Charlotte Berend-Corinth, "Vorwort," Lovis Corinth, *Selbstbiographie* (1926).

28. Commenting shortly after its publication, the cultivated German sculptor Adolf von Hilde-brand offered an ambivalent reaction: "Along with good ideas," he wrote a friend, "crazy, too." Hildebrand to Conrad Fiedler, January 23, 1890, *Adolf von Hildebrands Briefwechsel mit Conrad Fiedler,* ed. Günther Jachmann (n.d.), 294.

29. [Julius Langbehn], *Rembrandt als Erzieher, von einem Deutschen* (1890), 329, 26, 24, 162, 328.

30. Ibid., 21.

31. Albert Dresdner, *Der Weg der Kunst* (1904), 333–34.

32. Richter: diary entry, November 13, 1824, *Lebenserinnerungen eines deutschen Malers. Selbstbio-graphie nebst Tagebuchniederschriften und Briefen,* ed. Heinrich Richter (1885; 2nd ed., 1886), 363, 304–5.

33. William Vaughan, *German Romanticism and English Art* (1979), 63.

34. Nietzsche, *Jenseits von Gut und Böse. Vorspiel einer Philosophie der Zukunft* (1886), in *Werke,* ed. Karl Schlechta, 3 vols. (1966; 6th ed., 1969), III, 156 [par. 244].

SIX: The Common Touch

1. The Spirit of the Letter

1. See William Mills Todd III, *The Familiar Letter as a Literary Genre in the Age of Pushkin* (1976), 19, and W. H. Irving, *The Providence of Wit in the English Letter Writers* (1955), 44.

2. See Gellert, *Briefe, nebst einer praktischen Abhandlung von dem guten Geschmacke in Briefen* (1751).

3. Steinhausen: *Geschichte des deutschen Briefes. Zur Kulturgeschichte des deutschen Volkes,* 2 vols. continuously paginated (1889–91), II, 245, 302, 287 (2), 263; Austen: Jane Austen to Cassandra, January 3, 1801, *Selected Letters, 1796–1817,* ed. H. W. Chapman (1955; ed. 1985), 45.

4. Novalis, *Blüthenstaubfragment* no. 56, *Werke, Tagebücher und Briefe Friedrich von Hardenbergs,* ed. Hans-Joachim Mähl and Richard Samuel, 2 vols. (1978), II, 249.

5. Byron to John Cam Hobhouse and Douglas Kinnaird, January 19, 1819, *Byron's Letters and Journals,* ed. Leslie A. Marchand, 12 vols. (1973–82), VI, 92; Byron to [Mary Shelley], November 14, 1822, ibid., X, 32.

6. Achim von Arnim to Bettina von Arnim, September 26–27, 1815, *Achim und Bettina in ihren Briefen. Briefwechsel Achim von Arnim und Bettina Brentano,* ed. Werner Vordtriede, 2 vols. (1961), I, 21; Bettina von Arnim to Achim von Arnim [October 1815], ibid., 25; the same to the same, [probably beginning of 1815], ibid., 18; Achim von Arnim to Bettina von Arnim, March 2, 1818, ibid., 102; Bettina von Arnim to Achim von Arnim [ca. fall 1815], ibid., 36.

7. Stendhal to Prosper Mérimée, December 26, 1829, *Correspondance de Stendhal (1800–1842),* ed. Ad. Paupe and P. A. Cheramy, 3 vols. (1908), II, 508; the same to the same, December 23, 1826, ibid., 447.

8. Calvin Stowe to Harriet Beecher Stowe, February 14, 1847, quoted in Joan D. Hedrick, *Harriet Beecher Stowe: A Life* (1994), 180.

9. One favorite example is the substantial two-volume English offering *Love Letters of Famous Men and Women of the Past and Present Century,* ed. J. T. Merydew (1888); another, from Germany, *Dreihundert Briefe aus zwei Jahrhunderten,* ed. Karl von Holtei, 2 vols. (1872).

10. Hamerton, "Etty" (1875), *Portfolio Papers* (1889), 39.

11. [Eleanor C. H. Smyth], *Sir Rowland Hill: The Story of a Great Reform Told by His Daughter* (1907), 51.

12. Harriet Martineau, *A History of the Thirty Years' Peace, A. D. 1815–1846,* 4 vols. (1849; ed. 1878), IV, 12.

13. [Smyth], *Sir Rowland Hill,* 105.

14. See M. J. Daunton, *Royal Mail: The Post Office since 1840* (1985), 79–80.

15. Sir Rowland Hill, *Post Office Reform: Its Importance and Practicability* (1837), 67.

16. John Morley, *The Life of William Ewart Gladstone,* 3 vols. (1903), II, 57.

17. Catherine to Joseph Huntington, July 16, 1845, Selden Huntington Family Papers, box 3, Yale, Manuscripts and Archives.

18. Heinrich Kube, *Grosser deutscher Muster-Briefsteller* (1897), v.

19. J. D. Luddon to Joseph Huntington, April 25, 1843, Huntington Papers, box 3, Yale, Manuscripts and Archives.

20. See Todd, *Familiar Letter,* 204.

21. See among many others, entries for July 29, September 8, and September 10, 1886, Huntington Papers, box 1, Yale, Manuscripts and Archives.

22. Meyer Keyserling to Bertha Philippson, February 4, 1861, Meyer Keyserling Collection, AR 2004, Leo Baeck Institute (henceforth LBI), New York.

23. February 5, 1861, ibid.

24. Nanny Herzberg to Adolph Koritzer, May 20, 1856, Hanna de Mieses Collection, AR 4644, BII, LBI, New York.

25. Pauline Wengeroff, *Memoiren einer Grossmutter,* 2 vols. (1908–10; 2nd ed., 2 vols. in 1, 1913), II, 51–52. (In this autobiography, Wengeroff transliterated and annotated this letter written in Yiddish.)

26. Ulrich Levysohn to Clara Herrmann, August 16, 18[76], Clara Levysohn Collection, I, AR B. 377/3778, LBI, New York.

27. Marcus Pflaum to Emilie Hoeter, June 11, 1833; Emilie Hoeter to Marcus Pflaum, June 12, 1833; Marcus Pflaum to Emilie Hoeter, June 18, 1833, Mieses Collection, CI, LBI, New York.

28. Richard Cary Morse to his wife, August 23, 1849, Morse Family Papers, box 20, Yale, Manuscripts and Archives.

29. Mazzini and Macaulay: quoted in Denis Mack Smith, *Mazzini* (1994), 42–43; Carlyle: "To the Editor of the Times," written June 18 [1844] and published in the *Times* (London) the following day (p. 6).

30. Weld, "Some Thoughts on Letter Writing," *Godey's Lady's Book,* XLIV (January–June 1852), 252.

31. See also an anonymous American production of 1846: *The Letter Writer's Own Book; or, The Art of Polite Correspondence, Containing a Variety of Plain and Elegant Letters, on Business, Love, Courtship, Marriage, Relationship, Friendship &c, with Forms of Complimentary Cards, and Directions for Letter Writing, to Which Are Added Forms of Mortgages, Deeds, Bonds, Powers of Attorney, &c.*

32. *Otto Friedrich Rammlers Deutscher Reichs-Universal-Briefsteller oder Musterbuch zur Abfassung aller in den allgemeinen und freundschaftlichen Lebensverhältnissen sowie im Geschäftsleben vorkommenden Briefe, Dokumente und Aufsätze* (1834; 62nd ed., 1892), iii.

33. R. Turner, *The Parlour-Letter-Writer and Secretary's Assistant: Consisting of Original Letters on Every Occurrence in Life, Written in a Concise and Familiar Style, and Adapted to Both Sexes, to Which Are Added, Complimentary Cards, Wills, Bonds etc.* (1835), 18–19; Anon., *The Letter Writer's Own Book* (1846), xiv, xii; *Rammler,* 53.

34. Friend: G. J. Gladwin to Joseph Huntington, September 23, 1834, Huntington Papers, box 1; Proust to Robert Dreyfus, [August 28?, 1888], *Correspondance,* ed. Philip Kolb, 21 vols. (1970–93), I, 106.

35. *The Ladies' and Gentleman's Model Letter-Writer: A Complete Guide to Correspondence on All Subjects, with Household and Commercial Forms* (n.d.; 1871), 76, 77; *The Universal Letter-Writer; or, Complete Art of Polite Correspondence: Containing a Course of Interesting Letters on the Most Important, Instructive, and Entertaining Subjects* (1854), 104, 136.

36. *Rammler,* 95.

37. For detailed evidence, see Peter Gay, *The Bourgeois Experience,* vol. I, *Education of the Senses* (1984), passim.

38. Thomas R. Lounsbury to Jennie McNeil, March 3, 1862, Thomas R. Lounsbury Papers, ser. 1, box 14, Yale, Manuscripts and Archives.

39. For an instance of the first, see Nanny Herzberg to Adolph Koritzer, May 11, 1859, Mieses

Collection, BII, LBI, New York; for the second, Ulrich Levysohn to Clara Herrmann, August 20 [1876], Levysohn Collection, I, LBI, New York.

40. Nanny Herzberg to Adolph Koritzer, December 23, 1856, Mieses Collection, BII, LBI, New York.

41. Hermann Bahr to his father, Erich, March 13, 1883, *Briefwechsel mit seinem Vater,* ed. Adalbert Schmidt (1971), 15; the same to the same, March 11, 1883, ibid., 14; Erich Bahr to his son (no date, early spring 1883), ibid., 18.

42. Erich Bahr to his son, March 10, 1887, and June 11, 1890, ibid., 152, 276.

43. Selden Huntington to Joseph Huntington, November 21, 1833, Sheldon Huntington Family Papers, box 1, Yale, Manuscripts and Archives; Mrs. Huntington to Joseph Huntington, March 31, 1834, ibid.; cousin Sybil to Joseph Huntington, April 2, 1835, ibid.

44. Selden Huntington to Joseph Huntington, October 26, 1835, February 19 [1838], and April 7, 1841, ibid.; Mrs. Joseph Huntington to Joseph Huntington, September [28], 1836, ibid.; Joseph Huntington to Selden Huntington, September 13, 1842, ibid.

45. Barbey d'Aurevilly, "Balzac" (1876), *Littérature épistolaire* (1892), 1–2.

46. Henry A. Lounsbury to Thomas R. Lounsbury, July 2 [18]72, Thomas R. Lounsbury Papers, ser. 1, box 12, Yale, Manuscripts and Archives.

2. The Discreet Best Friend

1. De Guérin, April 20, 1834, *Journal, lettres, poèmes et fragments* (n.d., ca. 1911), 78.

2. Nietzsche, diary, December 26, 1856, *Werke,* ed. Karl Schlechta, 3 vols. (1966; 6th ed., 1969), III, 9.

3. See Mimi Sommer, "Designing Woman," *Connecticut Magazine* (March 1991), 75–83, quotation at 75.

4. Julie Manet, *Journal (1893–1899),* ed. Jean Griot (1979), 9.

5. Hebbel, diary, March 23, 1835, *Tagebücher, 1835–1863,* ed. Karl Pörnbacher, 3 vols. (1966–67; ed. 1984), I, 7.

6. Marie Bashkirtseff, *Journal* (in French), 2 vols. (1898), I, 5.

7. Jules Renard, *Journal* (1935), 256. The author died in 1910.

8. Reed: diary, 1818–49, from a partial typed transcription made by his son A. B. Reed (the original is lost; I owe these pages to Thomas A. Reed); Meyr: diary, September 6, [18]61, Meyriana, II, 2, Staatsbibliothek, Munich.

9. See "Letts, Thomas," *Dictionary of National Biography,* ed. Leslie Stephen and Sidney Lee, 21 vols. (1885–1900; repr. 1921–22), X, 1013.

10. Thackeray, "On Letts's Diary" (1862), *The Works of William Makepeace Thackeray,* Centenary Biographical Edition, ed. Lady Ritchie, 26 vols. (1910–11), XX, 177, 179.

11. To give but one instance of dry-as-dust, pedestrian entries, here is one from the diary of James Plumptre, English divine and censorious student of the licentious stage of his country since John Gay: "At Chapel / At Board at Hosp^l. / Mr Stevens elected Apothecary in the room of Mr. Gray. / Walked with Bonny and talked Latin." May 2 [1808], Cambridge University Library, Add. 5839.

12. Fanny Wood, August 25 [1835], *A Great-Niece's Journals, Being Extracts from the Journals of Fanny Anne Burney (Mrs. Wood) from 1830 to 1842,* ed. Margaret S. Rolt (1926), 64; August 8, 1835, ibid., 61.

13. See Theodore Dreiser, *American Diaries, 1902–1926,* ed. Thomas P. Riggio (1982), 3–4, 53 [introd.], 55–57 and passim [text].

14. Asa Fitch diary, August 16, 1839 (the event he recaptured had taken place on August 3), Asa Fitch Papers, box 2, Yale, Manuscripts and Archives.

15. September 1, 1839, ibid.

16. Waiblinger: *Tagebücher* (1956), 209; Macaulay: diary, January 7, 1856, quoted in George Otto Trevelyan, *The Life and Letters of Lord Macaulay*, 2 vols. (1876; World's Classics ed., 1932), II, 315; Wilde: *The Importance of Being Earnest* (1895), act II; Reed: diary, December 31, 1848.

17. Reed, diary, April 13, 1849.

18. *The Diary of Alice James,* ed. Leon Edel (1964), 25.

19. Amiel, *Journal intime,* ed. Bernard Gagnebin and Philippe M. Monnier, 8 vols. so far (1976–), V, 572. (Amiel's journal is even longer than the gigantic diary kept by the brothers Goncourt.)

20. *Journal of Emily Shore* (1891), 261.

21. Ibid., 1.

22. [Mid-September 1873], *The Diary of Beatrice Webb,* vol. I, *1873–1892: Glitter Around and Darkness Within,* ed. Norman and Jeanne MacKenzie (1982), 13.

23. September 16, 1825, *Aus Andersens Tagebüchern,* ed. and tr. Heinz Barüske, 2 vols. (1980), I, 31.

24. Tolstoy, March 17 [1847], *Tolstoy's Diaries,* ed. and tr. R. F. Christian, 2 vols. (1985), I, 4.

25. Bashkirtseff, *Journal,* I, 5.

26. Bashkirtseff: ibid.; Van Dyke: July 9, 1810, Diary, Special Collections Department, Rutgers University, Ac. 2981.

27. Shore, *Journal,* 263.

28. Julie Manet, October 28 [1897], *Journal,* 138–39.

29. January 8 [1898], ibid., 147; December 15 [1899], ibid., 285; January 8 [1898], ibid., 147; October 14 [1897], ibid., 135.

30. October 22 [1897], ibid., 137; December 22 [1898], ibid., 207.

31. November 14 [1899], ibid., 278; December 12 [1899], ibid., 284.

32. March 1 [1895], ibid., 52.

33. April 17 [1895], ibid., 52–53.

34. July 20, 1895, ibid., 54; December 5, 1896, ibid. (supplemental entry), 292.

35. December 15 [1896], ibid., 119; March 4 [1896], ibid., 83; October 28 [1897], ibid., 138–39.

36. Elizabeth Barrett, June 4, 1831, *Diary by E. B. B.: The Unpublished Diary of Elizabeth Barrett, 1831–1832,* ed. Philip Kelley and Ronald Hudson (1969), 1.

37. Barrett: ibid.; Gladstone: entry for September 16, 1841, *The Gladstone Diaries,* ed. M. R. D. Foot and H. C. G. Matthew, 14 vols. (1968–94), III, 140. See also Bashkirtseff, *Journal,* I, 5.

38. Delacroix, April 27, 1824, *Journal, 1822–1863* (1893; introd. André Joubin, 1980), 61–62.

39. "The progress of modern times is magnificent: inventions follow inventions, machines have prodigiously multiplied production, railroads and steamships have developed traffic to undreamt-of heights, millions of newspapers are read every year and billions of letters written; mighty progress has been achieved in all areas of cultural and intellectual life. . . ." Ferdinand Buomberger, "Massenelend und Kulturentwicklung," *Hochland,* I (March 1, 1904), 690. (This was not exactly meant as unconditional praise, for the author contrasts this progress with the persistence of poverty.) A few pages later, Dr. Josef Froberger broods on one of the most remarkable phenomena of the day: "mystical-religious tendencies are emerging ever more assertively and seem to find deep resonance in some circles." The "materialist world view" has in the last decades "lost its drawing power." In short, "in the long run, sober rationalism cannot satisfy aspiring spirits." And so, we are

getting "woolliness and lack of character." The age resembles the late Roman Empire, awash as it is in "Buddhism, occultism, demonism, religion of sentiment," down to the "all-German cult of Odin" and that of Isis. Perhaps the worst are the theosophists. "Moderner Mystizismus," ibid., 741–44.

BIBLIOGRAPHICAL ESSAY

This bibliographical essay, like its predecessors in this series, is selective rather than exhaustive, concentrating on texts that have contributed information, suggested interpretations, or invited contradiction. I have listed the major psychoanalytic studies on which I have drawn, as before, in *The Bourgeois Experience: Victoria to Freud,* vol. I, *Education of the Senses* (1984), 463–66 and 469, and will not repeat them here.

BOURGEOIS EXPERIENCES, IV:
The Art of Listening

William Sidney Mount (whose *The Power of Music* stimulated me to write this introductory essay), has been well dealt with in Alfred Frankenstein, *William Sidney Mount* (1975), and several contributions to *Catching the Tune: Music and William Sidney Mount,* ed. Janice Gray Armstrong (1984). Since Mount freely used black subjects in his oeuvre, comparative studies on the racial aspects of art proved of use; see Albert Boime, *The Art of Exclusion: Representing Blacks in the Nineteenth Century* (1990); and Hugh Honour, *The Image of the Black in Western Art,* vol. IV, *From the American Revolution to World War I* (1989). See also the instructive ch. 4 in Elizabeth Johns, *American Genre Painting: The Politics of Everyday Life* (1991).

The privileging of music without words after 1800 has been authoritatively expounded in Carl Dahlhaus, *The Idea of Absolute Music* (1978; tr. Roger Lustig, 1989). Dahlhaus, *Esthetics of Music* (1967; tr. William W. Austin, 1982), is an impressive summary sketch. Both explicate E. T. A. Hoffmann's epoch-making review of Beethoven's Fifth Symphony (1810) and his pioneering essay, "Gedanken über den hohen Wert der Musik," in *Fantasiestücke in Callots Manier* (1814). Although much work has been done on Hoffmann as music critic, including R. Murray Schafer, *E. T. A. Hoffmann and Music*

(1975), he could benefit from further study.* Among biographies, Rüdiger Safranski, *E. T. A. Hoffmann. Das Leben eines skeptischen Phantasten* (1984), seems the most rewarding. The massive collection by a foremost specialist, Friedrich Schnapp, *E. T. A. Hoffmann in Aufzeichnungen seiner Freunde und Bekannten* (1974), presents eyewitness evidence from contemporaries. Among surveys of musical history, Leon Plantinga, *Romantic Music: A History of Musical Style in Nineteenth-Century Europe* (1984), is notable for its good sense. The older history by Alfred Einstein, *Music in the Romantic Era* (1947), retains much authority. *The Early Romantic Era, between Revolutions: 1789 and 1848,* ed. Alexander Ringer (1990), explores the social dimension.

I have gleaned my evidence for the behavior—often misbehavior—of the public at concerts and recitals, and efforts to reform it, from musical journals, biographies (and autobiographies) of composers, and histories of orchestras. Helpful titles include *Thayer's Life of Beethoven,* rev. and ed. Elliot Forbes (1964; rev. ed., 1967); Herbert Weinstock, *Rossini: A Biography* (1968); *Mémoires de Hector Berlioz, comprenant ses voyages* (1870; many eds. since); *Offenbach en Amérique. Notes d'un musicien en voyage* (ca. 1876), a collection of Offenbach's letters to his wife; Howard Shanet, *Philharmonic: A History of New York's Orchestra* (1975); John H. Mueller, *The American Symphony Orchestra: A Social History of Musical Taste* (1951); Robert Elkin, *Royal Philharmonic: The Annals of the Royal Philharmonic Society* (1946); Richard Schickel, *The World of Carnegie Hall* (1960); Irwin Kolodin, *The Story of the Metropolitan Opera, 1883–1950: A Candid History* (1953). Michael Kennedy, *The Hallé Tradition: A Century of Music* (1960), is the biography of a bourgeois institution.

For Mozart's attitude toward his audiences, the letters to his father are most instructive, best read in the splendid edition, *Briefe und Aufzeichnungen. Gesamtausgabe,* ed. Wilhelm A. Bauer and Otto Erich Deutsch, 7 vols. (1962–75).

Several historians have taken profitable stabs at the social history of music. I have learned from the compact comparative study by William Weber, *Music and the Middle Class: The Social Structure of Concert Life in London, Paris, and Vienna* (1975). See also James H. Johnson, "Musical Experience and the Formation of a French Musical Public," *Journal of Modern History,* LXIV (June 1992), 216–26; Wilfred Dumwell, *Music and the European Mind* (1962); Cyril Ehrlich, *The Music Profession in Britain since the Eighteenth Century: A Social History* (1985); and E. D. Mackerness, *A Social History of English Music* (1964), esp. chs. 4–6. For Vienna, Eduard Hanslick, *Geschichte des Concertwesens in Wien,* 2 vols. (1869–70), is a classic—but to be read with some caution: Vienna's most influential critic, Hanslick was a proud bourgeois who overstates the significance of middle-class Viennese in the musical life of his city. There is a convenient, well-chosen anthology of his magisterial reviews, *Aus dem Tagebuch eines Rezensenten. Gesammelte Musikkritiken,* ed. Peter Wapnewski (1989), with a fine postscript by the editor. *Das "Museum." Einhundertfünfzig Jahre Frankfurter Konzertleben, 1808–1958,* ed. Hildegard

---

*Note the skeptical comments on the literature by Brigitte Feldges and Ulrich Stadler, *E. T. A. Hoffmann. Epoche—Werk—Wirkung* (1986), 243–44, an indispensable handbook for Hoffmann studies.

Weber (1958), is illuminating on a powerful local cultural institution.

For music during the decisive decades when ideals of conduct changed, see esp. Claude Laforêt [pseud. Flavien Bonnet-Roy], *La Vie musicale au temps romantique (salons, théâtres et concerts)* (1929), short and anecdotal; Léon Guichard, *La Musique et les lettres au temps du romantisme* (1955), more detailed, zeroing in on the relationship between music and literature; Arthur Ware Locke, *Music and the Romantic Movement in France* (1920), a short essay with good ideas but infected with Irving Babbitt's notion that romanticism was a kind of disease. For Beethoven as a cultural icon, see the exhaustive exploration by Alessandra Comini, *The Changing Image of Beethoven: A Study in Mythmaking* (1987).

The most important text, for me, detailing the relations of music to painting, has been Franzsepp Würtenberger, *Malerei und Musik. Die Geschichte des Verhaltens zweier Künste zueinander—dargestellt nach den Quellen im Zeitraum von Leonardo da Vinci bis John Cage* (1979). Though it focuses on the present, Leonard B. Meyer, *Music, the Arts, and Ideas: Patterns and Predictions in Twentieth-Century Culture* (1967), proved highly suggestive.

Amid the massive literature on Wagner, the titles most informative, and most relevant to my argument, have been Carl Dahlhaus, *Richard Wagners Musikdramen* (1971), terse but immensely thoughtful; Michael Karbaum, *100 Jahre Bayreuther Festspiele. Studien zur Geschichte der Bayreuther Festspiele* (1976); Geoffrey Skelton, "The Idea of Bayreuth," in *The Wagner Companion,* ed. Peter Burbidge and Richard Sutton (1979), 389–411; and Richard Beacham, "Adolphe Appia and the Staging of Wagnerian Opera," *Opera Quarterly,* L (Autumn 1983), 114–39. Frederic Spotts, *Bayreuth: A History of the Wagner Festival* (1994), a detailed account, arrived in time to be consulted.*

ONE: The Re-enchantment of the World

Romanticism, which occupies a pivotal position in my history of nineteenth-century inwardness, has spawned a monumental literature. We must begin with Arthur O. Lovejoy's devastating address of December 1923 to the Modern Language Association, demolishing every collective definition, still required reading: "On the Discrimination of Romanticisms," *PMLA,* XXXIX (1924), 229–53, conveniently available in Lovejoy, *Essays in the History of Ideas* (1948). It took a quarter of a century until René Wellek took up this formidable challenge to restore some scholarly repute to "romanticism" with "The Concept of Romanticism in Literary History," *Comparative Literature,* I (1949), 1–23, 147–72 (reprinted in Wellek, *Concepts of Criticism,* ed. Stephen G. Nichols, Jr. [1963], followed by a postscript, "Romanticism Re-examined"). The meanings and early usages of the word are laid out at enormous length (over 500 pages) in *"Romantic"*

---

*I have dealt with pertinent aspects of Wagner, his slaves and his enemies, in "Hermann Levi: A Study in Service and Self-hatred" (1975) and "For Beckmesser: Eduard Hanslick, Victim and Prophet" (1977), both of them available, revised, in *Freud, Jews and Other Germans: Masters and Victims in Modernist Culture* (1978); see also *The Bourgeois Experience: Victoria to Freud,* vol. II, *The Tender Passion* (1986), 264–69.

and Its Cognates: The European History of a Word, ed. Hans Eichner (1972).

Texts that have contributed to the debate on subjectivity most provocatively (not all of them confined to romanticism) include most prominently Lionel Trilling, *Sincerity and Authenticity* (1972); Henri Peyre, *Literature and Sincerity* (1963); and Georges Gusdorf, *La Découverte de soi* (1948). Isaiah Berlin, who has made the "counter-Enlightenment" his own, has necessarily confronted the romantics in several essays, notably "Giambattista Vico and Cultural History" (1983) and "The Apotheosis of the Romantic Will: The Revolt against the Myth of an Ideal World" (1975), both in *The Crooked Timber of Humanity: Chapters in the History of Ideas* (1991).

Paul van Tieghem, *Le Romantisme dans la littérature européenne* (1948), remains among the most serviceable histories; striving for objectivity and sweep, it includes in its pur-view "lesser" romantic movements in Scandinavia, the Netherlands, Italy. Mario Praz's classic, *The Romantic Agony* (1933; 2nd ed., tr. Angus Davidson, 1951), to whose knowl-edgeable anatomies of nineteenth-century eroticism I have often returned, again proved rewarding. Fritz Strich, *Deutsche Klassik und Romantik; oder, Vollendung und Unendlichkeit* (1922; 3rd ed., 1928), a bold attempt to contrast neoclassicism and romanticism, defying recent subtleties, is still provocative. M. H. Abrams has long been identified with this period; I am indebted to his influential *The Mirror and the Lamp: Romantic Theory and the Critical Tradition* (1953) and the no less important *Natural Supernaturalism: Tradition and Revolution in Romantic Literature* (1971). Both start with England but do not stop there. Abrams has also collected his shorter writings in *The Correspondent Breeze: Essays on English Romanticism* (1984). I am beholden to René Wellek's impressive *A History of Modern Criticism,* vol. II, *The Romantic Age* (1955), a learned, deliberately atomistic overview moving from critic to critic. The art historian Hugh Honour's *Romanticism* (1979) is an attractive, engagingly opinionated essay. Nicholas V. Riasanovsky, *The Emergence of Romanticism* (1992), surveys the birth of the romantic impulse in Britain and Germany in a slight book overloaded with long quotations. Eudo S. Mason, *Deutsche und englische Romantik. Eine Gegenüberstellung* (1959; 3rd ed., 1970), exploring the same theme, is far more satisfactory. H. G. Schenk's wide-ranging survey, *The Mind of the European Romantics* (1966), takes a position roughly similar to my own (he even uses the terms "enchantment" and "disenchantment"). *Romanticism in National Context,* ed. Roy Porter and Mikuláš Teich (1988), makes welcome discriminations. So do Lilian R. Furst's erudite publications, notably *Romanticism in Perspective* (1969; 2nd ed., 1979) and *The Contours of European Romanticism* (1979).

Jacques Barzun's polemic *Romanticism and the Modern Ego* (1943; rev. ed. with new title, *Classic, Romantic and Modern,* 1961) takes pride of place as a spirited defense of romantics against charges of obscurantist thinking and reactionary consequences; while my own sense of the romantics is rather darker than Barzun's, I have been held in check by his appeal. Michael G. Cooke, *Acts of Inclusion: Studies Bearing on an Elementary Theory of Romanticism* (1979), seeks a general theme in the romantics' defiance of precision and of rules. Barbara Fass, *La Belle Dame sans Merci and the Aesthetics of Romanticism* (1974), makes the seductive "fairy-mistress" central to her portrait. Robert Harbison, *Deliberate Regression* (1980), fastening on the least palatable manifestations of romantic thinking, follows what he considers the catastrophic consequences of its individualism from Rousseau to fascism. Romanticism seems to spawn such assaults. Gerald N. Izenberg's demanding comparative *Impossible Individuality: Romanticism, Revolution, and the Origins of Modern Selfhood, 1787–1802* (1992) concentrates, after a general introduction, on Friedrich Schlegel, Wordsworth, and Chateaubriand to trace two distinct concepts of individuality inherent in romantic thought. Jerome J. McGann, *The Romantic Ideology: A Critical Investigation* (1983), is an attempt to get clear of romantic presuppositions to offer criticisms in freedom.

German romanticism has been sparsely discussed in English; W. A. Willoughby, *The Romantic Movement in Germany* (1930), can still be consulted with profit. See also Glyn T. Hughes, *Romantic German Literature* (1979). Two articles by Arthur O. Lovejoy remain indispensable: "The Meaning of 'Romantic' in Early German Romanticism," *Modern Language Notes*, XXXI (1916), 385–96, and XXXII, 65–77, and "Schiller and the Genesis of German Romanticism," ibid., XXXV (1920), 1–10, 134–46, both reprinted in *Essays in the History of Ideas*. Germans have never settled the old debate whether their romanticism was a decline from the Age of Goethe (a view taken in Hermann A. Korff's widely cited but overrated *Der Geist der Goethezeit*, 4 vols. [1923–48]), or a summit of German literature, art, and thought. Georg Brandes, *The Romantic School in Germany* (1883; tr. 1906), vol. II of *Main Currents in Nineteenth Century Literature* (1872–94), though a century old and very personal, is spiced with sweeping insights. Another war-horse, Ricarda Huch, *Blütezeit der Romantik* (1899) and *Ausbreitung und Verfall der Romantik* (1902), published as *Die Romantik* in 1908 and often reprinted, is only a little younger and no less subjective than Brandes (neither troubles with footnotes or bibliographies) and equally perceptive. Rudolf Haym's solid, substantial *Die romantische Schule* (1870), too, has aged gracefully. Among recent titles *Die deutsche Romantik*, ed. Hans Steffen (1967; 2nd ed., 1970), is esp. helpful, offering chapters on individual *Romantiker* and topics like irony and fairy tales. And see the close, somewhat gnarled analyses in Werner Kohlschmidt, *Geschichte der deutschen Literatur von der Romantik bis zum späten Goethe* (1974), vol. III of *Geschichte der deutschen Literatur von den Anfängen bis zur Gegenwart*. Marianne Thalmann, *Romantiker entdecken die Stadt* (1965), is a stimulating essay on how German romantics learned to feel at home in Berlin. Theodore Ziolkowski's unconventional *German Romanticism and Its Institutions* (1990) delves into the professional activities of leading figures like Novalis (an administrator of salt mines in Saxony) or E. T. A. Hoffmann (a judge) to enrich the common two-dimensional portrait of these ostensibly unworldly dreamers. Nor can we dispense with Heinrich Heine's witty, idiosyncratic, and disparaging *Romantische Schule* (1833–35).

Exceedingly active in doing monographs about their romantics, Germans have not served them so well with biographies. Awakening an appetite for more, Ernst Behler, *Friedrich Schlegel in Selbstzeugnissen und Bilddokumenten* (1966), is an authoritative, if skeletal, introduction by a foremost scholar, chief editor of the definitive *Kritische Friedrich-Schlegel Ausgabe*. Hans Eichner, *Friedrich Schlegel* (1970), another brief study, is in English. Like his younger brother, August Wilhelm Schlegel has had no substantial biography. Josef Körner, *Die Botschaft der deutschen Romantik an Europa* (1929), is a short analysis that, for all its disquieting title, eschews all chauvinism; the German romantics' message to Europe turns out to be August Wilhelm Schlegel's theory of literature. The correspondence of the brothers may serve as a substitute: *Friedrich Schlegels Briefe an seinen Bruder August Wilhelm*, ed. Oskar Walzel (1890); *Briefe von und an Friedrich und Dorothea Schlegel*, ed. Josef Körner (1926); *Die Brüder August Wilhelm Schlegel und Friedrich Schlegel im Briefwechsel mit Schiller und Goethe*, ed. Josef Körner, with Ernst Wienecke (1926). (Once the *Kritische Ausgabe* of Friedrich Schlegel's writings is complete, its edition of his letters will become standard.) On the elder Schlegel's impact on French thought, see in addition to Körner, Chetana Nagavajara, *August Wilhelm Schlegel in Frankreich. Sein Anteil an der französischen Literaturkritik* (1966). J. Christopher Herold's gripping *Mistress to an Age: A Life of Madame de Staël* (1958), which has much to say about August Wilhelm Schlegel, is an admirable introduction to the early romantics, and subverting its racy title, learned, penetrating, and stylish.

For Friedrich von Hardenberg, we have Gerhard Schulz's short but informative *Novalis mit Selbstzeugnissen und Bilddokumenten* (1969) and Hermann Kurzke's attractive, equally short *Novalis* (1988). In English: John Neubauer, *Novalis* (1980). Friedrich Hiebel, *Novalis. Deutscher Dichter, Europäischer Denker, Christlicher Seher* (1951; 2nd much enlarged edition, 1972), has its own ideological agenda, which considerably limits its usefulness. The French *Germanist* Pierre Bertaud has specialized for decades in the fascinating and mysterious character of Hölderlin. In *Hölderlin und die französische Revolution* (1969), he underscores the poet's radicalism; in his bulky *Friedrich Hölderlin* (1978), deploying an array of documents, he develops a psychological profile to prove that Hölderlin was "different" but not mad, a plea that, however sensitive and well-informed, has not proved persuasive. For E. T. A. Hoffmann, see above, pp. 395–96. It is par for the course that the best biography of Tieck should be Roger Paulin, *Ludwig Tieck: A Literary Biography* (1985)—in English. For the inwardness of German philosophers and their conflict with the scientific world view, see Andrew Bowie, *Aesthetics and Subjectivity: From Kant to Nietzsche* (1990), erudite but problematic. J. Brändle, *Das Problem der Innerlichkeit. Hamann, Herder, Goethe* (1949), is a slender study of the prehistory of romantic inwardness.

They order these things better in England. Walter Jackson Bate, *From Classic to Romantic: Premises of Taste in Eighteenth-Century England* (1946), offers an elegant introduction to the emergence of romanticism in that country. Marilyn Butler, *Romantics, Rebels, and Reactionaries: English Literature and Its Background, 1760–1830* (1981), a brilliant overview (excessively modest in appearance), is in complete control of the material. M. H. Northrop Frye's terse *A Study of English Romanticism* (1968) is, as expected, a memorable performance, concentrating on the myths replaced and those invented, by analyzing Beddoes, Shelley, and Keats. *Romanticism and Consciousness: Essays in Criticism*, ed. Harold Bloom (1970), gathers a number of papers, many not easily accessible, that impinge on inwardness. Anne K. Mellor, *English Romantic Irony* (1980), elucidates with English instances a difficult concept, first introduced by Friedrich Schlegel. (See on this Helmut Prang, *Die romantische Ironie* [1972].) Marilyn Gaull, *English Romanticism: The Human Context* (1988), is a refreshing counterweight to an exclusive concern with high literature.* A similar contextual intention informs the well-designed *The Romantic Age in Britain*, vol. VI of *The Cambridge Cultural History of Britain*, ed. Boris Ford (1989), with essays on cities, the arts, music, graphic satire, and architecture, without skimping on poetry and the novel.

With individual romantics the English (and Americans) have particularly excelled. See Leslie A. Marchand's virtually definitive *Byron: A Biography*, 3 vols. (1957). Marchand's edition *Byron's Letters and Journals*, 12 vols. (1973–82), is admirable. Not surprisingly, Byron's dazzling letters have prompted anthologies, notably Marchand's own *Lord Byron: Selected Letters and Journals* (1982) and, earlier, *The Selected Letters of Lord Byron*, ed. Jacques Barzun (1953). *Byron: A Collection of Critical Essays*, ed. Paul West (1963), displays a wide spectrum of views. W. W. Robson's British Academy Lecture, *Byron as Poet* (1957), is suggestive. *Lord Byron and His Contemporaries*, ed. Charles E. Robinson (1982), puts the poet into his literary environment at home and abroad.

Walter Jackson Bate's exhaustive *John Keats* (1963) is the standard biography, and Douglas Bush, *John Keats: His Life and Writings* (1966), a tour de force of compression. Despite this formidable competition, Stuart M. Sperry, *Keats the Poet* (1973), remains worth reading; as does Christopher Ricks's witty *Keats and Embarrassment* (1974). In a fascinating monograph, *Romantic Medicine and John Keats* (1991), Hermione de Almeida has reread Keats from the perspective of his medical training. In *Shelley*, 2 vols. (1940), Newman I. White has thoroughly surveyed the poet's life; Richard Holmes, *Shelley, the Pursuit* (1974), is comprehensive and explicitly antisentimental. *The Letters of Percy Bysshe Shelley* have been well edited by Frederick L. Jones (1964).

Wordsworth has never lacked attention. The best recent lives are by Mary Moorman, *William Wordsworth: A Biography; The Early Years, 1770–1803* (1957), followed by *The Later Years, 1803–1850* (1965), and by Stephen Gill, *William Wordsworth: A Life* (1989), which packs an astonishing amount of information, judgments, and contemporary scholarship into one volume. Geoffrey A. Hartman, *Wordsworth's Poetry, 1787–1814* (1964; fifth printing, 1975, with an added essay, "Retrospect 1971"), gives a persuasive account of Wordsworth's maturation as he discovers the self and Nature. Hartman's essays, *The Unremarkable Wordsworth* (1987), are graceful visits to a favorite subject. The authoritative texts of Wordsworth's *Prelude* (the versions dating from 1799, 1805, and 1850) have been conveniently edited by Jonathan Wordsworth, M. H. Abrams, and Stephen Gill (1979). The *Letters of William and Dorothy Wordsworth* have been revised from the famous original edition of Ernest De Selincourt.† *The Age of William Wordsworth: Critical Essays on the Romantic Tradition*, ed. Kenneth R. Johnston and Gene W.

---

*"Most people in England during the opening decades of the nineteenth century," Marilyn Gaull writes on p. 1, "showed very little interest in the literature that we now consider important. Those who were literate and able to purchase literary works were primarily concerned with business, politics, war, trade, industry, fashion, sex, status, domestic comfort, horses, servants, marriage, and boxing matches."

†*The Early Years, 1787–1805*, by Chester L. Shaver (1967); *The Middle Years, 1806–1811*, by Mary Moorman (1969); *The Middle Years, 1812–1820*, by Mary Moorman and Alan G. Hill (1970); *The Later Years, 1821–1853*, 4 vols., by Alan G. Hill (1987–88).

Ruoff (1987), a collection of solid studies, travels from Wordsworth's relations to his sister and Keats to his fame abroad. Margaret Drabble, *Wordsworth* (1966), is remarkably meaty for so short an essay. Melvin Rader, *Wordsworth: A Philosophical Approach* (1967), evaluates the poet from an unconventional angle; John Jones, *The Egotistical Sublime: A History of Wordsworth's Imagination* (1954), is, in contrast, deliberately unphilosophical.

To judge from Richard Holmes's *Coleridge: Early Visions* (1989), his second volume will also do Coleridge the biographical justice he so eminently merits. Among earlier titles, Humphry House, *Coleridge* (1953), astute and succinct, is outstanding. And see Laurence S. Lockridge, *Coleridge the Moralist* (1977). A definitive edition, *The Collected Works of Samuel Taylor Coleridge,* ed. Kathleen Coburn et al., 16 vols. (1969–92), is an outstanding scholarly venture. The *Collected Letters of Samuel Taylor Coleridge,* ed. Earl Leslie Griggs, 6 vols. (1956–71), is a goldmine. Among commentaries, John Livingston Lowes, *The Road to Xanadu: A Study in the Ways of the Imagination* (1927), is a classic analysis of *Kubla Khan* and *The Rime of the Ancient Mariner.* Stephen Bygrave, *Coleridge and the Self: Romantic Egotism* (1986), speaks to the theme of this volume. As for Coleridge's plagiarisms—shall we say, borrowings?—Norman Fruman, *Coleridge: The Damaged Archangel* (1971), is caustic and still controversial.

For Hazlitt, there is above all *The Life of William Hazlitt* (1922; 2nd ed., 1947) by P. P. Howe, who has also edited *The Complete Works of William Hazlitt,* 21 vols. (1930–34), now standard. Herschel Baker's comprehensive *William Hazlitt* (1962) is particularly valuable for establishing the setting. David Bromwich, *Hazlitt: The Mind of the Critic* (1983), is demanding but worth the effort. Marilyn Butler, "Satire and the Images of Self in the Romantic Period: The Long Tradition of Hazlitt's *Liber Amoris,*" in *English Satire and the Satiric Tradition* (1984), 209–25, goes far beyond its brief—as so often, with this author, "brilliant" comes to mind. There is an interesting modern life of Scott by H. J. C. Grierson, *Sir Walter Scott, Bart.* (1938). Two defenses of the writer who helped to make the novel respectable yet is much less read today, A. O. J. Cockshut, *The Achievement of Walter Scott* (1969), and Alexander Welsh, *The Hero of the Waverly Novels with New Essays on Scott* (1963; rev. and enlarged ed., 1992), succeed in making a strong, the best possible, case. Grevel Lindop, *The Opium-Eater: A Life of Thomas De Quincey* (1981), is the most satisfactory account of this historic addict, a highly neurotic romantic who seems a case for the psychoanalyst; John Barrell, *The Infection of Thomas De Quincey: A Psychopathology of Imperialism* (1991), audaciously, perhaps too audaciously, connects his "patient's" obsessions to an unsavory racist ideology. The world of De Quincey's drug culture taking has been finely analyzed by Alethea Hayter, *Opium and the Romantic Imagination* (1968). And, to shift gears, that great anti-romantic Thomas Love Peacock has been fortunate in Marilyn Butler, *Peacock Displayed: A Satanist in His Context* (1979).

In France, romanticism flowered later and lived longer than elsewhere. Thus in the multivolume history of French literature, ed. Claude Pichois, Max Milner starts *Le Romantisme,* I (1973), in 1820 while Raymond Pouillart concludes vol. III (1968) in 1896. Among general treatments see Pierre Martino, *L'Epoque romantique en France,*

1815–1830 (1944; 6th ed., 1967), and Henri Peyre, *What Is Romanticism?* (1971; tr. Roda Roberts, 1977). Vol. V of Brandes's *Main Currents, The Romantic School in France* (1882; tr. 1906), is still worth consulting. So is Pierre Moreau, *Le Romantisme* (1932; 2nd ed., 1957), very substantial. Moreau's *Le Classicisme des romantiques* (1932) suitably complicates matters that others have oversimplified. Probably the most massive study of the French romantics is the series by Paul Bénichou, *Le Sacre de l'écrivain* (1973); *Le Temps des prophètes* (1977); and *Les Mages romantiques* (1989), which add up to a history of the French "romantic mind" with its grandiloquent, high-flown claims to virtually messianic stature.

Two exemplary introductions to French romantics in English are *French Literature and Its Background,* vol. IV, *The Early Nineteenth Century,* ed. John Cruickshank (1969), and the two-volume survey, *The French Romantics,* ed. D. G. Charlton (1984), both with excellent bibliographies. Margaret Gilman, *The Idea of Poetry in France: From Houdar de La Motte to Baudelaire* (1958), is a superlative survey analyzing the empiricists' struggle in behalf of prose and the romantics' counterattack.

Richard Switzer, *Chateaubriand* (1971), is a short introduction. Switzer has also edited an interesting commemorative symposium of 1968, published in 1970. Charles Augustin Sainte-Beuve's study *Chateaubriand et son groupe littéraire sous l'Empire,* 2 vols. (1849), by France's most perceptive and hardworking critic, remains eminently worth consulting. André Maurois, *René, ou la vie de Chateaubriand* (1956), follows his invariable recipe for his biographies: slick, easily digestible, but resting on research. Madame de Staël has been well served by Herold, *Mistress to an Age* (cited above, p. 400) On de Staël's defiance of the emperor, see Paul Gautier, *Madame de Staël et Napoléon* (1903).

Some of the most distinguished twentieth-century literary critics have occupied themselves with Stendhal. Significantly, Erich Auerbach, *Mimesis: The Representation of Reality in Western Literature* (1946; tr. Willard Task, 1953), Irving Howe, *Politics and the Novel* (1957), and Harry Levin, *The Gates of Horn* (1963), devote a chapter to him. And see Victor Brombert, *Stendhal et la voie oblique: L'Auteur devant son monde romanesque* (1954), an impressive analysis of his narrative strategies. For Stendhal the writer, see Georges Blin, *Stendhal et les problèmes du roman* (1953) and *Stendhal et les problèmes de la personnalité,* 2 vols. (1958–68), and that esteemed Beyliste, Henri Martineau: *L'Oeuvre de Stendhal: Histoire de ses livres et de sa pensée* (1945) and *Le Coeur de Stendhal: Histoire de sa vie et de ses sentiments,* 2 vols. (1952–53). The indefatigable editor, bibliographer, and organizer Vittorio Del Litto has expressed his own views in his thesis, *La Vie intellectuelle de Stendhal: Genèse et évolution de ses idées (1802–1821)* (1959). The most useful titles in English have been, for me, Robert M. Adams, *Stendhal: Notes on a Novelist* (1959), an informal essay; and Geoffrey Strickland, *Stendhal: The Education of a Novelist* (1974), a sound study. Gilbert D. Chaitin, *The Unhappy Few: A Psychological Study of the Novels of Stendhal* (1972), is that rare (and distrusted) bird, a psychoanalytic investigation of Stendhal's novels that reaches, I believe, credible results.

The principal representative of French romanticism in my text is Victor Hugo. Jean Bertrand Barrère, *Hugo: L'Homme et l'oeuvre* (1952; 2nd ed., 1961), is superior to facile lives published since then. For years, André Maurois's *Olympio: The Life of Victor Hugo* (1954; tr. Gerard Hopkins, 1956) has held the market but left room for more work. Some of that room has been taken up by Victor Brombert with *The Romantic Prison: The French Tradition* (1978), esp. ch. 6; and, even more central, *Victor Hugo and the Visionary Novel* (1984), which, undaunted, tackles Hugo's complex and confusing ideology.

In comparison with European versions, American romanticism seems somewhat marginal and derivative. Still, it deserves attention. Bryan Jay Wolf, *Romantic Re-vision: Culture and Consciousness in Nineteenth-Century American Painting and Literature* (1983), mixes literary and art history from a left-wing psychoanalytic perspective. The old symposium *Romanticism in America,* ed. George Boas (1940), has hardly dated. The pioneering text by Henry Nash Smith, *Virgin Land: The American West as Symbol of Myth* (1950; ed. 1970), inspired some of the best work in American studies, like Leo Marx, *The Machine in the Garden: Technology and the Pastoral Ideal in America* (1964); John William Ward, *Andrew Jackson: Symbol for an Age* (1955); Marvin Meyers, *The Jacksonian Persuasion: Politics and Belief* (1960). See also the delightful ch. 3, "Andrew Jackson and the Rise of Liberal Capitalism," in Richard Hofstadter, *The American Political Tradition and the Men Who Made It* (1948); Michael J. Hoffman, *The Subversive Vision: American Romanticism in American Literature* (1972), and Edward Halsey Foster, *The Civilized Wilderness: Backgrounds to American Romantic Literature, 1817–1860* (1975). All in one way or another tackle the paradox of a culture torn between romanticized wilderness and muscular capitalist expansion. Henry Nash Smith's impressive *Democracy and the Novel: Popular Resistance to Classic American Writers* (1978) confronts the harsh realities of American taste and the book-buying public, as does Michael T. Gilmore, *American Romanticism and the Marketplace* (1985).

Many of the texts already cited necessarily touch on the creative imagination, of which the romantics were so proud. I add C. M. Bowra's elegant *The Romantic Imagination* (1950), which stays with England, and I. A. Richards, *Coleridge on Imagination* (1934; 3rd ed., 1962), a pioneering analysis still worth reading. See also William Price Albrecht, *Hazlitt and the Creative Imagination* (1965), and Dietmar Kamper, *Zur Geschichte der Einbildungskraft* (1981). But in an important revisionist monograph, *The Creative Imagination, Enlightenment to Romanticism* (1981), James Engell has shown that the romantics' romance with the creative imagination had important forebears in the age of the Enlightenment.*

Like the romantic imagination, romantic politics has been touched upon in most titles mentioned before. Some texts carry the inquiry further: Crane Brinton, *The Political Ideas of the English Romanticists* (1926), rather dated now, has been largely super-

---

*This book helps to confirm, and extends, a point I have been making since working on the eighteenth century from the mid-fifties to the late sixties: the philosophes were anything but cold rationalists indifferent to passion. See Peter Gay, *The Enlightenment: An Interpretation,* 2 vols. (1966–69).

seded by Carl Woodring's *Politics in English Romantic Poetry* (1970). A. V. Dicey, collecting papers written much earlier, made himself Wordsworth's champion in *The Statesmanship of Wordsworth: An Essay* (1917). F. M. Todd, *Politics and the Poet: A Study of Wordsworth* (1957), is a tightly argued but not really convincing defense of Wordsworth's politics, its consistency and good sense. James K. Chandler, *Wordsworth's Second Nature: A Study of the Poetry and Politics* (1984), is subtler as it restores the poet to his cultural context. Alan Bewell, *Wordsworth and the Enlightenment: Nature, Man, and Society in the Experimental Poetry* (1989), sees Wordsworth's view of humanity—his anthropology—as a revision of Enlightenment ideas. John Colmer, *Coleridge: Critic of Society* (1959), is a brave (though, I think, not altogether persuasive) rescue operation pleading for the coherence and wisdom of Coleridge's political ideas. Carl Woodring, *Politics in the Poetry of Coleridge* (1961), is more balanced. Geoffrey Carnall, *Robert Southey and His Age: The Development of a Conservative Mind* (1960), explores a characteristic dramatic change of political front in mid-life. See also David Bromwich, "Keats's Politics," in *A Choice of Inheritance from Edmund Burke to Robert Frost* (1989), ch. 5, which documents, somewhat surprisingly, a political attitude in the presumably unpolitical poet.

For "right-wing" politics among German romantics, see Benedikt Koehler, *Ästhetik der Politik. Adam Müller und die politische Romantik* (1980). Reinhold Aris, *History of Political Thought in Germany, 1789 to 1815* (1936), is a workmanlike review of German ideas. Though apparently only marginal to romantic politics, Hajo Holborn, "Der deutsche Idealismus in sozialgeschichtlicher Beleuchtung," *Historische Zeitschrift*, CLXXIV (1959), 359–84, is right to the point. There are forceful chapters on German political romanticism (esp. 4–7) in Friedrich Meinecke, *Cosmopolitanism and the National State* (1907; tr. Robert B. Kimber, 1970); by an eminent German intellectual historian, the book is always intelligent, often astute, and seemed radical for German historiography when he wrote it, but rather complacent now with its patriotic bias. James J. Sheehan's superb *German History, 1770–1866* (1989) has a noteworthy chapter, "Culture in the Revolutionary Era." See also the thoughtful discussion by Thomas Nipperdey, "Auf der Suche nach der Identität: Romantischer Nationalismus," in *Nachdenken über die deutsche Geschichte* (1986), 110–25.

For French romantic politics, see Frank E. Manuel, *The New World of Henri Saint-Simon* (1956), a substantial treatment, and the brief study by Pierre Trahard, *Le Romantisme défini par "Le Globe"* (1924), an introduction to that influential newspaper, with a selection of articles appended. David Owen Evans, *Social Romanticism in France, 1830–1848* (1951), is a handy survey of the romantics' political side. And see H. J. Hunt, *Le Socialisme romantique et le romantisme en France* (1935). Ethel Harris, *Lamartine et le peuple* (1932), solidly canvasses the complicated career traversed by the poet's political ideas. For the restless political thought of the most articulate liberal writing in French, see Biancamaria Fontana, *Benjamin Constant and the Post-revolutionary Mind* (1991), and Stephen Holmes, *Benjamin Constant and the Making of Modern Liberalism* (1984). Both are illuminating, though the latter is too strenuously disposed to find consistency in that most volatile of theorists and activists.

Romantic religion is naturally a prime topic in all this literature. A few titles need to be added: David Jasper, *Coleridge as Poet and Religious Thinker* (1985), which, like other works on Coleridge, pleads for his elusive coherence. Fanny Imle, *Friedrich von Schlegels religiöse Entwicklung von Kant zum Katholizismus* (1927), follows the evolution of his religious thought. German theologians, notably Schleiermacher, played a significant role in formulating romantic religiosity. See Friedrich Wilhelm Katzenbach, *Friedrich Daniel Ernst Schleiermacher in Selbstzeugnissen und Bilddokumenten* (1967)—once again that popular series of short lives comes to the rescue. The uncompleted biography by the great German intellectual historian Wilhelm Dilthey, *Leben Schleiermachers,* vol. I (1870; 2nd ed., 1922), splendidly displays Dilthey's historical method. Stephen Sykes, *Friedrich Schleiermacher* (1971), is a brief introduction in English.

As for romantic love and the impress that it left on later generations, see, in addition to titles mentioned earlier, Paul Kluckhohn, *Die Auffassung der Liebe in der Literature des 18. Jahrhunderts und in der deutschen Romantik* (1922; 2nd ed., 1931), standard but (from my perspective) timid; *Shelley on Love: An Anthology,* ed. Richard Holmes (1980); Karen Lystra, *Searching the Heart: Women, Men, and Romantic Love in Nineteenth-Century America* (1989), an instructive monograph; Marion A. Kaplan, "For Love or Money—The Marriage Strategies of Jews in Imperial Germany," *Leo Baeck Yearbook XXVIII* (1983), 263–300, the very model of a paper, persuasively argued and amply documented; Bonnie G. Smith, *Ladies of the Leisure Class: The Bourgeoises of Northern France in the Nineteenth Century* (1981), which documents the ignorance of upper-class young Frenchwomen in sexual matters. Peter Gay, *The Tender Passion,* vol. II, *The Bourgeois Experience: Victoria to Freud* (1986), explores the varieties of nineteenth-century love in detail, with revisionist intentions and a sizable bibliography; the applicable psychoanalytic literature is at pp. 430–31, 434–36, 451–52.

While we have scores of specialized studies on the afterlife of romantics and how their message spread, they have not yet been brought together. Among the most instructive titles making at least a partial attempt is the excellent long essay by Virgil Nemoianu, *The Taming of Romanticism: European Literature and the Age of Biedermeier* (1984), which takes all of Europe as its province to demonstrate how the romantics' extravagant longing was adapted to respectable bourgeois ways. See also Donald D. Stone, *The Romantic Impulse in Victorian Fiction* (1980), almost as interesting as Nemoianu's volume; it describes the way that romanticism infiltrated the fiction written by English novelists from Disraeli to Meredith.

As an instance of the material that awaits synthesis, take that centering on Byron: for his reputation at home in his lifetime and beyond, there is Samuel C. Chew, *Byron in England: His Fame and After-fame* (1924), to be supplemented with *Byron's Political and Cultural Influence in Nineteenth-Century Europe: A Symposium,* ed. Paul Graham Trueblood (1981). See also Richard Ackermann, *Lord Byron. Sein Leben, seine Werke, sein Einfluss auf die deutsche Litteratur* (1901), and Walter J. Clark, *Byron und die romantische*

Poesie in Frankreich (1901). But to list such literature extensively would explode this bibliography.

TWO: Exercises in Self-definition

When I started on this project around 1970, agreeing with Oscar Wilde that "autobiography is irresistible," scholars were just beginning to find uses for modern autobiographies as historical material.* A century ago, the German historian Hans Glagau confronted autobiographers with a historian's outlook, in *Die moderne Selbstbiographie als historische Quelle. Eine Untersuchung* (1903), but did not influence scholars. One of very few students of the genre before 1914, Anna Robeson Burr, in *The Autobiography: A Critical and Comparative Study* (1909), offers revealing glimpses into the taste of a bygone era (pro-Rousseau for his sincerity, anti-Goethe for his evasiveness).

After the Second World War, Georges Gusdorf was one of the first to study written self-portraits: "Conditions et limites de l'autobiographie," *Formen der Selbstdarstellung,* ed. Günter Reichenkron and Erich Haase (1956), 105–23. Since then the topic has become downright fashionable. While I have benefited from a number of authors, this has largely been benefit through opposition: many are intent on documenting the self-construction, even self-creation, of the autobiographer who, to their mind, produces a special type of fiction. My own view is that, on the contrary, an autobiographer's every word is true, including distortions and outright lies. Literary critics have been deconstructing the usual suspects—St. Augustine, Rousseau, Goethe, J. S. Mill, Ruskin—and view them not as the recorders but as the architects of their recorded lives. Some of the most provocative exemplars are Avrom Fleishman, *Figures of Autobiography: The Language of Self-writing* (1983), which, bulky and ambitious, develops a typology of self-inventions; James Olney, *Metaphors of Self: The Meaning of Autobiography* (1972),

---

*On the other hand, historians had long paid attention to ancient and medieval autobiographies. For comparative purposes, I consulted Georg Misch, *A History of Autobiography in Antiquity,* 2 vols. (1907; 3rd ed., 1949–50; tr. E. W. Dickes in collaboration with the author, 1950), long regarded as authoritative if stodgy and, from our more "liberated" perspective, overly reticent. See also Paul Lehmann, "Autobiographies of the Middle Ages," *Transactions of the Royal Historical Society,* 5th ser., III (1953), 41–52; T. C. Price Zimmermann, "Confession and Autobiography in the Early Renaissance," *Renaissance Studies in Honor of Hans Baron,* ed. Anthony Molho and John A. Tedeschi (1971), 121–40; and L. D. Lerner, "Puritanism and the Spiritual Autobiography," *Hibbert Journal,* LV (1956–57), 373–86. Lerner analyzes the tremulous accounting that would have considerable impact on later writers looking into the spiritual mirror; on this point, see the fine study by Patricia Caldwell, *The Puritan Conversion Narrative: The Beginnings of American Expression* (1983). We must not forget Montaigne, the greatest autobiographer until Rousseau (and perhaps beyond). Two outstanding explorations are Donald M. Frame, *Montaigne's Discovery of Man: The Humanization of a Humanist* (1955), and Jean Starobinski, *Montaigne in Motion* (1982; tr. Arthur Goldhammer, 1985). Peter Burke, *Montaigne* (1981), is the best brief account.

which offers a Jungian slant from a similar standpoint; Regenia Gagnier, *Subjectivities: A History of Self-representation in Britain, 1832–1920* (1991), who, stating her allegiance in her title, adds to the familiar mix of working-class autobiographies and memoirs. One form that this skepticism about the dependability of the text takes is best represented in Jack Stillinger, *Multiple Authorship and the Myth of Solitary Genius* (1992); while Stillinger gives telling examples of hidden collaborators in Mill (his wife helped), or Coleridge (German philosophers helped, unwittingly), this does not make "solitary genius" a myth.* In two studies, *American Autobiography: The Prophetic Mode* (1979) and *Altered Egos: Authority in American Autobiography* (1989), G. Thomas Couser pursues what he considers the particular popularity of autobiography in the United States; the latter volume is indebted to post-structuralist theory. Linda H. Peterson, *Victorian Autobiography: The Tradition of Self-interpretation* (1986), states its thesis in the subtitle. Susanna Egan, *Patterns of Experience in Autobiography* (1984), sees autobiographies as inventions, beholden to the model of a pilgrimage, a journey, a climb. An influential exemplar of subjectivist scholarship which has spawned a school of "new historicists," Stephen Greenblatt's erudite *Renaissance Self-fashioning from More to Shakespeare* (1980) is eminently worth reading, even for those who dissent from his position. It is perhaps typical of this style of thinking that Herbert Leibowitz should title a perfectly sensible volume, *Fabricating Lives: Explorations in American Autobiography* (1989). Paul John Eakin, *Fictions in Autobiography: Studies in the Art of Self-invention* (1985), is the most radical representative of this school; though clearly written and often illuminating, it has not persuaded me.

One salutary exception to this modish view is Jerome Hamilton Buckley's accessible study of English exemplars, *The Turning Key: Autobiography and the Subjective Impulse since 1800* (1984).† See also A. O. J. Cockshut, *The Art of Autobiography in 19th & 20th Century England* (1984), which comes close to my own view of the autobiographical act. There is much wisdom in Karl Joachim Weintraub, *The Value of the Individual: Self and Circumstance in Autobiography* (1978), which moves through the centuries. Roy Pascal's impressive *Design and Truth in Autobiography* (1960) does much to clarify knotted issues. Jean Starobinski, "Le Style de l'autobiographie," *Poétique. Revue de théorie et d'analyse littéraires*, I (1970), 257–65; and Philippe Lejeune, *L'Autobiographie en France* (1971), a much quoted book, have left their traces on these pages. John Sturrock, *The Language of Autobiography* (1993), abounds in crisp judgments, normally fair-minded but at times, as with Rousseau, excessively harsh. William C. Spengemann, *The Forms of Autobiography: Episodes in the History of a Literary Genre* (1980), traces self-writing from St. Augustine to the mid-nineteenth century and adds an annotated bibliographical essay of nearly eighty

---

*The subjectivist view is not confined to studies of the nineteenth century. Consider John O. Lyons, *The Invention of the Self: The Hinge of Consciousness in the Eighteenth Century* (1978).

†"Autobiography is active, constructive, performative," writes J. Hillis Miller, ironically in a festschrift for Jerome Buckley. "It is a way of doing things with words, not a passive description of something already there. The fundamental tool of autobiography . . . is prosopopoeia, in this case the ascription of life to an effigy made of words." Miller, "Prosopopoeia and *Praeterita*," *19th-Century Lives: Essays Presented to Jerome Hamilton Buckley*, ed. Laurence S. Lockridge et al. (1989), 129.

pages. *When the Grass Was Taller: Autobiography and the Experience of Childhood* (1984), a fascinating monograph by Richard N. Coe, takes modern memoirs of youth across several continents.

For Rousseau, I used mainly the first volume of the splendid edition of his *Oeuvres complètes*, 4 vols., ed. Bernard Gagnebin, Robert Osmont, and Marcel Raymond (1959–69), which contains the *Confessions* and other autobiographical writings, tributaries to his masterpiece, and equipped with extensive, informative introductions, notes, and documents. His letters have been magnificently edited—a heroic task!—by R. A. Leigh, *Correspondance complète de Rousseau*, 45 vols. (1965–86). Jean Guéhenno wrote his exceptionally revealing two-volume biography, *Jean-Jacques Rousseau* (1962; tr. John and Doreen Weightman, 1966), without hindsight, trying to "relive Rousseau's life day by day" (I, xi). The late Maurice Cranston did not live to complete the third volume of his comprehensive biography; an impressive torso is left: *Jean-Jacques: The Early Life and Work of Jean-Jacques Rousseau, 1712–1754* (1982) and *Noble Savage: Jean-Jacques Rousseau, 1754–1762* (1991).

Several critical editions of Goethe's works provided access to *Aus meinem Leben. Dichtung und Wahrheit*. I relied mainly on the lavish, if too adoring, commentary by Erich Trunz, general editor of the *Werke*, 14 vols. (1948–60; 6th to 12th ed., 1981–86), vols. IX and X; other autobiographical writings appear in vol. X and XI. As Goethe himself insisted, *all* his works were fragments of a great confession, and so all stand to substantiate, expand, or correct *Dichtung und Wahrheit*. The letters in Goethe's correspondence, authoritatively edited by Karl Robert Mandelkow (though leaving a few minor gaps), *Briefe von und an Goethe*, 6 vols. (1962–69; 3rd and 4th eds., 1988), are so many commentaries. So are Goethe's copiously recorded conversations, elements in his self-analysis. His most memorable pronouncements were captured in Johann Peter Eckermann, *Gespräche mit Goethe in den letzten Jahren seines Lebens*, 3 vols. (1837–48; many editions). Amid the mountainous biographical literature, I single out Nicholas Boyle's scholarly, lucid *Goethe: The Poet and the Age*, vol. I, *The Poetry of Desire (1749–1790)* (1991), critical but not carping; its first three hundred pages cover the years of *Dichtung and Wahrheit*. Among earlier contributions, Barker Fairley, *Goethe as Revealed in His Poetry* (1932) and *A Study of Goethe* (1947), are masterly. More recently, Albrecht Schöne has made outstanding contributions to our understanding of Goethe, notably in *Götterzeichen, Liebeszauber, Satanskult. Neue Einblicke in alte Goethetexte* (1982; 3rd enlarged ed., 1993); *Goethes Farbentheologie* (1987); and *Fausts Himmelfahrt. Zur letzten Szene der Tragödie* (1994). K. R. Eissler, *Goethe: A Psychoanalytic Study, 1775–1786*, 2 vols. (1963), is an amazing production: an imaginative depth analysis of a decade in Goethe's life, awkwardly written and inclined to overargumentation but filled with startling gleams of insight. The long review of three-quarters of *Dichtung und Wahrheit* in the *Edinburgh Review*, XXVI (February–June 1816), 304–37, appreciative but not uncritical, is a good instance of German literature being taken seriously abroad—as long as it was Goethe.

Hans Christian Andersen's strange, significantly unreliable autobiography, deliberately titled to contrast with Goethe's in its claim to be more truthful than *Dichtung und Wahrheit,* may be corrected with Elias Bredsdorff, *Hans Christian Andersen: The Story of His Life and Work, 1805–75* (1975), which sees through Andersen's cheery and sentimental fictions.*

Georges Lubin has brought together and beautifully edited George Sand's voluminous autobiographical writings, *Ma vie* (1854–55) and related texts: *Oeuvres autobiographiques,* 2 vols. (1970–71). The same editor is responsible for a magnificent edition of Sand's almost literally countless letters: *Correspondance,* 25 vols (1964–91). For biographies, see (almost inescapably) André Maurois, *Lélia: The Life of George Sand* (1952; tr. Gerard Hopkins, 1977), and Joseph Barry, *Infamous Woman: The Life of George Sand* (1977). Barry has also edited a handy anthology: *George Sand in Her Own Words* (1979).

Peter Abbs's candid introduction to Edmund Gosse, *Father and Son: A Study of Two Temperaments* (1907; ed. 1983), raises the right questions. An admirable biography, Ann Thwaite, *Edmund Gosse: A Literary Landscape* (1984), shoulders the burden of "rewriting" Gosse's masterpiece, and largely replaces Evan Charteris, *The Life and Letters of Sir Edmund Gosse* (1931). As one might expect, a number of more general titles listed before (notably those by Peterson, Cockshut, and Buckley) feature *Father and Son.*

I was first alerted to Théodore Jouffroy by D. G. Charlton, *Secular Religions in France, 1815–1870* (1963), esp. 226–27. Jean Pommier, *Deux études sur Jouffroy et son temps* (1930), says the essential. The key texts include Jouffroy, "Comme les dogmes finissent" (written in 1823, published in 1825), *Le Cahier vert. Comment les dogmes finissent. Lettres inédites,* ed. Pierre Poux (1923), and above all "De l'organisation des sciences philosophiques," *Nouveaux mélanges philosophiques,* ed. Ph. Damiron (1842), both to be read with Pierre Leroux's energetic protest against the bowdlerizing of Jouffroy's texts: *De la mutilation d'un écrit postume de Théodore Jouffroy* (1843).

Darwin biographies keep coming; I have consulted Adrian Desmond and James Moore, *Darwin* (1991), and the shorter essay by Ernst Mayr, *One Long Argument: Charles Darwin and the Genesis of Modern Evolutionary Thought* (1991); the eclectic psychoanalyst John Bowlby weighed in with *Charles Darwin: A New Life* (1991). For Cardinal Newman, see esp. Meriol Trevor's two-volume life, *Newman: The Pillar of the Cloud* (1962) and *Light in Winter* (1963). Among sound specialized studies (which Newman seems to attract), I found C. F. Harrold, *John Henry Newman: An Expository and Critical Study of His Mind, Thought, and Art* (1945), most rewarding. Geoffrey Faber, *Oxford Apostles: A Character Study of the Oxford Movement* (1933; 2nd ed., 1956), is celebrated with good reason for its candor about the emotional—and erotic—life of Newman and his circle. An interesting Victorian effort to be fair is R. H. Hutton, *Cardinal Newman* (1891).

---

*I discovered Kjeld Heltoft, *Hans Christian Andersen as an artist* (1969), an extraordinary volume, after completing my text. A pity, for Andersen's landscapes, self-portraits, doodles, and paper cuts show a remarkable talent and (with their writers caught in a bottle, profiles stuffed to the brim with faces, Bosch-like caricatures, Rorschach blots, claustrophobic urban scenes, monstrous women with four pendulous breasts) call out for psychoanalytic interpretation.

With the completion of the definitive new edition of the *Collected Works of John Stuart Mill*, ed. J. M. Robson et al., 33 vols. (1963–91), one may hope for a weightier biography than Michael St. John Packe's *The Life of John Stuart Mill* (1954), which with all its genial qualities is not equal to its subject. There is much of interest in *The Early Draft of John Stuart Mill's "Autobiography,"* ed. Jack Stillinger (1961). The first to psychoanalyze Mill's breakdown was the analyst A. W. Levi, "The 'Mental Crisis' of John Stuart Mill," *Psychoanalysis and Psychoanalytic Review*, XXXII (1945), 86–101; his insight has been explored in detail in Bruce Mazlish, *James and John Stuart Mill: Father and Son in the Nineteenth Century* (1975), chs. 10–12. Two readable and reliable studies by Alan Ryan, *The Philosophy of John Stuart Mill* (1970) and *J. S. Mill* (1970), are essential for a general comprehension. Obviously, no study of Victorian autobiography has slighted Mill.

For comments on Theodor Fontane's *Meine Kinderjahre. Autobiographischer Roman*, see Walter Müller-Seidel, "Fontanes Autobiographik," *Jahrbuch der deutschen Schiller-Gesellschaft*, XIII (1969), 397–418; and Günter Niggle, "Fontanes 'Meine Kinderjahre' und die Gattungstradition," *Sprache und Bekenntnis. Sonderband des Literaturwissenschaftlichen Jahrbuches* (1971), 257–79. (I have not seen Brenda Doust's promising-sounding "An Examination of Theodor Fontane's Autobiographical Writings and Their Relation to His Prose Fiction with Special Reference to 'Meine Kinderjahre,' " M.Phil. thesis, London [1970].) Though devoted to the second volume of Fontane's autobiography, Lilian R. Furst, "The Autobiography of an Extrovert: Fontane's 'Von Zwanzig bis Dreissig,' " *German Life and Letters*, XII (1958–59), 287–94, has much to say about the first. So does Helmuth Nürnberger, *Der frühe Fontane. Politik, Poesie, Geschichte, 1840 bis 1860* (1967).

THREE: Usable Pasts

John A. Garraty, *The Nature of Biography* (1958), which offers a sketch history of biography and a full bibliography, is an informal introduction, sympathetic to what we now call "psychobiography." His earlier "The Interrelations of Psychology and Biography," *Psychological Bulletin*, LV (1954), 569–82, was a suitably tentative exploration. Leon Edel is emphatically in this camp; see *Literary Biography* (1957; ed. 1959), slight in bulk but rich in suggestions. (In an elegant, opinionated inaugural lecture, "Literary Biography" [1971; reprinted in *Golden Codgers: Biographical Speculations,* 1973], Richard Ellmann, one of the great biographers of our time, skeptically takes on Freudians like Edel.) James L. Clifford's anecdotal *From Puzzles to Portraits: Problems of a Literary Biographer* (1970), is far more cautious about Freud, and André Maurois, *Aspects of Biography* (1928; tr. S. C. Roberts, 1929), is downright hostile. So is Robert Gittings's brief *The Nature of Biography* (1978), which, though professing admiration for Freud (and, impartially, Jung), pronounces psychoanalytic biography a failure. More needs to be done on the possible uses of psychoanalysis for biography. The enterprise has been partly stymied by Freud's scathing comments about biography as an impossible genre, susceptible to distortions and lies.* A conference at Chapel Hill in 1981 produced *Introspection in Biography: The Biographer's Quest for Self-Awareness,* ed. Samuel H. Baron and Carl Pletsch (1985), which brings to bear psychoanalytic ideas on choosing, researching, judging, and writing a Life, and is a brave, inconclusive collective attempt.

Lytton Strachey, that nemesis of nineteenth-century biographers, has been satisfactorily covered in Michael Holroyd's exhaustive biography, *Lytton Strachey: The Unknown Years (1880–1910)* (1967) and *Lytton Strachey: The Years of Achievement (1910–1932)* (1968), esp. II, 261–325, which examines *Eminent Victorians,* its value and its failings, and the public response.

A. O. J. Cockshut, *Truth to Life: The Art of Biography in the Nineteenth Century* (1974), is sensible as usual; Ruth Hoberman, *Modernizing Lives: Experiments in English Biography, 1918–1939* (1987), reaches back into the years before the First World War in ch. 2, "The Revolt against Victorianism." Ira Bruce Nadel, *Biography: Fiction, Fact, Form* (1984), makes an original contribution, esp. in ch. 1, "Biography as an Institution." See also Helmut Scheuer, *Biographie. Studien zur Funktion und zum Wandel einer literarischen Gattung vom 18. Jahrhundert bis zur Gegenwart* (1979), a comprehensive and critical survey. In *Studies in Biography,* ed. Daniel Aaron (1978), accomplished biographers—Edward Mendelson, John Clive, James Clifford, Jean Strouse, and others—draw on their experience. In contrast, *Approaches to Victorian Biography,* ed. George P. Landow (1979), is fairly miscellaneous. *Victorian Muse: Selected Criticism and Parody of the Period,* ed. William E. Fredeman, Ira Bruce Nadel, and John F. Stasny (1986), collects a bouquet of nineteenth-century articles. On the vexed question of how biography relates to literary criticism, William Empson's last book, *Using Biography* (1984), penetrating and amusing as usual, brings together biographical essays on British poets and novelists.

John Morley, politician, editor, and indefatigable biographer, has little to say about the last in his *Recollections,* 2 vols. (1917). But see D. A. Hamer, *John Morley: Liberal Intellectual in Politics* (1968), John L. Kijinski, "John Morley's 'English Men of Letters' Series and the Politics of Reading," *Victorian Studies,* XXXIV (Winter 1991), 205–25, and Sidney Lee, Leslie Stephen's successor as editor of the *DNB, Principles of Biography* (1911). John T. Morse, Jr., recalls "Incidents Connected with the American Statesmen Series," *Proceedings of the Massachusetts Historical Society,* LXIV (October 1930–June 1932), 370–88. On the *DNB,* see David Cannadine, "The Dictionary of National Biography" (1981), in *The Pleasures of the Past* (1989), 275–84.

Carlyle's key text, *On Heroes, Hero-Worship, & the Heroic in History* (1841), has been admirably edited by Michael K. Goldberg et al. (1993). Sidney Hook, *The Hero in History: A Study in Limitation and Possibility* (1943), esp. chs. 1–3, is a pointed critique. See also Dixon Wecter, *The Hero in America: A Chronicle of Hero-Worship* (1941), a

---

*"Anyone who writes a biography," wrote Freud to Arnold Zweig, who wanted to do Freud's life, "commits himself to lies, concealments, hypocrisy, flattery and even to hiding his own lack of understanding, for biographical truth is not available, and if it were, it would be useless." May 31, 1936, Sigmund Freud–Arnold Zweig, *Briefwechsel,* ed. Ernst L. Freud (1968; ed. 1984), 137.

substantial, popularly written volume that ranges from the seventeenth to the twentieth century. On the scandal surrounding Froude's biography of Carlyle, which generated an embittered debate over candor or reticence in biography, see some violent reactions in endnotes above (p. 371); there were many more. The controversy between Froude and the Carlyle family is tersely covered in Garraty, *Biography*, 95–97 and 226. Fred Kaplan, *Thomas Carlyle: A Biography* (1983), focusing on the life rather than on the work, has ably dealt with the issue, pp. 542–47. The two biographies devoted to Carlyle's embattled biographer are at best moderately helpful: Herbert Paul, *The Life of Froude* (1905), idolizes its subject, and Waldo Hilary Dunn, *James Anthony Froude: A Biography*, 2 vols. (1961–63), though it takes its epigraph from Froude—"I have no respect for idealizing biographies"—weaves garlands around Froude's autobiographical texts. Edmund S. Purcell, "On the Ethics of Suppression in Biography," *19th Century*, XL (July–December 1896), 533–42, quotes Cardinal Newman: "another great subject . . . I mean the endemic perennial fidget which possesses us about giving scandal, facts are omitted in great histories, or glosses are put on memorable acts, because they are thought not edifying, whereas of all scandals such omissions, such glosses are the greatest."

For that hardworking moralist Samuel Smiles, who still awaits a full biography, see above all Asa Briggs's essay, "Samuel Smiles and the Gospel of Work," *Victorian People: A Reassessment of Persons and Themes, 1851–67* (1955), 116–39. Tim Travers, *Samuel Smiles and the Victorian Work Ethic* (1987), limits itself to the promise of the title. Parson Weems has been amply dealt with; chattily but adequately by Lewis Leary, *The Book-Peddling Parson* (1984). The bewildering diversity of biographers' and historians' attitudes toward Napoleon I has been persuasively reduced to order by Pieter Geyl, *Napoleon For and Against* (1945; tr. Olive Renier, 1949). The evolution of the Napoleonic legend is canvassed by Jean Tulard, *Napoleon: The Myth of the Saviour* (1987; tr. Teresa Waugh, 1984). For Nelson, see in addition to A. T. Mahan's long standard *The Life of Nelson: The Embodiment of the Sea Power of Great Britain* (1897; 2nd ed., 1899), Carola Oman's extensive, thoroughly documented *Nelson* (1946). Her *Admiral Nelson* (1954) is a short Life.

Elizabeth Gaskell's famous biography of Charlotte Brontë is discussed in Arthur Pollard, *Mrs. Gaskell: Novelist and Biographer* (1965), ch. 7, and Winifred Gérin, *Elizabeth Gaskell: A Biography* (1970), esp. ch. 15 (though her whole study is illuminating). An older analysis, by Clement K. Shorter, *Charlotte Brontë and Her Circle* (1896), intelligently appreciates Gaskell's *Charlotte Brontë*.

Justi's great biography of Winckelmann should be read with another important nineteenth-century document, Walter Pater's heated tribute in *The Renaissance: Studies in Art and Poetry* (1873; last enlarged ed., 1893). Henry C. Hatfield, *Winckelmann and His German Critics, 1755–1781* (1943), his *Aesthetic Paganism in German Literature, from Winckelmann to the Death of Goethe* (1964), esp. ch. 1, "Winckelmann and the Myth of Greece," and Hans Zeller, *Winckelmanns Beschreibung des Apollo im Belvedere* (1955), serve as correctives. Francis Haskell and Nicholas Penny, *Taste and the Antique: The Lure of Classical Sculpture, 1500–1900* (1981), has much of importance to say about Winckelmann. (This volume was in production when I came across Alex Potts, *Flesh and the Ideal: Winckelmann and the Origins of Art History* [1944].)

As historians increasingly made themselves into a profession, they became more self-conscious (in both senses) about their pedagogy, their leadership role (if any), and their theoretical orientation. G. P. Gooch, *History and Historians in the Nineteenth Century* (1913; rev. ed., 1959), holds up surprisingly well. Ernst Breisach, *Historiography: Ancient, Medieval & Modern* (1983), is sweeping, at times too hasty to judge (as in his dismissal of psychohistory). The unsurpassed ancient historian Arnaldo Momigliano occupied himself with nineteenth-century historical erudition through much of his life; some of his wonderful essays, collected in *A. D. Momigliano: Studies on Modern Scholarship,* ed. G. W. Bowersock and T. J. Cornell (1994), deal with Droysen, Grote, Burckhardt, Freeman, and others. Herbert Butterfield's erudite and rewarding *Man on His Past: The Study of Historical Scholarship* (1955) discusses the origins of modern historiography and some of its nineteenth-century giants.

France has been well served by William R. Keylor, *Academy and Community: The Foundation of the French Historical Profession* (1975), a model monograph. An early foreign appraisal was Henry E. Bourne, *The Teaching of History and Civics in the Elementary and Secondary Schools* (1902). Most prominent French historians, far more than historians elsewhere, were enmeshed in the debates about education; see Charles Seignobos, *L'Histoire dans l'enseignement secondaire* (1906); Ernest Lavisse, *L'Enseignement de l'histoire à l'école primaire* (1912); Louis Halphen, *L'Histoire en France depuis cent ans* (1914); and Charles Victor Langlois, *Les Etudes historiques* (1915). For a more recent appraisal, see Antoine Prost, *Histoire de l'enseignement en France, 1800–1967* (1968). Claude Bernard, *L'Enseignement de l'histoire en France au XIXe siècle* (1978), mainly anthologizes germane texts with (useful) commentaries. For French Catholic schools, see Jacqueline Freyssinet-Dominjon, *Les Manuels d'histoire de l'école libre, 1882–1959* (1969), to be contrasted with Phyllis Stock-Morton, *Moral Education for a Secular Society: The Development of "Morale Laïque" in Nineteenth Century France* (1988). French historians have enjoyed writing about their fellow professionals. See, for one, Alphonse Aulard, *Taine: Historien de la Révolution française* (1907). See also the first editor of the *Revue historique,* Gabriel Monod, appreciating his elders: *Les Maîtres de l'histoire: Renan, Taine, Michelet* (1894). Paul Farmer, *France Reviews Its Revolutionary Origins: Social Politics and Historical Opinion in the Third Republic* (1944), examines the critiques that French historians have lavished on that literally unforgettable event. (For its instructive English counterpart, see the account by the literary historian Barton R. Friedman of Blake, Scott, Hazlitt, Carlyle, Dickens, and Hardy, in *Fabricating History: English Writers on the French Revolution* [1988]—how they love words like "fabricating"!) See also Ann Rigney, *The Rhetoric of Historical Representation: Three Narrative Histories of the French Revolution* (1990). The historiography of the French Revolution has long been a test case of the way the historian's politics may guide his conclusions. In the 1890s, Lord Action already lectured on the subject: "Appendix: The Literature of the Revolution," *Lectures on the French*

Revolution (1910). *The French Revolution and the Birth of Modernity,* ed. Ferenc Fehér (1990), offers a variety of stances from the left, in Eric Hobsbawm, "The Making of a 'Bourgeois Revolution'" (30–48), to the right, in François Furet, "Transformations in the Historiography of the Revolution" (264–77, tr. Brian Singer). Rolf-Joachim Sattler, *Die Französische Revolution in europäischen Schulbüchern. Eine vergleichende Schulbuchanalyse* (1959), offers an interesting comparative account of what German, English, French, and Italian pupils learn about the Revolution.

Stanley Mellon moves into the early nineteenth century with *The Political Uses of History: A Study of Historians in the French Restoration* (1958). R. D. Anderson, *Education in France, 1848–1870* (1975), has perceptive pages on history teaching at mid-century. For the most impassioned, rhetorical, and once again influential French historian of the age, see *La 'voie royale': Essai sur l'idée du peuple dans l'oeuvre de Michelet* (1971), by Paul Viallaneix, editor of Michelet's massive *Journal.* Roland Barthes's selection from, and commentary on, *Michelet* (1954; tr. Richard Howard, 1987), and Arthur Mitzman's precise, uncompromising psychoanalytic study, *Michelet, Historian: Rebirth and Romanticism in 19th Century France* (1990), are enlightening, each in its own way. Lionel Gossman has written some highly instructive (though I think excessively subjectivist) essays on political French historians like Augustin Thierry: *Between History and Literature* (1990). Thierry, an activist though, he claimed, a fair-minded professional, raises the vexed issue of the "political historian," of whom the nineteenth century had its fair share. See esp. *Historians in Politics,* ed. Walter Laqueur and George L. Mosse (1974), which has informative essays on Tocqueville, Treitschke, Mommsen, Michelet, Lord Bryce, and others. And see the ambitious, disillusioned study by François Hartog, *Le XIXe siècle et l'histoire: Le Cas Fustel de Coulanges* (1988), which takes the "case" of a celebrated historian of the ancient world and of early France to show that scientific history and polemical intentions are hard to disentangle.*

For history as institution and idea in Germany, both before and after unification in 1871, see esp. Hartmut Boockmann et al., *Geschichtswissenschaft und Vereinswesen im 19. Jahrhundert. Beiträge zur Geschichte historischer Forschung in Deutschland* (1972) and *Deutsche Geschichtswissenschaft um 1900,* ed. Notker Hammerstein (1988). Ernst Weymar, *Das Selbstverständnis der Deutschen. Ein Bericht über den Geist des Geschichtsunterrichts der höheren Schulen im 19. Jahrhundert* (1961), is an excellent study of the fundamental convictions that animated the teaching of history in German schools and the texts pupils used. Wolfgang Hardtwig, *Geschichtskultur und Wissenschaft* (1990), collects some learned, highly recommended essays on the study of history in Victorian Germany, its growing "scientification," and the debates over the very nature of the discipline. There is also an interesting sociological study of historians, the first half of which is relevant here: Wolfgang Weber, *Priester der Klio: Historisch-sozialwissenschaftliche Studien zur Herkunft und*

---

*That the scientific ideal was powerful among late-nineteenth-century historians can be amply documented. See for one instance P. Lacombe's bulky *De l'histoire considérée comme science* (1894). A good introduction to the ongoing debate, amid a sizable literature, is Theodor Schieder, *Geschichte als Wissenschaft. Eine Einführung* (1965).

Karriere deutscher Historiker und zur Geschichte der Geschichtswissenschaft, 1800–1970 (1984).*
On the rise of historicism, with Ranke as its high priest—more on Ranke below (pp.
417–18)—see Friedrich Meinecke's last major work, *Historism,* 2 vols. (1936; tr. J. E.
Anderson, 1972), subtle, once compelling, but badly misleading, with its unhistorical
condescension to the historians of the Enlightenment, its excessive praise of Goethe as
an impulse to historical thinking, and its implicit claim to German superiority. A more
nuanced history of that perspective on the past is Friedrich Jaeger and Jörn Rüsen,
Geschichte des Historismus. Eine Einführung (1992). For fundamental ideas, see Georg G.
Iggers's clear-headed *The German Conception of History: The National Tradition of Historical Thought from Herder to the Present* (1968).

Thomas P. Peardon, *The Transition in English Historical Writing, 1760–1830* (1933),
sketches in the early background for British developments. In his authoritative *The
Victorian Mirror of History* (1985), A. Dwight Culler explores the way nineteenth-century
Englishmen—poets, historians, critics, theologians, painters—used their past. It may be
read with the charming, affectionate account by Frances J. Woodward, *The Doctor's
Disciples: A Study of Four Pupils of Arnold of Rugby* (1954), for Dr. Arnold's impact on his
pupils. J. W. Burrow, *A Liberal Descent: Victorian Historians and the English Past* (1981),
brilliantly analyzes four nineteenth-century historians: Macaulay, Stubbs, Freeman, and
Froude. *Some Modern Historians of Britain: Essays in Honor of R. L. Schuyler,* ed. Herman
Ausubel, J. Bartlet Brebner, and Erling M. Hunt (1951), gathers a handy collection of
short essays, ranging from John Lingard to Eileen Power. Some of England's most
important historians have been covered in texts already cited. See also George Otto
Trevelyan, *The Life and Letters of Lord Macaulay* (1876; enlarged ed., 1908), still worth
reading for details but largely superseded by Owen Dudley Edwards, *Macaulay* (1988),
terse and lively; and John Clive, *Macaulay: The Shaping of the Historian* (1973), celebrated
for its stylishness but closing before Macaulay started on his *History of England.* Sir
Charles Firth, *A Commentary on Macaulay's History of England,* ed. Godfrey Davies
(1938), is beautifully informed and just. H. E. Bell, *Maitland: A Critical Examination and
Assessment* (1965), and the more expansive C. H. S. Fifoot, *Frederic William Maitland: A
Life* (1971), tell the life of the great legal historian. G. R. Elton, *F. W. Maitland* (1985), is
a vehement essay. For the debate between J. B. Bury and G. M. Trevelyan over history
as art or science, see the excellent pages in David Cannadine, *G. M. Trevelyan: A Life in
History* (1992).

The greatest historian who never wrote a book has had several studies. See Gertrude
Himmelfarb, *Lord Acton: A Study in Conscience and Politics* (1962), and Hugh Tulloch,
Acton (1988), succinct and witty. Butterfield, *Man on his Past* (cited above, p. 414),
devotes two chapters to Acton and prints a number of exceedingly interesting, hitherto
unpublished passages from his writings. Valerie E. Chancellor, *History for Their Masters:
Opinion in the English History Textbook, 1880–1914* (1970), has gone to the sources from
which English pupils learned the facts—often less or more—about their past.

---

*I owe my reading of Boockmann and Weber to some fine discussions in James J. Sheehan,
German History, 1770–1866 (1989), 542–55, 841–51.

The first American to address the work of his profession was J. F. Jameson, in *The History of Historical Writing in America* (1891), a witness to his century as much as its historian. Michael Kraus's succinct *The Writing of American History* (1953) comes down to Charles Beard in less than four hundred pages. John Higham, with Leonard Krieger and Felix Gilbert, *History* (1965), is (not surprisingly, considering its authors) an authoritative survey. And see *Historical Scholarship in the United States, 1876–1901*, ed. W. Stull Holt (1938). David Levin has astutely canvassed four major American historians— Bancroft, Prescott, Motley, Parkman—in *History as Romantic Art* (1959); his comments on Motley proved particularly usable. Motley's outspoken letters are a significant source: *The Correspondence of John Lothrop Motley, D. L. C.,* ed. George William Curtis, 2 vols. (1889), and *John Lothrop Motley and His Family: Further Letters and Records,* ed. Susan St. John Mildmay (1910). Motley had vocal admirers in the bourgeois century; note for one prominent instance Ruth Putnam, *William the Silent, Prince of Orange: The Moderate Man of the Sixteenth Century,* 2 vols. (1895). But from the beginning, such major Dutch historians as Robert Fruin protested against Motley's onesidedness. Pieter Geyl, "Motley and His 'Rise of the Dutch Republic' " (1956), in *Encounters in History* (1963), sharp but fair, shows this to be the modern verdict, too. J. W. Smit, "The Present Position of Studies regarding the Revolt of the Netherlands," in *Britain and the Netherlands,* vol. I, ed. J. S. Bromley and E. H. Kossmann (1960), brings the controversy up to date. Geoffrey Parker, *Philip II* (1978), serves as counterweight to Motley's malicious portrait of the Spanish king. (John Lynch, *Spain under the Hapsburgs,* vol. I [1964; 2nd ed., 1981], works well for the same purpose.) For Prescott, C. Harvey Gardiner, *William Hickling Prescott: A Biography* (1969), is a serviceable modern life. Perhaps the best studies of Parkman are Otis A. Pease, *Parkman's History: The Historian as Literary Artist* (1953), an economical and pointed essay, and Mason Wade, *Francis Parkman: Heroic Historian* (1942). Wade has also edited *The Journals of Francis Parkman,* 2 vols. (1947). On Frederick Jackson Turner, see, above all, the chapters in Richard Hofstadter, *The Progressive Historians: Turner, Beard, Parrington* (1968) and *The Historical World of Frederick Jackson Turner, with Selections from His Correspondence,* narrative by Wilbur R. Jacobs (1968).

Ranke deserves even more attention than he has had. Eugen Guglia, *Leopold von Rankes Leben und Werke* (1893), slight and superficial, is still the only biography. Fortunately, it can be supplemented with excellent monographs: the thoughtful study by Rudolf Vierhaus, *Ranke und die soziale Welt* (1957), and Leonard Krieger, *Ranke: The Meaning of History* (1977), which, proceeding chronologically, profoundly canvasses Ranke's theoretical views, historical writings, and intellectual shifts. Theodore von Laue, *Leopold Ranke: The Formative Years* (1950), traces the emergence of historicism in Ranke's early work and conveniently publishes two important essays, "A Dialogue on Politics" and "The Great Powers." Carl Hinrichs, *Ranke und die Geschichtstheologie der Goethezeit* (1954), seeks to explain the evolution of the later Ranke's "theology of world history." *Leopold von Ranke: The Secret of World History: Selected Writings on the Art and Science of History,* tr. and ed. Roger Wines (1981), is a shrewdly arranged anthology that guided me to some little-known Ranke texts. The impact of Ranke on the next generation of German historians is persuasively expounded by Hans-Heinz Krill, *Die Ranke Renaissance. Max Lenz und Erich Marcks. Ein Beitrag zum historisch-politischen Denken in Deutschland, 1880–1935* (1962). After the Nazi calamity, a few German scholars returned to the master armed with a new critical stance. Ludwig Dehio, for some years editor of the *Historische Zeitschrift,* published there "Ranke and German Imperialism" (1950) (available in *Germany and World Politics in the Twentieth Century* [1955; tr. Dieter Pevsner, 1959]). The pugnacious if scrupulous Dutch historian Pieter Geyl exposed some consequential limitations in Ranke's ideology, esp. in "Ranke in the Light of the Catastrophe" (1952), in *Debates with Historians* (1955). One thoughtful symposium on Ranke discusses him as a world historian, his theories and style, his legacy and his influence: *Leopold von Ranke und die moderne Geschichtswissenschaft,* ed. Wolfgang J. Mommsen (1988).* On Ranke's reputation, see Georg G. Iggers, "The Image of Ranke in American and German Historical Thought," *History and Theory,* II (1962), 17–40. Last but by no means least, in his last book, *History: Politics or Culture? Reflections on Ranke and Burckhardt* (1990), Felix Gilbert returned to a subject that had long occupied him, and brilliantly explored the complex interaction between Ranke, the "political" historian, and Burckhardt, the "cultural" historian. In "What Ranke Meant," *The American Scholar,* LVI (Summer 1987), 393–97, he attempted to specify what Ranke had in mind with his untranslatable ideal of wanting to discover only "wie es eigentlich gewesen."

The psychological process of internalization, which I find crucial for the historian's proceedings, is, of course, a mainstay of psychoanalytic thinking since Freud. The best general commentary is Roy Schafer, *Aspects of Internalization* (1968).

FOUR: The Truths of Fiction

The literature on literature has become virtually unencompassable; hence the account of the sources I have consulted must be summary. On best-sellers, which involves the growth and division of reading publics, see, for France, Lise Queffélec, *Le Roman-Feuilleton français au XIXe siècle* (1989), terse but authoritative. Two close, precise analyses by James Smith Allen, *Popular French Romanticism: Authors, Readers, and Books in the 19th Century* (1981) and *In the Public Eye: A History of Reading in Modern France, 1800–1940* (1991), are pioneering studies. For Britain, recent scholarship has worked to undo the nostalgic, "aristocratic" perspective of Q. D. Leavis, *Fiction and the Reading Public* (1932). For a corrective, see R. K. Webb's meaty essay, "The Victorian Reading Public," in *The New Pelican Guide to English Literature,* vol. VI, *From Dickens to Hardy* (1958; 2nd ed., 1982), 198–219. See also Richard D. Altick, *The English Common Reader, 1800–1900*

---

*For Ranke as a "poet" see the chapter on him in Peter Gay, *Style in History* (1974). In that book, in which I take, in addition to Ranke, Gibbon, Macaulay, Burckhardt, and Mommsen as my exemplars, I argue that in the right hands, biases, preconceptions, even neurotic interferences may bring the historian closer to truth than he would have been without them.

(1957). The relevant volumes of the Oxford History of English Literature, W. L. Renwick, *English Literature, 1789–1815* (1963), and Ian Jack, *English Literature, 1815–1832* (1963), have much material. Peter Keating, *The Haunted Study: A Social History of the English Novel, 1875–1914* (1989), is gratifyingly sensitive to the complexities of the publishers' markets. Chs. 8–10 of J. W. Saunders, *The Profession of English Letters* (1964), are pertinent here. I have little space for the kind of social histories the British do so well and which usually include information on standards of living and literacy, and I mention only Harold Perkin, *The Origins of Modern English Society, 1780–1880* (1969), a fascinating (if not uncontested) study of the consolidation of modern class society; J. F. C. Harrison, *The Early Victorians, 1832–51* (1971; 2nd ed., 1979); G. F. A. Best, *Mid-Victorian Britain, 1851–75* (1971; 2nd ed., 1979); F. M. L. Thompson, *The Rise of Respectable Society: A Social History of Victorian Britain* (1988); and Asa Briggs, *The Age of Improvement, 1783–1867* (1959; corr. ed., 1962), older but durable.

In Germany, the social history of literature has only begun to take off; it tends to concentrate largely, but not wholly, on the lower middle classes and on what it calls, accurately if condescendingly, "trivial" literature. Two useful titles: *Das Triviale in Literatur, Musik und bildender Kunst,* ed. Helga de la Motte-Haber (1972), and *Trivialliteratur,* ed. Annamaria Rucktäschl and Hans Dieter Zimmermann (1976), have some first-rate contributions. The most comprehensive, much cited study is Rudolf Schenda, *Volk ohne Buch. Studien zur Sozialgeschichte der populären Lesestoffe, 1770–1910* (1970), massive, scholarly, disenchanted, with an impressive bibliography. Among Rolf Engelsing's trailblazing publications, the titles most appropriate to this volume include "Zur politischen Bildung der deutschen Unterschichten, 1789–1863," *Historische Zeitschrift,* CCVI (1968), 337–69, and *Massenpublikum und Journalistentum im 19. Jahrhundert in Nordwestdeutschland* (1966). *Das Buch zwischen gestern und morgen. Zeichen und Aspekte,* ed. Georg Ramsegger and Werner Schoenecke (1969), is very useful. Magdalene Zimmermann, *Die Gartenlaube als Dokument ihrer Zeit* (1963; abr. ed., 1967) offers an introductory essay and ample documentation from the pages of Germany's favorite family weekly. Hartmut Eggert, Hans Christoph Berg, and Michael Rutschky, "Die im Text versteckten Schüler. Probleme einer Rezeptionsforschung in praktischer Absicht," in *Literatur und Leser. Theorien und Modelle zur Rezeption literarischer Werke* (1975), is a suggestive program for further research. Much interesting theorizing on reception has been done by Wolfgang Iser, esp. in *The Act of Reading: A Theory of Aesthetic Response* (1976; tr. David Henry Wilson, 1978). For some illuminating dissections of readers' responses from a psychoanalytic point of view, see above all Norman N. Holland, *The Dynamics of Literary Response* (1968) and *5 Readers Reading* (1975).

For the United States, the already mentioned analysis by Henry Nash Smith, *Democracy and the Novel: Popular Resistance to Classic American Writers* (p. 404), confronts America's major novelists with the middle- and low-brow culture of their time. A good companion volume is Larzer Ziff, *Literary Democracy: The Declaration of Cultural Independence in America* (1981), a wide-ranging study taking in all of the middle and late nineteenth century, beyond the major authors to best-sellers. For the triumphant woman's journal *Godey's Lady's Book,* see esp. Frank Luther Mott, *A History of American Maga-*

zines, vol. I, *1741–1850* (1930), and vol. II, *1850–1865* (1938), for background and coverage.

The scholarship surrounding Karl May, Germany's unequaled teller of adventure tales, has become astonishing for its bulk and sobriety. A convenient and copious biographical guide, which adds information about the publishing, distribution, and afterlife of this sort of literature, is the *Karl-May-Handbuch,* ed. Gert Ueding, with Reinhard Tschapke (1987). It may be supplemented with *Karl May,* ed. Helmut Schmiedt (1983), which contains documents and individual essays. The best short biography is Hans Wollschläger, *Karl May. Grundriss eines gebrochenen Lebens* (1965). The amusing assault by the experimental German novelist Arno Schmidt, *Sitara und der Weg dorthin. Eine Studie über Wesen, Werk & Wirkung Karl Mays* (1963; corr. ed., 1985), which infuriated May's fan clubs, tries to prove that May's work is essentially the expressive outcome of homosexual fantasies (or experiences).

As for the best-selling author of *Les Trois Mousquetaires* and *Le Comte de Monte Cristo,* A. Craig Bell, *Alexandre Dumas* (1950), and André Maurois, *The Titans: A Three-Generation Biography of the Dumas* (1957; tr. Gerard Hopkins, 1957), say the essential. For Sue, see Jean Louis Bory, *Eugène Sue: Le Roi du roman populaire* (1962). German scholars, having taken to Sue with a will, have published informative, earnest monographs. See *Materialien zur Kritik des Feuilleton-Romans. "Die Geheimnisse von Paris" von Eugène Sue,* ed. Helga Grubitzsch (1977), which collects French, German, Russian, British, and American responses to Sue's greatest hit, and the very substantial *Als die Helden Opfer wurden: Grundlagen und Funktion gesellschaftlicher Ordnungsmodelle in den Feuilletonromanen "Les mystères de Paris" und "Le Juif errant" von Eugène Sue* (1985). Christophe Campos, "Social Romanticism," in *French Literature and Its Background,* ed. John Cruickshank, vol. IV, *The Early Nineteenth Century* (1960), 55–75, discovers Sue's place among social critics. Peter Brooks, *Reading for the Plot: Design and Intention in Narrative* (1984), has some fine pages on *Les Mystères de Paris* from a Lacanian psychoanalytic angle.

Hanns Sachs's interesting analysis of the way writers seduce readers through shared daydreams, *Gemeinsame Tagträume* (1924), takes off from Freud's pioneering, highly suggestive (and surely simplifying) talk of 1907, "Creative Writers and Daydreaming" (1908), *The Standard Edition of the Complete Psychological Works of Sigmund Freud,* ed. James Strachey et al., 24 vols. (1953–74), IX, 141–53.

For fairy tales, subjected to scholarly scrutiny for half a century, there are Max Lüthi, *The Fairytale as Art Form and Portrait of Man* (1975; tr. Jon Erickson, 1984); the famous study by Vladimir I. Propp, *Morphology of the Folk Tale* (1928; 2nd ed., tr. Laurence Scott, 1968); and Bruno Bettelheim, *The Uses of Enchantment: The Meaning and Importance of Fairy Tales* (1976), a vigorous plea from a psychoanalyst for their emotional utility. For the Grimms' tales, see Ruth B. Bottigheimer, *Grimms' Bad Girls & Bold Boys: The Moral & Social Vision of the "Tales"* (1987), which (a little hastily) rejects psychoanalytic readings as ahistorical and instead finds patterns in following edition after edition of the *Tales* with interesting results. Hermann Gerstner supplies the essential biographical details of the brothers in his brief *Brüder Grimm in Selbstzeugnissen und Bilddokumenten* (1973).

The first-person convention is perhaps best pursued through individual novelists. For a general treatment, see Bertil Romberg, *Studies in the Narrative Technique of the First-Person Novel* (1974). Jonathan Auerbach, *The Romance of Failure: First-Person Fictions of Poe, Hawthorne, and James* (1989), offers a close reading of three American writers using that strategy; see also the study of the authorial "I" by William R. Goetz, *Henry James and the Darkest Abyss of Romance* (1986), to be read with Laurence Bedwell Holland, *The Expense of Vision: Essays on the Craft of Henry James* (1964), which deeply analyzes James's "intimacy" with his characters. (For more on James, see just below.) Aylmer Maude, *The Life of Tolstoy*, 2 vols. (1930), remains the most distinguished biography among a rich harvest; see also, however, the intelligently managed *Tolstoy* (1988) by the English novelist and biographer A. N. Wilson. Henry Gifford, *Tolstoy* (1982), packs a great deal of thoughtful analysis into a narrow compass. I have found much use for *Tolstoy's Letters*, sel., ed., and tr. R. F. Christian, 2 vols. (1978), and his unbuttoned, disturbing self-revelations, *Tolstoy's Diaries*, tr. and ed. R. F. Christian, 2 vols. (1985). John Bayley's *Tolstoy and the Novel* (1966), deservedly acclaimed, has some excellent pages (83–92) on *Childhood*. Ronald Hingley, *Russian Writers and Society, 1825–1904* (1967), ably provides the social environment.

Gustave Rudler, *"Adolphe" de Benjamin Constant* (1935), is one of several serious treatments of Constant's only fiction; Paul Delbouille, *Genèse, structure et destin d' "Adolphe"* (1971), seems like erudite overkill, being some ten times as long as the text it analyzes. Martin Turnell, *The Novel in France* (1950), devotes some illuminating pages (79–122) to Constant's novel. Stephen Holmes, *Benjamin Constant and the Making of Modern Liberalism* (cited above, p. 405), draws on *Adolphe* to explicate Constant's social and cultural criticism. James Thompson and Barbara Wright, *La Vie et l'oeuvre d'Eugène Fromentin* (1987), is a sound biography; Camille Reynaud, *La Genèse de "Dominique"* (1937), traces Fromentin's way to his novel. See also Arthur R. Evans, Jr., *The Literary Art of Eugène Fromentin: A Study in Style and Motif* (1964), and Peter Gay, *The Bourgeois Experience: Victoria to Freud*, vol. II, *The Tender Passion* (1986), 144, 170–71. For the French tradition of self-revelation in literature, John Cruickshank, "The Novel of Self-Disclosure," in *French Literature and Its Background* (cited above, p. 403), 170–88, is thoughtful. P. Mansell Jones, *French Introspectives from Montaigne to Gide* (1937), touches on the dominant themes of this volume. Maurice Allem discusses Sainte-Beuve's only novel in *Sainte-Beuve et "Volupté"* (1935). (Titles dealing with Stendhal have been listed above, p. 403.)

Until recently, those without Russian had to make do with an old collection of Dostoevsky's correspondence, *Letters of Fyodor Michailovitch Dostoevsky to His Family and Friends*, tr. Ethel Colburn Mayne (1961). It has now been superseded by *Selected Letters of Fyodor Dostoevsky*, ed. Joseph Frank and David I. Goldstein, tr. Andrew R. MacAndrew (1987), and *Fyodor Dostoevsky: Complete Letters*, ed. and tr. David Lowe and Ronald Meyer, 5 vols. (1988–91); this last edition, though less elegant than its predecessor, is particularly open about Dostoevsky's virulent anti-Semitism. Frank, *Dostoevsky*, 3 vols. so far (1976, 1983, 1986), reaching to 1865, has a good claim to authoritative stature.

Konstantin Mochulsky, *Dostoevsky: His Life and Work* (1947; tr. Michael A. Minihan, 1967), hailed on its appearance as a classic, gives equal space to the prophet, the novelist, and the world-historical patient. Among recent authorities, I have learned most from several studies by Robert L. Jackson, chiefly *Dostoevsky's Quest for Form: A Study of His Philosophy of Art* (1966). And see Donald Fanger's excellent *Dostoevsky and Romantic Realism: A Study of Dostoevsky in Relation to Balzac, Dickens, and Gogol* (1965), which does not neglect Dostoevsky's *The Double*. The sophisticated contributors to the anthology *Dostoevsky: A Collection of Critical Essays,* ed. René Wellek (1962), is very helpful (it contains Freud's "Dostoevsky and Parricide" [1928], which Frank vehemently criticizes in an appendix to the first volume of his *Dostoevsky*). Karl Miller, *Doubles: Studies in Literary History* (1985), has a number of illuminating pages on Dostoevsky's obsession. Vladimir Nabokov's lecture "Fyodor Dostoevsky," in *Lectures on Russian Literature,* ed. Fredson Bowers (1981), a torrent of abuse, is interesting mainly as a curiosity.

The Henry James industry began to flourish only after his death in 1916. A pioneer in hailing James as a master was Percy Lubbock, in *The Craft of Fiction* (1921), which long remained a lonely, and is still an instructive, advocate. The boom in that industry seems almost like a concerted attempt to atone for the contemptuous dismissal of James as a snobbish and infertile *déraciné*, spread in the late 1920s by the populist, once commanding American literary historian Vernon L. Parrington.* He had been anticipated by Van Wyck Brooks's indictment, *The Pilgrimage of Henry James* (1925), which portrays James as a talented writer who had betrayed his gifts by living abroad. These verdicts now seem quaint, hopelessly philistine.

Leon Edel has made James his life's work. He has edited the *Complete Plays of Henry James* (1949), the *Complete Tales,* 12 vols. (1962–64), the *Letters,* 4 vols. (1974–84), individual stories and novels, and *The Diary of Alice James* (1964)—this last to be read with Jean Strouse's sensitive life, *Alice James: A Biography* (1980). Edel's biography, *Henry James,* 5 vols. (1953–72), reaching the proportions of a nineteenth-century Life, though somewhat thin on literary analysis, has been widely accepted as the standard account. (Edel has revised and abridged that biography, *Henry James: A Life* [1985].) *The Notebooks of Henry James,* ed. F. O. Matthiessen and Kenneth Murdock (1947), proved

---

*Parrington: "There is a suggestion of irony in the fact that one of our earliest realists, who was independent enough to break with the romantic tradition, should have fled from the reality that his art presumably would gird itself up to deal with. Like his fellow spirit Whistler, Henry James was a lifelong pilgrim to other shrines than those of his native land, who dedicated his gifts to ends that his fellow Americans were indifferent to. Life, with him, was largely a matter of nerves." Indeed, "he was never a realist. Rather, he was a self-deceived romantic, the last subtle expression of the genteel, who fell in love with culture and never realized how poor a thing he worshiped." In short, "the spirit of Henry James marks the last refinement of the genteel tradition, the completest embodiment of its vague cultural aspirations." A *"déraciné,"* he "lived in a world of fine gradations and imperceptible shades." Enough? *Main Currents in American Thought,* vol. III, *The Beginnings of Critical Realism in America* (1930; left incomplete at the author's death in 1929), 239–41.

an invaluable resource.* The high caliber of James's demanding prefaces to twenty-four volumes in the New York edition (*The Novels and Tales of Henry James,* 26 vols. [1907–17]; the posthumously published last two volumes edited by Percy Lubbock) was emphatically saluted by R. P. Blackmur in his edition *The Art of the Novel* (1934). The difficult last novels, long a stumbling block even for readers who enjoyed such middle-period novels as *The Portrait of a Lady* (1881), found their champion in F. O. Matthiessen, *Henry James: The Major Phase* (1944), brisk and convincing. Seymour Chatman, *The Later Style of Henry James* (1972), a highly technical linguistic monograph, buttresses Matthiessen's conclusions. See also Ruth Bernard Yeazell, *Language and Knowledge in the Late Novels of Henry James* (1976). James's interest in art has been canvassed more than once, most successfully in Adeline R. Tintner, *Henry James and the Lust of the Eyes: Thirteen Artists in His Work* (1993). Among numerous commentaries, Dorothea Krook, *The Ordeal of Consciousness in Henry James* (1962), has held up. *Henry James: The Critical Heritage* (1968), a volume in an established series, deserves to be singled out for its bulk and its informative research into James's income from his writings. For Henry James in his familial context, in addition to the biographies just cited, see above all R. W. B. Lewis, *The Jameses: A Family Narrative* (1991).

The fiction of Dickens, long and short, is available in several editions; whenever possible, I have used the handy volumes published by Penguin (under the collectives titles "English Library" and "Penguin Classics"), with good introductions and sparse, though helpful, notes. The magnificent Pilgrim Edition of *The Letters of Charles Dickens,* ed. Madeline House, Graham Storey, K. J. Fielding, et al., 7 vols. so far (1965–93), reaches to 1855. The pioneer biography, John Forster, *The Life of Charles Dickens,* 3 vols. (1872–74; ed. Andrew Lang, 2 vols., n.d.), by Dickens's closest associate, a mixture of frankness and delicacy, was the first to publish intimate materials and retains interest as a Victorian document. Edgar Johnson's well-meaning and widely appreciated *Charles Dickens: His Tragedy and Triumph,* 2 vols. (1952), is blemished by an uncritical reading of Dickens's fiction as increasingly admirable social criticism. Among many recent biographies, Fred Kaplan, *Dickens: A Biography* (1988), is the most gratifying: substantial, up-to-date in scholarship, and moving easily between life and literature. The reception of Dickens's work has been thoroughly canvassed to permit the historian to reconstruct this complicated and important story: see George H. Ford, *Dickens and His Readers: Aspects of Novel Criticism since 1836* (1955), supplemented by *The Dickens Critics,* ed. George H. Ford and Lauriat Lane, Jr. (1961), which offers a menu of critical essays, and *Dickens: The Critical Heritage,* ed. Philip Collins (1971). Susan R. Horton, *The Reader in the Dickens World: Style and Response* (1981), though an interesting technical experiment, has little to say about Dickens's popularity. K. J. Fielding has edited *The Speeches of Dickens* (1960), a valuable resource.

---

*This is the edition I used in writing this book, but there is now a more complete version: *The Complete Notebooks of Henry James,* ed. Leon Edel and Lyall H. Powers (1987).

Among overviews and more specialized studies, see above all Humphry House's powerfully argued *The Dickens World* (1941; 2nd ed., 1942), demonstrating how Dickens imaginatively reconstructed his time and place in his fiction, I have long gone to school to this little masterpiece. A. O. J. Cockshut, *The Imagination of Charles Dickens* (1961), is intriguing. Michael Slater, *Dickens and Women* (1983), covers the ground, though I am less critical of Dickens's heroines than he is. Two monographs by Philip Collins, *Dickens and Crime* (1962; 2nd ed., 1964) and *Dickens and Education* (1963; 2nd ed., 1965), are authoritative. So is John Butt and Kathleen Tillotson, *Dickens at Work* (1957). F. R. and Q. D. Leavis, *Dickens the Novelist* (1970), a gathering of essays written separately and published with the unexceptionable aim of showing Dickens to have been "one of the greatest of creative writers" (p. 9) is often penetrating but offputting with the authors' arrogance. I have derived instruction from the original, revisionist readings of Alexander Welsh in *The City of Dickens* (1971) and *From Copyright to Copperfield: The Identity of Dickens* (1987); but I dissent from his characterization of Agnes Wickfield, the heroine of *David Copperfield*, as a religious figure (see *City of Dickens*, 180–95). See my "The 'Legless Angel' of 'David Copperfield': There's More to Her Than Victorian Piety," *New York Times Book Review*, January 22, 1995, 22–24. Kathleen Tillotson's elegant essay *Novels of the Eighteen-forties* (1954) also covers Dickens. For good reasons, Dickens, particularly his semi-autobiographical *David Copperfield*, has attracted psychoanalytic interpretation; see esp. Leonard Manheim, "The Personal History of David Copperfield," *American Imago*, IX (1952), 21–45; E. Pearlman, "David Copperfield Dreams of Drowning," ibid., XXVIII (1971), 391–403; and Gordon D. Hirsch, "A Psychoanalytic Rereading of *David Copperfield*," *Victorian Newsletter*, no. 58 (Fall 1980), 1–5—all suggestive, though even more can be done. Harry Stone, *Dickens and the Invisible World: Fairy Tales, Fantasy, and Novel-Making* (1979), a detailed study of the relation of Dickens's work to fairy tales, sums up years of research.

FIVE: Images of the Mind

The history of self-portraiture needs more scholarship than it has enjoyed. Meanwhile we have Ludwig Goldscheider, *Fünfhundert Selbstporträts von der Antike bis zur Gegenwart* (1936), and Manuel Gasser, *Self-portraits: From the Fifteenth Century to the Present Day* (1961; tr. Angus Malcolm, 1963), to whom I owe the self-portrait of Barthélemy Menn; Sean Kelley and Edward Lucie-Smith, *The Self-portrait: A Modern View* (1987), which concentrates on English artists; Luba Gurdus, *The Self-portrait in French Painting from Neoclassicism to Realism* (1962); Georg M. Blochmann, *Zeitgeist und Künstlermythos: Untersuchungen zur Selbstdarstellung deutscher Maler der Gründerzeit: Marées, Lenbach, Böcklin, Makart, Feuerbach* (1991), a valiant attempt to rethink German artists of the early empire. The most instructive texts on the emergence of self-depiction in early-modern Europe include Gottfried Boehm, *Bildnis und Individuum. Über den Ursprung der Porträtmalerei in der italienischen Renaissance* (1985), John Pope-Hennessy, *The Portrait in the Renaissance* (1966), and Lorne Campbell, *Renaissance Portraits: European Portrait-Painting in the 14th,*

15th and 16th Century (1990), scholarly and historical in orientation. (Dürer and Rembrandt van Rijn will be treated separately below, pp. 427–29.)

Velázquez's celebrated *Las Meninas* has been much discussed; Jonathan Brown's masterly *Velázquez: Painter and Courtier* (1986), which makes most previous volumes redundant, frequently returns to this intricate painting. Svetlana Alpers, "Interpretation without Representation," *Representations,* I (February 1983), 31–42; Leo Steinberg, "Velázquez's *Las Meninas,*" *October,* XIX (1981), 45–54; and John R. Searle, *"Las Meninas* and the Paradoxes of Pictorial Representation," *Critical Inquiry,* VI (1980), 177–88, are interesting and characteristic for this age of paradoxes sought and valued.

Ekhart Berckenhagen has done a catalogue raisonné on the most prolific of eighteenth-century German face painters: *Anton Graff. Leben und Werk* (1967). For Mengs, whose series of self-portraits adds up to an honest effort to record the ravages of time on his face, see D. Honisch, *Anton Raphael Mengs und die Bildform des Frühklassizismus* (1965) and *Anton Raphael Mengs. Briefe an Raimondo Ghelli und Anton Maron,* ed. Herbert von Einem (1975).

Caspar David Friedrich, who did about ten acknowledged self-portraits, rediscovered after more than half a century of neglect through a major exhibition in 1906, has been victimized by tendentious right-wing readings. In retaliation, there have been left-wing responses: *Caspar David Friedrich und die deutsche Nachwelt* (1974), whose authors link his rediscovery to German imperialism and Nazism. Joseph Leo Koerner, *Caspar David Friedrich and the Subject of Landscape* (1990), happily avoids politicizing the painter in an impressive demonstration of Friedrich's romantic religious roots that does not slight him as an artist. In contrast, Helmut Börsch-Supan and Karl Wilhelm Jähning's curious *C. D. Friedrich. Gemälde, Druckgraphik und bildgemässe Zeichnungen* (1973), the harvest of exhaustive scholarly investigations, suffers from mechanical readings of Friedrich's allegories and symbolism. In an excellent overview, William Vaughan, *German Romantic Painting* (1980), more than a mere introduction, sensibly questions Börsch-Supan's reading of Friedrich. *Caspar David Friedrich, 1774–1840,* ed. Werner Hofmann (1974), concentrating on the landscapes, is a solid catalog. For materials, see *Caspar David Friedrich in Briefen und Bekenntnissen,* ed. Sigrid Hinz (1968; 2nd ed., 1984), and *Caspar David Friedrich—Unbekannte Dokumente seines Lebens,* ed. Karl-Ludwig Hoch (1985). Friedrich is a leading exhibit in an admirable essay by Otto von Simson, *Der Blick nach Innen: Vier Beiträge zur deutschen Malerei des 19. Jahrhunderts* (1986), which amply supports the thesis of this volume that *Innerlichkeit* was on the move in places, such as Spitzweg's genre pictures, where one least expected it. Eckart Klessmann's compact *Die deutsche Romantik* (1979), which links painting to literature, has been helpful to me.

For Rethel, maker of the modern dance of death, Josef Ponten, *Alfred Rethel. Des Meisters Werke in 300 Abbildungen* (1911), remains valuable. On the theme in general, see Gert Buchheit, *Der Totentanz* (1926). Heinrich Alfred Schmid suggests that the original model for all later representations was a political statement: "Holbeins Totentanz. Ein politisches Bekenntnis" (1928), in *Gesammelte kunsthistorische Schriften* (1933), 250–59.

Part of re-enchanting the world through inward experience was the nineteenth-century infatuation with landscape. The Victorians, of course, had admired ancestors, notably in the seventeenth century. There is much of interest in Max J. Friedländer, *Landscape, Portrait, Still-life: Their Origin and Development* (1947; tr. R. F. C. Hull, 1963). And see Wolfgang Stechow, *Dutch Landscape Painting of the Seventeenth Century* (1966), and *Masters of 17th Century Dutch Landscape Painting* (1988), a fine catalog edited by Peter C. Sutton. Lisa Vergara, *Rubens and the Poetics of Landscape* (1982), does justice to the work of a painter better known for masterpieces in other genres.

In the Victorian age, few landscapists, visionary though some of them were, joined Friedrich in producing works they wanted to see as religious in origin and—they hoped—in effect. John Constable offers a striking contrast. See Graham Reynolds, *Constable: The Natural Painter* (1965). *John Constable's Correspondence,* ed. R. B. Beckett, 6 vols. (1962–68), is so interesting that most writers on Constable have freely dipped into his letters and pronouncements. The first to explore that resource was C. R. Leslie, *Memoirs of the Life of John Constable Composed Chiefly of His Letters* (1843; enlarged ed., 1845, and repr. with plates by Jonathan Mayne, 1951), still much used. Basil Taylor, *Constable: Paintings, Drawings and Watercolours* (1973), has a long introduction and some captivating selections. Kurt Badt, *John Constable's Clouds* (1950), tackles a much discussed aspect of his art. T. S. R. Boase, *English Art, 1800–1870* (1959), places Constable into his world.

America's ambitious landscape painters have come to be appreciated only in the last half century. It was not until 1945 that the Art Institute of Chicago mounted an epoch-making exhibition, "The Hudson River School and the Early American Landscape Tradition." Since then, the revival has been fueled by increasingly voluminous catalogs. *Thomas Cole: Landscape into History,* ed. William H. Truettner and Alan Wallach (1994), provides good historical background. The earliest interpretation was by Louis L. Noble, *The Life and Works of Thomas Cole* (1852; ed. Eliot S. Vesell, 1964); Cole's followers, some of them gifted artists in their own right, have been captured in *American Paradise: The World of the Hudson River School,* a catalog, introduction by John K. Howat. Cole's great successor, Church, has been studied to splendid effect in *Frederic Edwin Church,* a catalog of 1989, by Franklin Kelly et al.

The French painters of the influential Barbizon school look tame only in comparison to the Impressionists. Jean Bouret, *The Barbizon School and 19th-Century French Landscape Painting* (1972; tr. 1973), is a convenient summary, compromised only by simplistic political notions about the "all-powerful" bourgeoisie (p. 10). (For Millet, see below, p. 427.) Norma Broude, *The Macciaioli: Italian Painters of the Nineteenth Century* (1987), has put a little-known school of Italian landscape painters on the map of the English-speaking world.

One of Böcklin's most vocal admirers, Fritz von Ostini, promoted his fame with "Arnold Böcklin," *Velhagen & Klasings Monatshefte* (March–August, 1893–94, vol. II), 31–51, followed by *Böcklin* (1904). Ferdinand Runkel edited Böcklin's diaries, memoirs, and correspondence: *Böcklin Memoiren. Tagebuchblätter von Böcklins Gattin Angela. Mit dem gesamten brieflichen Nachlass* (1910). The notes that the art historian Gustav Floerke took as Böcklin's Boswell, *Zehn Jahre mit Böcklin. Aufzeichnungen und Entwürfe* (1901; 3rd ed., under the title *Arnold Böcklin und seine Kunst. Aufzeichnungen,* 1921), have the aura of true intimacy. The diary entries of another admirer, *Arnold Böcklin. Aus den Tagebüchern von Otto Lasius (1884–1889),* ed. Maria Lina Lasius (1903), are also informative. Franz Hermann Meissner, *Arnold Böcklin* (1899), is typical for the idealizing publicity designed for the general educated public. Rolf Andree et al., take a far more nuanced view in *Arnold Böcklin, 1827–1901,* an exhibition catalog (1974). The famous assault on this bourgeois icon by Julius Meier-Graefe, Germany's most vehement advocate of Impressionism, *Der Fall Böcklin* (1905), remains a powerful statement. (For Meier-Graefe's role in German culture, see the interesting study by Kenworth Moffett, *Meier-Graefe as Art Critic* [1973].) The painting of Böcklin's that I have singled out in the text is the subject of Franz Zelger's very brief *Die Toteninsel. Selbstheroisierung und Abgesang der abendländischen Kultur* (1991). Jürgen Wissmann has briefly analyzed the popularity of this late romantic painter in *Arnold Böcklin und das Nachleben seiner Malerei. Studien zur Kunst der Jahrhundertwende* (1968). For Böcklin's being used in mouth-wash advertisements, see Henriette Väth-Hinz, *Odol. Reklame-Kunst um 1900* (1985), esp. 27–41, and *Der Spiegel,* May 10, 1993, 256–57—astonishing stuff. The "discoverer" of Hans Thoma, a painter interesting in part for his connection with the "Rembrandt-German" Julius Langbehn (for whom see below, p. 429), was the art historian Henry Thode: see his lectures *Böcklin und Thoma. Acht Vorträge über neudeutsche Malerei* (1905) and the heavy (in both senses) *Thoma. Des Meisters Gemälde in 874 Abbildungen* (1909).

Robert R. Herbert, Roseline Bacou, and Michel Laclotte, *Jean-François Millet (1814–1875)* (1976), is an exhaustive catalog showing the masterly hand of the first editor throughout. Among Herbert's most important articles on this topic, see "Millet Revisited," *Burlington Magazine,* CIV (July and September 1962), 294–305, and 377–85; "Millet Reconsidered," *Museum Studies,* I (1966), 29–65; and "City vs. Country: The Rural Image in French Painting from Millet to Gauguin," *Artforum,* VIII (February 1970), 44–55. See also *Jean-François Millet,* a formidable catalog, ed. Alexander R. Murphy (1984). Etienne Moreau-Nélaton, *Millet raconté par lui-même,* 3 vols. (1921), provides ample material. Alfred Trumble, *The Painter of the "Angelus": A Study of the Life, Labors, and Vicissitudes of Jean François Millet* (1889), is a good instance of this artist's impact on American art lovers. Estelle M. Hurll, *Millet: A Collection of Pictures with Introduction and Interpretation* (1900), is another. I am particularly indebted to "L'Alcove de l'Angelus," *Prosopopées,* V, ed. Jennifer Gough-Cooper and Jacques Caumont (November 1982), a ravishing and amusing, painstakingly illustrated, number showing the myriad decorative uses to which Millet's *Angelus*—towels, coffee grinders, plates, bellows—has been put. And see Christopher Parsons and Neil McWilliam on Millet's friend and patron, " 'Le paysan de Paris': Alfred Sensier and the Myth of Rural France," *Oxford Art Journal,* VI (1983), 38–58. Jean-François Millet was a powerful presence in those decades on both sides of the Atlantic, as much as Böcklin in German-speaking cultures.

Dürer has, of course, been exhaustively studied. The most learned modern biography remains Erwin Panofsky, *The Life and Art of Albrecht Dürer* (1943; 4th ed., 1955). Jane

Campbell Hutchison, *Albrecht Dürer: A Biography* (1990), is more centered on the life than on the art. Joseph Leo Koerner's erudite and appealing *The Moment of Self-portraiture in German Renaissance Art* (1993) goes beyond Dürer but always returns to him. Hugo Kehrer, *Dürers Selbstbildnisse und die Dürer Bildnisse* (1934), is authoritative. G. Kratzsch, *Kunstwart und Dürerbund* (1969), focuses on Ferdinand Avenarius, founder of the ambitious cultural bimonthly *Kunstwart* and the well-known *Dürerbund*—how better to foster Germany's artistic renewal than by appealing to the Master? Werner Oechslin, "Albrecht Dürer zwischen Kunstgeschichte und Ideologie," *Neue Zürcher Zeitung,* July 18, 1971, 40, ably analyzes the political temptations I have discussed in the text. I owe to Koerner the following two references for the self-portrait of 1500: Franz Winzinger, "Albrecht Dürers Münchener Selbstbildnis," *Zeitschrift für Kunstwissenschaft,* VIII (1951), 43–64, and on the significance of the year 1500 for Dürer and his world, Dieter Wuttke, "Dürer and Celtis. Von der Bedeutung des Jahres 1500 für den deutschen Humanismus: 'Jahrhundertfeier als symbolische Form,' " *Journal of Medieval and Renaissance Studies,* X (1980), 73–129. See also Jan Białostocki, *Dürer and His Critics, 1500–1971: Chapters in the History of Ideas including a Collection of Texts* (1986), to be read with the catalog *Dürers Gloria. Kunst. Kult. Konsum* (1971). *Dürer und die Nachwelt. Urkunden, Briefe, Dichtungen und wissenschaftliche Betrachtungen aus vier Jahrhunderten,* ed. Heinz Lüdecke and Susanne Heiland (1955), a well-selected anthology, led me to several sources.

After more than three centuries, Rembrandt's intentions remain a matter of debate. Jakob Rosenberg, *Rembrandt: Life and Work* (1948; rev. ed., 1964), concentrates on the painter, including his self-portraits, rather than on his culture. While I have problems with her conclusions about Rembrandt's self-revelations, I learned from the material that H. Perry Chapman has gathered in *Rembrandt's Self-portraits: A Study in Seventeenth-Century Identity* (1990). Ed. De Jongh, "The Spur of Wit: Rembrandt's Response to an Italian Challenge," *Delta: A Review of Arts, Life and Thought in the Netherlands,* XII (Summer 1969), 39–67, is interesting on the self-portraits. Georg Simmel, *Rembrandt. Ein kunstphilosophischer Versuch* (1917), ventures subtle observations. *Rembrandt,* ed. Ludwig Goldscheider (1960), handily reprints the three earliest Lives. The catalog of a 1969 exhibition at the Boston Museum of Fine Arts, *Rembrandt: Experimental Etcher,* naturally includes several of his etched self-portraits. On his masterpieces in that genre, see Christopher White, *Rembrandt as an Etcher: A Study of the Artist at Work* (1969). Egbert Haverkamp-Begemann's authoritative *Rembrandt: "The Nightwatch"* (1982), throws much light on the painter. Both Svetlana Alpers, *Rembrandt's Enterprise: The Studio and the Market* (1988), and, far more radically, Gary Schwartz, *Rembrandt: His Life, His Painting* (1985), have tried (as one expert put it) to "demystify" Rembrandt, Alpers I think more successfully than Schwartz. *Rembrandt und die Nachwelt,* ed. Susanne Heiland and Heinz Lüdecke (1960), is a convenient epitome of comments on the painter. For the early reception, see Seymour Slive, *Rembrandt and His Critics, 1630–1730* (1953). And see Jeroen Boomgaard and Robert Scheller, "A Delicate Balance—A Brief Survey of Rembrandt Criticism," in *Rembrandt: The Master & His Workshop,* a catalog, ed. Christopher Brown, Jan Kelch, and Pieter van Thiel (1991), 106–23. Julius Held, "Rembrandt: Truth and Legend" (1950), in *Rembrandt's "Aristotle" and other Rembrandt Studies* (1969), 130–38, has wise comments.

Langbehn, the "Rembrandt German," roused complicated feelings in his masses of readers. It has been asserted that some forty thousand copies of *Rembrandt als Erzieher* were sold in less than a year and a half, and that by 1909, nearly twenty years after publication, the book was in its forty-ninth printing. See Liselotte Voss, *Rembrandt als Erzieher und seine Bedeutung. Studie über die kulturelle Struktur der neunziger Jahre* (1929), useful for some facts but useless as cultural history. The kidnappers of Rembrandt were willing to go to any length. In 1943, in the midst of the Nazis' assault on the world in the name of the Nordic race, the German art historian Wilhelm Pinder published an inexpensive picture book, *Rembrandts Selbstbildnisse,* in which he insists that Rembrandt was a "man of the north" (p. 12), who unconsciously professed "the subordination of the individual figure to the All, in the sense of all Germanic art" (p. 18), and belonged to Beethoven's "racial and cultural world" (p. 7). (By 1950, this book had sold some 29,000 copies. *Karl Robert Langewiesche. 50 Jahre Verlagsarbeit,* ed. S. Langewiesche [1952].) By 1961, when Fritz Stern made Langbehn one of his three subjects in his well-known dissertation *The Politics of Cultural Despair: A Study in the Rise of the Germanic Ideology* (1961), the journalistic and scholarly literature on him was already sizable (for the latter, see ibid., 340–41). In a brilliant recent polemic, *Die Deutschen und ihre Kunst. Ein schwieriges Erbe* (1992), the eminent German art historian Hans Belting mentions Langbehn.*

SIX: The Common Touch

General histories of the mails are rare. Hermann Glaser and Thomas Werner, *Die Post in ihrer Zeit. Eine Kulturgeschichte menschlicher Kommunikation* (1990), offers a conspectus of postal communications, anecdotal, serious, and even "philosophical," and draws happily chosen illustrations from contemporary sources. Gerald Cullinan, *The United States Postal Service* (1973), is a straightforward account. For Britain, the country of the pioneering penny post, see Howard Robinson, *The British Post Office: A History* (1948), to be supplemented with M. J. Daunton, *Royal Mail: The Post Office since 1840* (1985). C. R. Perry, *The Victorian Post Office: The Growth of a Bureaucracy* (1992), concentrates on administrative matters. R. H. Super, *Trollope in the Post Office* (1981), pursues the novelist's long career as an innovative administrator. William Mills Todd III, *The Familiar Letter as a Literary Genre in the Age of Pushkin* (1976), goes beyond its title to offer historical observations. For Cicero and other ancient correspondents, there is Finley

---

*While the Nazis found Langbehn's Nordic notions congenial, during their reign a psychiatrist, Hans Bürger-Prinz, with Annemarie Segelke, published a psychiatric volume, *Julius Langbehn der Rembrandtdeutsche. Eine pathopsychologische Studie* (1940), that diagnosed him as a schizophrenic type. Probably so, though the authors give no room to Langbehn's fairly obvious sexual pathology. Bürger-Prinz's psychology is eclectic, superficial, and superstitious.

Hooper and Matthew Schwartz, *Roman Letters: History from a Personal Point of View* (1991). Nineteenth-century France is covered in *La Correspondance: Les Usages de la lettre au XIXe siècle,* ed. Roger Chartier (1991); Germany, in *Deutsche Postgeschichte. Essays und Bilder,* ed. Wolfgang Lotz (1989), both substantial accounts.

Georg Steinhausen, *Geschichte des deutschen Briefes. Zur Kulturgeschichte des deutschen Volkes,* 2 vols. (1889–91), is a document for its time as well as a rich history concluding with the letter-writing eighteenth century, which taught the nineteenth century so much. Walter Benjamin, *Deutsche Menschen. Eine Folge von Briefen* (1972), selects twenty-five extraordinary German letters from 1783 to 1883 and provides them with a commentary. See also, for England, Bruce Redford, *The Converse of the Pen: Acts of Intimacy in the Eighteenth-Century Familiar Letter* (1986). W. H. Irving, *The Providence of Wit in the English Letter Writers* (1955), quotes from a special public of accomplished English correspondents. James Aitken, *English Letters of the XIX Century* (1946), is a slender gathering.

Collecting letters of the great and the near-great has become a scholar's rewarding pursuit—it would be pointless to cite all the printed editions I have perused—but amiable selections used to be a popular gift to give in the nineteenth century. Two instances: for England, *Love Letters of Famous Men and Women of the Past and Present Century,* ed. J. T. Meryew (1888); for Germany, *Dreihundert Briefe aus zwei Jahrhunderten,* ed. Karl von Holtei, 2 vols. (1872). There were scores of others like them.

The inventor of the penny post, an impressive reformer if disagreeable man, has been celebrated by one close to him: [Eleanor C. H. Smyth], *Sir Rowland Hill. The Story of a Great Reform Told by His Daughter* (1907). See also Colin G. Hey, *Rowland Hill: Victorian Genius and Benefactor* (1989). He is naturally discussed in Robinson, Daunton, and Perry cited just above.

No doubt eighteenth-century authors of epistolary novels helped to set the stage for letter writing later. The genre has been explored by Laurent Versini, *Le Roman épistolaire* (1979). For a pioneering practitioner of the genre, see Carol Houlihan Flynn, *Samuel Richardson: A Man of Letters* (1982), and Janet Gurkin Altman, *Epistolarity: Approaches to a Form* (1982).

La Correspondance (édition, fonctions, signification), preface by Georges Ulysse (1984), records an interesting French-Italian colloquium ranging from individual correspondents to letter-writing manuals. Karl Heinz Bohrer, *Der romantische Brief. Die Entstehung aesthetischer Subjektivität* (1987), offers to my mind pretentious reflections on autonomy and subjectivity, but also usefully discusses romantic-letter writers.

The scholarship on diaries and journals is growing apace. Gustav René Hocke, *Europäische Tagebücher aus vier Jahrhunderten* (1963; ed. 1991), from whom many have borrowed, is a classic in the field; in a gigantic introductory essay, Hocke canvasses every possible meaning of diaries and journals, followed by an expansive anthology of snippets ranging from an entry by Cardinal Francesco da Fiesso of 1409 to one by Pope John XXIII dating from December 1961. Rüdiger Görner, *Das Tagebuch* (1986), is a brief introduction; Béatrice Didier, *Le Journal intime* (1976), also short, is suggestive; *Le Journal intime et ses formes littéraires,* ed. Vittorio Del Litto (1978), transcribes a wide-ranging colloquium held at Grenoble in 1975. Thomas Mallon, *A Book of One's Own: People and Their Diaries* (1984), is amusing, intelligent, and enlightening. For England, see Robert A. Fothergill, *Private Chronicles: A Study of English Diaries* (1974), which handily explores their inexhaustible variety. Arthur Ponsonby, *English Diaries: A Review of English Diaries from the 16th to the 20th Century, with an Introduction on Diary Writing* (1923), and its sequel, *More English Diaries: Further Reviews of Diaries from the 16th to the 19th Century, with an Introduction on Diary Reading* (1927), are a well-known pair of much used surveys. *Anthologie du journal intime avec une introduction et des notices,* ed. Maurice Chapelan (1947), does similar work for France. Emile Henriot, *La Manie du journal intime et le roman autobiographique* (1924), links diary writing to first-person fiction. Michèle Leleu, *Les Journaux intimes* (1952), offers psychological insights. The most interesting attempt by an educator-psychoanalyst to understand the motives of adolescents through their journals is Siegfried Bernfeld, *Trieb und Tradition im Jugendalter. Kulturpsychologische Studien an Tagebüchern* (1931).

Acknowledgments

Writing a book as wide-ranging as this one, I have called for, and cheerfully received, expert assistance. I am deeply grateful to it all.

As I have over the years, I once again tried out my ideas and formulations in lectures both at Yale and elsewhere. In a course on German culture, organized under the aegis of my colleague Cyrus Hamlin and run by Anette Schwarz, I was granted the opportunity to test my views of romanticism. Another came in the summer of 1993, in Berlin, at the Institut für Psychoanalyse, Psychotherapie und Psychosomatik, on "German romanticism as regression," which aroused a lively (I am tempted to say, vehement) debate that was highly instructive to me. In October 1994, I had the pleasure of delivering the first R. K. Webb lecture at the University of Maryland, Baltimore County, which honors the oldest of my friends, entitled "The Re-enchantment of the World," which gave me yet another chance to refine my definition of romanticism. I had more than one forum for "The Art of Listening," as I repeatedly revised this opening vignette, most agreeably a monthly colloquy that has been hospitable and profitable to me for years, the Muriel Gardiner Program on Psychoanalysis and the Humanities, at Yale.

Other encounters, too, helped me put finishing touches to this book. In 1994, in an NEH summer seminar on psychoanalysis and history, I had the interested and, happily, talkative company of a dozen college teachers with whom to argue out, and clarify, the way that psychoanalytic ideas may assist the writing of history without overwhelming it with jargon or ruining it with reductionism. Several months earlier, I spoke on the topic "History between Art and Science" at Bucknell University. I must mention one final, delightful rehearsal: the seven weeks I spent as a visiting professor at Georgetown University, giving fourteen lectures drawn from this text. In weekly sessions, some twenty graduate students regularly and vigorously assaulted my ideas, much to my benefit. My colleague in the course, Susan Pinkard, did more than steer me through the administrative mazes of her university (as did the acting chairman, Dorothy Brown); she made delightful opportunities for good talk. I appreciate Jeffrey von Arx and Sam Barnes's invitation. It is one of the dividends of such adventures that they bring the visitor new friends.

Old friends like Janet Malcolm and Gardner Botsford, Dick and Peggy Kuhns, Gladys Topkis with her consistent generosity, John Merriman as always, Stefan Collini invariably candid, Gaby Katwan on two continents all stood by with counsel, encouragement, and printed matter. This book would have been longer in the making and the poorer without them. I gladly acknowledge the ripe thinking of Vann Woodward and my frequent, long discussions with my former students and now close friends Mark Micale and Robert Dietle.

I note, with sincere thanks, the aid of others. Bob Herbert, with admirable, unfailing collegiality, gave me much-needed information about Millet and the Louvre, and steered me to Jennifer Gough-Cooper and Jacques Caumont, who furnished me with a hilarious bit of cultural history, an issue of the periodical they publish that displayed the almost unbelievable varied uses of Millet's *Angelus*. Wolfgang Hardtwig of the Humboldt University, Berlin, took up with me the vexed question of Ranke's readership. Edward Muir of Northwestern University exchanged letters about the same historian. I owe to Thomas A. Reed the excerpts from the diary of G. L. Reed. Dwight Culler shared his unsurpassed insight into the historical sense informing nineteenth-century England. Sherwin Simmons of the University of Oregon satisfied my curiosity about the ways of commercial advertisers with Arnold Böcklin's paintings. I talked Nietzsche with Randall Havas and the German romantics with Gail Newman of Williams College. Kay Kaufman Shelemay of Wesleyan College sent me an interesting dissertation. Frank Mecklenburg of the Leo Baeck Institute guided me through its rich holdings that proved to be a gold mine of love letters. My doctoral students Jennifer Hall and George Williamson made my work easier, by supplying information about the cost of hearing opera in nineteenth-century London and by talking about romantic mythmaking. Ingeborg Glier and Lore Segal clarified Grimms' fairy tales. Karen E. Ahlquist kindly lent me a dissertation. Marion Kaplan shared with me her impressive knowledge of German-Jewish cultural history. Peter de Bach went far beyond ordinary courtesy in enriching my knowledge of Dutch manners at concerts. Judith Schiff of Yale Manuscripts and Archives was forthcoming about collections of papers. Edward Skipworth at the Rutgers Special Collections saved me much time and effort by sending me relevant pages of Rachel Van Dyke's diary. With similar promptness, Carolyn A. Davis, Reader Services Librarian at the Syracuse University Library, supplied me with a portrait of Ranke. My former colleague Egbert Begemann, on whose broad, unmatched expertise in the history of art I have depended for years, canvassed with me the vexed issue of Rembrandt's intentions. Nancy Cott steered me to important titles in women's literature. Elizabeth Prelinger alerted me to the cultural consequences of Dürer and Rembrandt as printmakers. I recall pertinent and profitable conversations with Terry Pinkard, Danny Hofstadter, David Quint, and Benjamin Harshav. As a senior doing research for me, Christina Erickson dug up valuable material.

Norton proved, as before, an ideal publisher. I am indebted to Donald Lamm, publisher, editor, friend—see p. vii. Don's amiable assistants Amy Cherry, Jennifer DiToro, and Cecil Lyon eased my work with courtesy and dispatch. Ruth Mandel was most helpful with the illustrations. Otto Sonntag wielded a light pencil without overlooking my lapses.

I have always thanked my readers last not to slight them but to underscore how indispensable they have been to me. Leon Plantinga improved "The Art of Listening" with genial but pointed advice. David Bromwich, reading "The Re-enchantment of the World," challenged me to go beyond my text, as did Katie Snyder. Geoffrey

Hartman straightened me out on Wordsworth. Georges May gave "Exercises in Self-definition" an incisive reading. David Cannadine and Bob Webb energetically compelled me to rethink and, to a considerable measure, rewrite "Usable Pasts." Sandy Welsh and Cyrus Hamlin lent their expertise in nineteenth-century literature to "The Truths of Fiction," which profited from their reading. Joseph Koerner and Rick Brettell had impressive comments, which made me go back to my computer. And my wife, Ruth, with her accustomed generosity of spirit, set aside her own work to improve the manuscript by reading each chapter at least twice. Acting as Don Lamm's informal ally (far be it from me to allege a conspiracy!), she saw to it that the book got shorter—yes, it was longer once—and better. May they all soon have manuscripts of their own to show me, that I may in a practical way express my gratitude to them for all the extra work they made me do!

PETER GAY

INDEX